LIFE APPLICATION® BIBLE COMMENTARY

1 & 2 Corinthians

Bruce B. Barton, D.Min.
Greg Asimakoupoulos, M.Div.
Jonathan Farrar, M.A.
Linda Taylor
Dave Veerman, M.Div.
Neil Wilson, M.R.E.

General Editor:
Grant Osborne, Ph.D.
Series Editor:
Philip W. Comfort, Ph.D., D. Litt. et Phil.

Tyndale House Publishers, Inc.
WHEATON, ILLINOIS

Library of Congress Cataloging-in-Publication Data

1 & 2 Corinthians : life application commentary / Bruce B. Barton . . . [et al.] ; general editor, Grant Osborne.
    p. cm.—(Life application Bible commentary)
    Includes bibliographical references and index.
    ISBN 0-8423-2853-X (softcover : alk. paper)
    1. Bible. N.T. Corinthians—Commentaries. I. Barton, Bruce B. II. Osborne, Grant R. III. Title: 1 and 2 Corinthians. IV. Title: First & Second Corinthians.
V. Title: First and Second Corinthians. VI. Series.
BS2675.3.A18   1999

227′.2077—dc21   98-46122

Printed in the United States of America

05 04

7   6   5   4

CONTENTS

Gospels

MATTHEW:
MARK: between
LUKE:

Paul's Epistles

ACTS:
ROMANS: about 57
1 CORINTHIANS: about 55
2 CORINTHIANS: about 56–57
GALATIANS: about 49

EPHESIANS:
PHILIPPIANS:
COLOSSIANS:
1 THESSALONIANS: about 51
2 THESSALONIANS: about 51–52
1 TIMOTHY:
2 TIMOTHY:
TITUS:
PHILEMON:

General Epistles   JAMES: about 49

1 PETER:
2 PETER:

JUDE:

NEW TESTAMENT

AD 30	40	50	60

The church begins (Acts 1)

35 Paul's conversion (Acts 9)

46 Paul's first missionary journey (Acts 13)

Jerusalem Council and Paul's second journey (Acts 15)

54 Paul's third journey (Acts 18) Nero becomes emperor

58 Paul arrested (Acts 21)

64 Rome burns

61–63 Paul's Roman imprisonment (Acts 28)

between 60–65
55–65
about 60

JOHN: probably 80–85

about 63–65

about 61
about 62
about 61

about 64
about 66–67
about 64
about 61

HEBREWS: probably before 70

about 62–64
about 67

1 JOHN: between 85–90
2 JOHN: about 90
3 JOHN: about 90

about 65

REVELATION: about 95

TIMELINE

70	80	90	100

67–68
Paul and
Peter
executed

Jerusalem
destroyed

79 Mt. Vesuvius
erupts in Italy

68
Essenes hide
their library
of Bible
manuscripts
in a cave
in Qumran
by the
Dead Sea

About 75
John begins
ministry in
Ephesus

75
Rome begins
construction
of Colosseum

About 98
John's
death
at Ephesus

FOREWORD

The Life Application Bible Commentary series provides verse-by-verse explanation, background, and application for every verse in the New Testament. In addition, it gives personal help, teaching notes, and sermon ideas that will address needs, answer questions, and provide insight for applying the Word of God to life today. The content is highlighted so that particular verses and phrases are easy to find.

Each volume contains three sections: introduction, commentary, and reference. The introduction includes an overview of the book, the book's historical context, a timeline, cultural background information, major themes, an overview map, and an explanation about the author and audience.

The commentary section includes running commentary on the Bible text with reference to several modern versions, especially the New International Version, the New Revised Standard Version, and the New Living Translation, accompanied by life applications interspersed throughout. Additional elements include charts, diagrams, maps, and illustrations. There are also insightful quotes from church leaders and theologians such as John Calvin, Martin Luther, John Wesley, and A. W. Tozer. These features are designed to help you quickly grasp the biblical information and be prepared to communicate it to others. The reference section includes an index and a bibliography.

GENERAL INTRODUCTION

Lawsuit.
Split.
Scandal.

Tragically, contemporary headlines often trumpet bad reports from local churches. News of leaders' sexual escapades, disgruntled and disgraced members' lawsuits, unethical and irresponsible fiscal practices, and blatant heresies seems to parade weekly across television screens. Jesus had told the Twelve that his followers would be known by their love (John 13:35). Yet, today, many who claim to follow him are marked by anything but love. Instead of standing apart from the world, the church has taken the appearance of other, secular institutions and has blended in.

What would God say to these errant believers, to churches and individuals who have strayed from obeying his commands? He said it nearly 2,000 years ago through Paul to Christians in decadent Corinth, a city similar to many communities today. Paul wrote letters, now known as 1 and 2 Corinthians, urging believers to focus on Christ, forsake immorality, settle their differences, reject false teachers, unify, and . . . love. As you read these personal and powerful epistles written first to ancient Greeks, know that the words and principles apply to this generation as well.

PAUL'S MINISTRY IN CORINTH

On the dusty road to Damascus, Saul of Tarsus (later known as Paul) was stopped in his tracks (Acts 9:1-19). A blinding light from heaven knocked him straight to his knees. There, on that ordinary road, a voice from heaven called him to a radically different life than the one he had been leading. Before this encounter with Jesus, Paul had been a zealous Pharisee, studying under the most respected religious teacher of his day, Gamaliel. He had spent countless hours poring over the Law (Old Testament) so he could teach its minutiae (Acts 22:3)—every single law and all the accompanying oral tradition. As a devout Pharisee, he opposed, on principle, any group threatening traditional Judaism. This included the upstarts who worshiped Jesus as the Messiah—the early Christians.

The challenge that early Christians posed to the Jews brought
out his activist orientation, and he wouldn't let Judaism be undermined by a small group of Jesus-worshipers. So Paul obtained
the authority to imprison Christians and set out for Damascus. On
the way, he met Jesus in all his heavenly glory (Acts 9:3-6). This
divine encounter forever changed Paul. Instead of teaching the
details of tradition to fellow Jews, he spearheaded the preaching
of the gospel to the Gentiles. For two decades, this mission
would dominate his life. The task suited Paul, for he was a
Roman citizen, giving him special rights throughout the Empire.
Paul used those rights to advance the gospel (Acts 16:37-40;
22:24-29).

Instead of continuing to imprison Christian believers, Paul himself became imprisoned for preaching Christ (see Acts 16).
Instead of threatening Christ's followers, he endured harsh
threats and insults because of Christ (Acts 17:32). Paul's suffering, in fact, became the mark of his apostleship (see Christ's
words about Paul in Acts 9:16). These letters to the Corinthian
church recount Paul's sufferings, presented as his credentials, the
proof of his authority to preach Christ (1 Corinthians 4:9-13;
2 Corinthians 1:5-11).

Paul immediately began to preach about Jesus in Damascus
(Acts 9:20-22). This made him a target for harsh opposition—
from slander to flogging and stoning. The Jews of Damascus
were the first to oppose Paul, but they were not the last. Hearing
of their plot to murder him, Paul escaped in a basket, lowered
through a hole in the city wall (Acts 9:23-25). Paul returned to
Jerusalem, but he must have encountered vigorous opposition
from his former Jewish teachers. When he learned of a plot
against his life, Paul fled to his hometown, Tarsus (Acts 9:28-30).

After a couple of years, Barnabas recruited Paul to preach to
the Gentiles in Antioch (Acts 11:25-26). Soon the church in Antioch officially commissioned Paul and Barnabas as missionaries
to the Gentiles. For the next decade, the financial and spiritual
support of this church enabled Paul to travel throughout Asia
Minor and Greece, preaching the Good News of Jesus to everyone who would listen. On three separate missionary journeys,
Paul established a network of congregations in Macedonia,
Achaia, and Asia Minor (present-day Turkey and Greece).

Paul visited Corinth on his second missionary trip. At the time
of Paul's visit, Corinth was a bustling commercial city, a center
of Mediterranean trade. It is no wonder that Paul easily found
work as a tentmaker (most likely working with goat's-hair cloth,
a prominent trade of Paul's native region, Cilicia). In his spare

time, Paul began to speak about Christ to Jews at the local synagogue, but he received a cold reception. Undaunted by opposition, Paul began teaching next to the synagogue in Titius Justus's house. This infuriated the Jews. Paul's congregation probably included many God-fearing Gentiles who used to attend the synagogue right next door. Because these Corinthian Jews hated Paul, they presented an official complaint to Gallio, the governor of Achaia. Gallio refused to hear his case, however, because he viewed the early Christians as simply another sect of Judaism. Ironically, this mistaken perception protected the infant church from being rigorously persecuted by the Romans. With his opponents defeated, Paul was free to stay in Corinth for a year and a half (around A.D. 50–52), one of Paul's longest stays in any one city during his missionary journeys. Perhaps he envisioned Corinth as a center of evangelism for all of Greece.

The two letters to the Corinthians preserved in the Bible are evidence that Paul took special interest in the spiritual welfare of the Corinthian church. His long stay in the city made it painful for him to hear of the problems that had begun to plague the church there. Paul himself had established the church. He had endured much ridicule in order to preach the gospel. He had worked hard in order to preach free of charge. As these two letters make clear, however, the Corinthian church struggled in Paul's absence.

INTRODUCTION TO 1 CORINTHIANS

You've heard the jokes, no doubt, with the "good news/bad news" introduction. Typically they begin, "I have good news and bad news for you. The good news is . . ." and so on. Usually the punch line appears in the "bad news" section.

Paul's first letter to the church at Corinth follows the good news/bad news format, but it is no joke. The punch lines hit hard, with sharp commands and tough consequences.

After his customary greeting (1:1-3), Paul begins by affirming the great truths of the gospel: God had given the Corinthian believers grace through Christ Jesus (1:4); God had enriched them greatly (1:5); God had given them every spiritual gift (1:7); the Lord Jesus Christ would soon return (1:7); God would give them the power to be strong and blameless (1:8); God is faithful (1:9).

That's the good news.

But then Paul punches out the rest of the story, beginning with a discussion of the divisions among believers and a strong appeal for unity (1:10– 4:21). Next he moves swiftly to condemn a specific illicit relationship in the church (5:1-2), lawsuits between Christians (6:1-8), and sexual immorality (6:9-20). Then, Paul softens a bit as he teaches about marriage and the single life (7:1-40), the relationship between conscience and freedom in Christ (8:1–10:33), order in worship services (11:1-34), spiritual gifts (12:1–14:40), and the reality and power of the Resurrection (15:1-58). Each of these teachings, however, brings the implication of a problem. Evidently marriages were in trouble; strong and weak Christians were in conflict; worship, Communion, and spiritual gifts were being abused; and wrong doctrine was being introduced. So Paul says, "Do not be misled: 'Bad company corrupts good character.' Come back to your senses as you ought, and stop sinning; for there are some who are ignorant of God—I say this to your shame" (15:33-34 NIV).

Paul closes with a reminder of the collection for the church in Jerusalem (16:1-4), his plans to visit the Corinthians (16:5-9), and miscellaneous comments and encouragements (16:10-24).

As you read this first letter from Paul to the church at Corinth, look for yourself and your church in the text, and between the lines. If God were writing a letter specifically to you, what would

be your "good news" and "bad news"? Then look again; he has
something poignant to say to each one of us.

AUTHOR

Paul (Saul of Tarsus): former Pharisee, apostle, pioneer missionary of the church.

Paul's authorship of 1 Corinthians has never been seriously
questioned by Bible scholars. In the very first verse of 1 Corinthians, he identifies himself as the author and Sosthenes as his secretary (amanuensis). This evidence, along with the Pauline
emphasis on the believer's freedom in Christ (10:23-33), is
enough to convince most scholars. Even so, the writings of Clement of Rome provide more evidence. In A.D. 95, Clement
exhorted the Corinthian believers to reread the first part of Paul's
letter to them, and then he quoted from 1 Corinthians. Because
this evidence is dated within several decades of Paul's ministry to
the Corinthians, most scholars concede that the letter was written
by Paul. In fact, the critical Bible scholars who formed the
Tübingen school used 1 Corinthians (along with Romans,
2 Corinthians, and Galatians) to evaluate Pauline authorship of
other New Testament letters traditionally accepted as written by
him.

Although Paul's authorship of this epistle has gone virtually
unquestioned, a few critical scholars have suggested that 1 Corinthians may actually be two separate letters. They base their theories on what they believe to be inconsistencies in the text. These
so-called inconsistencies usually cannot stand up to close scrutiny. For example, one critical scholar has claimed that there is a
contradiction between Paul's claim that he is coming to Corinth
(4:19) and his statement that he will be staying in Ephesus (16:8).
But by reading the two passages within their contexts, the contra-
dictions are not nearly as apparent as they may seem at first. In
chapter 4, Paul was aggressively stating that he would come to
Corinth to discipline those who were arrogant and who were challenging his authority. Paul was stating that he would eventually
come, not that he would come immediately. In chapter 16, Paul
was giving the Corinthians the details of his travel plans. He
would stay in Ephesus for a while and then begin his journey to
Corinth.

On the other hand, the evidence for 1 Corinthians being one letter is more convincing. With its treatment of a series of topics
and its somewhat disjunctive nature, 1 Corinthians reads like a
letter that was written over a long period of time. Paul may have
been teaching his students in Ephesus when he wrote 1 Corinthi-

ans. Between classes he could have written a small portion of the letter, causing it to move abruptly from topic to topic and sometimes to repeat. It is a letter written by a busy teacher who wanted to address several issues in a troubled church.

DATE AND SETTING

Written from Ephesus around A.D. 55.

Near the end of 1 Corinthians, Paul reported the details of his recent travel plans and revealed that he was writing from the city of Ephesus (16:8). On his third missionary journey, Paul stayed in Ephesus for three years. Ephesus, a bustling seaport town in Asia Minor (present-day Turkey), was a strategic city for the spread of the gospel message in Asia Minor. Located at the intersection of two ancient overland routes (the coastal road running north to Troas and the western route to Colosse, Laodicea, and beyond), Ephesus became a customary stopping point for ships sailing through the Aegean Sea. Thus the city became known as the gateway to Asia. During the first century, however—the time period of Paul's ministry—the harbor began filling up with silt. This condition caused a slight economic downturn.

The numerous visitors who came to Ephesus every month kept revenue flowing into the town. The magnificent temple to Diana (the goddess of fertility, also called Artemis) was located in Ephesus. Four times larger than the Parthenon, this marble temple was considered one of the wonders of the ancient world. People from throughout the Roman Empire came to worship Diana there. In addition to the temple of Diana, Ephesus boasted an immense amphitheater that could seat twenty-five thousand and an equally huge stadium that hosted all types of gladiator fights. A sparkling marble street flanked by colonnades ran through the city, directing all visitors to the amphitheater. Because of its temples to pagan gods and goddesses, Ephesus was one of the great tourist capitals of the ancient world. It was no wonder that the craftsmen of that city became alarmed at the spread of Christianity among the populace (see Acts 19:21-41).

Perhaps it was because the city was such a center for tourism and trade that Paul spent three full years there—teaching the gospel in the lecture hall of Tyrannus. According to Luke, the author of Acts, this lecture hall became a gathering place for people from all over the province of Asia Minor who were interested in the Good News of Jesus Christ (see Acts 19:9-10). During this extended stay in Ephesus, Paul wrote 1 Corinthians.

AUDIENCE

The church in Corinth.

Along with Rome and Alexandria, Corinth was one of the major cities of the Roman Empire. Its prominence and wealth were derived from the extraordinary amount of shipping and commerce that passed through its harbors. The location of Corinth on a four-and-a-half-mile isthmus that connected mainland Greece and Achaia made it an ideal shipping hub. Ships were placed on wooden platforms and dragged across a stone road on the isthmus between the two ports of Corinth-Lechaeum and Cenchreae. A canal would have been ideal, but the Romans never built one. The lack of a canal, however, did not impede the ship traffic across the isthmus. It was easier and safer for a ship captain to pay the fees to have his ship dragged across the isthmus than to sail around Achaia, a two-hundred-mile journey known for its severe and unpredictable storms.

Although the Romans destroyed Corinth in 146 B.C. for taking a leadership role in a rebellion, Julius Caesar rebuilt the city in 46 B.C. The city quickly regained its former prominence, and by 27 B.C., it was named the capital of a senatorial province of Achaia. By the first century A.D., the city was the most influential commercial center in Greece. In addition to being a commercial center, Corinth was a manufacturing center for bronze, a metal used in the construction of many of the Roman amphitheaters. The prestige of Corinth was elaborately displayed at the biennial Isthmian games in that city (a series of games equivalent to the Olympic games). Paul drew upon the images of the athletes and awards in these games to illustrate the nature of the Christian life (9:24-27).

The wealth accompanying commercial success often breeds moral laxity; that certainly was the case in Corinth. Throughout the ancient world, the city was known for its moral decadence. Plato used the term "Corinthian girl" to refer to a prostitute; and Aristophanes used the verb "to act like a Corinthian" to refer to fornication. The magnificent temple of Aphrodite (the goddess of love, fertility, and beauty) stood on the mountain that overlooked Corinth as a monument to this immoral lifestyle. That temple was the center of many varieties of religious prostitution.

As a strong commercial center, Corinth drew a substantial number of people from every corner of the Roman Empire, so the city was ethnically and religiously diverse. In addition to the temple of Aphrodite, Corinth contained a temple for Asclepius, the Greek god of healing, as well as sites to venerate Issi, the Egyptian god of seafarers, and Poseidon, the Greek counterpart to Issi.

There is even archeological evidence of a Jewish synagogue dating back to the third century. The diversity of the city was reflected in the makeup of the Corinthian congregation (12:13).

Corinth was the last city Paul visited on his second missionary journey (Acts 18:1-18). He stayed in Corinth for eighteen months, establishing a church there. Apollos, who had been taught the basics of the Christian faith by Aquila and Priscilla in Ephesus, visited the church at a later time, encouraging the believers (1:12).

Unfortunately, the Corinthian church not only reflected the city's multiethnic character, but also its moral depravity. Paul's exhortations against incest (5:1-5) and against soliciting prostitutes (6:9-20) indicate that members in the church were struggling to resist the pervasive immorality of their city. But Paul wouldn't compromise the high standards of Christian conduct for the church in Corinth. Being surrounded by ubiquitous immorality did not make the Corinthians an exception. Instead, he called them to a pure life, set apart for God. He even compared their bodies to God's temple (6:18-20). Even with its numerous problems, the Corinthian body of believers became a strategic church for the propagation of the gospel. Its location on the major trade routes of the Roman Empire made it a key outpost for spreading the gospel in Achaia (present-day Greece).

OCCASION

To answer some questions about church order, to identify some problems in the Corinthian church, and to teach the believers how to live for Christ in a corrupt society.

In his travels throughout the Mediterranean world, Paul had visited numerous towns and seaports, establishing small cells of committed believers in almost every place he visited. During his travels Paul had dealt with a wide variety of people—from mad mobs to subtle philosophers—and with various situations—from fierce persecution to moral laxity. Throughout all this, he showed keen interest in the spiritual welfare of every person with whom he came in contact. His letters frequently recount how he wrestled in prayer for a church or an individual (2 Corinthians 13:7; 1 Thessalonians 3:10). This genuine concern prompted Paul to write letters to his converts, instructing them in the faith, and it compelled him to visit churches again and again. Corinth was no exception.

The very first letter that Paul wrote to the Corinthian believers has been lost. First Corinthians 5:9 mentions this previous letter. Obviously it could not have been 1 Corinthians. The exact contents of this letter are unknown; 1 Corinthians 5 implies that Paul had warned the Corinthians in that letter not to associate with so-called Christians who engaged in sexual immorality.

The problems in Corinth. Near the end of his stay in Ephesus, Paul wrote a second letter, the epistle entitled 1 Corinthians. He wrote this letter in response to a message delivered by Stephanas, Fortunatus, and Achaicus (16:17). Stephanas and his companions had asked Paul a series of questions, mostly concerning church order. In his long letter in response, Paul answered the questions related to Christian marriage (7:1-16), food sacrificed to idols (8:1-13), spiritual gifts (12:1-31), and the procedure for collecting money for the relief of the Jerusalem church (16:1-14). This is why 1 Corinthians is arranged topically. Instead of a theological treatise, with a central thesis and a number of arguments supporting the main point, 1 Corinthians is a practical letter addressing a variety of issues faced by the church.

In addition, Paul addressed problems that had surfaced in an unofficial report from Chloe's household in Corinth (see 1:11). According to that report, persistent problems had been plaguing the church. Specifically, members were quarreling with each other and forming cliques around various teachers—especially Paul, Peter, and Apollos (1:10-17). Corinthian believers were even suing each other (6:1) and arguing when they met to celebrate the Lord's Supper (11:17-22). Even more disturbing was the report of a case of incest in the church that had not been confronted by the church leaders (5:1). Paul responded to each of these very serious issues. In fact, 1 Corinthians seems to almost follow Chloe's report as an outline, as it answers the problems and issues raised.

The Gentile heritage. At first, many of the conflicts addressed in 1 Corinthians seem to be unrelated and disconnected. A careful analysis of all the problems and disputes, however, reveals a predominantly Gentile church. First, sexual permissiveness in the church would have been more a problem for Gentiles than for Jewish believers, who were already familiar with Old Testament restrictions on their sexual appetites (6:12-20). Second, numerous lawsuits would not have been a problem among Jewish Christians, for Jews were forbidden to use heathen courts and were expected to resolve their differences with the elders of the local synagogue (6:1-11). Only Gentile Christians would be inclined to sue each other in Roman courts. Third, Paul's extensive discussion on the wisdom of the Spirit compared to the foolishness of people confirms that his audience was primarily composed of Gentile Christians. Greek philosophers would demonstrate their so-called wisdom with lavish rhetoric. That's why Paul had to explain his reason for not presenting the gospel with "lofty words" but instead with the power of the Holy Spirit (2:1-4 NLT).

First Corinthians clearly shows that some of the philosophies of the Greek and Roman world were coloring the Corinthians' perception of their newfound faith in Jesus. This letter was written to a group of believers who were still influenced by philosophical dualism. Ever since Plato, much of Greek philosophy had been based on the belief that the spiritual and the material were completely separate spheres of human existence. According to this view, the material or physical side of human nature was inherently corrupt and doomed for destruction. By contrast, the spiritual side could gradually lose its connection to the material and ascend to God, the pure Spirit. This type of thinking was absorbed by Gnostics in the second century and probably formed the foundation of the Corinthians' denial of a bodily resurrection (see Paul's defense of Jesus' resurrection in 15:12-34).

Philosophical dualism led to two opposite extremes. Some people concluded that because the physical/material was irredeemable, what a person did in his or her body was irrelevant. Only the spirit mattered. This type of thinking justified all types of immorality. It would also explain why Paul had to emphasize to the Corinthians that their physical bodies were in fact members of Christ (6:12-20).

This dualism between body and spirit could also lead to asceticism. Some denied their physical bodies any pleasure in order to ascend to spiritual heights. This also is an emphasis in 1 Corinthians, where Paul had to confront the asceticism of some church members—those husbands and wives who were denying each other the physical joys of marriage (7:5).

Paul's relationship with the Corinthians. Tragically, Paul's passionate appeal for Christian love and holy living in 1 Corinthians fell on deaf ears. Paul must have been aware of the difficult situation that was developing in Corinth, for he sent his trusted assistant, Timothy, there (4:17; 16:10). Perhaps he hoped that Timothy would deal with some of the problems in person, explaining Paul's letter and modeling Christian love to the believers.

These efforts, however, must have been futile, for at the time that Paul wrote 2 Corinthians, about a year later, the situation had deteriorated even further. Paul had made a quick visit to Corinth, during which time some church members had challenged his authority (2 Corinthians 2:1; 12:14, 21; 13:1-4). After that trip, Paul may have written another letter to the Corinthians, a letter alluded to in 2 Corinthians 2:1-4; 7:8. In this letter, Paul sternly warned them to correct the abuses in the church. Around that time, he sent Titus to monitor the spiritual progress of the church.

Finally, in his fourth letter to the Corinthians (2 Corinthians),
Paul rejoiced in the good news brought to him by Titus. The
Corinthians had disciplined some of their members, as Paul had
instructed. Unfortunately, however, the reform was not completely sincere. Some members continued to challenge Paul's
authority to instruct them in Christ's ways. So Paul wrote 2 Corinthians to encourage them to continue in their obedience and to
warn those who were still opposing his authority.

The book of Acts reports that Paul finally did make it to Corinth on his third missionary journey (Acts 20:1-3). Perhaps at that
time, the tear in the relationship between Paul and the Corinthians was finally mended. Not much else is known about the Corinthian church until A.D. 95. In that year, Clement of Rome wrote
the Corinthians a letter urging them to stop arguing among themselves and to unite under Jesus' leadership. Clement's letter
reveals that the division in the Corinthian church had persisted,
despite Paul's severe warnings.

The central problem in Corinth. Why were there persistent
divisions among the Corinthians? One group, associated with one
teacher, wanted to achieve prominence in the church over another
group, associated with another teacher. The situation had deteriorated so much that church members were boasting about their
immorality. In Corinth, pride ran rampant. Even the display of spiritual gifts—teaching, preaching, and prophesying—had become an
occasion for competition and a subject of boasts (12:21-30). Paul
told the Corinthians to stop bragging and to love each other (12:1-
11; 13:1-13). Only when they put their differences aside and united
in a spirit of love would Jesus be able to use them for his holy purposes (1:2; 15:58). Today, that same lesson must be learned. Just as
in Corinth, many modern churches are divided. Conflicts over personalities, agendas, and even the color of the church carpet arise
from pride. One side will not give in to the other. Believers must
unify around Christ and love each other.

The history of the Corinthian church. The relationship between Paul and the Corinthian church had a long and torturous
history. The following chart outlines this history. Some of the
details are widely disputed among scholars (such as the date of
the "painful visit" and the "severe letter"), but most scholars
agree on the basic elements in this outline. For more on the
debates surrounding the chronology, consult the commentary on
2 Corinthians.

The Corinthian church was founded by Paul on his second missionary journey.

A.D. 52

Paul started teaching at Ephesus in the lecture hall of Tyrannus.

A.D. 52
Paul wrote his first letter to the Corinthians warning them
about Christians persisting in sexual immorality (see 1 Corinthians 5:9). Most believe this letter has not been preserved, but
some have suggested that 2 Corinthians 6:14–7:1 might be a fragment of this letter.

A.D. 54 or 55
Toward the end of his stay at Ephesus, Paul wrote his second
letter to the Corinthians, which is called 1 Corinthians today.

A.D. Spring 55
Paul most likely visited Corinth himself. During this painful
visit, he was challenged by one or more members.

A.D. Summer or Fall 55
After his painful visit, Paul wrote a severe letter to the Corinthians (see 2 Corinthians 2:1-4; 7:8). Most biblical commentators
consider this letter to be lost. Some scholars, however, have identified the letter as being the last four chapters of 2 Corinthians.
Other commentators have defended the traditional view that the
severe letter is actually 1 Corinthians.

A.D. Spring 56
Paul left Ephesus

A.D. Spring 56
Paul was in Macedonia

A.D. Summer 56
Titus came to Macedonia

A.D. Summer 56
Paul wrote the fourth letter to the Corinthians, what is called
today 2 Corinthians, in response to a report from Titus.

A.D. Fall 56

MESSAGE

Loyalties, Immorality, Freedom, Worship, Body of Christ, and
Resurrection.

Undoubtedly, Paul knew of the Greek philosophies behind
much of the Corinthians' behavior, but he did not use this pastoral and practical letter to rebut these philosophies. Paul believed
that the real cause of the Corinthians' problem was not errant philosophies but a lack of love for each other. Instead of unifying
around the gospel message, the Corinthians had created divisions
by asserting themselves in public worship and at the Lord's Supper. They had sided with one teacher over another.

To deal with this deeper issue, Paul encouraged the Corinthians to focus on Christ. As members of Christ's body, they should

be united to do Christ's work. If they could learn to love each other, they would grow in their faith.

Thus, the unifying theme of this corrective letter is the unity of Christians in Christ's body, the church (12:13). Paul's hope was that the Corinthians' love for Christ would motivate them to reform their own conduct according to Jesus' teachings to love each other (13:1-13). Loving each other as Christian brothers and sisters instead of fighting for positions of prominence within the church would unify them as God's holy people (1:2).

Loyalties (1:10-31; 2:1-5; 3:1-15; 4:1-21; 9:1-27). The Corinthians were rallying around various church leaders and teachers— Peter, Paul, and Apollos. Others, in an attempt at spiritual superiority, were claiming to "follow Christ." These loyalties led to intellectual pride and created a spirit of division in the church.

Importance for Today. Personal loyalty to human leaders or human wisdom must never divide Christians into camps. Believers should care for each other, not compete for prominence. Christ unifies those who trust in him; he doesn't divide believers from each other.

Like Christians in Corinth, contemporary believers often cluster around popular preachers and teachers. And the result is just as divisive as in the first century. Instead of dividing over personalities, worship styles, and theological minutiae, we need to focus on Christ. He will unify us.

Give your allegiance to no one but Christ. Let him lead you.

Immorality (1:8; 5:1-13; 6:1-20; 7:1-40; 9:24-27; 10:1-13; 16:13). Paul had received a report of rampant immorality in the Corinthian church: uncorrected sexual sin and lawsuits between believers. The people were indifferent to the immorality in their community and in the church and were thinking only of themselves. This blunted the witness of the church and led to misconceptions about Christian living, especially sexual freedom and marriage.

Highlighting the necessity for moral living and for bodies dedicated to serving God, Paul confronted the Corinthians with their sin and called them back to Christ-centered lives and marriages.

Importance for Today. Although contemporary culture denigrates marriage and promotes sexual promiscuity and frivolous lawsuits, Christians must keep their focus on God and his Word and never compromise with sinful ideas and practices. Believers should not blend in with society.

It won't be easy to go against the flow, but you should determine to live up to God's standard of morality. Refuse to condone immoral behavior, especially among believers.

Freedom (8:1-13; 9:19-27; 10:23-33; 11:1). Paul taught freedom of choice on practices not expressly forbidden in Scripture.

Some believers felt certain actions, such as buying meat taken from animals used in pagan rituals, were sinful by association. Others felt free from the law to do such actions. Paul taught that those who were stronger, who felt free to eat meat that had been offered to idols, should refrain from eating it in order to not become a stumbling block for a weaker believer. He also taught, however, that those with more sensitive consciences should not judge others and force them into a rigid "meatless" lifestyle.

Importance for Today. Although eating meat usually is not a controversial issue among believers today, other practices divide our churches. Paul clearly teaches that we are free in Christ, yet we must not abuse our Christian freedom by being inconsiderate and insensitive to others. We must never encourage others to do wrong by anything we do.

Whatever the behavior controversy in your church and community, let love be your guide. Avoid judging other believers, and be sensitive to those with more sensitive consciences.

Worship (11:2-34; 14:1-40). Paul addressed disorder in worship. People were taking the Lord's Supper without first confessing sin. And many were using it as an occasion to eat and drink to excess. In addition, there was misuse of spiritual gifts and confusion over the role of women in the church.

Paul gave explicit instructions for bringing order and focus back to their worship services. These instructions center around taking God's presence seriously.

Importance for Today. Certainly there is no greater privilege than to stand in the presence of almighty God. Thus, worship is an awesome and sacred task and should be carried out properly and in an orderly manner. Although worship styles will vary from culture to culture and church to church, all worship of God should be done in a manner worthy of his high honor.

Make sure that worship in your church is Christ-centered, harmonious, useful, and that it builds up all believers.

Body of Christ (12:1-31; 13:1-13; 16:1-3). Corinthian believers were confused about their roles in the church. And, evidently, many were seeking to possess the more noteworthy, public gifts (for example, preaching, teaching, speaking in tongues). But Paul emphasized that every member and every gift is essential for the life of the body of Christ. Just as with a physical body, the church has many parts, and each part has a special role to play; thus, God has given each member of the body a unique set of spiritual gifts. Instead of minimizing one's own role and usefulness or envying the more glamorous gifts that others may possess, each member should discover and use his or her own God-given spiritual gifts. Although great diversity exists in the body, expressed in the wide range of personalities and gifts, the church finds unity in Christ. And the greatest gift of all is love.

Importance for Today. Contemporary churches often divide over the exercise of specific spiritual gifts. Instead, believers should recognize that God gives all his children special gifts that should be used to build up and unify the church.

Analyze your giftedness in light of God's Word, and consult with fellow believers to discover your spiritual gifts. Don't worry if your gifts seem minor and insignificant; you have a vital role to play in the church. Use your gifts to build up the body and to glorify Christ. And above all else, reflect Christ's love.

Resurrection (15:1-58). Some people were denying that Christ had risen from the dead. Others taught that people would not physically be resurrected. Refuting these ideas, Paul proclaimed the reality of the Resurrection. In fact, Christ's resurrection assures believers that they will have new, living bodies after they die. The hope of the Resurrection gives Christians assurance and confidence to live for Christ daily.

Importance for today. Since we will be raised again to life after we die, our lives are not in vain. We must stay faithful to God in our morality and our service. We are to live today knowing we will spend eternity with Christ.

When you stand at the graveside of a loved one, or when you struggle with your own mortality, remember the Resurrection. Because he lives, you, too, shall live and be reunited with all the other believers who have gone before you.

VITAL STATISTICS

Purpose: To identify problems in the Corinthian church, to offer solutions, and to teach the believers how to live for Christ in a corrupt society

Author: Paul

To whom written: The church in Corinth, and Christians everywhere

Date written: About A.D. 55, near the end of Paul's three-year ministry in Ephesus, during his third missionary journey

Setting: Corinth was a major cosmopolitan city, a seaport and major trade center—the most important city in Achaia. It was also filled with idolatry and immorality. The church was largely made up of Gentiles. Paul had established this church on his second missionary journey.

Key verse: "Now, dear brothers and sisters, I appeal to you by the authority of the Lord Jesus Christ to stop arguing among yourselves. Let there be real harmony so there won't be divisions in the church. I plead with you to be of one mind, united in thought and purpose" (1:10 NLT).

Key people: Paul, Timothy, members of Chloe's household

Key places: Worship meetings in Corinth

Special features: This is a strong, straightforward letter.

OUTLINE

A. Paul Addresses Church Problems (1:1–6:20)

In Paul's absence, the Corinthian church had fallen into divisiveness and disorder. This resulted in many problems, which Paul addressed squarely. We must be concerned for unity and order in our local churches, but we should not mistake inactivity for order and cordiality for unity. We, too, must squarely address problems in our churches.

1. Divisions in the church
2. Disorder in the church

B. Paul Answers Church Questions (7:1–16:24)

The Corinthians had sent Paul a list of questions, and he

answered them in a way meant to correct abuses in the church and to show how important it is that they live what they believe. Paul gives us a Christian approach to problem solving. He analyzed each problem thoroughly to uncover the underlying issue and then explained the truths that should guide our actions.

1. Instruction on Christian marriage
2. Instruction on Christian freedom
3. Instruction on public worship
4. Instruction on the resurrection

1 CORINTHIANS

1 Corinthians 1

Through various sources, Paul had received reports of problems in the Corinthian church, including jealousy, divisiveness, sexual immorality, and failure to discipline members. Churches today also address many of the same problems. Believers can learn a great deal by seeing how Paul handled these delicate situations.

1:1 This letter is from Paul, chosen by the will of God to be an apostle of Christ Jesus, and from our brother Sosthenes.^{NLT} This man, *Paul,* also wrote many of the other letters included in the New Testament. His Hebrew name was Saul. Paul was a common Roman surname. It may have been a family name, or Paul may have chosen the name simply because of how close it sounded to his Jewish name. When Paul accepted the Christian faith and began his mission to the Gentiles, he identified with his listeners by using his Roman name. In all of his letters, he identified himself as Paul, linking himself with the Gentile believers to whom God had sent him with the gospel of Christ.

Paul was a Jew from the tribe of Benjamin and a descendant of Abraham (2 Corinthians 11:22). Born in Tarsus, he had been raised as a strict Pharisee and had been educated in Jerusalem under Gamaliel (Acts 22:3). Though born to Jewish parents, Paul was also a Roman citizen (Acts 22:27-28). Out of this diverse background, God fashioned a valuable servant, using every aspect of Paul's upbringing to further spread the gospel message across the Roman Empire. During Paul's ministry, he took three missionary journeys, covering thousands of miles as he carried the gospel across Asia and into Europe.

Following the style of first-century letters, Paul began his letter to the Corinthians by introducing himself as the writer: *This letter is from Paul.* Then he described himself as *chosen by the will of God to be an apostle of Christ Jesus.* God chose Paul for special work, saying that Paul would be his "chosen instrument to carry my name before the Gentiles and their kings and before the people of Israel" (Acts 9:15 NIV). Paul had not sought this apostleship; rather, God had chosen him. Thus, Paul could truthfully

say that he was an apostle "by the will of God." Paul was not one
of the original twelve disciples (later called apostles), but the
risen Christ Jesus had confronted him on the road to Damascus
and had called him to preach the gospel to both Jews and Gentiles (Acts 9:3-19). The apostles' mission was to be God's representatives: They were envoys, messengers, and delegates directly
under the authority of Jesus Christ. They had authority to set up
and supervise churches and to discipline them if necessary
(which Paul did in these two letters to the Corinthian church).

The *brother* named *Sosthenes* may have been Paul's secretary,
who had written this letter as Paul had dictated it. He was probably the Jewish synagogue leader in Corinth (Acts 18:17) who had
been beaten during an attack on Paul and then later became a
believer. Sosthenes was well known to the members of the Corinthian church, so Paul included his familiar name in the opening
of the letter.

CALLED
Paul was given a special calling from God to preach about
Jesus Christ. Each Christian has a job to do, a role to take, or a
contribution to make. One assignment may seem more
spectacular than another, but all are necessary to carry out
God's greater plans for his church and for his world (12:12-27).
Be available to God by placing your gifts at his service. Then as
you discover what he calls you to do, be ready to do it.

**1:2 To the church of God that is in Corinth, to those who are sanc-
tified in Christ Jesus, called to be saints, together with all
those who in every place call on the name of our Lord Jesus
Christ, both their Lord and ours.**[NRSV] Paul wrote this letter *to
the church of God that is in Corinth* while he was visiting Ephesus during his third missionary journey (Acts 19:1–20:1). Corinth
and Ephesus faced each other across the Aegean Sea. Paul knew
the Corinthian church well because he had spent eighteen months
in Corinth during his second missionary journey (Acts 18:1-18).
While in Ephesus, he had heard about problems in Corinth (1:11).
About the same time, a delegation from the Corinthian church
had visited Paul to ask his advice about their conflicts (16:17).
Paul's purpose for writing was to correct those problems and to
answer questions that church members had asked in a previous
letter (7:1).

Corinth, a giant cultural melting pot with a great diversity of
wealth, religions, and moral standards, had a reputation for being
fiercely independent and as decadent as any city in the world.
The Romans had destroyed Corinth in 146 B.C. after a rebellion.

EIGHT ISSUES IN THE FIRST LETTER TO THE CORINTHIANS

1. Paul's authority as an apostle had been challenged, so Paul defended his authority against the false teachers (chapters 2–4).

2. Paul rebuked the church for not disciplining the blatant sin of one of its members. The church's laxness in dealing with sin could become a severe problem (chapter 5).

3. Paul explained that the believers should not take one another to the civil courts but should handle their disputes among themselves (6:1-8).

4. Paul's teaching about freedom in Christ had been changed to the point that some thought that even fornication was allowable among believers. Paul corrected that error by explaining that freedom in Christ did not mean freedom to sin (6:9-20).

5. Paul answered the questions about marriage that the Corinthians had sent to him. Many new Christians were already married to unbelievers and did not know what to do. Other new Christians did not know whether or not they should marry. Paul gave forthright advice on the matter (chapter 7).

6. Paul answered questions about dealing with a world filled with idolatry. Surrounded by the pagan religious cults and immorality of Corinth, the new believers wondered about how to deal with the issue of eating food sacrificed to idols. Paul explained that they had freedom in Christ on this matter but that they should be careful not to offend those among them who had weak consciences about this matter (chapters 8–10).

7. Paul delineated matters of respect and order in worship services. Male and female roles needed to be understood in the context of this time period and culture (chapters 11–14).

8. Paul reminded the Corinthian believers of the resurrection of Jesus Christ because false teachers had caused them to doubt the reality of the Resurrection. Paul defended the Resurrection and explained that without it, their faith was worthless (chapter 15).

But in 46 B.C., Julius Caesar had rebuilt it because of its strategic seaport. By Paul's day (A.D. 50), the Romans had made Corinth the capital of Achaia (present-day Greece). It was a large city, offering Rome great profits through trade as well as the military protection of its ports. But the city's prosperity made it ripe for all sorts of corruption. Idolatry flourished, and there were more than a dozen pagan temples, employing at least a thousand prostitutes. On a hillside above the city sat the Temple of Aphrodite, which employed a thousand women who were there to fulfill "worshipers'" sexual pleasures. In the city, the Temple of Apollo employed young men whose job was to fulfill the sexual desires of male and female "worshipers." The gross immorality of the city made even pagans in other cities uncomfortable. To call

another person a sinner, one merely needed to call that person a
"Corinthian." No wonder Paul had come to this city "in weakness—timid and trembling" (2:3 NLT).

Yet out of this moral wasteland God formed a church through
Paul's ministry. Paul recognized this group of believers as *sancti-
fied in Christ Jesus, called to be saints.* To be "sanctified" means
to be cleansed of sin, separated from the world and belonging to
God. This can only happen through salvation "in Christ Jesus,"
for only his death on the cross could accomplish this for sinners.
Paul used "sanctified" as a metaphor for conversion. That only
God can sanctify a person stresses that this is not the work of the
Corinthians, but the work of God alone. Paul used the word
"saints" to refer to the believers in Corinth. These people were
not "saints" because of any merit of their own; they were "called
to be saints" because they were set apart by God to devote themselves to the highest moral living (see "called into the fellowship
of his Son," 1:9). "Called" means designated by God. God had
identified them to serve him and not to serve their own purposes.
Paul was emphasizing their dedication to God, not their personal
holiness.

FROM GOD TO US
As we read the opening words of Paul's letter, we may wonder:
How do these ancient words apply today? We are distanced
from the original readers by time, space, culture, and language.
But we do share five striking similarities with the Corinthian
Christians:
1. We are people equally needing God's truthful instruction.
2. We live in a similar aggressively pluralistic society that
   denies absolutes and makes personal rights absolute.
3. This claim to personal rights challenges the lordship of
   Jesus Christ within the church today, even as it did then.
4. The ancient philosophy that might and money make right
   continues to divide churches and destroy people's lives.
5. The resurrection of Jesus Christ remains the solid fact
   upon which our faith rests. To some, it will always be a
   stumbling block. So, in spite of the obvious differences between ourselves and the Corinthians, the points of similar-
   ity make it crucial that we read this letter as God's Word
   for our day.

By including a salutation to *all those who in every place call
on the name of our Lord Jesus Christ,* Paul was making it clear
that, although this letter was dealing with specific issues facing
the church at Corinth, all believers could learn from it. The Corinthian church must have included a great cross section of believers—wealthy merchants, common laborers, perhaps former

temple prostitutes, and middle-class families. Because of the
wide diversity of people and backgrounds, Paul took great pains
to stress the need for both spiritual unity and Christlike character.

A personal invitation makes a person feel wanted and welcome. Believers are "called to be saints," that is, called to be
holy. God personally invites men and women to be citizens of his
eternal kingdom. But Jesus Christ, God's Son, is the only one
who can bring them into this glorious kingdom because he is the
only one who removes sins. "Sanctified" means that believers are
chosen or set apart by Christ for his service. Individuals accept
God's invitation by accepting his Son, Jesus Christ, and by trusting in the work he did on the cross to forgive their sins.

**1:3 Grace to you and peace from God our Father and the Lord
Jesus Christ.**NKJV "Grace" means God's undeserved favor, his
kindness shown clearly in his free gift of salvation given in
Christ. Receiving it brings *peace* (see Romans 5:1), the peace
that Christ established between believers and God through his
death on the cross. In a world of noise, confusion, and relentless
pressures, people long for peace. Many give up the search, thinking it impossible to find, but true peace of heart and mind is available through faith in Jesus Christ. Paul used "grace and peace" as
a standard greeting in all of his letters (see, for example, Romans
1:7; 2 Corinthians 1:2; Galatians 1:3; Ephesians 1:2). He wanted
his readers to experience God's grace and peace in their daily living. "Grace" and "peace" are both standard greetings in Greek
and Jewish letters.

"God our Father and the Lord Jesus Christ" makes a distinction between two of the persons in the Trinity—the Father and
the Son. They are separate but equal in essence (see also 1 Thessalonians 3:11). See the commentary on 8:6.

PAUL THANKS GOD / 1:4-9

The problems in the Corinthian church shaped almost every word
Paul wrote in his letter. He realized that the believers were struggling with internal, as well as external, problems. They were forgetting to whom they belonged. They were overlooking the
source of the gifts and blessings over which they were arguing.
Other letters begin with Paul's thanksgiving to God for the believers; this one begins with Paul's gratitude for God's gifts. The
Corinthian believers were squabbling over gifts; he pointed them
to the Giver. From the start, Paul stressed that the Corinthians
belonged to God. He knew that if he could settle the issue of

ownership, God would continue to do a great work through the Corinthian church.

When correcting others, draw their attention to what God has already accomplished in them and for them. The same process can guide your own reflections on the condition of your relationship with God.

1:4 I give thanks to my God always for you because of the grace of God that has been given you in Christ Jesus.^{NRSV} In this letter, Paul would include strong words to the Corinthians, but he began on a positive note of thanksgiving. Paul affirmed their privilege of belonging to the Lord. Paul gave *thanks to . . . God* for the Corinthian believers because only by *the grace of God* can anyone come to believe and be accepted into God's family. That grace has been made available only *in Christ Jesus*—which is the essence of the gospel message. Paul usually would begin his letters with a word of thanks for the believers to whom he was writing (see, for example, Romans 1:8; Philippians 1:3-7; Colossians 1:3-8).

THANKSGIVING
Paul thanked God for the Corinthian believers. During the Thanksgiving holiday, we focus on our blessings and express our gratitude to God for them. But thanks should be expressed every day. We can never say thank you enough to parents, friends, leaders, and especially to God. When thanksgiving becomes an integral part of your life, you will find that your attitude toward life will change. You will become more positive, gracious, loving, and humble. Whom do you need to thank today?

1:5-6 For in him you have been enriched in every way—in all your speaking and in all your knowledge—because our testimony about Christ was confirmed in you.^{NIV} By God's grace, believers are accepted into his family (1:4); this grace, in turn, enables believers to be *enriched.* As a result of grace, God made them rich in every way. Evidently, the Corinthians were putting too much emphasis on possessing the gifts of the Spirit and not enough emphasis on God, who gave those gifts to them, or on Christ, who enabled them to have those gifts. They had been enriched in their *speaking* about God and in their *knowledge* of him. Greeks attached great importance to oratory and knowledge. For these believers, such abilities had been greatly enriched by God—notice Paul's use of the word "all" before each—*all* your speaking and *all* your knowledge. God's grace had increased their ability to speak about their faith, as well as their spiritual knowledge and understanding. These facts—both seen by Paul himself and reported to him by others—served to confirm his testimony about Christ to the Corinthian believers. The changed lives of these believers validated the truth of the gospel message that had been preached to them.

1:7 Now you have every spiritual gift you need as you eagerly wait for the return of our Lord Jesus Christ.NLT The Corinthian church members had all the spiritual gifts they needed to live the Christian life, to witness for Christ, and to stand against the paganism and immorality of Corinth. The word translated "spiritual gift" is *charisma,* a word used in three different ways in the New Testament: (1) for salvation (as in Romans 5:15); (2) for God's good gifts generally (as in Romans 11:29); (3) for special gifts given to believers by the Holy Spirit (as in chapter 12). Most likely, Paul was referring to the second option—God's good gifts generally. These gifts would help the church battle sin both inside the congregation and outside in the world. These believers in Corinth lacked nothing—they had every spiritual gift—and because of this they more eagerly looked forward in faith and hope to *the return of [the] Lord Jesus Christ.* This statement refers to the second coming of Christ. As part of the gospel message, the promise of Christ's ultimate return in triumph motivates all believers to live for him and eagerly await the time when they will live with him in his kingdom (see 1 Peter 4:7, 13). The spiritual gifts God has given to believers here on earth are merely a foretaste of what is to come.

THE BIG PICTURE
Before tackling the problems, Paul described his hope for the Corinthians. He guaranteed those believers that God would consider them "blameless" when Christ returns (1:8; see also Ephesians 1:7-10). This guarantee was not because of their great gifts or their shining performance, but because of what Jesus Christ accomplished for them through his death and resurrection. *All* who believe in the Lord Jesus will be considered blameless when Jesus Christ returns (see also 1 Thessalonians 3:13; Hebrews 9:28). Today's struggles, difficulties, and failures don't tell the whole story. Keep the big picture in mind. If you have faith in Christ, even if it is weak, you *are* and *will be* saved.

1:8 He will keep you strong to the end, so that you will be blameless on the day of our Lord Jesus Christ.NIV There will be an *end* to the eager waiting of believers (1:7), because Christ will return. Here, that second coming is called *the day of our Lord Jesus Christ.* Not only have the believers received gifts for building up the church and standing against sin, but Christ would also keep them strong until that "end" should come. Because Christ has died for believers, given them spiritual gifts, and promised to return for them, Paul guaranteed these believers that God would also consider them *blameless* (see Romans 8:33-34; Ephesians 1:7-10). This guarantee was not because of their great gifts or their shining performance, but because of what Jesus Christ accomplished for them through his death and resurrection.

1:9 God is faithful; by him you were called into the fellowship of his Son, Jesus Christ our Lord.NRSV Believers need never doubt God's grace, his gifts, or his promise to give them eternal life because *God is faithful.* God always does just what he says. God has promised, and because he cannot lie (Titus 1:2), believers can be certain that all of his promises will come true. God himself had *called* each of the Corinthian believers *into the fellowship of his Son,* and that call will never be rescinded. As Paul was chosen by God to be an apostle (1:1), so every believer has been chosen, or called, by God. As God called the believers, so he will complete his promises to them because he is faithful.

PAUL APPEALS FOR HARMONY / 1:10-17

In this large and diverse Corinthian church, the believers were favoring different preachers. Because the whole New Testament had not yet been written, the believers depended heavily on preaching and teaching for spiritual insight into the meaning of the Old Testament. However, they had split into factions—each following their favorite preacher or leader, even though the leaders spoke the same message and apparently had no knowledge of these factions. (Paul was away in Ephesus and did not even know of his own "group"; it is doubtful that Peter had ever been to Corinth; Apollos was a traveling preacher—see 16:12.)

Paul admonished the believers to remember the singular message that had brought them to faith, and to stop comparing messengers. Believers today should also focus on the truth of the message, not the style of the messenger.

1:10 Now, dear brothers and sisters, I appeal to you by the authority of the Lord Jesus Christ to stop arguing among yourselves. Let there be real harmony so there won't be divisions in the church. I plead with you to be of one mind, united in thought and purpose.NLT The phrase "brothers and sisters" emphasizes that all Christians are part of God's family. Believers share a unity that runs even deeper than that of blood brothers and sisters. Paul had founded the church in Corinth on his second missionary journey. Eighteen months after he had left, arguments and divisions had arisen, and some church members had slipped back into an immoral lifestyle. Paul wrote this letter to address the problems, to clear up confusion about right and wrong, and to remove the immorality among them. Because Paul was an apostle (1:1), he had the right to *appeal . . . by the authority of the Lord Jesus Christ.* This authority, however, had apparently been questioned by some—probably false teachers—so Paul would further explain his apostolic authority later in the letter. In reality, Paul was appealing to them, not even on the basis of his own authority but, rather, on that of the Lord Jesus Christ—the One who died for them and the One whom they worshiped.

Paul simply told the Corinthian believers to *stop arguing.* Paul had heard about these arguments through some members in the church (1:11). The arguments were between factions or *divisions* that had developed in the church itself, with various believers aligning themselves behind various teachers (1:12-13). Thus, Paul here was pleading with the believers to *let there be real harmony* and for them to *be of one mind, united in thought and purpose.* To be perfectly united does not mean that Paul required everyone to be exactly the same. Instead, he wanted them to set aside their arguments and focus on what truly mattered—Jesus Christ as Lord and their mission to take the light of the gospel into a dark world. The internal divisions would only cause strife and hinder the gospel, as well as make the church look ridiculous to those outside. For more on unity, see John 17:20-24 and Ephesians 2:14-19.

TIME-OUT!
Like a frustrated coach watching his team bicker on the court, Paul called for a time-out. He saw the danger of divisions and arguments. The Corinthian believers' lack of unity was obvious. They may have been playing in the same "uniform," but they were doing as much as the opposition to bring about their own defeat. The problems weren't so much differences of opinion as divided allegiances. They were arguing over which position on the team was most important in a way that made them ineffective as a unit. They were on the field, but out of the game.

Divisions between Christians work like brick walls and barbed-wire fences to undermine the effectiveness of the message that believers are to proclaim. Focus on your coach, Jesus Christ, and the purpose he has for you. Strive for harmony. Keep arguments about allegiances off the team.

1:11 **For some members of Chloe's household have told me about your arguments, dear friends.**NLT This woman named *Chloe* is unknown. Apparently, she was well-to-do, with servants *(members of [her] household)* traveling and handling the family's interests between Ephesus and Corinth. It is unknown if she was a believer, but some members of her household were. Paul was writing this letter from Ephesus, and Chloe may have lived in Ephesus with some of her servants having been to Corinth. There they would have heard about what was going on in the Corinthian church and would have reported this back to Paul. Or Chloe may have lived in Corinth; thus, when her servants had come to Ephesus, they had given Paul the details. In either case, these firsthand observers *told* Paul about the *arguments* that were going on in the Corinthian church. These arguments had to be dealt with; hence, Paul wrote this reprimanding letter to them.

1:12-13 **What I mean is this: One of you says, "I follow Paul"; another, "I follow Apollos"; another, "I follow Cephas"; still another, "I follow Christ." Is Christ divided? Was Paul crucified for you? Were you baptized into the name of Paul?**NIV The factions in the Corinthian church threatened to destroy it. These factious groups followed different preachers for different reasons.

Some of the believers followed *Paul,* who had founded their church. Although Paul was Jewish, he had been called as a missionary to the Gentiles, so he probably attracted many of the Gentile believers. Paul used great logical arguments but apparently did not have powerful speaking ability (2 Corinthians 10:10). Others chose to follow Peter *(Cephas).* A Jew and one of the twelve disciples of Jesus, Peter probably attracted many of the Jewish believers who had come to doubt Paul's apostolic authority. It is unknown whether Peter had ever been to Corinth, although some of the Jews may have heard him in Jerusalem at Pentecost (Acts 2). Or it is likely that the believers simply knew that Peter was the leader of the apostles. A third group chose to follow *Apollos,* an eloquent and popular preacher who had had a dynamic ministry in Corinth (Acts 18:24; 19:1; Titus 3:13). Apollos was from Alexandria and had become distinguished for his speaking ability. Oratory and eloquence were highly valued in the culture of the day, so Apollos probably attracted the highly educated and distinguished believers in the congregation. Finally, a fourth group claimed to *follow Christ.* This group may have boasted a special relationship to Christ, or they may have been positioning themselves above the fray, saying that they had chosen to follow Christ alone, not any human leader (see 2 Corinthians 10:7).

Paul used a series of rhetorical questions. First he asked whether Christ could be *divided*. This is a graphic picture of what happens when the church (the body of Christ) quarrels and argues. Christ is one; the church is one. No church ought to split into warring factions. Then Paul asked if he, himself, had been *crucified* for them. Again the answer is obviously no. Only One had been crucified for the believers—indeed, only One *could* be crucified to pay the penalty for sins. Third question: Were the believers *baptized into the name of Paul* (or even of Peter or Apollos)? Again, the answer was no. They were baptized into the name of the One who had been crucified for them. This whole idea of factions was wrong; Paul did not exempt those who desired to follow him, nor did he point out any flaws in the teachings of Peter and Apollos. They all taught the same thing—the gospel—but their demeanor and delivery were different. This had caused the cliques—and Paul refused to go along with any of it. Such divisions had to be stopped.

FAN CLUBS
Paul wondered whether the Corinthians' quarrels had "divided" Christ. This is a graphic picture of what happens when the church (the body of Christ) is divided. With so many churches and styles of worship available today, believers can get caught up in the same game of "my preacher is better than yours!" They follow personalities and even change churches based on who is popular. To act this way is to divide Christ again. But Christ is not divided, and his true followers should not allow anything to divide the church. Don't let your appreciation for any teacher, preacher, speaker, or writer lead you into intellectual pride. Believers' allegiance must be to Christ and to the unity that he desires.

1:14-16 I thank God that I did not baptize any of you except Crispus and Gaius, for now no one can say they were baptized in my name. (Oh yes, I also baptized the household of Stephanas. I don't remember baptizing anyone else.)NLT Paul's rhetorical question in 1:13, "Were you baptized into the name of Paul?" led him to note that he had baptized very few people in Corinth. He saw this as providential and thanked God that he had baptized only *Crispus* (perhaps the same man mentioned in Acts 18:8), *Gaius* (perhaps the same man noted in Romans 16:23), and *the household of Stephanas* (referring to the entire family, perhaps servants as well; see 16:15, 17). The parenthetical addition was simply part of his dictation to Sosthenes (see 1:1)—Paul had mentioned two men, and then remembered these others, and this was so noted as Paul spoke. While Paul certainly had many converts in the city, he had not baptized them all. Because he had baptized only a few, no one could say that *they were baptized in [Paul's] name*. No one could claim that Paul had been baptizing people in order to obtain their loyalty as their special leader. Clearly he was not attempting to make disciples for himself.

Ephesians 4:5 states that believers are united by "one baptism." Believers are not baptized "into" different preachers—they are baptized into the family of believers. Baptism replaced circumcision as the initiation rite of the new order, the new covenant. Christians need only "one baptism" by which they publicly acknowledge their one faith in one Lord. Paul wrote in 12:13, "For in the one Spirit we were all baptized into one body—Jews or Greeks, slaves or free—and we were all made to drink of one Spirit" (NRSV). This expression of faith through baptism brings unity to believers. Far from it being divisive, baptism is a key unifying factor in the church. While baptism was an important public sign of identification with Christ, it appears that the apostles focused on preaching and left the baptizing to others (see 1:17 and Acts 10:48), except in a few cases, such as the ones that Paul noted here.

1:17 For Christ did not send me to baptize, but to preach the gospel—not with words of human wisdom, lest the cross of Christ be emptied of its power.[NIV] When Paul said *Christ did not send me to baptize,* he was not minimizing the importance of baptism. Instead, he was pointing out that his gift was preaching, and that Christ had sent him *to preach the gospel* (see Acts 9:15). His primary task was to proclaim the message.

Even the preaching of the gospel could be cause for division, however. In fact, this was already happening in Corinth, with the believers lining up behind different preachers for different reasons. Paul pointed out that neither he, nor the other apostles and preachers, spoke *with words of human wisdom*. In his presentation of the gospel message, Paul did not depend upon the rhetoric or philosophical arguments so admired by the Greeks. To do so would have emptied the message, *the cross of Christ*, of *its power,* and it would have drawn people to the preachers rather than to the message of salvation in Christ. No rite or service in the church should be tied to a certain person. To do so can lead to favoritism. The cross gives power to these elements, not the wisdom or personality of the pastor.

STYLE AND SUBSTANCE
Some speakers use impressive words, but they are weak on
content. Some preachers make the Bible marginal in their
sermons in order to hold people's attention. Even Bible studies
give less focus to the Bible than they do to fellowship. Paul
stressed solid content and practical help for his listeners. He
wanted them to be impressed with his message, not just his
style (see 2:1-5). You don't need to be a great speaker with a
large vocabulary to share the gospel effectively. The persuasive
power is in the story, not the storyteller. Paul was not against
those who carefully prepare what they say (see 2:6), but
against those who try to impress others only with their own
knowledge or speaking ability. Make Christ the center of your
preaching, rather than trying to be impressive.

CHRIST BRINGS US LIFE FROM GOD / 1:18-31

The Greeks highly valued wisdom. Paul showed in the following
verses, however, that there is the kind of "wisdom" that the world
worships, and there is the true wisdom that comes from God
alone.

1:18 **I know very well how foolish the message of the cross sounds to
those who are on the road to destruction. But we who are being
saved recognize this message as the very power of God.**[NLT] Paul
had not come to Corinth to make disciples for himself; he had
come to "preach the gospel" (1:17). But this preaching was not
according to the world's wisdom or desires—it was not filled with
philosophical arguments or supernatural acts. Paul's preaching was
the message of the cross—Jesus Christ crucified on behalf of sinners. Such a message always has two results, for ultimately all of
humanity will end up in one of these two classes. (1) The gospel
message sounds *foolish . . . to those who are on the road to destruction.* For those who desire worldly wisdom, the message of the
cross seems stupid. "Who wants a crucified king?" they might ask.
(2) But for those *who are being saved . . . [the gospel message is]
the very power of God.* Paul wrote to the Romans, "For I am not
ashamed of the gospel of Christ, for it is the power of God to salvation for everyone who believes, for the Jew first and also for the
Greek" (1:16 NKJV). The gospel message is more than a true story
and a good way to live; it is "the very power of God." Only with
such power can the gospel message redeem sinful people and transform them into God's people.

1:19 **For it is written: "I will destroy the wisdom of the wise; the
intelligence of the intelligent I will frustrate."**[NIV] Paul summa-

HIGHLIGHTS OF 1 CORINTHIANS

The Meaning of the Cross (1:18–2:16)	Be considerate of one another because of what Christ has done for us. There is no place for pride or a know-it-all attitude. We are to have the mind of Christ.
The Story of the Last Supper (11:23-29)	The Last Supper is a time of reflection on Christ's final words to his disciples before he died on the cross; believers must celebrate this in an orderly and correct manner.
The Poem of Love (13:1-13)	Love is to guide all that believers do. Christians have different gifts, abilities, likes, dislikes—but they are called, without exception, to love.
The Christian's Destiny (15:42-58)	Christ, who died for sins, promised that just as he had come back to life after death, so believers' perishable bodies will be exchanged for heavenly bodies. They will live and reign with Christ.

rized Isaiah 29:14 to emphasize a point that Jesus often made: God's way of thinking is not like the world's way (normal human wisdom). "The wisdom of the wise" and "the intelligence of the intelligent" refer to world-centered wisdom and intelligence. These are not wrong, but they are worthless as a means of salvation. The context of the passage in Isaiah is that God hates those who "draw near with their mouths and honor me with their lips, while their hearts are far from me, and their worship of me is a human commandment learned by rote" (Isaiah 29:13 NRSV). Thus, God says he will destroy their wisdom and intelligence because it can never help them find him. People can spend a lifetime accumulating human wisdom and yet never learn how to have a personal relationship with God. They must come to the crucified and risen Christ to receive eternal life and the joy of a personal relationship with the Savior. Whether they use their "wisdom" and "intelligence" to search for God or to attempt to dismiss him, they will only find themselves doomed to frustration and, ultimately, to eternal separation from God.

1:20 So where does this leave the philosophers, the scholars, and the world's brilliant debaters? God has made them all look foolish and has shown their wisdom to be useless nonsense.[NLT] No human wisdom or intelligence can either discover or disprove

God. No human reasoning can bring salvation. So all those who have lived by their own wisdom—*the philosophers, the scholars, and the world's brilliant debaters*—will be left with nothing. God had already made them all look *foolish* and showed that their "wisdom" was no more than *useless nonsense.* Some have suggested that the "philosophers" (also translated "the wise ones") may have been an allusion to the Greeks. The "scholars" (also translated "scribes") may refer to the Jewish professionals who were skilled in God's law. The "brilliant debaters" (or "philosophers or disputers of this age") could refer to either Jews or Greeks who thought that any issue could be solved by human reasoning. Paul may have been thinking of such distinctions, or he may have been simply using three different terms to describe people who think they are learned. For all their learning, God would show them to be fools. Their wisdom would be "useless" because it could do nothing to provide salvation. That can come only through the cross.

1:21 Since God in his wisdom saw to it that the world would never find him through human wisdom, he has used our foolish preaching to save all who believe.[NLT] In his complete sovereignty and *in his wisdom,* God decided that people *would never find him through human wisdom.* Instead, he chose a crucified Savior and a message of salvation preached by weak and fallible human beings *to save all who believe.* This looks like absurdity to the "high and mighty" of this world. Many people of Paul's time, and many today, mocked the message of the gospel. In their human wisdom, they wanted to reason "above and beyond" and experience more than what they felt was offered in the *foolish preaching* of believers. In reality, the worldly wise will not find God; those who accept the message of the cross will find him and be saved.

1:22-24 For Jews demand signs and Greeks desire wisdom, but we proclaim Christ crucified, a stumbling block to Jews and foolishness to Gentiles, but to those who are the called, both Jews and Greeks, Christ the power of God and the wisdom of God.[NRSV] Many *Jews* considered the Good News of

> Evangelist, speaking to Christian after Christian's encounter with Worldly Wiseman: "I will now show thee who it was that deluded thee. . . . That man that met thee is one Worldly Wiseman; and rightly is he so called; partly because he savoreth only of the doctrine of this world (therefore he always goes to the town of Morality to church), and partly because he loveth that doctrine best, for it saveth him from the Cross."
>
> *John Bunyan in The Pilgrim's Progress*

Jesus Christ to be foolish because they thought the Messiah would be a conquering king who did many spectacular *signs* and miracles. Although Jesus had performed many miracles during his ministry on earth, many Jews who observed his miracles first-hand had refused to believe (Matthew 12:38-39; 16:1-4; Mark 8:11-12; Luke 11:16; John 6:30). Jesus had not restored David's throne in the way that they had expected. Besides, he had been executed as a criminal (Deuteronomy 21:23)—how could a criminal be the Savior? This proclamation of *Christ crucified* was a contradiction of all that they believed, and it became a *stumbling block* to them (see also Romans 9:33; 1 Peter 2:8).

SILLY, SUPERFICIAL, AND SIMPLE
Paul had literally been where no man had gone before. He had taken the gospel to uncharted territories and untested hearers. He understood rejection. When Paul mentioned audience reactions (1:21), he had the scars to prove just how violently some resisted the gospel. Problems in sharing the gospel were not theoretical for Paul.

Those who proclaim the gospel may find that others think they are ridiculous. If our message did not hold the answer to life and death it might seem silly and superficial. Though some ridicule it, the gospel remains the simple truth. Paul described the attitude we ought to have this way: "For I am not ashamed of this Good News about Christ. It is the power of God at work, saving everyone who believes—Jews first and also Gentiles" (Romans 1:16 NLT). Like Paul, we must proclaim the simple gospel.

The *Greeks* (also here called *Gentiles*) did not believe in a bodily resurrection; they did not see in Jesus the powerful characteristics of their mythological gods, and they thought no reputable person would be crucified. To them, death was defeat, not victory. It did not make sense—in their worldly wisdom—that any god would do such a thing as come to earth to be killed. The Greeks worshiped *wisdom* and revered their great thinkers and philosophers. To them, the gospel message just didn't measure up; to them, the proclamation of "Christ crucified" was *foolishness.*

While some Jews and Greek tripped over the message of "Christ crucified," it was a different story for *those who are called*—those who embraced and believed the gospel. Many people, *both Jews and Greeks,* will not stumble over the message but will find that the gospel of Christ crucified is *the power of God and the wisdom of God* (see 1:18).

MIXED REACTIONS
The Good News of Jesus Christ still sounds foolish to many
and offensive to others. It is foolishness to any who have
chosen another way to face their unavoidable appointment with
death and what comes after. It is offensive to those who
attempt to maintain a facade of self-righteousness or
self-confidence in the face of life's questions. Those who
cannot consider their own sinfulness will find that the gospel
offers a solution they insist they do not need. Our society
worships power, influence, and wealth. Jesus came as a
humble, poor servant, and he offers his kingdom to those who
have faith, not to those who work hard or improve themselves.
This may look ridiculous to the world, but Christ is our power,
the only way we can be saved. Make sure you know Christ
personally; then you'll have the greatest wisdom anyone could
desire.

1:25 For God's foolishness is wiser than human wisdom, and God's weakness is stronger than human strength.NRSV This verse provides the key to Paul's words in chapters 1–3. The message of Christ's death for sins sounds foolish to those who don't believe. They believe that they, by their own wisdom, can find the "ultimate reality" or make for themselves the best life; however, they will be woefully disappointed. Their wisest plans cannot even compare to God's most insignificant act. Paul's words do not imply that God could ever be foolish or weak; instead, he was making the point that *human wisdom* and *human strength* cannot begin to compare to God. What the world sees as foolishness (Christ's death for our sins as a display of God's power) is God's truth. The cross was reserved for criminals in Paul's day. How could such an act have any power? Yet this "foolishness" is wiser than any human plan that could have been laid, for through Christ's death alone comes salvation. Even an act that had appeared to be weakness (a human body dying on a cross) was far stronger than any human strength, for Christ would come back to life. Death seems to be the end of the road, the ultimate weakness. But Jesus did not stay dead. His resurrection demonstrated his power over death. And through what had appeared to be weakness, Christ accomplished what no amount of human strength could ever accomplish. By his death, people are saved from eternal death and given everlasting life—if they trust him as Savior and Lord. The "foolish" people who simply accept Christ's offer are actually the wisest of all, because they alone will live eternally with God.

1:26 Remember, dear brothers and sisters, that few of you were wise in the world's eyes, or powerful, or wealthy when God called you.[NLT] Having shown the difference between God's wisdom and what people of this world call wisdom, Paul urged his readers to *remember* that few of them had any worldly achievements *when God called* them. Few would have been considered *wise in the world's eyes* (Greek, *sophoi,* referring to the intellectuals or philosophers). Few were *powerful* or influential (Greek, *dunatoi,* referring to the politicians and decision makers in government). Few were *wealthy* (Greek, *eugeneis,* literally "those of noble birth," referring to the aristocracy). Among the earliest disciples, five were fishermen, one was a tax collector, and the careers of the rest are unknown. None had the status of education or wealth (though Matthew may have had some money, he had gotten it through tax collection, not high status by any means). By using these three terms, Paul was pointing out that intellectual, political, and social position are not necessary qualifications for being chosen by God. In fact, just the opposite was true. Yet they had been called by God. Clearly, God does not seek out the people whom the world admires; instead, he reveals himself to humble and searching hearts, regardless of their worldly position. God can use us no matter what our position or status. To the worldly wise, it would have made more sense for God to call the leaders and the influential people. But God does what seems foolish to the world—he calls those who do not have these characteristics and achievements. Paul explains why in 1:27.

> I expect to be amazed by three things when I first arrive in heaven. I will be delighted by those I find are actually there. I will be shocked to note who isn't there whom I assumed I would see. And then I will be speechless with wonder as I realize that by God's grace I am there!
> *Charles Spurgeon*

SURPRISED BY HUMILITY
Strangers who hear the gospel may think that Christians are claiming superiority over them. When the gospel exposes their sin, they may feel more vulnerable than they can stand. God's answer to those people must be given with plain humility, not just clever argument. This is why we must be clear about our own sinfulness as we speak to others (see Paul's testimony in 1 Timothy 1:15-18). We share the gospel with them because we both need it. The gospel is not a message we preach down to people. Share your message compassionately, as one who has also received God's kind and undeserved forgiveness.

1:27 But God chose what is foolish in the world to shame the wise; God chose what is weak in the world to shame the strong.^{NRSV} God "called" (1:26) and *God chose*—both of these works refer to conversion, God's "call" on a person that draws him or her to salvation. God's call and choice did not go out to the high and mighty; instead, God chose *what is foolish in the world to shame the wise. . . what is weak in the world to shame the strong.* Upon those "foolish and weak" people, God showered his mercy, giving them "Christ the power of God and the wisdom of God" (1:24). God would shame those thought to be wise and strong by the world by choosing not to reveal himself to them.

This sounds strange to the world. Why would God not choose leaders and influential people who could make sweeping reforms and be followed by the masses? God does not choose as people choose. His sovereign choice is not based on anything that people can do or achieve. No amount of human knowledge or influence can replace or bypass Christ's work on the cross.

CHRIST IS THE ANSWER
Paul said: "God made Christ to be wisdom itself" (1:30 NLT). This kind of claim strikes the world as boastful. It is. Paul himself used the word—"boast." His quote from Jeremiah 9:23-24 reveals the fact that everyone's ultimate belief comes across as a boast. God pointed out to Jeremiah that there are three widely accepted human sources of boastfulness—intelligence, strength, and wealth. Each turns out to be unworthy of our ultimate trust. But God, and God alone, is worth boasting about.

Our trust in God will sometimes open us to the accusation of acting superior. When that happens, we must calmly assert that our confidence is not in ourselves. Our unashamed confidence is in God. Live with confidence. Boast in Christ.

1:28-29 God chose things despised by the world, things counted as nothing at all, and used them to bring to nothing what the world considers important, so that no one can ever boast in the presence of God.^{NLT} God chose the foolish and the weak, the *things despised by the world,* so that those chosen can never *boast in the presence of God.* This choosing of ordinary people was a major theme of the Old Testament. God used Moses (Exodus 3), Deborah (Judges 4–5), Gideon (Judges 6–8), and many other people of humble origin to show that success came through his power, not theirs. The foolish and weak can never say that God chose them because of their talent or intelligence. Instead, God chooses those who are *counted as nothing at all* by the world and turns them into great people for him. People's abilities, social standing, or knowledge have nothing to do with God's choice. Skill and wisdom do not get a person into God's kingdom—faith in Christ does—so no one can boast that his or her achievements helped him or her secure eternal life. Salvation is totally from God through Jesus' death. No one can do anything to earn salvation; people need only accept what Jesus has already done for them.

1:30-31 He is the source of your life in Christ Jesus, who became for us wisdom from God, and righteousness and sanctification and redemption, in order that, as it is written, "Let the one who boasts, boast in the Lord."^{NRSV} Here Paul reminded the Corinthian believers that God alone *is the source of . . . life in Christ Jesus.* He used the word "your," speaking directly to his audience of believers. These believers in Corinth had received eternal life in Christ Jesus, *not* because of who they were or what they did but because of Christ Jesus alone, the "source of life." God is the source of believers' existence and the reason for their personal and living relationship with Christ. Their union and identification with Christ results in having God's *wisdom* and knowledge (Colossians 2:3), possessing right standing with God (*righteousness,* 2 Corinthians 5:21), being made holy (*sanctification,* 1 Thessalonians 4:3-7), and having the penalty for their sins paid by Jesus (*redemption,* Mark 10:45).

> The design of God in making wisdom, righteousness, sanctification, and redemption dependent on union with Christ, and union with Christ dependent, not on our merit, but on His own good pleasure, is that we should glory only in Him; that is, that our confidence should be in Him and not in ourselves, and that all the glory of our salvation should be ascribed to Him and not to us.   *Charles Hodge*

Because salvation is completely by God's grace, any boasting before God is sheer nonsense. If believers must boast, they must *boast in the Lord.* These words come from Jeremiah 9:23-24 and refer to saved people glorying in the Lord's acts on their behalf. So the redeemed people of the New Testament boast not in their salvation, but in God alone, who provided that salvation through his grace alone.

1 Corinthians 2

The Corinthians were confusing the gospel by creating artificial standards of faith. They were using wisdom as the gauge. The more wisdom someone claimed, the more spiritual that person became. Standards were determined by teachers. They were arguing and dividing over which teacher had the deepest spirituality. For Paul, the gospel—God's wisdom—was a pool of clear water. Believers were urged to go deeper, but they would find living water no matter how deep they dove.

2:1-2 When I came to you, brothers and sisters, I did not come proclaiming the mystery of God to you in lofty words or wisdom. For I decided to know nothing among you except Jesus Christ, and him crucified.NRSV The words "when I came to you" refer to Paul's first visit to Corinth during his second missionary journey (A.D. 51), when he founded the church (Acts 18:1-18). As Paul had explained in chapter 1, the gospel message, by its very simplicity, appears foolish to those who think themselves wise by human standards. Paul was a brilliant scholar and could have overwhelmed his audience in Corinth with intellectual arguments, *proclaiming the mystery of God . . . in lofty words or wisdom.* While this may have led to a measure of intellectual assent, it may not have led them to saving faith. Faith that depends on clever arguments and bright oratory can be undermined if another logical argument or better orator comes along. Faith grounded in the power of the Holy Spirit, however, cannot be undermined. So Paul decided instead to "know nothing among [them] except Jesus Christ, and him crucified." Paul shared the simple message of Jesus Christ, who had been crucified for the world's sins, and let that simple message move into the Corinthians' hearts by the power of the Holy Spirit (2:4). In sharing the gospel with others, believers should follow Paul's example and keep the message simple and basic. The power of the gospel message is not found in a preacher's eloquent use of words or ability to logically argue every detail. The power lies in the message itself: "Jesus Christ, and him crucified" for sin.

POWERFUL MESSAGE, POWERLESS MESSENGER
As Paul described his founding visit among the Corinthians
(Acts 18:1-18), he reminded them of his unimpressive personal
performance. His words had been plain and his physical
appearance less than forceful. He certainly remembered
himself as a person driven by a message, facing an intimidating
environment. He "kept it simple." The Corinthians had
responded. They were living examples of the power of the
gospel.

While believers cannot rival Paul's training or match his
experiences, they must still communicate the gospel in a
hostile world. When they try, they quickly learn about feeling
insignificant. The resistance is real. But Paul's example offers
two valuable lessons as we share the gospel. (1) Feelings of
confidence or insecurity should not be the motivation to
communicate. Personal gratitude and obedience to Christ as
well as compassion for others must drive our witnessing.
(2) The power of the gospel does not depend on the skill or
charisma of the speaker; it flows from God's Spirit, convincing
persons of the truth. Share what you know about Christ with
others and let the feelings take care of themselves.

2:3-4 **I came to you in weakness—timid and trembling. And my
message and my preaching were very plain. I did not use wise
and persuasive speeches, but the Holy Spirit was powerful
among you.**[NLT] Paul came to Corinth not as a powerful preacher
and debater ready to take on the city but, rather, *in weakness—
timid and trembling*. His attitude was not fearful, but utterly dependent upon God for the important task of bringing the gospel
into this wicked and idolatrous city. Prior to coming to Corinth,
Paul had faced many discouraging ministry events. At Philippi,
his ministry started strong but was nearly ruined by Jewish opposition (this also occurred in Thessalonica and Berea). In Athens,
Paul had very little positive results. It would have been very dis-
heartening. Paul's confidence was not in his keen intellect or
debating ability but in his knowledge that the Holy Spirit was
helping and guiding him. Paul was not denying the importance of
study and preparation for preaching—he had a thorough education in the Scriptures. He did not depend, however, on using *wise
and persuasive speeches* to change people's hearts. That would
happen only by the work of the *Holy Spirit* among them.

God is completely sovereign in this process that seems foolish
to the world—from the way God chose to accomplish salvation
(through the cross, 1:18-25), to the people he chose to draw to
himself (such as those hearing this letter, 1:26-31), and then to
the one who brought the message (Paul, 2:1-5). A "weak"
preacher with a *plain* message to an audience of "lower-class" or

"nonintellectual" people seemed like a recipe for disaster. But with God's sovereignty and the Holy Spirit's power, a body of believers grew up and stood up to the surrounding sinfulness and idolatry of Corinth.

Paul mentioned that the Holy Spirit had been powerful among them (Paul's preaching had come "with a demonstration of the Spirit's power," NIV). What exactly had occurred is unrecorded, but Paul may have been referring to their conversion, the receiving of the Holy Spirit upon conversion, and the gifts bestowed by the Holy Spirit on the Corinthian believers (the ability to speak in tongues, for example, as well as other gifts that Paul will discuss at length later in this letter). Paul's point was that the power of their conversion was not through him and his preaching but through the Holy Spirit.

2:5 I did this so that you might trust the power of God rather than human wisdom.NLT Paul deliberately chose *not* to use the style of persuasion and oratory that so fascinated those in the Greek world. Instead, he brought a simple message that depended upon the Holy Spirit's power for its effectiveness. Paul did not want his listeners focusing on the speech he gave, or how he presented it, or whatever other brand of *human wisdom* might have been used to persuade the Corinthians to believe. Instead, Paul wanted them to trust in the simple message and so *trust the power of God* for their salvation. See also Romans 1:16 for Paul's description of the gospel as God's "power." The Greek word translated "power" is *dunamei* in this verse; in Romans 1:16 it is *dunamis*.

SPIRITUAL LINEAGE
The Corinthian believers admired impressive teachers. Some had come to faith through the ministry of Paul. Others learned of salvation through Peter. Still others had been called to discipleship by the charismatic Apollos. But many of them were doing what Paul had tried to prevent when he first visited the city. He knew their faith must not "rest" on the all-too-weak vehicles that God had used to reach them but on God's power.

Believers honor those who have passed on to them the priceless Good News. New Christians, very much like newborns, rely heavily on those who have introduced them to Christ. But healthy spiritual growth depends on a faith rooted in Christ. Mature believers eventually become spiritual peers of their teachers. We continue to respect and appreciate those who brought us to Christ, but we also find ways to help them. How have you met specific needs of those who brought you the gospel?

2:6-7 Yet when I am among mature Christians, I do speak with words of wisdom, but not the kind of wisdom that belongs to this world, and not the kind that appeals to the rulers of this world, who are being brought to nothing. No, the wisdom we speak of is the secret wisdom of God, which was hidden in former times, though he made it for our benefit before the world began.NLT The Corinthians were accustomed to philosophical debate—whether engaging in it or simply listening to it. But, as Paul already noted, he did not come to them with philosophy, he came with the simple gospel message. When Paul did not entertain his listeners with *words of wisdom* (referring to philosophical debate), many criticized him, considering him unlearned and his message unimportant. Paul was not teaching a philosophy, however, nor was he debating speculative notions, for these never saved anyone. Such wisdom, wrote Paul, *the kind of wisdom that belongs to this world . . . the kind that appeals to the rulers of this world,* offers nothing. Who are "the rulers of this world"? Some have taught that these are demonic powers, or leaders who are demon inspired. Based on 2:8, however, this probably refers to those who participated in Jesus' crucifixion. Paul didn't bother with the worldly wisdom that would impress them.

Instead, when he was *among mature Christians,* Paul did *speak with words of wisdom,* but this was the highest wisdom because it came from God. The "mature" Christians were not those with advanced training but those who had been enlightened by the Holy Spirit and had received salvation, as contrasted with those who had rejected it (1:21-23; 2:14). Because of the Holy Spirit's guidance, believers could grasp this *secret wisdom of God, which was hidden in former times.* "Secret wisdom" refers to God's offer of salvation to all people made available through Jesus' death on the cross. This plan was "secret" because only through God's wisdom and the insight given by his Spirit can people begin to comprehend it. Attempting to understand this plan with human wisdom and through philosophical discussions will take people nowhere. Only God, through the Holy Spirit, can reveal it (2:10).

This plan had been *made . . . for our benefit before the world began.* In other words, God knew the entire cycle of the creation, fall, and salvation through his Son before he made the earth and placed Adam and Eve on it. This beneficial "secret wisdom" is literally "for our glory" (NIV). This reveals God's great plan for the human race—that despite the Fall, he would bring some to glory.

THE ORIGINAL PLAN
Paul understood that the Corinthians were fascinated with
wisdom. But he pointed out that their attraction was for the
current, popular, temporary "wisdom" rather than the timeless
wisdom of God.

The Corinthians mistakenly thought they could outgrow the
simple message of Christ. Worldly wisdom, which only
analyzes Jesus' life, halts at the cross. In that shortsighted
view, the great teacher had come to a tragic end. But God's
wisdom makes Christ, the cross, and the Resurrection central.

Beware of any teaching, no matter how fascinating, that
seeks to add to what Jesus accomplished. All that God has
revealed still begins and ends with Christ.

**2:8 None of the rulers of this age understood this; for if they
had, they would not have crucified the Lord of glory.**^{NRSV}
This "secret plan" had not been revealed to *the rulers of this
age* (those who are impressed by worldly wisdom, 2:6). "Rulers" refers to the rulers in Palestine (the Pharisees, Sadducees,
King Herod) and the Roman rulers (such as Pilate and the soldiers under his command). If these leaders had truly understood
who Jesus was and the eternal consequences of rejecting him,
they would not have crucified the Lord of glory. This is at the
heart of Paul's irony: The very ones who were trying to kill
Jesus were actually carrying out God's will. Thinking they
were getting rid of a nuisance—Jesus of Nazareth—they were
really crucifying the very Lord of glory, God incarnate. Jesus
was misunderstood and killed by those whom the world considered wise and powerful.

**2:9-10 However, as it is written: "No eye has seen, no ear has heard,
no mind has conceived what God has prepared for those who
love him"—but God has revealed it to us by his Spirit. The
Spirit searches all things, even the deep things of God.**^{NIV} The
phrase "as it is written" usually refers the reader to an Old Testament passage. Here, however, Paul seems more to have general-
ized an Old Testament theme, as references such as Psalm 31:20;
Isaiah 52:15; 64:4; 65:17 suggest. Paul's point is that human
senses and understanding cannot begin to comprehend *what God
has prepared for those who love him.* The future blessings that
believers will enjoy in heaven are beyond human understanding;
nevertheless, Christians believe and trust in these promises
because *God has revealed it to [them] by his Spirit.* Most likely,
the phrase "revealed it to us" refers to all believers who have
received the Holy Spirit and, thus, can understand from Scripture
the wonderful future that God is preparing for them.

Paul was explaining to the Corinthian believers that they had become very different from their unbelieving neighbors—essentially different because of the entrance of the Holy Spirit into their lives. The Holy Spirit, as God, reveals God to people. Human beings, through the Holy Spirit, can get some glimpses of what God has planned for his people.

Who is the Holy Spirit? God is three persons in one—the Father, the Son, and the Holy Spirit. God became a man in Jesus so that Jesus could die for our sins. Jesus rose from the dead to offer salvation to all people through spiritual renewal and rebirth. When Jesus ascended into heaven, his physical presence left the earth, but he promised to send the Holy Spirit so that his spiritual presence would still be among mankind (see Luke 24:49). The Holy Spirit first became available to the apostles on the day of the Resurrection (John 20:22) and then to more believers on the day of Pentecost (Acts 2). In the Old Testament, the Holy Spirit empowered specific individuals for specific purposes, but now all believers have the power of the Holy Spirit available to them. For more on the Holy Spirit, read John 14:16-28; Romans 8:9; 1 Corinthians 12:13; and 2 Corinthians 1:22.

The statement "the Spirit searches all things, even the deep things of God" means that only the Spirit can reveal to believers God's profound nature and wonderful plan, especially that formerly hidden mystery that is now revealed—salvation through Jesus' death and resurrection. That the Spirit "searches" these things means that he penetrates and is part of all the "deep things" of God (see 2:11).

BEYOND IMAGINATION

We cannot imagine all that God has in store for us, both in this life and for eternity. He will create a new heaven and a new earth (Isaiah 65:17; Revelation 21:1), and we will live with him forever. Until then, his Holy Spirit comforts and guides us. Knowing the wonderful and eternal future that awaits us gives us hope and courage to press on in this life, to endure hardship, and to avoid giving in to temptation. This world is not all there is. The best is yet to come.

We don't know the details of heaven. At best, God's Word provides a breathtaking glimpse. But we are confident that Christ has great blessings in store for all who trust him. We rightly reject any idea that makes heaven small, boring, gaudy, or trite. Instead, our thoughts of heaven begin with the fact that we will be with Christ (John 14:3). Challenge your mental picture of heaven with the footnote: Whatever I can imagine will be little more than a hint of what God can do.

**2:11 No one can know what anyone else is really thinking except
that person alone, and no one can know God's thoughts
except God's own Spirit.**^{NLT} Paul compared the Spirit's understanding of God with a person's understanding of himself or herself. Just as a person cannot penetrate another person's thought
processes, so *no one can know God's thoughts except God's own
Spirit.* The only way to know God is to know his Holy Spirit, to
have him in one's life. The only way to obtain the Holy Spirit is
to accept, by faith, the sacrifice of Christ on the cross. The Holy
Spirit is a distinct person, yet one in essence and function with
God the Father. The mystery of the Trinity—Father, Son, and
Holy Spirit—begins to unfold in verses such as this. Jesus told
his disciples, at the Last Supper:

> *"But I will send you the Counselor—the Spirit of truth. He will
> come to you from the Father and will tell you all about me. . . .
> It is actually best for you that I go away, because if I don't, the
> Counselor won't come. If I do go away, he will come because I
> will send him to you. And when he comes, he will convince the
> world of its sin, and of God's righteousness, and of the coming
> judgment. . . . When the Spirit of truth comes, he will guide you
> into all truth. He will not be presenting his own ideas; he will
> be telling you what he has heard. He will tell you about the
> future. He will bring me glory by revealing to you whatever he
> receives from me. All that the Father has is mine; this is what I
> mean when I say that the Spirit will reveal to you whatever he
> receives from me." (John 15:26; 16:7-8, 13-15* NLT)

KNOWING GOD
Paul challenged the Corinthians to consider the true source of
their knowledge and experience of God. They were arguing
over personalities and forgetting that God reveals himself to
people by the Spirit. They needed a renewed perspective.
     The greatest teachers never tell more about God than they
have received, nor do they stop being human themselves. They
are part of God's training program, but they cannot replace the
Spirit of God. The daily personal disciplines of the Christian
life—prayer, study of the Scriptures, obedient actions—all
require time and attention. But their effectiveness depends on
our reliance on God's Spirit. Ask the Holy Spirit to keep
reminding you of his presence.

**2:12 We have not received the spirit of the world but the Spirit
who is from God, that we may understand what God has
freely given us.**^{NIV} The word "we" contrasts the believers with

unbelievers. The rest of the verse contrasts their source of power and wisdom. Believers *have not received the spirit of the world.* The "spirit of the world" is contrasted with the Holy Spirit. This should not be interpreted to mean that there is a force equal and opposite to God or the Holy Spirit. Rather, this points out that the Holy Spirit's wisdom and power come from God, not from any earthly source. The "spirit of the world" has been taken to refer to Satan or a demon, but it refers to the wisdom of this age (2:6) and the wisdom of this world (1:20; 3:19), referring to human effort and philosophy. In context, this means both that believers do not depend on worldly wisdom and also that the Spirit they *have* received is not of this world. Instead, believers have received *the Spirit who is from God* (Galatians 3:5). Jesus had told his disciples that God would send the Spirit after his return to heaven. According to the Gospel of John (quoted above), Jesus had explained some of the reasons why the Spirit would come, including that believers would *understand what God has freely given* them. What God "freely gave" was salvation through the death of his Son. The understanding of the salvation that had been accomplished through Jesus' death would come to the believers as the Holy Spirit revealed it to them.

2:13 **When we tell you this, we do not use words of human wisdom. We speak words given to us by the Spirit, using the Spirit's words to explain spiritual truths.**[NLT] Paul may have had some critics in Corinth—the philosophers and orators who had been unimpressed with his message. Here Paul explained that the gospel message had not been given with *words of human wisdom* because no human wisdom can adequately explain God's wisdom. In order to speak the Spirit's message, believers must *speak words given to us by the Spirit.* In order to *explain spiritual truths,* believers must use *the Spirit's words.* Paul's words are authoritative because their source was the Holy Spirit. Paul was not merely giving his own personal views or his personal impression of what God had said. Under the inspiration of the Holy Spirit, he was writing the very thoughts and words of God. Today, all believers pass along the gospel message—trusting in God's Spirit to speak the spiritual truths. This was what Paul had preached, how the Corinthians had believed, and how they could spread the message.

2:14 **But people who aren't Christians can't understand these truths from God's Spirit. It all sounds foolish to them because only those who have the Spirit can understand what the Spirit means.**[NLT] The gospel sounded foolish to many in Corinth, just as it is scoffed at by many today. This should not come as a surprise. Non-Christians cannot fully understand God; thus they cannot grasp the concept that God's Spirit lives in believers. Just as a tone-deaf person cannot appreciate fine music fully, the person who rejects God cannot understand God's beautiful message. With the lines

> The unspiritual are out of court as religious critics; they are deaf men judging music.
>
> *Charles Finney*

of communication broken, a person is not able to hear what God is saying to him or her. Paul highlighted these truths about these nonbelievers: (1) They *can't understand these truths;* (2) the spiritual truths all sound *foolish to them;* and (3) they do not have the Spirit.

Unbelievers simply cannot comprehend Christ's work on the cross, see the beauty and compassion of God's divine plan, or desire to know God at all. These truths are "spiritually discerned" (NRSV). To "discern" means to examine and scrutinize. All of these mysteries remain as mere foolishness to them because the ability to comprehend, love, and glory in these realities comes directly from the Holy Spirit. For more on discernment, see Romans 8:5-9; Hebrews 5:14; James 1:5 .

SPIRITUAL DISCERNMENT
Everyone wants to be wise. Yet Paul taught the Corinthians that true wisdom or discernment requires the believer to be guided by the Holy Spirit. Because Satan's greatest impact on us occurs when he deceives us, we need the Holy Spirit's help. Spiritual discernment enables us to draw conclusions based on God's perspective, make wise decisions in difficult circumstances, recognize the activities of God's Spirit, distinguish the correct and incorrect use of Scripture, and identify and expose false teachers. Ask God to give you his discernment as you serve him. Let that discernment guide you in your daily walk.

2:15-16 **Those who are spiritual discern all things, and they are themselves subject to no one else's scrutiny. "For who has known the mind of the Lord so as to instruct him?" But we have the mind of Christ.**NRSV Because believers have the Spirit, they *discern all things.* They are able to make right judgments—not necessarily about all matters, but certainly about spiritual matters such as salvation or God's future blessings, and they will be able to make the necessary discernments regarding them. Believers *are themselves subject to no one else's scrutiny,* meaning that nonbelievers have no authority by which to judge what Christians believe. Nonbelievers can make no judgment of spiritual matters because they do not have the Spirit. Therefore, they can make no judgment of spiritual people for the same reason. Paul quoted from Isaiah 40:13 to show that a Christian is not subject to nonbelievers' judgments about spiritual matters: *"For who has known the mind of the Lord so as to instruct him?"* To judge believers' faith in salvation by the cross is to judge the Lord's wisdom. Paul wondered who was ready to take human wisdom up against God's wisdom. Who among the detractors knew the mind of the Lord so as to bypass the simple message of the cross?

In contrast to those who do not have the Spirit and do not know the mind of the Lord, believers do *have the mind of Christ.* Believers understand fully, as did Christ himself, the significance of the cross and what it meant for mankind's salvation.

No one can completely comprehend God (Romans 11:34), but through the guidance of the Holy Spirit, believers can understand spiritual truths. Believers have insight into some of God's plans, thoughts, and actions because, with the Spirit within, they have access to the mind of Christ. Through the Holy Spirit, believers can begin to know God's thoughts, talk with him, and expect his answers to their prayers. Paul could allow his detractors in Corinth to jeer at him, for they had no right to make judgments on him or his message—because he had the mind of Christ and they did not.

COMMUNICATING
Because non-Christians cannot understand God, they cannot grasp the concept that God's Spirit lives in believers. Don't expect most people to understand or approve of your decision to follow Christ. It all seems so silly to them. Just as a tone-deaf person cannot appreciate fine music fully, the person who rejects God cannot understand God's beautiful message. With the lines of communication broken, he or she won't be able to hear what God is saying to him or her.

We must not remain silent, using others' difficulty in understanding as an excuse. We are still one of God's communication channels. We must be alert to opportunities. Another person's question may be evidence that God's Spirit is drawing him or her to the point of decision. How would you respond today if someone asked you about your faith?

---

1 Corinthians 3

The Corinthians needed to mature in their spiritual lives. They were allowing themselves to be divided into factions regarding which preacher they liked better. These divisions in the church threatened the unity they would need in order to stand for the truth against false teachers and persecution.

GROWTH PATTERN
Paul called the Corinthians infants in the Christian life because they were not yet spiritually healthy and mature. The proof was that they were comparing themselves to one another and competing for recognition like children. This had led to divisions among Christians.

Immature believers often continue to live in "worldly" thought patterns, controlled by their own desires; mature believers are more in tune with God's desires. How much influence do your desires have on your life? To what degree have you allowed God's Word and God's Spirit to rewrite your personal desires? Seek to make God's desires your own. Being controlled by your own desires will stunt your growth.

3:1 Dear brothers and sisters, when I was with you I couldn't talk to you as I would to mature Christians. I had to talk as though you belonged to this world or as though you were infants in the Christian life.^{NLT} Continuing to speak to the believers in the church (the brothers and sisters), Paul reproved them for their lack of maturity in the faith. Instead of growing in the faith, they had let themselves be diverted into quarrels and factions so that Paul could not even talk to them as he *would to mature Christians* (literally, "spiritual"). He had to talk to them in his letters *as though [they] belonged to this world or as though [they] were infants in the Christian life.* Paul was not accusing the Corinthians of being carnal (or "worldly"); he was saying that their behavior was sinful in comparison to that of the mature believers. They were indwelt by the Spirit, for they could not be Christians without the Holy Spirit (see Romans 8:9; Galatians 3:2-3). But these "infants"

had not grown in the faith because they were acting like the
world around them. The proof was that they quarreled like children, allowing divisions to distract them—as noted in the following verses.

**3:2-3 I had to feed you with milk and not with solid food, because
you couldn't handle anything stronger. And you still aren't
ready, for you are still controlled by your own sinful desires.
You are jealous of one another and quarrel with each other.
Doesn't that prove you are controlled by your own desires?
You are acting like people who don't belong to the Lord.**NLT
These believers in Corinth should have long since grown out of
the "infant" stage and been maturing in their faith. Instead, they
were still acting like "infants" (3:1), so Paul had to *feed* them
(teach them) *with milk and not with solid food*—meaning that he
had to continue to give them the basics of the faith instead of
being able to teach them deeper truths (Hebrews 5:12; 1 Peter
2:2). Just as babies drink only milk because they cannot eat solid
food, so these "baby Christians" had to keep relearning the basics
and *couldn't handle anything stronger.* He had to teach them
according to their spiritual capacity. Paul longed to teach them
deeper truths, but he realized that they weren't ready because
they were still influenced by the world. For *sinful desires* (also
translated "carnal desires"), Paul used the term *sarkikos,* from
sarks, meaning "flesh" or "selfish human nature," to indicate that
their mind-set was worldly, characterized by selfish desires and
not the desires of the Spirit. Their jealousy and quarreling proved
it. Instead of acting different from the world because of their salvation through Christ, they continued to act *like people who don't
belong to the Lord.* They were believers, but they were spiritually
immature. By remaining immature and allowing that immaturity
to divide them, they were wreaking havoc on the church. To the
Galatians, Paul wrote, "So I say, live by the Spirit, and you will
not gratify the desires of the sinful nature" (Galatians 5:16 NIV).
James wrote, "What causes fights and quarrels among you?
Don't they come from your desires that battle within you?"
(James 4:1 NIV). Paul would not allow divisions and quarreling to
destroy the church in Corinth; thus, he did not shrink from rebuk-
ing it.

**3:4-5 When one of you says, "I am a follower of Paul," and another
says, "I prefer Apollos," aren't you acting like those who are
not Christians? Who is Apollos, and who is Paul, that we
should be the cause of such quarrels? Why, we're only servants. Through us God caused you to believe. Each of us did
the work the Lord gave us.**NLT As already mentioned in 1:12-13,

the cause of the divisions and quarrels had to do with loyalty to
different teachers. In 1:12, Paul also mentioned Peter; here he
focused on the two men who had actually preached and taught in
Corinth—himself and Apollos (for more about Apollos and why
the believers had splintered into these factions, see commentary
on 1:12). The believers had split up, some being followers of
Paul, others preferring Apollos. Paul was pointing out that to act
that way was to act *like those who are not Christians.* Apollos and
Paul were no more than servants of God who brought the message of salvation to the Corinthians. Both men *did the work the
Lord gave* them to do, and through their preaching, *God caused
[the Corinthians] to believe.* As mere servants of the Lord, they
had pointed the people toward Christ, not toward themselves.
Neither Paul nor Apollos wanted a party of followers; they
wanted the people to believe in Jesus Christ for salvation and to
grow up to maturity in faith. That is the goal of any good
preacher.

TEAMWORK
God's work requires many different individuals with a variety of
gifts and abilities. There are few superstars; instead, many
team members are needed to serve in their special roles. The
effectiveness of one member depends in a large way on the
effectiveness of all. We may see only partial results from our
individual efforts. We can even misunderstand God's purposes
or overemphasize our role. Only God, who makes things grow
(3:6), sees the whole picture.
   We can become useful members of God's team by not
seeking personal acclaim for what we do. Don't seek the praise
that comes from people—it is comparatively worthless. Instead,
seek approval from God.

**3:6-7 My job was to plant the seed in your hearts, and Apollos
watered it, but it was God, not we, who made it grow. The
ones who do the planting or watering aren't important, but
God is important because he is the one who makes the seed
grow.**[NLT] Part of the reason for the factions may have been the different jobs Paul and Apollos had done in Corinth ("the work the
Lord" gave them, 3:5). Paul planted the seed of the gospel message in the believers' hearts. He was a missionary pioneer, the
first to bring the message of salvation, and the founder of the
church in Corinth. Apollos's role was to water—to help the
believers grow stronger in the faith. Paul had founded the church
in Corinth; then Apollos had built on that foundation. Unfortunately, some of the believers in Corinth had split into factions

that pledged loyalty to Paul, the "planter," or to Apollos, the "waterer."

Paul explained to these loyal believers that they had misplaced their loyalties. Paul and Apollos had only done what God had told them to do. Paul had planted the seed and Apollos had watered it; but they did not make the "seed of faith" grow— *it was God . . . who made it grow.* In fact, compared to God's role in the process, *the ones who do the planting or watering aren't important, but God is important because he is the one who makes the seed grow.* Paul, Apollos, Peter, and any missionary or minister of the gospel is nothing more than God's instrument. God alone brings the seed to fruition. Thus, there is no room for pride on the part of these leaders, and there is no room for divisive loyalty toward these leaders on the part of the followers.

GOD'S SERVANTS
After the preachers' work is completed, God keeps on making Christians grow. Christian leaders should certainly be respected, but we should never place them on pedestals that create barriers between people or set them up as a substitute for Christ. If one pastor or minister was instrumental in your coming to Christ, thank the Lord. If another who has taken his place doesn't seem as exciting or treat you with special attention, thank God for the work God gave each minister to do. Focus on God, not on his servants.

3:8-9 **The one who plants and the one who waters work as a team with the same purpose. Yet they will be rewarded individually, according to their own hard work. We work together as partners who belong to God. You are God's field, God's building—not ours.**[NLT] While each servant has various functions—Paul planted (originally brought the gospel message) and Apollos watered (continued in teaching)—each one was a team member with a common goal. Their goal was the same— to bring people into God's kingdom and to see them mature in their faith. Yet, that being said, each servant is still individually responsible for his or her work—*they will be rewarded individually, according to their own hard work.* For more on how God rewards our work, see 1 Corinthians 4:5. Paul will explain this comment in more detail in the following verses. For more on how God rewards believers, see 4:5; Ephesians 6:8; Colossians 3:23; Hebrews 11:6. For Jesus' words on rewards, see the chart in Matthew 16:27 in the Life Application Commentary *Matthew.*

Paul and the other preachers and teachers of the true gospel message worked together *as partners who belong to God.* Their ministry belonged not to them, but to God. For more on "partners" *(sunergoi),* see 2 Corinthians 8:23; Philippians 2:25; Colossians 4:11; 1 Thessalonians 3:2. For more on *God's building,* see 3:17.

3:10-11 According to the grace of God given to me, like a skilled master builder I laid a foundation, and someone else is building on it. Each builder must choose with care how to build on it. For no one can lay any foundation other than the one that has been laid; that foundation is Jesus Christ.[NRSV] Paul had been called by God to be an apostle and to take the gospel message to the Gentiles (see 1:1; Acts 9:15). God gave him the grace for this message, and, *like a skilled master builder,* he was doing what God had called him to do. He *laid a foundation,* meaning that he took the message of Jesus Christ to these people. The foundation of the church—of all believers—is *Jesus Christ,* and *no one can lay any foundation other than the one that has been laid.* Paul had carefully laid that foundation, having taught the truth of the gospel message (as already described in chapters 1–2). On that foundation, *someone else* (referring to Apollos) was *building on it.* Because each of God's workers will be rewarded individually according to his or her own hard work (3:8), *each builder must choose with care how to build on* that foundation. Paul will discuss this further in 3:12-13. Paul was not criticizing Apollos but was explaining that any builder must be careful. All true believers have the gospel message as their foundation, and each one is building on that foundation. This "building" probably refers to the church, to sound teaching, and to each individual's Christian character. Only the truth can build strong character in the believers and thus build a strong church. The foundation may be strong, but a variety of materials might be chosen in the building process, as Paul describes further.

> If you wish to be a leader you will be frustrated, for very few people wish to be led. If you aim to be a servant you will never be frustrated. *Frank F. Warren*

Jesus ended his Sermon on the Mount with the same picture Paul used here (Matthew 7:24-27). Jesus compared two kinds of life: one constructed on the knowledge and application of his words; the other constructed without regard for Christ. Both houses can be built, but only one will stand up to the winds and storms of life.

LASTING FOUNDATION
The foundation of the church—of all believers—is Jesus Christ. Nothing and no one else will do, wrote Paul. A building with no foundation, or one poorly constructed, will not last. The finest materials used to construct a home quickly rot and fall apart if they are resting on the ground. And a building is only as solid as its foundation. The foundation of our lives is Jesus Christ; he is our base, our reason for being. Everything we are and do must fit into the pattern provided by him. Are you building your life on the only real and lasting foundation, or are you building on a faulty foundation such as wealth, security, success, or fame? Be careful how you build.

3:12-13 **Now anyone who builds on that foundation may use gold, silver, jewels, wood, hay, or straw.**[NLT] The foundation for the building is Jesus Christ (3:11); Christians build on this foundation with a variety of materials of different quality. There is little value in attempting to find a meaning behind each of the materials Paul mentioned; most likely, he was dividing the materials into two basic classes— the valuable building materials, which were imperishable (here called *gold, silver,* and *jewels*), and the worthless building materials, which probably symbolize worldly wisdom (here called *wood, hay,* and *straw*). A workman who recognizes the quality of the foundation will build with valuable materials so that the building is beautiful, strong, and lasting. A workman who does not value the foundation will not care about the quality or longevity of the building and so will build with worthless materials. Paul was particularly speaking to church leaders or ministers who were responsible to build their churches with the truth of Christ, as opposed to teachings based on the values and desires of the world.

CONSTRUCTION MATERIALS
While some have applied these verses to personal spiritual growth, Paul's teaching has to do with ministry to others. What do we do to build others up? Do we build on Christ as foundation? Do we build with perishable materials? The Corinthians could construct their church with lasting, eternal teaching or with the changing, temporary wisdom of the day.
Paul's words challenge our methods of discipleship. Do we attach others to ourselves as the foundation, or to Christ? Do we use our abilities and spiritual gifts to build up others in the church or keep them tied to us? Do we use Bible-based teaching or merely adaptations of worldly wisdom?

But there is going to come a time of testing at the judgment day to see what kind of work each builder has done. Every-

one's work will be put through the fire to see whether or not it keeps its value.^{NLT} This "time of testing" that is coming "at the judgment day" refers to Christ's second coming. At that time, believers will be separated from unbelievers, with believers receiving their promised reward in heaven (1 Thessalonians 5:2-9). Believers will not be judged regarding their salvation—their salvation is sure—but they will be judged *to see what kind of work* they have done. *Everyone's work will be put through the fire to see whether or not it keeps its value.* "Fire" pictures a scorching test that will reveal the value of the "building." Those made with gold, silver, and precious gems will stand up to this test; those thrown together with wood, hay, and straw will go up in flames and be destroyed.

Christ will evaluate each minister's contribution to the life of the church, and the judgment day will reveal the sincerity of each person's work. God will determine whether or not each person has been faithful to Jesus' instructions. Good work will be rewarded; unfaithful or inferior work will be burned up. In the church built on Jesus Christ, each member will be mature, spiritually sensitive, and doctrinally sound. The Corinthian church, however, was filled with those whose work was "wood, hay, or straw," members who were immature, insensitive to one another, and vulnerable to wrong doctrine (3:1-4).

LOST IN THE MAZE
It is so easy for churches and ministries to build on Christ's solid foundation with faulty methods and materials. Christian leaders rush to incorporate secular principles and philosophies to try to run the church. While we must be open to modern methods of communication, stewardship, and leadership, we must not be enthralled with modern information and methods too quickly. Test these principles against God's Word; use discernment to assess the validity of all that you teach.

3:14-15 If what has been built on the foundation survives, the builder will receive a reward. If the work is burned up, the builder will suffer loss; the builder will be saved, but only as through fire.^{NRSV} Because the foundation is Jesus Christ, everyone who builds on that foundation *will be saved.* But these believers will present to God the lives that they have lived for him. Some of them will present lives of gold, silver, and jewels—lives built on the truth of the gospel and spent in sacrifice and service to God. These builders *will receive a reward* (see 3:8). Some will present lives that amount to no more than wood, hay, and straw, and all that they did and accomplished in this world will be *burned up.*

These builders *will be saved, but only as through fire,* as if they jumped out of a burning building and lost everything but their lives. They will enter heaven but will not receive the same reward as those who built well.

3:16 **Do you not know that you are the temple of God and that the Spirit of God dwells in you?**NKJV God's people, all believers in Jesus Christ, *are the temple of God.* Not only that, but *the Spirit of God dwells in* them. While it is true that each individual is a "temple of the Holy Spirit" (6:19), Paul was teaching here about the nature of the church or Christian community. This is a common theme in the New Testament (verses quoted from NIV, italics ours):

- "What agreement is there between the temple of God and idols? For we are the *temple* of the living God. As God has said: 'I will live with them and walk among them, and I will be their God, and they will be my people'" (2 Corinthians 6:16).
- "And in him you too are being built together to become a *dwelling* in which God lives by his Spirit" (Ephesians 2:22).
- "But Christ is faithful as a son over God's house. And we are his *house,* if we hold on to our courage and the hope of which we boast" (Hebrews 3:6).
- "You also, like living stones, are being built into a *spiritual house* to be a holy priesthood, offering spiritual sacrifices acceptable to God through Jesus Christ" (1 Peter 2:5).

GOD'S WORK SITE
We are accustomed to reading these phrases ("you are the temple of God" and "the Spirit of God dwells in you") as if the grammar were singular. Perhaps a southern expression would help us get the point—"y'all are God's temple." Paul wanted the Corinthians to think more as a unified assembly and less as a collection of competing interests or independent individuals. He was emphasizing the intent of Jesus' prayer in John 17:21-23 that believers be unified in God. What actions could you take this week to strengthen your ties to fellow Christians in the church of Jesus Christ?

Corinth boasted many pagan temples and shrines, but there was only one temple for God—the Corinthian Christians were it! The "Spirit of God" is the Holy Spirit, whom Jesus promised would come and live in his followers (John 14:17-20; 16:7). The Holy Spirit draws all believers together as Christ's body on earth; he provides the unity that should characterize them. Because every believer is a temple for the Holy Spirit (a dwelling place for him),

the believers ought not be dividing into warring factions because
that destroys the temple, as the following verses emphasize.

**3:17 If anyone destroys God's temple, God will destroy that per-
son. For God's temple is holy, and you are that temple.**^{NRSV} In
the Old Testament, the penalty for defiling God's dwelling
(whether the tabernacle or the temple) was death (Leviticus
15:31) or separation from the nation (Numbers 19:20). The penalty for destroying God's spiritual temple—found in his people
individually and in the church collectively—is no less severe. *If
anyone destroys God's temple,* wrote Paul, *God will destroy that
person* because God's temple is holy. Anyone who destroys it
will face God's judgment. How might anyone attempt to destroy
God's temple? False teaching that undermines believers' faith,
rivalry that creates dissension and rips churches apart, and weak
discipleship that promotes easy-believism are all problems that
weaken the church's foundation. In 3:15, Paul wrote of the
builder who, though he or she builds shoddily on the foundation,
will yet be saved. This verse focuses on those who, already
unsaved, set out to destroy those who are saved—such as the
false teachers. God will destroy them because of their sin.

**3:18 Stop fooling yourselves. If you think you are wise by this
world's standards, you will have to become a fool so you can
become wise by God's standards.**^{NLT} Thus far, most of Paul's letter has focused on the difference between the world's wisdom
and God's wisdom (see 1:17–2:16). Some of the Corinthian
believers had been fooled into thinking that they needed special
knowledge or deeper wisdom in order to be saved—that Jesus'
death wasn't enough for salvation. Paul admonished them to *stop
fooling* themselves. If they continued to think that they were *wise
by this world's standards,* they were fooling themselves.

     Some people have used Paul's teaching here to rail against any
study of philosophy or even higher learning in general. But Paul
was not promoting the abandonment of reason. Paul was counter-
ing the Corinthians' use of rhetoric and debate (the "world's standards") to uphold their own divisive positions. He was warning
them that God's way of thinking is infinitely more valuable, even
though it may seem foolish to the world (1:27). They would need
to empty themselves of their pride in human wisdom in order to
be filled with God's wisdom.

**3:19-20 For the wisdom of this world is foolishness in God's sight. As it
is written: "He catches the wise in their craftiness"; and again,
"The Lord knows that the thoughts of the wise are futile."**^{NIV} In
1:18, Paul had stated that "the message of the cross is foolishness to

those who are perishing" (NIV); here he stated the flip side—*the wisdom of this world is foolishness in God's sight.* Two Old Testament Scriptures are used to back up his statement. The first comes from Job 5:12, where God is the one who *catches the wise in their craftiness.* In this case, the "wise" were the worldly-wise. The other reference comes from Psalm 94:11, again speaking of the worldly-wise ones, warning them that *the Lord knows that the thoughts of the wise are futile.* No matter how wise a human being may appear, God is far wiser. Nothing that a "wise" human being can do is beyond God's understanding. God knows the thoughts of everyone. What these wise people will accomplish is futile because it concerns this world alone and will pass away.

3:21-23 So don't take pride in following a particular leader. Everything belongs to you: Paul and Apollos and Peter; the whole world and life and death; the present and the future. Everything belongs to you, and you belong to Christ, and Christ belongs to God.NLT Therefore, the Corinthian believers ought not *take pride in following a particular leader,* such as *Paul and Apollos and Peter* (see also 1:11-12; 2:4-7). Believers must not place their faith in human leaders; instead, they must follow Christ Jesus alone. The phrase "everything belongs to you" underscores the fact that all believers have everything because they have Christ. They need not boast about following any particular leader because they would be limiting themselves. Indeed, *all* those leaders already belonged to them because, Paul exclaimed, *the whole world and life and death; the present and the future . . . everything belongs to you.* They owned it all by association—everything belonged to them because they *belong to Christ, and Christ belongs to God.*

The "whole world" refers to the physical world, not to the ethical system (as in 1:20). Believers have true "life" because life only has meaning when lived for Christ. While nonbelievers are victims of life, swept along by its current and wondering if there is meaning to it, believers can use life well because they understand its true purpose. Even "death" belongs to believers because it holds no terrors. Nonbelievers can only fear death. Believers, however, know that Christ has conquered death; death is the entranceway into an eternity with God. The present and the future belong to believers because they belong to the One who holds the present and the future.

Believers ought never settle for faithfulness to a human leader or human ideas; they ought never break into factions quarreling over their respective loyalties. And this should especially not occur since believers have been given *everything* from God's gracious hand.

1 Corinthians 4

PAUL COUNSELS HIS BELOVED CHILDREN / 4:1-21

The discussion in chapter 3 regarding the status of ministers of the gospel led Paul to further explain how believers should regard their ministers. The leaders (himself, Apollos, Peter, or others) were never to be the focus of anyone's loyalty. They do not have supernatural powers, nor do they advance their own doctrines. Their authority is given and limited by the Master—Jesus Christ.

TRUSTWORTHY
Paul and the other church leaders were "servants of Christ" (4:1). Christ's true servants prove themselves through their personal character and the content of their teaching. Over a period of time, servant-leaders must demonstrate both aspects of their calling. Paul knew that leaders in the church played crucial roles in God's plan, but he also knew the difference between ability and usability. The Corinthians were arguing over credentials; Paul wanted them to listen to those who were actually serving them in Christ's name. He wasn't worried about his declining popularity. He was concerned about the true spiritual health of fellow Christians he loved.

How does someone get your attention as a Christian leader? Are you more impressed by a person's image or the evidence of personal integrity? What servant-leader for Christ has made the deepest impact on your life? Take time to thank God for that person.

4:1-2 Think of us in this way, as servants of Christ and stewards of God's mysteries. Moreover, it is required of stewards that they be found trustworthy.^{NRSV} The believers ought not to be boasting about "their" leader (3:21). Instead, Paul wrote, *think of us in this way, as servants of Christ and stewards of God's mysteries.* As "servants of Christ," these leaders served their Master and did exactly what he told them to do. As "stewards of God's mysteries," these leaders acted as managers of a household, caring for the members and dispensing the provisions as needed. Wealthy households often would have stewards who managed the family resources and ran the home. Certainly, a person with that much responsibility should *be found trustworthy.* The same was true with these "stewards" of God's message of salvation. A steward worked under the authority of the master and reported directly to the master. Ministers of the gospel message are merely God's servants.

Paul and the other leaders had been entrusted with "God's mysteries." The word "mysteries" refers to "God's secret wisdom, a wisdom that has been hidden and that God destined for our glory before time began" (2:7 NIV)—the mystery of the plan of salvation. These mysteries cannot be discovered or comprehended by human wisdom, but they have been entrusted to God's workers to be carefully and responsibly taught to others.

WHAT DOES CHRIST THINK?
Paul rejected human judgments on his ministry. This may appear odd at first. Was he that self-confident? Didn't he care what others thought? Actually, Paul cared far more about what Christ might say about his ministry than about anyone else's evaluation—even his own self-evaluation. He wasn't claiming unaccountable authority. Rather, he was telling the Corinthians that his faithfulness, as well as theirs, eventually would be measured by Christ himself.

Paul's candor clarifies two significant temptations to be resisted by anyone in ministry. The first is to rely too heavily on the approval or disapproval of others. The second is to rely too heavily on self-rationalizations. We can justify almost any behavior. With the support of others, we may even behave scandalously. But final accountability comes from Christ. When facing criticism or praise, pray for the capacity to see things from God's perspective.

4:3-4 **I care very little if I am judged by you or by any human court; indeed, I do not even judge myself. My conscience is clear, but that does not make me innocent. It is the Lord who judges me.**^{NIV} The Corinthians battled over the preacher whom *they* judged to be the best or the message that *they* liked most, but Paul dismissed their judgment entirely. Human judgment was as worthless before God as human wisdom (2:6). Because he had been called by God to serve, Paul owed allegiance to God alone, and he looked to God alone to judge his performance. As a steward serves the master of the estate, so Paul served God. Paul did not concern himself with what any group of people thought of his teaching style or his message. Paul did not even depend on his own self-evaluation—*I do not even judge myself.* When he did look within, Paul could honestly say that he had a clear conscience, but that did not mean

PLEASING GOD

The New Testament illustrates the importance of pleasing God, not people. The secret to pleasing God is faith, obedience, and service. (Verses are quoted from NLT.)

Reference	Key Phrase	Significance
John 8:29	"Jesus said, 'When you have lifted up the Son of Man on the cross, then you will realize that . . . I do nothing on my own, but I speak what the Father taught me.'"	Believers are to follow totally, just as Christ did.
2 Corinthians 5:9	"So our aim is to please him always, whether we are here in this body or away from this body."	Believers should aim always to please God in their words and actions.
Galatians 6:8	"Those who live to please the Spirit will harvest everlasting life from the Spirit."	Believers are assured of great reward when they live to please and honor God.
Ephesians 5:10	"Try to find out what is pleasing to the Lord."	Believers will be shown what God wants them to do if they ask him.
Colossians 1:9-10	"We ask [God] to make you wise with spiritual wisdom. Then the way you live will always honor and please the Lord, and you will continually do good, kind things for others."	Believers can ask God for wisdom to help them live to honor and please him.
1 Thessalonians 2:4	"Our purpose is to please God, not people. He is the one who examines the motives of our hearts."	Believers must always focus on pleasing God; then even if they don't please people, they know that their consciences are clear.
1 Thessalonians 4:1	"Finally . . . we urge you in the name of the Lord Jesus to live in a way that pleases God."	Believers are urged to please God because of what Jesus has done for them.
Hebrews 11:6	"It is impossible to please God without faith."	The most important ingredient to pleasing God is faith that trusts him for salvation.

he was *innocent*. The Lord alone could make that pronouncement. Paul was accountable to God and would be judged by God alone.

4:5 So be careful not to jump to conclusions before the Lord returns as to whether or not someone is faithful. When the Lord comes, he will bring our deepest secrets to light and will reveal our private motives. And then God will give to everyone whatever praise is due.^{NLT} The Corinthian believers had expended much energy on making judgments concerning various leaders. Paul explained that God alone could judge the leaders because he alone knows the *deepest secrets* and *private motives*. Human beings cannot do that, so they should *be careful not to jump to conclusions before the Lord returns as to whether or not someone is faithful*. People can see only the outside, but God can discern a person's heart (1 Samuel 16:7). A minister may appear to be a faithful servant but be harboring pride in his heart. At the same time, another minister may not be flamboyant or outwardly successful yet be a sincere person of God. One group of believers may appear to be sincere, all the while harboring envy and dissension. Other believers may not appear to have much in the world's estimation yet be filled with God's Spirit and manifest his gifts.

> Blessed is God's ambassador who is not in bonds—bonds of habit, shackling sins of flesh or spirit, bonds within or bonds without, in his own family or church or among the ecclesiastics over him, bonds that quench the Spirit and stifle his message until he is a parrot instead of a prophet.   *Vance Havner*

Believers, therefore, ought not be making such judgments. This will happen *when the Lord comes,* and then *God will give to everyone whatever praise is due* (see also 2 Corinthians 5:10). At the Second Coming, those who have been faithful, as judged by God himself, will receive praise and reward from him.

THE RIGHT JUDGE
It is tempting to judge fellow Christians, evaluating whether or not they are good followers of Christ. But only God knows a person's heart, and he is the only one with the right to judge. Paul's warning to the Corinthians should warn us today. We are to confront those who are sinning (see 5:12-13), but we must not judge who is a better servant for Christ. When you judge someone, you invariably consider yourself better—and that is arrogant.

4:6 Dear brothers and sisters, I have used Apollos and myself to illustrate what I've been saying. If you pay attention to the Scriptures, you won't brag about one of your leaders at the expense of another.^{NLT} Because the Corinthians had split into various cliques, each following its favorite preacher, Paul used their loyalties to himself and Apollos to illustrate what he was saying about God's ministers. The groups were not to boast about being tied to a particular preacher because each preacher was simply a humble servant who had suffered for the same message of salvation in Jesus Christ. No preacher of God has more status than another. If they would *pay attention to the Scriptures,* focusing on what God has said, they wouldn't be bragging about one leader over another. If they read and understood the Scriptures and what they say about God's sovereignty and the role of spiritual leaders, the factions would dissolve.

BEYOND LOYALTY
It is easy for us to become attached to a spiritual leader. It's natural to feel loyalty to one who has been helpful. But Paul warned about pride in favorite leaders that divides the church. Any true spiritual leader is a representative of Christ and has nothing to offer that God hasn't given him or her. Don't let your loyalty cause strife, slander, or broken relationships. Make sure that your deepest loyalties are to Christ and not to his human agents. Those who spend more time debating church leadership than declaring Christ's message don't have Christ as their top priority.

4:7 What makes you better than anyone else? What do you have that God hasn't given you? And if all you have is from God, why boast as though you have accomplished something on your own?[NLT] Paul's words about God's ministers merely illustrate the larger truth that believers ought not make judgments about one another either. Apparently each faction that followed a different leader also placed itself above the others. But Paul asked the rhetorical questions so they could see the silliness of their prideful positions against one another. No one was

> A proud man is always looking down on things and people; and, of course, as long as you're looking down, you can't see something that's above you.   *C. S. Lewis*

better than anyone else. Everything they had, everything they accomplished, every gift they received—all came from God. Therefore, wrote Paul, *if all you have is from God,* how can anyone possibly boast about being better than anyone else, as if they *accomplished something* on their own? The obvious answer is that no one has any right to boast about anything.

4:8 Already you have all you want! Already you have become rich! You have become kings—and that without us! How I

wish that you really had become kings so that we might be kings with you![NIV] With biting sarcasm, Paul derided the rampant pride in the Corinthian church. The believers proclaimed loyalties and set themselves against one another, and many looked down even on the apostle Paul for his lack of wealth or great oratory (see 2:1-5). These believers apparently already had all they wanted. They thought they had the kingdom's riches, and they reigned in their little groups as though they had *become kings.* Believing that they possessed all the great wisdom and knowledge they needed, they felt qualified to judge others. Paul marveled that they were able to accomplish all of this apart from those who had brought the gospel truth to them. With great irony, Paul explained that he wished he could be a king along with them, for apparently they had surpassed the apostle in wisdom and knowledge and had already reached full maturity.

REALITY CHECK
While Jesus was still on earth, the disciples had held heated discussions on the subject "Who's the greatest?" (see Luke 9:46-48; 22:24-30). Later followers of Jesus have continually faced that same temptation. Jesus' original answer still stands: Those who are truly greatest don't know and don't care. They are too busy serving others to give much thought to rank.

Paul's emphatic comparisons between the experiences of the apostles and the claims of the Corinthians were clearly intended to shatter their arrogance. Paul wasn't complaining about apostolic suffering; rather, he was concerned about the Corinthian self-sufficiency. He didn't question the believers' "spiritual wealth." Instead, he sought to puncture their inflated sense of importance. How easily good gifts like talents and experiences become twisted into causes for pride rather than tools for greater service. Do you use your material blessings to help others or to feel superior to them?

4:9 But sometimes I think God has put us apostles on display, like prisoners of war at the end of a victor's parade, condemned to die. We have become a spectacle to the entire world—to people and angels alike.[NLT] While some of the Corinthian believers lived as though they were kings, the apostles apparently had been passed up for such honor. How odd that the apostles, who had been called to minister the gospel message across the world, were not reigning as kings but instead were *on display . . . prisoners . . . condemned to die . . . a spectacle.* For almost all of the apostles, that was in fact what happened. James, the son of Zebedee, was the first to be martyred (Acts 12:2). According to tradition, Peter may have been crucified by Nero. John was exiled. Paul was put to death by Nero, and

Andrew was crucified in Achaia, near Corinth. While these new Christians were attempting to reign, their spiritual leaders were facing an entirely different sort of life—one filled with suffering for the sake of the gospel.

4:10 **We are fools for Christ, but you are so wise in Christ! We are weak, but you are strong! You are honored, we are dishonored!**NIV Surely Paul's sarcasm shamed his readers. He pointed out the strangeness of their supposed wisdom, strength, and honor while God's apostles were considered as foolish, weak, and without honor.

4:11-13 **To the present hour we are hungry and thirsty, we are poorly clothed and beaten and homeless, and we grow weary from the work of our own hands. When reviled, we bless; when persecuted, we endure; when slandered, we speak kindly. We have become like the rubbish of the world, the dregs of all things, to this very day.**NRSV To further elaborate on the warped viewpoint of the proud Corinthian believers, Paul described the hardships that he and the other apostles continued to face in their ministry. Far from being honored for their preaching and fawned over as kings, they faced severe suffering. Not worrying about even the necessities of life, they were *poorly clothed* and *homeless*. They had to forego many necessities at various times in order to do the work they had been given. How many Christians today are willing to take up the cause of Christ under these circumstances? They had been *beaten* (see Acts 14:19). They worked hard with their *own hands* so that they would not become a burden to the people to whom they ministered. In Corinth, Paul had worked as a tentmaker (see Acts 18:1-3), which was something the Greeks looked down upon. They did not value manual labor but considered it to be the work of slaves. Throughout his ministry, Paul faced being *reviled, persecuted,* and *slandered,* yet the Spirit within him helped him to *bless, endure,* and *speak kindly.* To endure when persecuted, bless when reviled, and respond kindly when slandered reflects the teaching of Christ (Matthew 5:38-45; 23:8-12; Mark 8:34-38; 10:42-45; Luke 6:27-36). To respond as Paul did requires restraint that the Holy Spirit can provide. Paul was modeling for us the attitude we should show as we serve Christ today.

Even so, the world saw these men as no more than *rubbish . . . the dregs,* because they did not meet up to worldly standards of success. Paul willingly took this abuse in order to bring the message of eternal life to any and all who would believe. Most Christians today want careers that give them comfort, money, and prestige. Very few are willing to accept work that takes away "necessary" comforts, earns little money, and/or causes people to look down on them—even if it is for the cause of the gospel.

4:14-16 **I am not writing these things to shame you, but to warn you as my beloved children. For even if you had ten thousand others to teach you about Christ, you have only one spiritual father. For I became your father in Christ Jesus when I preached the Good News to you. So I ask you to follow my example and do as I do.**[NLT] Paul's previous sarcasm had not been meant to *shame* these believers *but to warn* them because they were his *beloved children* in the faith. The word "warn" refers to a parental instruction given for the benefit of the children. Paul gave this warning because he wanted the Corinthians to turn from their sin, to change their arrogant behavior for service and obedience to God.

Many teachers might come and teach about Christ, but Paul portrayed a special affection for these believers—he was their *spiritual father.* In an attempt to unify the church, Paul appealed to his relationship with them. By "father," Paul meant that he was the church's founder because he had originally *preached the Good News* to them. Because Paul had started the church, he could be trusted to have its best interests at heart, and he had the authority to warn them of their sinful ways. Paul's tough words were motivated by love—like the love a good father has for his children (see also 1 Thessalonians 2:11). Because the church could trust him, they could also imitate him, so he boldly explained that they could follow his example (see also 1 Corinthians 11:1; Ephesians 5:1; Philippians 3:17; 1 Thessalonians 1:6).

IMITATION
Paul was confident, even forceful, in his unique relationship with the Corinthian church. He had introduced many of them to Jesus Christ. He told the Corinthians to imitate him. He was able to make this statement because he walked close to God, spent time in God's Word and in prayer, and was aware of God's presence in his life at all times. God was Paul's example; therefore, Paul's life could be an example to other Christians. Paul wasn't expecting others to imitate everything he did, but they should imitate those aspects of his beliefs and conduct that were modeling Christ's way of living.

Make it a point to identify Christlike character traits in the people you allow to shape your life. Influences you cannot trace back to Christ cannot truthfully claim your commitment.

4:17 **That is the very reason I am sending Timothy—to help you do this. For he is my beloved and trustworthy child in the Lord. He will remind you of what I teach about Christ Jesus in all the**

SET AN EXAMPLE

Throughout Scripture, setting an example is stressed as an important element of discipleship. (Verses are quoted from NLT.)

- *Matthew 11:29—"Take my yoke upon you."*
  Jesus told his followers to learn from his example of gentleness and humility.

- *Philippians 3:17—"Pattern your lives after mine."*
  Paul urged believers to follow his example of enthusiasm, perseverance, and maturity.

- *1 Thessalonians 1:6-7—"You imitated both us and the Lord. . . . You yourselves became an example."*
  The new Christians at Thessalonica received training in discipleship from Paul, and even in suffering they expressed what they had learned.

- *1 Timothy 1:16—"But that is why God had mercy on me, so that Christ Jesus could use me as a prime example of his great patience with even the worst sinners."*
  Paul used his unworthiness to receive Christ as an example of grace so that no one would hold back from coming to Christ.

- *1 Peter 5:3—"Don't lord it over the people assigned to your care, but lead them by your good example."*
  Peter taught Christian leaders to lead by example, not by commands.

Paul told the Corinthian believers to follow his example. As the body of Christ, believers must show Christ to the world by being examples. Nonbelievers should be able to see Christ in believers and be so drawn to what they see that they seek Christ and his salvation. What kind of example are you?

---

churches wherever I go.NLT Timothy had accompanied Paul on his second missionary journey (see Acts 16:1-3) and was a key person in the growth of the early church. Timothy probably arrived in Corinth shortly after this letter (see 16:10)—the bearers of the letter possibly being Stephanus, Fortunatus, and Achaicus (see 16:17). It is clear that Timothy was not with Paul at this letter's writing because he is not mentioned in either the greeting or the closing. Most likely Timothy was notified by Paul to travel on to Corinth from Macedonia (Acts 19:22). Timothy's role was to *remind* the Corinthians of the faith they had received—the same message that Paul was teaching *about Christ Jesus in all the churches.* Apparently the Corinthians had forgotten both their faith and how to live it. Paul did not leave the Corinthians to figure it out on their own; he sent a *beloved and trustworthy child in the Lord* to help them. Afterward, Timothy was to return to Paul and report on the church's progress. (See also Life Application Commentaries: *John* on John 14:26 and *1, 2 Timothy and Titus* on 2 Timothy 2:2.)

4:18-19 I know that some of you have become arrogant, thinking I will never visit you again. But I will come—and soon—if the Lord will let me, and then I'll find out whether these arrogant people are just big talkers or whether they really have God's power.^{NLT} In their eagerness to set themselves up as leaders, the false teachers had said that Paul would not be coming back to Corinth—probably pointing out weakness, fear, or some other inadequacy (see 9:1-3; 2 Corinthians 1:17; 10:10). They assumed, therefore, that they could do as they pleased. But Paul explained that he had every intention of going back to Corinth *soon,* if this were the Lord's will. At that time, Paul would expose the *arrogant people* for who they really were. They were *big talkers,* but did *they really have God's power?* The answer would be obvious to everyone.

It is not known whether Paul ever returned to Corinth, but it is likely. In 2 Corinthians 2:1, he wrote that he decided not to make "another painful visit," implying that he had had a previous painful confrontation with the Corinthian believers.

4:20 For the Kingdom of God is not just fancy talk; it is living by God's power.^{NLT} Being a big talker is one thing, but *living by God's power* is quite another. Some people talk a lot about faith, but that's all it is—talk. They may know all the right words to say, but their lives don't reflect God's power. Paul says that the *Kingdom of God is not just fancy talk,* it is to be lived. There is a big difference between knowing the right words and living them out. The "Kingdom" refers not to the future reign of Christ but to the present reign of God in believers' lives. A person can live only by God's power when he or she has the Holy Spirit within (see John 3:3-8; 2 Corinthians 5:17).

4:21 Which do you choose? Should I come with punishment and scolding, or should I come with quiet love and gentleness?^{NLT} Paul wrote that when he came—and he would come, barring divine intervention (4:19)—he would come with his authority from God as their spiritual father. Far from being afraid or weak, he would arrive ready to deal with the situation as it was. This letter would precede him, and the Corinthian believers would have time to *choose* to continue in their arrogance and therefore receive *punishment and scolding,* or to make the necessary changes and therefore receive *love and gentleness.* It would be up to them.

1 Corinthians 5

PAUL CONDEMNS IMMORALITY IN THE CHURCH / 5:1-13

The pride that characterized the Corinthian church (see 4:10, 18) had so blinded the believers that they were allowing flagrant sexual immorality to take place in their fellowship. Their pride may have been such that they refused to admit this sin and deal with it, or they may have been proud that this man was one of their spiritual people, honored for his "knowledge" or "wisdom." Paul condemned the believers for allowing this sin to go on unchallenged in their midst. Believers today can learn from this passage about how the church must deal with flagrant and unrepented sin.

5:1 I can hardly believe the report about the sexual immorality going on among you, something so evil that even the pagans don't do it. I am told that you have a man in your church who is living in sin with his father's wife.^{NLT} A report had been delivered to Paul regarding *sexual immorality going on* among the believers in Corinth. The Corinthian church had been unwilling to discipline this man. When Paul heard this, he could *hardly believe the report.*

Paul prefaced his pronouncement of knowledge of this situation by saying that the problem was *so evil that even the pagans don't do it*—quite an indictment on these believers. Most of the believers knew about the sinful relationship already, but apparently they had been unwilling to admit it, so Paul described the sin point-blank: *A man in your church . . . is living in sin with his father's wife*. This man was having an affair, already a sinful act deserving discipline. But his sexual activity outside of marriage had taken place with his "father's wife" (probably his stepmother). Whether the man had seduced this woman away from his father, or whether the woman was divorced or widowed is unclear. In any case, even the pagans would have shuddered at this, but the church members were trying to ignore the situation. The Jews definitely considered this against the law (Leviticus 18:8; 20:11) and the Romans had laws against it, according to

Cicero. Although Romans and Greeks had notoriously immoral sexual standards, this act was forbidden.

MORAL UNDERTOW
Lifeguards know that as scary as large waves near the beach may look, the hidden undertow kills far more people. A strong current beneath the surface can pull a weak or unprepared swimmer underwater and out to sea. Paul was concerned about the "waves" being made by the Corinthians over leadership. But he also knew that beneath the surface issues were sins pulling like a spiritual and moral undertow in the life of the church.

The watching world seldom understands theological storms. Doctrinal breakers don't impress them. But they do note the way believers treat each other. They have "hypocrisy radar." They have heard about the undertow. When our lives contradict our words, they see it. When obvious sins are rationalized or ignored, the world knows. Often, some within the church are pulled under.

A proper response to sin in the church includes grief and action. Those who refuse to recognize sin are not practicing love. Until we can grieve and repent for sin (both our own and that of people who "hide in plain sight" in the church), we will not be in a place where God can direct our actions.

5:2 And you are so proud of yourselves! Why aren't you mourning in sorrow and shame? And why haven't you removed this man from your fellowship?[NLT] The problem of arrogance in the Corinthian church had spilled over to the point where they were tolerating flagrant sin. Instead of being proud of themselves, they should have been *mourning in sorrow and shame*. Then, they should have *removed this man from [their] fellowship*. The church must discipline flagrant sin among its members—such sins, left unchecked, can divide and paralyze a church. This "removal" of the person was not meant to be vengeful but to help bring about a cure.

Today, tolerance has become such a battle cry in the media and in political and educational circles that it has affected even the church. It is very difficult for people to discipline sin in church members because everyone is trying to be accepting of others. People say, "Who am I to judge? I have sin in my life." So they want all sin excused, including their own. We must not let modern-day low standards determine what is true and right for the church.

5:3 Even though I am not physically present, I am with you in spirit. And I have already passed judgment on the one who

did this, just as if I were present.NIV While those in the Corinthian church had failed to do anything about this man's sin, Paul himself, *not physically present* (in fact, hundreds of miles away), would tell them what had to be done.

After hearing of this situation, he *already passed judgment on the one who did this, just as if [he] were present.* Paul had weighed the matter and had passed judgment in his heart and mind, yet this phrase carries more punch than merely saying, "I have given this some thought." As an apostle and the spiritual father of this church (4:15), Paul had the authority to deal with the matter. Although this is not the same as a church council, Paul intended his opinion to carry the same weight of his leadership and influence as an apostle "as if" he were actually there. Because he was with them *in spirit,* he understood exactly what was going on; he also understood the danger to the church if the sin were to remain undisciplined.

> Maybe the most significant thing we can learn from such a text is how far many of us are removed from a view of the church in which the dynamic of the Spirit was so real that exclusion could be a genuinely redemptive action.
>
> *Gordon Fee*

JUDGMENT
People who otherwise ignore the Bible readily quote the phrase, "Do not judge," as Jesus' complete statement on passing judgment on others. Curiously, their application of the phrase often sounds as though they are passing judgment on someone's "judgmental" behavior. Did Jesus mean there could be no discernment or proper discrimination among his followers? The context of the phrase (Matthew 7:1-6) answers the question. Jesus brought the Golden Rule to the area of good judgment. Let any discernment applied to someone else's life be tempered by the following considerations:

- Judge as you want to be judged.
- Realize that in some way, the same demands you make on others will be made on you.
- Remember that your sensitivity to someone else's sin may be an indication of the same sin in you.
- After dealing with sin in your own life, you will be better able to help others deal with sin in theirs.

The refusal to exercise wise judgment is much more often evidence of a lack of personal self-examination than an example of genuine concern for others.

5:4-5 When you are assembled in the name of our Lord Jesus and I am with you in spirit, and the power of our Lord Jesus is present, hand this man over to Satan, so that the sinful nature

may be destroyed and his spirit saved on the day of the Lord.^{NIV} Paul had already passed judgment and decided what the church needed to do immediately in order to handle this sin. The church needed to take responsibility in dealing with this man. Three elements needed to be present in order to handle this discipline adequately:

1. *When you are assembled* . . . the whole congregation needed to witness and support the action.
2. *And I am with you in spirit* . . . refers to Paul's indictment as an authoritative apostle.
3. *The power of our Lord Jesus is present* . . . referring to spiritual action.

Paul wrote that the next time they were "assembled in the name of our Lord Jesus," they should discipline the man. This should be done with the whole congregation present. Paul, the founder and father of the church, would be with them in spirit, and they would all be under the power of the Lord Jesus. These three elements were important in dealing with the discipline in this situation. Apparently the whole congregation knew about this man, so they all needed to witness the discipline. But this concurrence of the three elements would not occur without Paul present in spirit. The entire situation was under the mighty power of the Lord Jesus to deal with the man's spirit and to bring him to repentance.

Paul explained the discipline that should be carried out: *Hand this man over to Satan.* This would mean excluding him from the fellowship of believers (see 1 Timothy 1:20). Without the spiritual support of Christians, this man would be left alone with his sin and Satan, and hopefully this emptiness would drive him to repentance. This amounted to excommunication from the worship, ministry, and fellowship of the church. The church had not literally given him to Satan, for only God can consign a person to eternal judgment. It was meant to force him to see the consequences of sin by living in Satan's sphere of influence—the world apart from Christ and the church.

The phrase "that the sinful nature may be destroyed" can also be translated "for the destruction of the flesh" (see NRSV). Thus, there are two basic interpretations of this statement: (1) that the man would be subject to sickness leading to death; (2) that the man would experience some kind of severe discipline that would crucify his sinful nature. According to the first interpretation, Satan would afflict the man physically and thus bring him to God. In Job 2:4-10, God is portrayed as allowing Satan to test Job with suffering. Paul also saw his thorn in the flesh (2 Corin-

thians 12:7) as administered by Satan. In this man's case, he
would have to die physically (see 1 Corinthians 11:30-32; cf.
Acts 5:1-10), but his spirit would be saved as a result of the process. According to the second interpretation, Paul was saying that
the exclusion from the fellowship (and there would be suffering
in that) would help the man to face his sinful, selfish nature
(flesh), repent, and return to the church. Paul wanted this sinner
to experience the crucifixion of his sinful nature (Romans 7:5-6;
Galatians 5:24). It may take such drastic measures to deal with
the sinful nature, but how much more important for the man that
he face this and repent in order that *his spirit [be] saved on the
day of the Lord.* Paul hoped that this harsh disciplinary action
might be of eternal benefit to the man.

Churches today need the spiritual determination to deal with
sins such as these that affect the whole church. But excommunication as a form of discipline should be used rarely and carefully. It
should be an action of the church body, not just one or two
people. Its purpose should be redemptive and restorative, not
vengeful or vindictive.

DECISIVE DISCIPLINE
Paul used the case of the incestuous relationship to confront
the Corinthians with their obvious lack of true maturity. Although
they claimed great spiritual health (1:7), he regarded this
situation as a gangrenous limb. It was too late for preventive
treatments or normal surgery. The disciplinary actions Paul
directed were spiritual crisis intervention. They ought to be
applied carefully in church discipline. Paul was dealing with a
scandal, while at the same time making it clear that the
Corinthian behavior had allowed incest to become acceptable.
Even today, discipline of people within the church must begin
with repentance by all the church.

**5:6-7 Your boasting is not good. Don't you know that a little yeast
works through the whole batch of dough? Get rid of the old
yeast that you may be a new batch without yeast—as you
really are. For Christ, our Passover lamb, has been sacrificed.**[NIV] Paul was writing to those who wanted to ignore this
church problem. They boasted, but they had no grounds to boast
because they were allowing a horrible sin to exist in their fellowship. Believers in any congregation have a responsibility to one
another. Yeast makes bread dough rise; a little bit affects the
whole batch. Sins left uncorrected, no matter whether secret or
blatant, affect the entire congregation, just as *a little yeast works
through the whole batch of dough.*

Believers should encourage, pray for, and build up one another, but they must also be intolerant of sin that jeopardizes the spiritual health of the church. They had to expel this sinful man from the fellowship, just as a cook would get rid of old yeast, so that they might be pure *(a new batch without yeast—as you really are)*. This "purity" did not mean that without this man they would be sinless (Paul would address other problems in the rest of this letter). Instead, Paul understood that this particular sin, left unchecked, would work evil in the church; thus, it needed to be disciplined by excommunication so that the believers could see the serious consequences of sin.

Indeed, they ought not forget that Christ gave his life so that people could deal with sin. By not dealing with this man's sin, they were making Christ's death of no effect. They should remember, said Paul, that *Christ, our Passover lamb, has been sacrificed.* The reference to the Passover refers to the time when the Hebrews prepared for their exodus from slavery in Egypt. They were commanded to prepare bread without yeast because they didn't have time to wait for it to rise. And because yeast also was a symbol of sin, they were commanded to sweep all of it out of the house (Exodus 12:15; 13:7). In preparation for their flight from Egypt, the Hebrews followed God's instructions by placing the blood of a lamb on the doorframes of their homes. That night, the firstborn son of every family who did not have blood on the doorframes was killed. The lamb had to be killed in order to get the blood to protect them. Christ is the Passover lamb, the perfect sacrifice, who gave his blood for the sins of all who believe. Because he has delivered his people from the slavery of sin, they should have nothing to do with the sins of the past ("old yeast"). Continuing in sin shows disregard for Christ's sacrifice.

DISCIPLINE TODAY
Paul's firm response to blatant sin in the church meets hardened resistance today. Discipline and accountability are sorely lacking in churches. Often, sinful members, when confronted, simply move to another church without recognizing that the attempted discipline was love in action rather than judgmentalism. These times are as desperate as those Paul faced in Corinth. Ask the Lord to fill the leaders in your church with wisdom and courage so that they can set the pace of faithfulness for all the members.

5:8 Therefore let us keep the Festival, not with the old yeast, the yeast of malice and wickedness, but with bread without yeast, the bread of sincerity and truth.[NIV] The words "let us keep the

Festival" are not a command to keep the Jewish Passover but a figurative way of picturing what Christ is to believers. In Paul's day, the Passover was celebrated with a ceremonial search throughout one's home for yeast and then destroying the yeast before the Passover lamb was slain in the temple. Because Christ, the Passover Lamb, has already been sacrificed, all yeast (that is, all evil) should be removed from among his people. The old life *(with the old yeast)* was characterized by *malice and wickedness;* these have no part in Christ's church. Believers, characterized by being born again, have cleansed the evil from their lives and are like *bread without yeast,* living in *sincerity and truth.* Paul wrote to the Romans, "Don't copy the behavior and customs of this world, but let God transform you into a new person by changing the way you think. Then you will know what God wants you to do, and you will know how good and pleasing and perfect his will really is" (Romans 12:2 NLT).

GOOD BREAD
Passover was a corporate, or community, festival. Paul illustrated and taught that Christians may have individual roles within the church, but the life of the church is corporate, not individualized. Believers are connected to Christ and to each other. A small piece of fermented dough eventually affects the whole loaf. Boasting as well as immorality hurt the whole church. Christianity is not a private lifestyle.

How do you experience your connection with other Christians? To what degree do you include in your decisions the thought that you represent both Jesus Christ and fellow believers? Live each day with truth and integrity. Don't let sinful desires contaminate your life.

5:9-11 **When I wrote to you before, I told you not to associate with people who indulge in sexual sin. But I wasn't talking about unbelievers who indulge in sexual sin, or who are greedy or are swindlers or idol worshipers. You would have to leave this world to avoid people like that. What I meant was that you are not to associate with anyone who claims to be a Christian yet indulges in sexual sin, or is greedy, or worships idols, or is abusive, or a drunkard, or a swindler. Don't even eat with such people.**[NLT] The words "when I wrote to you before" refer to Paul's earlier letter to the Corinthian church, often called the "lost letter" because it has not been preserved. In that letter, he had told the Corinthians *not to associate with people who indulge in sexual sin.* Either the Corinthians had misunderstood what Paul meant, or they had avoided his command by pointing out the impossibility of not associating with sinners in a sinful world. So Paul made it clear here that he *wasn't talking about unbelievers,* for they, by nature, are involved in sexual sin, greed, swindling, and idol worship. Believers cannot disassociate themselves completely from unbelievers—they *would have to leave this world to avoid people like that.* In addition, with no contact with unbelievers, believers would not be able to carry out Christ's command to tell them about salvation (Matthew 28:18-20).

Paul meant that believers were *not to associate with anyone who claims to be a Christian* and yet has a sinful lifestyle. Paul listed a few sins such as sexual sin, greed, idol worship, abuse, drunkenness, or swindling (stealing by violence, extortion). Believers must separate themselves from those who claim to be Christians yet indulge in sins explicitly forbidden in Scripture and then rationalize their actions. By rationalizing their sin, these "believers" harm others for whom Christ died and they tarnish the image of God in their lives. A church that includes such people is hardly fit to be the light of the world because it distorts the picture of Christ that it presents to the world. The church has a responsibility to rebuke, correct, and restore those in the fellowship who claim to be believers but live like unbelievers.

5:12-13 It isn't my responsibility to judge outsiders, but it certainly is your job to judge those inside the church who are sinning in these ways. God will judge those on the outside; but as the Scriptures say, "You must remove the evil person from among you."NLT The difference between believers and nonbelievers lies in their relationship to Jesus Christ, but a difference also exists in how believers are to relate to those inside and outside the church. The *outsiders* (referring to nonbelievers) are to be met where they are (even in their sinful lifestyles, 5:9-11) and offered the gospel message. Yet the believers are not responsible to *judge* them because *God will judge those on the outside.*

In the church, however, believers have the *job to judge those . . . who are sinning in these ways.* The Bible consistently says not to criticize people by gossiping or making rash judgments. At the same time, however, believers are to judge and deal with sinners "who are sinning in these ways," referring to blatant, unrepented sin as described in 5:9-11. Paul's instructions for this sinful man—*you must remove the evil person from among you* (5:1-2)—come from Deuteronomy 17:7. This instruction should not be used to handle trivial matters or to take revenge; nor should it be applied to individual problems between believers.

CHURCH DISCIPLINE

The church, at times, must exercise discipline toward members who have sinned. But church discipline must be handled carefully, straightforwardly, and lovingly.

Steps (Matthew 18:15-17)

1. Go to the brother or sister who sinned; show the fault to him or her in private.

2. If he or she does not listen, go with one or two witnesses.

3. If he or she refuses to listen, take the matter before the church.

After these steps have been carried out, the next steps are:

1. Remove the one in error from the fellowship (1 Corinthians 5:2-13).

2. The church gives united disapproval, but forgiveness and comfort are in order if he or she chooses to repent (2 Corinthians 2:5-8).

3. Do not associate with the disobedient person, and if you must, speak to him or her as one who needs a warning (2 Thessalonians 3:14-15).

4. After two warnings, reject the person from the fellowship (Titus 3:10).

These verses are instructions for dealing with open sin in the church, with a person who claims to be a Christian and yet who sins without remorse. The church is to confront and discipline such a person in love.

1 Corinthians 6

In chapter 5 Paul explains what to do with open immorality in the congregation. In chapter 6 he explains how the congregation should handle smaller problems between believers.

6:1 When you have something against another Christian, why do you file a lawsuit and ask a secular court to decide the matter, instead of taking it to other Christians to decide who is right?NLT While there are certain cases that, by law, have to be submitted to the legal authorities, disputes between Christians should be handled by qualified Christian leaders in the church. Paul declared that disagreeing Christians should not have to *file a lawsuit and ask a secular court* to resolve differences among them. Why did Paul make this point? (1) If the judge and jury were not Christians, they would not likely be sensitive to Christian values. (2) The basis for going to court is often revenge; this should never be a Christian's motive. (3) Lawsuits make the church look bad, causing unbelievers to focus on church problems rather than on its purpose.

ANOTHER LOOK
For Paul, reconciliation was serious business. Christians were to demonstrate their understanding of reconciliation with God by the way they handled conflicts with each other. Yet the Corinthian Christians were taking each other to court. In the face of their spiritual pride, Paul held up the jarring mirror of their spiritual misbehavior.

Few of us enjoy facing our inconsistencies. But we certainly need to hear the truth about ourselves. If we don't know any other Christians willing to tell us the truth—in spite of how we might react—we are missing valuable guidance. So, what kind of people can give us that kind of help? They will be people whose words and lives are filled with Jesus' words and actions. They will be open about their own failures. And, like Paul did with the Corinthians, they will continue to love us even while they correct us. Sound like someone you already know? Identify those people. They will give valuable counsel along the way.

6:2 Don't you know that someday we Christians are going to judge the world? And since you are going to judge the world, can't you decide these little things among yourselves?^{NLT} The phrases "don't you know" or "don't you realize" occur six times in this chapter, indicating that Paul was pointing out to these believers facts that they should have already known and understood (see also 6:3, 9, 15-16, 19). By going to pagan authorities to settle disputes, the Christians were acting beneath their dignity. They should be able to settle these disputes among themselves because *someday* (at the Second Coming) *Christians* (who are coheirs with Christ) *are going to judge the world* (see also 2 Timothy 2:12; Revelation 3:21; 20:4). Because of this truth, believers should not take their disputes into the world, because it would be a poor witness and would show a lack of unity in the church. Instead, believers should be able to *decide these little things among* themselves.

RESOLUTIONS
Because of all that Christians have been given and because of the authority that they will have in the future to judge the world and the angels, they should be able to deal with disputes among themselves.

Think of the prospect of spending eternity with folks we haven't learned to get along with on earth. That in itself should drive our efforts to resolve problems with other believers. When we do, God is honored, and others gain a fresh perspective of the transforming truth of the gospel. We practice evangelism when we settle differences. Jesus said, "By this everyone will know that you are my disciples, if you have love for one another" (John 13:35 NRSV).

6:3 Don't you realize that we Christians will judge angels? So you should surely be able to resolve ordinary disagreements here on earth.^{NLT} Having just stated that Christians will eventually judge the world (6:2), Paul added that *we Christians will judge angels.* The use of the word "angels" without an article leaves the meaning unclear. This could mean that Paul was referring to Christians' part in judging the devil and his demons (evil angels) at Christ's second coming (see 2 Peter 2:4; Jude 1:6; Revelation 19:19-20; 20:10). Or it could mean that the Christians will "judge angels" in the sense that they will preside over angels when they (the Christians) reign with Christ. Paul's point was that, in light of the privilege that will belong to believers in the future, they *should surely be able to resolve ordinary disagreements here on earth.*

6:4-6 **If you have legal disputes about such matters, why do you go to outside judges who are not respected by the church? I am saying this to shame you. Isn't there anyone in all the church who is wise enough to decide these arguments? But instead, one Christian sues another—right in front of unbelievers!**NLT Repeating his concern stated in 6:1, Paul asked why the Corinthian Christians were taking their disputes *to outside judges.* They were "outside" because they were not Christians. That they *are not respected* does not mean that the believers were showing no respect for pagan judges. Instead, these pagan judges lived by an entirely different standard than the Christians; therefore, their judgments could not be in accordance with the spiritual laws by which the Christians lived. *The church* then could not respect the judgments made by these judges. The pagan judges judged by their human beliefs and ultimately had a short tenure; believers use God's wisdom to judge and ultimately will judge the world (6:2).

Some versions of the Bible translate 6:4 to sound as though believers should appoint judges from among themselves because even people of "little account" (NIV) in the church would be better judges than pagan judges. The translation above, however, focusing on outside judges, seems to make the most sense in context.

Paul asked these questions to *shame* them. Compare this to 4:14, where he stated that he did not intend to shame but to warn them regarding their divisions. Here, however, Paul *did* intend to shame these believers. They should be ashamed if they couldn't find *anyone in all the church . . . wise enough to decide* their disagreements. Apparently they had been acting with great pride (4:8), yet they couldn't handle their own disagreements. This surely should have shamed them. Instead of using the wisdom and discernment from the Holy Spirit, which was available to them as believers, they were suing each other, *right in front of unbelievers.* What kind of witness was this for the church? To take their private disputes into the public and pagan domain gave ammunition to those who opposed the church and did not make the church seem like an inviting place. How much better for the believers to live "above" such matters, dealing with them in their own congregation with the help of respected leaders, so that nothing would hinder their witness for Christ in the world. The Christian Legal Society and other associations have taken great steps to provide legal resolution between Christians and between churches. Many Christian organizations place third-party arbitration clauses in their contracts to ensure there will be peaceful settlement of conflicts.

6:7-8 In fact, to have lawsuits at all with one another is already a defeat for you. Why not rather be wronged? Why not rather be defrauded? But you yourselves wrong and defraud—and believers at that.NRSV The basic problem went back to the Corinthian congregation. If they had been maturing in their faith, they would not have become so riddled with sin that the believers would actually have to bring lawsuits against one another. That these believers had to resort to lawsuits to settle disputes among them was *already a defeat* for them. It showed that they were still immature. Paul explained the direction in which they needed to grow—they needed to willingly *be wronged* and *defrauded* if that would mean protecting the church. Believers should never be wronged and defrauded by other believers in the first place. Mature believers would not act in that manner. If they were wronged by other believers, mature believers should be willing to "turn the other cheek" (Matthew 5:39).

HUMBLING ALTERNATIVE
Offenses and disagreements too often become contests of will. The original issues get buried under the win-or-lose mind-set that takes over. Desperation invites ruthless tactics. Paul was dismayed that the Corinthians would treat one another so poorly. What would he think of the state of church discipline and unity today?

Paul challenged the Corinthians to keep the bottom line in mind. His questions "Why not rather be wronged?" and "Why not rather be defrauded?" were not rhetorical. He was serious. Paul made it clear that it is always easier to see and react to someone else's offense than it is to see and regret our own. We claim we want life to be fair, then we say that fairness is present only when we win. But when one side deliberately puts down its weapons in this kind of family conflict, God often works wonders. In your relationships with other Christians, do you carry a heavy arsenal, or do you travel unarmed?

USE YOUR BODY TO GIVE GOD GLORY / 6:9-20

If the Corinthian church truly realized their high calling, they would live in a completely different manner, and they would not have the problems involving lawsuits (6:7-8). Paul seized upon this opportunity to remind the Corinthian believers that their lives must change. They should not practice such evil acts because evil people cannot inherit the kingdom of God.

6:9-10 Do you not know that the wicked will not inherit the kingdom of God? Do not be deceived: Neither the sexually immoral

nor idolaters nor adulterers nor male prostitutes nor homosexual offenders nor thieves nor the greedy nor drunkards nor slanderers nor swindlers will inherit the kingdom of God.^{NIV} In these verses, Paul gives a strong proclamation about those who will not inherit God's kingdom: the *sexually immoral, idolaters, adulterers, male prostitutes, homosexual offenders, thieves, greedy, drunkards, slanderers,* and *swindlers.* The Christians could not call themselves followers of Jesus and allow any kind of evil to permeate their lives. By saying that none of these people *will inherit the kingdom of God,* Paul was referring to people who persist in their evil practices with no sign of remorse. Such people—if they think they are believers—need to reevaluate their lives to see if they truly believe in Christ.

WHAT ABOUT HOMOSEXUALITY?
Paul wrote that "homosexual offenders" will not "inherit the kingdom of God." There are so many different opinions in our world today regarding homosexuality. Some believe that they can be Christian homosexuals. Some believe that homosexuality is an inborn trait, just like a person is born white or black. Some believe that homosexuality is merely an alternative lifestyle to be accepted. Some think homosexuals ought to be able to "get married," "have kids," and be treated as a "family." So what should Bible-believing Christians think?
    What Christians need to understand is that homosexual acts *are* sin—pure and simple. The Bible says so. Homosexuality is not a lifestyle, an inborn trait, or something to be treated as normal. Homosexual activity is sin. Yet it is not unforgivable. God loves homosexuals just as much as he loves other sinners. Jesus' death on the cross paid for the sin of homosexuality, just as it paid for the sins of lying, greed, lust, hate, and pride. It has been said—and it is true—that the church is a hospital for sinners, not a showcase for saints. It is a place where those caught in homosexual behavior can be freed and forgiven. It is a place where believers who have committed the sins of hatred, prejudice, and self-righteousness toward homosexuals need to go to ask the Lord for forgiveness and healing. Homosexuals, like all sinners, stand guilty before God. Rather than spreading hatred, spread the word that there is hope for sinners of all kinds through the life, death, and resurrection of Jesus Christ. He is the one who sets people free, regardless of their sins.

"Male prostitutes" *(arsenokoitai)* refers to those who practice homosexuality. Some attempt to legitimize homosexuality as an acceptable alternative lifestyle. Even some Christians say that people have a right to choose their sexual preference. But the Bible specifically calls homosexual behavior sin (see Leviticus 18:22-29; Romans 1:18-32; 1 Timothy 1:9-11). Christians must be careful, however, to condemn only the practice, not the people. Those who commit homosexual acts are not to be feared, ridiculed, or hated. They can be forgiven, and their lives can be transformed. The church should be a haven of forgiveness and healing for repentant homosexuals without compromising its stance against homosexual behavior.

6:11 And that is what some of you were. But you were washed, you were sanctified, you were justified in the name of the Lord Jesus Christ and by the Spirit of our God.^{NIV} The list of sins may seem unduly long (6:9-10), but apparently Paul was being complete in listing what kinds of lives and lifestyles from which the Corinthian believers had come. Paul listed sexual sins such as immorality, idolatry (pointing to the sexual content of some forms of idol worship), adultery, male prostitution (the temple of Apollo employed young men whose job was to fulfill the sexual desires of male and female "worshipers"), and homosexuality. Even the writings of pagan authors and historians attest to the rampant immorality in the city of Corinth. Many of the believers had come out of a lifestyle where sexual perversion was part of their "worship!" Paul also listed other sins such as stealing, greed, drunkenness, slander, and swindling. These sexual sins and other personal sins described *what some of [the Corinthian believers] were.* When Paul had come to Corinth, he met people with the lowest morals. Yet the power of Jesus Christ had changed them.

Paul stressed that there is no kind of sin that cannot be forgiven. When the Corinthians received Jesus Christ, they *were washed.* This refers to a cleansing process that had washed away their sins through the blood of Jesus (Hebrews 10:22; Revelation 7:14). They *were sanctified,* meaning that they had been set apart by God (John 17:17; 1 Corinthians 1:2; 1 Thessalonians 4:3; 5:23). And they *were justified,* meaning that God had declared that these believers were righteous and just in his sight. Believers are justified *in the name of the Lord Jesus Christ.* The "name" refers to the character and nature of the One who justifies—he was perfect and sinless. Because Jesus took their punishment, sinners are able to come to God. With the full name as given here, "the Lord Jesus Christ," comes the full title of the One who is God, who became a man, and who then returned to heaven to reign forever. The phrase "Spirit of our God" reminded the believers that the Holy Spirit draws people to God and fills them when they believe. "We were all baptized by one Spirit into one body—whether Jews or Greeks, slave or free—and we were all given the one Spirit to drink" (12:13 NIV). In this verse, the Trinity is represented—God the

Father, Jesus Christ the Son, and the Holy Spirit all taking part
in transforming people from their sinful lives to a new way of
living in obedience to God.

THE WAY WE WERE
The list of the disinherited that Paul included in 6:10 served
very much like a well-known Old Testament parable. God had
sent the prophet Nathan to confront David about his sin with
Bathsheba (2 Samuel 12:1-14). Nathan's parable about the rich
man who had stolen the poor man's only lamb and then had
killed the lamb enraged the king. At that point, Nathan pointed
out that the case they were discussing was David's own
behavior.
  Paul used a similar tactic. He reminded the Corinthians of the
behaviors that are evidence of sin. He appealed to their shared
conviction that such lives, if left unchanged, would not lead to
eternal life. Then, as they nodded their heads in agreement, he
stated the punch line: "And that is what some of you were" (6:11).
  Any time Christians downplay or forget their condition without
Christ, there are two negative results: (1) It makes them value
the freedom they have in Christ less; and (2) it makes them
less compassionate about people who have never heard the
gospel.

6:12 **"Everything is permissible for me"—but not everything is
beneficial. "Everything is permissible for me"—but I will not
be mastered by anything.**[NIV] The phrase "everything is permissible for me" appears to have been a catchphrase, as it appears
twice in this verse and twice again in 10:23. Apparently the Christians in Corinth had been using this phrase as a license to live any
way they pleased. Perhaps Paul had used the statement when he
preached to them about their freedom in Christ, but they had
wrongly interpreted it. By "freedom in Christ," Paul never meant
disregarding basic Christian morality and ethics. Some Christians
in Corinth apparently were using this to excuse their sins, saying
Christ had taken away all sin, so they had complete freedom to
live as they pleased; or what they were doing was not strictly forbidden by Scripture.
  Paul answered both of these excuses:

1. While Christ has taken away sin, this does not mean that
   everything is beneficial and that believers can do what they
   know is wrong. The New Testament specifically forbids many
   sins (see 6:9-10) that were originally prohibited in the Old
   Testament (see Romans 12:9-21; 13:8-10); however, not every
   possible sin is recorded. While some actions may not be
   specifically forbidden in Scripture, believers should know that

these actions and their results would not be beneficial to themselves or to the church. Believers should be using their Christian freedom to share the gospel and show love for others instead of looking for ways to gratify themselves.

2. Some actions are not sinful in themselves, but they are not appropriate because they can control believers' lives and lead them away from God. Believers should not do these actions because they do not want to *be mastered by anything*.

Freedom is a mark of the Christian faith—freedom from sin and guilt, and freedom to use and enjoy all things that come from God. But Christians should not abuse this freedom and hurt themselves or others. Drinking too much leads to alcoholism, gluttony leads to obesity. But we can also be mastered (enslaved or empowered) by money, sports, television, or any one thing that controls our life or robs our devotion to Christ or service to others. Many people have misinterpreted the phrase today to mean, "I will not be mastered by any rule of ethics, law, or Bible principle," rather than, "I will not be mastered by any besetting sin." Christians who have been in the church for many years can easily excuse sins such as gossip, bitterness, an unforgiving spirit, lust, or withholding money from God's work. We must be on alert for those desires that can master us. What God has allowed his children to enjoy must not grow into a bad habit that controls them. For more about Christian freedom and everyday behavior, read chapter 8.

RADICALLY DIFFERENT
Paul would have a lot to be angry about in our permissive society. In a permissive society it is easy for Christians to overlook or tolerate some immoral behaviors (greed, drunkenness, gluttony, etc.) while remaining outraged at others (homosexuality, idolatry, thievery). We must not participate in sin or condone it in any way, nor may we be selective about what we condemn or excuse. Staying away from more "acceptable" forms of sin is difficult, but it is no more difficult for us than it was for the Corinthians.

God expects his followers in any age to have high standards. This is most clearly seen, not in the measuring stick we hold up against society, but in our humble commitment to pursue holiness and our transparency about God's ongoing work of grace in our lives.

6:13 You say, "Food is for the stomach, and the stomach is for food." This is true, though someday God will do away with both of them. But our bodies were not made for sexual immo-

rality. **They were made for the Lord, and the Lord cares about our bodies.**^{NLT} Another saying, *Food is for the stomach, and the stomach is for food,* had apparently been used as an illustration to explain the Corinthians' warped understanding of Christian freedom. They seemed to believe that because the physical activity of eating and digesting food had no effect on one's Christian life, neither would other merely physical activities—such as *sexual immorality.*

Paul stated that it was *true* that what one eats does not affect the spiritual life. In fact, so transitory is this physical realm that one day *God will do away with both* stomachs and food. However, he also stated that one could not compare eating to sexual activity. Humans are a combination of material and spiritual. Just as the spirit affects the body, so too the physical body affects the spirit. People cannot commit sin with their bodies without damaging their souls because their bodies and souls are inseparably joined. While the stomach was made for food, people's *bodies were not made for sexual immorality.* Stomachs and food will pass away, but believers' bodies will be transformed and glorified.

DESTRUCTIVE POWER

Paul challenges us to a higher purpose than merely fulfilling our sexual desires. Sexual immorality is a temptation that is always before us. In movies and on television, sex outside marriage is treated as a normal, even desirable, part of life, while marriage is often shown as confining and joyless. People can even be looked down on by others if they are suspected of being pure. But God does not forbid sexual sin just to be difficult. He knows its power to destroy a person physically and spiritually. No one should underestimate the power of sexual immorality. It has devastated countless lives and destroyed families, churches, communities, and even nations. God wants to protect us from damaging ourselves and others, and so he offers to fill us—our loneliness, our desires—with himself.

The Greek word for body used here *(soma)* refers to the whole being and personality, not to the worldly flesh (the Greek word for that is *sarx*). These bodies *were made for the Lord, and the Lord cares about our bodies.* Many of the world's religions teach that the soul or spirit is important but not the body; Christians have sometimes been influenced by these ideas. In truth, however, Christianity takes very seriously the realm of the physical. God created a physical world and pronounced it good. He promises a new earth where real people have transformed physical lives. At the heart of Christianity is the story of God himself tak-

ing on flesh and blood and coming to live with people, offering
both physical healing and spiritual restoration.

6:14 **And God both raised up the Lord and will also raise us up by
His power.**NKJV God's care and concern for the physical bodies of
his children began at Creation. Jesus was put to death, but God
raised up the Lord. Coming back to life from death is an impossibility in this world; however, God, who controls everything,
brought his Son back to life and *will also raise us up by His
power.* That God would bring his Son back in a body shows the
value that God places on his children's physical bodies. Paul
made this point to prepare for the following discussion of why
the Corinthian believers must not use their bodies for sexual
immorality (6:13).

6:15-16 **Do you not know that your bodies are members of Christ?
Should I therefore take the members of Christ and make
them members of a prostitute? Never! Do you not know that
whoever is united to a prostitute becomes one body with her?
For it is said, "The two shall be one flesh."**NRSV This teaching
about sexual immorality and prostitutes was especially important
for the Corinthian church because the temple of the love-goddess
Aphrodite was in Corinth. This temple employed more than a
thousand prostitutes, and sex was part of the worship ritual. Paul
clearly stated that Christians should have no part in sexual immorality, even if it is acceptable and popular in the surrounding culture.

His reason? Because the believers' *bodies are members of
Christ.* Chapter 12 describes the church: "Now all of you
together are Christ's body, and each one of you is a separate and
necessary part of it" (12:27 NLT). Because believers are part of
the very "body" of Jesus Christ on earth, they obviously should
never think of taking *the members of Christ and [making] them
members of a prostitute.* Sex is more than a mere physical act;
instead, it unites a man and a woman in such a way that they
become *one body.* This was true for Adam and Eve, because God
had planned that *the two shall be one flesh* in marriage (Genesis
2:24).

Paul was not denying the beauty of sex between a married man
and woman, nor was he saying that any sexual union is an exact
comparison of believers' union with Christ. Paul wanted his readers to see the perversion of using their God-given bodies for such
wickedness as sexual sin with a prostitute (perhaps even a temple
prostitute, thus making the sexual sin a form of idol worship).
These sins are not merely physical, having no effect on a person's
spiritual life. They are deeply emotional and even mystical, in the

case of the union created between sexual partners. This must not be taken for granted. But for the person who has sexually sinned in the past, there is forgiveness, healing, and renewal. Becoming one in an illicit sexual relationship is not unforgivable.

SEX
The parallels of Paul's descriptions with our own times are striking. But we've taken the distortion much further. The Corinthians faced pagan religions that used sex in worship. Modern culture has made a religion out of worshiping sex. It permeates every part of our lives. Paul clearly stated that Christians are to have no part in sexual immorality, even if it is acceptable and popular in our culture. The decision to look at life and live life under God's direction will require obedience every day. How easy it is to rationalize away God's requirement when it comes to books, movies, television, and personal fantasies.

6:17 But the person who is joined to the Lord becomes one spirit with him.NLT A person who commits sexual sin with a prostitute is "united" (joined) with him or her. By contrast, *the person who is joined to the Lord becomes one spirit with him*. The same verb is used both times in the Greek, describing the oneness that believers have with the Lord who is spirit (see 2 Corinthians 3:17-18).

6:18 Run away from sexual sin! No other sin so clearly affects the body as this one does. For sexual immorality is a sin against your own body.NLT Sexual sin is a violation of one's own body. Paul described it as a sin that affects the body like no other, a sin that *is against [one's] own body*. As in 6:13, the word "body" refers not to the flesh, but to the whole being and personality. This sin has disastrous effects. But what an enticement it can be for all people, and believers are not exempt. Clearly other sins also affect the body, such as gluttony or drunkenness, but no other sin has the same effect on the memory, personality, or soul of a person as sexual sin. Paul argues that in intercourse, people are united (6:16-17). Their spirits are not involved in quite the same way in other sins. Also Paul argues that our bodies are the temple of God (6:19-20). In sexual sin, a person removes his or her body from God's control to unite with someone not in his plan. Thus, those people violate God's purpose for their bodies. Satan gladly uses sexual sin as a weapon, for he knows its power to destroy. Thus, Paul says, don't walk, but *run away from sexual sin*. Believers need to exercise alertness and awareness to stay away from places where temptation is strong, and they need to use strong, evasive action if they find themselves entrapped.

GOOD SEX
Christians are free to be all they can be for God, but they are not free *from* God. God created sex to be a beautiful and essential ingredient of marriage, but sexual sin—sex outside the marriage relationship—*always* hurts someone. It hurts God because it shows that we prefer following our own desires to the leading of the Holy Spirit. It hurts others because it violates the commitment so necessary to a relationship. It often brings disease to the body. And it deeply affects our personalities, which respond in anguish when we harm ourselves physically and spiritually.

Although Satan would have us believe the contrary, sex within God's guidelines offers pleasure, satisfaction, fascination, intimacy, health, and wholeness. The best way *is* God's way. He invented sex. We can express our gratefulness to God in prayer and by being faithful to his guidelines.

6:19-20 **Do you not know that your body is a temple of the Holy Spirit, who is in you, whom you have received from God? You are not your own; you were bought at a price. Therefore honor God with your body.**[NIV] Paul asked for the sixth time in this chapter *Do you not know?* indicat-ing that this was a fact the Corinthians should have known but apparently had missed or forgotten. The words "your body" in this verse refer not to the cor-porate "body of Christ," but to each believer's individual, physical body. How should the Corinthian believers think about their bodies? Paul explained that each should view his or her body as *a temple of the Holy Spirit,* who was living in them.

The believers' physical bodies belonged to God. In them, his Spirit lived; through them, he would accom-plish his work on earth. One day they will be resurrected. Jesus Christ died to pay the *price* that purchased sinful people's freedom (Ephesians 1:7; 1 Peter 1:18-19). His blood provided the sacrifice that made believers accept-able to God. Because of Jesus' death

> The presence of the Spirit means that God himself, who created us with bodies in the first place, has taken keen interest in our whole life, including the life of the body. The creation of the body was pronounced *good* in the beginning; it has now been purchased by Christ and is sanctified by the presence of God himself through his Holy Spirit. We must therefore "sanctify" it as well . . . by living the life of the Spirit, a life of holiness.
>
> *Gordon Fee*

and resurrection, the Holy Spirit came to indwell those who believed in him—he took up residence *in* their bodies. The principle "you are not your own" has to be learned before believers can honor God with their bodies. Most people today treat their bodies as a personal convenience for doing what they want. They can wreck them with bad health practices or use them for fulfilling sinful desires. But Paul claims the body for God. Jesus had told his disciples, "The world at large cannot receive [the Holy Spirit], because it isn't looking for him and doesn't recognize him. But you do, because he lives with you now and later will be in you" (John 14:17 NLT). This Holy Spirit had come into them when they had believed, having *received* him *from God*. The believers, therefore, ought to *honor God* with their bodies. Just as the temple was a place for worship, sacrifice, prayer, and communion with God, so should our bodies be used to implement these high purposes.

The believers seemed to have thought that the presence of the Spirit within them negated the value of their bodies; Paul told them just the opposite—the body as the Spirit's temple affirms its importance to God. Christians cannot indulge their bodies because they are unimportant, nor can they punish their bodies in order to be saved or become more spiritual. They must "honor God with their bodies" by showing their gratefulness for Jesus' sacrifice by their worship, obedience, and service (see Romans 12:1-2).

OWNERSHIP
What did Paul mean when he said that our bodies are not our own but belong to God? Many people say they have the right to do whatever they want with their own bodies. Although they think that this is freedom, they are really enslaved to their own desires. When we become Christians, the Holy Spirit fills and lives in us. Therefore, we no longer own our bodies. "Bought at a price" refers to slaves purchased at auction. Christ's death freed us from sin but also obligates us to his service.

If you live in a building owned by someone else, you try not to violate the building's rules. Because your body belongs to God, you must not violate his standards for living. Make it your practice to have an occasional body checkup in prayer. Reflect on how you are treating your body and ask God to point out any thoughts or behaviors that need change or improvement.

---

1 Corinthians 7

After discussing disorder in the church, Paul moved to the list of questions that the Corinthians had sent him, including those on marriage, singleness, eating meat offered to idols, propriety in worship, orderliness in the Lord's Supper, spiritual gifts, and the resurrection. Questions that plague churches today are remarkably similar, so we can receive specific guidance in these areas from this letter. The first section (7:1-16) applies to those who are presently married or who have been married.

MUTUAL MONOGAMY
In the verses that follow, Paul makes his basic position very clear: Marriage involves two people, a man and a woman, working out their life for a lifetime. Even a casual reader notes the balance. What is really good for the man is really good for the woman. What is really good for the wife is really good for the husband. Marriage itself is good. In spite of sinfulness and societal attitudes that have devalued and twisted marriage, God's original design remains the ideal. A mutual commitment to God's ways in marriage can make even the most difficult union survive. Base your convictions on what God says, not on society's distortions.

7:1 Now about the questions you asked in your letter. Yes, it is good to live a celibate life.[NLT] The Corinthian believers had written to Paul, asking him several questions, or perhaps even taking issue with some of his principles, relating to the Christian life and problems in the church. Apparently this first question regarded whether people should stay married or if those previously married should remain celibate. Christians in Corinth were surrounded by sexual temptation. The city had a reputation even among pagans for sexual immorality and religious prostitution. To this sexually saturated society, Paul was delivering these instructions on sex and marriage. The Corinthians needed special, specific instructions because of their culture's immoral standards. Some believers were teaching total sexual abstinence within marriage because of a mistaken notion that sexual relations were sinful; some were proposing sepa-

rating from or divorcing spouses in order to stay pure. To the first
question, Paul answered that *it is good to live a celibate life* ("It is
well for a man not to touch a woman," NRSV). At first glance this
may seem to contradict God's words in Genesis 2:18, "It is not
good for the man to be alone" (NLT). Paul maintained a high view
of marriage (Ephesians 5:25-33). In 7:1, Paul was not stating an
absolute; rather, he was simply explaining that celibacy was normal, and that it may be God's will for some to remain single. Paul's
advice may have been directed at the "present crisis" referred to in
7:26; he thought it would be easier to face persecution as a single
person. But, as Paul would explain later in this chapter, his words
do not mean that married couples should divorce or that Christians
ought not marry. For those whom God calls to celibacy (such as
Paul himself), the lifestyle is in accordance with God's will for
them. They should see it as a gift to be used to further God's kingdom (7:7).

MARRIAGE SEMINAR
Much of what Paul wrote about marriage was based on its
lifelong nature. First Corinthians serves as a "mini" marriage
seminar for Christians. The Corinthian church was in turmoil
because of the immorality of the culture around them. Some
Greeks, in rejecting immorality, rejected sex and marriage
altogether. The Corinthian Christians wondered if this was what
they should do also, so they asked Paul several questions:
"Because sex is perverted, shouldn't we also abstain in
marriage?" "If my spouse is unsaved, should I seek a divorce?"
"Should unmarried people and widows remain unmarried?"
Paul answered many of these questions by saying, "For now,
stay put. Be content in the situation where God has placed you.
If you're married, don't seek to be single. If you're single, don't
seek to be married."

The main teaching points in Paul's advice about marriage
include the following:
- Choosing to remain unmarried can be good if the unmarried
  person uses the extra time to serve God.
- Married people belong to each other, and they should live
  that relationship out fully.
- A Christian husband and wife ought to find a way to stay
  together.
- A marriage partner who becomes a Christian may not use
  his or her faith as an excuse for divorce and may have to
  accept rejection by his or her non-Christian partner.
- Believers should be content in the roles God has given them.
- Marriage can either complicate or clarify a person's commitment to Christ.
- Believers should always be available to the Lord, regardless of their status in life.

7:2 **But because there is so much sexual immorality, each man should have his own wife, and each woman should have her own husband.**NLT After saying that living the celibate life is acceptable and good, Paul quickly added that he did not mean that being married was bad. God created marriage, so it cannot be bad. Those who can remain celibate should do so, but the believers in Corinth ought not deprive themselves of being married and try to enforce celibacy. That would set them up for failure *because there is so much sexual immorality.* As noted above, sexual immorality was pervasive in Corinth, invading even the worship of some of their gods and goddesses. Many of the believers had come out of very immoral lifestyles. Paul advised, therefore, that those men and women not given the gift of celibacy from God should go ahead and marry. Then they would be able to fulfill their sexual desires in the God-honoring institution of marriage.

7:3 **The husband should not deprive his wife of sexual intimacy, which is her right as a married woman, nor should the wife deprive her husband.**NLT In the same way that God created marriage, he also created sex with which the human race could procreate as well as find great enjoyment. Just as with anything else that God created, however, sinful humanity can find a way to dirty it. God created sex to occur only between a man and a woman, and only within the confines of the marriage commitment, but humans have used sex wrongly. The Corinthians were surrounded by sexual temptations. Such temptations can be difficult to withstand because they appeal to the normal and natural desires that God has given to human beings.

Some people in the ancient world reacted against the extreme immorality by doing just the opposite—becoming ascetics and abstaining from sex altogether. Apparently, some married people, who saw or experienced the evil of sex wrongly used, began to believe that all sex was immoral, so they should abstain even in their marriages. While celibacy should be the rule for those who choose to remain single (7:1), Paul explained that it should not have any place in the marriage relationship. Marriage provides God's way to satisfy natural sexual desires and to strengthen the partners against temptation. Married couples have the responsibility to care for each other; therefore, husbands and wives should not *deprive* each other but should fulfill each other's needs and desires. Notice that Paul did not emphasize that one partner can demand sex from the other but rather that neither should withhold it. Both partners need to listen to God in this matter and do what is best for the union. Paul's reference to the wife's *right as a married woman* as being equal to the man's right was revolution-

ary in this culture of male domination. Paul stressed equality of
men and women in their rights as marriage partners to give and
receive from each other.

MISAPPLICATION
The Corinthians had a lot to learn about Bible application.
Apparently, some were teaching that the easiest way to apply
God's guidelines about marriage and sexuality was to avoid
marriage and sex completely. Principles designed to protect
were being used to destroy marriage. Walls erected to make
marriage a safe and wonderful place were being described as
undesirable enclosures.
    Today's popular description of marriage commitment as little
more than worthless ink stains on a piece of paper presents a
parallel misunderstanding. When lifelong, mutual commitment
is ruled out as the basis for marriage, the relationship is left
without foundation. God did not design marriage to be part-time
or short-term. The results that people desire in marriage
(intimacy, trust, unity, security, joy) are never instant. In order to
grow, they require the time that only a lifelong commitment
provides. Patiently apply God's principles to your marriage.
God will bless your faithfulness.

**7:4 The wife's body does not belong to her alone but also to her
husband. In the same way, the husband's body does not
belong to him alone but also to his wife.**[NIV] A person's body
belongs to God when that person becomes a Christian because
Jesus Christ bought that person by paying the price to release
him or her from sin (see 6:19-20). Physically, their bodies
belong to their spouses. God designed marriage so that through
the union of husband and wife two become one. The sexual
relationship makes two people "one flesh" (6:16; also Genesis
2:24). The sexual act causes a mystical and intimate union such
that *the wife's body* no longer belongs just to her *but also to her
husband.* In the same way, *the husband's body* no longer
belongs to him alone *but also to his wife.* The unity given to the
married couple through their sexual relationship makes them no
longer independent beings; they have become "one flesh." So
Paul said to these married believers that sex is not immoral
because God created it; therefore, they should not deprive their
spouse.

**7:5-6 Do not deprive one another except perhaps by agreement
for a set time, to devote yourselves to prayer, and then come
together again, so that Satan may not tempt you because of
your lack of self-control.**[NRSV] The only time the spouses
should *deprive one another* of sexual intimacy would be if they

mutually agree, *for a set time,* to abstain from sex in order to *devote [themselves] to prayer.* Times of devoted prayer to God are vital for all believers; some may feel that they want to do this with total focus on God and so would abstain from sex or even food if it were a time for fasting. This is laudable, but Paul also explained that it should not be a habit. Because those married are already "one flesh," they must maintain that union and *come together again.* Otherwise, they would leave themselves open for Satan's temptations with sexual immorality because of a possible *lack of self-control.*

This I say by way of concession, not of command.^{NRSV} Some scholars think that this statement most likely refers to all that Paul had said thus far concerning his answer to their marriage question (7:1). Marriage is desirable, and certainly needful in order to procreate under God's guidelines, but marriage is not commanded by God. However, this statement could just as easily conclude his statement in 7:5-6—which he doesn't want to them to understand as if it were a command.

7:7 I wish everyone could get along without marrying, just as I do. But we are not all the same. God gives some the gift of marriage, and to others he gives the gift of singleness.^{NLT} Paul made a personal note, further explaining that celibacy is acceptable, by stating that he wished *everyone could get along without marrying* just as he did. Paul well knew that his life-style—itinerant travel, difficult work, not having a permanent home, danger, often being mocked and ridiculed, sometimes being beaten and jailed, all for the sake of the gospel—was not one that he could easily adhere to with a wife and children along. He would feel the need to protect them; he would worry about them as any good husband and father would. So Paul thanked the Lord for his gift of being able to remain celibate by doing what God wanted him to do with the freedom that a married man would not have. He wished that others could serve the Lord with such complete abandon.

Paul also realized, however, that if everyone remained unmarried, there would be no Christian children and no furthering of the Christian faith to the next generation. Thus all believers are not *the same.* To some *God gives . . . the gift of marriage,* and they can serve God well in that capacity. To others *he gives the gift of singleness* so they can fulfill other roles in the furthering of his kingdom. Because these are gifts from God, one should not try to force either one on anyone's life.

VALUED ROLES
Both marriage and singleness are gifts from God. One is not morally better than the other, and both are valuable for accomplishing God's purposes. It is important for each believer, therefore, to accept his or her present situation. When Paul said he wished that all people were like him (that is, unmarried), he was expressing his desire that more people would devote themselves *completely* to the ministry without the added concerns of spouse and family, as he had done. He was not criticizing marriage—after all, marriage and sex are God's created way of providing companionship and populating the earth.

Are you married? Seek to honor God with your marriage commitment by honoring your spouse. Seek to serve God in whatever situation, position in life, or surroundings that you and your spouse share. If your spouse is not a believer, pray that your life and faithfulness will lead him or her to faith in Jesus Christ.

Are you single? Seek to honor God with your singleness. Do not feel that you are less of a person, alone in a world of couples. Instead, see your singleness as a gift from God. Ask him how he would have you serve him with that gift. You may find opportunities available to you that might never have been possible if you were married.

Trust God with your life. Seek to serve him with the gifts he has given.

7:8 To the unmarried and the widows I say that it is well for them to remain unmarried as I am.NRSV Paul laid down the general principles regarding marriage in the previous verses; here he began to speak to various people's situations specifically. First, he wrote instructions *to the unmarried and the widows* (and widowers). Paul's single-minded focus was always on God's kingdom and service for it, so his advice to these believers in Corinth is couched in his concern for their ability to bear up under persecution for their faith and to serve the Lord wholeheartedly (see 7:26, 32-35). (Note that in a different place and situation, Paul counseled the younger widows to marry. See 1 Timothy 5:14.) So he suggested to those presently not bound in marriage that it would be *well for them to remain unmarried* as he himself was.

It is unknown whether Paul was ever married, if his wife left him (perhaps when he became a Christian), or if he was widowed. Some believe he was probably married at one time because marriage was required of Jewish men in positions of leadership among the Jews, as Paul had been before he became a Christian.

7:9 But if they cannot control themselves, they should marry, for it is better to marry than to burn with passion.NIV The Corinthians seemed to have a problem with self-control—as suggested by

the kind of sexual immorality so common in the city. The believers came out of that lifestyle, yet probably many still were struggling with their sinful natures in that area. Paul did not suggest
enforced celibacy on such people. Instead, he told married people
to give themselves to each other (7:3-4); he told single people to
try to use their singleness as an opportunity to give all to the Lord
(7:7-8). Yet, he also understood that those who struggled with
self-control should not put themselves in the position of enforced
celibacy, for Satan would use many temptations right there in the
city to bring them down. Instead, Paul said these people *should
marry, for it is better to marry than to burn with passion.* This is
not a put-down of marriage as being no more than a legitmate
way to release sexual pressure; instead, it is tied with the gifts of
marriage and singleness that Paul had mentioned in 7:7. Those
who do not have the gift of singleness, and thus have a passion
that will need a proper release, ought to marry. It would be difficult to live with such a desire without having been given the
grace to do so.

PREMARITAL DECISION MAKING
Sexual pressure is not the best motive for getting married, but it
is better to marry the right person than to "burn with passion."
Some in Corinth taught that all sex was wrong, so engaged
couples may have been deciding not to get married. In this
passage, Paul was telling couples who wanted to marry that
they should not frustrate their normal sexual drives by avoiding
marriage. This does not mean, however, that people who have
trouble controlling themselves should marry the first person
who comes along. It is better to deal with the pressure of desire
than to deal with an unhappy marriage.

**7:10-11 To the married I give this command (not I, but the Lord): A
wife must not separate from her husband. But if she does, she
must remain unmarried or else be reconciled to her husband.
And a husband must not divorce his wife.**NIV Having spoken to
the unmarried people in 7:8-9, Paul here turned his attention *to
the married.* He explained to the Corinthian believers the Christian view of divorce, given as a *command,* not from Paul himself,
but from *the Lord,* referring to Jesus Christ. Jesus had taught
about divorce during his time on earth (see Matthew 5:31-32;
19:3-9; Mark 10:2-12; Luke 16:18), saying that married people
were not meant to be divorced. While divorce was permitted as a
concession, it was not God's plan for married people. Paul either
had received this teaching by divine inspiration, or he may have
heard it in one of his conversations with the disciples.

WHAT THE BIBLE SAYS ABOUT MARRIAGE

Genesis 2:18-24	Marriage is God's idea.
Genesis 24:58-60	Commitment is essential to a successful marriage.
Genesis 29:10-11	Romance is important.
Jeremiah 7:34	Marriage holds times of great joy
Malachi 2:14-15	Marriage creates the best environment for raising children.
Matthew 5:31-32	Unfaithfulness breaks the bond of trust, the foundation of all relationships.
Matthew 19:6	Marriage is permanent.
Romans 7:2-3	Ideally, only death should dissolve marriage.
1 Corinthians 7	In marriage, the husband and wife belong to each other.
Ephesians 5:21-33	Marriage is based on the principled practice of love.
Ephesians 5:23-32	Marriage is a living symbol of Christ and the church.
Hebrews 13:4	Marriage is good and honorable.
1 Peter 3:1-7	In marriage, each partner has responsibilities in caring for the other.

Paul explained, therefore, that *a wife must not separate from her husband.* Apparently it was possible in the Greco-Roman culture for a wife to leave her husband (in Jewish culture, divorce laws focused on the husband separating from his wife). If a woman has already separated from her husband, *she must remain unmarried or else be reconciled to her husband.* She does not have the option to marry another man. In the same way, the *husband must not divorce his wife.* Although Paul gave an exception in 7:15, the ideal remains.

7:12-13 Now, I will speak to the rest of you, though I do not have a direct command from the Lord. If a Christian man has a wife who is an unbeliever and she is willing to continue living with him, he must not leave her. And if a Christian woman has a husband who is an unbeliever, and he is willing to continue living with her, she must not leave him.NLT Next, Paul turned his attention to *the rest of you*—the people who were married but felt "single" because their spouses were unbelievers. Undoubtedly, there were many such couples in the Corinthian church. About this particular situation, Paul said he did *not have a direct command from the Lord.* So he did what all believers must do when Scripture doesn't state exactly what must be done in a particular situation—he inferred what should be done from what Scripture *does* say. Scripture has plenty to say about marriage. The "command" about the permanence of marriage (7:10) comes from the Old Testament (Genesis 2:24) and from Jesus (as noted above). Paul based his advice on God's commands about marriage and applied them to the situation the Corinthians were facing.

MAY A DIVORCED PERSON REMARRY?
By forbidding divorced persons from remarrying, Paul was upholding the teaching of Jesus in Matthew 5:31-32; 19:3-9; Mark 10:11-12; and Luke 16:18. Jesus' main point was to teach that the divorce laws should not be used to dispose of one partner in order to get another one.

The nagging question for Christians remains: May a divorced person, who truly repents of a sinful past and commits his or her life to God, remarry?

We long for a simple, direct reply to that question, but there is none. Rather, we need to consider the intent of Jesus' message on marriage. We have Jesus' high view of marriage and low view of divorce recorded in the Gospels. Jesus proclaimed new life—full forgiveness and restoration—to all who would come to God in repentance and faith. Spiritual discernment is essential here, but the gospel—God's promise of wholeness and full healing—includes the sacred bond of marriage. Thus, it seems right for churches to allow a repentant, formerly married person to marry another believer.

Because of their desire to serve Christ, some people in the Corinthian church thought they ought to divorce their pagan spouses and marry Christians. But Paul affirmed the marriage commitment. God's ideal is for marriages to stay together— even when one spouse is not a believer. To leave the marriage— even for the noblest of goals in serving the Lord—would actually be to disobey God's express command regarding marriage (Mark 10:2-9). Instead, the believing spouse should try to win the other to Christ (7:16). It would be easy to rationalize leaving; however, Paul makes a strong case for staying with the unbelieving spouse and being a positive influence on the marriage. Paul, like Jesus, believed that marriage is permanent. Paul commanded this for the believers in the church whose unbelieving spouses were *willing to continue living with* them. He gave other advice to those whose unbelieving spouses wanted to dissolve the marriage *because* the husband or wife had become a Christian (see 7:15).

7:14 **For the unbelieving husband has been sanctified through his wife, and the unbelieving wife has been sanctified through her believing husband. Otherwise your children**

would be unclean, but as it is, they are holy.^{NIV} The church
included individuals who had become believers but whose
spouses had not. Paul had already stated that these believers
must remain with their unbelieving wife or husband. He
explained that the unbelieving spouse *has been sanctified* by
the believing spouse. The word "sanctify" can mean to cleanse,
make pure, regard as sacred. It is used in the Old Testament to
describe the items that become holy because of their relationship to something already deemed holy by God. For example,
the temple sanctified the gold connected with it, or the altar
sanctified the gift laid on it (see Matthew 23:17, 19). There are
two views of how "sanctified" is applied to the unbeliever. One
view is that there is a moral influence on the unbeliever as the
Christian spouse bears witness to Christ and lives obediently to
God. The other view is that the Christian, now blessed by God,
includes his or her spouse in the promised blessings of the covenant as they overflow to the unbeliever. "Sanctification" does
not carry the meaning of "salvation"; that is, the unbelieving
husband is not "saved" through his wife's salvation. That
would make no sense because of Paul's words in 7:16 about the
desired conversion of these pagan partners. More likely, the
Corinthians had heeded Paul's advice in 5:9-11 not to associate
with unbelievers. They had interpreted Paul to mean that sex
with an unbelieving marriage partner would defile them. Paul
affirmed the opposite. When believers have sexual relations
with their unbelieving spouse, the unbelievers are blessed in a
certain way. The marriage and its sexual relations set up or lead
into the possibility of the conversion of the unbeliever.

In this context, Paul pictured the unbelieving husband or wife,
although remaining pagan, would assume "sanctification" in the
eyes of God because of his or her intimate relationship with a
believer. An unbelieving husband, as guardian and caretaker of a
home and of his Christian wife, is sanctified by God due to the
man's role in the life of one of God's chosen ones. The same is
true of the wife.

The blessings that flow to believers don't stop there but extend
to others. Among those most likely to receive benefits from
God's work in believers' lives are their spouse and children. God
regards the marriage as "sanctified" (set apart for his use) by the
presence of one Christian spouse. The other partner does not
receive salvation automatically but is helped by this relationship.
The unbeliever is in a relationship with one upon whom God has
his hand and whom God will use for his service. This will have
an effect because of the close relationship and love between the
partners that presumably already exist.

Paul calls the children of such a marriage *holy* because of
God's blessing on the family. Many feel that the blessing given to
the Christian parent extends to the children (though this is not
expressly stated in Scripture), and they are to be regarded as
Christian until they are old enough to decide for themselves.
"Holy" here means dedicated to God by the believing parent. But
the believing parent, called upon to raise his or her children in the
faith, will hopefully have such an influence that the children will
accept salvation for themselves.

**7:15 But if the unbeliever leaves, let him do so. A believing man
or woman is not bound in such circumstances; God has
called us to live in peace.**^{NIV} While the believing spouse must
not leave the marriage if the unbeliever wants to stay married
(7:12-13), the opposite may also happen. The unbeliever may
decide that, because his or her spouse has become a Christian,
the marriage should be dissolved. In this case, the believer's
only choices would be to deny faith in Jesus Christ in order to
maintain the marriage, or maintain faith in Christ and let the
marriage be dissolved. As difficult as it might be, and as much
as marriage is sanctified by God, the high calling of God must
not be denied for any reason. So the believer must let the unbeliever go. When a divorce happens for this reason, *a believing
man or woman is not bound in such circumstances* to God's law
regarding divorce. This may be the second exception to remar-
riage, along with adultery (see Matthew 5:31-32). So the Christian man or woman can allow the divorce to happen and not be
disobeying God. Another reason to not block this divorce is
that *God has called us to live in peace*—a situation that would
be impossible in a home where the unbeliever felt hostile
toward the believer. It would be better for such a marriage to be
dissolved.

**7:16 You wives must remember that your husbands might be con-
verted because of you. And you husbands must remember
that your wives might be converted because of you.**^{NLT} Another
reason for believers to try not to dissolve their marriage to an
unbeliever is that they can be a good influence on their spouse.
The intimacy and day-to-day-ness of marriage provide ample
opportunity for the Christian to be a powerful witness to his or
her spouse. So powerful can it be, Paul reminded them, that the
unbelieving wife or husband *might be converted* because of the
faithful testimony of the believing wives and husbands. For those
couples who can stay together "in peace" (7:15), this would be
the most joyous result of all.

BELIEVERS SHOULD BE CONTENT WHERE THEY ARE / 7:17-24

Paul had just finished explaining to the believers who were married to unbelievers that they should stay in their situation peacefully if at all possible and live for Christ in their marriage. This passage expands his thought on that topic, explaining that just because people become Christians, this does not call for wholesale changes in every part of their outward lives.

7:17-19 **You must accept whatever situation the Lord has put you in, and continue on as you were when God first called you. This is my rule for all the churches. For instance, a man who was circumcised before he became a believer should not try to reverse it. And the man who was uncircumcised when he became a believer should not be circumcised now.**NLT Christ makes changes from within and calls people from all walks of life. While some changes are made in behavior and attitudes, the believers ought not make some kinds of changes. For example, they ought not change marriage partners. They need not even try to change jobs (unless the job was dishonoring to God). Instead, *accept whatever situation the Lord has put you in, and continue on as you were when God first called you* because God can use his faithful followers in all areas of life. This was not Paul's advice just to the church in Corinth but his *rule for all the churches.*

For instance, Paul wrote, *a man who was circumcised before he became a believer should not try to reverse it.* The ceremony of circumcision was an important part of the Jews' relationship with God. In fact, before Christ came, circumcision was commanded by God for those who claimed to follow him (Genesis 17:9-14). But after Christ's death and resurrection, circumcision was no longer necessary (Acts 15; Romans 4:9-11; Galatians 5:2-4; Colossians 2:11). For the Jews, circumcision was the sign of their covenant with God; the Greeks, however, looked down upon it as the mark of lowly people. Some Jews, in an attempt to become more acceptable in Greek culture, could attempt to surgically reverse the marks of a circumcision. To add to the confusion, the Judaizers (a group of false teachers) were claiming that Gentiles had to be circumcised before they could become Christians. Paul pointed out that, in God's kingdom, **circumcision is nothing and uncircumcision is nothing, but keeping the commandments of God is what matters.**NKJV Jewish Christians did not need to reverse their circumcisions, and Gentile Christians did not need to be circumcised (Romans 2:25, 29; Galatians 5:6). Instead, they should stay exactly as they were when they became believers; any outward change would make no difference. The inner change is all that matters. They should focus on *keeping the commandments of God,* desiring to conform their heart and will in obedience to him.

START WHERE YOU ARE
Apparently the Corinthians were ready to make wholesale changes without thinking through the ramifications. Paul was writing to say that people should be Christians where they are. You can do God's work and demonstrate your faith *anywhere.* If you became a Christian after marriage, and your spouse is not a believer, remember that you don't have to be married to a Christian to live for Christ. Don't assume that you are in the wrong place or are stuck with the wrong person. You may be just where God wants you (see 7:20).

7:20 You should continue on as you were when God called you.[NLT] Paul repeated what he had said in 7:17 for emphasis and because he had said this was his rule for all the churches. The believers *should continue on* as they were *when God called* them. This refers to examples such as marriage, circumcision or uncircumcision (as noted above), job, or station in life (slave or free, 7:21-23). Obviously, it does not refer to one's spiritual, inward life; that should be growing and changing every day as believers draw closer to and learn more about God.

STAY THERE
Often we are so concerned about what we *could* be doing for God somewhere else that we miss great opportunities right where we are. Paul says that when someone becomes a Christian, he or she should usually continue with the work he or she has previously been doing—provided it isn't immoral or unethical. Every job can become Christian work when you realize that the purpose of your life is to honor, serve, and speak out for Christ. Because God has placed you where you are, look carefully for opportunities to serve him there. After all, if God found you there, God can certainly use you there!

7:21 Are you a slave? Don't let that worry you—but if you get a chance to be free, take it.[NLT] From religious variations in the church (between those circumcised and those uncircumcised), Paul moved on to the varied social states of the believers. The church in Corinth also included people from every station in life—many of them slaves. Therefore, if a believer was a slave when he became a Christian, he could continue as a Christian slave, doing his work as for the Lord (Ephesians 6:5-9). The key phrase is "don't let that worry you." The slaves should not feel that because they became Christians they could no longer serve as slaves because they deserved freedom. Unfortunately, they might have to keep living as slaves, but they should serve Christ wholeheartedly in their position. Of course, they also were free to seek to better themselves, for Paul says, *if you get a chance to be free, take it.* Obedience to God, as always, is what matters most (7:19). For more on Christianity and slavery, see the following Life Application Bible Commentaries: *Ephesians* (Ephesians 6:5-9), *Colossians* (Colossians 3:22–4:2), and *1 & 2 Timothy and Titus* (Titus 2:9-10).

7:22-23 **And remember, if you were a slave when the Lord called you, the Lord has now set you free from the awful power of sin. And if you were free when the Lord called you, you are now a slave of Christ. God purchased you at a high price. Don't be enslaved by the world.**[NLT] Slavery was common throughout the Roman Empire, so many of the believers in Corinth were slaves *when the Lord called [them].* Paul said that although the Christian slaves remained enslaved to other human beings, they were *free from the awful power of sin* in their lives (Romans 6:18, 22). These slaves had been made free. In the same way, if a person was free when the Lord called him, he was *now a slave of Christ.* The free people had become servants of the Savior who *purchased [them] at a high price,* higher than any rich person ever paid for a slave, for the Savior had paid with his blood (6:20; Romans 5:9; 2 Corinthians 5:21).

Because God paid a great price to bring his people to himself, he has complete authority over their lives. Believers' lives and service come under his control; all that they do is for his kingdom and his glory. Because believers are servants of God, they should no longer *be enslaved by the world.* They live in the world, but they are not of it, looking forward to a future citizenship in heaven.

SET FREE
People are slaves to sin until they commit their lives to Christ, who alone can conquer sin's power. Sin, pride, and fear no longer have any claim over them, just as a slave owner no longer has power over slaves who have been sold. The Bible says that people become Christ's slaves when they become Christians (Romans 6:18), but this actually means that they gain freedom, because sin no longer controls them. Don't let the society around you dictate the rules. Make Christ your final authority.

7:24 So, dear brothers and sisters, whatever situation you were in when you became a believer, stay there in your new relationship with God.^{NLT} This passage repeats Paul's statement of 7:17 and 7:20. God can use people from all areas of life, so *whatever situation* God found them in, they should *stay there in [their] new relationship with God.* Because believers have been set free from sin and are free to live for God, they ought not feel either pride or shame in their station in life. Instead, they should serve God from that position, seeking to share the gospel with those who might not otherwise hear it. For further discussion on living with unbelievers, see the Life Application Bible Commentary *1 & 2 Peter and Jude* (1 Peter 3:1-7).

QUESTIONS ABOUT SINGLENESS / 7:25-40

Throughout this chapter, Paul has been telling believers not to seek to change their situations but to remain where they are and to seek to serve the Lord there. A person should not make drastic changes during difficult times. Paul wanted the believers to focus on making the most of their time before Christ returns—sharing the faith so that many more can become believers. Paul's urgency and single-minded focus on God's kingdom come through in the advice he gives to married and single people in these verses. As always, he did not want anything to hinder their work for the advance of God's kingdom.

7:25-26 Now, about the young women who are not yet married. I do not have a command from the Lord for them. But the Lord in his kindness has given me wisdom that can be trusted, and I will share it with you. Because of this present crisis, I think it is best to remain just as you are.^{NLT} The words "now, about" indicate that at this point Paul began addressing another matter about which the Corinthian church had asked. In their culture, a young woman's parents usually would make the decision about whether or not their daughter would marry. So these parents had written wondering what decisions to make regarding their daughters—the *young women who are not yet married.*

Paul clearly stated that he had no specific *command from the Lord* for the believers on this subject; that is, he did not have a direct teaching from Jesus to draw from. This does not mean, however, that Paul's words here should be taken as any less inspired. Paul offered them this advice because he knew that *the Lord in his kindness [had] given [him] wisdom that can be trusted.* Paul shared that wisdom with the believers when they asked such questions as this.

Paul advised the young women to *remain* as they were, unmarried. He reasoned that it would be easier on them to be single than married during *this present crisis*. There has been discussion among scholars regarding the nature of this "crisis." Some have suggested that Paul expected the Lord's return and was referring to the certain calamities that would take place prior to the Second Coming. Most likely, however, Paul foresaw the impending persecution that the Roman government would soon bring upon Christians. He gave this practical advice because being unmarried would mean less suffering and more freedom to throw one's life into the cause of Christ (7:29), even to the point of fearlessly dying for him. Paul's advice reveals his single-minded devotion to spreading the Good News. He wanted these unmarried believers to consider the times in which they were living and how well they could follow the will of God for them in their unmarried state as compared to being married.

7:27 Are you married? Do not seek a divorce. Are you unmarried? Do not look for a wife.[NIV] Speaking to the young women not yet married, Paul had explained that "it is best to remain just as you are." This means that it would be best for them not to put their energies into worrying about getting married. Paul expanded his advice for everyone, both men and women, married and single. A *married* person should *not seek a divorce; an unmarried* man should not *look for a wife*. Paul's reasoning rested with what he had said in 7:26. It would be difficult to be a Christian in the Roman Empire in coming days. Paul was advising church members to stay focused on the Lord and on the business of sharing the gospel.

7:28 But if you do get married, it is not a sin. And if a young woman gets married, it is not a sin. However, I am trying to spare you the extra problems that come with marriage.[NLT] Lest he be misunderstood, Paul explained that he was not saying that it would be sinful for these young unmarried women to get married. That would be inconsistent with all of Scripture. Instead, Paul was *trying to spare [them] the extra problems that come with marriage*. Life holds plenty of difficulties—and in the first-century Roman world, one of those difficulties would be persecution of Christians. Paul wanted the believers in Corinth to be able to let go of everything in their faithfulness to God—that would be much easier without the attachment of marriage. Thus, he advised the unmarried to remain that way. If they chose to marry, however, that would not be wrong.

MARITAL LIMITATIONS
Many people naively think that marriage will solve all their
problems. Here are some problems marriage *won't* solve:
- Loneliness
- Sexual temptation
- Satisfaction of one's deepest emotional needs
- Elimination of life's difficulties

Marriage alone does not hold two people together, but
commitment does—commitment to Christ and to each other
despite conflicts and problems. As wonderful as it is, marriage
does not automatically solve every problem. Whether married
or single, be content with your situation and focus on Christ,
not on loved ones, to help address your problems.

**7:29-30 Now let me say this, dear brothers and sisters: The time that
remains is very short, so husbands should not let marriage be
their major concern. Happiness or sadness or wealth should not
keep anyone from doing God's work.**[NLT] As Paul had challenged
the unmarried to consider their situation in light of the call of God
on their lives and their brief time on earth to accomplish it, so he
challenged all the brothers and sisters to look at life and realize that
the time that remains is very short. Paul probably did not have the
Second Coming in mind here; rather, he probably was thinking of
coming persecutions and the resulting curtailment of the believers'
freedom to witness for their faith. Paul urged the believers not to
regard marriage, home, or financial security as the ultimate goals of
life. As much as possible, they should live unhindered by the cares
of this world, not getting involved with burdensome mortgages,
budgets, investments, or debts that might keep them from doing
God's work. Married men and women, as Paul pointed out (7:33-
34), must take care of earthly responsibilities—but they should
make every effort to keep them modest and manageable. They
must live for the Lord in their marriages. If life brings them *happiness or sadness or wealth,* they should not be bound up in any of it;
these situations must *not keep [them] from doing God's work.*

Paul's focus, as always, was that believers make the most of
their time before Christ's return. Every person in every generation should have this sense of urgency about telling the Good
News to others. Life is short—there's not much time!

**7:31 Those in frequent contact with the things of the world should
make good use of them without becoming attached to them,
for this world and all it contains will pass away.**[NLT] Believers
must live detached from this world. Those who have been
blessed with *the things of the world should make good use of
them without becoming attached to them.* Material blessings can

be used to further God's kingdom. Jesus commended the unbelievers in his day who used money wisely, and he encouraged the
disciples to learn from them: "I tell you, use your worldly
resources to benefit others and make friends. In this way, your
generosity stores up a reward for you in heaven" (Luke 16:9
NLT). All of our possessions and opportunities can be shared with
those in ministry or put to good use. Our homes can be opened,
our cars loaned out, and our possessions shared. Believers who
have been blessed with material wealth must always remember
that they have been blessed in order to bless others. Paul did not
want the believers to be "attached" to anything in this life as if
that were all there is—to do so would be to forget that *this world
and all it contains will pass away* (see also 1 John 2:8, 17).

7:32-34 **In everything you do, I want you to be free from the concerns
of this life. An unmarried man can spend his time doing the
Lord's work and thinking how to please him. But a married
man can't do that so well. He has to think about his earthly
responsibilities and how to please his wife. His interests are
divided. In the same way, a woman who is no longer married or
has never been married can be more devoted to the Lord in
body and in spirit, while the married woman must be concerned about her earthly responsibilities and how to please her
husband.**NLT Marriage is a tremendous responsibility for each of
the spouses involved. For a marriage to be successful, husband and
wife must work at their relationship—they will both have to be concerned about *earthly responsibilities* and about *how to please* each
other. This is good and important for those who are married. Paul
was not saying that this was wrong in any way; he was simply
pointing out that unmarried people can focus their energies elsewhere. For example, *an unmarried man can spend his time doing
the Lord's work and thinking how to please him,* and an unmarried
woman *can be more devoted to the Lord in body and in spirit.* As
Paul had noted in 7:28, his advice rests on his desire that these
believers *be free from the concerns of this life.* Later, Paul would
uphold the privilege of marriage (9:3-5), but this was his advice to
those who had asked about their personal situations.

THE GIFT OF SINGLENESS
Some single people feel tremendous pressure to be married.
They think their lives can be complete with a spouse. But Paul
underlines one advantage of being single—the potential of a
greater focus on Christ and his work. If you are unmarried, use
your special opportunity to serve Christ wholeheartedly.

7:35 I say this for your own benefit, not to put any restraint upon you, but to promote good order and unhindered devotion to the Lord.^{NRSV} Paul gave the advice in the previous verses for their *benefit,* but *not to put any restraint* upon the believers. These were not regulations that the churches had to follow. Instead, this advice came from Paul's heart, to help the struggling believers in Corinth to be able *to promote good order and unhindered devotion to the Lord.* This would be helpful as they lived their Christianity in the midst of the gross immorality of Corinth and as they anticipated persecution for their faith.

7:36-37 If anyone thinks he is acting improperly toward the virgin he is engaged to, and if she is getting along in years and he feels he ought to marry, he should do as he wants. He is not sinning. They should get married. But the man who has settled the matter in his own mind, who is under no compulsion but has control over his own will, and who has made up his mind not to marry the virgin—this man also does the right thing.^{NIV} The phrase "getting along in years" means past the prime age for marriage. In their culture at that time, a young woman was considered "fully developed" and ready for marriage at eighteen to twenty years old. The young man should marry if *he feels he ought to marry.* But if he *has made up his mind not to marry,* he should let the young woman go. In so doing, this young man *also does the right thing.* That he *is under no compulsion* means that he does not have outside pressure such as from parents or through a prior agreement. Such a man *has control over his own will* and can thus make his own decision.

7:38 So the person who marries does well, and the person who doesn't marry does even better.^{NLT} When Paul wrote that *the person who doesn't marry does even better,* he was referring to the potential time available for service to God. The single person does not have the responsibility of caring for a spouse and raising a family. Singleness, however, does not ensure service to God— involvement in service depends on the commitment of the individual.

7:39 A woman is bound to her husband as long as he lives. But if her husband dies, she is free to marry anyone she wishes, but he must belong to the Lord.^{NIV} The Bible teaches that marriage is a lifelong contract between a man and a woman—"as long as they both shall live." Therefore, a married woman *is bound to her husband as long as he lives.* The relationship was not to be dissolved for any reason. If the woman's husband were to die, however, the marriage contract would be void, and *she is free to* *marry anyone she wishes,* providing that this person were a Christian *(he must belong to the Lord).* This also applied to men whose wives had died.

There may have been some teaching in either Jewish or Greek society stating that a widowed woman could not remarry because she was bound forever to her husband, even if he had died. Paul stated clearly that this was not to be the case. But the widow or widower should still be very careful about whom he or she chooses to get married to—that part *is* prescribed by God, for he would not have them marry unbelievers.

7:40 But in my opinion it will be better for her if she doesn't marry again, and I think I am giving you counsel from God's Spirit when I say this.NLT While the widow *can* remarry (7:39), that doesn't necessarily mean that she *should.* In fact, Paul's opinion was that *it will be better for her if she doesn't marry again* for the same reasons he said that the unmarried people might think about remaining single (7:25, 28, 32-34).

When Paul stated *I think I am giving you counsel from God's Spirit when I say this,* there was nothing tentative in his meaning. At times he gave these believers commands from the Lord because he could bring words directly from Jesus or from the Old Testament; at other times, he gave them his "advice" or "counsel," but this still carried the weight of divine inspiration. Paul's advice came from the Holy Spirit, who gave him the words he needed to answer the Corinthian church's questions.

WISE COUNSEL
Although Paul's words were written almost two thousand years ago, his counsel rings true. Struggling marriages, quick divorces, and lonely singles are not a modern invention. Life in a fallen world is difficult. Paul's responses to the Corinthian questions and mistakes are filled with wisdom, realism, truth—the evidences of inspiration by God's Spirit. Some of his guidelines may not apply directly to us personally; others may be difficult to understand. But neither of those points relieves us from acting on what does apply and what we do understand. Take the clear steps of obedience, and much of the ambiguity will fall away.

---

1 Corinthians 8

The discussion regarding whether the Corinthian believers should eat food that had been offered to idols begins here and continues through 11:1. Most likely, this first section deals with meals served in the pagan temples, and the discussion in 10:23–11:1 deals with food purchased in the marketplace and served in private homes. The Corinthians had written to Paul with questions regarding these issues, but their exact questions are unknown. The believers concluded that their knowledge of God and the fact that the idols had no power allowed them to continue to eat meals in the temple. Paul dealt with that issue in this first section.

8:1 Now concerning food sacrificed to idols: we know that "all of us possess knowledge." Knowledge puffs up, but love builds up.[NRSV] The Corinthian believers had sent another question to Paul (see 7:1)—this one regarding *food sacrificed to idols*. Their question pertains to the idolatry with its sacrifices that permeated the Greek and Roman cultures of the day. (Paul also dealt with this issue in his letter to the Roman believers—see Romans 14.) One might think that believers should obviously not have contact with idolatry in any form. Paul had prohibited such contact in 5:9-11, and the Jerusalem council had forbidden the Christians to eat meat offered to idols (Acts 15:29). For believers in Corinth, however, staying clear of any contact with idolatry was nearly impossible for two main reasons. First, people often ate meals in temples or in places associated with idols. This was accepted social practice for public or private

> Knowledge, or at least a high conceit of it, is very apt to swell the mind, to fill it with wind, and so puff it up. This tends to do no good to ourselves, but in many instances is much to the hurt of others. But true love, and tender regard to our brethren, will put us upon consulting their interest, and acting as may be for their edification.
>
> *Matthew Henry*

gatherings. To cut oneself off from such gatherings would be like not attending weddings or other social celebrations today. So this caused much concern for the believers. At such gatherings, a sacrifice was made to the idol. When such meat was sacrificed, the priest would divide it into three portions: One would be burned up, one would be given to the priest, and one would be given to the offerer. If the priest did not use his portion, it would be sent to the marketplace. This caused the second concern for the believers. The meat, after being sacrificed to an idol and sold in the market, would then be bought and served in private homes. So the Corinthian believers wondered if the meat had been contaminated by its having been offered on a pagan altar, and, if by eating it, they would be participating in idol worship. Paul answered both of these concerns; most likely, the advice in 8:1-13 deals with temple-sponsored meals, while 10:23–11:1 deals with meat sold in the marketplace.

The words "all of us possess knowledge" may have been a quote from the Corinthians' letter to Paul. This "knowledge" probably refers to knowledge that there is one true God and knowledge that idols are worthless and have no power.

The conclusion, then, is that believers can eat anything because God created it, so a ceremony offering food to an idol could do nothing to contaminate the food. Since they didn't believe in idols, and God doesn't regard idols, Corinthian believers could eat with their friends without problems. Some believers understood this fact. Others, however, felt very strongly that to eat such meat would be wrong; their consciences bothered them.

> In our salutary emphasis on truth and knowledge, we must never succumb to an intellectual arrogance that assigns small importance to self-denying love for those who do not know as much. *D. A. Carson*

This must have become a divisive issue, because the question had come to Paul.

Paul took the opportunity to tell them that *knowledge puffs up, but love builds up.* While these believers had a certain amount of knowledge leading to freedom, it would be of no value if they did not deal with their fellow believers in a spirit of love. Those who might be taking pride in their knowledge of Christ would only be "puffed up" and could end up dividing the church. Those who took their knowledge and used it lovingly among the believers were "building up" the church. In this situation, acting on knowledge alone—even accurate knowledge—without love for other believers, would harm the church.

Paul maintained his stance that eating meat sacrificed to

idols was wrong. He upheld the decision of the Jerusalem council. But he would go on to explain (what the Corinthians probably observed) why he would eat meat in private homes with Gentiles.

KNOWLEDGE AND LOVE
Love outranks knowledge. Knowledge can make us look good and feel important, but it can also give us an arrogant, know-it-all attitude. Apparently, the Corinthians were treating one another based on the "it's who and what you know that matters" philosophy. Paul saw that they were actually lacking love for God and each other. Their specific problems and questions formed a veneer over their failure to love (see chapter 13 for Paul's beautiful answer).
   Knowledge places the emphasis on the "knower;" love draws attention to the one who is loved. Knowledge attempts to define love; love makes use of knowledge to refine its actions. Knowledge serves love. This is not to say that Christians are lovingly ignorant. We do seek to know more, especially about God. We ought to hunger for the kind of knowledge that will help us love the Lord and our neighbor better.

8:2-3 Anyone who claims to know all the answers doesn't really know very much. But the person who loves God is the one God knows and cares for.^{NLT} Because "knowledge puffs up," people with knowledge might even claim *to know all the answers*. No one can know everything, however, and a person who claims to know it all shows that he or she *doesn't really know very much*. By contrast, *the person who loves God* has found the truth and also has discovered that he or she cannot be God and know all the answers. To love God is to submit to him. Love for God, then, naturally leads to love for other believers.

   Knowledge without love leads to a pride that will eventually fall under its own weight. Love without knowledge, however, can lead to sentimentalism, wherein people love everyone without regard for truth. Knowledge of God goes hand in hand with love, for God is love (1 John 4:8). The following verses explain that true knowledge of God leads Christians to willingly support and help weaker believers so as not to cause them to stumble—in this context by not eating food sacrificed to idols. But the principle can apply to any situation in the modern world where some believers experience freedom in certain areas and others do not.

8:4 So now, what about it? Should we eat meat that has been sacrificed to idols? Well, we all know that an idol is not really a god and that there is only one God and no other.^{NLT} After dealing with any root issue of pride in this matter (8:1-3), Paul returned to the question at hand, *Should we eat meat that has been sacrificed to idols?* The believers in Corinth had come to believe *that there is only one God and no other* out of a culture that embraced many gods. These gods had to be pleased and appeased—often their "power" would be used against those who displeased them or for those who did all that they wanted. These believers knew that *an idol* was *not really a god.* Not only are idols powerless, they are imaginary. They have no substance, authority, power, or ability to curse or bless. The believers' knowledge was the basis for this argument. They knew that the idols were worthless. Paul agreed with them, but this statement set the stage for what he would say about eating meat offered to idols.

IDOL FOOD
Paul's counsel about food offered to idols may seem foreign today. Although the specific issues change, the underlying struggle remains. Nonbelievers are in and of the world. Believers, however, are no longer of the world but do remain in it (see John 15:19; 17:14-16). We are surrounded by the old ideas, habits, and values of life without Christ. We now look at even common things like food, entertainment, and friendships with a new set of priorities. All believers will experience the same ongoing enticement from the old life. Some may have to consciously avoid those things that had a particular hold on them in the past. Pagan addictions are not transformed into harmless hobbies when people become Christians.
  Paul pointed out that freedom in Christ does not work itself out in the same way for everyone. Those differences should not cause jealousy or insensitivity toward other Christians. As we love others, we must think about how our words and actions will affect them. Be patient with other Christians.

8:5-6 **For even if there are so-called gods, whether in heaven or on earth (as indeed there are many "gods" and many "lords"), yet for us there is but one God, the Father, from whom all things came and for whom we live; and there is but one Lord, Jesus Christ, through whom all things came and through whom we live.**[NIV] The idols themselves were phony, but they represented *so-called gods* to the many people who worshiped them, whether their abode was thought to be *in heaven or on earth.* Paul acknowledged that many people believed the gods to be real. Idolatry takes away from God the worship he is due. Satan is behind all attempts to thwart God; therefore, the "power" behind idolatry is the demons, the *"gods"* and *"lords"* of the spirit world (Ephesians 6:12). Demons exist, but they are subordinate to the *one God, the Father, from whom all things came and for whom we live*. God created everything—even the metal, wood, and stone from which people fashion their idols. The pagans divided creation up among the various gods who ruled their own spheres, but the one true God created everything. Those who believe in God live their lives *for* him and his glory.

There is one God and *there is but one Lord, Jesus Christ, through whom all things came and through whom we live*. Paul's statement of "one God" and "one Lord" places the uniqueness and living reality of God the Father and Jesus Christ against the false Corinthian deities. This characterizes God the Father as the source and fulfillment (destiny) of all creation, and God the Son, Jesus Christ, as the mediator. God is "Father," signifying his love and desire to relate to his people. God is creator. He is not himself part of the cosmos but is the source of everything created. God is also every believer's fulfillment or destiny. Their existence meets his purposes. Next Paul wrote of the nature and work of Christ. He called Christ "Lord," a name that the Old Testament uses only in reference to God. Through Jesus Christ, God created and redeemed the world.

8:7 However, not all Christians realize this. Some are accustomed to thinking of idols as being real, so when they eat food that has been offered to idols, they think of it as the worship of real gods, and their weak consciences are violated.[NLT] Basic Christian theology focuses on the fact that there is one God, who created everything, and that idols are nothing. *However,* wrote Paul, *not all Christians realize this*. They believe in the all-powerful God of the Christian faith but are not thoroughly convinced that the other gods do not exist at all. In their hearts and consciences, they have difficulty because they are *accustomed to thinking of idols as being real*. Therefore, when they eat meat that had been sacrificed as part of a religious ceremony, they cannot separate the meat from the ceremony. Eating such meat causes them to *think of it as the worship of real gods*. This brought pangs of conscience. Paul said they had *weak consciences*. A "weak" conscience regards as wrong an act that is not wrong, or is still unclear about whether it is wrong or not. The possibility exists for new converts to fall back into old obsessions by seeing other believers exercise their freedom. Old patterns may link the activity (such as playing cards) with an old obsession (such as gambling). The Corinthians' weak consciences could not discriminate between right and wrong regarding food offered to idols, so when they ate such meat, they *violated* their consciences and so believed that they were sinning against God.

STRONGER AND WEAKER BELIEVERS

Paul advises those who are more mature in the faith about how they must care about their brothers and sisters in Christ who have more tender consciences. The "weaker" brothers and sisters are advised concerning their growth; and pastors and leaders are instructed on how to deal with the conflicts that easily could arise between these groups.

Advice to:

Stronger believer	Don't be proud of your maturity; don't flaunt your freedom. Act in love so you do not cause a weaker believer to stumble.
Weaker believer	Although you may not feel the same freedom in some areas as in others, take your time and pray to God, but do not force others to adhere to your stipulations. You would hinder other believers by making up rules and standards for how everyone ought to behave. Make sure your convictions are based on God's Word and are not simply an expression of your opinions.
Pastors and leaders	Teach correctly from God's Word, helping Christians understand what is right and wrong in God's eyes and helping them see that they can have varied opinions on other issues and still be unified. Don't allow problems to cause splits and divisions.

8:8-9 **But food does not bring us near to God; we are no worse if we do not eat, and no better if we do. Be careful, however, that the exercise of your freedom does not become a stumbling block to the weak.**[NIV] Food is neutral—neither good nor evil, regardless of whether or not it has been sacrificed in a pagan temple to an idol. There would be nothing inherently wrong with eating such meat because food has nothing to do with one's relationship with God—it cannot *bring us near to God,* nor can it take us farther away. Therefore, it is really a matter of indifference. Yet because it is merely a matter of indifference, Paul said that the strong believers should not push the weak but, instead, be willing to love the weak. These "strong" believers (as opposed to those whom Paul described as "weak") knew Scripture and stood strong on God's commands and prohibitions but were free from minor, legalistic constraints. Yet, they must *be careful . . . that the exercise of [their] freedom does not become a stumbling block to the weak.* Since it really doesn't matter what kind of food believers eat, the strong believers should live on the side of love for the sake of the weaker believers.

A "stumbling block" refers to something that might cause someone to trip or fall into sin. The strong but insensitive Chris-

tian may flaunt his or her freedom, be a harmful example, and
thus offend the consciences of others. The overscrupulous but
weak Christian may try to fence others in with petty rules and regulations, thus causing dissension. Paul wanted his readers to be
both strong in the faith and sensitive to others' needs. Because all
believers are strong in certain areas and weak in others, they constantly need to monitor the effects of their behavior on others.

DESTRUCTIVE FREEDOM
Freedom without boundaries or direction quickly takes on the
form of slavery. A distraught mental patient who had completely
wrecked her life in the exercise of "freedom" expressed a
life-changing principle when she asked her counselor, "You
mean I don't have to do what I want to do?"

Superficial freedom insists we can do anything we want to
do. True freedom understands that personal desires don't rule
wisely. We don't always want what is best.

Paul reminded his friends in Corinth that if the practice of
their freedom hurt others, they ought to reconsider their
actions. The three central controls over our freedom in Christ
are (1) Christ's commands and example; (2) our awareness of
the indwelling Holy Spirit; and (3) our commitment to love
others.

8:10 **You see, this is what can happen: Weak Christians who think
it is wrong to eat this food will see you eating in the temple of
an idol. You know there's nothing wrong with it, but they will
be encouraged to violate their conscience by eating food that
has been dedicated to the idol.**NLT Paul offered an example of
what might happen. The *weak Christians* (those with "weak consciences" as explained in 8:7) think that *it is wrong to eat* food
that has been sacrificed to an idol. Strong Christians *know there's
nothing wrong with* eating such food, so they go to *the temple of
an idol* and eat there. As noted in 8:1, this would not have been
an uncommon occurrence, for most social and cultural events
happened in the temples. When weak believers see their fellow
Christians eating in the idol temple, the weak believers would *be
encouraged to violate their conscience* by doing the same. If a
weak believer does something that he or she is not sure is right or
wrong, that action will bring condemnation. As Paul wrote to the
Romans, "Those who have doubts are condemned if they eat,
because they do not act from faith" (Romans 14:23 NRSV).

If one believer has no scruples about where meat comes from
or how it is prepared but flaunts his or her belief in order to cause
one who is concerned to be distressed, then that stronger individual is not acting in love. The conduct of stronger believers is not

to be decided by what they feel is their better insight into the
Scriptures or what they feel would "strengthen" those weaker
ones. Rather, it is to be decided by love and sensitivity. Paul was
pointing out how the strong believers ought to use their freedom
in public—the situation he described here was very public. If
these strong believers ate meat that had been offered to idols in
the privacy of their homes because they knew such meat was not
tainted in any way, they could do so with liberty and without concern for the scruples of the weaker believers. Strong Christians
ought to, at times, restrain their freedom for the sake of the weak,
but they need not come into bondage to the consciences of weak
believers.

BOUNDARIES
Christian freedom does not mean that "anything goes." It
means that salvation is not determined by good deeds or
legalistic rules but by the free gift of God (Ephesians 2:8-9).
Christian freedom, then, is inseparably tied to Christian
responsibility. New believers are often very sensitive to what is
right or wrong, what they should or shouldn't do. Some actions
may be perfectly all right for us to do but may harm a Christian
brother or sister who is still young in the faith and learning what
the Christian life is all about. If someone came out of
alcoholism, it would be unwise to use or offer alcoholic
beverages around him or her. We must be careful not to offend
a sensitive or younger Christian or, by our example, to cause
him or her to sin. When we love others, our freedom should be
less important to us than disturbing the faith of a brother or
sister in Christ.

**8:11 So by your knowledge those weak believers for whom Christ
died are destroyed.**[NRSV] The stronger believer must not let what
he or she wants to do (when it is a minor matter such as whether
to eat meat or not) become a stumbling block that could destroy a
weaker brother or sister. The strong believers know they are free
from concern about meat offered to idols, but that *knowledge*
must not cause them to harm other believers. The Greek verb
translated "destroyed" *(apollumi)* often means "to bring about
destruction." It could also mean a "ruin" of one's conscience if
the weaker believer goes against his or her scruples. To ruin a person's conscience would be total destruction. Therefore, strong
Christians are to act in love. That other person, no matter how
much the strong believer disagrees with him or her, is still someone for whom Christ died. If Christ willingly gave up his life,
Christians ought to be willing to give up their freedoms occasion-
ally so as not to harm another.

Mature Christians shouldn't flaunt their freedom. They should be sensitive to younger converts whose faith can be destroyed by such freedom. For example, a young Christian addicted to gambling may be damaged by the strong Christian's freedom to play cards. Some activities may be all right in and of themselves but not around weaker new converts. Weak believers ought not do anything against their consciences, but they must grow in the faith and, at the same time, not pass judgment on their stronger brothers and sisters.

CLEAR CONSCIENCE
All believers try to steer clear of actions forbidden by Scripture. But what do we do when Scripture has nothing to say about a particular issue? We should follow our conscience. To go against a conviction will leave a person with a guilty or uneasy conscience. When God shows us that something is wrong for us, we should avoid it. But we should not look down on other Christians who exercise their freedom in those areas.

8:12 And you are sinning against Christ when you sin against other Christians by encouraging them to do something they believe is wrong.^{NLT} Throughout this passage, Paul has been addressing stronger believers. So when he wrote *and you,* he was referring to these people. If they were insensitive to their weaker brothers and sisters *by encouraging them to do something they believe is wrong,* then they would be sinning both *against Christ* and *against other Christians.* Because all believers are temples of the Holy Spirit (6:19), no one believer has the right to sin against any other believer—to do so would be to sin against Christ himself.

8:13 If what I eat is going to make another Christian sin, I will never eat meat again as long as I live—for I don't want to make another Christian stumble.^{NLT} Paul willingly followed his own advice, stating that if what he ate would *make another Christian sin,* he would never eat meat again. Strong believers can restrict their freedoms for the sake of others.

In areas of disagreement, Paul counseled the believers to keep their beliefs between themselves and God. The brother or sister who believes in certain freedoms should not be trying to influence others with scruples to "loosen up." Those bothered by some actions should not be judging or condemning those with freedom, nor should they be trying to force their scruples on the entire church. Instead, all believers should seek to have a clear conscience before God.

1 Corinthians 9

At the end of chapter 8, Paul said that he would gladly give up his right to eat meat if that would help a weaker believer not to stumble. What follows in this chapter is Paul's defense of his apostleship and of his freedom to exercise, or not to exercise, his rights as a believer who is free in Christ.

Interestingly, what reads like a relentless demand for recognition (Paul used at least sixteen rhetorical questions in a row) turns into another teaching opportunity. He hoped the Corinthians could learn something of spiritual value by understanding his attitude toward his ministry. He could have rightfully demanded many things from the Corinthians; instead, he gave them real freedom in Christ. He didn't want them dependent on others, or even on himself; he wanted them dependent on Christ.

9:1-2 Am I not free? Am I not an apostle? Have I not seen Jesus our Lord? Are you not the result of my work in the Lord? Even though I may not be an apostle to others, surely I am to you! For you are the seal of my apostleship in the Lord.^{NIV} In defending his apostleship, Paul reestablished his authority for some in Corinth who doubted that they should listen to him (9:3). So Paul presented his credentials as *an apostle*. In Greek, these four questions are rhetorical—they expect a "yes" answer.

Only a small group of believers were "apostles." In order to have the authority of an apostle, the person had to show the following three evidences:

1. A commission directly from Jesus Christ in the sight of witnesses, or confirmed by others. To qualify as a true "apostle," a person had to have personally seen the Lord Jesus after his resurrection. For Paul, this occurred in Acts 9:3-18 (see also 1 Corinthians 15:8). He reminded the believers, *Have I not seen Jesus our Lord?*
2. Signs, wonders, and mighty acts. One example of this is recorded in Acts 13:9-12. For Paul's account of his visit in Corinth, see 2 Corinthians 12:12.

3. Successful ministry. In 3:5-7, Paul had described his work among the Corinthians. See also Acts 18:1-17. Paul spoke of that ministry in these verses: *Are you not the result of my work in the Lord? . . . For you are the seal of my apostleship in the Lord.*

Such credentials make the advice he gives in this letter more persuasive. Second Corinthians 10–13 defends Paul's apostleship in greater detail.

Paul had served in Corinth, and many had become believers through his ministry. If the believers doubted his authority, then they would have to doubt their faith as well. The fact that his readers had accepted Christ testified to Paul's authority among them. They were the "seal," or authentication, of his apostleship. The Corinthians' relationship with Paul was different from their relationship with any other teacher. Paul did not plant all the churches that existed, but *surely* he had planted the one in Corinth. Paul did not want these believers to forget that!

9:3-4 **This is my answer to those who question my authority as an apostle. Don't we have the right to live in your homes and share your meals?**NLT Earlier in this letter, Paul rebuked the Corinthians for their factions and their overly zealous loyalty to different preachers (3:1-22). Those who were *not* loyal to Paul apparently had been questioning his authority. It seems that they questioned Paul because he was not taking advantage of the rights accorded to apostles. Evidently in the Greco-Roman world of Paul's day, it was quite an issue how missionaries, traveling teachers, or philosophers were supported. They could charge fees, beg, work, or accept gifts by patrons. In Philippi, Paul accepted Lydia's support (Acts 16:15), but since then had abandoned that practice. Because other church leaders continued to accept patronage, the issue arose: Maybe Paul did not get support because his status as an apostle was in question. Paul was asserting his right to get support (which he had voluntarily laid aside so as not to bring the gospel under suspicion).

Paul gave them his *answer* by asking a series of questions. Paul indeed had the authority of an apostle, but he would not exercise his rights as an apostle if doing so would cause a stumbling block to anyone. Yet he also explained, through these questions, that the churches ought to willingly accord these rights to those who deserved them. If Paul waived these rights at various times, this was a personal decision based on his zeal for the gospel.

First he asked, *Don't we have the right to live in your homes and share your meals?* Many in that day did not understand the concept of the church being a self-supporting unit, collecting

money to pay its full-time leaders, eventually to care for buildings and to give to missionary efforts and those in need. Church
leaders deserve to be paid by those in their charge. The apostles,
as they traveled to spread the Good News, also had a right to hospitality from the churches—meals and a place to stay.

Paul had waived this right, however; he willingly worked hard
in order to pay for his own lodging and food. In Corinth, he had
worked as a tentmaker or leatherworker (Acts 18:3). He did not
want to receive money from the believers in Corinth because this
could hinder his work for the gospel (9:11-12).

**9:5 Don't we have the right to bring a Christian wife along with
us as the other disciples and the Lord's brothers and Peter
do?**NLT That the apostles had *the right to bring a Christian wife
along* means that they had the right to have their wives travel
along with them, supported financially by the churches. Paul's
mention of "the other disciples and the Lord's brothers and
Peter" refers to others in the church who were considered to be
apostles and who also had wives who had come to believe in
Jesus. The brothers of Jesus (referring to Jesus' physical half
brothers) had not believed in Jesus at first (John 7:3-5), but
after the Resurrection, they believed and attained leadership status in the church at Jerusalem (Acts 1:14). James (one of the
"Lord's brothers"), for example, led the way to an agreement at
the Jerusalem council (Acts 15) and wrote the book of James.
Peter was a prominent apostle in the early church; his wife is
not mentioned elsewhere, but the Gospels record a time when
Jesus healed Peter's mother-in-law (Matthew 8:14-15; Mark
1:30; Luke 4:38).

SETTING ASIDE
Paul used himself as an illustration of giving up personal rights.
Paul asserted his right to hospitality, to be married, and to be
paid for his work. But he willingly gave up these rights to win
people to Christ. When your focus is on living for Christ, your
rights become comparatively unimportant. What rights in your
life should you set aside in order to serve and love others?

**9:6-7 Or is it only Barnabas and I who have no right to refrain
from working for a living? Who at any time pays the
expenses for doing military service? Who plants a vineyard
and does not eat any of its fruit? Or who tends a flock and
does not get any of its milk?**NRSV *Barnabas* had traveled with
Paul during the first missionary journey (Acts 13:1–14:28).
When they prepared to embark on a second journey, a dispute

between them caused them to separate, effectively creating two
teams (Acts 15:36-41). Barnabas was also considered to be an
apostle (Acts 14:3-4, 14). This may mean that Paul and Barnabas were the only apostles who made it a habit to work and
earn their living as they traveled to spread the gospel (4:12;
Acts 18:2-3). Because these two men had refrained from taking
money from the churches, some were saying that they were not
apostles (see 9:3-4). Also, tentmaking was regarded as lowly
work, fit primarily for slaves. They questioned whether Paul
had the same authority as other apostles because they looked
down on him for working with his hands. Paul asserted that he
and Barnabas had the authority of apostles, even though they
did not take advantage of the rights they deserved—having
waived them of their own free will. Paul also made it clear in
the following series of questions, however, that he was not putting himself above the other apostles. They all had a right to
support from the churches—just as a man who serves in the military has his expenses covered, or one who plants a vineyard
can enjoy its fruit, or a shepherd can drink some of the milk
from his flock. All were fed by their occupation. This should be
no different for apostles. The same holds true for Christian
workers (see 9:10). They should not have to toil in the service
of Christ at their own expense.

9:8-10 **Do I say this merely from a human point of view? Doesn't the
Law say the same thing? For it is written in the Law of
Moses: "Do not muzzle an ox while it is treading out the
grain." Is it about oxen that God is concerned?**[NIV] While
Paul's argument made sense from a *human point of view,* he did
not need to end there, for his words held the authority of Scripture. The *Law of Moses* states, in Deuteronomy 25:4, *"Do not
muzzle an ox while it is treading out the grain."* In ancient times,
grain was often "threshed" by placing sheaves on a hard surface
and then allowing oxen to drag something heavy back and forth
across it. The law said that the oxen should be allowed to eat
some of the grain while they worked. This law was not made to
protect oxen but to illustrate a point. God's people were to care
for their animals by allowing oxen to eat while they worked, but,
Paul asked, **Wasn't he also speaking to us? Of course he was.
Just as farm workers who plow fields and thresh the grain
expect a share of the harvest, Christian workers should be
paid by those they serve.**[NLT] God's ministers deserve to be cared
for by those to whom they minister, just as farm workers share in
the harvest.

WAGES FOR WORK
Jesus said that workers deserve their wages (Luke 10:7). Paul echoed this thought and urged the church to pay Christian workers. People serving in these specialized roles shouldn't have to argue or claim their right to pay. Believers have the responsibility to care for pastors, teachers, and other spiritual leaders. It is our duty to see that those who serve us in the ministry are fairly and adequately compensated. When the annual budget comes up for review, support a proper salary for your ministers and staff.

9:11-12 If we have sown spiritual seed among you, is it too much if we reap a material harvest from you? If others have this right of support from you, shouldn't we have it all the more? But we did not use this right. On the contrary, we put up with anything rather than hinder the gospel of Christ.NIV The comparison with ministers of the gospel and farm workers sharing in the harvest (9:10) prompted Paul to use the illustration of sowing *spiritual seed among* the people of Corinth (see also 3:6). Those who had sown this "spiritual seed" would not have been expecting *too much* in wanting *a material harvest* from the Corinthian believers.

Then, added Paul, *if others have this right of support* (perhaps Peter or Apollos had received support from this church), then most certainly those who originally had brought the gospel message to these believers should *have it all the more.* Paul and others (perhaps Barnabas; see 9:6) had not demanded their right for support, however; they had worked to earn their own living and not be a burden to the church. Paul was not required to work this way, but he chose to *put up with anything rather than hinder the gospel of Christ.* Some may have implied that because Paul did not take gifts, he was implicitly recognizing his inferiority. "Not so," said Paul. His only reason for not taking support from this church was his concern that some might not accept his message. So he chose to forego that support. He put up with the hardships of "working two jobs" so that no pagan inquiring about Christianity would be put off by the financial obligation of supporting a missionary. "Rather than hinder" implies breaking up a road to prevent the enemy's advance. Paul wanted a clear road for evangelism. In this section, Paul set up his argument for 9:15-18.

9:13 Don't you know that those who work in the temple get their food from the temple, and those who serve at the altar share in what is offered on the altar?NIV The phrase "don't you know" implies that the readers should have known and understood the fact that Paul was presenting. Paul returned to the argument of 9:7 and gave two more examples of his right to receive support. It was everywhere understood that those who had sacred jobs (such as serving *in the temple* or *at the altar*) were "working" and therefore derived their livelihood from the job. They did not have to go elsewhere. As part of their pay, priests in the temple would receive a portion of the offerings as their food (see Numbers 18:8-24). This was true in the pagan temples, as well.

9:14 **In the same way, the Lord gave orders that those who preach the Good News should be supported by those who benefit from it.**NLT Paul's explanation that God's ministers should be supported by the churches came as an order from the Lord. This argument will be repeated in 9:17. Probably Paul was alluding to Jesus' command in Luke 10:7, "Don't hesitate to accept hospitality, because those who work deserve their pay" (NLT; see also 1 Timothy 5:18). The churches were required to honor *those who preach the Good News,* and those who served among the believers should be supported by *those who benefit from* their ministry. This command from God allowed traveling missionaries and local ministers to focus entirely on the spread of the gospel and the growth of the church, and not be concerned about making money.

9:15 **But I have not used any of these rights. And I am not writing this in the hope that you will do such things for me. I would rather die than have anyone deprive me of this boast.**NIV The churches were commanded to support God's ministers, and the ministers had a right to expect such support. Paul noted here and in 9:12, however, that he had *not used any of these rights* in Corinth because he felt that doing so would hinder the spread of the gospel in that city. Paul *did* accept gifts from some churches, such as the Philippian church (see Philippians 4:14-19). He must have felt, however, that to take any money in Corinth would have caused some to think he was after money instead of souls! Paul wanted the Corinthians to see in him integrity and self-denial for the sake of the gospel. So Paul willingly set aside his rights as an apostle, giving up the easier path of voluntary support for hard work, in order to bring more people in Corinth to the Lord. Paul was single-minded—his entire life was focused on advancing God's kingdom.

Paul hastened to add that he was not writing all this in the hopes that now the Corinthians *would* begin to give him support. Instead, he wanted them to know that he would continue to preach without expecting support (this was his *boast*) when it seemed necessary to do so. Paul planned to visit Corinth again, and he wanted to be able to face those who opposed him with the fact that he had unselfishly served among them without having

ever accepted financial support from them. They could not claim
that his motives were impure.

NO HINDRANCE
These verses concerning Paul's rights and the church's
responsibility have a two-part challenge for the church today.
First, the church must support its workers in a fair and equitable
way. That is the church's responsibility. It can research pay
scales, examine the standard of living in its community, and do
what is right and fair. Second, Christian workers must not let
their attitude about pay and benefits hinder the gospel. It is too
easy for desire for more pay to enter into a person's mind and
distract from serving. Ministers need Paul's attitude: "I have not
used any of these rights."

9:16 **Yet when I preach the gospel, I cannot boast, for I am compelled to preach. Woe to me if I do not preach the gospel!**^{NIV}
Paul may have "boasted" in his desire to serve the Corinthian
believers freely, but he could not boast about that service. Paul
had been called to *preach the gospel,* and he did so, not by his
own choice. In fact, he was *compelled to preach;* he had to
preach, for God had called him to do so. *Woe* to Paul if he didn't!
The word "woe" referred to some undescribed calamity that
would befall him should he *not preach the gospel.* This compulsion did not mean that Paul did not enjoy this duty (see Romans
1:5; 11:13; 15:15-16; Galatians 1:15-16); instead, it means that,
like a slave serving a beloved master, Paul served his Lord by
faithfully doing the duties God had given him (see Acts 9:15-16).

PERSISTENT GIFT
God chose Paul. Preaching the gospel was Paul's gift and
calling. He admitted he couldn't stop preaching even if he had
wanted to. Paul was driven by the desire to do what God
wanted, using his gifts for God's glory.
    Paul's admission offers a clue to discovering our spiritual
gifts. What do you find yourself doing over and over? In what
very specific way do you have a habit of serving others and
enjoying it? Give other Christians permission to observe you
and offer feedback. Make it a point to discover what special
gifts has God given you.

9:17 **If I were doing this of my own free will, then I would deserve
payment. But God has chosen me and given me this sacred
trust, and I have no choice.**^{NLT} Paul perceived his call by God as
a *sacred trust;* therefore, he felt that he could freely serve God as
an apostle without expecting *payment.* Far from not deserving to

be paid, as his detractors were saying, Paul did not feel that he deserved payment for an honored duty that he had been commanded to do. In this matter, he felt that he had *no choice* but to serve these believers without financial support.

9:18 What then is my reward? Just this: that in preaching the gospel I may offer it free of charge, and so not make use of my rights in preaching it.^{NIV} God would not give Paul any special *reward* for preaching to the Corinthians without charge; that had been Paul's choice. Besides, Paul was merely doing what God had called him to do. But Paul *did* have a reward in being able to *offer* his preaching of the salvation message *free of charge,* and in not having to *make use of [his] rights* as an apostle *in preaching it.* His reward came in being able to show the genuineness of his love and concern for these Corinthian believers.

9:19 For though I am free with respect to all, I have made myself a slave to all, so that I might win more of them.^{NRSV} In 9:19-22, Paul asserted that he was *free* to yield certain rights in matters that did not compromise the gospel message. In such a way, he could vary the style of his message or other minor matters, becoming a *slave* to his audience *so that [he] might win more of them.* Paul's goals were to glorify God and to bring people to Christ. Thus he stayed free of any philosophical position or material entanglement that might sidetrack him while he strictly disciplined himself to carry out his goals. In 9:24-27, he emphasized a life of strict discipline. For Paul, both freedom and discipline were important tools to be used in God's service.

CULTURAL ADAPTATION
By being a slave to all, Paul was communicating the heart of his mission strategy. He had a willingness to accommodate and adjust to different settings. When with Jews, he ate kosher food; when with Gentiles, he ate regular food. In Philippi, he accepted support; in other places, he did not. Was Paul a chameleon, merely adapting to each environment? In some ways, he was; but his principles were higher than self-protection. He wanted people of all cultures and backgrounds to listen to the gospel. Whenever missionaries go to another culture, they should consciously embrace and adapt to every element in that culture that doesn't hinder the gospel or violate biblical ethics.

9:20 To the Jews I became like a Jew, to win the Jews. To those under the law I became like one under the law (though I myself am not under the law), so as to win those under the law.^{NIV} Paul never compromised the doctrines of Scripture, never changed God's Word in order to make it more palatable to people in any given place. He never went against God's law or his own conscience. In matters that did not violate any principle of God's Word, however, Paul was willing to *become like* his audience in order *to win* them to Christ. Three groups are mentioned in these verses: Jews, Gentiles, and those with weak consciences. By saying, *to the Jews I became like a Jew,* Paul was stating that, when necessary, he conformed his life to the practices of *those under the law* even though he himself was no longer *under the law* (because of his freedom in Christ; see Acts 16:3; 18:18; 21:20-26). If, however, Paul had gone into a Jewish synagogue to preach, all the while flouting the Jewish laws and showing no respect for their laws and customs because of his "freedom in Christ," he would have offended the very people he had come to tell about Jesus Christ. But by adapting himself to them, by conforming to their regulations and restrictions (Paul had been a Pharisee), he had gained an audience so that he might *win those under the law.* Again, Paul was careful never to violate any of God's commands in his attempts to serve his listeners. He never conceded that those regulations had to be kept in order for people to become believers, but he conformed to the laws to help the Jews come to Christ. The line was a difficult one to walk, for the book of Galatians records a time when Paul rebuked Peter for acting like a Jew among the Gentiles (see Galatians 2:11-21).

9:21 To those not having the law I became like one not having the law (though I am not free from God's law but am under Christ's law), so as to win those not having the law.NIV As Paul conformed himself to the Jews, he also conformed to *those not having the law,* referring to Gentiles. Paul met them on their own turf, becoming *like one not having the law.* This did not mean that Paul had thrown aside all restraints and was living like a pagan in hopes of winning the pagans to Christ! As he explained, he always remembered that he was *not free from God's law but [was] under Christ's law.* Paul lived according to God's law and his conscience, but he did not put undue constraints on his Gentile audiences. Unlike some false teachers of the day, called Judaizers, Paul did not require the Gentiles to follow the Jewish laws in order to become believers (see Acts 15:1-21). Instead, he spoke a message that would *win those not having the law* (see, for example, Acts 17:1-34).

9:22-23 To the weak I became weak, so that I might win the weak. I have become all things to all people, that I might by all means save some.NRSV "The weak" refers to those with a weak conscience, a subject Paul had discussed in chapter 8. In that chapter,

Paul had explained that believers who were free in Christ ought to set aside certain freedoms in the presence of another believer with a more sensitive conscience. Paul followed his own advice, saying that he *became weak* when with such people (meaning that he had set aside his freedoms and had lived by their restraints for a time) so that he *might win the weak.* The "weak" were already believers, but they needed to grow into a deeper knowledge of Christ and a deeper understanding of their freedom in Christ. Paul did this delicately, becoming as they were in order to gain their listening ears. He chose to *become all things to all people* (the Jews, the Gentiles, and those with weak consciences, 9:20-22) in order to *save some.* Paul never compromised the gospel truth, God's law, or his own conscience; in other matters, however, Paul was willing to go to great lengths to meet people where they were. He had one focus: **I do all this for the sake of the gospel, that I may share in its blessings.**[NIV] Paul's life focused on taking the gospel to an unbelieving world. He did not preach with pride, counting the numbers of converts; instead, he preached with love for the gospel and for people, so that in the end, he and all believers could *share* together in the *blessings* of knowing Christ.

STRATEGY
First Corinthians 9 reveals several basic principles for effective ministry: find common ground with others; avoid a know-it-all attitude; make others feel accepted; be sensitive to others' needs and concerns; and look for opportunities to tell about Christ. These principles are just as valid today as they were then. Which of these were used by those who brought you to Christ? Which ones need more conscious attention in your own efforts to introduce your friends, neighbors, and coworkers to Christ?

9:24-25 **Remember that in a race everyone runs, but only one person gets the prize. You also must run in such a way that you will win. All athletes practice strict self-control. They do it to win a prize that will fade away, but we do it for an eternal prize.**[NLT] Paul's exhortations in the previous verses—for the believers to give up their own rights, to think of others first, to be wholehearted in their focus on bringing others to Christ—called upon the Christians to deny themselves as they looked forward to future reward. Paul compared this to *a race,* picturing the ancient "games." The Olympics were already operating in Paul's time. Second in popularity only to the Olympic games, the Isthmian games were celebrated every two years at Corinth. Athletes would come from all over Greece, and the winners of the games were accorded the highest honor. To get into the games, and especially to emerge as victors, required that each athlete prepare diligently with self-denial and dedication. Typically, for ten months prior to the games, the athletes-in-training denied themselves many ordinary pleasures in order to prepare and be in top condition for the competition. Each put forth his greatest effort during the contest, setting aside all else in order to win the prize. *Everyone runs, but only one person gets the prize.* The coveted prize, and the honor accorded with it, meant the world to these athletes. They would give up everything else in order to obtain it.

THE LONG RUN
Paul immediately practiced his strategy of identifying with his audience by using an athletic lesson. Because Corinth was the site of the Isthmian Games, Paul knew that the Corinthians would be able to understand that winning a race requires purpose and discipline. Paul used this illustration to explain that the Christian life takes hard work, self-denial, and grueling preparation. As Christians, we are running toward our heavenly reward. The essential disciplines of prayer, Bible study, and worship equip us to run with vigor and stamina. Don't merely observe from the grandstand; don't just jog a couple of laps each morning. Train diligently—your spiritual progress depends upon it.

When Paul told the believers to be like those athletes, he did not mean that the believers were all running against each other with only one actually winning. Instead, he wanted every believer to *run in such a way that you will win.* In other words, every believer should be putting out the kind of effort for the reward of God's kingdom that an athlete puts out to merely win a wreath. The athletes practiced *strict self-control* so as to *win a prize that will fade away.* (For more on self-control, see Galatians 5:22; Titus 2:11; 1 Peter 4:7; 5:8.) Believers, therefore, ought to willingly practice self-control with a focus on bringing others to Christ because they are running toward *an eternal prize.* They have all already "won"; the prize is not dependent on how they run the race. Because they already are assured of the prize, they should live for God with as much focus and enthusiasm as did the ancient runners at the games.

Paul pointed to the self-control of runners. They must make choices between good and bad. Christians' choices are not always between good and bad. At times we must even give up something good in order to do what God wants. Each person's special duties determine the discipline and denial that he or she must accept.

Without a goal, discipline is nothing but self-punishment. With the goal of pleasing God, denial seems like nothing compared to the eternal, imperishable reward.

9:26-27 **So I run straight to the goal with purpose in every step. I am not like a boxer who misses his punches. I discipline my body like an athlete, training it to do what it should. Otherwise, I fear that after preaching to others I myself might be disqualified.**^{NLT} Paul not only preached the gospel message and encouraged the believers to self-discipline and self-denial, he also practiced what he preached. He too had to live by the gospel, and he too practiced self-denial like the athletes just described. Paul did not run the race aimlessly, nor was he like a boxer who *misses his punches.* Instead, he kept his eyes focused on *the goal,* running *straight* for it, *with purpose in every step.* He did not allow himself to be sidetracked and he did not waste time becoming lazy. He kept on, disciplining and *training* his body. Paul pictured life as a battle. Believers must not become lazy—for Satan seeks to cause them to stumble, sin continues to buffet, and sorrow and pain are a daily reality (see Romans 7:14-25). Instead of being bound by their bodies, believers must diligently discipline themselves in their Christian lives in order to stay "in shape."

SELF-CONTROL
Whatever happened to self-control? Many books and speakers guide wandering souls to self-fulfillment, self-satisfaction, and self-awareness. Not many tackle self-control.

Self-control requires an honest look at your strengths and weaknesses, with emphasis on the latter. It means building the will to say no when a powerful appetite inside you screams yes.

- No to friends or situations that will lead you away from Christ.
- No to casual sex, saving intimacy for marriage.
- No to laziness in favor of "can do" and "will do."

Self-control is a long, steady course in learning attitudes that do not come naturally, and channeling natural appetites toward God's purposes. Where are your weak points? Pray with a friend for God's help to redirect weakness into strength.

When Paul said *otherwise, I fear that after preaching to others I myself might be disqualified,* he did not mean that he feared losing his salvation, only that he would be disqualified from receiving rewards from Christ. This passage describes the spiritual maturation process, the period of growth during believers' lives on earth when they are living "in" the world while not being "of" it. The time between a person's acceptance of Christ

WHY WE DON'T GIVE UP

Perseverance, persistence, the prize! Christ never promised us an easy way to live. These verses (9:26-27) remind us that we must have a purpose and a plan because times will be difficult and Satan will attack. We must be diligent, all the while remembering that we never run alone. God keeps his promises.

Reference	The Purpose	The Plan	The Prize
1 Corinthians 9:24-27	Run to get the prize.	Deny yourself whatever is potentially harmful.	A crown that will last forever
	Run straight to the goal.	Discipline your body, training it.	
Galatians 6:7-10	Don't become weary in doing good.	Sow to please the Spirit.	Reap eternal life.
	Don't get discouraged and give up.		
	Do good to everyone.		
Ephesians 6:10-20	Put on the full armor of God.	Use all the pieces of God's armor.	Holding your stance against the devil's schemes
	Pray on all occasions.		
Philippians 3:12-14	Press on toward the day when you will be all God wants you to be.	Forget the past; strain toward the finish line ahead.	The prize for which God calls you heavenward
2 Timothy 2:1-13	Entrust these great truths to people who will teach them to others.	Endure hardship like a soldier and don't get involved in worldly affairs.	You will live with Christ; you will reign with him.
	Be strong in Christ's grace, even when your faith is faltering.	Follow the Lord's rules, as an athlete must do in order to win.	
		Work hard, like a farmer who tends his crops for the harvest. God always remains faithful to you and always carries out his promises.	

as Savior and his or her death is the only time when growth in Christ can occur. Paul wanted to grow diligently and receive a reward from Christ at his return. Paul did not want to be like the person who builds his or her life with shoddy materials, only to be saved "like someone escaping through a wall of flames" (3:15 NLT).

1 Corinthians 10

In chapter 9 Paul used himself as an example of a mature Christian who disciplined himself to better serve God. Chapter 10 presents Israel as an example of spiritual immaturity, shown in their overconfidence and lack of self-discipline.

10:1 **I don't want you to forget, dear brothers and sisters, what happened to our ancestors in the wilderness long ago. God guided all of them by sending a cloud that moved along ahead of them, and he brought them all safely through the waters of the sea on dry ground.**^{NLT} This chapter continues Paul's argument concerning the lifestyle of the believers and the need for self-discipline, as recorded in chapters 8 and 9. At the end of chapter 9, Paul had described his own self-discipline and had warned about the danger of being "disqualified." The Christian life is a struggle, precisely because it is "Christian." It is a struggle to obey God, face persecution, exercise self-control and self-discipline, and deal with sin in one's life. When people are "saved," they grow in their relationship with Christ and want to become more like him. They will not become perfect in this life, but they desire to work toward holiness. Some of the Corinthian believers thought that because they had professed faith, went to church, and joined in the Lord's Supper, they could then live as they pleased. But this was a false belief, as Paul would show through the example he used from Israel's history.

A perfect Old Testament example of believing the false notion that one can be saved and then live a faithless, God-less life can be seen in *what happened to* the Jews' *ancestors in the wilderness long ago.* The book of Exodus contains the record of their miraculous escape from slavery in Egypt by the intervention of God (see Exodus 1–12). God gave them a leader (Moses), set them free (through great miracles), and then *guided all of them* as they moved out of Egypt and headed toward the land God wanted to give them (the Promised Land). "A cloud" refers to God's presence in the form of a cloud by day and fire by night (Exodus 13:21-22). Their guide was God himself in a physical form, directly in front of them! When they came to the Red Sea, God *brought them all safely through the waters of the sea on dry ground.* This event is recorded in Exodus 14.

The emphasis in 10:1-4 is on the word "all," which Paul used four or five times. Paul was making the point that *all* of the Israelites experienced the miracles of God's protection and guidance. Yet, later, so many turned away. Many thought that their place among God's people assured them the Promised Land. Assuming themselves secure, they refused the life of self-discipline, self-denial, and obedience to God. Because of that, many were "disqualified" from entering the Promised Land.

GENERAL BLESSINGS
From the example of his own life (chapter 9) Paul turned to the subject of the Exodus. God's power in freeing his people from bondage in Egypt provides countless insights into God's grace and integrity. The people were liberated en masse. Many walked out of slavery physically, but their hearts, minds, and wills remained captive. Freedom from oppression did not lead them to grateful living. Though all benefitted, many nullified those benefits by persistent unbelief.

Christians today have a marvelous heritage of God's faithfulness. We also have a lengthy history of human sinfulness. How tragic it is when, through ignorance of the past, we repeat many of the same mistakes that spiritually crippled and limited the spread of the gospel. When we read in God's Word about the failures of others, do we respond, "That couldn't happen to me"? If so, we may be falling into the same danger.

10:2 **They were all baptized into Moses in the cloud and in the sea.**^NIV This verse at first seems very difficult to understand. But it must be understood that "baptism" here is used for comparison, not as an exact equivalent. And "into Moses" is used as being analogous to the Christian experience of being baptized "into Christ" (see Romans 6:3; Galatians 3:27). The Israelites were baptized in that they shared the blessing and gracious deliverance of God with and through Moses' intervention and leadership. By their experience of passing through the Red Sea, they were united and initiated together under Moses' leadership. "When the people of Israel saw the mighty power that the LORD had displayed against the Egyptians, they feared the LORD and put their faith in him and his servant Moses" (Exodus 14:31 NLT). The *cloud* represented God's presence and glory among them (Exodus 14:19-22), indicating his leadership and protection. The *sea* represented God's salvation of his people through the Red Sea as they crossed safely to escape the Egyptians. *All* of the Israelites experienced this "baptism." However, the common experience of this baptism did not keep most of them faithful to God in the days that followed.

10:3-4 **They all ate the same spiritual food and drank the same spiritual drink; for they drank from the spiritual rock that accompanied them, and that rock was Christ.**^{NIV} Further miracles sustained the Israelites as they journeyed through the desert. God provided *spiritual food* in the form of "manna" that came from heaven (Exodus 16:4, 14-31). Paul called it "spiritual" because God had provided it for them. The *spiritual drink* referred to the water Moses obtained from a rock, again a provision directly from God. Moses got water from a rock both at the beginning and at the end of Israel's journey (Exodus 17:1-7; Numbers 20:2-13). This had given rise to a rabbinic interpretation of Numbers 21:16-18 that a well, known as Miriam's Well and shaped like a *rock,* had *accompanied them,* providing water wherever they went. Paul referred to *Christ* as *that rock* who had actually accompanied and sustained the people, meeting their needs during their travels. The Old Testament often refers to God as a "rock" (see, for example, Genesis 49:24; Deuteronomy 32:4; 2 Samuel 22:32). Paul's reference to Christ as the spiritual "rock" would have connected Christ with Yahweh of the Exodus, thereby indicating the deity of Christ.

10:5 **Yet after all this, God was not pleased with most of them, and he destroyed them in the wilderness.**^{NLT} God had performed great miracles for his people—setting them free from slavery, guiding them through a sea, and giving them food and drink in a barren wilderness. *Yet after all this,* most of the people rebelled against God. The word "most" is actually an understatement; of the thousands who stood at the very edge of the Promised Land, only two men had faith enough in God to enter (Numbers 14:5-12). Because of their lack of faith, God caused the people to turn back from the land and wander for forty years in the wilderness. God *destroyed them in the wilderness* by causing them to wander until they died. Only Joshua and Caleb lived long enough to enter the land (Numbers 14:30). The rest died without ever having entered the Promised Land—this was God's punishment on them for their disobedience and rebellion against him. See Hebrews 3–4, where the wilderness example is also used as a warning.

10:6 **Now these things occurred as examples for us, so that we might not desire evil as they did.**^{NRSV} Far from being irrelevant to New Testament Christians, the stories of people in the Old

Testament provide *examples* from which the believers can learn.
In particular, the story of the Israelites' escape from Egypt
teaches believers to *not desire evil as they did.* Clearly, the Israelites' status as God's people and recipients of his love and provision did not mean that all of them loved and served God in
return. Instead, many actually desired evil and turned away from
God, as the following verses describe.

LESSONS
As Paul wrote about the history of his people, he highlighted
God's directions, warnings, and examples. It turns out that
events transpired and were recorded for future purposes. Twice
in this chapter, he pointed out that "these things occurred as
examples" for us (10:6, 11). The examples were specific
behaviors: idolatry, sexual immorality, testing the Lord, and
complaining. In each case, the consequences were death.
Each also represents a real temptation toward "setting our
hearts on evil things" (NIV).
   Instead of obeying the One who gave them freedom, God's
people rebelled. We rebel against God when we give in to our
cravings to put pleasures ahead of service to God. Don't let
anything come between you and God.

**10:7 Do not be idolaters, as some of them were; as it is written:
"The people sat down to eat and drink and got up to indulge
in pagan revelry."**NIV This incident, when *"the people sat down
to eat and drink and got up to indulge in pagan revelry,"*
occurred when the Israelites made a golden calf and worshiped it
in the wilderness (Exodus 32). Paul was quoting Exodus 32:6.
The people became *idolaters,* worshiping an image rather than
God, who had brought them out of Egypt. The Israelites claimed
to be worshiping God (Exodus 32:5); however, God was dishonored by what they were doing—both by their idol (a golden calf)
and then by their "pagan revelry." "Revelry" refers to singing,
shouting, and dancing that promote sexual immorality. This also
shows that the problem addressed in 8:1-13 was idolatry, not
merely eating marketplace meat. If those people who had witnessed the miracles of the escape from Egypt could so easily be
tempted to turn to idolatry, then the Christians in Corinth, who
were surrounded by idols, should also be on their guard. The
Corinthian believers needed to remember that God is completely
separate from idolatry. They could not participate in idol festivals
or celebrations and claim that they were really worshiping God
through them. This dishonored God. He does not overlook sin,
nor does he take it lightly. Neither should his followers.

GOD OR IDOLS

Why did people continually turn to idols instead of to God?

Idols were:	*God is:*
Tangible	Intangible—no physical form
Morally similar—had human characteristics	Morally dissimilar—has divine characteristics
Comprehensible	Incomprehensible
Able to be manipulated	Not able to be manipulated
Worshiping idols involved:	*Worshiping God involves:*
Sexual immorality	Purity and commitment
Doing whatever a person wanted	Doing what God wants
Focusing on self	Focusing on others

10:8 **And we must not engage in sexual immorality as some of them did, causing 23,000 of them to die in one day.**^{NLT} This incident, when *23,000 of* the Israelites died *in one day* is recorded in Numbers 25:1-9. The Israelites worshiped a god of Canaan, Baal of Peor, and engaged in *sexual immorality* with Moabite women. Part of the worship of this god, Baal, involved sexual immorality; the Israelites had engaged in actions clearly against their own laws in order to "worship" an idol. This occurred during the wanderings in the wilderness, so it involved the same group of people who had left Egypt and had already been punished for worshiping the golden calf (10:7). Many continued in sin, without regard for the God to whom they claimed to belong. Because of their sin, God punished them harshly. For the believers in Corinth, the comparison would have been inescapable. Much of the idol worship there focused on ritual prostitution and sexual immorality of all kinds. God would not go lightly on those

IDOLATRY
Today we can allow many things to become gods to us. Money, fame, work, or pleasure can become gods when we concentrate too much on them for personal identity, meaning, and security. No one sets out with the intention of worshiping these things. But by the amount of time we devote to them, they can grow into gods that ultimately control our thoughts and energies. Letting God hold the central place in our lives keeps these things from turning into gods.

who claimed to be his but still engaged in idol worship or sexual immorality.

Sexual sin is powerful and destructive. That is why God has so many laws about sexual sins. Instructions about sexual behavior would have been vital for 3 million people on a forty-year camping trip. But they would be equally important when they entered the Promised Land and settled down as a nation. Paul recognized the importance of strong rules about sex for believers, because sexual sins have the power to disrupt and destroy the church (see also Colossians 3:5-8). Sins involving sex are not innocent dabblings in forbidden pleasures, as is so often portrayed, but powerful destroyers of relationships. They bring confusion and tear down the respect and trust so essential for solid marriages and secure children.

10:9 **Nor should we put Christ to the test, as some of them did and then died from snakebites.**^{NLT} Other versions (such as the NIV), following some manuscripts, read "the Lord" instead of "Christ." But "Christ" has the better manuscript support and is the reading that scribes would be tempted to change because it is difficult to imagine the Israelites tempting Christ in the wilderness. But Paul had already affirmed that Christ, as the spiritual Rock, accompanied them in their wilderness journeys (see 10:4 and discussion). This verse affirms Christ's deity and preexistence.

This verse also recalls Israel's complaining about having been brought out into the wilderness. The people complained, "Why have you brought us out of Egypt to die here in the wilderness? . . . There is nothing to eat here and nothing to drink. And we hate this wretched manna" (Numbers 21:5 NLT). The people even complained about the manna—the miracle food that God had provided (see Exodus 16:31-32). They were testing the Lord's patience to see what he would do, and he punished them for their complaining attitudes by sending poisonous snakes among them. Many were killed by the snakes. Those who claim to be God's people will not test the Lord to see how much they can get away with. True believers will seek to stay near to God in order to constantly live in obedience to him (see also Hebrews 3–4).

10:10 **And don't grumble as some of them did, for that is why God sent his angel of death to destroy them.**^{NLT} This incident of grumbling occurred when the people complained against the leadership of Moses and Aaron—an event that actually happened several times. The phrase "God sent his angel of death to destroy them" could refer to when the Israelites grumbled at Kadesh, refusing to enter the Promised Land. God punished them with a plague (Numbers 14:2, 36-37). This could also refer to the inci-

dent recorded in Numbers 16 when a group rebelled against
Moses, and God sent a plague that killed the rebels. In both
cases, the assumption is that the plague that resulted came
through God's angel of death. This angel is first mentioned in
Exodus 12:23, with the last plague that came upon Egypt. Grumbling against God or against his leaders results in divine punishment. God does not take this sin lightly either. This was another
problem that the Corinthian church was facing (3:1-9).

UNFULFILLED DESIRES
Paul warned the Corinthian believers not to grumble. We start
to grumble when our attention shifts from what we have to what
we don't have. The people of Israel didn't seem to notice what
God was doing for them—setting them free, making them a
nation, giving them a new land—because they were so
wrapped up in what God wasn't doing for them. They could
think of nothing but the delicious Egyptian food they had left
behind (Numbers 11:5).
   Before we judge the Israelites too harshly, it's helpful to think
about what occupies our attention most of the time. Are we
grateful for what God has given us, or are we always thinking
about what we would like to have? Don't allow your unfulfilled
desires to cause you to forget God's gifts of life: food, health,
work, and friends.

**10:11 These things happened to them as examples and were written
down as warnings for us, on whom the fulfillment of the ages
has come.**NIV The Old Testament stories *were written down as
warnings* for believers of the first century, and for today. When
the Israelites disobeyed, they received punishment. Likewise,
when people who claim to be Christians sin with no repentance,
no desire to change, and no concern for God's laws, they too will
receive punishment. When Christ came, everything changed. The
ages past reached their *fulfillment,* and now their lessons,
recorded in the pages of Scripture, can be understood in the light
of God's mercy and salvation in Jesus Christ.

**10:12 So, if you think you are standing firm, be careful that you
don't fall.**NIV The Israelites had received numerous pictures of
God's grace and witnessed many miracles performed before their
very eyes. Yet they gave in to temptation and fell away from
God. Paul warned the Corinthian Christians to *be careful.* If they
began to take pride in their faith, if they began to take it for
granted, if they thought they were *standing firm,* that was the
time to be most careful not to *fall.* The Corinthians were very
sure of themselves, almost prideful. Paul said that if the Israelites

fell into idolatry, so could some in the Corinthian church. No
human being is ever beyond temptation while he or she is on this
earth. Paul warned the believers not to let down their guard.
Those most liable to fall are those who think they won't.

DECEPTIVE COMPARISONS
Most of us can list people who are moral, ethical, and spiritual
"failures." We may become proud of ourselves as "standing
firm" by comparison. We ought to take their failures as sober
warnings of our own vulnerability to sin. Such comparisons
demonstrate neither compassion for others nor concern for the
danger of false confidence. Place your confidence in God
rather than in your personal effort.

10:13 **But remember that the temptations that come into your life
are no different from what others experience. And God is
faithful. He will keep the temptation from becoming so strong
that you can't stand up against it. When you are tempted, he
will show you a way out so that you will not give in to it.**NLT
Temptations come into every believer's life—no one is exempt.
Temptation is not sinful; the sin comes when the person gives in
to temptation. Believers must not be shocked or discouraged, or
think that they are alone in their shortcomings. Instead, they
should realize their weaknesses and turn to God to resist the temptation. Enduring temptation brings great rewards (James 1:12).
Yet God does not leave his people to Satan's whims. God is not a
spectator; he does not leave his children alone to face whatever
temptations Satan can throw at them. Instead, *God is faithful.* He
will not always remove the temptation, because facing it and
remaining strong can be a growing experience; however, God
does promise to *keep the temptation from becoming so strong
that you can't stand up against it.* This means that there exists no
temptation that a believer cannot resist. But the believer must
resist and stand against it. Each temptation can be resisted
because God made it possible to resist it. The secret to resisting
temptation is to recognize the source of the temptation and then
to recognize the source of strength in temptation. God promises
to give his people the strength to resist.
   Not only that, but God also promises to *show you a way out so
that you will not give in* to the temptation and fall into sin. It will
take self-discipline to look for that "way out" even in the middle
of the temptation and then to take it when it is found. The way
out is seldom easy and often requires support from others. One of
the God-given ways of escape from temptation is common sense.
If a believer knows that he will be tempted in certain situations,

then he should stay away from them. Another way out of temptation is through Christian friends. Instead of trying to deal with temptation alone, a believer can explain her dilemma to a close Christian friend and ask for support. This friend can pray, hold the person accountable, and give valuable insights and advice.

The truth is that God loves his people so much that he will protect them from unbearable temptation. And he will always give a way out. Temptation need never drive a wedge between believers and God. Instead, a believer ought to be able to say, "Thank you, God, for trusting me that much. You know I can handle this temptation. Now what do you want me to do?"

BATTLE PLAN
In a culture filled with moral depravity and sin-inducing pressures, Paul gave strong encouragement to the Corinthians about temptation. He said:
- Wrong desires and temptations happen to everyone, so don't feel as though you have been singled out.
- Others have resisted temptation and so can you.
- Any temptation can be resisted because God will help you resist it.

God gives you a way to resist temptation by helping you
- recognize people and situations that give you trouble;
- run from anything you know is wrong;
- choose to do only what is right;
- pray for his help; and
- seek friends who love God and can support you when you are tempted.

Running from a tempting situation is your first step on the way to victory (see 2 Timothy 2:22).

10:14-15 **Therefore, my dear friends, flee from idolatry. I speak to sensible people; judge for yourselves what I say.**[NIV] The Corinthian believers needed to be aware that any dabbling at the edges of their former lives of idol worship might lead them back into sin. How much wiser, instead, to *flee from idolatry*. No believer should think that he or she can withstand any temptation, for such pride can lead to a fall (10:12). The Corinthian believers needed to be wise enough to know that, because of past association, they should run from some temptations. It might not be wise for believers to go to feasts where meat had been offered to idols, because it could draw them back into former sins. Even if one person were strong against such temptation, he or she might be a stumbling block for a weak person—actually becoming a temptation for someone who might not be as strong against the temptation to return to idolatry (see 8:9). Because they were *sensible* *people,* Paul trusted that they could *judge* what he had to say and realize that it would be the best course of action.

FAMILIAR IDOLATRY
Paul told the Corinthian believers to "flee from idolatry" (10:14). Idol worship was the major expression of religion in Corinth. There were several pagan temples in the city, and they were very popular. The statues of wood or stone were not evil in themselves, but people gave them credit for what only God could do, such as provide good weather, crops, and children. Idolatry is still a serious problem today, but it takes a different form. We don't put our trust in statues of wood and stone but in paper money and plastic cards. Trusting anything for what God alone provides is idolatry. Our modern idols are those symbols of power, pleasure, or prestige that we so highly regard. When we understand contemporary parallels to idolatry, Paul's words "flee from idolatry" reveal a choice we must make every day.

10:16-17 Is not the cup of thanksgiving for which we give thanks a participation in the blood of Christ? And is not the bread that we break a participation in the body of Christ? Because there is one loaf, we, who are many, are one body, for we all partake of the one loaf.[NIV] Christians participate in Christ's once-for-all sacrifice when they share *the cup of thanksgiving* (symbolizing Christ's blood) and eat *the bread* (symbolizing his body). The "cup of thanksgiving" or "cup of blessing" probably referred to the third cup drunk at the Passover meal. Jesus instituted the Lord's Supper and spoke of this communion with him through the cup and the bread in Matthew 26:17-30 (see also Mark 14:12-26; Luke 22:7-23). Sharing in this meal signified *participation in the blood of Christ* and *in the body of Christ.* Since the early days of the church, believers have celebrated this special meal. Taking part in sharing the *one loaf* with other believers symbolized their unity in *one body* with Christ. (Paul would write in more detail about this ceremony in 11:17-34.)

10:18 Consider the people of Israel: Do not those who eat the sacrifices participate in the altar?[NIV] In Old Testament days, when Jews offered a sacrifice, they ate a part of that sacrifice as a way of restoring their unity with God, against whom they had sinned (Deuteronomy 12:17-18; 14:22-27). By offering the sacrifice and then eating a portion of the gift that had been offered, they were participating *in the altar*—that is, they were fellowshiping with God, to whom they had brought their gifts.

VISIBLE UNITY
Christian unity begins in the heart of individual believers. Are
we willing to be unified with others who may be completely
different from us other than the fact that we both follow Jesus
Christ?

Unity in Christ grows as local church groups practice Christ's
teachings. This unity can expand as groups of local churches
discover that they can practice larger efforts in obedience to
Christ. Because Satan's power is directly challenged by these
examples of unity, we can expect resistance. We can also
expect simple resistance from people who confuse human
loyalties and traditions with the command to obey Jesus. To
achieve Christian unity, we need Christ's help and the Holy
Spirit's restraining power.

To promote unity in Christ, take these steps:

1. Focus on the nature, attributes, splendor, and holiness of
   God. Filling our minds with God will keep us from being
   occupied with ourselves.
2. Keep mind, heart, and ears open while keeping the mouth
   closed longer. Realize that not all believers use the same
   terms, nor speak the same "language." Impulsive conclusions can prevent us from getting along with those who
   share allegiance to Jesus Christ.
3. Steer clear of persons who closely measure everyone
   else by their standards. We may be the next to be "dissected" and judged.
4. Remember that Jesus died for persons, not principles or a
   system.
5. Stay out of endless arguments over various denomina-
   tional methods and church traditions. Satan uses these to
   distract the church from obeying its commission. Better to
   fail as we obey than to neither fail nor obey!

10:19-20 **What am I trying to say? Am I saying that the idols to whom
the pagans bring sacrifices are real gods and that these sacrifices are of some value? No, not at all. What I am saying is
that these sacrifices are offered to demons, not to God. And I
don't want any of you to be partners with demons.**[NLT] Because
both Christian communion and the Jewish system of sacrifice provided a mystical relationship between God and the participants,
then, by extension, to take part in a pagan sacrificial feast would
provide a similar mystical union—not with idols (for they are
nothing but wood and stone), but with the demons that the idols
represent (see commentary on 8:5-6). Satan and his demons are
behind all idolatry, for idolatry turns people away from the true
God. That is always Satan's goal. Demons use people's openness
and willingness to believe to deceive them. Demons are fallen
angels who joined Satan in his rebellion against God and are now

evil spirits under Satan's control. They help Satan tempt people to sin and have great destructive powers.

Paul's advice here seems to focus on believers taking part in actual religious celebrations (not mere social functions) at an idol's temple. Paul wanted the Corinthian believers to "flee from idolatry" (10:14) and never set foot in an idol temple in order to take part in a religious ceremony or to eat food offered to that idol through such a ceremony. He reiterated that this was not because the idols had any reality or that the *sacrifices are of some value.* Instead, when people sacrificed to idols, they were actually offering their sacrifices *to demons, not to God.* Therefore, taking part in such a religious ceremony was not a neutral activity; it amounted to them becoming *partners with demons.*

10:21-22 **You cannot drink the cup of the Lord and the cup of demons too; you cannot have a part in both the Lord's table and the table of demons. Are we trying to arouse the Lord's jealousy? Are we stronger than he?**^{NIV} Eating at the Lord's table means communing with Christ and identifying with his death (10:16-17). Eating at the demons' table means identifying with Satan by worshiping or promoting pagan (or evil) activities (10:19-20). Obviously, the Christian cannot do both. It would be a contradiction to try to *have a part in both the Lord's table and the table of demons.* To do so is to *arouse the Lord's jealousy.* When ancient Israel turned to idols, God punished them severely (10:7-8). The question "Are we stronger than he?" implies a negative answer. Because believers are not stronger than God, they should not think that they can withstand the Lord's anger for their sin of idolatry (see Deuteronomy 32:21).

UNDIVIDED
Followers of Christ must give him total allegiance. They cannot, as Paul explains, have a part in "both the Lord's table and the table of demons." Eating at the Lord's table means communing with Christ and identifying with his death. Eating at the demons' table means identifying with Satan by worshiping or promoting pagan (or evil) activities. Are you trying to lead two lives, following the desires of both Christ and the crowd? The Bible says that you can't do both at the same time.

10:23-24 **"All things are lawful," but not all things are beneficial. "All things are lawful," but not all things build up. Do not seek your own advantage, but that of the other.**^{NRSV} Paul was responding to the quote of the Corinthians. He was not himself teaching that *all things are lawful.* Obviously, believers are not free to disobey Christ or God's moral law. This argument was a misinterpretation of Paul's view of freedom in Christ. The issue of eating meat offered to idols led Paul to three conclusions in the matter. These conclusions can be applied to the broad spectrum of Christian liberties:

DEFERENCE

It's difficult to know when to defer to weaker believers. Sometimes it's even more difficult to spot them. Their existence can be used as a tool for control. Note that Paul's example doesn't include the "helpful" third party—someone who takes it upon themselves to say, "You shouldn't do that; there might be a weaker believer around." Paul's example (10:25-31) limits responsibility to direct awareness. One believer says to another, "I'm uncomfortable with what you're about to do" (or, "Do you know where that meat came from?"). The response gives an opportunity for compassion.

Paul describes a simple rule of thumb to help in making the decision—we should be sensitive and gracious. The goal here is not a general hypersensitivity that worries about what others might possibly think. Rather, it is a genuine awareness of others and a willingness to limit what we do when there is a real possibility of misunderstanding and offense.

Some actions may not be wrong, but they may not be in the best interest of others. We have freedom in Christ, but we shouldn't exercise our freedom at the cost of hurting a Christian brother or sister. We are not to consider only ourselves; we must also consider the needs and perspective of others.

- While eating such meat is essentially unimportant to one's faith, and while it is *lawful* (not against God's law, see also 6:12), it may not necessarily be *beneficial* to the believer. The Christian has the freedom to eat such meat because he or she knows it doesn't matter (8:6-8). Just because something is not against the law, however, doesn't mean that it is helpful.
- While believers are free to practice their freedom in Christ in matters that are *lawful,* some practices of freedom do not necessarily work to *build up* individual believers, others, or the church.
- Therefore, Christians are to use their freedoms, not to their *own advantage, but* to *that of the other.* As Paul had concluded at the end of chapter 8, all Christians, free in Christ, should humbly set aside their freedoms in order to win more people for the kingdom. Nothing should ever impede a believer's witness for Christ. It is always more important to avoid unhelpful actions than to assert freedoms.

10:25-26 Here's what you should do. You may eat any meat that is sold in the marketplace. Don't ask whether or not it was offered to

**idols, and then your conscience won't be bothered. For "the
earth is the Lord's, and everything in it."**[NLT] Regarding the specific example of meat offered to idols, Paul offered this advice.
First of all, the believers should feel free to *eat any meat that is
sold in the marketplace.* As noted in the commentary on 8:1,
meat that arrived for sale in the marketplace may have been left
over from a sacrifice at a pagan altar. But it was impossible to
know if such meat had been part of a sacrifice. Paul told the
believers, *Don't ask whether or not it was offered to idols, and
then your conscience won't be bothered.* It doesn't matter (that
has already been decided) because *the earth is the Lord's, and
everything in it* (quoted from Psalm 24:1). Whatever happened to
the meat in a pagan temple, the believers knew that all food was
created by God and is a gift from God. Therefore, the Christians
were free to eat anything. And if they didn't ask, then they
wouldn't know whether it was offered to idols. Then they
wouldn't have to worry about their consciences.

LIVING FREE
The Corinthians' struggle against sin brings to light a recurring
problem. In a world where everything seems tainted by evil,
how shall we live? Paul gave one answer to the dilemma—to
buy whatever meat is sold at the market without asking
whether it was offered to idols. It doesn't matter anyway, and
no one's conscience would be troubled. When we become too
worried about every action, we become legalistic and cannot
enjoy life. Everything belongs to God, and he has given us all
things to enjoy. If you know something is a problem, then you
can deal with it, but don't go looking for problems.

**10:27 If some unbeliever invites you to a meal and you want to go,
eat whatever is put before you without raising questions of
conscience.**[NIV] In the same way as suggested in 10:26, if the
believers were invited to the home of an unbeliever for dinner,
they could go. In the homes of unbelievers, the Christians might
well be served meat that had been offered to idols. Paul's advice,
as with buying meat in the market (10:25-26) is to *eat whatever
is put before you without raising questions of conscience.* It
would probably have been a breach of hospitality to ask about the
food and then to refuse to eat it. How much better to just enjoy
the host's hospitality and be a witness to his family than to raise
questions of conscience and so lose that opportunity.

**10:28-31 But suppose someone warns you that this meat has been
offered to an idol. Don't eat it, out of consideration for the
conscience of the one who told you. It might not be a matter**

of conscience for you, but it is for the other person.^{NLT} But the situation could arise that several believers are eating a meal at the home of an unbeliever. One of these believers (the *someone* referred to here, who was a "weaker" believer, see 8:10) *warns* his fellow believers that the meat they had been served had been *offered to an idol.* At that point, then, the stronger believers, although they know that this really makes no difference, should refrain from eating the meat *out of consideration for the conscience* of that weaker believer because of the clear association with temple worship. (This weaker believer feels that in eating that meat, the Christians would be sanctioning idol worship.) This is the same advice Paul gave in chapter 8. While *it might not be a matter of conscience* for the strong believer, if *it is for* another, then the strong believer must refuse to eat the meat for the sake of the weak in this context.

HARM TO NONE
Why should we be limited by another person's conscience? Simply because we are to do all things for God's glory, even our eating and drinking. Nothing we do should cause another believer to stumble. We do what is best for others, so that they might be saved. We should also be sensitive to the meaning of our actions to new Christians who are sorting out how to renounce sinful ways from the past and live for Christ.

However, Christians should not make a career out of *being* the offended people with oversensitive consciences. Believers must not project their standards onto others. Many believers who have been Christians for years are still oversensitive and judgmental of others. Instead of being the offended weaker brothers and sisters, they are no more than offended "Pharisees."

Christian leaders and teachers should carefully teach about the freedom Christians have in matters not expressly forbidden by Scripture. New or weak Christians should not remain in a weak or sensitive state but grow into maturity and discernment lest they prove to be an unnecessary burden on others' freedom.

Now why should my freedom be limited by what someone else thinks? If I can thank God for the food and enjoy it, why should I be condemned for eating it? Whatever you eat or drink or whatever you do, you must do all for the glory of God.^{NLT} Paul's question here, taken in context of his discussion regarding strong believers acquiescing to weaker believers in matters of conscience, means that Christian freedom, because it is freedom, should never be *limited* or *condemned* by another. The only real way to hold on to that freedom is to use or not use it freely, depending on the situation. Strong believers must not allow their freedom to be limited or condemned by weaker believers, so they should not use their freedom when that could happen.

Simply because these strong believers can *thank God for the food and enjoy it,* no matter where it came from, they should not allow themselves to be condemned for using that freedom. It is better, said Paul, to set aside one's freedom in those situations. The bottom line is that all believers do should be done *for the glory of God.* If these strong believers had to set aside their liberties in order to win others to Christ, they should do so because this would bring glory to God.

10:32-33 **Do not cause anyone to stumble, whether Jews, Greeks or the church of God—even as I try to please everybody in every way. For I am not seeking my own good but the good of many, so that they may be saved.**[NIV] Paul wanted these believers to understand that the liberty God gave them was not to be used to *cause anyone to stumble* and turn away from faith; rather, as Paul described in 8:13, his entire life focused on winning others to Christ. If need be, he would never eat any meat again if it would keep others from stumbling. In things that did not really matter, Paul tried *to please everybody in every way*—whether they were *Jews, Greeks or the church of God.* In 9:19-22, Paul had described how he served among the Jews, the Gentiles, and those weaker believers in the church, becoming "all things to all people, that I might by all means save some" (9:22 NRSV). Always, Paul's focus was not to seek his *own good but the good of many, so that they may be saved.* Nothing, not even liberty in Christ, should cause believers to lose sight of their desire to win others to Christ.

FREEDOM CHOOSES
Paul's criterion for all his actions was not what he liked best but what was best for those around him. Other possible attitudes would be
- being insensitive and doing whatever, no matter who is hurt by it;
- being oversensitive and doing nothing, for fear that someone may be displeased; or
- being a "yes person" by going along with everything, trying to gain approval from people rather than from God.

Each of these other options actually destroys our freedom in Christ. In this age of "me first" and "looking out for number one," Paul's startling statement is a good standard. If we make the good of others one of our primary goals, we will develop a serving attitude that pleases God.

MAKING CHOICES IN SENSITIVE ISSUES

Every person makes hundreds of choices every day. Most choices have
no right or wrong attached to them—like what a person wears or eats.
But many decisions carry a little more weight. You don't want to do wrong,
and you don't want to cause others to do wrong, so how can you make
such decisions? Ask yourself the following questions.

If I choose one course of action:	
	. . . does it help my witness for Christ? (9:19-22)
	. . . am I motivated by a desire to help others to know Christ? (9:23; 10:33)
	. . . does it help me do my best? (9:25)
	. . . is it against a specific command in Scripture and would thus cause me to sin? (10:12)
	. . . is it the best and most beneficial course of action? (10:23, 33)
	. . . am I thinking only of myself, or do I truly care about the other person? (10:24)
	. . . am I acting lovingly or selfishly? (10:28-31)
	. . . does it glorify God? (10:31)
	. . . will it cause someone else to sin? (10:32)

11:1 Imitate me, just as I also imitate Christ.NKJV This verse belongs at
the conclusion of chapter 10, not at the beginning of chapter 11,
where it has been traditionally placed. Paul had just told the Corinthians that his goal was to seek the good of others, not himself. In
this regard, Paul called upon them to imitate him. Elsewhere Paul
had encouraged the believers to *imitate* him. In 4:15-16, he had
stated, "For even if you had ten thousand others to teach you about
Christ, you have only one spiritual father. For I became your father
in Christ Jesus when I preached the Good News to you. So I ask
you to follow my example and do as I do" (NLT, see commentary
on 4:14-16; see also Ephesians 5:1; 1 Thessalonians 1:6; 2:14). As
in chapter 4, Paul's words were not prideful. He had just spent three
chapters explaining how the Corinthian believers needed to deal
with the issue of eating meat that had been offered to idols. His conclusion of the matter balanced freedom in Christ with responsibility
to love the "weaker" believers. All Christians should be so focused
on bringing others to Christ that nothing stands in the way of that
goal. Paul followed his own advice (see 8:13; 10:33) and encouraged the believers to follow his example. The reason they could do
so? Because he followed Christ's example—*just as I also imitate
Christ.*

The New Testament places strong emphasis on imitating leaders. It also gives strong words to those leaders that they be worthy of emulation (Scripture quotations are from the NIV):

- Matthew 11:29—"Take my yoke upon you and learn from me." Jesus told his followers to learn from his example of gentleness and humility.
- Philippians 3:17—"Join with others in following my example." Paul urged believers to follow his example of enthusiasm, perseverance, and maturity.
- 1 Thessalonians 1:6-7—"You became imitators of us and of the Lord. . . . And so you became a model to all the believers." The new Christians at Thessalonica received training in discipleship from Paul, and even in suffering, they modeled before others what they had learned.
- 1 Timothy 1:16—"In me . . . Christ Jesus might display his unlimited patience as an example for those who would believe on him." Paul used his unworthiness to receive Christ as an example of grace so that no one would hold back from coming to Christ.
- 1 Peter 5:3—"Not lording it over those entrusted to you, but being examples to the flock." Peter taught Christian leaders to lead by example, not by commands.
- See also 1 Corinthians 4:16 and Hebrews 6:12.

Christians owe much to others who have taught them and have modeled for them what they need to know about the gospel and Christian living. They should continue following the good examples of those who have invested themselves in them by investing their own lives through evangelism, service, and Christian education. They, in turn, become models worth imitating.

IMITATION
Why did Paul say, "Imitate me" (11:1)? Paul wasn't being arrogant—he did not think of himself as sinless. He had already introduced them to the Messiah; now he wanted them to follow his example.

The Corinthian believers did not know much about the life and ministry of Christ. Paul could not tell them to imitate Jesus because the Gospels had not yet been written, so they knew little of what Jesus was like. The best way to point these new Christians to Christ was to point them to a Christian whom they trusted (see also Galatians 4:12; Philippians 3:17; 1 Thessalonians 1:6; 2:14; 2 Thessalonians 3:7, 9). Paul had lived in Corinth almost two years and had built a relationship of trust with many of these new believers.

Even today, God's Spirit still uses the faithful lives of Christians alongside the Scriptures to help people understand and follow Christ. Watch how faithful Christians live and, in the light of Scripture, pattern your conduct after theirs.

1 Corinthians 11

This section focuses primarily on proper attitudes and conduct in worship, not on the marriage relationship or on the role of women in the church. While Paul's specific instructions may be cultural (women covering their heads in worship), the principles behind his specific instructions are timeless—for they instruct believers to show respect for their spouse and to have reverent behavior in worship. If a believer's actions offend members and could divide the church, then the believer should change his or her ways to promote church unity. Paul told the women who were not wearing head coverings to wear them, not because it was a scriptural command, but because it kept the congregation from dividing over a petty issue that took people's focus off Christ.

11:2 I am so glad, dear friends, that you always keep me in your thoughts and you are following the Christian teaching I passed on to you.^{NLT} Apparently, in their letter to Paul, the Corinthian believers had told him that they were *following the Christian teaching* that Paul had *passed on to* them. This "teaching" was what Paul had received from Jesus Christ himself, as well as from the other apostles. It was truth, not anything Paul had thought up on his own (which the false teachers did), so the believers could trust and follow it.

11:3 Now I want you to realize that the head of every man is Christ, and the head of the woman is man, and the head of Christ is God.^{NIV} Paul commended the Corinthian believers' faithfulness to the teaching that he had passed on to them (11:2), but apparently they were facing problems regarding men and women in worship. In this area, they were not properly keeping the tradition that Paul had taught. No specifics are given. The details were in the letter he received from the Corinthians. Paul had been answering specific questions; apparently a question had arisen about head coverings in worship—see 11:10, "For this reason, and because of the angels, the woman ought to have a sign of authority on her head" (NIV). The Corinthians may have adopted cultural patterns of male-female relationships into their worship that (as some scholars argue) had blurred the distinction between males and females. It may have been customs of dress regarding hair coverings, or perhaps it involved issues of hairstyle (short or long hair for men and women). Paul began to answer the Corinthians' question by first giving the general principle of how relationships should be regarded in the church. Paul wanted them to *realize* important facts about relationships as they had been instituted by God: *The head of every man is Christ, and the head of the woman is man, and the head of Christ is God.*

The words translated "head of" can mean origin, source of, or authority. Traditionally, many scholars have interpreted *kephale* ("head") to be used in the same way as *exousia* ("authority"). Thus, they take the word to mean "chief" or person of highest rank. Other scholars see *kephale* to mean "source of life," conveying relational sense—as in the account that man was the source of woman's existence (Genesis 2:22-23; see 11:7-9). In the language of 11:9-12, the focus is on the relationship. Paul was not concerned, as some have argued, for the submission of women, but rather that the completeness or glory of the relationship not be diminished (see 11:7).

How then is Christ "the head of every man"? There are two ways to consider Christ as "the source of life": (1) Because Christ was present at Creation, he is the Creator of every man; and (2) Christ is every believer's source of life in the new creation. Paul wrote in 2 Corinthians, "Therefore, if anyone is in Christ, he is a new creation; the old has gone, the new has come!" (5:17 NIV). Most likely, Paul was speaking of believers' spiritual relationship in Christ, so the second meaning is more probable.

In the phrase "the head of Christ is God," Paul was not teaching that Christ was inferior to God or lesser in any way (see 8:6). Nor was he thinking that Christ was the offspring of God with regard to his eternal being. Paul was referring to the incarnation of Christ. Through Christ's coming to earth, believers receive forgiveness and are united with God and with one another (3:22-23). From this theological base, Paul will address the issue of head coverings.

11:4-5 Every man who prays or prophesies with his head covered dishonors his head. And every woman who prays or prophesies with her head uncovered dishonors her head—it is just as though her head were shaved.[NIV] In this section Paul's main concern is irreverence in worship. The praying and prophesying mentioned here were in the context of public worship. When a

man prayed or prophesied, he was to do so *without* his head covered. In contrast, when a woman prayed or prophesied, she was
to do so only *with* her head covered. We do not know conclu-
sively what the historical situation was. A woman uncovering her
head could have meant (1) that she was not wearing a veil; (2)
that she was not wearing a shawl or true head covering; or (3)
that her hair was loosened and hanging down.

Remember that Paul gave these instructions in response to a
question that had been sent to him by the Corinthian believers.
Paul explained that the men were not to cover their heads
because they are "the image and glory of God" (11:7); to do so
would be to shame their head—Christ. So in worship, the men
should not veil themselves because that would dishonor God.
Women were allowed to pray and prophesy in public *(and every
woman who prays or prophesies)*; Paul's only stipulation for the
Corinthian women was that they should cover their heads when
doing so.

While the general principle of propriety and distinctions between men and woman still stands, the cultural advice given here
about head coverings need not be considered as binding to all the
churches for all time. Indeed, when Paul wrote to Timothy with
advice about the women in the church in Ephesus, he did not tell
Timothy to make sure the women covered their heads. Instead,
his advice focused on modesty in their dress (see 1 Timothy 2:9-
10). The situation in Corinth may have been that women were
coming to church with their heads uncovered and this was causing disruption. Although the reason for the problem is unknown,
we can gather that Paul's concern was that nothing disrupt worship. So he advised the Corinthian women to cover their heads in
public worship much as he advised the Christians not to eat meat
offered to idols in public situations. The women were certainly
free to not cover their heads just as they were free to eat meat
offered to idols. Neither of these mattered regarding their salvation. However, Paul always advised that Christians show defer-
ence to others in order to promote unity.

The statement that for a woman to have her head uncovered in
worship would be *just as though her head were shaved* is cultural
and, again, the reason for the statement is unknown, although
11:6 hints that a shaved head was a disgrace. Some commentators
believe that a woman with a shaved head may have been a
temple prostitute or the dominant mate in a lesbian couple. Such
women who became Christians not only needed to grow out their
hair (11:15) but also to cover their heads in worship in recognition of their relationship to God and to their Christian brothers
under God.

A modern example might be a Christian woman living in an Eastern culture. While that Christian is certainly "free" to wear shorts and a T-shirt (and would not have any problem doing so in the United States), she should set aside that freedom out of respect for the culture in which she lives. She should dress modestly and cover what should be covered. She will have far more acceptance by doing that than by flaunting her freedom to dress in a certain way that would be acceptable elsewhere.

"Praying" refers, as noted above, to public prayer during worship. "Prophesying" refers not just to telling of future events as revealed to a person by God but also to public speaking about religious truths, witnessing for Christ, and bringing God's word of encouragement to the congregation (see 14:31). Both men and women could do this in the early church. (See, for example, Philip's daughters in Acts 21:9.) Women prophesying fulfilled the words of the prophet Joel, "Your sons and daughters will prophesy" (Joel 2:28 NIV). The spiritual gifts, given by the Holy Spirit, do not discriminate between men and women.

11:6 If a woman does not cover her head, she should have her hair cut off; and if it is a disgrace for a woman to have her hair cut or shaved off, she should cover her head.NIV To further make the point that women should cover their heads in public worship, Paul wrote that *if a woman does not cover her head, she should have her hair cut off.* In other words, if she refuses to cover her head, thus disgracing herself, then she might as well cut or shave off all of her hair because that too was *a disgrace.* Therefore, if the "uncovered" head (short or shaved hair) is a disgrace, then she ought to willingly cover her head during worship. Paul was not here referring to the woman's hair as her covering; the covering was a sort of veil worn over the head.

11:7-9 A man ought not to cover his head, since he is the image and glory of God; but the woman is the glory of man. For man did not come from woman, but woman from man; neither was man created for woman, but woman for man.NIV The reason that *a man ought not to cover his head* in worship is because *he is the image and glory of God*—he represents and reflects God himself. Women are also made in the image of God, for Genesis 1:27 says, "So God created humankind in his image, in the image of God he created them; male and female he created them" (NRSV). But *the woman is the glory of man.* By praying and prophesying with her head uncovered, she would be dishonoring and shaming man whose glory she was supposed to be. Paul does not say what he means by using the word "glory" here. It could be that man and woman together reflect the image of God (glory) and that by uncovering her head, the woman was taking something away from the identity of the man, thus depleting his part in the reflection of God's glory. Paul reasoned this back to the order of creation. Man was created first, and then woman. "So the Lord God caused the man to fall into a deep sleep; and while he was sleeping, he took one of the man's ribs and closed up the place with flesh. Then the Lord God made a woman from the rib he had taken out of the man, and he brought her to the man" (Genesis 2:21-22 NIV). Genesis also explains that man was not created for woman, *but woman for man:* "The Lord God said, 'It is not good for the man to be alone. I will make a helper suitable for him'" (Genesis 2:18 NIV).

11:10 For this reason, and because of the angels, the woman ought to have a sign of authority on her head.[NIV] *For this reason,* because God's people are to glorify him, the women *ought to have a sign of authority on* their heads. There are two basic views of this verse: (1) that the head covering represents the woman's submission to male authority; or (2) that the head covering represents the God-given authority (enablement) for a woman to function this way in the church. Most likely, Paul meant the second option. It is important to understand that while the stipulation of head covering is upheld in Corinth, the main point is that these Christian women had an equal status with men because of their union with Christ. They were free in Christ, equal before God, and able to pray and prophesy in the worship services. They were no longer to be regarded as inferior, which would have been their previous status in both Greek and Jewish cultures (see Galatians 3:27-28). The head covering was not a sign of subjection but a sign of women's willingness to be under the authority of God, just as men were under the authority of God.

The other reason for women wearing this sign of authority is *because of the angels.* It was proper for women to wear head coverings in the worship of God because the angels would be present during this worship. Hebrews 1:14 states that angels watch over believers and care for them. Because the angels observe God's people at worship, his people should be sensitive to follow God's commands in worship. The angels live to serve God; likewise God's people, who have been saved by his grace, should live in obedience to his commands.

11:11-12 But in relationships among the Lord's people, women are not independent of men, and men are not independent of women. For although the first woman came from man, all men have been born from women ever since, and everything comes from God.[NLT] Paul acknowledged women's roles in praying and prophesying, and their authority in doing so. But he reminded the Corinthians that all people relate to each other and to God. Clearly God created men and women as interdependent: *Women are not independent of men, and men are not independent of women.* Even though Adam was created before Eve, and even though Eve came from Adam (*the first woman came from man,* 11:8), ever since then *all men have been born from women.* No one is completely independent. Finally, *everything comes from God,* who is the Source of all that exists.

NO CONTEST
God created roles and relationships in order for his created world to function smoothly. Although there must be lines of authority in the church, there should *not* be lines of superiority. God created men and women with unique and complementary characteristics. Competition doesn't improve relationship. One sex is not better than the other. We must not let the issue of authority and submission become a wedge to destroy oneness in church or in marriage. Instead, we should glorify God by utilizing all the capacities he has given us.

11:13-15 **Judge for yourselves: Is it proper for a woman to pray to God with her head uncovered? Does not the very nature of things teach you that if a man has long hair, it is a disgrace to him, but that if a woman has long hair, it is her glory? For long hair is given to her as a covering.**[NIV] Paul called upon the Corinthian believers to *judge for* themselves, considering that they should act in accordance with *the very nature of things.* Paul's point in these verses is that men and women are different; they were created differently. When Paul referred to the "nature of things," he was referring to custom, propriety, and the way culture operates. Men should live as and look like men; women should live as and look like women. Women have been naturally given a "covering" of hair, and they should wear their hair long. The distinctions between men and women ought not be blurred. Men and women were created alike in that they are loved by God and saved by him, and both are created in the image of God (Genesis 1:26). Anything that blurs their God-given distinctions in the culture or ruins their ability to share their faith has to be put aside. In the culture of Corinth, long hair on a man was disgraceful, while short hair on a woman was equally disgraceful. No one knows the details as to why, except that this may have had to do with the looks of heathen priests and priestesses, homosexuals, or temple prostitutes.

AVOID SPLITTING HAIRS
In talking about head coverings and length of hair, Paul was
saying that believers should look and behave in ways that are
honorable within their own culture. In many cultures, long hair
on men is considered appropriate and masculine. In Corinth, it
may have been thought a sign of male prostitution in the pagan
temples. And women with short hair may have been labeled
prostitutes. Paul was saying that in the Corinthian culture,
Christian women should keep their hair long. If short hair on
women was a sign of prostitution, then a Christian woman with
short hair would find it even more difficult to be a believable
witness for Jesus Christ. Paul wasn't encouraging Christians to
adopt all the practices of the culture, but to avoid appearances
and behavior that detract from the goal of being believable
witnesses for Jesus Christ as we demonstrate our Christian
faith.

11:16 **But if anyone wants to argue about this, all I can say is that**
we have no other custom than this, and all the churches of
God feel the same way about it.^{NLT} In this statement Paul
admonished the contentious ones at Corinth to behave appropriately in church meetings. Calling upon the other churches as
examples of such orderliness, Paul urged anyone who might
argue with him that the other churches would stand with Paul in
this matter.

ORDER AT THE LORD'S SUPPER / 11:17-34

A second abuse of worship existed in the Corinthian church
regarding how to celebrate the Lord's Supper. Apparently, there
was a division between the rich and the poor during both the love
feast and the celebration of Communion itself. The rich despised
the poor at the accompanying meal and disregarded their needs
(11:21-22). It was common for the church to meet in the homes
of wealthier members and to have a fellowship meal ("love
feast") before Communion. Since the dining area could seat only
a few, the host most likely selected those who ate with him while
the rest ate in the open court or atrium. Where a person ate
became a distinction of class. This lack of unity caused the believers to lose the real meaning behind what they were remembering—the sacrifice of Jesus' body on the cross.

11:17 **In the following directives I have no praise for you, for your**
meetings do more harm than good.^{NIV} At the beginning of the
last section (11:2), Paul commended the Corinthians for remembering what he had taught them. Concerning this next issue in his

letter, however, he had *no praise for* them. In this situation, their
meetings were doing *more harm than good.*

11:18-19 **For, to begin with, when you come together as a church, I**
hear that there are divisions among you; and to some extent I
believe it. Indeed, there have to be factions among you, for
only so will it become clear who among you are genuine.NRSV
Paul allowed that there would be differences and divisions
among church members. In some cases that would be natural—
genuine believers would naturally be separate from those who
were not true believers. However, when the people in a church
develop into self-willed divisions (such as class distinctions, or
the factions described in 3:4), these are destructive to the congregation. Apparently, Paul was referring to class (economic) distinctions here, because these *divisions* were hurting a time of
fellowship that should have been drawing the believers together,
not separating them.

11:20-21 **When you come together, it is not the Lord's Supper you eat,**
for as you eat, each of you goes ahead without waiting for any-
body else. One remains hungry, another gets drunk.NIV The
Lord's Supper was instituted by Jesus before he died. In a private
meal with his disciples, often called the
Last Supper, Jesus spoke to his disciples about the significance of this last
meal: "While they were eating, Jesus
took bread, gave thanks and broke it,
and gave it to his disciples, saying,
'Take and eat; this is my body.' Then he
took the cup, gave thanks and offered it
to them, saying, 'Drink from it, all of
you. This is my blood of the covenant,
which is poured out for many for the
forgiveness of sins. I tell you, I will not
drink of this fruit of the vine from now
on until that day when I drink it anew
with you in my Father's kingdom'"
(Matthew 26:26-29 NIV). Jesus and his
disciples ate a meal, sang psalms, read Scripture, and prayed.
Then Jesus took two traditional parts of the Passover meal, the
passing of bread and the drinking of wine, and gave them new
meaning as representations of his body and blood. He used the
bread and wine to explain the significance of what he was about
to do on the cross.

The Lord's Supper was celebrated from the earliest days of the
church. Acts 2:41-42 says, "Those who accepted [Peter's] mes-

> Next to the Blessed
> Sacrament itself, your
> neighbour is the holiest
> object presented to your
> senses. If he is your
> Christian neighbour, he is
> holy in almost the same
> way, for in him also
> Christ *vere latitat*—the
> glorifier and the glorified,
> Glory Himself—is truly
> hidden.   *C. S. Lewis*

sage were baptized, and about three thousand were added to their number that day. They devoted themselves to the apostles' teaching and to the fellowship, to the breaking of bread and to prayer" (NIV). "Breaking of bread" refers to Communion services that were celebrated in remembrance of Jesus; they were patterned after the Last Supper that Jesus had held with his disciples before his death.

When the Lord's Supper was celebrated in the early church, it included a feast or fellowship meal followed by the celebration of Communion. At the fellowship meal in the church in Corinth, it seems that people brought food to share, with the rich bringing more food than the poor. Instead of sharing equally among everyone, the rich ate among themselves with their own food, leaving the poor with little or nothing. And when the people ate and drank excessively, *without waiting for anybody else,* this also caused people to go hungry. There was little sharing and caring. Therefore, Paul said that they were not preparing themselves to share *the Lord's Supper,* but they were merely satisfying their hunger, as they would at any meal. The feast did not demonstrate the unity and love that should characterize the church, nor was it a preparation for Communion. Approaching the Lord's Supper (Communion) with some of the church members *hungry,* while others had gotten *drunk,* made a mockery of what was to be a holy and unifying time for the believers. Paul condemned these actions and reminded the church of the real purpose of the Lord's Supper.

11:22 Don't you have homes to eat and drink in? Or do you despise the church of God and humiliate those who have nothing? What shall I say to you? Shall I praise you for this? Certainly not![NIV] Some in the Corinthian church had turned the fellowship meal into a gluttonous feast where some ate too much and others got nothing. This had made a mockery of the Lord's Supper. In addition, by the rich separating themselves from the poor who could not bring as much food, the rich were humiliating those who had nothing. Obviously there was nothing for Paul to praise in this behavior. Instead, he advised the believers to eat and drink at home. Then, when they came to share in the feast, no one would be ravenous, but they could, with self-control, wait for one another and eat only a little so there would be enough for everyone (11:33-34).

11:23-24 For I received from the Lord that which I also delivered to you: that the Lord Jesus on the same night in which He was betrayed took bread; and when He had given thanks, He broke it and said, "Take, eat; this is My body which is broken

for you; do this in remembrance of Me."NKJV Paul could not praise their actions, and he reminded them that he had *delivered to* them what he had *received from the Lord* regarding the celebration of the Lord's Supper. Paul received the following instructions from the Lord. This probably does not mean that he had a divine, direct revelation because the tradition of the Lord's Supper had been in circulation among the churches through the teaching of the apostles ever since the church first began. The same words of Jesus that Paul quotes are also quoted by the Gospel writers (Matthew 26:26; Mark 14:22; and Luke 22:19). Thus, it seems clear that Paul and the Gospel writers drew upon the same apostolic tradition.

Christians pose several different possibilities for what Christ meant when he said, *"This is My body. . . . This is My blood" :* Some believe that the wine and bread actually become Christ's physical blood and body (transubstantiation). Others believe that the bread and wine remain unchanged, but Christ is spiritually present with the bread and wine (consubstantiation). Still others believe that the bread and wine symbolize Christ's body and blood (symbolization). Christians generally agree, however, that participating in the Lord's Supper is an important facet of Christian worship and that Christ's presence, however they understand it, strengthens them spiritually. By eating "the body of Christ," believers receive, through faith, the power and benefits of Christ's body broken for sin and glorified forever. Because the Lord's Supper is commemorated *in remembrance* of the body and blood of Jesus given for the redemption of sinful people, it must never be taken lightly. Hence, Paul's instructions in the remainder of the chapter.

REMEMBER
Jesus asked the disciples to eat the broken bread "in remembrance of me." He wanted them to remember his sacrifice, the basis for forgiveness of sins, and his friendship that they could continue to enjoy through the work of the Holy Spirit. Although the exact meaning of Communion has been strongly debated throughout church history, Christians still take bread and wine in remembrance of their Lord and Savior, Jesus Christ. Do not neglect participating in the Lord's Supper. Let it remind you of what Christ did for you.

11:25 In the same manner He also took the cup after supper, saying, "This cup is the new covenant in My blood. This do, as often as you drink it, in remembrance of Me."NKJV As Jesus had taken the bread, had given thanks, and had broken it (11:23-24), *in the same manner He also took the cup.* The "cup" represented *the new covenant in [Jesus'] blood.* What is this new covenant? In the old covenant (the promise of God with his people before Christ came), people could approach God only through the priests and the sacrificial system. God would forgive people's sins if they would bring animals for the priests to sacrifice. When this sacrificial system was begun, the agreement between God and human beings was sealed with the blood of animals. The people of Israel first entered into this agreement after the Exodus from Egypt (Exodus 24). But animal blood did not in itself remove sin (only God can forgive sin), and animal sacrifices had to be repeated day by day and year after year.

Jesus' death on the cross ushered in the new covenant (or agreement) between God and humanity. This concept is key to all New Testament theology. Under this new covenant, Jesus died in the place of sinners. Unlike the blood of animals, Jesus' blood truly removed the sins of all who put their faith in him. And Jesus' sacrifice will never have to be repeated; it is good for all eternity (Hebrews 9:23-28). The new covenant completes, rather than replaces, the old covenant, fulfilling everything the old covenant looked forward to (see Jeremiah 31:31-34). Now people can personally approach God and communicate with him. Eating the bread and drinking the cup shows that God's people are remembering Christ's death for them and renewing their commitment to serve him.

TWO-WAY REMEMBERING
Jesus said, "Do this, as often as you drink it, in remembrance of me." How do we remember Christ in the Lord's Supper? By thinking about what he did and why he did it. Further, the remembering has both a backward and forward look. We remember Christ's death, and we remember that he is coming! If the Lord's Supper becomes just a ritual or a pious habit, it loses its significance. But when we appreciate what Christ has done and anticipate what he will do when he returns, the Lord's Supper takes on a profound sense of purpose. Take time to prepare yourself spiritually for Communion. Gratefully recall Christ's loving sacrifice for you. Let the reality that your sins are forgiven motivate you to love and serve him better.

11:26 **For as often as you eat this bread and drink this cup, you proclaim the Lord's death till He comes.**[NKJV] The eating of the bread and drinking of the cup are to be done on a continual basis in the churches until the return of Christ *(till He comes).* By observing this special meal, the believers *proclaim the Lord's* *death.* By partaking of the body and blood of Christ, they person-ally show their participation in the Christian community and their faith in the Lord Jesus Christ as Savior. The periodic, solemn cel-ebration of the Lord's Supper among believers reminds them of Christ's suffering on their behalf and of his imminent return when he will take them with him.

11:27-28 Whoever, therefore, eats the bread or drinks the cup of the Lord in an unworthy manner will be answerable for the body and blood of the Lord. Examine yourselves, and only then eat of the bread and drink of the cup.[NRSV] The solemn occasion of the Lord's Supper was to be celebrated carefully and entered into with spiritual readiness. When Paul said that no one should take the Lord's Supper *in an unworthy manner,* he was speaking to church members who were rushing into it without thinking of its meaning and, thus, were "not honoring the body of Christ" (11:29 NLT). Those who did so would be *answerable for the body and blood of the Lord.* To treat the symbols of Christ's ultimate sacrifice irreverently is to be guilty of irreverence toward his body and blood shed on sinners' behalf. Instead of honoring Christ's sacrifice, those who ate unworthily were sharing in the guilt of those who crucified him.

CAUTIONS
Paul gives specific instructions on how the Lord's Supper should be observed:

- We should take the Lord's Supper thoughtfully, because we are proclaiming that Christ died for our sins (11:26).
- We should take it worthily, with due reverence and respect (11:27).
- We should examine ourselves for any unconfessed sin or resentful attitude (11:28). We are to be properly prepared, based on our belief in and love for Christ.
- We should be considerate of others (11:33), waiting until everyone is present and then eating in an orderly and uni-fied manner.

Ironically, the realization that we are not worthy (that we don't deserve a place at the Lord's Table) is the very position from which Christ welcomes us to the feast. We are the guests whom the host has graciously invited. Humility must be the engraving on our invitation.

We should prepare ourselves for Communion through healthy introspection, confession of sin, and resolution of differences with others. These actions remove the barriers that affect our relationship with Christ and with other believers. Awareness of your sin should not keep you away from Communion but should drive you to participate in it.

In reality, no one is "worthy" to take the Lord's Supper. All believers are sinners saved by grace. But because they are saved, believers can celebrate this solemn rite as given to them by the Savior.

The very nature of the rite calls for introspection. Therefore, Paul told the believers to *examine* themselves. No one should partake of the Lord's Supper who had not accepted Jesus' sacrifice on the cross for salvation. Neither should they come to the table drunk, angry with others, or with known but unrepented sin in their lives. Coming to the Lord's table "in an unworthy manner" means to come without a solemn understanding of what is being remembered, and without a repentant and humble spirit before the Lord.

11:29-30 **For all who eat and drink without discerning the body, eat and drink judgment against themselves. For this reason many of you are weak and ill, and some have died.**NRSV The seriousness of the matter is revealed in these words. To *eat and drink without discerning the body* means coming to the Lord's table and not honoring the body of Christ sacrificed for our sins. Some versions, following inferior manuscript support, exhibit the interpolation "body of the Lord," in an attempt to distinguish Christ's body from the body of believers, the church. According to superior manuscript evidence, the reading is "the body," which can be interpreted as either the body of Jesus offered on the cross or the body of believers or both.

The Corinthians had two problems: (1) They did not distinguish this special meal from all others; and (2) they did not discern their interrelationship as believers—the body of Christ. Regarding the second problem, the Corinthians had become divided at the Lord's Supper between the rich and the poor. But any such divisions had to be done away with if they were to truly come together as the body of Christ, remembering Christ's sacrifice on their behalf. To not come to the table in unity and acceptance of fellow believers revealed arrogance and ungratefulness for what Christ had done.

To take the Lord's Supper—to eat the bread and drink the wine—as though it were no more than a regular meal to assuage hunger is to miss the sanctity of this special rite. Those who did so were eating and drinking God's *judgment against themselves.* This "judgment" was severe, one of the most severe in the New Testament. The judgment was disciplinary in nature (11:32); that is, this did not refer to eternal judgment, but it was severe enough as to cause *many* of the believers to be *weak and ill,* while some had even *died.* That some of the people had died may have been a special supernatural judgment on the Corinthian church. This type of disciplinary judgment highlights the seriousness of the Communion service. The Lord's Supper is not to be taken lightly; this new covenant cost Jesus his life. It is not a meaningless ritual, but a sacrament given by Christ to help strengthen believers' faith.

11:31 But if we judged ourselves, we would not come under judgment.^{NIV} If the believers *judged* themselves—that is, if they took time to examine themselves (11:28) before taking the Lord's Supper and so came to it with humble and repentant hearts—they *would not come under judgment.* This "judgment" refers to what Paul had just described in 11:29-30. While no one can come to the Lord's Supper "worthy" of Christ's redemptive work, all believers can come with the right attitude and the right motivation to thank and praise God for what he has done.

11:32 When we are judged by the Lord, we are being disciplined so that we will not be condemned with the world.^{NIV} Paul hastened to add that the judgment of 11:29-30 was disciplinary in nature and not eternal. The judgment sent by God is meant to bring believers back to a right understanding of the Lord's Supper so they can celebrate it correctly. The discipline will draw them back so that they can worship the Lord and *not be condemned with the world.* The world will face eternal condemnation because it has rejected Christ.

11:33-34 So, dear brothers and sisters, when you gather for the Lord's Supper, wait for each other. If you are really hungry, eat at home so you won't bring judgment upon yourselves when you meet together.^{NLT} To solve the problem in Corinth, Paul advised the believers, when they gathered to celebrate the Lord's Supper, to *wait for each other.* They should come to this meal desiring to fellowship with other believers and to prepare for the Lord's Supper to follow, not to fill up on a big dinner. The phrase "If you are really hungry, eat at home" means that the people should eat dinner beforehand, so they would come to the fellowship meal in the right frame of mind. As Paul had already explained, to come with the wrong attitude would *bring judgment* upon themselves. How sad to turn a blessed time of unity and thanksgiving into a time of division and judgment. Paul did not want this to be the case in Corinth.

I'll give you instructions about the other matters after I arrive.^{NLT} Apparently there were other questions that needed Paul's *instructions,* but these questions were not urgent enough for him to take up in this letter. He would talk with the believers about these when he arrived in Corinth.

1 Corinthians 12

Spiritual gifts had become symbols of spiritual power, causing rivalries in the church because some people thought they were more "spiritual" than others because of their gifts. This was a terrible misuse of spiritual gifts because their purpose is always to help the church function more effectively, not to divide it. We can be divisive if we insist on using our gift our own way without being sensitive to others. We must never use gifts as a means of manipulating others or promoting our own self-interest.

SPIRITUAL GIFTS FOR THE CHURCH
The prophet Joel prophesied about "spiritual gifts":

> Then after I have poured out my rains again, I will pour out my Spirit upon all people. Your sons and daughters will prophesy. Your old men will dream dreams. Your young men will see visions. In those days, I will pour out my Spirit even on servants, men and women alike. (Joel 2:28-29 NLT)

The apostle Peter quoted from that prophecy from Joel in his great sermon at Pentecost as he explained to the amazed listeners how the group of believers were speaking in many different languages:

> And everyone present was filled with the Holy Spirit and began speaking in other languages as the Holy Spirit gave them this ability. . . . Then Peter stepped forward with the other apostles and shouted to the crowd . . . "What you see this morning was predicted centuries ago by the prophet Joel." (Acts 2:4, 14, 16 NLT)

Clearly, the Holy Spirit gave that small group of believers a great gift, needed at that time, to establish the church. Jews from many lands heard the gospel in their own language (Acts 2:5-6), and three thousand of them were baptized that very day (Acts 2:41).

The Holy Spirit gives "different kinds of spiritual gifts" (12:4) to be used in serving the church and building up the body of Christ. This chapter does not give an exhaustive list of spiritual gifts (for other lists, see Romans 12:4-8; Ephesians 4:11-13; 1 Peter 4:10-11). Believers have different gifts, and some believers have more than one gift. All spiritual gifts come from God, and their purpose is to build up Christ's body, the church.

12:1 **Now concerning spiritual gifts, brothers and sisters, I do not want you to be uninformed.**^{NRSV} The words "now concerning" introduce another question that the Corinthians had apparently asked Paul to answer. The words "spiritual gifts" refer to special abilities given by the Holy Spirit to every believer that are to be used to minister to the needs of the body of believers. The word "gifts" in Greek is *charismata;* it comes from the same root wood as the word "grace" *(charis).* Freely bestowed by God, the gifts are special endowments given to believers to enable them to do extraordinary work for God. Paul did not want the believers to be *uninformed* about these gifts, but, rather, to understand and use them for God's glory.

12:2 **You know that when you were pagans, somehow or other you were influenced and led astray to mute idols.**^{NIV} To contrast the work of the Holy Spirit, Paul reminded the believers of the influence of evil spirits (see 10:20-21). When they *were pagans* (sometimes the word refers to "non-Jews," but here it means "non-Christians"), they had been *influenced and led astray to mute idols.* Evil spirits had done the "influencing" and "leading astray" and had led the people to idols, which could tell the people nothing. Evidently, in the cult religions, evil spirits "spoke" through their followers in what was called "ecstatic" or "inspired" speech. Evil forces were at work in the world, and the Corinthians would need to understand that what they had experienced as "tongues" or "inspired speech" in their pagan religion was completely different from the "speaking in tongues" that the believers might experience through the Holy Spirit.

12:3 **Therefore I tell you that no one who is speaking by the Spirit of God says, "Jesus be cursed," and no one can say, "Jesus is Lord," except by the Holy Spirit.**^{NIV}
The way to know whether a person exhibiting "inspired words" actually was filled with the Holy Spirit was to listen to what he or she said about Jesus Christ. Those who said *Jesus be cursed* or who blasphemed Jesus in any way obviously were not *speaking by the Spirit of God.* Those who proclaimed and believed that *Jesus is Lord,* however, were speaking by the Spirit, for only *by the Holy Spirit* can a person acknowledge the lordship of Christ. Some false teachers might be able to say those words and not mean them, but the

> The ultimate criterion of the Spirit's activity is the exaltation of Jesus as Lord. Whatever takes away from that, even if they be legitimate expressions of the Spirit, begins to move away from Christ to a more pagan fascination with spiritual activity as an end in itself. *Gordon Fee*

truth would eventually come out. The Holy Spirit within believers helps them to truly believe and publicly confess Jesus Christ
as Lord. The words "Jesus is Lord" formed the earliest Christian
confession of faith. When Peter confessed that Jesus was "the
Messiah, the Son of the living God," Jesus responded, "You are
blessed, Simon son of John, because my Father in heaven has
revealed this to you. You did not learn this from any human
being" (Matthew 16:16-17 NLT). All who truly have the Holy
Spirit will be able to say that Jesus is Lord of their lives.

CREDENTIALS
Anyone can claim to speak for God, and the world is full of
false teachers. Paul gives a test to help believers discern
whether or not a messenger is really from God: Does he or she
confess Jesus Christ as Lord? Does the confession ring
genuine with detail, and is it backed up with action? Don't
naively accept the words of all who claim to speak for God; test
their credentials by finding out what they teach about Christ.

12:4-6 **Now there are different kinds of spiritual gifts, but it is the
same Holy Spirit who is the source of them all. There are different kinds of service in the church, but it is the same Lord
we are serving. There are different ways God works in our
lives, but it is the same God who does the work through all of
us.**NLT The answers that Paul has given to the Corinthians' questions thus far in this letter have focused on unity among believers, order in the church, and exaltation of Jesus Christ. So with
the concern about spiritual gifts, Paul was concerned that the
Corinthians' focus on any particular gift, such as "tongues," or
ecstatic speech, would tear them apart. While the specific question is unknown, Paul clearly wanted the believers to understand
that tongues had their place but should not be sought by everyone. In the broad context of spiritual gifts, the gift of tongues was
just one gift. *There are different kinds of spiritual gifts . . . different kinds of service in the church . . . different ways God works in
our lives.* God's people receive many kinds of gifts, and no one
gift is better than another. This may also have been a problem in
Corinth—some believers may have been belittling some gifts.
This chapter explains that all the gifts come from one source and
are to be used for one purpose. The one source is the Trinity—
God the Father, the *Lord* Christ, and the *Holy Spirit.* The one purpose is the building up of the body of Christ—which happens as
the gifts are used to their fullest potential, as the people serve the
Lord and one another, and as God works through his people.
    These gifts are just that—gifts. They are not earned. They are

not given to believers asking for a specific one. They are not chosen by people. God alone administers the gifts among his people. God, not believers, controls the gifts. Each believer, then, is responsible to seek God's guidance in discovering his or her particular gift(s) and then discovering how best to use them for God's purposes.

SPECIALIZATION
God is completely involved in the giving, using, and empowering of gifts. Specific gifts, places of service, and activities vary, but they all have their best effects when they build up the body of Christ—the church. God creates a unique place in the body for every believer. Gifts and ministries may overlap, but each believer has a specialized, God-designed role. Part of the exciting adventure of following Christ involves discovering one's service contribution and then making it available to God. Make serving God and his people your motive as you utilize your gifts.

12:7 A spiritual gift is given to each of us as a means of helping the entire church.[NLT] Every believer has at least one spiritual gift—*a spiritual gift is given to each of us*. The gifts are not to cause division among the believers, jealously regarding who received a particular gift when another person desired it, or rivalry over the use of similar gifts. Instead, God graciously gives spiritual gifts *as a means of helping the entire church*. Spiritual gifts are not for private use or as a badge to be worn proudly; instead, they are to be used publicly to build up the church. Some gifts help those in the church to grow closer to Christ. Other gifts bring outsiders into the church. Others help to encourage those in the church who are carrying burdens. All these gifts are needed, for different needs require different kinds of service. (See also the Life Application Bible Commentary *Ephesians,* 4:7-12.)

Some people have interpreted this verse to imply that each person must have a gift; therefore, each believer must identify it and insist on using it. It may be true that every believer has a gift (12:11), but this statement was meant to counter those in Corinth who believed that every person *had* to speak in tongues. Such a view is wrong. What Paul stressed was the manifestation of the Spirit, the great variety and diversity of the gifts of the triune God (12:4-6), and the importance of using the gifts to help others.

12:8 To one there is given through the Spirit the message of wisdom.[NIV] To illustrate that there are a wide variety of gifts from the Holy Spirit, Paul gave a list. This list was not meant to be exhaustive; it merely illustrates many of the different kinds of spiritual gifts. The Spirit gives many gifts; the Bible contains no definitive list of all the gifts.

To one person, explained Paul, the Spirit gives *the message of wisdom.* The problem of wisdom (human versus divine) was a hot topic in Corinth. At the beginning of this letter (1:17–2:16), Paul spent several paragraphs explaining the difference between God's wisdom and human "wisdom."

All believers are given wisdom from the Spirit (2:15-16), but some are given the ability to give the "message of wisdom." This may refer to the promise of Christ (see Luke 21:15) that the Spirit would give special wisdom to those facing adversaries and persecution. Based on Paul's argument in chapter 1, it most likely refers to recognizing Christ crucified as the basis of God's true wisdom, and proclaiming Christ in this way. That this particular gift does not occur on any of the other lists of gifts has led some scholars to think that this gift was especially important (and more prominent) for the believers in the Greek city of Corinth, where the issue of "wisdom" was causing much discussion.

GIFT LIST
Like other lists of spiritual gifts in the New Testament (see 12:27-31; 14; Romans 12:4-8; Ephesians 4:11-13), it appears that Paul meant this list to be suggestive rather than exhaustive. The list provides us with a starting point. We must recognize, however, that God's purpose in giving gifts has little to do with self-esteem. We cannot ask for gifts in order to feel more powerful, important, or significant (James 4:3). When we make it our goal to be available to God and to seek to serve others for Christ's sake, our spiritual gifts will come to the surface. We may need the insight of others to recognize our specific gifts. Consider these steps:
1. Ask God to increase your usefulness.
2. Seek opportunities of service.
3. Observe how other believers serve.
4. Ask those you've served and those who serve with you to help you discern your spiritual strengths.
5. Practice those gifts even more.

To another the message of knowledge by means of the same Spirit.NIV Another person might be given *the message of knowledge.* As with "wisdom," the Corinthians also believed they had special "knowledge." People may think they have all kinds of wisdom and knowledge, which leads to pride, but true wisdom and knowledge are found in Christ alone. But to some people *the same Spirit* gives extraordinary knowledge. This could mean a special

knowledge of spiritual realities (see 13:2, 8-12; 14:6) or knowledge
given to teachers who are training others in Christian truth.

12:9 The Spirit gives special faith to another.^{NLT} All Christians have
faith because the faith that brings a person to salvation is the
work of the Holy Spirit. "God saved you by his special favor
when you believed. And you can't take credit for this; it is a gift
from God" (Ephesians 2:8 NLT; see also Galatians 5:22; 1 Timothy 4:12-14). Some people, however, have the spiritual gift of
faith, which is an unusual measure of trust in the Holy Spirit's
power. In 13:2, Paul describes this gift further: "If I had the gift
of faith so that I could speak to a mountain and make it move
. . ." (NLT). This kind of faith is a supernatural trust in God's
miraculous power for specific situations. While the next two
gifts, healing and doing miracles, are listed separately, this gift of
faith is surely connected to the ability to do such acts through the
Holy Spirit. This gift of faith could also be manifested in believers' willingness to face persecution and martyrdom without
renouncing what they believed.

To another gifts of healing by that one Spirit.^{NIV} The next two
gifts (healing and miracles) are visual manifestations of the
Spirit. The *gifts of healing* had been manifested through Peter,
Paul, and the other apostles (see, for example, Acts 3:6-8; 5:15-
16; 9:33-34; 14:8-10). The gift of healing is given, not to the person healed, but to the person who does the healing. Some people
want to say they have received the gift of healing for an illness
they have, but the gifts are given to be used to benefit others.

12:10 He gives one person the power to perform miracles.^{NLT} As
with the gifts of healing (12:9), the Spirit will give to some an
extraordinary power to *perform miracles.* While performing a
healing would be considered a miracle, the inclusion of this gift
separately from healings refers to other miraculous manifestations of the Spirit (see Galatians 3:5).

And to another the ability to prophesy.^{NLT} The rest of the gifts
mentioned in this passage focus on verbal manifestations of the
Spirit. To some people, the Spirit gives a special *ability to prophesy.* "Prophesy" does not just refer to predicting the future; it can
also mean giving a message received from God to the community
of believers: "One who prophesies is helping others grow in the
Lord, encouraging and comforting them" (14:3 NLT). The prophet
Joel had written the words of the Lord, "I will pour out my Spirit
upon all people. Your sons and daughters will prophesy" (Joel
2:28 NLT). As with the gift of faith, the ability to share one's faith
with power is available to everyone (see 14:1-5), but to some the

Spirit gives a special measure of this gift. Paul wrote in Romans, "God has given each of us the ability to do certain things well. So if God has given you the ability to prophesy, speak out when you have faith that God is speaking through you" (Romans 12:6 NLT). Some have interpreted "prophecy" to be fulfilled in various sermons throughout church history. Others, however, say that prophecy is not a sermon, but a spontaneous, Spirit-inspired message that is orally delivered in the congregation for the edification and encouragement of the body of Christ.

He gives someone else the ability to know whether it is really the Spirit of God or another spirit that is speaking.^{NLT} Because there are many false teachers who claim to "prophesy" for God, some in the church are given *the ability to know whether it is really the Spirit of God or another spirit that is speaking.* While some believers have a special gift to discern what is really from God's Spirit and what is not, all believers are expected to have discernment: "Dear friends, do not believe every spirit, but test the spirits to see whether they are from God, because many false prophets have gone out into the world" (1 John 4:1 NIV; see also 1 Thessalonians 5:20-21). But since the gift mentioned here is also described in 14:29 ("Let two or three prophesy, and let the others evaluate what is said"; NLT), this kind of spiritual discernment pertains specifically to oracular manifestations in Christian meetings. Paul's mention of this shows his concern for the protection of the truth in the worship service. Those given the gift of special discernment can help separate truth from error.

Still another person is given the ability to speak in unknown languages, and another is given the ability to interpret what is being said.^{NLT} Opinions differ over exactly what Paul meant by *unknown languages.* Some believe that this refers to earthly languages that a person did not know before (the same as the gift described in Acts 2:4, 7-8). Other scholars say that this refers to an "ecstatic" language, a "heavenly" language. Most likely the second view is correct. Probably the only time that the word "tongues" refers to other earthly languages is when describing Pentecost (Acts 2:4, 7-8). The rest of the time in the New Testament, the word refers to ecstatic languages unknown to anyone—"tongues of angels" (13:1). Speaking in tongues *is* a legitimate gift of the Spirit. The exercise of the gift demands some guidelines (as noted in chapter 14) so that the *purpose* of the gift—to help the body of Christ—is not lost. Those who speak in tongues should follow the guidelines; those who do not speak in tongues ought *not* seek the gift as a sign of salvation or as a sign of special closeness with God, for it is neither. It is a gift of God, given only to whomever God chooses. If a person has not experienced the gift of tongues, he or she ought not seek it but seek what gifts God *has* given.

12:11 It is the one and only Holy Spirit who distributes these gifts. He alone decides which gift each person should have.^{NLT} This verse repeats the point made in 12:1, 4-6—that the source of all the gifts *is the one and only Holy Spirit.* The Holy Spirit gives *these gifts* (again emphasizing the diversity), but they are to be used for God's divine purpose. Because the Holy Spirit *alone decides which gift each person should have,* there is no place for rivalry, jealousy, or pride among believers regarding their gifts. God, through his Spirit, gives to every person in the community of believers exactly the right gifts for him or her to provide the needed services for the church and for God's kingdom.

Whatever the practice of different churches, believers must realize that the Holy Spirit does not submit to any view of methodology. He cannot be limited or confined to cultural or contemporary views of propriety. All believers need to be open to God's gracious power in their lives and in their worship.

THE GIFT GIVER
No matter what gift(s) a person has, all spiritual gifts are distributed by the Holy Spirit. The Holy Spirit decides which gifts each believer should have. We are responsible to use and sharpen our gifts, but we can take no credit for what God has freely given us.

Note that discussions about spiritual gifts usually create difficulties when two central points are overlooked: (1) Properly used, spiritual gifts are not self-serving but serve the whole body of Christ (cf verse 7); (2) each gift becomes practically useless when used without love (as Paul will make clear in chapter 13). As we seek to identify and utilize the gifts, let us make the love of God and the love of fellow Christians our highest motives.

BELIEVERS ARE THE BODY OF CHRIST / 12:12-31

Using the analogy of the body, Paul emphasized the importance of each church member. If a seemingly insignificant part is taken away, the whole body becomes less effective. Thinking that one's gift is more important than someone else's is an expression of spiritual pride. Devaluing the gift offends the Giver. We should not look down on those who seem unimportant, and we should not be jealous of others who have impressive gifts. Instead, we should use the gifts we have been given and encourage others to use theirs. If we don't, the body of believers will be less effective.

12:12 **The body is a unit, though it is made up of many parts; and though all its parts are many, they form one body. So it is with Christ.**[NIV] Paul followed his section describing the diversity of gifts that the Holy Spirit gives to the church by providing an analogy of a *body* (see also 10:17). Some take this following section to be an argument for unity despite diversity (and so it could be), but the context reveals Paul's more pressing concern in the Corinthian church—that they accept diversity in their *one body.* Just as a body *is made up of many parts,* so the church is made up of many people with different gifts. It seems that the Corinthians all wanted to speak in tongues or desired more spectacular manifestations of the Spirit's power. Paul explained, however, that while not everyone has the same gift, they still *form one body*— the body of Christ.

BODY LANGUAGE
Paul compares the body of Christ to a human body. Each part has a specific function that is necessary to the body as a whole. The parts are different for a purpose, and in their differences they must work together. Diversity can maintain unity as long as all submit to one Lord. Christians must avoid two common errors: (1) being too proud of their abilities; and (2) thinking they have nothing to give to the body of believers. Instead of comparing ourselves to one another, we should use our different gifts, together, to spread the Good News of salvation. We speak Christ's "body language" when we practice our unique gifts under his sole authority.

12:13 **For we were all baptized by one Spirit into one body— whether Jews or Greeks, slave or free—and we were all given the one Spirit to drink.**[NIV] What gives believers their unity is the *one Spirit*—the very same Spirit who also gives their diversity through the many and varied gifts. As believers live out their diversity through the gifts, they must never forget the basic fact that unites them—they *were all baptized by one Spirit into one body.* All believers receive the same Holy Spirit at the time of their conversion. This distinguishes them from nonbelievers and unites them with one another. This "receiving" of the Spirit is here called being "baptized by" the Spirit. The metaphor pictures baptism and compares believers' experience of water baptism (see 1:13-16) to being set apart by the Holy Spirit. Not only that, but the Holy Spirit also lives within believers (6:19). The phrase "we were all given the one Spirit to drink" means that the same

Holy Spirit completely fills all believers' innermost beings (Ephesians 5:18-20). The indwelling Holy Spirit unites all believers who might otherwise be as different as *Jews* from *Greeks* (Gentiles) or as a *slave* from a *free* person (see also Galatians 3:23; Colossians 3:11).

BASIS FOR UNITY
The church is composed of many types of people from a variety of backgrounds with a multitude of gifts and abilities. It is easy for these differences to divide people, as was the case in Corinth. Despite the differences, however, all believers have one thing in common—faith in Christ. On this essential truth the church finds unity. All believers are baptized by one Holy Spirit into one body of believers, the church. We don't lose our individual identities, but we have an overriding oneness in Christ. When a person becomes a Christian, the Holy Spirit takes up residence, and that person is born into God's family. As members of God's family, we may have different interests and gifts, but let us pursue a common goal—deep unity in Christ.

12:14-15 **Indeed, the body does not consist of one member but of many. If the foot would say, "Because I am not a hand, I do not belong to the body," that would not make it any less a part of the body.**^NRSV Having established that the church, the worldwide community of believers, is indeed one body—the body of Christ—Paul went on to show the necessary diversity in that body. A human body *does not consist of one member but of many.* For a body to function, such diversity is essential. Individual members cannot separate themselves without harming the body. Just as a *foot* cannot decide to leave the body because it is not a *hand,* so a believer who does not have a particular gift cannot decide that he or she is not a part of the church. Not having a particular gift would *not make [that person] any less a part of the body.* Apparently, some believers in Corinth were discouraged that they did not have a particular gift—probably one of the more spectacular gifts, such as the gift of tongues—so they believed that they could not truly be a part of the body unless they experienced that particular gift. But Paul explains, through this metaphor, that all the different gifts given by the Spirit to believers must be utilized in order for the church to function well. Likewise, the gifts are interdependent. Like the body, they cannot function without each other.

12:16 **And if the ear would say, "Because I am not an eye, I do not belong to the body," that would not make it any less a part of the body.**^NRSV As with the foot and the hand (12:15), so it is with the ear and the eye. The parts of the body should desire to perform only the functions for which they were made, not seeking other parts. The *ear* may prefer to be able to see, like the *eye,* but that does not mean that the ear is *any less a part of the body.* The ear will no more be changed into an eye or given the ability to see than a believer will be able to exchange one gift for another. Instead, each believer should discover his or her spiritual gift and then use it to its fullest capacity for the Lord.

12:17 If the whole body were an eye, where would the sense of hearing be? If the whole body were an ear, where would the sense of smell be?[NIV] Every spiritual gift from the Holy Spirit is vital to the functioning of the body. Thus, the gifts are not given at whim and will not be changed according to people's preferences. If everyone wanted to be *an eye,* then the body might see very well, but it would not be able to hear. *If the whole body were an ear,* there would be no *sense of smell.*

EYE REVOLT
Those who conclude that the New Testament has little humor actually are admitting they have little imagination. We respond to the mental picture of an eyeball's declaration of independence from the rest of the body with a chuckle. A conference between body parts would make one thing laughably clear: As important as any one part might be to the whole, their reliance on the rest, even to accomplish their vital role, is far more crucial.
    The idea that Christians can somehow function and flourish outside of the body of Christ sounds as ludicrous as a rebellious ear or foot. Solitary Christianity has no basis in God's Word. We need the church, and we are needed by other Christians.

12:18-20 But God made our bodies with many parts, and he has put each part just where he wants it. What a strange thing a body would be if it had only one part! Yes, there are many parts, but only one body.[NLT] As God created human bodies to function with their *many parts* working together, so the body of Christ—the church—needs all the various gifts working in harmony. The picture of a body with *only one part* illustrates the absurdity of a church with everyone trying to have the same gift. It would not be a body at all, and it would be unable to function. While *there are many parts,* there is *only one body,* because God ordained it that way, putting *each part just where he wants it.* All believers—those with the spectacular gifts and those with the quieter gifts—are placed right where God wants them so that they might serve effectively together. They are one body with many parts, because God made it that way.

12:21 **The eye cannot say to the hand, "I don't need you!" And the head cannot say to the feet, "I don't need you!"**[NIV] Not only should each individual part realize its own importance, but all the other parts should realize their interdependence as well. One part of the body *cannot say* it doesn't need another part. Those in the church who have the more spectacular gifts should not look down on or dismiss those with other gifts because, in reality, all are needed.

12:22 **On the contrary, the members of the body that seem to be weaker are indispensable.**[NRSV] The more honored members must not look down on the more humble members (12:21); in fact, those who *seem to be weaker are indispensable.* These "weaker" members are those who appear to be less important in the body. These people may not be always visible, always up front exercising their gifts, but they are in the background. If they are using their God-given gifts, they are actually indispensable to the body. Those with the visible gifts could not function to their full capacity without the other indispensable members utilizing their gifts. The pastor in a church may be well versed and eloquent, but he will not be effective if the other members are not utilizing their gifts to greet newcomers warmly, to make sure the building is maintained and clean, to plan the worship service, to make sure equipment is working properly, to follow up on people with needs, or to pray faithfully for the ministry. The church needs the visible members, but it needs everyone. In reality, the less-visible members are the "indispensable" ones.

DISCOUNTS
Paul argued for diversity of gifts and acceptance of the full range of gifts that God gives to his people. No one should feel superior about his or her gift; instead, all should use their gifts to willingly serve. Too often the "up-front" gifts, like speaking or teaching, are more highly regarded than the "behind-the-scenes" gifts, like helping and serving. No one should discount the contribution of another person, no matter how insignificant it may seem. We should not be dissatisfied with the gift God has given us but be eager to serve. Nor should we envy those who seem to have more gifts than we do. In love, treat everyone's gift, yours included, as valuable to God.

12:23-24 **And the parts we regard as less honorable are those we clothe with the greatest care. So we carefully protect from the eyes of others those parts that should not be seen, while other parts do not require this special care. So God has put the body together in such a way that extra honor and care are**

given to those parts that have less dignity.NLT The play on words in this verse is difficult to bring out from the Greek to the English. "The parts we regard as less honorable" refers to the sexual parts of the body, the parts that *we carefully protect from the eyes of others.* The point of this verse is that appearances are deceiving; all parts of the body are necessary, even the ones that *should not be seen* and the *parts that have less dignity.* No one should dismiss anyone else as unimportant in the body of Christ; neither should undue prominence be given to anyone. The reason for this is explained in 12:25.

CONNECTED
What is your response when a fellow Christian is honored? How do you respond when someone is suffering? We are called to rejoice with those who rejoice and weep with those who weep (Romans 12:15). Too often, unfortunately, we are jealous of those who rejoice and apathetic toward those who weep. When that happens, we have overlooked our connection with them in Christ.

Believers are in the world together—there is no such thing as private Christianity. Christ makes us one, even when we wish otherwise. When we follow Christ, we find ourselves in mixed company. We shouldn't stop with enjoying only our own relationship with God; we need to get involved in the lives of others. That's also the best way to break through our mere human reactions to them.

12:25-26 **This makes for harmony among the members, so that all the members care for each other equally. If one part suffers, all the parts suffer with it, and if one part is honored, all the parts are glad.**NLT The *harmony* Paul wanted *among the members* had already been discussed in 1:10: "Now, dear brothers and sisters, I appeal to you by the authority of the Lord Jesus Christ to stop arguing among yourselves. Let there be real harmony so there won't be divisions in the church. I plead with you to be of one mind, united in thought and purpose" (NLT). Such harmony happens only when all the members—the weak and the strong, the flamboyant and the quiet, the up-front and the behind-the-scenes—use their gifts, appreciate one another, and *care for each other equally.* Such caring is demonstrated as they share in one another's joys and sorrows. As with the physical, human body, one part's suffering causes every part to suffer. When the head aches, the whole body suffers. When a thumb is hit with a hammer, the whole body knows it. In the body of believers, therefore, *if one part suffers, all the parts suffer with it.* Believers should share one another's burdens in order to help lighten them. Like-

wise, *if one part is honored, all the parts are glad.* There is no
room for jealousy or strife when one person receives praise;
instead, all should be glad.

Believers need to be able to empathize with others—to join in
with their feelings as if they were experiencing the feelings themselves. Christians should rejoice with others, with no hint of jealousy; and they should suffer with them, offering kindness,
concern, compassion, and a shoulder to cry on if needed. Following Jesus will mean that believers will have a wide variety of
experiences. Christianity neither denies life's hardships nor dulls
life's excitements. Both laughter and tears are appropriate before
God. Identifying with the joys and heartaches of others is an
important way for believers to show love and unity.

**12:27 Now all of you together are Christ's body, and each one of
you is a separate and necessary part of it.**NLT The words "all
of you together" refer to all believers across the world. All
believers together *are Christ's body.* As new believers come to
salvation in Jesus Christ, they join that body, receive a gift
from the Holy Spirit, and are used by God. Therefore, each and
every believer in the body of Christ *is a separate and necessary
part of* that body. No believer is unimportant—each one has a
gift to share in order to make the body function that much more
effectively.

**12:28 And in the church God has appointed first of all apostles,
second prophets, third teachers, then workers of miracles,
also those having gifts of healing, those able to help others,
those with gifts of administration, and those speaking in different kinds of tongues.**NIV Having established believers' unity
in their diversity, Paul went on to describe this diversity by a
list (not complete) of various offices and gifts. These gifts are
given to *the church* by *God,* who *has appointed* those whom he
has chosen to serve in various capacities. The order of these
gifts in this verse is important. The first three gifted people
listed are those who proclaim the gospel and teach the truth—
apostles, prophets, and teachers (see also Ephesians 4:11).
These are important gifts, for there would be no church without
those who bring the message and teach the truth. Thus Paul specifically ranked them as *first, second, third* to show their prime
importance above all the other gifts.

The *apostles* include the eleven men Jesus called (without
Judas Iscariot), plus others who are called apostles—such as Paul
himself (Romans 1:1), Matthias (Acts 1:26), Barnabas (Acts
14:14), Jesus' brother James (Galatians 1:19), Silas (1 Thessalonians 2:6), and Andronicus and Junias (Romans 16:7). It seems that

the qualifications for being an apostle were to have seen the risen Christ, to have been sent out by Christ to preach the gospel, and to work on behalf of the kingdom, building its foundation. Paul also noted "signs, wonders and miracles" as marks of a true apostle (2 Corinthians 12:12 NIV). There were only a few apostles who brought the gospel message to the world.

God also appointed *prophets* to the church. These people had special gifts in ministering God's messages to his people. At times they would foretell the future (Acts 11:28; 21:9, 11), but more often they exhorted, encouraged, and strengthened God's people (Acts 15:32; 1 Corinthians 14:29). God spoke through prophets, inspiring them with specific messages for particular times and places.

While the apostles and prophets had a universal sphere of function (the church as a whole), the *teachers* probably served in the local churches. They needed to be trustworthy and faithful stewards of the truth of the gospel. People in that day did not have their own Bibles to read, so the teachers in the local congregations continued to teach the believers in the truth after the apostles had moved on to other cities.

The rest of this list reveals other gifts. Some of these have been noted earlier in this chapter. Some are appointed as *workers of miracles* (12:10), some have *gifts of healing* (12:9), some are *able to help others* (perhaps unusual compassion and caring), and others have *gifts of administration* to help the church run smoothly. It is significant that Paul places last the gift of *speaking in different kinds of tongues*. This was the one gift that seemed to have caused so much consternation and division in the Corinthian church (12:1-3, 10). Paul placed it as a relatively unimportant gift when compared with those who share the gospel or serve in more tangible ways.

12:29-30 **Are all apostles? Are all prophets? Are all teachers? Do all work miracles? Do all have gifts of healing? Do all speak in tongues? Do all interpret?**[NIV] These rhetorical questions demand a "no" answer. Not everyone in any church falls into one of these categories. Not *all* were *apostles;* in fact, only a few could ever claim that office. Not *all* were *prophets* or *teachers* either, for God gifted some for those offices while he gave others the various other gifts, some of which are listed here. Chapter 14 discusses the subject of speaking in and interpreting tongues in more detail. Not everyone in the church has the same gift, nor can anyone claim to have all the gifts. Believers in the church must see themselves, not as individual plants, but as an entire garden under the cultivation of God's Spirit. His purpose involves not simply the production of a single gift but all the gifts, each becoming ripe as it is needed. No one person can perfectly exemplify all the gifts. Each person depends on the faithful ministry of everyone else.

This list of gifts is representative, not exhaustive. It would be difficult for one person to embody all these gifts. A prophet might not make a good administrator, and a helper might fail as a teacher. When people identify their own gifts and their unique combination of gifts (this list is far from complete), they should then discover how they can use their gifts to build up Christ's body, the church. At the same time, they should realize that one or two gifts can't do all the work of the church. Believers should be thankful for each other, thankful that others have gifts that are completely different. In the church, believers' strengths and weaknesses can balance each other. Some people's abilities compensate for other people's deficiencies. Together all believers can build Christ's church. But all these gifts will be worthless if they are used begrudgingly, out of duty, or if they are exercised without love (see also 13:1-3).

ADVENTURE
The "most helpful" gifts are those that are more beneficial to the body of Christ. Paul has already made it clear that one gift is not superior to another, but he urges believers to discover how they can serve Christ's body with the gifts God has given them. Your spiritual gifts are not for your own self-advancement. Discovering them can be an adventure in service. Those gifts were given to you for serving God and enhancing the spiritual growth of the whole body.

12:31 And in any event, you should desire the most helpful gifts. First, however, let me tell you about something else that is better than any of them!NLT The believers *should desire the most helpful gifts,* or "seek the greater gifts." In other words, in the desire to be helpful in the body of Christ, they should seek the power of the Spirit. Too often this verse is only applied individually when the emphasis should be on the church as a body. The church ought to desire the most helpful gifts so that it can function well. It would be incorrect to interpret Paul as saying "desire the most helpful gifts" to mean "seek the gifts from the top of the list" (12:27-28). Paul had been stressing diversity of gifts and the necessity for the gifts to be interactive within the body. He could not have thereby excluded healing or tongues as lesser gifts. In addition, he could not have meant for the people to desire to be apostles—that was impossible, because only a few chosen men could claim that title.

The believers should earnestly desire gifts that benefit everyone (as opposed to an unintelligible tongue that, without interpretation, helps no one but the speaker). The Corinthians had to get their focus off of the gift of speaking in ecstatic languages; instead, they needed to see the value in all the gifts, especially those that helped others. Paul's saying "let me tell you about something else that is better than any of them" leads into chapter 13.

1 Corinthians 13

In chapter 12, Paul gave evidence of the Corinthians' lack of love in the utilization of spiritual gifts; chapter 13 defines real love; and chapter 14 shows how love works. While spiritual gifts are important to the functioning of the body (12:12-31), they lose their value if love is not behind them. Love is more important than all the spiritual gifts exercised in the church body; love is the "most excellent way" (12:31 NIV) for believers to use their gifts.

THE ULTIMATE
According to 1 Corinthians 13, love provides the basis for all the spiritual gifts exercised in the church body. Love connects every act with God and makes our actions and gifts useful. Although people have different gifts, expressing God's love should be the ultimate purpose of every gift. When you ask God for more love, realize that part of the answer comes in the form of spiritual gifts. When you ask God to show you your spiritual gifts, his answer will include a new awareness of the people around you who need his love.

13:1 If I could speak in any language in heaven or on earth but didn't love others, I would only be making meaningless noise like a loud gong or a clanging cymbal.^{NLT} Great faith, acts of dedication or sacrifice, miracle-working power, or the ability to *speak in any language in heaven or on earth* will produce very little without *love*. This phrase is also translated "the tongues of men and of angels" (NIV). The Corinthians believed that they had the angels' language when they spoke in tongues. But their knowledge led to pride, which stripped them of love and consideration for others. Love makes believers' actions and gifts useful. Although people have different gifts, love is available to everyone. Without love, speaking in another language, although a gift of the Spirit, becomes nothing more than *meaningless noise*. A *cymbal* was often used in ecstatic rites in pagan worship. The gift of tongues, used without love, is as valueless as pagan worship. Without love, the gifts do not build up other believers, so they are useless. Christians must not exalt gifts over character. Love is far more important.

The word for love used here is *agape*. The Greeks had different words that described different kinds of love. The word *agape* connotes a deep, abiding, self-sacrificing love—the kind that looks out for the other person first. God requires his people to have *agape* love for one another.

13:2 And though I have the gift of prophecy, and understand all mysteries and all knowledge, and though I have all faith, so that I could remove mountains, but have not love, I am nothing.[NKJV] Three gifts are mentioned in this verse: prophecy, knowledge, and faith. The *gift of prophecy* was described in the commentary on 12:10 as a gift that not only enables the person to see events in the future but also to bring God's message to the church under the direction of the Holy Spirit (see also 14:1-25; 1 Thessalonians 5:19-20). Paul explains in 14:3 that "The one who prophesies is helping others grow in the Lord, encouraging and comforting them" (NLT). While all believers ought to study in order to understand more and be able to teach others about what they believe, some people have been given a special measure of this gift with the ability to *understand all mysteries and all knowledge* ("knowledge" was another gift). Such understanding and even the ability to share it with others, however, are worth nothing without love.

> God requires mercy and love "from the heart," not sacrifice, not the exercising of gifts. We must remember that Satan is a master at mimicking the gifts of the Spirit, but he cannot mimic the heart. He can set up a puppet teacher who is endowed with great knowledge, but he cannot give that person love for God and love for other Christians. This is solely a Christian grace and can only come by the Spirit of Christ.
>
> *R. C. Sproul*

The gift of *faith* was described in 12:9. This does not refer to saving faith, whereby people come to believe in Jesus Christ as Savior; instead, this is an unusual measure of trust in the Holy Spirit's power to do mighty works, much like Elijah received in 1 Kings 18. If a person has faith that *could remove mountains* but does not have love, the faith is worth *nothing*.

13:3 If I gave everything I have to the poor and even sacrificed my body, I could boast about it; but if I didn't love others, I would be of no value whatsoever.[NLT] There is a significant textual variant in this verse. Attached to the words "if I give my body that" some manuscripts read *kauthasomai* ("I may be burned"), but other manuscripts (including the three earliest) read *kauxasomai* ("I may boast"). In the Greek, there is but a one-letter difference between the first reading and the second. Good arguments have been advanced by scholars in support of each reading. But those who support the second reading point to the earlier attestation in the manuscripts and to the fact that martyrdom by burning was a phenomenon yet unknown to the original readers of this epistle. Furthermore, in Clement of Rome's letter to the church in Corinth (c. A.D. 96), Clement spoke of those who delivered themselves to bondage in order to ransom others. This could very well be what Paul was referring to—unless Paul was thinking about the fiery ordeal of Shadrach, Meschach, and Abednego (see Daniel 3), in which case the first reading would be the one he wrote. Whatever the reading, the verse says that love produces willingness to give sacrificially and to suffer. Acts of charity and self-sacrifice can be done for the sake of an ideal or with pride as a motivation. But they are of no value for the kingdom, wrote Paul, unless they are done from the foundation of love for others.

13:4 Love is patient.[NIV] Because love is so important among the believers, Paul went on to describe that love in more detail. How does such love look when lived out in the lives of believers? First of all, *love is patient*. The expression "is patient" *(makrothumei)* is the opposite of being short-tempered. Patience (sometimes translated "long-suffering" or "slow to anger") is an attribute of God (see Exodus 34:6; Numbers 14:18; Romans 2:4; 1 Peter 3:20). In many places, God's people are called upon to be patient (see, for example, Ephesians 4:2; Colossians 3:12; 1 Thessalonians 5:14). Patience is a fruit of the Spirit (Galatians 5:22).

What does patient love among believers look like? Such love bears with certain annoyances or inconveniences without complaint. Such love does not lose its temper when provoked. Such love steadily perseveres. Without love, no matter how wonderful the gifts in the church, people will be impatient with one another, short-tempered, and irritable.

Love is kind.[NIV] The Greek word translated "is kind" *(chresteuetai)* occurs

> Before we rush to trivialize these words about love by assuming they can easily fit us, let's stop to consider that they actually describe God's character. These are not sugary claims. They are hard-edged descriptions of God's perfection-in-relationship. The Holy Spirit inspired the apostle to write a breathtakingly beautiful description of the nature of God. Only God can put His character in us.
>
> *Neil Wilson*

only here in the New Testament. ("Kindness," *chrestotes,* occurs in Galatians 5:22.) It probably means the same as a similar word (also translated as "kind") in Ephesians 4:32: "Be kind to each other, tenderhearted, forgiving one another, just as God through Christ has forgiven you" (NLT). Kindness takes the initiative in responding generously to others' needs. The psalms and writings of the prophets say much about God's kindness (Psalm 18:50; Isaiah 54:8; Jeremiah 9:24). Because believers have received kindness, they ought to act with kindness toward others.

How does "kind love" look among believers? Such love is considerate and helpful to others. Kind love is gentle and mild, always ready to show compassion, especially to those in need. Without love, even the great gifts cannot be exercised with an eye to helping others.

It does not envy.[NIV] "Envy" refers to strong jealousy of another person. The envious person desires what another person has. This seems to have been a particular problem in Corinth—those with "lesser" gifts envied those with "greater" gifts. The seed of envy can lead to seething anger and hatred. Those who are too busy envying each other's gifts are unlikely to be using their own gifts in loving service to God and others. Envy stagnates the church, causing the envious believers to remain self-centered and self-focused, feeling sorry for themselves, and not fulfilling their God-given role. When there is love, believers will gladly use whatever gifts they have been given to work together for the advance of God's kingdom. They will be glad that others have different gifts so that the entire job can get done.

GENUINE LOVE
Society confuses love and lust. Often, so do believers. Unlike lust, God's kind of love is directed outward toward others, not inward toward one's self. It is utterly unselfish. This kind of love goes against natural inclinations. It is possible to practice this love only if God helps us set aside our own desires and instincts so that we can give love while expecting nothing in return. Thus the more we become like Christ, the more love we will show to others.

It does not boast, it is not proud.[NIV] While some believers may have a problem with envy, those with the "greater" gifts might have a problem with boasting or pride. Again, it seems that this may have been a problem in Corinth. When spectacularly gifted believers begin to *boast,* they have directed their energy toward themselves. The gift becomes not a tool of service for the king-

dom but a way of self-advancement. Such believers are *proud*.
While some pride can be positive, this kind of pride takes credit
for an undeserved gift. Gifted believers who are caught up in
pride and boasting over their gifts are unable to serve. Without
love, they may feel that by using their gifts, they are doing someone a favor, that others should be grateful to them, and that they
are far superior.

13:5 It is not rude.NIV The word translated "is rude" *(aschemonei)*
refers to actions that are improper. Also translated as "love does
not behave in an unseemly way," this means that love does not
behave impolitely, discourteously, or crudely. Believers who use
their gifts with love will be careful to act in a manner worthy of
their calling before God. They will never humiliate others. This
may also have been a problem in Corinth, especially in their worship services (see 11:2-16).

It is not self-seeking.NIV People who are *self-seeking* always
want their own way. They are selfish, self-centered, wanting
what they think is best for them. This is the opposite of love.
Love *(agape)* looks out for others, seeks their best interests,
willingly gives up its own for the sake of another. A self-seeking person may use his or her gifts but not with a serving
attitude or a desire to build the kingdom. Instead, the gifts are
only used if they can somehow benefit the self-seeking person.
This is not God's way. Instead, because of love, the believers
use their gifts to benefit others first, without "self" or selfish
desires getting in the way.

It is not easily angered.NIV The word for "easily angered" could
also be translated "touchy," "irritable," or "sensitive to slights."
Such people let things get on their nerves. One believer, in the
process of exercising his or her gifts, may irritate another
believer. These "easily angered" believers may not like the style
or manner in which these others exercise their gifts. Or they may
get easily angered at anyone who crosses them. This is not the
way of love. When believers exercise their gifts in love, they will
be able to give one another some latitude to follow God as they
see fit. They will not let themselves be easily provoked over disagreements, but they will be able to always respond in a loving
manner. This does not mean that anger is wrong, for anger can be
a motivating factor when directed against wrongs or injustices.
People who are "easily angered," however, are usually upset
about personal affronts or minor issues. This stifles their service
for God and the use of their gifts.

IRRITABILITY
Paul says that true love isn't easily angered. Sometimes we're irritated or angered by others, and we don't know why. Not all irritability stems from sinful or selfish motives, although the irritable treatment of others surely is wrong. Much irritability comes from a love of perfection, a deep desire that programs, meetings, and structures be run perfectly. A desire to run things perfectly can erupt into anger at events or people who get in the way or ruin that desire. Those who are easily irritated need to remember that perfection exists only in God. We need to love him and our fellow Christians, not the visions we have for perfection here on earth.

It keeps no record of wrongs.[NIV] Believers must not allow themselves to become easily angered, and they must not keep *record of wrongs.* Such people will remember every offense against them as though it were written in a book and tallied. These "wrongs" are not sins that need to be dealt with in the congregation (such as that described in chapter 5) but minor offenses or misunderstandings between believers. Those who keep record of these wrongs and personal injuries will harbor resentment against other believers. Love, however, makes allowances for people's foibles and flaws and willingly forgets when wrongs were done. This frees all believers to grow and mature in Christ and to grow in their ability to serve and use their gifts. When mistakes are made, love overlooks them and allows believers to continue to serve with the gifts God has given them. God does not keep a record of believers' wrongs (2 Corinthians 5:19).

13:6 Love does not delight in evil but rejoices with the truth.[NIV] When believers show love, they do not *delight in evil,* either by showing superior morality over it or by taking pleasure in another's fall. Love does not take pleasure in any kind of evil. Instead, love does the exact opposite—it *rejoices with the truth.* Through their relationship with Jesus Christ, believers possess the one and only truth (John 14:6). Those who love should remain untainted by evil. Instead, they ought to always seek truth, desire that truth win out, protect the truth, and proclaim the truth whenever possible.

13:7 It always protects, always trusts, always hopes, always perseveres.[NIV] After explaining what love does not do (13:4b-6), Paul listed four positive attributes of love. First of all, love *always protects.* The word in Greek, *stego,* means "cover" or "hide by covering." This does not refer to hiding hurtful sin but to protecting someone from embarrassment, gossip, or any other such harm.

When believers love one another, they refuse harmful gossip and protect one another from those who would try to inflict harm.

Love *always trusts*. This means both that love never loses faith and that it is willing to think the best of others. It does not mean that believers must be gullible, trusting everyone; instead, it means that they are willing to think the best as opposed to the worst of others. Love gives the benefit of the doubt. With real love, believers can deal with conflict lovingly. When everyone willingly thinks the best of everyone else, people are freed to be honest and open.

Love *always hopes*. Believers who love look forward, not backward. They seek for growth and maturity in the church, knowing that God is working in every person. They know that failure is not the end, and they trust in God who promises "that all things work together for good for those who love God, who are called according to his purpose" (Romans 8:28 NRSV).

Love *always perseveres*. Believers who love are active and steadfast in their faith. They hold on, no matter what difficulties they face. Hardship and pain do not stop love. When believers persevere, they face suffering within the body. They face persecution. They hang on when the going gets tough. They strive to save their marriages despite disappointment, to continue to trust God despite setbacks, and to continue to serve God despite fear or sorrow. When believers truly persevere, nothing can stop them.

13:8 Love never fails. But where there are prophecies, they will cease; where there are tongues, they will be stilled; where there is knowledge, it will pass away.[NIV] All the spiritual gifts will eventually pass away, but *love never fails*. Love is permanent. There will be no end to love. Spiritual gifts will end because they are given to build God's kingdom. When Jesus Christ returns, the kingdom will be established and the "building up" will no longer be necessary. Therefore *where there are prophecies* (12:10; 13:2), *they will cease*. This gift was to be used for speaking the gospel message boldly, telling the future, and helping others grow in the Lord. One day, evangelism will no longer be necessary, all prophecies will be fulfilled, and all believers will be made perfect in Christ (1 John 3:2).

For the same reason, *where there are tongues* (12:10; 13:1), *they will be stilled*. Tongues are meant for blessing or instruction in the church when an interpreter is present, but in eternity all will understand the same language. Finally, *where there is knowledge* (12:8; 13:2), *it will pass away*. No one will need teachers because everyone will be given perfect knowledge of all that God has done.

Some have used this verse as the central passage for teaching that speaking in tongues came to an end in its usefulness with the

death of the apostles and the writing of the New Testament. Therefore, they say, the focus today should be on the written word, not
on tongues or prophecy. "When the end comes" (13:10), that is,
when believers will be made perfect, "special gifts will all disappear." These same scholars take "perfection" to mean the close of
the New Testament canon or the completion of all the authentic
New Testament books. This view is upheld by various groups and
denominations. Others believe that the perfection will happen at the
return of Christ; thus, these gifts (prophecies, tongues, and knowledge) still have a place. It is incongruous to argue that tongues have
no value now while affirming that prophecy and knowledge are
still important. Most likely, therefore, Paul was not teaching the ces-
sation of tongues but the priority of love. "When the end comes"
(13:10) is linked to seeing Christ face to face (13:12), and not to the
completion of the New Testament.

13:9-10 **Now we know only a little, and even the gift of prophecy
reveals little! But when the end comes, these special gifts will
all disappear.**NLT On this earth, outside of heaven, everything is
imperfect. No matter how much people may know, they *know
only a little*. No matter how much prophecy is given, it still
reveals little. Not until the arrival of God's kingdom *(the end,* in
Greek, *teleion)* will everything be made perfect and complete. At
that time, all the *special gifts* of the Spirit will *disappear* (see
13:7-8). Because gifts are given for the building up of the body
of Christ, they will no longer be needed. The body will be complete, and God's kingdom will have arrived. Yet love will continue (13:8), because love is the very essence of God himself.
"God is love," wrote John (1 John 4:8, 16). God's love caused
him to reach out to undeserving humanity and send a Savior. His
love saved people and will bring them into his kingdom to be
with him forever. The kingdom rests on God's love.

COMPLETE
When Paul wrote of the coming end, he was referring to when we
must see Christ face to face. God gives believers spiritual gifts for
their lives on earth in order to build up, serve, and strengthen fellow
Christians. The spiritual gifts are for the church. In eternity, we will be
made perfect and complete and will be in the very presence of God.
We will no longer need the spiritual gifts, so they will come to an
end. Then, we will have a perfect understanding and appreciation
for one another as unique expressions of God's infinite creativity.
We will use our differences as a reason to praise God! Based on
that perspective, let us treat each other with the same love and unity
that we will one day share.

13:11 **It's like this: When I was a child, I spoke and thought and reasoned as a child does. But when I grew up, I put away childish things.**^{NLT} The contrast between believers' spiritual
understanding now, when they know only a little, and their lives
in the future kingdom, when everything will be made clear, is
illustrated in human terms. A child talks, thinks, and reasons like
a child. His or her understanding is incomplete. But when a child
grows up, he or she matures in speech, thought, and reason, putting *away childish things.* So now believers know only a little,
like children, but one day they will be able to put their present understanding behind them because they will understand clearly.

13:12 **Now we see but a poor reflection as in a mirror; then we shall
see face to face. Now I know in part; then I shall know fully,
even as I am fully known.**^{NIV} By way of further metaphor,
believers' present spiritual understanding is like *a poor reflection
as in a mirror.* They see very poorly now, compared to what they
will understand when they *see* God *face to face.* Right now, they
only *know in part;* at the time of Christ's return, they *shall know
fully.* The understanding will be complete, as is God's present understanding of each individual. While believers' knowledge is
still growing and maturing, God already knows each person *fully.*
Instead of boasting about their spiritual gifts, the Corinthian
believers should realize that these gifts were nothing compared to
what they would experience in heaven.

13:13 **And now abide faith, hope, love, these three; but the greatest
of these is love.**^{NKJV} In other places in Scripture, faith, hope, and
love are presented together (see Romans 5:1-5; Galatians 5:5-6;
Ephesians 4:2-5; Colossians 1:4-5; 1 Thessalonians 1:3; 5:8;
Hebrews 6:10-12; 10:22-24; 1 Peter 1:3-8). Most likely, Paul was
showing that love is a spiritual reality of a different kind, like
hope and faith, and not to be considered as one of the spiritual
gifts. In eternity, the gifts will drop away in significance, but
faith, hope, and love will remain.

"Faith" sometimes refers to a spiritual gift (12:9; 13:2) or to
saving faith that God has forgiven sins. In this context, it refers to
trust in the goodness and mercy of the Lord. Such trust will see
believers through until they live face to face in God's presence.
Believers also *hope;* they look forward to the arrival of God's
promised kingdom in its fullest form, knowing that God will
deliver them in times of suffering.

Paul added that while these three remain, *the greatest of these
is love.* How is love "the greatest"? Paul already had established
that love would abide forever (13:8). Love is the greatest because
it is one quality of the Christian life that will be fully active both

in the present and for eternity. Believers' faith in God will be realized when they see God face to face—for where there is sight, faith is no longer needed. Similarly, the believers' hope will be fully realized. Love will endure forever as those in the new heaven and new earth continue to love God and his people.

THESE THREE

Paul wrote that love endures forever. In morally corrupt Corinth, love had become a mixed-up term with little meaning. Today, people are still confused about love. Love is the greatest of all human qualities and is an attribute of God himself (1 John 4:8). Love involves unselfish service to others. *Faith* is the foundation and content of God's message; *hope* is the attitude and focus; *love* is the action. *Faith* informs action; *hope* influences action; *love* is action. When faith and hope are in line, you are free to love completely because you understand how God loves. Does your faith fully express itself in loving others?

1 Corinthians 14

The gift of speaking in unknown tongues was a concern in the
Corinthian church. The use of the gift had caused disorder in worship. Apparently, the Corinthians had a knack for turning even
good gifts into divisive issues.

Speaking in tongues is one of the legitimate gifts of the Holy
Spirit, but the Corinthian believers were using it as a sign of spiritual superiority rather than as a means for giving spiritual unity.
When spiritual gifts are properly used, they help everyone in the
church. Much of the controversy over spiritual gifts today comes
from the vacuum that has been created because the gifts have
been abused in some Christian circles (strikingly similar to the
Corinthian problems), while at the same time they have been
almost completely ignored in other Christian groups. In your
church, seek balanced biblical teaching.

14:1 **Let love be your highest goal, but also desire the special abilities the Spirit gives, especially the gift of prophecy.**^{NLT} The previous chapter, known as the "love chapter," is nestled purposefully
into this section on tongues. As beautiful as it is standing alone,
chapter 13 serves as a transition from chapter 12 (regarding the various gifts of the Spirit) to chapter 14 (focusing on the abuse of one
particular gift, the gift of tongues). Having described love as the
most valuable of all the gifts given by the Holy Spirit, Paul concluded here that believers should *let love be [their] highest goal.*
Then, from that foundation, they should *desire the special abilities
the Spirit gives.* This repeats the statement of 12:31, "eagerly desire
the greater gifts" (NIV), desiring to be helpful in the body of Christ
by seeking the gifts that benefit everyone. To "desire" the gifts
means literally "to pursue, strive for, seek after, aspire to." Elsewhere, Paul used the word to refer to spiritual effort (see Romans
9:30-31; 12:13; 14:19; Philippians 3:12; 1 Thessalonians 5:15;
1 Timothy 6:11; 2 Timothy 2:22). The tense of the verb implies con-
tinuous action; that is, it could read, "keep on desiring."

The "greater gifts" or "special abilities" that Paul wanted the

PROPHETS IN NEW TESTAMENT TIMES

The word *prophets* refers to those who speak for God. The New Testament gives us many of the characteristics and activities of those called prophets.

The early believers saw the Spirit come at Pentecost, fulfilling the prophet Joel's prediction that all God's people would prophesy.	Acts 2:17
Prophets ranked second in importance only to the apostles.	1 Corinthians 12:28-31; Ephesians 4:11
Some people are given a special gift of prophecy.	1 Corinthians 12:29; 13:2
Prophets are called "pneumatics" (spiritual ones).	1 Corinthians 14:37
Prophets played a foundational role in the early church.	1 Corinthians 12:28-31; Ephesians 2:20; 4:11
Prophets function primarily in the worship of the church.	Acts 13:1-2
Prophets may sometimes predict the future.	Acts 11:28; 20:23; 27:22-26
Prophets may announce judgments.	Acts 13:11; 28:25-28
Prophets may act symbolically.	Acts 21:10-11
Prophets may receive visions.	Acts 9:10-16; 2 Corinthians 12:1
Prophets may identify a specific person for specific Christian tasks, even at times equipping this person with the spiritual gifts necessary to carry out the tasks.	Acts 11:27-28; 13:1-2; 1 Timothy 4:14
Prophets may preach messages or explain passages of the Bible.	Luke 1:67-79; Acts 15:32; Romans 11:25-36; Ephesians 3:5
Prophets are saturated in the Old Testament Scriptures, and their words are influenced by the language of the Bible.	Romans 11:27 with Isaiah 27:9; 1 Corinthians 15:51, 54-55 with Isaiah 25:8 and Hosea 13:14
Prophets use phrases such as *the Lord says* or *the Holy Spirit says* as introductory formulas for prophetic insight.	Acts 21:11; Hebrews 3:7
Prophecy in the New Testament included prophetic words given for the benefit of the body of believers.	1 Corinthians 14:3-4
Prophecy in the New Testament also included the work of the Spirit on the prophet, whereby the Spirit revealed to the prophet a word from Christ.	John 16:12-14; Revelation 1:10; 4:1-2

Corinthians to seek were those that edified the church. *The gift of prophecy* (see also 12:10) had not so much to do with predicting future events as it had to do with bringing some message from God under the direction of the Holy Spirit to the body of believers. This gift provides insight, warning, correction, and encouragement (see 14:3). The Corinthians were eager for gifts, especially tongues, but Paul wanted them to be eager for the gifts that edify—namely, prophecy. The Reformers (Calvin, Luther) believed that sermons are the exercise of the gift of prophecy. Other scholars say that "prophecy," as used here by Paul, means spontaneous, Spirit-inspired messages that are orally delivered in the congregation for the edification and encouragement of the body of Christ.

14:2 For if your gift is the ability to speak in tongues, you will be talking to God but not to people, since they won't be able to understand you. You will be speaking by the power of the Spirit, but it will all be mysterious.[NLT] The gift of prophecy should be desired more than the gift of tongues because the *ability to speak in tongues* does not help other people since *they won't be able to understand you.* The "tongues" mentioned are not earthly languages (such as the gift described in Acts 2:4-12). Instead, this refers to an "ecstatic" or heavenly language, unknown to the speaker or to anyone else. Through this special gift, the believer talks *to God but not to people;* talking to God primarily involves prayer and praise. Because "tongues" is a true spiritual gift, the speaker is *speaking by the power of the Spirit,* but the words cannot be understood—*it will all be mysterious.*

As wonderful as this gift is, Paul wanted the Corinthian believers, in particular, to stop overemphasizing it. They needed to keep its value in perspective. Paul's goal, as always, was the unity and edification of all the believers.

Paul made several points about the gift of speaking in tongues:

- The gift of speaking in tongues is a spiritual gift from the Holy Spirit (12:28; 14:2, 39).
- Speaking in tongues is a desirable gift, but it is not a requirement of salvation or of being filled with the Spirit (12:30-31).
- The gift of tongues is less important than prophecy and teaching (14:4).
- The gift of tongues must be accompanied by some rules regarding its best use in public settings (14:26-28).

14:3-4 But one who prophesies is helping others grow in the Lord, encouraging and comforting them. A person who speaks in tongues is strengthened personally in the Lord, but one who

speaks a word of prophecy strengthens the entire church.^{NLT} Although Paul himself spoke in tongues (14:18), he stressed prophecy because it benefits the whole church. In context, speaking in tongues primarily benefits the speaker. Public worship must be understandable and edifying to the whole church. The purpose of "prophecy" is *helping others grow in the Lord, encouraging and comforting them,* and the one who *speaks a word of prophecy strengthens the entire church.* Through prophecy, believers are taught more about the Lord and their faith so they can grow as a body.

The *person who speaks in tongues,* however, *is strengthened personally in the Lord.* Such personal edification is truly a blessing for the one who has received this gift, but a person who prays in a tongue for personal edification should not be doing so in public worship because, while it strengthens him or her, it does not strengthen anyone else. Paul would give some guidelines for the use of tongues in public worship later in this chapter.

TO SPEAK OR NOT
The use of tongues in the modern church has continued despite conflicting teaching regarding the legitimacy of this gift. There are at least four distinct approaches to spiritual gifts:

1. *Studious or ignorant neglect*—the subject of spiritual gifts is avoided or simply unknown.

2. *Rejection by historical limitation*—the teaching that spiritual gifts only functioned during the apostolic age and ended with the writing of the New Testament.

3. *Emphatic approval*—spiritual gifts are central to Christian experience, sometimes even insisting the presence of a single gift (i.e. tongues) as the mark of genuine belief.

4. *Cautious acceptance*—seeking to avoid the problems described in Scripture while at the same time acknowledging the Holy Spirit's freedom and power to act within the church and through Christians.

The first three approaches fail to take Scripture seriously. Each makes a judgment about spiritual gifts that is ultimately based on issues outside of the Bible. These are issues that each church must deal with in order to ensure orderly worship. But they are best handled by being open and not limiting the Holy Spirit's work. Keep open to other Christians who regard tongues differently than you do.

14:5 **I wish you all had the gift of speaking in tongues, but even more I wish you were all able to prophesy. For prophecy is a greater and more useful gift than speaking in tongues, unless someone interprets what you are saying so that the whole church can get some good out of it.**^{NLT} Paul never wrote disparagingly of the gift of tongues, only the Corinthians' overemphasis of it. In fact, he even wished that they *all had the gift of speaking in tongues,* for the gift has great value for individuals in their private communication with God. But the issue at hand was that the Corinthian believers were seeking that gift above all others, when other gifts were actually more helpful to the church as a whole. Repeating his emphasis in 14:1, Paul stated that *prophecy is a greater and more useful gift than speaking in tongues.* The one who prophesies helps others to grow and encourages and comforts them (14:3). The one speaking in tongues realizes a wonderful relationship with the Lord but has edified no one else *unless someone interprets* what has been said *so that the whole church can get some good out of it.* (For more on interpretation, see 12:30; 14:13, 22-25.) With interpretation, therefore, the gift of tongues *can* edify the church. Apparently, the Corinthian believers were exhibiting the gift of tongues in public worship without interpretation, and that was helping no one.

ABLE TO PROPHESY
Paul's words to the Corinthians about tongues and prophecy have much to say to our generation. Many Christians struggle with the discussion of tongues. Paul would clearly say that no one should put down those Christians who speak in tongues, and those who speak in tongues should not disparage those who do not. Believers need unity and love. The enemy is not each other but the sinful world, Satan, and our selfish, sinful desires. But Paul would have another word for today: "I wish you were all able to prophesy." Paul would encourage us to be so in tune with the Spirit that his messages of comfort, encouragement, and edification would be heard in our congregations today. Make sure your actions are encouraging and edifying.

14:6 Dear brothers and sisters, if I should come to you talking in an unknown language, how would that help you? But if I bring you some revelation or some special knowledge or some prophecy or some teaching—that is what will help you.[NLT] In Corinth, the gift of tongues was being used as a barometer of spirituality. Therefore, Paul described the natural inferiority of a gift that does not edify. For example, if, on his next visit to the Corinthian church, he *should come . . . talking in an unknown language,* would that help the young church grow in Christ? Would the believers be edified, encouraged, or comforted? Obviously not. However, if he were to come to them with *some revelation, special knowledge, prophecy,* or *teaching,* then any one of those would be helpful to them. What Paul meant specifically by each of these words is unknown. He probably was not referring to four different types of information given by speaking but to various names of the speaking done with the help of the Spirit for the benefit of the believers. The common factor is that all of these, to be helpful, would have to be done in a language understood by the hearers.

14:7 Even in the case of lifeless things that make sounds, such as the flute or harp, how will anyone know what tune is being played unless there is a distinction in the notes?[NIV] Paul argued his point with three different pictures. First, musical instruments, *such as the flute or harp,* make only noise if no one can distinguish the *tune* or *a distinction in the notes.* If an instrument is to make beautiful sounds that benefit the listener, the sounds must make sense.

14:8 And if the bugler doesn't sound a clear call, how will the soldiers know they are being called to battle?[NLT] The bugler was important in a battalion of soldiers. With different note combinations, the bugler would sound the call to wake up, to retire for the evening, or the call to battle. *If the bugler doesn't sound a clear call,* however, the soldiers would be left in confusion, not knowing whether or not *they are being called to battle.* That would be disastrous if they were being attacked! Mere sounds are not beneficial; only sounds that make sense and are understood by the hearers are helpful. (See Ezekiel 33 for an Old Testament example of the watchman's responsibility to give a clear call.)

HIGHER GOAL
Paul confronted the self-oriented use of the gift of tongues. Spiritual people must be careful not to pursue self-development at the expense of broken, lost people. Giving too much attention to our own needs, ideas, and spiritual expression, we may push aside the Spirit's true desire and abandon those who need encouragement. Follow Paul's advice and make encouraging and edifying others the highest goal.

14:9 And it's the same for you. If you talk to people in a language they don't understand, how will they know what you mean? You might as well be talking to an empty room.[NLT] People from many lands converged in a busy city like Corinth. The residents were certainly familiar with foreigners who could not speak their language. As mere sounds mean nothing without some sort of plan and pattern of understanding (14:7-8), so human language, when not understood, accomplishes nothing. Trying to communicate in a language to a person who does not understand it would be *talking to an empty room.* Whatever is said would not benefit the hearer at all because he or she would not be able to understand the words. The language would be no more than noise to the hearers.

14:10-12 **Undoubtedly there are all sorts of languages in the world, yet none of them is without meaning. If then I do not grasp the meaning of what someone is saying, I am a foreigner to the speaker, and he is a foreigner to me. So it is with you. Since you are eager to have spiritual gifts, try to excel in gifts that build up the church.**^{NIV} Just because someone doesn't understand a certain language doesn't mean that the language has no meaning. In fact, *there are all sorts of languages in the world,* and all of them have meaning. But when two people who speak different languages attempt to communicate, one is not be able to *grasp the meaning* of what the other is trying to say. They are foreigners to each other. *So it is with you,* concluded Paul. Just as two foreigners cannot understand each other's language, so those speaking in tongues cannot be understood by the congregation. Thus, their speaking is not beneficial to the church.

Because the Corinthians had been so *eager to have spiritual gifts,* Paul admonished them to *try to excel in gifts that build up the church* (see Ephesians 4:12). Paul was speaking to the church as a whole, not to individuals. The literal translation of 14:12 is, "since zealots you are of spiritual things, be zealous that you may abound in the edification of the church." The church as a whole should strive to have the gifts that build up its members. It should support those who serve in those capacities, and it should redirect its zeal from a desire to speak in tongues to a desire to serve the Lord in the best way that will build up the church. No one should seek merely the personal experience. God does not give us gifts for private, selfish use. The gifts are for helping others.

14:13-14 **So anyone who has the gift of speaking in tongues should pray also for the gift of interpretation in order to tell people plainly what has been said. For if I pray in tongues, my spirit is praying, but I don't understand what I am saying.**^{NLT} The simple conclusion to the matter is that *anyone who has the gift of speaking in tongues should pray also for the gift of interpretation* of what he or she says in the unknown language. Up to this point, Paul had been explaining that the gift of speaking in tongues was of no value to the congregation as a whole, only to the person who speaks to God in the unknown tongue. But if the person also has the gift of interpretation, the tongue could be used in public

worship if the one praying (or someone else with the gift of interpretation) would then interpret *in order to tell people plainly
what has been said*. That way, the entire church would be edified
by this gift.

Paul intimates in 14:2 and 14:4 that the gift of speaking in
tongues provides a person with glorious communion with God.
Most likely, however, this communion results not from understanding what the person is saying but from drawing closer to
God through the power of the Spirit. Yet the person who prays
that way is not expected to then be able to interpret his or her
own words immediately. Paul wrote, *if I pray in tongues, my
spirit is praying, but I don't understand what I am saying*. That is
part of the mysterious beauty of this particular gift—it does not
engage the intellect in order to use it. It is a gift filled with fervor
and passion for the Lord. Yet even as the person prays, he or she
does not understand his or her own words. The phrase "my spirit
is praying" probably refers to both the spirit and the Spirit—the
person's inner spirit prays to and praises God with words given
by the Holy Spirit.

While the spiritual fervor of one speaking in tongues has merit,
wrote Paul, this ought not be the end in itself. Fervor is important, but people's minds must be engaged in order for them to be
edified. This can only be done if the words prayed to God are
interpreted for everyone else. Thus, the gift of interpretation is
required when tongues are used in the assembly.

14:15 **So what shall I do? I will pray with my spirit, but I will also
pray with my mind; I will sing with my spirit, but I will also
sing with my mind.**[NIV] Paul states in 14:18 that he himself
speaks in tongues, so he wrote in the first person here, including
himself in this situation. His answer is that he will do both—he
will *pray* and *sing* in tongues with his spirit, and he will pray and
sing in his own language so as to also engage his *mind*. Praying
in tongues was, for Paul, a practice that edified him even if he did
not understand what he was saying (see 14:13-14 commentary).
Praying with the spirit (see "spiritual songs," Ephesians 5:19)
may be charismatic singing in the Spirit or singing spontaneously
to previously composed songs.

In addition to that, however, he would pray and sing with his
intellect and understanding in his own language—this would
edify both himself and others. In praying and singing, both the
mind and the spirit are to be fully engaged. When believers sing,
they should also think about the meaning of the words. When
they pour out their feelings to God in prayer, they should not turn
off their capacity to think. True Christianity is neither barren intel-

lectualism nor thoughtless emotionalism. (See also Ephesians
1:17-18; Philippians 1:9-11; and Colossians 1:9.) Paul may also
have had in mind a private/public distinction. In his private
prayers and singing, he could do so in tongues. In public, however, he would speak in Greek so that the congregation would
understand and be edified.

14:16-17 **If you are praising God with your spirit, how can one who
finds himself among those who do not understand say
"Amen" to your thanksgiving, since he does not know what
you are saying?**[NRSV] Paul just stated that he intended to continue
to pray and sing in tongues (privately) and in his own language
(publicly). The believers in Corinth should do the same. Those
with the gift of tongues could continue to speak in tongues privately, but they needed to focus more on praying and singing in
their own language in corporate worship. The reason is simple. If
they were *praising God* with their spirits (meaning in an
unknown tongue), *how can one who finds himself among those
who do not understand say "Amen" to [their] thanksgiving?*
"Those who do not understand" refers to the rest of the people in
the congregation who do not have the gift of tongues or of interpretation; thus, they do not understand what is being said. These
may be other believers or people interested in Christianity who
have not yet made the commitment. Most likely this refers to
other believers because only they would be able to "say 'Amen'"
to particular words of thanksgiving. To say "amen" means to
agree with or endorse what has been said (1 Chronicles 16:36;
Nehemiah 5:13; 8:6; Galatians 1:5; Ephesians 3:21). If the rest of
the people in the congregation have no clue what a tongues-
speaker has said, how can they express agreement with it? The
effect of the thanksgiving is lost because no one has understood
the words. Paul continued, **You will be giving thanks very
nicely, no doubt, but it doesn't help the other people present.**[NLT] The bottom line on the corporate use of a spiritual gift is
that it should *help the other people present.* That is the purpose of
corporate worship, and believers must be sensitive to one another
in that context—keeping out anything that would interfere with
spiritual growth. Certainly the one speaking in tongues is *giving
thanks very nicely,* but what is needed in the assembly of believers is intelligibility. Only then are the rest of the listeners edified.
Corporate worship is just that—corporate. As a unified body, the
believers come together to praise God, offer thanks, and learn. If
various individuals attempt to continue their own private edification by speaking in tongues without interpretation, they will do
so at the expense of others. Instead, they should worship that way

privately. In public worship, everyone should be able to understand and participate.

14:18-19 I thank God that I speak in tongues more than all of you. But in the church I would rather speak five intelligible words to instruct others than ten thousand words in a tongue.^{NIV} Paul had been downplaying the value of tongues because of the Corinthian overemphasis on that particular gift, but he added that he himself had that gift. Paul used the gift consistently in private prayer, saying that he spoke *in tongues more than all of* the believers in Corinth. Up to this point in the letter, the Corinthians may have been thinking that Paul was putting down the gift of tongues because he did not possess it. Paul explained, however, that not only did he have the gift but that he used it more profitably than the rest of them. Then he pointed them back to the issue at hand—what was happening in the assembly. Paul understood the limitations of the gift of tongues when it came to edifying the body of believers. Instead of impressing people with the gift of tongues that he, like many of them, had received, Paul said that he *would rather speak five intelligible words to instruct others than ten thousand words in a tongue* because only words that are understood can instruct. The implication is that the believers in Corinth who were gifted with tongues should do the same.

UNDERSTANDABLE WORSHIP
Just as musical instruments must sound each note in order for the music to be clear, so Paul says that words preached in the hearers' language are more clear and helpful. There are many languages in the world (14:10), and people who speak different languages can rarely understand each other. It is the same with speaking in tongues. Although this gift is helpful to many people in private worship and in public worship with interpretation, Paul wrote that he would rather speak five words that his hearers can understand than ten thousand that they cannot (14:19). Paul's argument confronts all Christians with basic questions: Do we pay attention in worship? Do we seek to be clear in what we say? Are we sensitive to making worship always understandable to others?

14:20 Dear brothers and sisters, don't be childish in your understanding of these things. Be innocent as babies when it comes to evil, but be mature and wise in understanding matters of this kind.^{NLT} In 3:1-3, Paul had explained to the Corinthian believers his concern that they were still "infants in the Christian life" (NLT) and had to be dealt with like little children. Here he once again reprimanded them for their wrong thinking regarding the use of the gift of tongues in the assembly of believers. He had explained how they should view that gift in 14:1-19, and here had written that they should not *be childish in [their] understanding of these things,* but, instead, they should *be mature and wise in understanding matters of this kind.* Children prefer excitement to instruction, but adults ought to know better. The Corinthians had been acting like children, enjoying the excitement that tongues offered in their assembly without realizing that they were obtaining no solid instruction from them. It is all right to be as *innocent as babies when it comes to evil,* but there is no place for constant immaturity in the Christian life. Believers are to be growing and maturing so that they can understand these issues for themselves and make wise decisions concerning them.

14:21 In the law it is written, "By people of strange tongues and by the lips of foreigners I will speak to this people; yet even then they will not listen to me," says the Lord.[NRSV] Paul's use of Scripture comes from Isaiah 28:11-12. He may have been adapting the passage or generalizing from it, since it is not an exact quote from either the Greek (Septuagint) nor the Hebrew text available at that time. He may have been quoting from another Greek text that no longer exists. Paul's point in quoting this passage was to set up his conclusion in 14:23. The people in Isaiah's time did not listen to the prophets who spoke in their language, and when people of other languages spoke to the Jews, they still did not listen. So Paul was saying that speaking in tongues will convince no one. Those outside the church who might enter and hear the Corinthian believers speaking in tongues (with no one to explain the meaning) would think that the Christians were crazy. That reaction would fulfill the Old Testament words that tongues will not draw unbelievers into the church. On the contrary, it will turn them away and leave them to judgment. Unbelievers need the gospel message spoken clearly and intelligibly, not tongues.

14:22 Tongues, then, are a sign, not for believers but for unbelievers; prophecy, however, is for believers, not for unbelievers.[NIV] The Corinthians argued that speaking in tongues was supposed to be a *sign* to unbelievers, as it was in Acts 2. But Paul argued that after speaking in tongues, believers were supposed to explain what was said and give the credit to God. The unsaved people would then be convinced of a spiritual reality and be motivated to look further into the Christian faith. This is one way to reach unbelievers, but clear communication of God's message is better (14:5). *Tongues* are a sign for unbelievers in the same way that Old Testament signs were understood.

14:23 **So if the whole church comes together and everyone speaks in tongues, and some who do not understand or some unbelievers come in, will they not say that you are out of your mind?**^{NIV} The way the Corinthians were speaking in tongues was helping no one. *If the whole church comes together and everyone speaks in tongues,* the result will be chaotic noise. (Such disorderliness may have been the case, considering Paul's further instructions in 14:27-28.) Even if they were speaking one at a time, without interpretation of the words spoken, other believers *who do not understand* and *unbelievers* who *come in* will say that the Christians are out of their minds. They will not sound as though they are praising and praying, but rather one would think that they are all insane. This will edify no one, scare off unbelievers, and hurt the witness of the church.

THE USUAL
Unusual or unexpected spiritual events have a fascination all their own, but mere curiosity must be secondary to God's purposes. God's truth and power can be found in both the extraordinary and the ordinary. We don't need to ask God to get our attention in some strange new way; instead, we need to ask for fresh attention to the amazing ways God has already made himself known. Instead of looking for something new, follow what God has clearly communicated to you.

14:24-25 **But if all of you are prophesying, and unbelievers or people who don't understand these things come into your meeting, they will be convicted of sin, and they will be condemned by what you say.**^{NLT} Paul had already stated the value of *prophesying* over speaking in tongues (14:1-6) because prophecy "is helping others grow in the Lord, encouraging and comforting them" (14:3 NLT). Prophecy also speaks forth the word of truth. This was probably the type of speaking to which this verse refers because of how it affects those who heard and understood it. The *unbelievers* and the believers not gifted with speaking in tongues would come into the meeting and learn something. Here Paul highlighted the specific speaking that would help lead people to repent of their sins. *They will be convicted of sin.* "Convicted" means reproved or rebuked through the probing work of the Holy Spirit, who exposes and convinces people of sin (Ephesians 5:12-13; 1 Timothy 5:20; 2 Timothy 4:2). Unbelievers would also be *condemned,* meaning "judged," "held to account," "examined."

As they listen, their secret thoughts will be laid bare, and they will fall down on their knees and worship God, declaring,

"God is really here among you."[NLT] Having one's *secret
thoughts . . . laid bare* will lead both to conviction and condemnation. Obviously, the Corinthian believers would be far less convicted to have everyone speaking in tongues. They all would feel
very spiritual, with no one having to face any sin. But when
Spirit-inspired, intelligible words of truth are spoken, those who
truly *listen* will find God right there among the congregation. His
presence will be made known. The listeners *will fall down on
their knees and worship God* (see Isaiah 45:14; Zechariah 8:23).
And that is ultimately what the church should desire—to reach
out and draw in the unbelievers, bringing them to saving faith in
Jesus Christ and then helping them grow to maturity.

WORSHIP IN AN ORDERLY WAY / 14:26-40

Paul reviews the guidelines for tongues and prophecy as exercised
in corporate worship. He restates the importance of everyone being
able to understand, of orderliness, and of edifying each participant.

14:26 **Well, my brothers and sisters, let's summarize what I am saying. When you meet, one will sing, another will teach, another
will tell some special revelation God has given, one will speak
in an unknown language, while another will interpret what is
said. But everything that is done must be useful to all and
build them up in the Lord.**[NLT] When believers meet, *one will
sing* (an ability not mentioned in chapter 12 but a large part of
worship going back to the Old Testament and the psalms; see also
Ephesians 5:19; Colossians 3:16), *another will teach* (12:29;
Romans 12:7; Colossians 3:16), *another will tell some special
revelation God has given* (this could be an aspect of the gift of
prophecy—12:10, 29; 13:2; 14:1), *one will speak in an unknown
language* (12:10, 28, 30), *while another will interpret* (12:30).

PARTICIPATION
Everything done in worship services must be beneficial to the
worshipers. Every worshiper ought to consider herself or
himself a contributor. These principles touch every
aspect—singing, preaching, and the exercise of spiritual gifts.
Contributions to the service (by singing, speaking, reading,
praying, playing instruments, giving) must have love as their
chief motivation. As you prepare and participate in worship,
seek to strengthen the faith of other believers.

This verse is not to be taken as Paul's recommendation of an
order of service; his point is that various activities can happen in
corporate worship. While all of this occurs, however, *everything*

WHAT THE BIBLE TEACHES ABOUT WORSHIP
(Verses are quoted from NLT.)

Worship is first and foremost an encounter with the living and holy God.

"'Do not come any closer,' God told him. 'Take off your sandals, for you are standing on holy ground'" (Exodus 3:5).

God is our friend, but he is also our sovereign Lord. To approach him frivolously shows a lack of respect and sincerity. When you come to God in worship, do you approach him casually, or do you come as though you were an invited guest before a king?

Worship is only as real as the involvement of those participating.

"The Lord gave these instructions to Moses on Mount Sinai when he commanded the Israelites to bring their offerings to the Lord in the wilderness of Sinai" (Leviticus 7:38).

All the rituals in Leviticus were meant to teach the people valuable lessons. But over time, the people became indifferent. When your church appears to be conducting dry, meaningless rituals, try rediscovering the meaning and purpose behind them. Your worship will be revitalized.

A true worship experience is often a direct result of preparation for worship.

"The Lord said to Moses, 'Give these instructions to the people of Israel: The offerings you present to me by fire on the altar are my food, and they are very pleasing to me. See to it that they are brought at the appointed times and offered according to my instructions'" (Numbers 28:1-2).

Following these rituals took time, and this gave the people the opportunity to prepare their heart for worship. Unless your heart is ready, worship is meaningless. God is delighted when you are prepared to come before him in a spirit of thankfulness.

Believers should take advantage of every opportunity and praise God.

"Sing praises to God, our strength. Sing to the God of Israel. Sing! Beat the tambourine. Play the sweet lyre and the harp. Sound the trumpet for a sacred feast when the moon is new, when the moon is full" (Psalm 81:1-3).

Israel's holidays reminded the nation of God's great miracles. Remember the spiritual origin of the holidays you celebrate, and use them as opportunities to worship God for his goodness to you, your family, and your nation.

Worship and music go hand in hand.

"David and the army commanders then appointed men from

David instituted music for the temple worship services. Worship should involve the whole the families of Asaph, Heman, and Jeduthun to proclaim God's messages to the accompaniment of harps, lyres, and cymbals" (1 Chronicles 25:1).

person, and music helps lift a person's thoughts and emotions to God. Through music you can celebrate God's greatness.

Worship is bringing the best believers have to Christ.	"They entered the house where the child and his mother, Mary, were, and they fell down before him and worshiped him. Then they opened their treasure chests and gave him gifts of gold, frankincense, and myrrh" (Matthew 2:11).	The wise men brought gifts and worshiped Jesus for who he was. This is the essence of true worship—honoring Christ for who he is and being willing to give to him what is valuable to you. Worship God because he is worthy of the best you have to give.
Genuine worship results in submission and obedience to Jesus.	"But even as he said it, a bright cloud came over them, and a voice from the cloud said, 'This is my beloved Son, and I am fully pleased with him. Listen to him'" (Matthew 17:5).	Jesus is more than just a great leader. He is the Son of God. When you understand this profound truth, the only adequate response is worship. When you have a correct understanding of Christ, you will obey him.
Everything done in corporate worship must be beneficial to the worshipers.	"Since you are so eager to have spiritual gifts, ask God for those that will be of real help to the whole church" (1 Corinthians 14:12).	This principle touches every aspect of worship. Those contributing to a worship service must speak useful words or participate in a way that will strengthen the faith of other believers.
In worship, everything must be done in harmony and with order.	"Be sure that everything is done properly and in order" (1 Corinthians 14:40).	Even when the gifts of the Holy Spirit are being exercised, there is no excuse for disorder. When there is chaos, the church is not allowing God to work among believers as he would like. Make sure that what you bring to worship is appropriate, but also make sure that you participate.

that is done must be useful to all and build them up in the Lord.
Also, all believers should show love (chapter 13), and everything
should edify (14:1-25).

14:27-28 **If anyone speaks in a tongue, two—or at the most three—
should speak, one at a time, and someone must interpret.**^{NIV}
Because all activities done in corporate worship must be done to
help and build up all the believers, Paul described how tongues can
still be useful. He had already argued that tongues are not beneficial without interpretation (14:5) and certainly not when everyone
is speaking at once (14:23). Tongues can be edifying to everyone, if
a few simple rules are followed. First, *if anyone* in the congregation
has the gift and can speak *in a tongue,* then only *two—or at the
most three—should speak, one at a time.* In other words, not everyone with the gift of tongues should speak at every service—only
two or three should speak. That Paul should have to say that they
should speak "one at a time" seems to be a corrective—apparently
they were not doing so. Not only were the Corinthians overemphasizing this gift, but they were allowing it to dominate their
church gatherings. Thus, Paul corrected this error. In addition, the
gift of tongues should not so dominate a person that he or she cannot control the impulse to speak. It was possible for the believers to
exercise this gift in a controlled, appropriate, and orderly way. The
believers who had come out of pagan cults certainly had witnessed
the ecstatic mania often associated with pagan worship rites. The
gifts given to believers were radically different than the demon-
induced "religious" frenzy performed by those in the cults.

The other stipulation for use of tongues in public worship is
that *someone must interpret.* Either the person speaking can interpret for himself or herself (if he or she has the gift, see 14:13), or
another person with that gift should interpret what was said into a
known language (12:30; 14:26). Because there must be an interpreter, Paul continued: **But if there is no one to interpret, let
them be silent in church and speak to themselves and to
God.**^{NRSV} If those with the gift of tongues know that they do not
have the gift of interpretation, and if no one else in the congregation is known to have that gift, then they should *be silent in
church.* Paul was not forbidding believers from using their gift,
but instructing them to pray silently, speaking *to themselves and
to God.* That way they would be blessed by the use of their gift,
but they would not in any way hinder the assembly.

14:29 **Two or three prophets should speak, and the others should
weigh carefully what is said.**^{NIV} Having just explained certain
regulations on the use of tongues in the assembly, Paul also
placed regulations on prophetic speaking. Although this was

the particular gift that Paul had recommended to the believers
(14:1-5), he also realized that its use had to be regulated by
love, edification, and order. Just as only two or three people
should be allowed to speak in tongues (14:27-28), so only *two
or three prophets* (those who have been given that gift, 12:10,
28-29; 13:2) *should speak.* It is unclear who *the others* are—
they could be "others" who also have the gift but exercise it at
that time, not by speaking but by weighing *carefully what is
said.* Or "the others" could refer to the congregation as a
whole, discussing a prophet's words to make sure that they
agreed with Scripture. People in the church should never accept
the words of any person, gifted or not, without careful discernment and personal knowledge of God's Word; otherwise, false
teachers could easily obtain a hearing and lead people astray.

14:30-32 **And if a revelation comes to someone who is sitting down, the
first speaker should stop. For you can all prophesy in turn so
that everyone may be instructed and encouraged. The spirits
of prophets are subject to the control of prophets.**[NIV] In order
for the worship service to continue in an orderly manner (14:40),
further guidelines were needed. These words might have been
directed at those who would have a tendency to dominate. One
who is speaking should willingly defer to another who has
received a prophecy. That *a revelation* would come suddenly to a
person describes this gift and its use in a worship service. It, too,
could get out of control if the speakers were not careful to take
turns and defer to one another as the Spirit leads each to speak.
The phrase "for you can all prophesy" does not mean that everyone in the congregation has the gift of prophecy, but that those to
whom the gift is given and to whom the Spirit gives a message
must be allowed to speak *in turn so that everyone may be
instructed and encouraged* (14:3-6). As always, the worship service should be for the edification of the believers.

The phrase "the spirits of prophets are subject to the control of
prophets" means that "the people who prophesy are in control of
their spirit and can wait their turn" (NLT). In other words, this
gift, like the gift of tongues, does not send people out of control,
unable to stop their mouths. The message, given by the Spirit, is
"subject" to the person's spirit. He or she can control when to
speak and when to defer to another. This gift could also be exercised in a controlled, appropriate, and orderly way.

14:33 **For God is not a God of disorder but of peace, as in all the
other churches.**[NLT] The reason that the church service must be controlled and orderly is that *God is not a God of disorder but of
peace.* In worship, everything must be done in harmony and with

order. Even when the gifts of the Holy Spirit are being exercised, there is no excuse for disorder or disturbances. In order to please God in their worship, believers are not to be wild and out of control. Instead, they should be using their gifts in an appropriate manner, always seeking to edify others. To contradict God's own character in worship does not honor him. When everyone in the Christian assembly is truly in tune with the Holy Spirit, there will not be disorder, but harmony and "peace" that pleases God and encourages his people. This was not Paul's instruction for the Corinthian church alone; indeed, *all the other churches* must exhibit the character of the one they worship. When the Corinthians did so, they would be in line with what God expects of all his people.

ORDER
Paul stated that God is not a God of disorder but of peace. Note that the preferred alternative to disorder is "peace." Too often, in resisting disorder, Christians have opted for rigid, predictable, and unvarying forms of worship in which God's presence is as difficult to find as in disorderly gatherings. When there is chaos, the church is not allowing God to work among believers as he would like. Peaceful order should not, however, rule out God's creativity, joy, and unpredictability. Do your part to have worship be a joyful, peaceful, winsome experience that draws people into it.

14:34-35 **Women should be silent during the church meetings. It is not proper for them to speak. They should be submissive, just as the law says. If they have any questions to ask, let them ask their husbands at home, for it is improper for women to speak in church meetings.**NLT Does this mean that women should not speak in church services today? It is clear from 11:5 that women often prayed and prophesied in public worship. It is also clear in chapters 12–14 that women are given spiritual gifts and are encouraged to exercise them in the body of Christ. So what did Paul mean? It would be helpful to understand the context and the use of the word "silent."

In the Greek culture, women were discouraged from saying anything in public, and they were certainly not

In all likelihood what was uppermost in [Paul's] mind was the lax moral state of Corinth and the feeling that nothing, absolutely nothing, must be done which would bring upon the infant Church the faintest suspicion of immodesty. It would certainly be very wrong to take these words of Paul out of the context for which they were written.
William Barclay

allowed to confront or question men publicly. Apparently, some of the women who had become Christians thought that their Christian freedom gave them the right to question the men in public worship. This was causing division in the church. In addition, women of that day did not receive formal religious education as did the men.

The Greek word for "silent" used here is also used in 14:28, referring to the silence commanded on the one who desired to speak in tongues but without an interpreter present. Obviously, that did not mean that this person was never to speak in the church, only to remain silent when certain conditions were not met so that the church service would not be disrupted. The same Greek word is also used in 14:30 for the prophet who is asked to stop speaking ("be silent" in the Greek) when another has been given a revelation. Again, this obviously does not mean that the prophet was never to speak. This would negate his or her gift. Because women as well as men were gifted with tongues, interpretation, or prophecy, they would need to speak in order to exercise their gifts.

The "speaking" to which Paul referred was the inappropriate asking of questions that would disrupt the worship service or take it on a tangent. Therefore, the women *should be silent during the church meetings,* not because they were never to speak, but because they were not to speak out with questions that would be ineffective in edifying the entire church. *If they have any questions,* says Paul, *let them ask their husbands at home.* That they *should be submissive* compares with Paul's words in 11:7-12—to keep the believers in obedience with God's commanded lines of authority *(just as the law says).* There is no clear reference to an Old Testament passage. Paul may have been referring to a generally accepted interpretation of Genesis 3:16. Apparently, the women believers in Corinth, newly freed in Christ to be able to learn and take part in worship, had been raising questions that could have been answered at home without disrupting the services. In this entire chapter, Paul had been dealing with various forms of disorder and confusion taking place in the Corinthian church in particular. His words are corrective. In this instance, Paul was asking the Corinthian women not to flaunt their Christian freedom during worship. The purpose of Paul's words was to promote unity, not to teach about the role of women in the church.

14:36 Did the word of God originate with you? Or are you the only people it has reached?[NIV] This entire chapter corrects the Corinthian believers regarding their insistence on the gift of tongues as a sign of being "filled with the Spirit" and allowing it to overtake their church services. In their letter to Paul, they may even have questioned his spirituality since they had never heard him speak in tongues (hence his comment in 14:18). They have been guilty of taking off on a tangent and leaving the gospel behind. So Paul asked, sarcastically, *Did the word of God originate with you? Or are you the only people it has reached?* Were they the apostles? Were they the ones who learned directly from Jesus Christ? The answer is no. Then why did they think they could decide on their own what would constitute salvation and how they should worship? The Corinthian church was out of line with what was acceptable behavior in the churches (14:33), and they needed to make some changes. The Corinthians needed to recognize that all true believers are filled with the Spirit at the moment of salvation, and that they all will manifest different gifts. This variety was the strength of the church, for it provided them with all the necessary "parts" (as in a "body," 12:12-31) in order to function properly.

14:37-38 **Anyone who claims to be a prophet, or to have spiritual powers, must acknowledge that what I am writing to you is a command of the Lord. Anyone who does not recognize this is not to be recognized.**^{NRSV} The authority of Paul's words was not to be questioned. As an apostle, Paul was writing *a command of the Lord,* and they all should treat his words as such. Any true prophet among them would *acknowledge* this; anyone who claimed to be a prophet but did *not recognize* Paul's words as authoritative was *not to be recognized.* The lines of authority went from "apostles" to "prophets" (12:28). Paul was an apostle, so his authority was not to be questioned. Those who claimed to be "prophets" would prove it by their acceptance of Paul's words.

14:39-40 **So, dear brothers and sisters, be eager to prophesy, and don't forbid speaking in tongues. But be sure that everything is done properly and in order.**^{NLT} With the words "dear brothers and sisters," Paul closed his answers to their questions about worship on a friendly note. He truly loved these believers and sought to correct their errors so that they could continue to grow in the Lord and not be sidetracked by anything. They were to *be eager to prophesy* (14:1) because that is the more powerful tool for the edification of the believers, but they should not *forbid speaking in tongues* because that is a bona fide gift of the Holy Spirit. They must *be sure that everything is done properly and in order*—and that would happen if they followed his instructions as outlined in this chapter.

Worship services should be intelligible and marked by mutual respect and proper behavior. They should be organized in a way to enhance communication but not so as to stifle the spontaneous work of the Spirit.

 WORSHIP
Paul urged the Corinthians to conduct their worship in an orderly way. Worship is vital to individuals and to the whole church. The quality of our worship forms a powerful expression of the reality of our conversion. Having been loved by God, we seek to love God back with our whole being. Our gatherings should be conducted in an orderly way so that we can worship, be taught, and be prepared to serve God. Believers should be encouraged to prepare for the expected in worship but also to anticipate God's ability to do the unexpected. Those who are responsible for planning worship should make sure it has order and direction rather than chaos and confusion. Opportunity for the expression of many gifts should be included.

---

1 Corinthians 15

The truth never loses its power. People, however, often lose their grip on truth. The struggles in the Corinthian church made it clear to Paul that they needed to refocus their attention on the gospel. He brought his letter to a close with a vigorous proclamation of the resurrection of Jesus Christ. They were wandering; Paul called them back to the center. Like the Corinthians, we can't afford to stray from Christ. Every claim about Christianity has roots in his resurrection. What we believe about this life and the afterlife depends on what Jesus did with death. God's Word calls us back to the center.

15:1-2 Now, brothers, I want to remind you of the gospel I preached to you, which you received and on which you have taken your stand. By this gospel you are saved, if you hold firmly to the word I preached to you. Otherwise, you have believed in vain.^{NIV} In this final section of the letter, Paul gave a masterly defense of the resurrection of Christ and its importance to the Christian faith. The gospel message that he had *preached to* them, that they had *received,* on which they had taken their stand was the message that had *saved* them. Paul wanted to remind them of that gospel, because apparently some (probably false teachers) had been distorting it. In fact, some of the Corinthians had come to believe

> The Gospels do not explain the Resurrection; the Resurrection explains the Gospels. Belief in the Resurrection is not an appendage to the Christian faith; it *is* the Christian faith.
>
> *John S. Whale*

that there would be no resurrection of the dead (15:12). Not only was the church in Corinth having problems with unity (as Paul tried to clear up in the previous chapters), it was also dealing with basic problems of theology. This, too, would tear apart the church. As an apostle who had himself seen the risen Christ (15:8), Paul took these Corinthian believers back to the basics of the message that they had welcomed and received. Because

WHY BELIEVE THE RESURRECTION?

acceptance of that gospel had saved them, they should *hold firmly* to it. To do otherwise would mean that they had *believed in vain*. If they could be so easily swayed to other messages, tangents, and untruths, then perhaps what they claimed as belief was not belief at all. If the faith they thought they had could not assure them of salvation, then that faith was worthless.

15:3-4 **For what I received I passed on to you as of first importance: that Christ died for our sins according to the Scriptures, that he was buried, that he was raised on the third day according to the Scriptures.**^{NIV} Paul had *received* the gospel message from Christ himself, as had all the other apostles; then he *passed on to* all his listeners that same message. These words indicate the careful and literal way that Christian teachers passed on tradition from one generation to the next.

The central theme of the gospel is given here. It is the key text for the defense of Christianity. The three points that are *of first importance* are as follows:

1. *Christ died for our sins according to the Scriptures.* Without
the truth of this message, Christ's death was worthless, and
those who believe in him are still in their sins and without
hope. However, Christ as the sinless Son of God took the
punishment of sin, "dying for sin" so that those who believe
can have their sins removed. The phrase "according to the
Scriptures" refers to the Old Testament prophecies regarding
this event, such as Psalm 16:8-11 and Isaiah 53:5-6. Christ's
death on the cross was no accident, no afterthought. It had
been part of God's plan from all eternity in order to bring
about the salvation of all who believe.

MIXED HARVEST
Paul restated the gospel because there were unbelievers in the
Corinthian church. Most churches contain people who do not
yet believe. Some are moving in the direction of belief, and
others are simply pretending. Impostors, however, are not to be
removed (see Matthew 13:28-29), for that is the Lord's work
alone. The Good News about Jesus Christ will save us *if* we
firmly believe it and faithfully follow it. The preaching of the
gospel, then, accomplishes two purposes: (1) The message
offers salvation to those who have not yet responded; and
(2) the message challenges believers to remain faithful.
    Pray for the communicators in your church. Perhaps you are
one yourself. Remember that every believer is a living sermon.
Pray that the gospel will be heard and understood clearly in
your fellowship.

---

2. *He was buried.* The fact of Christ's death is revealed in the
fact of his burial. Many have tried to discount the actual
death of Christ, from the false teachers of Paul's day to false
teachers today. But Jesus Christ did die on the cross and was
buried in a tomb. (For more information on the facts of
Jesus' death, see the Life Application Commentary *Mark,* in
Mark 16:9, the chart called "Evidence that Jesus Actually
Died and Arose.")
3. *He was raised on the third day according to the Scriptures.*
Christ "was raised" permanently, forever; his Father raised
him from the dead. He came back to life from being a dead
person in a grave "on the third day" as noted in the Gospels
(Friday afternoon to Sunday morning—three days in Jewish
reckoning of time). This also occurred "according to the
Scriptures." Jesus had quoted the prophet Jonah: "For as
Jonah was three days and three nights in the belly of a huge
fish, so the Son of Man will be three days and three nights in
the heart of the earth" (Matthew 12:40 NIV; see also Jonah

1:17) to show the connection to "three days" as prophesied in the Old Testament. Psalm 16:8-11 and Psalm 110 also foretell the resurrection of the Messiah.

15:5 He was seen by Peter and then by the twelve apostles.ᴺᴸᵀ
Jesus made several appearances to various people after his resurrection, some of which Paul included here. He first mentioned the appearance to *Peter,* noted in Luke 24:34 (see also Mark 16:7). Peter had denied his Lord and then had wept bitterly (Mark 14:72). Jesus forgave Peter and still considered him to be one of his disciples. Jesus had great responsibilities for Peter to fulfill in the church that had not yet been born.

Jesus had also been seen *by the twelve apostles.* The expression "twelve apostles" was a title for the original disciples—sometimes they are called "the Twelve." But this title doesn't always signify that twelve apostles were present. By the time of the Resurrection, Judas Iscariot and another apostle, Thomas, were not present at Christ's first appearance. These appearances are recorded in Mark 16:14; Luke 24:36-43; John 20:19-31.

REBEL HOLDOUTS
There will always be people who say that Jesus didn't rise from the dead. Those who seek to deny the Resurrection are neither courageous nor novel in their thinking. They have nothing but hopelessness and despair to offer those who believe them. Their efforts simply highlight the importance of Christ's victory.

Paul wrote that many people saw Jesus after his resurrection: Peter; the disciples (the Twelve); more than five hundred Christian believers (most of whom were still alive when Paul wrote this, although some had died); James (Jesus' brother); all the apostles; and, finally, Paul himself. The Resurrection is an historical fact. Don't be discouraged by doubters who deny the Resurrection. Be filled with hope because of the knowledge that one day you, and they, will see the living proof when Christ returns.

15:6 After that, he was seen by more than five hundred of his followers at one time, most of whom are still alive, though some have died by now.ᴺᴸᵀ This event is recorded nowhere else. It most likely occurred in Galilee, and the sheer number of eyewitnesses, *more than five hundred,* should cause doubters to stop and think before dismissing the Resurrection accounts of a few followers. All these people saw him *at one time,* and at the time of Paul's writing, *most of* them were *still alive.* Paul could appeal to their testimony to back up his own.

JESUS' APPEARANCES AFTER HIS RESURRECTION

Jesus appeared to

1. Mary Magdalene . . . . Mark 16:9-11; John 20:11-18
2. The other women at the tomb. . . . . Matthew 28:8-10
3. Peter in Jerusalem . . . . Luke 24:34; 1 Corinthians 15:5
4. The two travelers on the road . . . . . Mark 16:12-13; Luke 24:13-35
5. Ten disciples behind closed
   doors . . . . Luke 24:36-43; John 20:19-25
6. All eleven disciples
   (including Thomas). . . . . Mark 16:14; John 20:26-31;
                                             1 Corinthians 15:5
7. Seven disciples while fishing
   on the Sea of Galilee . . . . John 21:1-14
8. Eleven disciples on a
   mountain in Galilee . . . . Matthew 28:16-20; Mark 16:15-18
9. More than 500 believers . . . . 1 Corinthians 15:6
10. Jesus' brother James . . . . 1 Corinthians 15:7
11. Those who watched Jesus
    ascend into heaven . . . . Mark 16:19-20; Luke 24:50-53;
                                             Acts 1:3-9

15:7 Then he appeared to James, then to all the apostles.NRSV This *James* is Jesus' brother (actually, half brother), who at first did not believe that Jesus was the Messiah (John 7:5). After seeing the resurrected Christ, he became a believer (as did Jesus' other brothers, Acts 1:14). James ultimately became a leader of the church in Jerusalem (Acts 15:13). He also wrote the New Testament book of James. (For more information on James, see the Introduction to the Life Application Commentary *James.*) This next mention of *all the apostles* must describe an event separate from that recorded in 15:5, as well as designating the James mentioned here from the two apostles of that name.

15:8 Last of all, I saw him, too, long after the others, as though I had been born at the wrong time.NLT One of the credentials to be an apostle was to have been an eyewitness of Jesus Christ. Paul could call himself an apostle (1:1) because he had seen Jesus *last of all . . . long after the others.* This event is recorded in Acts 9:3-6. The phrase "as though I had been born at the wrong time" (literally, "miscarriage") means that Paul's opportunity to see Jesus Christ was a special case. The other apostles saw Christ before the Resurrection; they lived and traveled with him for nearly three years. Paul was not one of the original twelve apostles, yet Christ appeared to him.

15:9 For I am the least of the apostles and do not even deserve to be called an apostle, because I persecuted the church of God.^{NIV} As a zealous Pharisee, Paul had been an enemy of the Christian church—even to the point of capturing and persecuting believers (see Acts 9:1-3). Here Paul reminded the Corinthian believers of the magnificent grace of God in drawing sinners out of sin and into his kingdom. By calling himself *the least of the apostles,* Paul was not putting himself down (see 2 Corinthians 11:5; Galatians 2:11). Instead, he realized that although all of the apostles had been drawn from sin, Paul had actively *persecuted the church of God.* He fully realized the depth of the error and sin from which he had been saved, so much so that he knew he did *not even deserve to be called an apostle.* Only God's grace had handed him such a privilege and responsibility.

APOSTOLIC ATTITUDE
Paul felt unworthy to be called an apostle of Christ. Though undoubtedly the most influential of the apostles, Paul was deeply humble. He knew that he had worked hard and accomplished much, but only because God had poured kindness and grace upon him. True humility is not convincing yourself that you are worthless but recognizing God's work in you. Take God's perspective on who you are and acknowledge his grace in developing your abilities.

15:10-11 But by the grace of God I am what I am, and his grace to me was not without effect. No, I worked harder than all of them— yet not I, but the grace of God that was with me. Whether, then, it was I or they, this is what we preach, and this is what you believed.^{NIV} Neither Paul nor any of the apostles could take credit for achieving the position of apostle. They had all been called to that position *by the grace of God.* Only by God's "grace"—his undeserved favor poured out on sinners—was Paul saved and enabled to serve. And Paul certainly did so! He wrote of having *worked harder than all of* the other apostles. This was not an arrogant boast because he knew that his hard work was a result of *the grace of God that was with* him. Because of his previous position as a Pharisee (Acts 23:6; Philippians 3:5) and his previous occupation of persecuting Christians, Paul's conversion made him the object of even greater persecution than the other apostles; thus he had to work harder to preach the same message. He wrote to Timothy, "The saying is sure and worthy of full acceptance, that Christ Jesus came into the world to save sinners—of whom I am the foremost. But for that very reason I received mercy, so that in me, as the foremost, Jesus Christ might display the utmost patience, mak-

ing me an example to those who would come to believe in him for
eternal life" (1 Timothy 1:15-16 NRSV).

Whether, then, it was I or they who brought the gospel message,
they all brought the same message as noted in 15:3-4. *This is what
we preach,* explained Paul, and the apostles never strayed from that
message. *This is what you believed,* he reminded them, so they
must not stray from the message that had brought them salvation.

THE RESURRECTION OF THE DEAD / 15:12-34

Christians attempting to share their faith are often shocked by the
world's denial of the possibility of Resurrection. The gospel
remains an irritating and upsetting challenge to the commonly
held views of life and death. Christians are convinced that Jesus'
resurrection *did* happen, and that it changed everything. The
Christian faith comes from Christ's experience, not people's individual feelings or desires. The conviction of the Resurrection
gives believers hope for the future.

**15:12 But if it is preached that Christ has been raised from the
dead, how can some of you say that there is no resurrection of
the dead?**^NIV The gospel message the Corinthians had received
and believed included the basic facts recorded in 15:3-4: "For
what I received I passed on to you as of first importance: that
Christ died for our sins according to the Scriptures, that he was
buried, that he was raised on the third day according to the
Scriptures" (NIV). The words "if it is preached" mean "since it
was preached." The Corinthian believers had accepted the message of the gospel because of the promise of the Resurrection—a
fact central to the Christian faith. In order to believe in their own
resurrection, they had to believe that *Christ has been raised from
the dead.* If they had believed that, why then were some of them
saying *that there is no resurrection of the dead?* Such a belief
contradicted the entire gospel message.

The exact beliefs of those who stated this "no resurrection" are
unknown. They may have held the Greek view that matter was evil
and, therefore, no physical body would rise. Most Greeks did not
believe that people's bodies would be resurrected after death. They
saw the afterlife as something that happened only to the soul.
According to Greek philosophers, the soul was the real person,
imprisoned in a physical body, and at death the soul was released.
There was no immortality for the body, but the soul entered an eternal state. Or they may have taken an overly spiritualized view of
the present state as Christians. They were "spiritual people," so the

body would be unnecessary. Christianity, by contrast, affirms that the body and soul will be united after resurrection.

WHY IS THE RESURRECTION SO IMPORTANT?
The resurrection of Jesus from the dead is the central fact of Christian history. On it, the church is built; without it, there would be no Christian church today. Jesus' resurrection is unique. Other religions have strong ethical systems, concepts about paradise and afterlife, and various holy Scriptures. Only Christianity has a God who became human, literally died for his people, and was raised again in power and glory to rule his church forever.
Why is the Resurrection so important?

- Because Christ was raised from the dead, we know that the kingdom of heaven has broken into earth's history. Our world is now headed for redemption, not disaster. God's mighty power is at work destroying sin, creating new lives, and preparing us for Jesus' second coming.
- Because of the Resurrection, we know that death has been conquered, and we too will be raised from the dead to live forever with Christ.
- The Resurrection gives authority to the church's witness in the world. Look at the early evangelistic sermons in the book of Acts: The apostles' most important message was the proclamation that Jesus Christ had been raised from the dead!
- The Resurrection helps us find meaning even in great tragedy. No matter what happens to us as we walk with the Lord, the Resurrection gives us hope for the future.
- The Resurrection assures us that Christ is alive and ruling his kingdom. He is not legend; he is alive and real.
- God's power that brought Jesus back from the dead is available to us so that we can live for him in an evil world.

Christians can look very different from one another, and they can hold widely varying beliefs about politics, lifestyle, and even theology. But one central belief unites and inspires all true Christians—Jesus Christ rose from the dead!

The church at Corinth was in the heart of Greek culture. Thus many believers had a difficult time believing in a bodily resurrection. Paul wrote this part of his letter to clear up this confusion about the resurrection.

15:13-14 **If there is no resurrection of the dead, then not even Christ has been raised. And if Christ has not been raised, our preaching is useless and so is your faith.**NIV Paul argued that if the resurrection is not possible, then Jesus is still in the grave. If Jesus is still in the grave, then the apostles' *preaching is useless* because they

> Our Lord has written the promise of the resurrection, not in books alone, but in every leaf in springtime. *Martin Luther*

preached a risen Savior. *If Christ has not been raised,* believers' faith is also useless. Why believe in a dead "Savior"? If Jesus is still dead, then his sacrifice did not appease God for believers' sin, and believers have no advocate with the Father (Hebrews 7:25; 8:1). They also have no Comforter in the Holy Spirit, for he was to come when Christ returned to glory (John 16:5, 13-15). They have no hope of eternal life if not even their Savior gained eternal life. They have no reason to believe a gospel message, centered on Resurrection, *if there is no resurrection of the dead.*

CONFIRMATION
The bodily resurrection of Christ is the center of the Christian faith. Because Christ rose from the dead, as he promised, we know that what he said is true and that he is God. The Resurrection affirms the truthfulness of Jesus' life and words. The Resurrection confirms Jesus' unique authority to say, "I am the resurrection and the life" (John 11:25). Because he rose, we have certainty that our sins are forgiven. Because he rose, he lives and represents us before God. Because he rose and defeated death, we know we will also be raised. Christ's resurrection guaranteed both his promise to us and his authority to make it. We must take him at his word and believe.

15:15-16 More than that, we are then found to be false witnesses about God, for we have testified about God that he raised Christ from the dead. But he did not raise him if in fact the dead are not raised. For if the dead are not raised, then Christ has not been raised either.[NIV] If Christ has not been raised from the dead, not only would the apostles' preaching be "useless" (15:14), but the apostles themselves would be considered liars—*false witnesses about God*—because they had been preaching *about God that he raised Christ from the dead.* The apostles had been telling people that God raised Christ from the dead. However, if resurrection is impossible, *if the dead are not raised,* then Christ was not raised. This point is repeated from 15:13 to drive home the point. The Corinthians had to understand the logical implications of the position they had chosen. To no longer believe in the physical resurrection was to throw away the entire gospel message. They could not claim to be Christians without believing in the Resurrection.

15:17 And if Christ has not been raised, then your faith is useless, and you are still under condemnation for your sins.[NLT] Again Paul proclaimed that *if Christ has not been raised, then your faith is useless* (see 15:14). They have no reason to have faith if they take the Resurrection out of that faith. In addition to taking away the hope of future life with God, refusing to believe that Jesus rose from the grave means that Christians are *still under condemnation for [their] sins*. If Jesus died and was never raised, then his death did nothing to accomplish justification. God raising him from the dead showed acceptance of Christ's sacrifice. If God left Jesus in the grave, then the sacrifice was not accepted and no one has received cleansing from sin. The condemnation for sin is death (Romans 6:23). To still be under condemnation means that all people will be given the ultimate penalty for their sins.

HARD TRUTH
Why does Paul say believers should be pitied if there were only earthly value to Christianity? In Paul's day, Christianity often brought a person persecution, ostracism from family, and, in many cases, poverty. There were few tangible benefits from being a Christian in that society. It was certainly not a step up the social or career ladder. Even more important, however, is the fact that if Christ had not been resurrected from death, Christians could not be forgiven for their sins and would have no hope of eternal life.

In many places in the world today, those who believe in Christ still pay a heavy price. Some are dying for their faith. But for many, Christianity is little more than a convenient faith. If following Christ doesn't place you at odds with the world around you in some way, examine the depth of your roots.

15:18-19 **In that case, all who have died believing in Christ have perished! And if we have hope in Christ only for this life, we are the most miserable people in the world.**^{NLT} Christians carry with them, even through persecution and death, the promise of eternal life with God. Yet if Christ was never raised from the dead, and if there is no hope of resurrection, then *all who have died believing in Christ have perished!* If all the preachers lied (15:15) and no one will be raised, then not only is faith meaningless for this life, it is meaningless in death. Those who believed in Christ believed a lie; those who died because of persecution for their faith perished for no reason. The consequences of believing the lie that there will be no resurrection shake the very foundations of the Christian faith. Paul pointed out the silliness of the argument—*if we have hope in Christ only for this life, we are the most miserable people in the world*. If the only promise of the Christian faith applies to this life, then why believe in it? Why believe in a faith that brought—in this culture and even still in many places in the world—persecution, sorrow, death, ostracism, separation? Without the resurrection, there would be no hope for final judgment and justice or hope for a final dwelling place with

EVIDENCE THAT JESUS ACTUALLY DIED AND AROSE

This evidence demonstrates Jesus' uniqueness in history and proves that he is God's Son. No one else was able to predict his own resurrection and then accomplish it.

Erroneous Expla-nations for the Empty Tomb	Evidence against These Explanations	References
Jesus was only unconscious and later revived.	A Roman soldier told Pilate that Jesus was dead.	Mark 15:44-45
	The Roman soldiers did not break Jesus' legs because he had already died, and one of them pierced Jesus' side with a spear.	John 19:32-34
	Joseph of Arimathea and Nicodemus wrapped Jesus' body and placed it in the tomb.	John 19:38-42
The women made a mistake and went to the wrong tomb.	Mary Magdalene and Mary the mother of Joses saw Jesus placed in the tomb.	Matthew 27:59-61; Mark 15:47; Luke 23:55
	On Sunday morning, Peter and John also went to the same tomb.	John 20:3-9
Unknown thieves stole Jesus' body.	The tomb was sealed and guarded by Roman sol-diers.	Matthew 27:65-66
The disciples stole Jesus' body	The tomb was guarded and sealed.	Matthew 27:66

God. There would be nothing but death to look forward to. If the end is the same for everyone, why not live like the pagans in sensual pleasure (15:32)? Why deny oneself? Why be miserable if the other choices bring the same result?

15:20 But the fact is that Christ has been raised from the dead. He has become the first of a great harvest of those who will be raised to life again.NLT However, the above argument is moot because *the fact is that Christ has been raised from the dead.* The hypothetical "if" statements in the previous verses concede to the certain facts of history. Christians may indeed face difficulty, but the fact of the Resurrection changes everything. Because Christ was raised from the dead, *he has become the first of a great harvest of those who will be raised to life again.* The "first of a great harvest" (also called the firstfruits) was the first part of the harvest that faithful Jews would bring to the temple as an offering (Leviticus 23:10). Although Christ was not the first to rise from the dead (he raised Lazarus and others), he was the first to be raised to never die again. He is the forerunner for those who believe in him, the proof of their eventual resurrection to eternal life.

15:21-22 **So you see, just as death came into the world through a man, Adam, now the resurrection from the dead has begun through another man, Christ. Everyone dies because all of us are related to Adam, the first man. But all who are related to Christ, the other man, will be given new life.**NLT *Death came into the world* as a consequence of the sin of one man, *Adam* (Genesis 3:17-19). Adam sinned against God and brought alienation from God and death to all humanity. Sin resulted in death. All human beings are *related to Adam* and have two characteristics in common: They are sinners; and they will die. By capitulating to sin, Adam allowed the whole human race to succumb to death. Death is inescapable; it comes to every living thing. And the reign of death over creation began because of Adam's sin. Paul contrasted the roles of two single agents: Adam and Christ. Adam's sin brought condemnation and death to all; Christ's sinless sacrifice and resurrection brought *resurrection from the dead* to all who *are related to Christ* through accepting his sacrifice on their behalf. Those who believe in him *will be given new life.* This same idea is explained in Romans 5:12-21.

DEATH AND LIFE
Adam's sin allowed death to claim every human's life; Christ's death challenged that claim and nullified it in the Resurrection. Adam "gave" us all death; Christ offers life to all. In other words, real life can only be found in Christ. At conception, we receive as part of our human inheritance the gift of death; at conversion, we receive Christ's gift of eternal life. The choice is between death and life. How tragic that so many make the wrong choice. What will *you* choose—life or death?

15:23 **But there is an order to this resurrection: Christ was raised first; then when Christ comes back, all his people will be raised.**NLT Paul wanted to clarify, however, that *there is an order to this resurrection.* It had not already happened, as perhaps some of the false teachers were claiming. Rather, *Christ was raised first,* three days after his crucifixion, and he is the "first of a great harvest" (15:20 NLT). That "harvest" will be taken in *when Christ comes back* at his second coming. At that time, *his people,* those who believed in him as Savior, *will be raised* from death to eternal life.

15:24-25 **Then the end will come, when he hands over the kingdom to God the Father after he has destroyed all dominion, authority and power. For he must reign until he has put all his enemies under his feet.**[NIV] The words "then the end will come" did not mean that the end would come (or had come) immediately after Christ's resurrection. This is an unspecified time of an event still to occur. At the time of Christ's second coming, "the end will come," and the resurrected Christ will conquer all evil, including death. (See Revelation 20:14 for words about the final destruction of death.) Christ will destroy *all dominion, authority and power* that oppose God and then hand *over the kingdom to God the Father.* At Christ's resurrection, Christ began the destruction of Satan and all his dominion. At the resurrection of the dead, all Satan's power will be broken. Christ *must reign* because God has ordained it so; what God has said cannot be changed. The word "must" has the sense of "will definitely without a doubt"; Christ will reign as the ultimate ruler, having *put all his enemies under his feet.* This phrase is used in the Old Testament to refer to total conquest (see Psalm 110:1).

Because the resurrection of Christ is an accomplished fact and because the promise of the resurrection is a future fact, the promise of Christ's ultimate and final reign can be trusted as fact and anticipated by every believer.

TEAMWORK
Although God the Father and God the Son are equal (Philippians 2:6), each has a special work to do and an area of sovereign control (15:28). Christ is not inferior to the Father, but his work is to defeat all evil on earth. First, he defeated sin and death on the cross, and in the last days, he will defeat Satan and all evil. World events may seem out of control, and justice may seem scarce. But God is in control, allowing evil to remain for a time until he sends Jesus to earth again. Then Christ will present to God a perfect new world.

We, too, have special roles to play in God's plan. Much of Christ's work is done *in* us, and requires our cooperation and obedience. To also participate in Christ's work, we must allow his words and presence to direct our relationships and decisions.

15:26 **The last enemy to be destroyed is death.**[NRSV] While the enemies in 15:25 were not named, one *last enemy* was here named— *death.* Death is every living being's enemy, the common fate of all humanity. Death is the last enemy that always wins. But

Christ will destroy death! At the Cross and through the Resurrection, Christ has already defeated death. Yet people still die. For those who believe in Christ, however, death is merely a doorway into eternal life. Finally one day, there will be no more death. John proclaimed this in the book of Revelation: "And death and the grave were thrown into the lake of fire" (20:14).

15:27 For he "has put everything under his feet." Now when it says that "everything" has been put under him, it is clear that this does not include God himself, who put everything under Christ.[NIV] As noted in 15:24-25, the one ultimately in charge is God the Father. This verse sounds very much like Psalm 8:6: "You made him ruler over the works of your hands; you put everything under his feet" (NIV). The first "he" refers to God, who *"has put everything under [Christ's] feet."* Because God did this, *it is clear* (or should have been to Paul's readers) that the word "everything" *does not include God himself.* God gave the Son supreme authority over everything, except God himself.

15:28 When he has done this, then the Son himself will be made subject to him who put everything under him, so that God may be all in all.[NIV] *When he has done this,* when the Son has toppled all evil powers and when God has placed everything under the Son's feet, *then the Son himself will be made subject to* God. "God" here refers to "God the Father." No one can take God's place, not even the Son. This must happen *so that God may be all in all.* Some have used this verse to attempt to prove the inferiority of Christ (that he was not equal with God). But this verse is not about the person, nature, or being of God (his essence) as it relates to Christ. Instead, this verse is speaking of the work or mission of Christ, whereby he willingly obeyed the Father by subjecting the government of the world first to himself, then symbolically and willingly placing it under God's control. In these words, Paul was not attempting to take the three persons of the Trinity and decide their relative importance. Their essential nature is always one and the same; however, the authority rests through the work each has accomplished. God sent the Son; the Son will finish the work and then will turn redeemed humanity back over to God.

15:29 Now if there is no resurrection, what will those do who are baptized for the dead? If the dead are not raised at all, why are people baptized for them?[NIV] To further emphasize his point about the fact of the resurrection, Paul returned to his conditional "if" clauses. *If there is no resurrection,* he asked, *what will those do who are baptized for the dead?* Apparently, some believers had been baptized on behalf of others who had died unbaptized. Nothing more is known about this practice, but it obviously affirms a belief in resurrection. Corinthian believers may have been practicing a sort of vicarious baptism for the sake of believers who had died before being baptized. The "dead" certainly referred to those who had come to faith, not to unbelievers who had died, or Paul would have condemned the practice. Paul was not promoting baptism for the dead; he was continuing to illustrate his argument that the resurrection is a reality. (Certain groups, such as Mormons, who encourage baptism for the dead today, do so on very flimsy biblical grounds.) Paul's apparent lack of concern over this situation probably means that, though theologically incorrect, the practice was basically harmless. Paul could have written disapprovingly of this practice, but pointing out the glaring inconsistency of their rejecting the afterlife while baptizing for the dead was sufficient. Paul had deeper theological issues to straighten out—at this point, the fact of the resurrection. If there is a resurrection, then all believers will be raised (and all who truly believed will be saved whether they have been baptized or not). If there is no resurrection, however, as some had contended, then why bother with this ritual?

LIFE CONSISTENCY
If death ends it all, enjoying the moment would be all that matters. But Christians know that life continues beyond the grave and that life on earth is only a preparation for our life that will never end. What you do today matters for eternity. In light of eternity, sin is a foolish gamble. Your belief in the resurrection will affect your view of the future. It ought to also affect how you live today.

15:30-31 **And why are we putting ourselves in danger every hour? I die every day! That is as certain, brothers and sisters, as my boasting of you—a boast that I make in Christ Jesus our Lord.**NRSV If there is no resurrection, believers are indeed the "most miserable people in the world" (15:19 NLT). Why should the apostles bother to put themselves *in danger every hour,* dying *every day* for the sake of the gospel message. To suffer and face danger for the sake of a message that only has "benefits" for this life would be foolish indeed. "I die every day" refers to Paul's daily exposure to danger. Why would any sane person do this for the sake of a gospel that only ends in death, just like anything else? This constant danger *is as certain . . . as [Paul's] boasting* about the Corinthians. Despite all that Paul had to correct and rebuke in them, he genuinely loved the

Corinthian believers and boasted of their faith. He could *make* that boast *in Christ Jesus our Lord,* knowing that Christ had saved them and that Paul had been their spiritual father (4:15). See also 2 Corinthians 11:23-27.

15:32 **And what value was there in fighting wild beasts—those men of Ephesus—if there will be no resurrection from the dead? If there is no resurrection, "Let's feast and get drunk, for tomorrow we die!"**ᴺᴸᵀ Some have taken the reference to *fighting wild beasts* to literally mean that Paul had been placed in the arena—a vicious form of entertainment where prisoners would be placed in a stadium and wild beasts sent in to tear them apart. Paul probably meant this metaphorically, however, as noted in the translation above, referring, instead, to *those men of Ephesus.* The human enemies that Paul had faced in Ephesus had been as vicious as wild beasts (see Acts 19). When Paul was in Ephesus, Demetrius stirred up people against Paul. Paul preached against Artemis, the goddess of fertility, and was disrupting Demetrius's silver business (he made idols). Demetrius caused a furious riot against Paul.

Paul repeated the question, *If there will be no resurrection from the dead,* then *what value was there in* standing up for his faith against those in Ephesus who wanted to kill him (Acts 19:31)? Why bother standing for anything at all? If there is nothing more to look forward to than simply to one day die and return to dust, then why deny oneself? Instead, it would make far more sense for everyone to *feast and get drunk* (see also Isaiah 22:13). Life with no meaning leaves one with the need to simply indulge oneself and get all one can for enjoyment here and now.

15:33 **Don't be fooled by those who say such things, for "bad company corrupts good character."**ᴺᴸᵀ Those who denied the resurrection could not possibly be true believers, for this entire chapter explains why the resurrection is central to the Christian faith. Paul told the Corinthian believers not to *be fooled by those who say such things*—those who denied the resurrection and told the believers to "feast and get drunk" (15:32). This is quoted from a proverb in a comedy by the Greek playwright Menander, titled *Thais;* it was used by Paul to make a point to his Greek audience. The bit of worldly wisdom, *"bad company corrupts good character,"* means that keeping company with those who deny the resurrection will corrupt true believers and hurt the testimony of the church.

15:34 **Come to your senses and stop sinning. For to your shame I say that some of you don't even know God.**ᴺᴸᵀ Paul's final words about this issue were simply that the Corinthians should *come to [their] senses* (literally, "to wake up out of a drunken stupor"). If they would take the time to think about it, they would realize, as Paul had argued earlier, that it would be senseless to live for a faith that offered nothing after death. To deny the resurrection amounted to *sinning,* for it denied the truth of the claims of Christ and the promises of God. It was to their *shame* that some among them did not *even know God.* To not understand and believe the doctrine of the resurrection meant to not understand anything about God, for the doctrine is central to all that God has done for sinful humanity.

THE RESURRECTION BODY / 15:35-58

Our present bodies have been wonderfully designed for life in this world, but they are are perishable and prone to decay. In a sense, each person lives as a prototype of his or her final body version. Our resurrection bodies will be transformed versions of our present bodies. Those spiritual bodies will not be limited by the laws of nature. This does not necessarily mean we will be superpeople, but our bodies will be different from and more capable than our present, earthly bodies. Our spiritual bodies will not be weak, will never get sick, and will never die. The very possibilities inspire anticipation, excitement, and praise to the God who can do all things!

15:35-37 **But someone may ask, "How will the dead be raised? What kind of bodies will they have?" What a foolish question! When you put a seed into the ground, it doesn't grow into a plant unless it dies first. And what you put into the ground is not the plant that will grow, but only a dry little seed of wheat or whatever it is you are planting.**[NLT] Paul had already argued for the truth of the resurrection. Those who might still be skeptical may have further questions about this resurrection, so Paul asked two such questions himself in order to answer them: (1) *How will the dead be raised?* (2) *What kind of bodies will they have?* How could it be possible for a dead body to come back to life; and if it could do so, then what kind of body would it be?

To Paul, these were *foolish* questions. The answers should have been obvious from nature itself. Paul compared the resurrection of believers' bodies with the growth in a garden. A seed placed into the ground *doesn't grow into a plant unless it dies first.* The plant that grows looks very different from the seed because God gives it a new "body." Jesus had given the same metaphor for his own death in John 12:24, "Unless a grain of wheat falls into the earth and dies, it remains just a single grain;

but if it dies it bears much fruit" (NRSV). Jesus was referring to
what his death would accomplish, but his analogy was the same
as Paul's. Both show the necessity of death before new life. Just
as *a dry little seed,* such as a seed of wheat, *doesn't grow into a
plant unless it dies first,* so new bodies will not be obtained until
the earthly bodies have died. And those new bodies will be different from the present bodies.

OUTCOME
Paul launched into a discussion about what believers'
resurrected bodies would be like. If you could select your own
body, what kind would you choose—strong, athletic, beautiful?
Paul explained that believers will be recognized in their
resurrected bodies, yet they will be better than ever imagined,
for they will be made to live forever. People will still have
personalities and individualities, but these will be perfected
through Christ's work. The Bible does not reveal everything that
resurrected bodies will be able to do, but they will be perfect,
without sickness or disease (see Philippians 3:21). Every guess
on our part must be tempered by the knowledge that God will
do better than we can imagine!

**15:38-39 But God gives it a body as he has chosen, and to each kind of
seed its own body. Not all flesh is alike, but there is one flesh
for human beings, another for animals, another for birds, and
another for fish.**NRSV There are different kinds of bodies—for
people, animals, fish, birds. Paul was preparing the foundation
for his point that bodies before the resurrection can be different
from bodies after the resurrection.

**15:40-41 There are also heavenly bodies and there are earthly bod-
ies; but the splendor of the heavenly bodies is one kind, and
the splendor of the earthly bodies is another. The sun has
one kind of splendor, the moon another and the stars
another; and star differs from star in splendor.**NIV Furthermore, the *heavenly bodies* (the sun, moon, and stars) differ
greatly from *earthly bodies.* Each kind of body has its own kind
of substance created and controlled by God. Each is appropriate to its sphere of existence, and each has its own kind of
splendor or radiance. God made many different types of bodies; certainly he can arrange and govern the existence of the resurrection body.

**15:42-44 So will it be with the resurrection of the dead. The body that
is sown is perishable, it is raised imperishable; it is sown in
dishonor, it is raised in glory; it is sown in weakness, it is
raised in power; it is sown a natural body, it is raised a spiri-**

tual body. If there is a natural body, there is also a spiritual body.NIV God's creation power will continue as dead bodies are resurrected and transformed into new bodies. Paul's continued use of the term "is sown" shows that he still has the seed from 15:36-37 in mind. Like a seed that is sown and then grows into a glorious new plant, *so it will be with the resurrection of the dead.* Believers' present physical bodies will be different from their resurrection bodies.

First, physical bodies are *perishable,* but *raised* bodies will be *imperishable.* Every human's physical body is going to "perish" (die). Death eventually takes everyone. Those raised with Christ, however, will have bodies that will never die. These eternal bodies will live forever.

Physical bodies are *sown in dishonor* but *raised in glory.* A dead body, by its very nature, has nothing honorable about it. But the raised body will have a "glory" that far surpasses the beauty of a flower (as compared to its seed). It will not be a raised corpse like what one might see in horror movies; it will be a remade body, far more glorious than the physical body had ever been.

Physical bodies are *sown in weakness* but *raised in power.* While the Greeks might have honored those with perfectly trained, muscular bodies, when death strikes, every body is rendered completely weak and powerless. But the raised body will be raised by the power of God himself and will have power given to it by God.

Every physical body *is sown a natural body* but *raised a spiritual body.* The "natural" body *(soma psuchikon)* is suited to life in the present world; however, such a body is not fit for the world to come. That future world, where Christ will reign in his kingdom, will require a "spiritual" body *(soma pneumatikon).* Paul did not mean that this will be "spiritual" as opposed to physical or material, for that would contradict all that Paul has just written about resurrected bodies. Believers will not become "spirits." Instead, "spiritual" refers to a body that suits a new, spiritual life, just as our present bodies (Greek *psuchikon*) suit our lives as "souls" *(psuche).* Each believer will no longer have *a natural body,* like Adam, designed to live on this earth; instead, each will have *a spiritual body,* like Christ had after his resurrection (15:48-49).

15:45 The Scriptures tell us, "The first man, Adam, became a living person." But the last Adam—that is, Christ—is a life-giving Spirit.NLT Paul quoted *the Scriptures* to point out the difference between these two kinds of bodies. Genesis 2:7 speaks of *the first* *man, Adam,* becoming *a living person.* Adam was made from the dust of the ground and given the breath of life from God. Every human being since that time shares the same characteristics. However, *the last Adam—that is, Christ—is a life-giving Spirit.* Just as Adam was the first of the human race, so Christ is the first of those who will be raised from the dead to eternal life. Because Christ rose from the dead, he is "a life-giving spirit" who entered into a new form of existence. He is the source of the spiritual life that will result in believers' resurrection. Christ's new glorified human body now suits his new, glorified, spiritual life—just as Adam's human body was suitable to his natural life. When believers are resurrected, God will give them transformed, eternal bodies suited to eternal life.

15:46-47 **The spiritual did not come first, but the natural, and after that the spiritual.**NIV People have *natural* life first; that is, they are born into this earth and live here. Only from there do they then obtain *spiritual* life. Paul may have been contradicting a particular false teaching by this statement. He illustrated this point by continuing: **Adam, the first man, was made from the dust of the earth, while Christ, the second man, came from heaven.**NLT The natural man, *Adam,* came first on this earth and *was made from the dust of the earth.* While it is true that Christ has existed from eternity past, he is here called *the second man* because he *came from heaven* to earth many years after Adam. Christ came as a human baby with a body like all other humans, but he did not originate from the dust of the earth as had Adam. He "came from heaven."

15:48-49 **Every human being has an earthly body just like Adam's, but our heavenly bodies will be just like Christ's. Just as we are now like Adam, the man of the earth, so we will someday be like Christ, the man from heaven.**NLT Because all humanity is bound up with Adam, so *every human being has an earthly body just like Adam's.* Earthly bodies are fitted for life on this earth, yet they have the characteristics of being limited by death, disease, and weakness (15:42-44). Believers can know with certainty, however, that their *heavenly bodies will be just like Christ's*—imperishable, eternal, glorious, and filled with power (15:42-44). At this time, all are *like Adam;* one day, all believers will be *like Christ* (Philippians 3:21). The apostle John wrote to the believers, "Dear friends, now we are children of God, and what we will be has not yet been made known. But we know that when he appears, we shall be like him, for we shall see him as he is" (1 John 3:2 NIV).

PHYSICAL BODIES AND RESURRECTION BODIES

All people have bodies—each looks different; each has different strengths
and weaknesses. But as physical, earthly bodies, they are all alike. All
believers are promised life after death and bodies like Christ's
(15:45-49)—resurrection bodies.

Physical Bodies	Resurrection Bodies
Perishable	Imperishable
Sown in dishonor	Raised in glory
Sown in weakness	Raised in power
Natural	Spiritual
From the dust	From heaven

15:50 **What I am saying, dear brothers and sisters, is that flesh and
blood cannot inherit the Kingdom of God. These perishable
bodies of ours are not able to live forever.**NLT After describing
the different natures of the two types of bodies—those before resurrection and those after—Paul explained his point. The resurrected bodies have to be different from these present, physical
bodies because *flesh and blood cannot inherit the Kingdom of
God.* These bodies cannot go into God's eternal kingdom because
these present bodies were not made *to live forever*—otherwise
they would. So God has prepared new bodies that will live forever. The resurrection is a fact; new bodies ready for life in eternity is also a fact.

REASON FOR HOPE
Everyone faces limitations. Those who have physical, mental,
or emotional disabilities are especially aware of this fact. Some
may be blind, but they can see a new way to live. Some may
be deaf, but they can hear God's Good News. Some may be
lame, but they can walk in God's love. In addition, they have
the encouragement that those disabilities are only temporary.
All believers will be given new bodies when Christ returns. And
these bodies will be without disabilities, never to die or become
sick. Let this truth give you hope in your suffering.

15:51-52 **Listen, I tell you a mystery: We will not all sleep, but we
will all be changed—in a flash, in the twinkling of an eye, at
the last trumpet. For the trumpet will sound, the dead will
be raised imperishable, and we will be changed.**NIV With
great emphasis Paul passed on to these Corinthians *a mystery*—
knowledge given to him by divine revelation from Christ. This
information should transform their lives as they look forward to

what God had promised them. If flesh and blood cannot inherit the kingdom (15:50), then what about those who are still alive at the return of Christ? Paul answered the implicit question. The phrase "we will not all sleep" means that some Christians will still be alive at the time of Christ's return. They will not have to die before they get their new resurrection bodies. (For further discussion of these new bodies, see 2 Corinthians 5:1-10.) Instead, they *will all be changed,* transformed immediately, *in the twinkling of an eye* (see 1 Thessalonians 4:13-18). A trumpet blast will usher in the new heaven and earth (Revelation 11:15). The Jews would understand the significance of this because trumpets were always blown to signal the start of great festivals and other extraordinary events (Numbers 10:10). At that time, when the trumpet sounds and Christ returns, *the dead will be raised imperishable,* out of the graves with their new bodies. Those still alive *will be changed,* also receiving their new bodies. This change will happen instantly for all Christians, whether they are dead or alive. All will be made ready to go with Christ.

15:53 For our perishable earthly bodies must be transformed into heavenly bodies that will never die.NLT Because "flesh and blood cannot inherit the Kingdom of God" (15:50 NLT), and because Christians are promised eternal life in God's kingdom, then their present *perishable earthly bodies must be transformed into heavenly bodies that will never die.* The perishable bodies will not be thrown away or abandoned; instead, they will be "transformed." Each person will still be recognizable, will still be the person God created him or her to be, but each will be made perfect with a body that will be able to live forever in the kingdom.

15:54-55 When this happens—when our perishable earthly bodies have been transformed into heavenly bodies that will never die—then at last the Scriptures will come true: "Death is swallowed up in victory. O death, where is your victory? O death, where is your sting?"NLT The ultimate enemy of every human body is *death.* It takes every person; it cannot be escaped. For those who have no hope in Christ, death is the end of everything, the ultimate nothingness, the reason for living as one pleases in this life. Christians have been given an entirely different perspective. For believers, death is not the end; it is merely a doorway into eternal life. Most Christians will experience death; some who are alive at the time of Christ's return will not themselves face death but will have known plenty who did. But *when our perishable earthly bod-*

WHAT WE KNOW ABOUT ETERNITY

The Bible devotes much less space to describing eternity than it does to convincing people that eternal life is available as a free gift from God. Most of the brief descriptions of eternity would be more accurately called hints, since they use terms and ideas from present experience to describe what we cannot fully grasp until we are there ourselves. These references hint at aspects of what our future will be like if we have accepted Christ's gift of eternal life.

Reference	Description
John 14:2-3	A place prepared for us
John 20:19, 26	Unlimited by physical properties (1 Corinthians 15:35-39)
1 John 3:2	We will be like Jesus.
1 Corinthians 15	We will have new bodies.
1 Corinthians 2:9	Our experience will be wonderful.
Revelation 21:1	A new environment
Revelation 21:3	A new experience of God's presence (1 Corinthians 13:12)
Revelation 21:4	New emotions
Revelation 21:4	There will be no more death.

---

ies have been transformed into heavenly bodies that will never die, then the final victory over death will have been accomplished. Death was defeated at the resurrection of Christ, but total victory over death will not be accomplished until human beings—made from the dust of the earth, just like Adam— are given bodies that defy death. When this happens, *the Scriptures will come true.* Paul quoted from Isaiah 25:8 and Hosea 13:14—God's promises that one day death itself will no longer carry *victory* or *sting* because death will be no more (Revelation 21–22).

15:56-57 The sting of death is sin, and the power of sin is the law. But thanks be to God! He gives us the victory through our Lord Jesus Christ.[NIV] If it were not for *sin,* then there would be no *sting of death.* If it were not for *the law,* then sin would have no *power.* But the law declares sin, and the wages of sin is death (see Romans 6:23; 7:7-20). Because the law set standards that cannot be reached, all people are condemned as sinners. For those who have not had their sins pardoned at the cross of Christ, death is not a passage to eternal life but an enemy with a terrible "sting." It is not annihilation or nothingness, it is the doorway to judgment. But for those who have come to Christ

as Savior, who have laid their sins at the cross and been pardoned, they can say *thanks be to God.* They have been given
victory over sin and death *through [the] Lord Jesus Christ.* Paul
wrote to the Romans:

> *For when we died with Christ we were set free from the*
> *power of sin. And since we died with Christ, we know we*
> *will also share his new life. We are sure of this because*
> *Christ rose from the dead, and he will never die again.*
> *Death no longer has any power over him. He died once to*
> *defeat sin, and now he lives for the glory of God. . . . For*
> *the wages of sin is death, but the free gift of God is*
> *eternal life through Christ Jesus our Lord. (Romans*
> *6:7-10, 23 NLT)*

COUNTERVICTORY
Satan seemed to be victorious in the Garden of Eden (Genesis
3) and at the cross of Jesus. The trophy was death. But God
turned Satan's apparent victory into defeat when Jesus Christ
rose from the dead (Colossians 2:15; Hebrews 2:14-15). Thus
death is no longer a source of dread or fear. It has ceased to
be the proof of Satan's power. Christ overcame it, and one day
we will also. The law will no longer make sinners out of us who
cannot keep it. Death has been defeated, and we have hope
beyond the grave.

**15:58 Therefore, my beloved, be steadfast, immovable, always
excelling in the work of the Lord, because you know that in
the Lord your labor is not in vain.**[NRSV] Because of these promises—of future resurrection, of living eternally in the kingdom,
of preparation for that kingdom with new bodies that will be
fashioned by God himself—believers have motivation and
responsibilities for life now lived in their perishable bodies.
The time on earth is valuable—we have much work to do for
the kingdom. Others must be invited to join; believers must be
taught to grow in the Lord. Because of the promise of the
future, life is not meant to be spent as a self-indulgent party,
where people "eat, drink, and be merry." Every job done for the
Lord *is not in vain.* It is not a fruitless exercise that ends in
death like everything else. Work *in the Lord* will result in taking part in the great promises and rewards of God's kingdom.
So believers should *be steadfast* in their faith, not wavering or
doubting; they should be *immovable,* not listening to the whims
of false teachers but standing firm; and *always excelling in the*

work of the Lord, serving him to the utmost, knowing that great reward awaits.

KEEP ON
Because of the resurrection, nothing believers do for the Lord is in vain. Sometimes we hesitate to do good because we don't see any results. But if we can maintain a heavenly perspective, we will understand that we often will not see the good that comes from our efforts. If we truly believe that Christ has won the ultimate victory, that belief must affect the way we live right now. Don't let discouragement over an apparent lack of results keep you from working. Do the good that you have opportunity to do, knowing that your work will have eternal results.

---

1 Corinthians 16

Paul had just said that no good deed is ever in vain (15:58). In this chapter, he mentions some practical deeds that have value for all Christians. The Corinthians had been asked to join with Christians in other areas to support the church in Jerusalem. Paul could hardly have found a more practical example of the unity of the body of Christ (12:12-13) than in his desire that all the churches give to help a suffering body of believers.

16:1 Now about the money being collected for the Christians in Jerusalem: You should follow the same procedures I gave to the churches in Galatia.NLT The words "now about" indicate that this was another topic about which the Corinthians had asked (see also 7:1; 8:1; 12:1). Paul must have spoken or written to them earlier about this, so that they knew they would be giving and to whom. Their questions apparently focused on how to go about collecting the funds. They apparently wondered how to handle *the money being collected for the Christians in Jerusalem.*

The Christians in Jerusalem were suffering from poverty. While the reason is unknown, it may have had to do with a famine, such as the one mentioned in Acts 11:28-29 when the believers in Antioch had sent help to the church in Jerusalem. That collection had been carried by Paul himself and Barnabas (Acts 11:30). Apparently, the Jerusalem church was still suffering, so Paul continued to collect money from other churches to send to Jerusalem (see Romans 15:25-31; 2 Corinthians 8:4; 9:1-15). Paul advised the Corinthian believers to *follow the same procedures* that he had given *to the churches in Galatia.* This collection was a widespread effort involving many of the churches. The procedures given to the churches in Galatia are outlined in the following verses, for Paul explained that the Corinthians would be asked to follow the same plan. He suggested that the believers set aside a certain amount each week and give it to the church until he arrived to take it on to Jerusalem. Paul had planned to go straight to Corinth from Ephesus, but he changed his mind

(2 Corinthians 1–2). When he finally arrived, he took the gift and delivered it to the Jerusalem church (Acts 21:18; 24:17).

Paul may have had another purpose in mind for the collection. He probably saw it as a way to provoke the unbelieving Jews in Jerusalem to belief that the Messiah had come. Paul believed that the conversion of the Gentiles would bring the Jews to Christ (see Romans 11:11-24). The Jews would see the gift as a fulfillment of Isaiah 2:2-4; 60:6-7, 11; and Micah 4:13, where it was promised that the Gentiles would bring gifts to Jerusalem.

PRACTICAL GENEROSITY

Paul's simple instructions about giving still apply today. We tend to think of generosity as spontaneous giving. Often, it is. But generosity can also be demonstrated by the commitment to give regularly to those needs that are ongoing. Certain projects may require a single gift. A struggling church or group of believers may need temporary help over several months. Pastors, missionaries, and others can do so only as other believers give financial and prayer support for those ministries. In what ways have you made giving a regular part of worship?

16:2 On every Lord's Day, each of you should put aside some amount of money in relation to what you have earned and save it for this offering. Don't wait until I get there and then try to collect it all at once.[NLT] The first procedure that the Corinthian believers should implement right away was to ask each person (or family) to *put aside some amount of money . . . and save it for this offering.* This was to be done *on every Lord's Day.* Some have suggested that this offering was to be kept at home, but Paul's mention of setting it aside on Sunday (the day when the believers met together for worship—see Acts 20:7) probably means that the believers were to bring the amount that had been set aside that week and place it in a special offering at church. That offering, in turn, would be held until Paul's arrival. Paul stipulated that everyone must give *(each of you)*; no one was exempt. But he did not stipulate how much everyone should give; instead, each should give *in relation to what* he or she had earned.

By implementing this plan, the money would be ready and waiting whenever Paul arrived (which at this point was still an uncertain date). Paul would not have to personally make any sort of appeal; he did not really want to be there when the collections were made. Paul did not want to have anyone concerned about what might appear to be his own interest in the money. He also did not want the church to be reduced to having to *try to collect it all at once.* Instead, the entire effort would be well planned and appropriately carried out so as to help the Christians in Jerusalem as generously as possible.

THE POOR
Believers are expected to act on behalf of the poor. Here are eight common excuses for not helping the poor:
1. They don't deserve help. They got themselves into poverty; let them get themselves out.
2. God's call to help the poor applies to another time.
3. We don't know any poor people.
4. I have my own needs.
5. Any money I give will be wasted, stolen, or spent on other things. The poor will never see it.
6. I may become a victim myself.
7. I don't know where to start, and I don't have the time.
8. My little bit won't make any difference.

Instead of making lame excuses, ask what can be done to help the poor. Does your church have programs that help the needy? Could you volunteer to work with a community group that fights poverty? As one individual, you may not be able to accomplish much, but join up with similarly motivated people and watch mountains begin to move.

16:3-4 **When I come I will write letters of recommendation for the messengers you choose to deliver your gift to Jerusalem. And if it seems appropriate for me also to go along, then we can travel together.**NLT To further distance himself from the offering, Paul suggested that the Corinthian church choose their own *messengers . . . to deliver* the gift to Jerusalem. These men are listed in Acts 20:4. Paul would *write letters of recommendation for* those messengers, so that when they arrived at the Jerusalem church their mission would be heralded by Paul himself and the church could readily welcome them. Paul might end up traveling with them *if it seem[ed] appropriate* (or "advisable"; NIV).

▧ *PAUL'S FINAL INSTRUCTIONS / 16:5-24*

As the Corinthians awaited Paul's next visit, they were directed to be on their guard against spiritual dangers, stand firm in the faith, behave courageously, be strong, and do everything with kindness and in love. This list could be called a Christian's job description. Today, as believers await the return of Christ, they should follow the same instructions.

16:5-6 **I will visit you after passing through Macedonia—for I intend to pass through Macedonia—and perhaps I will stay with you or even spend the winter, so that you may send me on my**

way, wherever I go.^{NRSV} Paul was writing this letter near the end
of his three-year ministry in Ephesus (see Introduction and Introductory Map). It may have been tempting for Paul to take the
next ship across the Aegean Sea from Ephesus to Corinth in order
to deal with the problems and squelch those who said he was
avoiding them (4:18); however, Paul explained that he would
indeed visit with them *after passing through Macedonia* (see
Acts 20:1-2). Because Paul had intended to go to Macedonia, he
would do so. In the meantime, he would send Timothy (4:17;
16:10) and Titus (2 Corinthians 7:13). But when he did arrive, he
would *stay* with them for a time, perhaps even spending the
entire *winter* there. This would not be a "passing visit" (16:7);
these were not the words of a man afraid to deal with the problems in Corinth. Then he would let them send him on his way—
by providing both encouragement and provisions for his next
journey, *wherever* that might take him.

16:7 **I do not want to see you now and make only a passing visit; I
hope to spend some time with you, if the Lord permits.**^{NIV}
Paul knew that if he were to go immediately to Corinth, it would
by necessity be *only a passing visit,* and he did not want to do
that. He preferred to *spend some time* with them and would do so
if the Lord permitted it. Paul made plans, but he always knew
that at any moment God could intervene and make changes. Paul
would go wherever God sent him (16:6).

OBSTACLES AND OPPORTUNITIES
Paul certainly didn't confuse God's guidance and the "easy
way." He understood that open doors may well include many
adversaries. In a sense, he kept his eyes on the trail and didn't
worry that it went uphill. He could see that the opportunities in
Ephesus were greater than the obstacles he would have to
overcome. His attention was focused on opportunities to
minister, and he sensed God's guidance. We tend to focus on
the obstacles to ministry and find ourselves confused and
without guidance. We mistake obstacles (or adversaries) for
closed doors. Practicing Paul's approach will improve our
sense of direction.

16:8-9 **But I will stay on at Ephesus until Pentecost, because a great
door for effective work has opened to me, and there are many
who oppose me.**^{NIV} Paul was writing from Ephesus and wanted
to *stay* there until *Pentecost.* That meant that Paul was planning
to stay well into the spring in Ephesus, travel through the summer
in Macedonia (16:5), and then spend the winter in Corinth (16:6).
Paul wanted to go to Corinth, but he had pressing work in Ephe-

sus and knew that he needed to be there to take advantage of *a great door for effective work* that had been *opened to* him. Oddly enough, Paul also wanted to stay in Ephesus because of many who were opposing him. Who these were is unknown, although Acts 19 gives a clear picture of the opposition he faced in Ephesus. Paul was not afraid of the opposition; instead, because God had opened the door, Paul would stay to complete the ministry God had given.

16:10-11 **If Timothy comes, see to it that he has nothing to fear while he is with you, for he is carrying on the work of the Lord, just as I am. No one, then, should refuse to accept him. Send him on his way in peace so that he may return to me. I am expecting him along with the brothers.**^{NIV} As Paul was writing, Timothy (and another believer named Erastus) were traveling ahead of him through Macedonia (Acts 19:22). Paul expected Timothy to also arrive ahead of him at Corinth (4:17). Paul respected Timothy and had worked closely with him (Acts 16:1-3; Philippians 2:22; 1 Timothy 1:2). Although Timothy was young, Paul encouraged the Corinthian church to welcome him because he was *carrying on the work of the Lord.* With all the problems that had been brewing in the Corinthian church, Paul wanted to make sure that the young Timothy would have *nothing to fear* during his visit in Corinth and that *no one . . . should refuse to accept him.* Timothy often traveled as Paul's emissary, going ahead or staying behind in order to help the churches (see Acts 17:10-15; Philippians 1:1; 2:19; 1 Thessalonians 3:2). Paul stated that Timothy should be accepted by the churches in the same way that they would accept Paul himself. After Timothy stayed among the Corinthians for a while, they should *send him on his way in peace so that he may return to* Paul *along with the brothers.* The identity of these men is unknown, although one of them may have been Erastus, who had been sent along with Timothy on this particular trip (Acts 19:22). Paul knew of the tensions in the church and had sent Timothy to remind the church of his instructions in case any animosity toward him would spill over to Timothy. Paul did not want Timothy to be mistreated.

16:12 **Now concerning our brother Apollos, I strongly urged him to visit you with the other brothers, but he was not at all willing to come now. He will come when he has the opportunity.**^{NRSV} The phrase "now concerning" indicates that this was another question posed by the Corinthians. Perhaps they wondered about Apollos and wanted him to come and visit. *Apollos,* who had preached in Corinth, was doing evangelistic work in Greece (Acts 18:24-28). Apollos *was not at all willing* to go to Corinth right away, but he would do so when he had the chance. Perhaps Apollos's reluctance had to do with the factions in the Corinthian church (1:12; 3:4-5) and a desire not to make the problem any worse. Paul could "send" Timothy, but he could only "strongly urge" Apollos, who apparently worked independently of Paul although preaching the same message (3:5-6; 4:1).

SHARED MINISTRY

This letter was designed to pave the way for Paul's next visit to Corinth. But Paul didn't present himself as God's sole faithful messenger. These verses mention five others—Timothy, Apollos, Stephanas, Fortunatus, and Achaicus—who, in one way or another, served the Corinthians and Paul. Paul was eager to receive help from others who were genuine servants of God.

We serve a God of unlimited means, yet we must be humble in claiming the effectiveness of our service. We should encourage others, work alongside them, and ask for and accept their help. To do so illustrates teamwork in the marvelous spiritual organism called the church of Jesus Christ.

16:13-14 Be on guard. Stand true to what you believe. Be courageous. Be strong. And everything you do must be done with love.^{NLT}
Paul's final words to the church in Corinth sum up what he has written in this letter.

- They were to *be on guard.* They were to be constantly watchful or alert for spiritual enemies that might slip in and threaten to destroy them, whether it be divisions (1:10-17; 11:18), pride (3:18-21), sin (5:1-8), disorder (14:40), or erroneous theology (15:12). (See also 1 Thessalonians 5:6, 10; 1 Peter 5:8.)
- They needed to *stand true to what* they believed—that is, the gospel that they had been taught in the beginning, the gospel that they had accepted, the gospel that had brought them salvation (15:1-2).
- They had to *be courageous* so that they could stand against false teachers, deal with sin in the congregation, and straighten out the problems that Paul had addressed in this letter.
- They should *be strong* with the strength given by the Holy Spirit.
- They should do *everything . . . with love* (13:1-13), because without love, they would be no more than prideful noisemakers.

16:15-16 You know that Stephanas and his household were the first to become Christians in Greece, and they are spending their lives in service to other Christians. I urge you, dear brothers

and sisters, **to respect them fully and others like them who
serve with such real devotion.** NLT *Stephanas and his household*
were mentioned in 1:16 as people whom Paul had baptized. Paul
held up this "household" as an example of Christian living.
Exactly what they were doing is unknown, but Paul made it clear
that they were *spending their lives in service to other Christians.*
They were doing exactly what Paul had been talking about in this
letter. From his words, *I urge you . . . to respect them fully,* it
sounds as though they had, perhaps, even been treated with disre-
spect—Paul wanted to correct this. But these people *and others
like them* were serving the Lord *with such real devotion.* These
people were examples to the rest of the believers in Corinth,
exhibiting practical Christian faith.

16:17-18 **I am so glad that Stephanas, Fortunatus, and Achaicus have
come here. They have been making up for the help you weren't
here to give me. They have been a wonderful encouragement to
me, as they have been to you, too. You must give proper honor
to all who serve so well.** NLT *Stephanas* himself had come to Ephesus to see Paul, along with two other men, *Fortunatus* and *Achaicus,* who are mentioned only here. These men may have delivered
the letter that contained all the questions that Paul had been answering (see 7:1). These words give a glimpse into Paul's genuine joy at
being able to commune with other believers. Apparently, Paul truly
missed the believers in Corinth and would have loved to go immediately to see them if it had been possible, but these men made up
for that absence by their presence. That they brought a letter with
questions for the apostle to answer also shows that the church was
seeking Paul's advice, which was a good sign. These men were *a
wonderful encouragement* to Paul as representatives of the larger
congregation. Paul wanted them to be treated with *proper honor* as
well. They had taken time to serve the church by finding Paul and
getting the answers to questions so that the church could deal with
some difficulties. These men's concern for the church in Corinth
was honorable indeed.

16:19 **The churches in the province of Asia send you greetings.
Aquila and Priscilla greet you warmly in the Lord, and so
does the church that meets at their house.** NIV Just as all the
churches were working together to collect funds for the church in
Jerusalem (16:1-4), so all the churches stood united as they
greeted one another from distant places. As Paul had traveled
across the Roman Empire, he started churches in many cities.
Although far apart geographically, the churches were united in
their relationship to Jesus Christ, and Paul emphasized this unity
each time he would send greetings from one church to another.

The phrase "the churches in the province of Asia" would have referred to the Roman province of Asia located in what is now part of Turkey. There were churches in Ephesus (Ephesians 1:1), Colosse, Laodicea, and Hierapolis (Colossians 1:2; 4:13, 16).

Paul also sent greetings from *Aquila and Priscilla.* The church in Corinth would have known this married couple, for they had lived in Corinth. Both were tentmakers (or leatherworkers) whom Paul had met during his stay in Corinth (Acts 18:1-3). Aquila and Priscilla had followed Paul to Ephesus and had lived there with him, helping to teach others about Jesus. They even risked their lives for Paul, although the exact event is unknown (Romans 16:3-5). The great preacher Apollos, whom so many of the Corinthian believers admired, had been taught the Christian faith by this couple (Acts 18:26).

The early churches would meet in homes. Because of sporadic persecution and the great expense involved, church buildings were not constructed at this time (church buildings were not built until the third century). Many congregations were so small that the entire church could meet in one home. At other times, especially in large cities such as Ephesus or Rome, smaller groups of believers would meet regularly in various private homes (see Romans 16:5; Philemon 1:2). Apparently, Aquila and Priscilla had opened their home for just such a gathering, and this "church" also sent its greetings to Corinth.

16:20 **All the brothers and sisters send greetings. Greet one another with a holy kiss.**[NRSV] Finally, Paul sent *greetings* from *all the brothers and sisters.* The word "all" is comprehensive; perhaps this indicates that all the house churches in Ephesus, not just the one that met at Aquila and Priscilla's home, sent greetings to all the Christians in Corinth.

THE KISS
Paul encouraged the "holy kiss" as a way for Christians to greet each other, and a way to help break down the divisions in this church. This custom was carried over from Jewish society, where a kiss was a normal greeting. In our day, a handshake or hug conveys the same warmth, genuineness, and respect. To a church mired in a pattern of divisiveness and personal competitiveness, Paul issues a simple order: Show the world you appreciate each other. Make sure your greetings are heartfelt and enthusiastic.

To *greet one another with a holy kiss* was encouraged by Paul as a way to greet Christians, and a way to help break down the divisions in this church. Kissing was a normal way of greeting each other in Paul's day. This "holy kiss" or "kiss of love" expressed the love and unity among the believers. Paul wanted his readers to express their love and unity to one another. Paul used the same expression in Romans 16:16; 2 Corinthians 13:12; and 1 Thessalonians 5:26. Peter also recommended the "holy kiss" to the believers (1 Peter 5:14).

16:21 I, Paul, write this greeting with my own hand.NRSV Usually Paul would dictate his letters to a scribe, and often he would end with a short note in his own handwriting (see also Galatians 6:11; Colossians 4:18; 2 Thessalonians 3:17; Philemon 1:19). This is similar to adding a handwritten postscript (P.S.) to a typewritten letter. This *greeting with [Paul's] own hand* assured the recipients that false teachers were not writing letters in Paul's name (as apparently had been a problem—see 2 Thessalonians 2:2; 3:17). It also gave the letters a personal touch.

16:22 If anyone does not love the Lord, that person is cursed. Our Lord, come!NLT Paul had addressed many problems in this letter, hoping to help the believers straighten out their attitudes and actions and then to bring them back in line with the truth. Some of the problems existed because of pretenders in the church, people who did *not love the Lord*. Paul's final word for such people is that they be *cursed*. The word means to be placed under God's wrath (see also commentary on 12:3). These words were written in Paul's own handwriting (16:21), adding emphasis to these serious words toward any who would attempt to hurt the church of God.

As always, Paul's focus was on the coming kingdom, so he added the Aramaic word *maranatha* (translated for modern readers as "Our Lord, come!"). The word *maranatha,* although in the Aramaic language, must have been picked up in the Greek-speaking world as a way of expressing the hope of the Second Coming (see also Revelation 22:20). Paul never wanted believers to forget that this was what they were looking forward to and working toward. It was part of the foundation of their faith. Without Christ and the future bodily resurrection, the faith would be meaningless. (Read Paul's argument about this in chapter 15.)

16:23-24 May the grace of the Lord Jesus be with you. My love to all of you in Christ Jesus.NLT As Paul began this letter (1:3), so he ended it. Paul's final prayer was for *the grace of the Lord Jesus* to remain with them. Paul often ended his letters this way, asking his readers to continue to experience God's undeserved kindness and love every day of their lives and then to pass along that grace to others.

Although this had been a difficult letter to write, with many issues to be handled and sins to be corrected, Paul closed by reaffirming his *love* for these believers *in Christ Jesus*. Through Christ alone they had all been saved from the darkness and brought into the light; through him alone they had been joined together in his service. Paul loved these believers, cared for them, prayed for them, and longed to see them.

MARANATHA
The Lord Jesus Christ is coming back to earth again. To Paul, this was a glad hope, the very best he could look forward to. He was not afraid of seeing Christ—he could hardly wait! His brief prayer combines the excitement of a cheer and the urgency of a welcome. Do you share Paul's eager anticipation? Those who love Christ are looking forward to that wonderful time of his return (Titus 2:13). As for those who did not love the Lord, however, Paul says to let them be cursed.

2 CORINTHIANS

INTRODUCTION TO 2 CORINTHIANS

Educational background, personal experience, completed projects, satisfied customers, special qualifications—people list a variety of credentials to prove their competency and reliability. Credentials are important. Before hiring a plumber or entrusting your life to a surgeon, you want to make sure the crucial person is well qualified. Not to do so would be foolish or irresponsible.

But credentials can seem superfluous, especially in a close relationship. You probably wouldn't ask a friend for proof of his reliability, nor would you ask a relative for references. You know the person well, and that's good enough.

It comes as a surprise, then, to find Paul presenting his credentials to the believers at Corinth. He had lived among them, had led many of them to Christ, and had established the church in that important Greek city. But false teachers had infiltrated the church and were trying to undermine his authority. They questioned his apostleship and veracity, especially considering the harsh words of his previous correspondence.

So Paul reiterated his qualifications, refuting phony preachers (2:17), false teachers (3:1), and false apostles (11:5, 13) in the process. This was awkward for Paul, but it was necessary to regain the Corinthians. Paul cared for the church, and he knew it was vital that they follow his Spirit-led instructions.

Second Corinthians reveals the heart of a concerned pastor. Paul had heard of the Corinthians' problems. They had even sent him a delegation with questions about church order. With concern similar to a father who is sending his son to college for the first time, Paul wrote a long letter that he hoped would put the Corinthian church on track. He had invested so much of himself into them that he couldn't bear to see the church disintegrate over petty matters and lax discipline.

As you read 2 Corinthians, consider what you would say to counteract the lies of false teachers today, using the power and authority of this inspired letter and the rest of God's Word.

AUTHOR

Paul (Saul of Tarsus): Pharisee, apostle, pioneer missionary of the church. (See the discussion under Author in the introduction to 1 Corinthians on pages 2–3.)

Questions about Authorship and Unity. Second Corinthians
is, for the most part, an autobiographical letter. In it, Paul
described to the Corinthians the details of his recent missionary
trip. The letter includes intriguing specifics about Paul's life, such
as the time he faced his imminent death in Asia Minor (1:8-10)
and his irritating "thorn in the flesh" (12:7). These explicit details
substantiate the fact that Paul wrote 2 Corinthians, for no other
person could provide such an intimate portrait. Furthermore, in
2 Corinthians, Paul made the concept of God's grace central
(God's grace in Paul's preaching—1:12; God's grace to the Corinthians—9:8, 14; God's grace in Paul's weakness—12:9) as he did
in his other well-known letters (see, for example, Galatians 1:6).
For these reasons, no one has effectively challenged Paul's
authorship of 2 Corinthians as stated in the first line of the letter:
"This letter is from Paul" (1:1 NLT).

Although Paul's authorship has gone unchallenged, scholars
have debated whether 2 Corinthians is actually one letter.
Because of the fluctuations in tone and word choice, some Bible
commentators have asserted that 2 Corinthians is actually two,
three, or even four letters placed together by an editor. In their
zeal to divide 2 Corinthians, these scholars have overlooked the
overall consistency of the letter. As just mentioned, grace remains
a central theme of the letter. Furthermore, there is a focus
throughout on Paul's authority to preach the gospel (for example,
1:3-23; 2:14-17; 10:1-18) and his sufferings for the cause of
Christ (for example, 6:3-13; 11:16-33). The obvious changes in
tone in 2 Corinthians can be explained without suggesting that
the book is actually a *series* of letters. For instance, a change in
tone could reflect a lengthy pause in Paul's writing, at which time
he received additional information on the state of the Corinthian
church. A more detailed explanation of some of the theories surrounding 2 Corinthians follows:

Second Corinthians 10:1–13:13. Some Bible commentators
point to the difference in tone between the first nine chapters of
2 Corinthians and the last four chapters as evidence that 2 Corinthians was originally two separate letters written by Paul. The
first nine chapters have a joyous tone. Paul rejoiced over the
Corinthians' obedience to his latest directives (2:5-11; 7:2-15)
and even gave the believers detailed instructions about gathering
an offering for the Christians in Jerusalem (8:1-24). This would
suggest that Paul and the Corinthian church had been reconciled,
despite the problems of the recent past (7:7-10). The last four
chapters of Corinthians, however, contain a dramatic change of
tone. Here Paul passionately defended his authority against his
opponents in the church (10:13-18), exhorted the Corinthians to

remedy the problems in their church before he arrived to do it himself (10:1-2; 13:2, 10), and instructed believers to bring their disputes to him only if they had two or three witnesses (13:1-2). Because of these differences, some have asserted that the last four chapters of 2 Corinthians form the severe letter to which 7:8 alludes (for more information, see the section titled "Occasion and Purpose").

Although this theory has become popular in certain circles, there are other ways to explain the dramatic change of tone in 2 Corinthians. One approach is to view the change as Paul's strategy to win the hearts and minds of the Corinthian believers. By first commending them for their obedience to his previous instructions, Paul was preparing them to accept the more severe aspects of his letter—the fact that he was coming to discipline those who were opposing his authority (13:1-3). Another approach proposes that the change of tone reflects an extended pause in the writing of the letter. During this time, Paul may have picked up the pen from the scribe to whom he was dictating and dealt with some of the difficult issues that had suddenly come to his attention.

Second Corinthians 6:14–7:1. Although the vast majority of scholars agree that Paul wrote 2 Corinthians, some have speculated whether 6:14–7:1 was inserted by a later editor. These scholars believe that Paul's plea to the Corinthians to open their hearts to him (see 6:13; 7:2) was interrupted with an editor's insertion of the passage on spiritually separating oneself from unbelievers (see 6:14–7:1).

Although this may be plausible, no early manuscript has ever omitted this section from 2 Corinthians. This theory, therefore, has no concrete evidence on which to stand. Furthermore, most scholars believe that this section (6:14–7:1) explains why there is a "lack of love" between the Corinthians and Paul (6:12 NLT). The believers had not separated themselves from those who were opposing Paul and the truth of his teachings. Viewed in this light, the section is integral to Paul's appeal to the Corinthians to open their hearts to him (6:13; 7:2).

Additional Passages in Question. Second Corinthians is one of the books that Bible scholars have analyzed and dissected again and again. As a result, scholarly theories abound. Some believe that chapters 8 and 9 of 2 Corinthians are also separate letters— chapter 8 being a letter of commendation for Titus to the Corinthian church and chapter 9 being a letter of commendation to the churches in the rest of Greece. Others have wondered whether 2:14–7:4 might comprise another letter written to the Corinthian church. The evidence for such editorial changes in 2 Corinthians is slim, however, especially since no early manuscript of 2 Corinthians ever omits those verses.

In conclusion, 2 Corinthians can be viewed as a single, unified letter written by Paul to a troubled and divided church. The church at Corinth needed both encouragement to continue doing what was right and exhortation to discipline those who were still misleading people in the congregation. Second Corinthians is a passionate letter from a pastor who was extremely concerned about his congregation. Paul rejoiced in the triumphs of his congregation, but he expressed sorrow over the problems that persistently plagued them.

DATE AND SETTING

Written from Macedonia around A.D. 55–57.

In this letter, Paul repeatedly stated that he was writing from Macedonia (7:5; 8:1; 9:2). The exact city is unknown, but the subscriptions on some ancient manuscripts of 2 Corinthians read "written from Philippi." (The subscriptions were introductory comments inserted at the beginning of ancient letters.) There is no way to verify whether Paul was actually at Philippi, however; and this location has been questioned by a number of scholars.

What is known for certain is that Paul was in Macedonia. This region—along with Corinth in Greece—was evangelized on Paul's second missionary trip. Congregations were established in Philippi, Thessalonica, Berea, and Athens. On his third missionary journey, Paul stayed in Ephesus for a little over two years. During that time he wrote 1 Corinthians. After the riot at Ephesus (Acts 19:21-41), Paul traveled through Asia Minor and into Macedonia, encouraging the congregations he had established on his second missionary journey. In Macedonia, Paul experienced severe persecution, the type of hardship the churches in that region were already experiencing (see 2 Thessalonians 1:3-12 for Paul's earlier encouragement of a Macedonian church to stand firm in the faith in the face of persecution). In Macedonia, however, Paul's thoughts were not only on the horrible conditions there (see 1:8-9; 7:5) but on the spiritual battles the Christians at Corinth were fighting. Titus, Paul's assistant, was supposed to meet him in Troas with the news from Corinth. Somewhere in Macedonia, they got together. There Titus delivered a mixed report. The church in Corinth had obeyed Paul's earlier directives to discipline some of its members, but at the same time some were questioning his authority (by delaying his visit, 1:12-24, and by not confronting them in person, 10:1).

Thus, in Macedonia—in the middle of troubles and difficulties—Paul wrote this letter to the divided congregation at Corinth. He praised the believers for their obedience, but he also reasserted his authority to preach the gospel to the Gentiles. Paul warned them that he was on his way to Corinth. Then he sent Titus ahead with the letter to prepare the congregation for his visit (8:16; 13:1-3). When Paul finally did make it to Corinth, he stayed in that region for three months (see Acts 20:1-3).

AUDIENCE

The church in Corinth. (See the discussion under "Audience" in the introduction to 1 Corinthians on pages 4–5.)

OCCASION AND PURPOSE

To affirm Paul's ministry, defend his authority as an apostle, and refute the false teachers in Corinth.

Every letter has a context. A mother in her letter to a daughter may allude to the girlfriend they were discussing in the previous letter. The same is true for letters preserved in the Bible. Second Corinthians is no exception. To understand 2 Corinthians, it is useful to understand the long and complicated relationship between Paul and Corinth, a relationship that has taken some time for scholars to unravel. In fact, some of the details surrounding Paul's painful visit (2:1) and his severe letter to the Corinthians (2:1-4; 7:8) are still debated by scholars. It is possible, however, to sketch an outline of Paul's torturous relationship with the Corinthians.

1. Evangelizing Corinth. On Paul's second missionary journey, Paul traveled into what is known today as Greece. After a cold reception by the philosophers and thinkers who gathered in Athens, Paul went on to Corinth (Acts 18). Initially, Paul worked with Aquila and Priscilla as a tentmaker. But eventually he received enough financial support from Macedonian Christians to preach the gospel full time. After being rejected by many of the Jews, Paul focused his missionary work on the Gentiles and stayed with the Gentile God-fearer Titus Justus. In a vision one night, God encouraged Paul to keep on preaching in Corinth (Acts 18:9-11), so he stayed for a year and a half (A.D. 50–52).

2. Paul's stay at Ephesus. Around A.D. 52, Paul left Corinth to report back to his home church in Antioch and the elders in Jerusalem (Acts 18:18-22). On his next missionary journey, Paul made his headquarters at Ephesus, at the lecture hall of Tyrannus (Acts 19:8-10). There, he preached for a little over two years. Evidently, he sent many of his students to the surrounding region, for

Luke reported in Acts "that people throughout the province of Asia—both Jews and Greeks—heard the Lord's message" (see Acts 19:10 NLT). It was at Ephesus that Paul wrote several letters to the Corinthians.

3. The first letter to the Corinthians. Around this time, Paul wrote his first letter to the Corinthians. This is the letter to which Paul alluded in 1 Corinthians 5:9. Evidently the letter warned the Corinthians not to associate with those who called themselves Christians and yet persistently participated in sexual immorality (1 Corinthians 5:9-13). Although some scholars consider 6:14–7:1 to be a fragment of that letter, most believe that this letter was not preserved.

4. The second letter to the Corinthians. Toward the end of his stay at Ephesus (around A.D. 54–55), Paul wrote his second letter to the Corinthians, known today as 1 Corinthians. Earlier Paul had received a letter from the Corinthian church delivered by Stephanas, Fortunatus, and Achaicus (1 Corinthians 16:17). This letter had been filled with questions about church order. In 1 Corinthians, Paul answered these questions. The questions involved Christian marriage (1 Corinthians 7:1), food sacrificed to idols (1 Corinthians 8:1), spiritual gifts (1 Corinthians 12:1), and the collection of money for the relief of Christians in Jerusalem (1 Corinthians 16:1). In addition to these questions, Paul addressed a number of concerns arising from the unofficial report from Chloe's household. In particular, he was concerned with the reports of incest (1 Corinthians 5:1), lawsuits between members of the church (1 Corinthians 6:1), and drunkenness, gluttony, and arguments at the Lord's Supper (1 Corinthians 11:17-22).

5. Paul's painful visit. Shortly after sending 1 Corinthians, Paul most likely visited Corinth himself. The situation with the church concerned him so much that he traveled there to rectify the problems that had emerged. According to what can be gathered from 2 Corinthians, Paul's authority was challenged by a particular church member (perhaps leading others) during this visit. In response, Paul warned the church to discipline its immoral members before he had to do it himself (see 2:1; 12:14, 21; 13:1-4).

6. The severe letter to the Corinthians. After this painful visit, Paul wrote a "severe letter" to the Corinthians, evidently encouraging the Corinthians to discipline their errant member and/or members (see 2:1-4; 7:8). Most Bible commentators consider this letter to be Paul's third letter to the Corinthians, which is now lost. It has become generally accepted that 1 Corinthians was not the "severe letter," primarily because 1 Corinthians as a whole does not reflect the extreme sorrow that Paul described as being behind his severe letter.

Yet traditionally this "severe letter" has been identified as 1 Corinthians. Proponents of this theory identify the sinner who Paul forgave in 2:5-11 with the incestuous man of 1 Corinthians 5:1-5. Other scholars have identified the "severe letter" as being the last four chapters of 2 Corinthians, citing the extreme difference in tone and subject matter between the first nine chapters and the last four. The change in tone can just as easily be explained, however, by a hiatus in writing the letter. For any number of reasons, Paul may have paused in dictating 2 Corinthians. When he began dictating again or picked up the pen himself, his tone had changed. Perhaps he had received more distressing news about his opponents in the Corinthian church.

Most likely, the "severe letter" to which 2:1-4; 7:8 alludes has not been preserved.

7. The fourth letter to Corinthians. In A.D. 55, Paul left Ephesus for an evangelism trip to Troas (Acts 20:1-6). Evidently, he was supposed to meet Titus there in order to receive a report on the Corinthian church. Although there were some promising opportunities to share the gospel in Troas, Paul went on to Macedonia to find Titus because of his concern about the spiritual condition of the Corinthians (2:12-13). He met Titus somewhere in Macedonia and heard the good news that the Corinthians had disciplined the offender just as Paul had instructed (2:5-11; 7:2-16). Titus gave Paul a report that was, on the whole, encouraging (2:14; 7:5-7). However, other problems were surfacing in Corinth. Many were grumbling about Paul—the fickleness of his travel plans (1:12–2:4) and whether he truly possessed the authority of an apostle (3:1-18).

Paul wrote his fourth letter, 2 Corinthians, to encourage the Corinthians in their obedience (7:8-15), to defend his own authority (10:1-18), and to refute the false teachers that were still among them (11:1-15). In this letter, he revealed his earnest concern for the Corinthians. False teachers were trying to steal them away from Christ's teaching and from Paul himself. With a passion unmatched in any of his other letters, Paul revealed his entire life to the Corinthians. Even though he was reluctant to do so, he paraded his suffering for the cause of Christ as his official credential as Christ's ambassador to them (6:3-13). Would the Corinthians open their hearts to him, the person who had told them about Christ in the beginning? That was Paul's fervent plea (6:13). If they didn't remedy the problems in their church, Paul warned that he would come to do so himself (13:1-10). But his wish was to build them up in Christ instead.

MESSAGE

Trials, Church Discipline, Hope, Giving, and Sound Doctrine.

Trials (1:3-11; 2:1-11; 6:1-13; 12:1-10). Paul experienced great suffering, persecution, and opposition in his ministry. He even struggled with a personal weakness—a "thorn in the flesh." Through it all, Paul affirmed God's faithfulness. Despite the pain, he trusted in his loving Father and stayed true to his call.

Importance for Today. God is faithful. His strength is sufficient for any trial. When trials come, they keep us from pride and teach us dependence on God. He comforts us so we can comfort others. When persecuted or pressured, it is easy to lose heart or to doubt. When struggling with pain, it is easy to question God's goodness. Like Paul, however, we must focus on God's faithfulness and love and then persevere.

Regardless of what you are going through, God is with you. Keep focused on him and his love.

Church discipline (2:1-17; 5:11-21; 7:2-16; 10:1-18; 11:1-33; 12:1-21; 13:1-4). Paul defended his role in church discipline. And because of mounting opposition to his leadership, Paul presented his credentials as an apostle of Christ. Neither immorality nor false teaching could be ignored, so Paul hit the issues head-on. The church was to be neither lax nor too severe in administering discipline. The church was to restore the corrected person when he or she repented.

Importance for Today. The goal of all discipline in the church should be correction, not vengeance. For churches to be effective, they must confront and solve problems, not ignore them. In everything, we must act in love.

We must also beware of those who would rationalize sinful behavior or unjustly criticize spiritual leaders. We must clearly present God's Word, live by it personally, and hold the church to it corporately.

If you are a church leader, don't neglect church discipline, but do so with care. Also, submit yourself to the discipline of your church.

Hope (3:7-18; 4:1-18; 5:1-10). To encourage the Corinthians as they faced trials, Paul reminded them that they would receive new bodies in heaven. This would be a great victory in contrast to their present suffering. Surely this world is not the final home of the believer. What a profound and life-changing truth.

Importance for Today. To know we will receive new bodies offers us hope. No matter what adversity we face, we can keep going. Our faithful service will result in triumph.

We must also resist becoming too tied to this world and its values. Hope can be found *only* in Christ. That's our salvation and our message. Find your hope in Christ. In him and him alone is life.

Giving (8:1-24; 9:1-15). Paul organized a collection of funds for the poor in the Jerusalem church. Many of the Asian churches gave money. Paul explained and defended his beliefs about giving. And Paul was not shy about asking for money, as he urged the Corinthians to give generously and follow through on their previous commitment.

Importance for Today. God's work should be supported by his people. In addition, believers should take the lead in helping the needy, feeding the hungry, and curing the sick. Like the Corinthians, we should follow through on our financial commitments. Our giving should be generous, sacrificial, according to a plan, and based on need. Our generosity not only helps those in need but enables them to thank God.

Give generously to support your local church and God's work all over the world. And look for ways to reach out to needy folks in your community.

Sound Doctrine (6:14-18; 7:1; 13:5-14). False teachers were challenging Paul's ministry and authority as an apostle. So Paul listed his credentials and asserted his authority in order to preserve correct Christian doctrine. His sincerity, his love for Christ, and his concern for the people were his defense.

Importance for Today. We should share Paul's concern for correct teaching in our churches. But in so doing, we must share his motivation—love for Christ and people. For us, sound doctrine begins with a study of the Bible, God's Word.

VITAL STATISTICS

Purpose: To affirm Paul's ministry, defend his authority as an apostle, and refute the false teachers in Corinth

Author: Paul

To whom written: The church in Corinth, and Christians everywhere

Date written: About A.D. 55–57, from Macedonia

Setting: Paul had already written three letters to the Corinthians (two are now lost). In 1 Corinthians (the second of these letters), he used strong words to correct and teach. Most of the church had responded in the right spirit; there were, however, those who were denying Paul's authority and questioning his motives.

Key verse: "We are Christ's ambassadors, and God is using us to speak to you. We urge you, as though Christ himself were here pleading with you, 'Be reconciled to God!'" (5:20 NLT).

Key people: Paul, Timothy, Titus, false teachers

Key places: Corinth, Jerusalem

Special features: This is an intensely personal and autobiographical letter.

OUTLINE

In responding to the attacks on his character and authority, Paul explains the nature of Christian ministry and openly shares about his ministry. This is an important letter for all who wish to be involved in any kind of Christian ministry, because it has much to teach us about how we should handle our ministries today. Like Paul, those involved in ministry should be blameless, sincere, confident, caring, open, and willing to suffer for the sake of Christ.

1. Paul explains his actions (1:1–2:11)
2. Paul defends his ministry (2:12–7:16)
3. Paul defends the collection (8:1–9:15)
4. Paul defends his authority (10:1–13:13)

2 Corinthians 1:1–2:4

Paul wrote this letter to the Christians in Corinth from Macedonia. He had suffered great persecution in Asia Minor—perhaps in the city of Ephesus—and he was on the way to visit the Corinthians. He was traveling through all of Greece—through both Macedonia in the north and Achaia in the south—to collect a donation for the poor Christians in Jerusalem. Paul sent this letter on ahead of him to tell the Corinthians how they should handle some of the problems that were plaguing them; he especially focused on the problem of the false teachers who had infiltrated the church. A significant group of believers had been influenced by these false teachers. Paul wrote 2 Corinthians to reassert his apostolic authority among the Corinthians.

This letter was probably one of the more difficult letters for Paul to write. Although Paul wanted to rejoice with the Corinthians in their spiritual growth, he didn't shrink from asserting his authority and disciplining those who needed it.

1:1 Paul, an apostle of Christ Jesus by the will of God.[NIV] Right from the start, Paul identified himself as *an apostle*. It was appropriate for Paul to mention his apostleship here, for his authority is a major theme of this letter. A group of false apostles (literally "pseudo-apostles"; see 11:13) had infiltrated the Corinthian church. This distressed Paul greatly because he had founded the church himself on his second missionary journey. To gain a foothold in Corinth, these false apostles had systematically discredited Paul's missionary work. Paul wrote 2 Corinthians to defend his apostolic authority and to refute the false teachers and their accusations.

What does it mean to be an "apostle"? The Greek word *apostolos* literally means "one sent forth." An apostle was "sent forth" by *Christ Jesus* with the mission to make disciples in his name (Matthew 28:18-20). The disciples—the Twelve who followed Jesus during his earthly ministry, learning from him and witnessing his miracles—became the apostles. Yet Paul was also included among the apostles because Jesus himself had called

Paul to preach the Good News to the Gentiles. Although Paul had been a zealous Pharisee who persecuted Christians, Jesus appeared to him on the Damascus road, calling him to a radically different life. Paul was an apostle *by the will of God* because God himself chose him for that work: "Saul is my chosen instrument to take my message to the Gentiles and to kings, as well as to the people of Israel" (Acts 9:15 NLT; "Saul" is Paul's Hebrew name). This vision of Christ changed Paul forever, making him not only a devoted follower of Christ but also an apostle sent by Christ to make disciples among the Gentiles. Jesus' calling gave Paul the authority to establish churches throughout the known Mediterranean world and to teach the believers who gathered in these churches. Paul's apostleship was confirmed by the apostles in Jerusalem (Acts 9:28), and his message was confirmed at the Council of Jerusalem (Acts 15:1-21).

Paul's extensive training in the Law under the well-known teacher Gamaliel made him a skilled apologist for Christianity. In all of Paul's letters, however, including this one, Paul never relied on his credentials or his education for his authority as an apostle. Instead, he relied on the testimony of changed lives and the power of the Spirit in his teaching. It was the Spirit of God who had established a network of Christian churches throughout Asia Minor and Greece within a few decades. It was the Spirit's message—not Paul's own—that Paul preached.

And Timothy our brother.NIV Timothy was Paul's assistant. He had grown up in Lystra, a city in the province of Galatia. Paul had visited Galatia on his first missionary journey (Acts 14:8-21). During that trip, he most likely met Timothy's mother, Eunice, and his grandmother, Lois (2 Timothy 1:5). On his second visit to Lystra, Paul asked young Timothy to travel with him (Acts 16:1-5). Evidently, Paul saw in Timothy a willingness to cooperate with Christ's plan and an enthusiasm for the gospel. These were necessary characteristics for an early Christian missionary. Timothy agreed to join Paul and, subsequently, traveled all over the Mediterranean world with him, helping to establish churches wherever they went. Timothy courageously shared Paul's sufferings and ridicule. Although Paul had other helpers, such as Titus, he developed a special relationship with Timothy, calling him a son in Christ (Philippians 2:22).

At times, Paul would commission Timothy as an emissary to a specific church. Timothy had visited the church at Philippi (Philippians 2:19), the church at Thessalonica (1 Thessalonians 3:2), and other Macedonian churches (Acts 19:22) in that role. He had also functioned as Paul's emissary to the Corinthians. In 1 Corinthians, Paul not only informed the Corinthians that Timothy would come to them, he also endorsed Timothy's message: "He will remind you of my way of life in Christ Jesus" (1 Corinthians 4:17 NIV). Apparently Paul was slightly apprehensive of sending Timothy to the Corinthians, so he reiterated in that letter that they should treat Timothy with due respect (1 Corinthians 16:10). It becomes clear in 2 Corinthians that the Corinthian church—or some group within the church—had rejected Paul's authority, so some scholars have suggested that Timothy was the one who was rejected. Because Timothy represented Paul and his message, Paul interpreted their rejection of Timothy as a rejection of his own message. Whatever the case, it is clear that the Corinthian church and Paul had a rocky relationship. Inevitably, Timothy, as Paul's assistant and emissary, would have received the brunt of the Corinthians' criticism. In 2 Corinthians, Paul took special care to identify Timothy's message as the same as his own message (1:19). It is significant, therefore, that Paul mentions Timothy at the outset of his letter. Although at other times Paul identifies Timothy as a "son" (Philippians 2:22), here Paul identifies him as a *brother* in Christ—a person on an equal level, instead of a subordinate. Paul may have done this to bolster Timothy's authority among the Corinthians.

We are writing to God's church in Corinth.NLT Paul founded the Corinthian church around A.D. 50 on his second missionary journey. The core of this church was a group of Gentiles who would gather at Titius Justus's house to hear Paul preach. Since Justus's home was right next to the Jewish synagogue in Corinth, it can be reasonably assumed that many of the Gentiles were God-fearers—in other words, Gentiles who had attended the services in the local synagogue before Paul started preaching. The fact that the Corinthian Jews actively opposed Paul's preaching supports this assumption (see Acts 18:6). These Jews were probably reacting to a loss of membership at their synagogue. They were so enraged over Paul's preaching that they took action, filing a formal complaint with Gallio, the governor of the province of Achaia (see Acts 18:12-17). But Gallio refused to hear their complaint. He thought these Jews were merely presenting a feud between two different sects of Judaism before him. With Jewish opposition thwarted in Corinth, Paul was free to stay in the city for a year and a half. He spent that time preaching and teaching so that the Corinthians would be firmly established in the truths of Christ.

Together with all the saints throughout Achaia.NIV In the first century, the southern portion of Greece functioned as a political

unit called *Achaia.* It was a province of the Roman Empire. The
northern portion of Greece was governed separately and was
called Macedonia.

Paul addressed this letter to all the Christians in Achaia
because he viewed Corinth as the center of Christianity for that
province. Most likely, Christians throughout Achaia were aware
of the situation in the Corinthian church. By addressing this letter
to all the Achaians, Paul would make it clear to every Christian in
that region what his stance was with respect to the controversial
issues in the Corinthian church. Furthermore, Paul wrote this letter with general spiritual principles in mind. Paul's passionate
defense of his apostolic authority (10:1-18) and his eloquent comparisons of the new covenant to the old covenant (2:12–3:18)
could benefit all Christians.

Paul commonly called Christians *saints.* The Greek word for
"saints" is *hagioi,* meaning "those set apart" or "holy ones." That
is, Christians are set apart *from* evil and *to* God's righteous purposes. In the Old Testament, the nation of Israel was described in
that fashion, a holy nation set apart for God and distinct from the
nations and their wicked practices (compare Exodus 19:6 with
1 Peter 2:9). Thus, when Paul used the word "saints" to describe
Christians, he wasn't suggesting that they were perfect. The content of 1 and 2 Corinthians makes it abundantly clear that the congregation had many serious faults (1 Corinthians 5:1-12;
2 Corinthians 2:5-17). Paul did not consider them saints because
of their behavior but because God had chosen them as his own
people. The Corinthian Christians were dedicated to God and to
the constant struggle of separating themselves from evil to do the
will of God. They were God's holy people.

**1:2 Grace to you and peace from God our Father and the Lord
Jesus Christ.**NKJV This was the standard greeting Paul used in his
letters. It was a Christian adaptation of the common letter-writing
practice of his day. After identifying to whom a letter was
addressed, a writer would write "greetings," in Greek, *chairein*—
a word that functioned much like our word "hello." Paul christianized this common greeting by using the Greek word *charis,*
commonly translated "grace." Grace is God's undeserved favor.
God's graciousness is preeminently shown by the fact that he sent
his own Son, Jesus Christ, to die on the cross. At the same time
God showers on people undeserved favor every day—by providing everything from rain for crops to sunlight for illuminating our
days. His graciousness is even more pronounced to Christians,
who enjoy his Spirit, who guides them to do what is right.

The Greek word for "peace" is based on the common Hebrew

greeting *shalom*. For Jews, *shalom* did not mean absence of conflict, as it does for us when we say, "there is peace in the Middle East." Instead, *shalom* connotes well-being, wholeness, and inner tranquillity. Peace is "the way things ought to be." For Paul, Christ's death on the cross was the only event that restored true peace.

By identifying *God* the *Father* and the *Lord Jesus* together, Paul was asserting that both the Father and the Son had granted these wonderful gifts of grace and peace. Paul was pointing to Jesus as a full person in the Godhead. Both God the Father and the Lord Jesus together provide Christians with grace and peace. Paul used the same expression in his introductory remarks to the Romans (Romans 1:7), to the Galatians (Galatians 1:3), to the Ephesians (Ephesians 1:2), and to the Philippians (Philippians 1:2). During his ministry on earth, Jesus had consistently identified God as his Father (John 10:29), and he even declared that he and the Father were one (John 10:30). The early church adopted Jesus' terminology, calling God the Father (Acts 2:33). In his letter to the Romans, Paul explained why Christians considered God as their true Father. Jesus had given Christians the Spirit of sonship, which made them truly children of God (see Romans 8:15).

WE PASS ON GOD'S COMFORT TO OTHERS / 1:3-11

Paul would typically begin a letter by thanking God for the believers to whom he was writing. In his letter to the Romans, he praised the Romans for their faith (Romans 1:8-9). In Ephesians, he praised the Ephesians for their love for others (Ephesians 1:15). The Thessalonians were praised for their faithful work and their hope in Jesus' second coming. Finally, the Colossians were praised for their trust in Jesus (Colossians 1:3). Even in 1 Corinthians, Paul praised God for giving the Corinthians spiritual gifts of eloquence and knowledge. But in 2 Corinthians, Paul had no praise for the Corinthians. In its place, however, he did not blame them; rather, he tried to encourage them.

1:3 Blessed be the God and Father of our Lord Jesus Christ.NRSV This section began with a common phrase from first-century synagogue liturgies. "Blessed be God" was a declaration of praise used by the worshipers of the Old Testament and a phrase that typically began a worship service in a synagogue (see Psalm 66:20; 68:35). The exact expression appears at the beginning of one of Peter's letters (1 Peter 1:3). The prevalent use of this phrase in New Testament letters (see also Ephesians 1:3) indicates that the phrase may have become a common expression in worship, perhaps a "call to worship" for early churches.

Paul, however, didn't adopt worship expressions from synagogues without significant changes. He typically christianized Jewish expressions, by clearly articulating whose God he was worshiping. Worship and praise were owed *only* to the God who had sent Jesus to die on the cross for our salvation. Paul used the Greek word for "Lord," which means "master" or "owner," with the name "Jesus," to express Jesus' complete authority over believers. "Christ," on the other hand, was the Greek word for "Messiah." Thus with the phrase "Lord Jesus Christ," Paul was identifying Jesus as both his Master and the promised Messiah of the Old Testament. God was the *Father* of Jesus in the sense that Jesus had come from God the Father, not that Jesus had been created by God the Father.

With this "call to worship," the early church—and Paul in this letter—clearly were identifying the God whom they were worshiping. Their God was the One who had graciously sent his Son as the promised Savior of his people. This was the only God who was indeed worthy of worship.

THE COMPASSIONATE GOD
For some people, the mere mention of God's name triggers a fearful or guilty response. He is viewed as an austere distant deity unconcerned with what concerns us. But that is not the God of the Bible. Paul wasted no time in the first chapter of this letter introducing his readers to the Father of compassion (1:3). Our definition of what it means to be compassionate derives from God himself. He invented compassion. Compassion is the heartbeat of his character. If he is indeed our Father, we will resemble the One to whom we are related. To whom is it easy for you to show compassion? To whom is it more of a challenge? Identify someone you will treat compassionately today and then follow through.

The Father of compassion.[NIV] The prayer that introduces the confession of faith in a Jewish synagogue service praises God for his compassion: "O our Father, merciful Father." Here, Paul followed this synagogue pattern of worship, but he didn't stick to the words of this Jewish rite. Paul had dramatically experienced God's mercy in his recent travels through Asia. He was introducing his testimony of God's compassionate character in his own life with a worship phrase that many of the Corinthians would have known. They had probably recited it in their house churches. Those Christians who were Jews or Gentile God-fearers before their conversions had dutifully recited it in the synagogue. But here Paul injected this meaningful phrase with new life by calling God *the Father of compassion.* By telling the Corinthians how God had mercifully worked in his life, Paul was encouraging the Corinthians to remember God's mercy to them when they recited this phrase in worship.

And the God of all comfort.NIV Many translations use the word "comfort" for the Greek word *paraklesis* here, but the word does not mean ease and relaxation. The meaning of this Greek word is closer to "encouragement." The word does not imply that God rescues his people from every discomfort but that he gives them the tools, the necessary training, and the essential guidance to endure the problems of this life. That is why Jesus used this word—the *Paraclete*—for the Holy Spirit (see John 14:16). The Holy Spirit is the "Encourager."

HANG ON
Paul had experienced both trouble and comfort (1:4). It's a principle of life that we receive in order to give encouragement. Paul applied this principle to the help God offers us when we are dealing with hardships. As a result, no sorrow in our lives needs to be wasted. Our ability to empathize with another comes from our firsthand experiences of life. Through those experiences, we discover the handles for hanging on during hard times. Make a list of difficult times in your last year when you experienced "handles" you know were God-sent. Identify how God came through for you. How can you help someone with a problem you've experienced?

1:4 He comforts us in all our troubles so that we can comfort others. When others are troubled, we will be able to give them the same comfort God has given us.NLT Paul had an extremely difficult letter to write to the Corinthians. Although they had not necessarily been hard-pressed by external persecution, the Corinthian church had gone through a lot of internal dissension. Opposing sides were vying for their points of view (1 Corinthians 1:10-17), and people were even suing each other (1 Corinthians 6:1-7). Instead of focusing on these persistent problems, Paul began his letter by focusing on God and his comfort. God would encourage—and even admonish—the Corinthians through these difficult times. When the troubles passed and the Corinthians emerged faithful, then they would be able to encourage others who needed the same encouragement.

For Paul, times of trials and difficulty were not a time to despair (1:8-10; 4:7-12; 11:23-29). Instead, they were to be seen as opportunities to reveal the true self and to experience God's love even more. Trials are never easy. But it is through trials that God can shape and mold our character. Often, it is only through trials that we can learn about God's loving care for us.

1:5 For just as the sufferings of Christ flow over into our lives, so also through Christ our comfort overflows.^{NIV} Paul expected to suffer, just as Christ had suffered on this earth, enduring the ultimate humiliation—a criminal's death on a cross (John 19:19-37). Jesus had warned his disciples that they could expect the same: "'No servant is greater than his master.' If they persecuted me, they will persecute you also" (John 15:20 NIV). His warning was an apt one, for the early church experienced strong opposition and persecution. The first Christian martyr was Stephen (Acts 7:57-60), commencing a long list of martyrs for the Christian faith (see Acts 12:2; Revelation 7:14-17).

> Suffering is nature's way of indicating a mistaken attitude or way of behavior, and to the nonegocentric person every moment of suffering is the opportunity for growth. People should rejoice in suffering, strange as it sounds, for this is a sign of the availability of energy to transform their characters. *Rollo May*

Although he had been a traveling evangelist for less than a decade, Paul had already experienced much hardship and suffering for the cause of Christ. He had been insulted (Acts 13:45); chased out of towns, villages, and cities by angry mobs (Acts 17:8-10); beaten and thrown into dank, dark prisons (Acts 16:22-23); stoned and left for dead (Acts 14:19-20); and he was even the object of murderous plots (Acts 14:5).

It was clear to Paul that God doesn't protect his people from *suffering*. Instead, he allows them to experience ridicule, rejection, and abuse. Today, people don't expect suffering and don't tolerate it when it occurs in their lives. People expect instant relief and instant cures. And in the case of unrelenting pain, some have suggested that people have the right to end their lives. According to this type of thinking, suffering must be stopped at any cost—even life itself.

Paul had a radically different view of suffering. According to Paul, suffering—especially trials and discomfort associated with the advancement of Christ's kingdom—is God's way of allowing Christians to become more like Jesus—to suffer for the gospel just as Jesus suffered for it (Philippians 1:29; 3:10). Peter agreed with Paul: Christians should rejoice when they suffer, for in their own suffering they will in some small way experience what it meant for Jesus to suffer for their sins (1 Peter 4:12-13).

In addition to drawing people closer to Christ, suffering can
also help them grow in their faith. God uses suffering to improve
his people and shape them into better Christians. In fact, suffering should be thought of as the necessary pain that accompanies
spiritual growth. In Romans, Paul noted that suffering produces
perseverance, which, in turn, produces Christian character
(Romans 5:3-4; see also James 1:3-4; 2 Peter 1:6; Revelation 2:2,
19). This passage highlights another benefit to suffering: It
teaches the sufferer how to encourage others who are also suffering (see 1:6-7).

Understanding these truths about suffering can help believers
look beyond their difficult situations to the ultimate goal: moving
closer to Christ. This doesn't make the sufferings, trials, and difficulties any easier. But it does inspire God's people to endure
those difficult times. There is a God-given purpose for suffering—even though that purpose may be totally hidden at the time
of the trial. In the midst of difficulties, Christians can be confident that God is present. He knows their pain (Christ experienced
great agony and death on the cross; Philippians 2:8; Hebrews
12:2), but he also has all of eternity in view. God has a good purpose for pain and suffering; and he works out that good purpose
in believers' lives (Romans 8:28), giving them enough comfort in
order to persevere through any hardship.

**1:6 So when we are weighed down with troubles, it is for your
benefit and salvation! For when God comforts us, it is so that
we, in turn, can be an encouragement to you.Then you can
patiently endure the same things we suffer.**NLT Here Paul was
explaining to the Corinthians why he was recounting his suffering and trials in Asia. He was emphasizing that the church was
not composed of individuals but was a body with its members
thoroughly interrelated. Paul had already taught the Corinthians:
"If one member suffers, all suffer together with it; if one member
is honored, all rejoice together with it" (1 Corinthians 12:26
NRSV). This letter relates Paul's own suffering for the cause of the
gospel in order to remind the Corinthians of their unity with Paul
as a fellow Christian. Paul and his fellow travelers had been
weighed down with troubles, but this resulted in the Corinthians'
benefit and salvation. Because Paul and his fellow travelers had
been comforted by God, they could *be an encouragement to* the
Corinthians. True empathy should be found in the church, where
all members are united in Christ (1 Corinthians 12:12-31). This
life will bring suffering and trials, but Christians should encourage the suffering person. And when the sufferer perseveres, that
person will gain renewed insight, which will enable that person

to encourage others who experience similar difficult situations. Then those people *can patiently endure the same things.*

In the case of Paul and the Corinthians, this was even more true. Paul was not suffering the common problems of everyday life. He was being persecuted for identifying with Christ and preaching the gospel message. Paul's God-inspired courage in the face of difficulties had enabled him to preach in Corinth in the first place. Thus, the Corinthians had a strong connection with Paul, their mentor and founder. But 2 Corinthians reveals that some of the Corinthian Christians were rejecting their connection to Paul (10:1-18). Thus, Paul took pains at the start of his letter to emphasize his relationship with the Corinthians.

1:7 And our hope for you is firm, because we know that just as you share in our sufferings, so also you share in our comfort.NIV Despite all the problems the Corinthians had experienced—from acrimonious division in the church to shocking cases of immorality, Paul expressed his complete and unshakable confidence in them—*our hope for you is firm.* He knew the Corinthian church was struggling and suffering, but his confident hope was that their struggles were for the cause of the gospel, just as he was struggling for the advancement of the gospel in Asia Minor. Their steadfastness to the gospel of truth and their perseverance through difficulties would enable them to enjoy God's encouragement and strength—a reward that was worth the agonizing struggle.

1:8 For we do not want you to be ignorant, brethren, of our trouble which came to us in Asia: that we were burdened beyond measure, above strength, so that we despaired even of life.NKJV Next, Paul moved from the general principle—that God encourages Christians in their trials—to his particular situation. He didn't explain to the Corinthians the details about what happened to him in Asia, only that it involved fearing for his life. Commentators have suggested a number of different scenarios: (1) Paul was afflicted with a serious illness, perhaps loosely connected to his "thorn in the flesh" (see 12:1-10). (2) Paul was imprisoned in Ephesus, an event to which Paul might have been alluding when he wrote of fighting "wild beasts in Ephesus" (see 1 Corinthians 15:23-31). (3) Paul had feared for his life during the riot instigated by the Ephesian silversmiths (see Acts 19:31).

Of course, Paul's trouble associated with the Ephesian riot is the most documented of the three possibilities. This very well could have been the life-threatening situation to which Paul was referring, but this is not certain. All we know for sure is that Paul *despaired even of life.* He was *burdened beyond measure,* just like a ship weighted down to the point of sinking. Paul's despair was real. He was dealing with a profound depression.

PRESSURE, STRESS, AND DEPRESSION
Paul knew a great deal about trouble. Being a follower of Christ doesn't exempt a person from pressure, stress, and depression. Many believers believe Christians should never be depressed. But here Paul—a champion of the early church—was dealing with that very problem. In the case of the apostle Paul, pressure came with the territory of discipleship. He candidly wrote that the pressure was so great that at times, he despaired of life itself (1:8). Evidently, he wondered if he would even escape the vise-grip of opposition. No doubt you have marks to prove that you've been there too. When you spend time in quiet conversation with the Lord today, honestly admit the pressure and anxiety currently consuming you from the inside out. Ask him to undergird you as you chip away at situations you feel are beyond your ability. Celebrate the promise Paul gave to his friends at the church in Philippi. "I can do all things through Christ who strengthens me" (Philippians 4:13 NKJV).

1:9 Indeed, we felt that we had received the sentence of death so that we would rely not on ourselves but on God who raises the dead.NRSV Some commentators have interpreted the *sentence of death* as implying that Paul had received an official verdict while in jail. Others have insisted that the Greek word for "sentence" can be translated "answer." Thus, Paul might have been picturing himself in this passage as a humble petitioner for his life. The answer he received to his earnest cry for mercy was death. There was no hope. No person could save him. Paul's only hope was in God.

But Paul's hope was well placed. Only God *raises the dead.* God's power to raise from the dead was a doctrine some of the Corinthians were doubting (see Paul's extended explanation of the doctrine of the resurrection in 1 Corinthians 15:1-56). In 2 Corinthians, Paul repeatedly emphasized the temporary nature of human existence (4:16; 5:1) in order to highlight the importance of the Christian hope in eternal life. Without a confident hope in the resurrection, the Christian faith would be useless (see 1 Corinthians 15:14).

Paul wrote that any amount of suffering is worth enduring, for suffering makes God's people realize that God is the only One on whom they can *rely.* It is worse to enjoy the comforts of this world and remain deceived. Depending on oneself ultimately leads to destruction, because people cannot rescue themselves from death. If suffering in your life produces nothing more than a fervent dependence on God and a renewed prayer life, then in God's eyes the suffering may have been well worth the pain.

1:10 And he did deliver us from mortal danger. And we are confident that he will continue to deliver us.[NLT] Paul's hope in God was vindicated. God, who holds the ultimate power between life and death, had rescued him. His prayer was answered. The same God who raised Jesus Christ from the dead delivered Paul *from mortal danger.* God had not only protected Paul from death, but he had also given Paul the courage to endure the pressures of the situation.

The Lord's deliverance of Paul during this especially difficult time gave Paul the courage to believe that God had been planning his rescue from the beginning and would *continue to deliver* him in the future. Just like Paul, we should recount the times God has rescued and delivered us in the past. These incidents will provide the evidence that God is—at the moment, in the midst of our struggles—planning our miraculous rescue. Remembering that our God is a deliverer should evoke unspeakable joy and gratitude.

1:11 He will rescue us because you are helping by praying for us. As a result, many will give thanks to God because so many people's prayers for our safety have been answered.[NLT] Paul showed an untiring belief in the effectiveness of intercessory prayer. Often he would ask churches to pray for him (see Romans 15:30-32; Ephesians 6:18-20).

> Prayer is a shield to the soul, a sacrifice to God, and a scourge to Satan.
> *John Bunyan*

Here Paul thanked the Corinthians for *praying for* him. In Greek, Paul literally wrote that the Corinthians "were working together to support" him in prayer. Paul used that type of language to encourage the Corinthians to work together in their church and with him. Their joint effort in prayer would make him an effective minister of the gospel. Paul knew that the cure for the divisions that plagued the church (see 1 Corinthians 1:10-17) was bowing together in prayer. If all the church would humble themselves before God, many of their differences would fade in comparison to the all-important cause of Christ.

Just as in verse 7, this verse eloquently highlights the interdependence of the members of the church with each other (a truth Paul had already illustrated in his metaphor of the body—see 1 Corinthians 12:12-30). This interdependence is illustrated with a situation in Paul's life. Reports of Paul's suffering had driven the Corinthians to prayer. In response to their prayers, God had delivered Paul. This deliverance gave Paul the opportunity, in turn, to write a letter to share not only the news of his deliverance but how God had encouraged him. In turn, this encouragement—perhaps even exhortation—from Paul would strengthen the Corinthians to face any difficulties they might encounter. This type of reciprocity was what Paul was trying to illustrate with his recent trial. There is no such thing as a self-reliant Christian. The whole church is inextricably joined together in its spiritual growth toward God. Because God had delivered him, Paul could encourage the Corinthians to *give thanks to God because* their *prayers for* the *safety* of Paul and his companions had been answered. The Corinthians' praise would inspire many others and teach them of God's faithfulness.

SAFETY FIRST
Paul encouraged believers to pray for his safety (1:11). Prayer isn't limited to church. It's a vehicle God has given to get us (and those we love) safely through life's hazards. Paul requested prayer for himself and his companions as they traveled to spread God's Word. He knew from experience that the prayers of people in congregations he had served had moved God's hands to bail him out when he was imprisoned literally and figuratively. He knew exactly what to say when people asked how they could be of assistance to him. Pray. Pray. Pray. If Paul and his associates needed prayer support, so do those who provide spiritual leadership in your life. Satan will challenge those who identify with Christ and his church. Pray for your pastors, Sunday school teachers, seminary professors, missionaries, and others you know who are extending the borders of Christ's kingdom.

PAUL'S CHANGE OF PLANS / 1:12–2:4

After praising God for the comfort the Lord had shown him in his most recent trials, Paul started to explain his most recent travel plans to the Corinthians. In 1 Corinthians, Paul had told the Corinthians that he would visit them after traveling through Macedonia (see 1 Corinthians 16:5-7). Since that time, he had altered his travel plans. He planned to visit Corinth twice, stopping there first before traveling through Macedonia and then again on his way back east (see 1:15-16). Paul made the first of these two visits. But since this visit was extremely "painful," Paul decided not to return to Corinth immediately. Instead, he most likely went straight to Ephesus from Macedonia. There, he wrote a "severe letter" to address the difficult issues that the Corinthian church had to handle (see 2:3).

From the evidence of 1 and 2 Corinthians, we can piece together what happened on Paul's "painful visit." Some false teachers had infiltrated the church at Corinth and attempted to discredit Paul's authority. This had caused the church to divide into factions that supported one teacher over another (see 1 Corinthians 3:1-23). In addition to these divisions, these false teachers had begun to attack Paul's character. They questioned his authority as an apostle, giving a variety of reasons—including his lack of eloquence, his refusal to accept financial support, and even some of the setbacks and trials he had endured as an evangelist. Apparently, on Paul's last visit someone had publicly challenged his authority (see 13:3). Paul sternly warned the Corinthians (13:2) during that visit and then continued on his journey through Macedonia. Instead of returning to Corinth, however, he went straight to Ephesus. He canceled his second visit and instead wrote a letter (his third one to them) that exhorted the church to resolve some of the problems in their community (2:3). Paul outlined the first step they had to make: They had to discipline the member who had caused Paul so much trouble on his last visit (2:5-11).

After spending much of the first chapter of 2 Corinthians highlighting how he and the Corinthians were intimate coworkers for the cause of Jesus, Paul dove into a full defense of his own sincerity, something that was suffering a full-scale attack at Corinth.

1:12 Now this is our boast: Our conscience testifies.[NIV] Second Corinthians speaks more of boasting than any of Paul's other letters (see 1:12, 14; 10:8, 13, 16-17; 11:12, 18, 21, 30; 12:5-6, 9) because Paul had to counter the boasts of his opponents in Corinth. Essentially, the Greek word for "boast" means "confidence." Sometimes Paul would use the word in a negative sense to describe those who placed confidence in their own abilities (11:12). At other times, Paul used the word for a well-placed confidence, or hope, in God and the power God freely gives to all Christians (10:17). In this way, Paul could boast in God because it ultimately brought glory to the Lord.

Paul might have spoken of his *conscience* here because it was a term frequently used by the Corinthians. The Stoics were known for referring to their conscience as the voice of God within them. Paul did not use the term in the same sense, however; instead, he seemed to be identifying the conscience as a human ability to judge whether an action was correct. But Paul made it clear that even his conscience was judged by God (see

1 Corinthians 4:4-5). In the end, a person's conscience will not justify him or her before the Almighty. God—and God alone—will judge each person's actions. Although Paul appealed to his conscience, he knew that his conscience would ultimately be vindicated before Jesus Christ (1:14).

We have conducted ourselves in the world, and especially in our relations with you, in the holiness and sincerity that are from God.NIV Paul did not want to bring reproach on the gospel with his behavior. For this reason, he was extremely careful. Paul tried to be completely sincere, and he tried to act in a way that was beyond criticism. In this way, he would draw attention to the truthfulness of his message instead of to his own behavior. In the first century, there were many wandering preachers. Some of them used despicable ways to garner financial support. Paul tried to distance himself from such messengers by supporting himself in Corinth, working alongside Priscilla and Aquila as a tentmaker. Paul was reminding the Corinthians of this type of ethical scrupulousness.

We have done so not according to worldly wisdom but according to God's grace.NIV In addition to his conduct, Paul pointed to the reason for his good behavior and the source of his teaching: It did not come from *worldly wisdom,* but from *God's grace.* Paul had already delineated the difference between human wisdom and God's wisdom in 1 Corinthians. Although most people look either for eloquent speeches or awe-inspiring signs to authenticate the truth of a message, God chooses to use foolish and weak messengers to shame the wise with his powerful message of truth (1 Corinthians 1:18–2:14). Perhaps it was because the Corinthians were continuing to admire eloquent speakers among them that Paul alluded to his discussion of the superiority of God's message to human wisdom in 1 Corinthians.

The Greek word *charis,* translated in this verse as "grace," means God's undeserved favor. In this context, it means God's gifts that enabled Paul to preach the gospel. In other words, Paul wasn't relying on his own wisdom and knowledge when he visited Corinth with the truth of the gospel. Instead, he was relying on God's enabling power—something that should have been clear to all the Corinthians.

1:13-14 **For we do not write you anything you cannot read or understand. And I hope that, as you have understood us in part, you will come to understand fully that you can boast of us just as we will boast of you in the day of the Lord Jesus.**NIV Although the Greek here could mean that Paul wasn't writing anything the Corinthians didn't already know, it is more probable that Paul was denying that he didn't write anything the Corinthians couldn't understand. Apparently, the Corinthians were questioning Paul's sincerity. Some in the church were claiming that he wrote one thing and then said another (see 10:9-10). Here Paul defended his sincerity, especially his honesty in his previous letters.

If the Corinthians were not convinced of his genuine intentions, Paul could only *hope*—that is, confidently expect—that his sincere intentions would be revealed on the day of the Lord Jesus. That day is the day Jesus will come back to this earth. The Old Testament prophets referred to this day as "the day of the Lord" (see Isaiah 13:6; Joel 1:15; Amos 5:18). Paul added Jesus' name to this Old Testament phrase in order to make clear who the prophets were looking for. They were anticipating the day when Jesus would bring justice to the earth and deliver the righteous from their oppressors. On that day, Paul expected that his actions and words would be shown for what they were: blameless and true. Indeed, the genuineness of the Corinthians' faith would be a matter of great joy for Paul on that day. They would be able to *boast* (or take pride) in having had Paul as their teacher, and he would then *boast of* having had them as his converts. Just as the faith of the Thessalonians would bring joy to Paul when Jesus came back, the Corinthians, too, would fill him with joy (see 1 Thessalonians 2:19). The Corinthians, in turn, would be able to rejoice in the accomplishments of Paul because they had become his fellow workers by faithfully praying for his ministry (1:11).

SIMPLICITY
The key to missionaries' effectiveness is learning the language of those to whom they are communicating God's Word. If they share the gospel in language and concepts that people don't understand, their well-intentioned words can fall to the ground. They are useless. Paul knew this cross-cultural principle and took special care to communicate to the Corinthians in words and images they could understand. Paul worked at making his words understandable. Although Paul was probably more educated than most of the people who read and heard his letters, he placed the canister of kingdom truths on the bottom shelf, within easy reach of the least educated. Those who preach and teach would do well to follow Paul's example. How adept are you at communicating a simple biblical concept?

1:15-16 Because I was confident of this, I planned to visit you first so that you might benefit twice. I planned to visit you on my way to Macedonia and to come back to you from Macedonia, and

then to have you send me on my way to Judea.[NIV] Paul had
based his travel plans on his confidence that the Corinthians were
taking pride in him, just as he was in them (see 1:14). He had
made a quick, unscheduled visit to Corinth. But when he had
arrived, he had found quite a different atmosphere at that church.
At least a portion of its members had rejected him and repudiated
his authority. Paul would later call this a "painful visit"—one that
caused a breach in the Corinthians' intimate relationship with
him (see 2:1). This "painful visit" was quick because Paul had to
hurry on to visit the churches in Macedonia. But while he was in
Corinth, he had promised to visit the Corinthians on the way
back.

Paul changed his travel plans, however. Instead of visiting Corinth on the way back through Macedonia and Achaia (present-
day Greece), Paul most likely sailed directly to Ephesus. Paul had
made his original plans thinking that the church had solved most
of its problems. When the time came for Paul's scheduled trip to
Corinth, however, the crisis had not been fully resolved (although
progress was being made in some areas; see 7:11-16). So Paul
wrote a letter instead (2:3-4; 7:8). He believed that another visit
would only make matters worse.

The fact that Paul first made an unscheduled visit and then canceled his second scheduled visit to Corinth gave his opponents
another reason to criticize him. He had not come through on his
promises. Subsequently, in 2 Corinthians, Paul spent much of the
letter defending his honesty to the Corinthians (1:12).

The Greek words that Paul used in these verses emphasize his
sincerity. First, he wanted to communicate that he had made his
plans with care. Paul used a Greek word for "planned" that conveys a strong act of will—basically, a thought-out decision. Second, Paul wanted to emphasize the motives behind his actions.
The root of the Greek word for "benefit" is *charis,* the word commonly translated as "grace." Paul used *charis* in this context to
mean "joy," "kindness," "pleasure," or "benefit." Thus, Paul was
saying that he would have two opportunities—because of the two
visits—to show kindness to the Corinthians. In contrast, the meeting turned out not to be a joy but a burden and a source of pain.

With his careful choice of words, Paul was trying to express
his motives clearly to the Corinthians. He had made intentional
plans for their mutual spiritual *benefit.* The abrupt changes in
Paul's travel plans were for the same reason: He canceled his
visit to Corinth because he wanted the best for them.

The Corinthians had misread Paul, and in this letter he had to
explain his motives. Paul's predicament is a clear warning to all
Christians. Christians not only must pursue what is right in all cir-

cumstances, but they also should make sure their course of action effectively communicates their sincere motives.

1:17 When I planned this, did I do it lightly? Or do I make my plans in a worldly manner so that in the same breath I say, "Yes, yes" and "No, no"?NIV Paul's change of plans had given his accusers at Corinth reasons to complain about his conduct— and even to criticize his authority. By criticizing him for his erratic travel plans, Paul's opponents were implying that he couldn't be trusted. If Paul couldn't be trusted, then how could they believe his message?

The Greek construction Paul used for the word "lightly" implies that he was quoting the charge of his opponents. The word connotes a person who makes promises that he or she doesn't intend to keep—a person who is fundamentally untrustworthy.

After his first rhetorical question in this verse, Paul asked another rhetorical question that again quoted the accusations of his opponents. The allegation that Paul made his plans *in a worldly manner* was repeated by Paul in this letter (in 10:2). According to Paul, the "world" sharply contrasts with the Spirit (see Galatians 5:16-17). By the phrase "worldly manner," Paul meant the standards and mores of this world—that is, human self-interest that governs the behavior of many people. A person governed by pure self-interest and selfish desires would say yes when it was convenient, but then renege on that promise when some other better opportunity afforded itself. This is the predictable behavior of a person who doesn't say no to his or her own selfish desires.

Throughout his writings, Paul contrasted a person's worldly desires with being controlled by the Spirit. The Spirit of God living within Christians helps them to break free from their own selfishness. The Spirit transforms Christians from within, giving them the motivation to act according to a higher standard and not mere self-interest. The higher standard is obedience to God. Paul had come to the Corinthians with the message of the Spirit—not merely a human message. He had proven his sincere motives by refusing to take money from them. Paul wasn't acting out of self-interest. He wasn't preaching to them for his own financial benefit. Instead, Paul—empowered by the Holy Spirit—was preaching a divine message, the refreshing truth in a world of falsehoods.

Paul's opponents at Corinth had used Paul's own sharp distinction between the world and the Spirit against him. They had labeled his actions as being motivated by the world's standards.

This accusation was in direct contradiction to Paul's own claim in 1 Corinthians that his preaching was not from himself or any other human authority but from the Spirit of God (see 1 Corinthians 2:4). Labeling his actions as coming from worldly reasoning was a direct assault on Paul's spiritual authority. These serious accusations circulating in Corinth were the reason why Paul had to write 2 Corinthians. In essence, this letter is a passionate defense of Paul's apostolic authority and the truth of his message.

STRAIGHT TALK
A Christian's words should be clean and decent. Paul refers in 1:17 to a worldly manner of decision making. When people decide as people of the world do, they speak out of both sides of their mouth—saying one thing and doing another. Christians are to be in the world but not "of the world" (John 17:14-16). The "world" is the system of values that completely ignores biblical wisdom. We Christians are tempted to think as worldly people do because we live in the world. When we purposely resist the world's influence and evaluate our motives and goals by God's Word, we can be certain about our choices and plans. The confidence that Paul knew is the confidence that God wants us to have as we face our future and commit to responsibilities within his church. Christian leaders must communicate their intentions and follow through on what they say.

1:18-19 **As surely as God is faithful, our word to you has not been "Yes and No." For the Son of God, Jesus Christ, whom we proclaimed among you, Silvanus and Timothy and I, was not "Yes and No"; but in him it is always "Yes."**[NRSV] Instead of immediately answering his opponents' criticisms of his behavior, Paul addressed the fundamental problem at Corinth: The believers in Corinth were questioning the veracity of Paul's message to them. Paul clearly saw what was at stake. Questioning the motives and honesty of the messenger would eventually lead to questioning the truth of the message.

Instead of defending himself, Paul reminded the Corinthians of God's faithfulness. There was no duplicity in God. His promises would be fulfilled. There would be no wavering between "yes" and "no." Jesus Christ was the premier example of this. All of God's promises concerning the Messiah, or the Savior of Israel, were fulfilled in Christ. Thus "in him it is always 'Yes.'" Jesus was completely faithful in his ministry, fulfilling every promise God had made. He never sinned (1 Peter 3:18). He faithfully and obediently died for all of humanity (Hebrews 2:9). And now he faithfully intercedes for all who believe (Romans 8:34; Hebrews 4:14, 15). Jesus is the embodiment of God's faithfulness.

After reminding the Corinthians of Jesus' faithfulness in everything, Paul employed a common line of argument in the first century, an argument from the greater to the lesser. If Jesus had
proved himself faithful, then Jesus' appointed messengers—Paul,
Timothy, and Silas—would certainly be faithful and trustworthy.
Paul had shown his faithfulness as a messenger of Christ by not
wavering in his preaching. He had *always* preached Christ to the
Corinthians. The fact that Paul consistently preached Christ—as
he had with them—meant he would be trustworthy in the smaller
things—such as travel plans.

**1:20 For in him every one of God's promises is a "Yes." For this
reason it is through him that we say the "Amen," to the glory
of God.**^{NRSV} This verse reiterates Paul's point: Christ has fulfilled
all of God's promises. His earthly ministry is an example of
God's faithfulness to his people. God had promised he would provide a Savior, and he did. Christ obediently and faithfully said
"yes" to God and his great promises.

As he did in the beginning of this letter (1:3), Paul once again
quoted from first-century liturgy. This time it is the *Amen*. The frequent use of this Old Testament Hebrew word in the letters of the
New Testament indicates that first-century Christians used this
word in their worship services (see 1:20; Romans 1:25; 9:5; 11:36;
15:33; 16:20, 27; 1 Corinthians 14:16; 16:24; Galatians 1:5). The
Hebrew word *amen* conveys a firm agreement with what has been
said. The Israelites used this word to express their agreement to
God's law and its blessings and curses (see Deuteronomy 27:15). In
this verse Paul explained why Christians use the word. It is the way
Christians acknowledge that Jesus has fulfilled all of God's promises. Jesus is the great "Amen" (Revelation 3:14) because he has
been faithful to God. When Christians say "Amen," they are joining Jesus in saying "Yes" to God. By doing this, Christians everywhere bring *glory* to God. They give God the proper respect and
honor that he deserves. With this type of reasoning, Paul made it
clear that his own integrity stood on Christ's integrity because his
message was consistently Christ's gospel.

Paul's approach with his opponents in Corinth is instructive. In
the beginning of the letter, he resisted the temptation to defend
his actions and attack his opponents. Instead, he began his letter
by praising God (see 1:3-11). With these praises, Paul spoke of
the Corinthians. It was only because of Jesus that they were connected in the first place (1:6, 14). Christ had joined Paul and the
Corinthians together in the struggle to preach and live out the
truth of the gospel. Their fervent prayers benefited him, and his
sufferings for the gospel in Asia in turn would benefit them (1:6,

11). Their lives were inextricably intertwined in order to bring praise and glory to God. In other words, Paul—in this troublesome situation—emphasized the common ground between him and the Corinthians: Jesus Christ and his message. Paul refused to address the differences between them until he had reminded the Corinthians of the greater cause of Christ to which they were both dedicated.

Differences will occur in any church. Disputes will break out. In mediating these disputes, the first thing to do is to focus on the primary purpose of the church in the beginning: to spread the gospel and bring glory to God. Many times when church members resolutely focus on their common Savior, differences begin to fade into the background. The church becomes what it was made to be: a community of believers who consciously bring glory to God.

KEEP YOUR WORD
Paul stressed integrity in communication (1:20). The expression "you have my word on it" increases confidence. The people offering a product or a service are staking their reputation to stand behind the advertised quality and performance. According to John 1:1, Jesus is the Word (the *Logos*). He is the expressed communication of the Creator's love and redemptive plan. But he is more. According to this text, Jesus is the guarantee of all God has advertised in biblical history. In Jesus' virgin birth, his ministry of miracles, his atoning death, and his supernatural resurrection, we read the fine print of God's warranty of salvation. In Jesus, God has given his word.

To whom have you recently given your word that you would do something? A son or daughter? A parent? Someone on the church staff? A member of your small group? Have you neglected your promise? Are you consistently late for an agreed-on time to meet? Confess your neglect. Ask forgiveness. When possible, start again. Follow Christ's example.

1:21-22 Now it is God who makes both us and you stand firm in Christ.[NIV] In these two verses, Paul described how he, his coworkers—Timothy, and Silas—and the Corinthians themselves were all tied together. They had all received God's Spirit, an indication they all belonged to God through Christ. It was God's undeniable work in the lives of all of them that guaranteed Paul's trustworthiness in such things as his travel plans (see 1:23).

These verses use four key terms to describe how God made them all part of his family.

1. The first, "stand firm," is derived from legal terminology. In the first-century Mediterranean world, this was a technical word for

a legal guarantee that would confirm a sale as valid. All terms of the sale would be carried out as promised. In the New Testament, the word is used for the miraculous signs and spiritual gifts that confirmed that God was indeed working at that time and place (see Mark 16:20; 1 Corinthians 1:6). Here Paul used the word to express that it is God himself who guarantees the salvation of those who believe in Jesus. Having the guarantee or confirmation of God Almighty would be the greatest amount of security a person could ask for—especially since the Lord God had already proven his faithfulness to his promises in the life of Jesus Christ.

The next three terms are found in these words:

He anointed us, set his seal of ownership on us, and put his Spirit in our hearts as a deposit, guaranteeing what is to come.NIV

2. The second word, "anointed," was derived from an Old Testament concept. In the Old Testament, prophets, priests, and kings were anointed to signify their commission to be representatives of God to the Israelites (see Exodus 28:41; 1 Samuel 15:1; 1 Kings 19:16). The Hebrew word for "anointed" was *masiah* (the English word "Messiah" is derived from this word). The Hebrew word was eventually used to refer to the promised Savior of the Israelites. The Greek translation of the Hebrew word *masiah* is the word *christos,* or in English, "Christ." So when Christians speak of Jesus as the Christ, they are confessing him as the promised Messiah of the Old Testament. Here Paul used the Greek verb *chrio* for "anointed" to speak of the anointing of God's Spirit. Luke, the author of Acts, used this Greek word in the same way: to speak of the Spirit's power coming on a person (see Luke 4:18; Acts 10:38).

3. The third word Paul used for salvation, "seal," was derived from the commercial language of the first century. The Greek word for "seal" referred to the practice of sealing letters so that they would not be tampered with. A seal would identify whose letter it was and also guarantee the authenticity of that letter. In the first century, a seal might also be used for the packages containing money. A first-century seal was similar to the present-day brand that is burned on the hide of an animal. The brand identifies the owner of the animal and warns others against tampering with this animal. Many people do essentially the same thing when they engrave serial numbers into their valuables as a mark of their ownership of those items.

Paul used this image of a seal or brand for Christians also. God himself has sealed, or stamped on us, his mark of ownership when he gave us his Spirit to live in us (see Paul's use of this word in Ephesians 1:13; 4:30).

4. Paul used yet another legal term of his day, "deposit." The Greek word for "deposit" refers to the down payment that a buyer will give a seller to declare the intent of paying the full amount. In our credit-driven modern society, we pay down payments or earnest money on everything from a house to a coat placed on layaway. Here and in Ephesians 1:14, Paul used this word to refer to the Holy Spirit. God gives his Spirit to his children as a down payment. It is only a foretaste of the glorious joy they will experience in heaven—the full payment that God has promised.

With these four key terms, Paul reiterates again and again to whom he, along with the Corinthians, belong. They are owned by God, who has not only placed the down payment of his own Spirit in their hearts but also has guaranteed, sealed, and anointed them in Christ. These four assurances are the basis for a believer's certainty that he or she is saved and will live with God forever in heaven. It is the Spirit of God, not a Christian's works, that guarantee a believer's salvation.

1:23-24 **I call God as my witness that it was in order to spare you that I did not return to Corinth.**[NIV] Paul had planned to visit the Corinthians twice (see 1:15-16). But after experiencing the brunt of his opponents' attacks on his last "painful visit" (2:1 NLT), he, instead, wrote a letter to give them a chance to change their ways (7:8-9). Paul didn't want to visit and repeat the same advice for the same problems. Instead, he wanted to visit them at a time when he could encourage them in their faith.

This verse has a common legal expression, "I call God as my witness," that was used to summon a witness to a trial. In other words, Paul was subpoenaing God as his *witness*. Since no other person could testify to his motives, Paul was appealing to God as a witness to his innocence. In a number of his New Testament letters, Paul called on God as witness to his intentions (see Romans 1:9; Philippians 1:8; 1 Thessalonians 2:5, 10). Paul saw his whole life—including his innermost thoughts—as an open book to God.

In this case, Paul wanted to make it clear that his decision to cancel his second visit to Corinth had been made out of consideration for the spiritual welfare of the Corinthians. He hadn't made the decision for selfish reasons, as his opponents had claimed (1:17). He wasn't simply a fickle person. Instead, his motive had been to *spare* the Corinthians the sorrow that another visit would produce. Apparently, Paul wanted to give the Corinthians time to resolve some of the problems that had surfaced on his last "painful visit."

Not that we lord it over your faith, but we work with you for your joy, because it is by faith you stand firm.^{NIV} In the beginning of 2 Corinthians, Paul was very careful not to offend the Corinthians. Instead, he repeatedly emphasized their unity in Christ. Through Jesus, Paul and the Corinthians had been joined (see 1:6, 11, 14, 21). Paul and the Corinthians were even working together to further the cause of the gospel: The Corinthians' prayers were strengthening Paul in his trials; in turn, Paul was encouraging them. On the day when Jesus would return, the Corinthians would be able to take pride in Paul's work; Paul, in turn, would take pride in the Corinthians' faith (1:14). Paul took great pains to emphasize how they were working together, in order to avoid any "us-versus-them" attitudes.

This verse protects Paul from any misunderstanding with the Corinthians by explaining what he meant by "spare." It qualifies his previous statement. Paul wasn't acting as a judge or governor *over* the Corinthians' *faith* in Christ. Paul couldn't give them their faith—that is, their confident belief in God and in Jesus, their Savior—much less control it. Their faith was a gift from God (Romans 12:3; Ephesians 2:8), not subject to anyone's control except God's. In this respect, the Corinthians were subject to no one except the ultimate Judge (Romans 14:1-4). As a result of this gift of faith, the Corinthians were to *stand firm*. This means to endure and persevere in the face of opposition and pressure from the world (see notes in the Life Application Commentary *Hebrews* 12:1; 12:11-13).

STANDING FIRM
Endurance grows out of commitment to Jesus Christ. In Matthew 10:22, Jesus predicted that his followers would be severely persecuted by those who hated what he stood for. In the midst of terrible persecutions, however, they could have hope, knowing that salvation was theirs. Times of trial serve to sift true Christians from false or fair-weather Christians. When you are pressured to give up and turn your back on Christ, don't do it. Remember the benefits of standing firm and continue to live for Christ.

Standing firm to the end is not a way to be saved but the evidence that a person is really committed to Jesus. Persistence is not a means to earn salvation; it is the by-product of a truly devoted life.

Instead of describing his apostolic role as being a master, Paul carefully described his job as an apostle as working with the Corinthians for their ultimate *joy* in Christ. It could only be in Christ because it would only be *by faith* in him that they could *stand firm*. Paul wasn't their taskmaster. Instead, he was a fellow worker, pointing out how they could experience the joy God wanted to give them. This is a potent image for any spiritual leader—from a pastor to a Sunday school teacher. A spiritual leader should be less of a master and more of a friend—a person who works beside, always pointing to the path that leads to the joy that can be found only in God.

2:1-2 So I made up my mind that I would not make another painful visit to you.[NIV] Paul didn't recount exactly what had happened on this painful visit in this letter. That would have been inappropriate since Paul had already addressed it previously (see 2:3). But this letter gives some clues to what happened. From the two letters that have been preserved—1 and 2 Corinthians—we know that the Corinthians not only had problems with incest (1 Corinthians 5:1-2) and adultery (1 Corinthians 6:9), but they were also troubled by incessant arguing (1 Corinthians 1:10), disruptions during the worship service (1 Corinthians 11:17-22), and even lawsuits between believers (1 Corinthians 6:1-8). Moreover, a group of false teachers were preoccupied with criticizing Paul's actions and authority (11:1-11). Apparently, on Paul's last visit, a member of the Corinthian church had publicly challenged Paul (2:5). Paul issued a severe warning to those who were persistently sinning in the church (13:2).

For if I grieve you, who is left to make me glad but you whom I have grieved?[NIV] This rhetorical question reiterates Paul's point that his ministry is to work with the Corinthians for their mutual joy (see 1:24). Many of Paul's letters describe the joy and encouragement he had received from other Christians—from the Romans (Romans 15:32), the Philippians (Philippians 1:25), and the Thessalonians (1 Thessalonians 2:19). The steadfast faith of these Christians encouraged Paul to continue in his evangelistic labors. Later in this letter, Paul would describe how Titus's promising report of the Corinthians' faith encouraged him to endure persecution (see 7:4, 7).

Thus, Paul decided not to visit the Corinthians because he didn't want to cause unnecessary sorrow. He had already rebuked the church on his last visit (13:2). He wanted to give them more instruction on how to correct some of the abuses in the church (see Paul's description of his letter in 2:3-4), but he also wanted to give them some time to resolve the issues amongst themselves, for their faith would ultimately stand on God—not on Paul or his efforts to reform them (see 1:24). Appropriately, Paul gave the Corinthians some time to work out what putting their faith in action meant.

2:3 That is why I wrote as I did in my last letter, so that when I do come, I will not be made sad by the very ones who ought to give

me the greatest joy. Surely you know that my happiness depends on your happiness.NLT The identity of Paul's *last letter* has been a subject of much scholarly debate. Traditionally, the letter Paul referred to here was considered 1 Corinthians. Proponents of this theory identified the sinner who Paul forgave in the next passage (2:5-11) with the incestuous man of 1 Corinthians 5:1-5.

It has become generally accepted, however, that 1 Corinthians is not the "last letter," primarily because 1 Corinthians as a whole does not reflect the extreme sorrow described by Paul in these following verses. Furthermore, the details described in the next passage (2:5-11) do not seem to fit the situation with the incestuous man of 1 Corinthians 5:1-5 but instead someone who had personally offended Paul on his last trip to Corinth (see 2:5). For these reasons, many Bible commentators consider the letter referred to in this verse to be lost. Apparently Paul wrote this "severe letter" to the Corinthians soon after his "painful visit" with them. In this lost letter, he had exhorted the Corinthians to discipline their errant members—specifically, the ones who were publicly opposing his authority (see 2 Corinthians 2:1-4; 7:8). God, according to his sovereign plan, preserved all of Paul's letters he wanted to include in the Bible—God's inspired Word. According to his plan, this letter was not preserved for later generations to read and study.

This verse reiterates that Paul's own *joy* depended on the spiritual condition of the Corinthians. The first part of 2 Corinthians emphasizes the interdependence of Paul and the Corinthians—the community of the faith that existed between them (see 1:11-14). Paul's own spiritual success was intimately connected with the Corinthians' spiritual success. This verse (2:3) again emphasizes that the Corinthians provided part of Paul's motivation. In fact, their strong faith and their *happiness* was one of the reasons he could courageously face the trials of an evangelist (see 7:4).

The interdependence of Christians was a truth Paul had already told the Corinthians about (see 1 Corinthians 12:12-29). Christians, together, form one body, joined by Christ to glorify God the Father. As all part of one body, believers are to work together for the gospel of Christ. Each member should do his or her part, according to the spiritual gifts God has given that person. Paul had to stress this truth again and again—*surely you know that my happiness depends on your happiness.* In Ephesians, Paul underscores the unity of Gentiles and Israelites in Christ (Ephesians 3:6). In Romans, Paul encourages each Christian to enthusiastically use his or her unique spiritual gift for the benefit of the entire church (Romans 12:4-8). In Colossians, he encourages all to pursue peace with one another since they are all part of the same body (Colossians 3:15).

TIMELY LETTERS
Paul wrote letters—lots of them. He understood the importance of maintaining contact with those with whom he was in relationship and those for whom he was a spiritual parent. Paul took the time to communicate even when the content of his letters challenged ungodly behavior and attitudes. In today's fast-paced, jam-packed lifestyles, the art of letter writing has almost become extinct. Telephone calls and electronic communication have replaced the written word and have increased the speed of information. Still, schedules and commitments often crowd out those who need spiritual input. A letter can be an important ministry tool. Who are those who need a letter from you? How can you share what they need to hear in a way they know you care for them?

2:4 How painful it was to write that letter! Heartbroken, I cried over it. I didn't want to hurt you, but I wanted you to know how very much I love you.ᴺᴸᵀ Paul passionately expressed how he felt when he wrote *that letter,* the "severe letter." Although he was sorry that his letter would *hurt* the Corinthians, he had sent it anyway. In 7:8-12, Paul explains his reasons in more detail. His severe reprimand in this letter was aimed at securing a change of heart in the Corinthian believers. He knew it would cause much sorrow, but he was hoping that it would provoke "godly sorrow" (7:10 NIV), a sorrow that leads to repentance. That is why Paul claimed here that his motive was *love*. Sometimes the most loving action a person can do for a fellow Christian is to confront him or her with the truth. The truth often hurts. Confronting a person in the wrong with the truth, however, can be the best thing a friend can do.

TOUGH LOVE
Paul did not enjoy reprimanding his friends and fellow believers, but he cared enough about the Corinthians to confront them with their wrongdoing (2:4). Proverbs 27:6 says: "Wounds from a friend are better than many kisses from an enemy" (NLT). Sometimes our friends make choices that we know are wrong. If we ignore their behavior and let them continue in it, we won't be showing love to them. We show love by honestly sharing our concerns in order to help these friends do and be their very best for God. When we don't make any move to help, we show that we are more concerned about being well liked than about what will happen to them.

2 Corinthians 2:5-17

After explaining in general terms why he had delayed his visit
to Corinth (see 1:12–2:4), Paul addressed the specific confrontation that most likely had led to his decision to cancel his visit.
Paul doesn't name the offender who had caused the trouble the
last time he was in Corinth, but he does instruct the church on
how to handle this man. As this letter will explain later, the
Corinthians had obeyed Paul's previous instructions in the letter Paul had written with tears (see 2:1-4; 7:8-10). They had
accepted responsibility for the offense. Truly sorry for their initial mismanagement of the unfortunate event, they had punished the offender.

Paul was concerned for the offender's spiritual welfare. He
interrupted his explanation of his recent travel plans (compare
2:1-4 with 2:12-13) to instruct the church on how to treat this
man. This reveals Paul's pastoral concern. Although the primary
purpose of 2 Corinthians is to reassert Paul's apostolic authority
in the face of mounting criticism, Paul didn't want the spiritual
condition of anyone in the church to be jeopardized—even if it
was the man who had offended him personally (see 2:5). He
explained that it was time to forgive the man. Paul had probably
heard from Titus that the punishment by the entire church had
driven the man to sorrow (see 7:6-7). If given the chance, his sorrow could be transformed into the godly sorrow that would lead
to repentance (see Paul's description of godly sorrow in 7:10-13).
The offender needed forgiveness, acceptance, and comfort. Paul
was concerned that undue severity would give Satan a foothold
in the church by permanently separating the man from the congregation of believers. It was essential, therefore, that the church act
quickly to forgive and restore this man, while he was still repentant. Church discipline should always seek the restoration of the
offender. Two mistakes in church discipline should be avoided—
being too lenient by not correcting mistakes and being too harsh
by not forgiving the sinner. There is a time to confront and a time
to comfort.

2:5 But if anyone has caused pain, he has caused it not to me, but to some extent—not to exaggerate it—to all of you.^{NRSV} These verses emphasize that the reason Paul was concerned about this man's offense was not to correct an injury Paul had suffered. If that had been the case, then Paul might take his own instructions to heart: to simply ignore the injustice (see 1 Corinthians 6:7). Instead, Paul's point is that the whole church *(all of you)* had suffered because of this man.

Most likely, the offender's actions had amounted to a direct attack on Paul's apostolic authority. The teachings of the "false apostles," who had infiltrated the Corinthian church and had started discrediting Paul's authority, might have inspired this man to challenge Paul's authority in public (see Paul's censure of these "false apostles" in 11:1-15). Paul would perceive this not only as an attack on his authority but also an insult to the entire church, which had been founded on the gospel message that Paul had delivered to them. If Paul were fundamentally untrustworthy, then his message couldn't be trusted either (see Paul's defense of his message in 1:19-20). This would be an offense with broad implications.

Paul's concern in all of this was to assure the Corinthians that he wasn't trying to defend himself. This wasn't a personal vendetta; instead, it touched on the foundations of the Christian faith. The distinction expressed in this verse should be made in churches today. Personal agendas or preferences should not block the clear proclamation of the gospel. But when an issue touches on the authority of Jesus or the truth of the gospel, that issue must be taken seriously, for it affects the life of the entire church. We, too, need to muster the courage to pass judgment on quarrelsome, selfish ambition in our churches, just as Paul did in the first century (see Philippians 2:3; James 3:14).

2:6 He was punished enough when most of you were united in your judgment against him.^{NLT} Paul's stern letter had produced the desired effect. The majority of the Corinthians had realized that tolerating this man and the sin he encouraged would ruin the congregation. They couldn't function as the holy people of God with such a rebel among them.

The Greek word Paul used for "punished" is only used here in the New Testament. In the first century, Greek words derived from this root were used for legal sanctions or commercial penalties. But these words might also indicate a simple rebuke. It is not entirely clear what action the Corinthian church took against this offender. Most likely, they had excluded him from partaking of the Lord's Supper, a punishment that Paul himself had suggested in 1 Corinthians: "If anyone eats this bread or drinks this cup of the Lord unworthily, that person is guilty of sinning against the body and the blood of the Lord" (1 Corinthians 11:27 NLT). The main point is that *most* of the believers in the church *were united in . . . judgment against* this man. This united front showed the man the seriousness of his sin and, no doubt, helped lead him to repentance (for more on church discipline, see notes on 2:11 and 1 Corinthians 5:1-13).

2:7-8 So now instead you should forgive and console him, so that he may not be overwhelmed by excessive sorrow. So I urge you to reaffirm your love for him.NRSV Evidently, the reproof that the Corinthians had meted out was sufficient—at least, Titus had reported that it was (see 7:8-10). The unnamed offender had realized the seriousness of his actions. Paul was extremely concerned that the Corinthians *forgive and console* the offender at the appropriate time. He did not want the offender to be *overwhelmed by excessive sorrow.* The Greek verb for "overwhelmed" was used in Greek writings to describe engulfing waves. Thus Paul's image here was of the disciplined person drowning in sadness. Paul wasn't concerned for his own vindication in this distressing incident but instead for the offender's spiritual welfare.

Just as on his last visit, Paul had passionately urged the Corinthians to punish the offender (13:2), here he encouraged the Corinthians to *reaffirm* their *love for* the offender. The intent of church discipline should be reform, not punishment. The goal should be to bring the offender to repentance.

God is the ultimate judge and the ultimate punisher of every person's deeds (James 4:12). On this earth, however, the church has the responsibility to discipline members who are straying from the truth of the gospel or the righteous life that God demands. In this situation, the discipline had promoted genuine repentance. Thus, the Corinthians were to restore the man who was being disciplined, showing him genuine Christian love. The Greek word for "reaffirm" here suggests a legal act, such as a ratification of an appointment. The fact that Paul used here a legal term with the Greek word *agape,* a word that means "selfless love," is remarkable. Paul was asking the Corinthian church to confirm the membership of this man in the community of love— that is, the church—in a public and official manner. Paul doesn't quote Jesus on this matter, but he was, in effect, following Jesus' own instructions: "If another believer sins, rebuke him; then if he repents, forgive him" (Luke 17:3 NLT).

Knowing the appropriate time to rebuke and the appropriate

time to forgive is the key to compassionate church discipline. In his letters to the Corinthians, Paul was teaching the Corinthian church to discern the proper occasion for both (see 13:1-5; 1 Corinthians 5:1-5). This type of discernment is crucial for a church plagued with problems, as the Corinthian church was. Christians in position of authority must consistently check their motives when it comes to church discipline. They must ask: Am I keeping the spiritual welfare of my church members—especially that of the offender—in mind?

2:9 The reason I wrote you was to see if you would stand the test and be obedient in everything.[NIV] Paul reiterated his reason for writing the "severe letter" to the Corinthians. First of all, he hoped the letter would rectify the troublesome situation before he arrived (see 2:3). When he visited them, he wanted to encourage them in their faith instead of correcting then. Second, he wanted to *test* their obedience.

After taking pains to emphasize how he was working with the Corinthians for their joy instead of tyrannically controlling their faith (1:24), Paul praised their obedience to the gospel. As Paul explained to the Romans, God had assigned him the apostolic task of calling people to obedience to God, which comes out of faith in Christ (see Romans 1:5). Later in 2 Corinthians, Paul unequivocally would assert his authority as an apostle to punish disobedience. He had been empowered by Christ with apostolic authority (10:4-6). But Paul's authority didn't involve commanding obedience to himself but, instead, to Christ and the gospel. Paul explained this thoroughly to the Galatians. His message was the gospel revealed to him by Jesus Christ himself. A preacher of any other gospel than the one he preached would be eternally condemned (Galatians 1:6-12). In 1 Corinthians, Paul maintained that he had preached only the message of Christ crucified. He had added nothing to it. Although both Jew and Gentile considered it foolish, the message possessed the power of God. Paul did possess the authority to command obedience to this message and to the God of this gospel. He announced his authority to the Thessalonians (1 Thessalonians 4:2). When Paul defended his apostolic authority to the Corinthians, he was careful to explain that he possessed the authority to build up the church, not to tear it down (see 10:8; 13:10).

The good news was that the Corinthians were obedient to the gospel. Titus's report from Corinth revealed that they had listened to Paul's rebuke and had obeyed his instructions. Their complete obedience in these matters caused Paul to rejoice (7:13-16).

2:10 **If you forgive anyone, I also forgive him. And what I have forgiven—if there was anything to forgive—I have forgiven in
the sight of Christ for your sake.**[NIV] The Greek word for "forgive" is *charizomai*. Although Paul
used other Greek words to express forgiveness, he generally favored this
word because it was derived from the
Greek word for "grace," *charis*. For
Paul, forgiveness was the central point
of the gospel. Out of his own free will,
God forgives those who believe in his

> Everyone says
> forgiveness is a lovely
> idea, until they have
> something to forgive.
> *C. S. Lewis*

Son (Romans 3:24; 5:15). It is only through God's grace—that is,
his undeserved favor—that anyone is saved at all (Ephesians 2:5,
8). So the Corinthians' forgiveness of the offender among them
was fundamentally based on Christ's forgiveness of them (Ephesians 4:32; Colossians 3:13).

This verse downplays Paul's own part in the entire incident.
Paul didn't want to imply that he was governing the Corinthians'
faith (see Paul's denial of any motive like that in 1:24). Hence, he
phrased the pronouncement of forgiveness in the opposite way as
would be expected. Since the offense was primarily directed
against Paul (see 2:5), he should have been the first to pronounce
forgiveness. Instead, he emphasized that it was the Corinthians
who should forgive. He would merely agree with their verdict. In
this self-deprecating manner, Paul even suggested that he didn't
have anything to forgive. In this way, he was reiterating the point
that the offense had been against the entire church, not merely
himself (see note at 2:5).

The Greek phrase for "in the sight of Christ" is literally "in the
face of Christ." Paul was making the point that all of the delibera-
tions of the church were in Christ's presence. Jesus saw everything—even the motives and thoughts of every person. In
downplaying his own authority in this situation, Paul was pointing to the ultimate authority: Christ himself. It was before Christ
that the church would forgive the offender, and it was before
Christ that Paul—hundreds of miles away—would forgive the
same offender.

2:11 **In order that Satan might not outwit us. For we are not
unaware of his schemes.**[NIV] Paul spoke of *Satan* more in his letters to the Corinthians than in any other of his New Testament letters. He saw the telltale signs of a demonic attack on the church
at Corinth. Second Corinthians unambiguously identifies the
"false apostles" in the Corinthian church with the clever deceptions of *Satan* (see 11:14). Moreover, Paul identifies Satan as the

THE CHRISTIAN'S ARMOR AGAINST SATAN

Satan devises schemes against believers because they are not on his side anymore. They are in God's army. The following is a list (derived from Ephesians 6:11-17) of the armor that God gives every believer.

Piece of Armor	*The Believer's Defense against Satan*
Belt of truth	Study Scripture so that Satan cannot deceive you.
Breastplate of righteousness	Ask God for the ability to resist Satan's temptations.
Shoes that are ready to spread the gospel	Ask God to give you an opportunity to tell unbelievers about Jesus.
Shield of faith	Ask God to increase your faith in him.
Helmet of salvation	Continually remind yourself that Jesus has saved you from your sins.
Sword of the Spirit, which is the Word of God	Ask the Spirit to help you understand the Bible's message.

one who was tempting some in the church into sexual immorality (see 1 Corinthians 5:1-5; 6:12-20) and others to participate in the idolatrous feasts of their pagan neighbors (see 1 Corinthians 10:18-22).

This passage identifies another one of Satan's evil schemes. In their zeal to purge the church from sin, the Corinthians were punishing the offender without keeping in mind the purpose of discipline: to inspire repentance and promote reconciliation to God. Under Satan's influence, the offender's sorrow could easily be turned into resentment (see 2:7) instead of repentance (see Paul's comparison of godly sorrow with worldly sorrow in 7:10). Paul pleaded with the Corinthians to guard against such a tragic outcome (see note on 1 Corinthians 5:1-13).

2:12 Now when I went to Troas to preach the gospel of Christ and found that the Lord had opened a door for me.[NIV] *Troas* was a large seaport on the Aegean Sea, ten miles away from the well-known, ancient city of Troy. It was near the straits of Dardanelles, which led to the Black Sea. Founded by Antigonus, a successor of Alexander the Great, in 334 B.C., this city was ruled by the Seleucid dynasty after Alexander the Great's death in 323 B.C. In 300 B.C. the city was renamed Alexandria Troas after Alexander the Great and became a prominent seaport that connected

Asia Minor to cities in Macedonia and Thrace (present-day northern Greece). When Rome gained control of the city in 133 B.C.,
the Romans seriously considered making it a capital for the surrounding region.

WITH LOVE
Church discipline should be used to help keep the church pure
and to help wayward people repent. But Satan tries to harm the
church by tempting it to use discipline in an unforgiving way
(2:14). One of Satan's most powerful weapons is deception,
and the sooner we, like Paul, unmask his lies, the better. Often,
Satan deceives those who are exercising discipline so that they
think they are more pure than the person being disciplined.
This causes bitterness to take root in the congregation. The
disciplined person may even leave the congregation. Believers
must remember that the purpose of church discipline is to
"restore" a person to fellowship with God, not to destroy that
person. Be cautious not to vent personal anger under the guise
of church discipline.

Paul had visited this bustling seaport on his second missionary
journey. He most likely had met Luke, the author of Luke and Acts,
at that time. In this city, Paul had a vision of a Macedonian man
asking him to share the gospel with him. Paul took this as sign from
God and immediately went to Philippi, a prominent town in Macedonia (see Acts 16:9-10). But Paul is not referring to this visit to
Troas in this letter. Paul wrote 2 Corinthians on his third missionary
journey, not his second. Apparently, while Paul was traveling
through Asia Minor on his third missionary journey, *the Lord had
opened a door for* Paul to preach the gospel. First Corinthians uses
the same metaphor for the opportunities for evangelism in Ephesus.
Paul stayed in Ephesus for two years. There he preached the gospel
in the lecture hall of Tyrannus, where students from all over Asia
Minor gathered. Ephesus eventually became a center for the evan-
gelization of the entire region. Paul probably expected Troas to be
the same type of center for evangelism.

In Troas, Paul had an opportunity *to preach the gospel of Christ.*
Paul used the Greek word *euangelion* for "gospel." The word
means "good news," and Paul used the word sixty times in his New
Testament letters. Paul summarized his life mission as the task of
preaching the gospel to Gentiles (see Galatians 1:11-16; 2 Timothy
1:10). What was the gospel message that he preached? By the word
"gospel," Paul meant the wonderful message of God's salvation
freely given to all those who believe in his Son, Jesus Christ (Galatians 3:6-14; Colossians 1:21-23). This message was the very Word
of God (see the interchangeable use of the word "gospel" and "the

Word of God" in 4:2-4). For this reason, it would be a serious matter to mutate this message or accept a different message, a different gospel (see 11:4; Galatians 1:6). That would be tantamount to completely rejecting God's offer of salvation. That was why Paul passionately and courageously defended the purity of the gospel from false teaching (see 11:1-6). His zeal for the purity of the gospel led him to confront the apostle Peter's actions (see Galatians 2:14-15). But his mission to further the gospel was for building up and not tearing down, as he would indicate to the Corinthians later in this letter (13:10). For this purpose, Paul traveled all over the Mediterranean world, preaching the gospel in every city where he found an opportunity. Apparently he had found such an opportunity in Troas.

2:13 I still had no peace of mind, because I did not find my brother Titus there. So I said good-by to them and went on to Macedonia.[NIV] This is the first time that Paul mentioned Titus's role in the complex relationship between Paul and the Corinthians. As it becomes clear in this letter, *Titus* placed a crucial role in reconciling the two (see 2:13; 7:6, 13-14; 8:6, 16-17, 23; 12:18). Titus was a Greek convert whom Paul greatly loved and wholeheartedly trusted (Galatians 2:3). Titus most likely had come to faith in Christ through Paul's ministry. Paul and Titus enjoyed a spe-

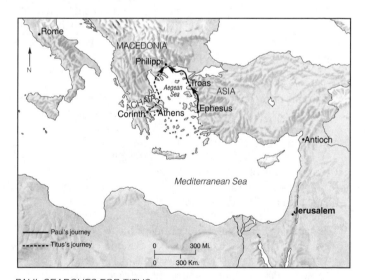

PAUL SEARCHES FOR TITUS
Paul had searched for Titus, hoping to meet him in Troas and receive news about the Corinthian church. When he did not find Titus in Troas, Paul went on to Macedonia, most likely to Philippi, where he found him.

cial relationship. Paul called Titus a "true son" (Titus 1:4 NIV) and a "partner" in Paul's work (8:23 NIV).

Titus must have had a resolute faith in Christ, for Paul chose to present him to the elders in Jerusalem as an example of the faith among the Gentiles (Galatians 2:1-5). Evidently Paul used Titus as a representative to some of the more difficult churches. It is clear from Paul's letter to him (the book of Titus) that Paul had sent Titus to a region known for violence and immorality—the island of Crete—in order to "straighten out what was left unfinished" (see Titus 1:5 NIV). Titus was not only to appoint elders in every church, but he also had the tasks of silencing rebellious talkers in the churches (Titus 1:1-12) and warning divisive people (3:10). Second Timothy 4:10 reveals that while Paul was in prison, he had sent Titus to another difficult region, Dalmatia. According to church tradition, Titus would eventually return to Crete to live out his remaining years.

Paul had already sent Timothy to Corinth, where, apparently, Timothy had run into some difficulties (see the note on 1:1). So after being personally and publicly challenged during his visit to Corinth, Paul had sent Titus with his "severe letter." Apparently Titus had the courage and resolve to go to this rebellious church with a letter from Paul commanding them to correct the abuses in their church. Paul was anxiously awaiting word on how his stern letter had affected the troublesome situation in Corinth. This was the same letter that he had cried over, so it was natural that he would have *no peace of mind* (literally, "no relief in my spirit") over it. Uncharacteristically, Paul abandoned an opportunity for evangelism at Troas because he was so troubled about the situation in Corinth.

But this short visit to Troas wouldn't be the last time Paul would visit that city. He would stop at Troas again before traveling back to Jerusalem (Acts 20:6-12). At that time, he would spend seven days there. On the Sunday of that visit, he spoke to the entire congregation at Troas until dawn of the next day. On this visit, Paul was determined to give the Christians in Troas everything they needed to stand firm in their faith in the gospel.

Apparently Paul had made some arrangements to meet Titus in Troas. So when Paul *did not find* him there, he became worried for Titus's safety and left the city to search for him in *Macedonia,* the northern province of present-day Greece. Later in this letter, Paul told the Corinthians that he did meet Titus in Macedonia. Titus's encouraging report of the situation at Corinth brought Paul great joy. Titus had achieved some success in reforming the church, as Paul would write later in this letter (see 7:5-16). Paul

was so overjoyed by the progress among the Corinthians that he
sent Titus back to Corinth with this letter we call 2 Corinthians
(8:6, 16-17).

BROTHERS
Paul called Titus his brother (2:13), although Titus wasn't his
actual brother. They were siblings in Christ, part of the family of
God. Paul loved Titus like a brother. When Paul was unable to
connect with Titus in Troas as planned, he was beside himself
with concern. Paul was concerned about his fellow worker in
Christ. Just as Paul did, we must take responsibility for the
safety and welfare of those whose name we share (Christian).
We take responsibility for being aware when those to whom we
are regularly related in Christ are absent from worship or other
gatherings. We are not content to go on with life as usual. Who
haven't you seen at church for a while? What action can you
take to make sure you show them your concern?

THE FRAGRANCE OF CHRIST / 2:14-17

Paul spent the first two chapters of 2 Corinthians chronicling his
recent ministry. It was quite depressing. He had suffered severe
affliction in Asia, even despairing of his own life (1:8-10). Criticism of his integrity plagued him in Corinth (1:17-20). The situation was so bad that some person had publicly confronted Paul
during a visit. In response, with sorrow and tears, Paul had to
write a stern letter of warning (2:1-4). Then, because he was
plagued with concern over Titus's welfare and the status of the
Corinthian church, Paul had to pass over a definite opportunity to
preach the gospel in Troas (2:12-13). Most missionaries would
hesitate to write such a report to their supporters. Opposition, conflict, and distress faced Paul at every turn.

Paul interrupted this sad tale with a burst of heartfelt praise.
Because of Paul's sudden change of tone in 2:14 and the fact that
he resumed his story of meeting Titus in 7:5, many scholars have
speculated whether the passage beginning in 2:14 and ending at
7:4 may either be another letter from Paul to the Corinthians
inserted at 2:14 or even an insertion of an anonymous editor. On
closer examination, the connection between this section of Paul's
letter and the previous section can be seen. One of the clear
emphases of 2 Corinthians is God's ability to transform Paul's
suffering and weakness into victory for the gospel. This theme
already surfaced in Paul's insistence that his suffering in Asia
would result in people praising and glorifying God (1:8-11). The
most explicit expression in this letter occurs in 12:9:

> *"My grace is sufficient for you, for my power is made perfect
> in weakness." Therefore I will boast all the more gladly about
> my weaknesses, so that Christ's power may rest on me. (*NIV*)*

The best way to interpret the drastic change of tone that occurs
at verse 14 of this chapter is to view this section as reiterating
one of the fundamental points of 2 Corinthians: God loves to
work through weakness in order to bring glory to himself. Hence,
Paul's trials and his faltering speech didn't disqualify him from
preaching the gospel. Instead, such weakness and suffering made
him a perfect conduit for God's grace, God's message, and God's
power (for Paul's extensive descriptions of his sufferings in
2 Corinthians, see 6:3-13; 11:16-27).

2:14 **But thanks be to God, who always leads us in triumphal procession in Christ and through us spreads everywhere the fragrance of the knowledge of him.**[NIV] In a Roman *triumphal
procession,* a Roman general would drive his captives and the
spoils of war before him down the main thoroughfare of Rome.
He would be greeted by the loud cheers of Romans citizens, and
a cloud of incense would be burned for the gods as they paraded
to the temple of Jupiter. To the Romans, the aroma was the sweet
smell of victory. To the captives in the parade, it was the smell of
abject slavery and perhaps even death.

Though it is clear that this verse alludes to this Roman practice, the exact nature of Paul's analogy has been widely disputed.
It is unclear whether Paul was implying that Christians are victorious partners with Christ or whether he was implying that they
are God's willing captives. Some commentators insist that "leads
us in triumphal procession" means that Christians are like the
Roman soldiers being led by the victorious general. These commentators point to the context of the passage. Paul was emphasizing God's power to triumph over Paul's weaknesses. The triumph
was God's and the gospel's. Other commentators insist that the
Greek word for "lead in triumphal procession" means "to lead
someone as a captive in a procession." As such, Paul was comparing himself and all Christians to the captives in a Roman triumphal procession. He, along with all Christians, were former
enemies of God. Hence, when Christians become believers, God
takes them as captured enemies.

In the final analysis, the general meaning seems to be that
Christ will eventually triumph over all evil. No opponent, set-
back, or weakness can stop Christ's victory. It has already been
accomplished on the cross. The triumphal procession of Christ is
on its way.

2:15-16 Our lives are a fragrance presented by Christ to God. But this fragrance is perceived differently by those being saved and by those perishing.^{NLT} These verses expand the analogy of the Roman processional incense. Here Paul used the Greek word *euodia* (translated "fragrance"), which connotes only agreeable smells. The incense at these processionals would be burned for the enjoyment of the god being worshiped. In the case of the Roman triumphal procession, incense was burned to Jupiter. But Paul's Jewish readers, steeped in Old Testament language, would immediately recognize Paul's language as being similar to Leviticus 23:18, where the burnt offerings are said to be "an aroma pleasing to the Lord."

Unlike these settings, where physical smells were presented to God (or in the Roman case, Jupiter), Paul told the Corinthians that the holy lives of Christians please God the most (see Romans 12:1)—not the thoughtless animal sacrifices of some of the Old Testament Israelites. The same truth is taught in Proverbs 21:3: "To do what is right and just is more acceptable to the Lord than sacrifice" (NIV). A heart and life wholeheartedly devoted to God is the most acceptable sacrifice to him.

To the one a fragrance from death to death, to the other a fragrance from life to life.^{NRSV} In addition to being something that pleases God, a holy life dedicated to God brings glory to him. Through Christians *(those being saved),* the precious aroma of God's grace is spread throughout the world. When Christians preach the gospel message, however, it is good news to some *(a fragrance from life to life)* and bad news to others *(a fragrance from death to death).* Those who are being drawn by the Spirit immediately recognize the life-giving power of the message. Those who stubbornly refuse to believe, however, smell something foul—the judgment of death that awaits them.

The idiom "from death to death" expresses something in progress. It is an aroma that not only smells of death but also leads to death. These people are on the pathway to eternal destruction, and every step they take brings them closer to their ultimate death. The idiom "from life to life" has the opposite connotation. It expresses an aroma that originates in the genuine life of the believer and spurs the believer closer and closer to its goal: the glory of eternal life.

Paul painted a stark contrast. There is no middle ground. There is the pathway to life and the pathway to death. Although the paths may appear to be parallel, the farther one walks on the path leading to death, the farther one deviates from the goodness, truth, and love that characterize the path of life. This is a consistent theme of Scripture. Jesus presented the same stark contrast: "Wide is the gate and broad is the road that leads to destruction, and many enter through it. But small is the gate and narrow the road that leads to life, and only a few find it" (Matthew 7:13-14 NIV). Moses spoke of the same contrast to the Israelites: "Today I have given you the choice between life and death, between blessings and curses. I call on heaven and earth to witness the choice you make. Oh, that you would choose life, that you and your descendants might live!" (Deuteronomy 30:19 NLT).

And who is adequate for such a task as this?[NLT] The Greek word for "adequate" means "competence" or "authority." Apparently, some of the preachers and teachers in Corinth had been boasting of their competence in spiritual matters and denigrating Paul's abilities. Chapter 11 of this letter is a full-scale defense of Paul's apostolic authority against these opponents.

The answer to the rhetorical question posed here is not entirely clear. Paul didn't answer the question *"Who is adequate for such a task?"* Paul might have been implying that he, as an apostle commissioned by Christ himself, was qualified. The verse after this one implies this answer, for Paul began to explain how he, unlike many others, did not have mixed motives when he preached. Paul preached the message with all sincerity, not trying to make money off the gospel (see 2:17–3:1). However, the implied answer may be that no one is competent for the task. God was the One who commissioned Paul (Acts 9:1-22) and empowered him to be an ambassador to the Gentiles (Galatians 2:7; Ephesians 3:8); he made Paul competent for the enormous task of preaching the gospel (3:5; 1 Corinthians 15:10). In the same way, believers can ready themselves for their God-given tasks by relying on God's power instead of their own competence. Serving Christ requires focusing on what Jesus can do through us, not what we can do for him.

2:17 For we are not peddlers of God's word like so many; but in Christ we speak as persons of sincerity, as persons sent from God and standing in his presence.[NRSV] After questioning whether anyone is adequate for the task of preaching the gospel, Paul indirectly criticized his opponents at Corinth for being *peddlers of God's word.*

This criticism is in response to Paul's critics, who had disparaged Paul's ministry in Corinth because he had not demanded payment for his services. Today, this would be equivalent to accusing a person of not being a professional but instead a dabbler or dilettante. While in Corinth, Paul had supported himself as a tentmaker (Acts 18:1-4). His critics saw this work as Paul's profession, and his preaching as the inarticulate thoughts of a mere tentmaker. These opponents of Paul considered themselves professional preachers, trained in the Jewish law and in public speaking (see 11:6, 22). They possessed the necessary credentials and, on the surface, were certainly competent to lead the Corinthian church.

Paul saw the situation in a totally different light, however. No one was competent to preach the gospel message. God did not need anyone's professional services. No one could claim to be qualified for the task of handling God's truth. Paul saw these high-priced preachers—later he would call them "false apostles" and would imply that they were tools of Satan (11:13-15)—as mere "peddlers," or merchants, of the divine treasures of God's Word. Because of the common tricks of petty traders, the Greek word for "peddlers" Paul used here had negative connotations. The word implied that these preachers watered down the gospel message with their greed, just as petty traders would water down wine.

It is obvious from 1 Corinthians that Paul did not object to preachers earning a living wage for their work in sharing the gospel. He had gone to great lengths to defend the right of preachers to ask for money in 1 Corinthians 9:3-10. On the other hand, Paul himself passed up that right. He strove to present the gospel free of charge in order to show his *sincerity*. Paul wasn't trying to build a following that would financially support him. He wasn't preaching what people wanted to hear. He was preaching the unadulterated truth, the glorious message of salvation through Jesus Christ.

HUCKSTERS
Paul contended that he was not like a "peddler." Like many communicators in his day, Paul was accused of being a peddler of God's Word. The image is of a door-to-door salesman hawking the truth of God's prophets for profit or to gain popularity. What they said and how they said it was shaped by who was listening (and how much money they had). In the apostle's time, and today, many will sit under our teaching who will question our motives and falsely label us. Our confidence and humility come in the knowledge that we speak as those called by God in the presence of God. Take time to reflect on your call to ministry as a salaried (or voluntary) servant of Christ. What difference should it make in your preparation or delivery of a sermon or a lesson if God himself is your primary audience?

Three parallel phrases reiterate Paul's profound sense of responsibility when it came to preaching. He had been *sent,* or commissioned, *from God* himself to preach the truth. Moreover, it was *in Christ,* or as Christ's representative, that Paul had spoken in the first place. He had been commissioned by Christ on the Damascus road to preach the gospel, not only to the Israelites but also to the Gentiles and even to kings (see Acts 9:1-15). Like a loyal servant, Paul took his commission seriously. He spoke his message in God's *presence,* or in God's sight. He consciously left his message and his life open to God's intense scrutiny. He dared not preach or speak anything that he would be ashamed to speak before God Almighty. Paul knew that he would be held accountable for his speech and his actions. This was in sharp contrast to *many* preachers, whose primary motive was profit.

2 Corinthians 3

Résumés, references, and letters of recommendation—all of these are tools of modern job hunting. In Paul's day, a letter of commendation from a reputable person could guarantee the success of one's endeavors. Traveling Christian evangelists in the first century, according to the custom of the day, carried letters of recommendation. With these, a poor preacher would be given, at least, a place to stay, a meal, and an opportunity to speak to the congregation. Apparently some false teachers had gained access to the Corinthian church with such letters. But instead of using their influence to further the cause of the gospel, these teachers had criticized Paul's message and his authority. Part of that criticism was his lack of letters of recommendation.

Paul responded to these criticisms reluctantly. It seemed foolish to defend his ministry and authority to a church he had established himself. But as the criticisms grew louder, Paul spoke up. It should have been clear from the beginning that his ministry among the Corinthians had been empowered by the Holy Spirit. The testimony of those whose lives had been forever changed by Paul's gospel and the Spirit who empowered that gospel should have been more than enough proof of his authority.

Paul's reasoned defense of his ministry in this passage quickly turns to a lengthy comparison of his ministry of the Spirit with Moses' ministry of the law. This probably indicates that the false teachers who had infiltrated the Corinthian church were holding up Moses as a godly model. Paul insisted that the Holy Spirit's work within the lives of believers had greater power than Moses and the law.

As you read and study this passage, notice *how* Paul countered the arguments of his critics in Corinth. They were attacking his authority, his credentials, and even his abilities. These were, indeed, harsh critics. Paul, however, did not reply with a passionate self-defense. He freely admitted that his competence didn't come from his own abilities. But he did claim that his apostolic authority had been given to him by Jesus to plant churches and lead those churches in the Christian faith. Proof of his authority lay in the clear work of the Holy Spirit through his ministry. In this way, Paul steered the dispute back to the ultimate issue: whether the Corinthians would submit to Christ's authority in their lives.

3:1 **Are we beginning again to tell you how good we are?**[NLT] Paul showed a great deal of sensitivity to the charge of praising himself or recommending himself to the Corinthians. He categorically denied doing the actions suggested here (see also 5:12 and 10:18). Obviously, Paul did not want to appear as if he were bragging about his accomplishments in the ministry (see 11:17). Instead, he was making a conscious effort to brag only about how Christ's strength was apparent in his weaknesses (see 11:30).

The Corinthians were putting Paul in a difficult situation. He, along with his coworkers Silas and Timothy, had founded the church. Paul didn't need to defend himself to the Corinthians: Their existence as a church was due to his Spirit-empowered preaching. Instead of questioning those preachers who came after him, the Corinthians had begun to question their own spiritual father. In essence, they were demanding that Paul present his qualifications to preach. This is apparent, for right at the start of 2 Corinthians, Paul had to speak in his own self-defense, defending his recent travel plans (1:12-17). He did this so that the Corinthians would not be misled by the false teachers.

Or do we need, like some people, letters of recommendation to you or from you?[NIV] Just as people use résumés today to introduce themselves to a prospective employer, in Paul's day traveling preachers and evangelists introduced themselves with *letters of recommendation* from various churches. Paul had written letters of recommendation on behalf of Phoebe (Romans 16:1-2) and Timothy (1 Corinthians 16:10-11). These letters helped Paul's trusted companions and friends find a welcome in various churches.

Apparently some false teachers had started using letters of recommendation to gain a speaking platform in the Corinthian church (see 11:13-15). These traveling peddlers of the Word of God, as Paul called them (2:17), had come *to* Corinth with these letters—perhaps authentic, perhaps forged—and were asking the Corinthians to recommend them to other churches. The letters gained for them hospitality from members of other churches, an opportunity to speak, and even reimbursement.

Apparently some of these false teachers had begun to criticize Paul's authority by subtly asking if he had presented any letters of recommendation. Justifiably, Paul was annoyed that he would

have to explain his apostolic credentials to the church he had
founded.

3:2-3 **But the only letter of recommendation we need is you yourselves! Your lives are a letter written in our hearts, and everyone can read it and recognize our good work among you.**^{NLT}
In a clear and forceful way, Paul stated that he did not need any
letters. The changed lives of the believers to whom he and his
companions had preached were recommendation enough. Any
discipleship program should be judged by the quality of those
who have been discipled.

Paul claimed that the changed lives of the Corinthian believers
were *a letter written in our hearts.* Some ancient manuscripts
read "your hearts" instead; therefore, some have interpreted this
verse as saying that the Corinthians' own hearts, their own
changed lives by the Holy Spirit, testified to Paul's apostolic
authority to all those who saw it. But this affirmation is made by
Paul in the next verse. Thus, the reading with "our hearts,"
though more difficult to interpret, is probably original. Paul
might have been trying to express his own participation in the
lives of the Corinthians (a theme of this letter, see 1:6-7, 11; 2:5-
6). As an evangelist to them, Paul was inextricably intertwined
with them. Their success was his; their sorrows were also his. In
this way, their lives of faith were etched in his heart and the
hearts of his coworkers, Silas and Timothy. Just as the lives of the
Corinthians were an open book to all, the intimate connection between the Corinthians and their founder, Paul, was manifest to
all. So anything that the Corinthians did would also reflect on
Paul and his ministry, and vice versa.

**And you show that you are a letter of Christ, prepared by us,
written not with ink but with the Spirit of the living God, not
on tablets of stone but on tablets of human hearts.**^{NRSV} If the
Corinthians were Paul's letter of recommendation, then this letter
was from Jesus *Christ* himself. This emphasizes that Paul's
authority as an apostle came from Jesus. Christ himself had confronted Paul on the road to Damascus and had commissioned him
as an apostle and an evangelist (see Acts 9:1-20). Paul's heavenly
commission was also confirmed by the apostles in Jerusalem and
eventually by the elders at the church at Antioch, who had sent
him and Barnabas to evangelize the Gentiles (see Acts 9:26-28;
13:1-2). For the Corinthians' benefit, Paul underscored his divine
calling. Although Paul had reputable Christians who would stand
behind him and recommend him, he did not emphasize that fact.
In contrast to the false teachers at Corinth, Paul's ministry was

authorized by Jesus. Paul's letter of recommendation had been written by Christ himself.

This "letter" of Christ had been delivered by Paul and his coworkers; they were messengers for God and his glorious Good News of salvation. It was written by the *Spirit of the living God* (the Holy Spirit) on the hearts and lives of those who believed. The Holy Spirit, who was working in the Corinthians' hearts and was a guarantee of the Corinthians' glorious inheritance in heaven, affirmed the authenticity of Paul's message.

Next, Paul compared this letter from Christ written on the Corinthians' hearts to the Ten Commandments written by the finger of God on *tablets of stone*. Paul's point is clear: The signs of the Spirit's work in a person's life are superior to any kind of writing, whether it was a church's recommendation or the law of God etched on stone (see Exodus 31:18).

The imagery of writing on *tablets of human hearts* comes from the prophet Ezekiel. This Old Testament prophet had predicted that one day God himself would remove Israel's heart of stone and replace it with a heart of flesh, a heart that would follow God's decrees because God himself had written his law on it:

> *And I will give you a new heart with new and right desires, and I will put a new spirit in you. I will take out your stony heart of sin and give you a new, obedient heart. And I will put my Spirit in you so you will obey my laws and do whatever I command. (Ezekiel 36:26-27* NLT*)*
>
> *"But this is the new covenant I will make with the people of Israel on that day," says the Lord. "I will put my laws in their minds, and I will write them on their hearts. I will be their God, and they will be my people." (Jeremiah 31:33* NLT*)*

THE OPEN BOOK
The Corinthian congregation received correspondence from the apostle, and, to Paul, they were themselves correspondence to a nonbelieving world. What he taught them about Christ and godly living is observable and understandable. Their lifestyle was a witness without the need for words. What is important to us can be read and evaluated by those who watch us. We are the only Gospel some people will ever read. Review your personal datebook and checkbook. What kind of a message does your life present?

Paul was declaring to the Corinthians that the day Ezekiel had predicted had come. The Holy Spirit was writing God's law on their hearts and changing them on the inside. The new covenant of which Ezekiel spoke centuries ago was the gospel Paul preached. Paul's allusion to Ezekiel's prophecy begins his extended explanation in this chapter of the difference between the new covenant and the old covenant (3:6-18).

3:4-5 Such is the confidence that we have through Christ toward God. Not that we are competent of ourselves to claim anything as coming from us; our competence is from God.NRSV Paul did not want to have anything to do with vain boasting (see 3:1; 5:12; 10:18). Yet he expressed his confidence and assurance (see 1:15; 5:6, 8) in his own ministry, not because of his own eloquence or sophistication, but because God *through Christ* had commissioned Paul as an apostle on the Damascus road (see Acts 9:15-19).

Paul had asked who was competent (or adequate) for the task of preaching the Good News (2:16). In this verse, Paul answered his own question: Only those who are called by God are *competent,* for their *competence* lies in God. This might have been a slight snub to Paul's opponents in Corinth. They had boasted of their wisdom (see 1 Corinthians 2:1), their eloquence (11:6), their superior Jewish ancestry (11:12), and, as it has become clear in this passage, their letters of recommendation. In contrast, Paul refused to boast in himself. Instead, he boasted in Christ's strength, which had become evident through his weaknesses (11:30) and the trials he had endured for the cause of Christ (11:16-27; see also Ephesians 3:7-8; 1 Thessalonians 2:4; 1 Timothy 1:12, 14).

BRAGGING RIGHTS
Paul was not boasting; he gave God the credit for all his accomplishments. The false teachers boasted of their own power and prestige, but Paul expressed his humility before God. No one is adequate without God's help. No one is competent to carry out the responsibilities of God's calling on his or her own strength. Without the Holy Spirit's enabling, natural talent can carry a person only so far. To test your attitude, ask yourself—when your ministry starts succeeding—who is getting the credit: you or Christ?

Paul's strategy with his opponents was ingenious. He refused to stoop to arguing over his own abilities. He freely admitted he was inadequate and incompetent for the delicate task of communicating the Good News faithfully. He knew he preached and ministered in the presence of Christ himself (2:10). No one could take such a task lightly. Paul's humility about his own qualifications for the ministry exposed his critics for what they were: loud boasters. At the same time, Paul did not relinquish his authority to these false teachers. He pointed to his commission from Christ—*our competence is from God*—to preach the Good News as the source of his competence and his authority.

3:6 He has made us competent as ministers of a new covenant—not of the letter but of the Spirit.^{NIV} After explaining that he wasn't boasting in himself, Paul declared that God had *made* him and his companions *ministers of a new covenant,* or servants of the new covenant. This is one of the two times that Paul used the Greek words for "new covenant." The other reference to the new covenant is Paul's quote of Jesus' words concerning the cup of the new covenant (1 Corinthians 11:25). Most likely, Paul was using the terminology of Jeremiah 31:31-33 in this passage. The prophet Jeremiah spoke of a new covenant when God would write his law on his people's hearts (see 3:2).

For the letter kills, but the Spirit gives life.^{NIV} This verse ends with a short adage—*the letter kills, but the Spirit gives life.* The Corinthians must have been familiar with this saying, for Paul used it as a support for his own ministry and did not entirely explain it. "The letter" refers to the Old Testament Scriptures, the summary of the law of Moses. Paul's letter to the Romans shows that Paul unequivocally denied that following the law can achieve salvation. Instead, the law only makes people conscious of their sin, the sin which ultimately leads to death (Romans 2:29; 3:19-20; 6:23; 7:6). Trying to be saved by keeping Old Testament laws will end in death. Only by believing in the Lord Jesus Christ can a person receive eternal life through the Holy Spirit. No one but Jesus has ever fulfilled the law perfectly; thus, the whole world is condemned to death. The law makes people realize their sin, but it cannot give life. Under the new covenant, eternal life comes from the Holy Spirit. The Spirit gives new life to all who believe in Christ. The moral law (the Ten Commandments) still points out sin and shows Christians how to obey God, but forgiveness comes only through the grace and mercy of Christ (see Romans 7:10–8:2).

3:7-8 Now if the ministry that brought death, which was engraved in letters on stone, came with glory, so that the Israelites could not look steadily at the face of Moses because of its glory, fading though it was, will not the ministry of the Spirit be even more glorious?^{NIV} Paul used the story of the giving of the Ten Commandments to illustrate the difference between his ministry and the ministry of Moses.

The story can be found in Exodus 34:29-35. After receiving

THE OLD AND NEW COVENANTS

Like pointing out the similarities and differences between the photograph of a person and the actual person, the connection between the old Mosaic covenant and the new Messianic covenant proves that the old covenant was a shadow of the real Christ.

The Old Covenant under Moses	The New Covenant in Christ	Application
Gifts and sacrifices by those guilty of sin	Self-sacrifice by the guiltless Christ	Christ died for you.
Focused on a physical building where one goes to worship	Focuses on the reign of Christ in the heart	God is directly involved in your life.
A shadow	A reality	Not temporal but eternal
Limited promises	Limitless promises	We can trust God's promises to us.
Failed agreement by people	Faithful agreement by Christ	Christ has kept the agreement where people couldn't.
External standards and rules	Internal standards—a new heart	God sees both actions and motives—we are accountable to God, not rules.
Limited access to God	Unlimited access to God	God is personally available.
Based on fear	Based on love and forgiveness	Forgiveness keeps our failures from destroying the agreement.
Legal cleansing	Personal cleansing	God's cleansing is complete.
Continual sacrifice	Conclusive sacrifice	Christ's sacrifice was perfect and final.
Forgiveness earned	Forgiveness freely given	We have true and complete forgiveness.
Repeated yearly	Completed by Christ's death	Christ's death can be applied to your sin.
Human effort	God's grace	Initiated by God's love for you
Available to some	Available to all	Available to you

the Ten Commandments written by God himself, Moses came down from Mount Sinai with the tablets. Although Moses did not realize it, his *face* was radiant and glowing—full of *glory*. Moses had spoken to God on the mountain. The word "glory" *(doxes)*, from which we derive the word "doxology," refers to the wonderful, awe-inspiring, indescribable presence of God himself. People tend to think of "glory" in terms of brightness, but it is certainly more than that. It is utter wholeness, completeness.

When Moses returned to the Israelite camp, the people saw his radiant face and were afraid to approach him. Moses called the people to gather around him so he could tell them all that God had commanded them to do, so he put a veil over his face. Whenever Moses would enter the Most Holy Place in the tabernacle to be in the Lord's presence, he would take the veil off his face to speak with God. Then, he would stand before the people with his face uncovered and tell them what God had commanded. After he finished speaking, Moses would once again slip the veil over his face.

If the law that leads to death was glorious, how much more glorious is God's plan to give life through his Spirit. The sacrifice of Jesus Christ is far superior to the Old Testament system of sacrifice (see the Life Application Bible Commentary *Hebrews* chapters 8 and 10 for a more complete discussion). If Christianity is superior to the Judaism of the Old Testament, which was the highest form of religion on earth, it will surely be superior to any other contemporary religion. Because God's plan is wonderful by comparison to any other, we dare not reject it or treat it casually.

Paul seized Moses' habit of putting a veil over his face and then taking it off as a symbol of the difference between the old and new covenants, the *ministry that brought death* versus the *ministry of the Spirit*. The old covenant had brought condemnation because it pointed out sin and its tragic consequence: death. In contrast, the new covenant brings life. It is a "ministry of the Spirit" because it was, from the start, accompanied by the signs of the Spirit. On the day of Pentecost, the Spirit had empowered the disciples to speak boldly of God's salvation (see Acts 2:4-21). On that day, Peter had preached to those listening, urging them to repent and believe in Jesus so that they, too, could receive the Holy *Spirit* (Acts 2:38). Integral to the new covenant was the promise of the Spirit of God living within the believer to guide and empower him or her.

Paul's New Testament letters underscore the importance of Jesus' gift of the Holy Spirit to believers (Romans 5:5; Galatians 3:2-8). The Spirit was the guarantee—the first deposit—of their salvation. Believers were new creations because of the Spirit's work in their lives. As such, believers had to live according to the dictates of the Spirit, instead of reverting back to their old, sinful ways (Romans 7:6). In his first letter to the Corinthians, Paul took care to prove that his ministry had been empowered by the Spirit. As such, it was far superior to worldly wisdom (1 Corinthians 2:10-14). This letter compared Paul's ministry of the Spirit to Moses' ministry of the law. It was more glorious—literally, reflecting more of the brilliance of God—than the law. To make his point even more forceful, Paul described the glory of Moses' face as a *fading* glory. The Old Testament passage does not record this fact. It seems that Paul interpreted Moses' action of covering his face with a veil as an effort on Moses' part to divert attention from the fading brilliance of his own face in order to focus the people's attention on the law. Paul saw this fading glory as another sign of the temporary nature of the old covenant.

GLORY AHEAD

Paul recalled the stone tablets on which God had written the old covenant. He identified the law, although lethal, as nonetheless glorious because it is God's provision and proof of his intervention in the life of his people. But that which was summarized on stone is nowhere near as glorious as what is yet to come. The Spirit creates a new life in us. He is the Holy Spirit who was present at the creation of the world as one of the agents in the origin of life itself (Genesis 1:2). He is the power behind the rebirth of every Christian and the one who helps us live the Christian life. By his power, we will be transformed into Christ's perfect likeness when he returns. Thank God for the fact that the best is yet to be.

3:9 If the old covenant, which brings condemnation, was glorious, how much more glorious is the new covenant, which makes us right with God.^{NLT} In this passage, Paul labels the *old covenant* as the ministry *which brings condemnation,* and the *new covenant* as the ministry *which makes us right with God.* Paul took it for granted that the Corinthians knew the reasoning behind his argument here. After all, he had spent a year and a half teaching them.

Paul's letter to the Romans, however, explains in detail how the old covenant brings condemnation. The law carries a verdict of guilty because it points out sin in people's lives (Romans 3:19-20; 5:12-13). In contrast, the new covenant makes people right with God. This phrase uses the Greek word *dikaiosune,* the word commonly translated "righteousness." In his New Testament letters, Paul used this Greek word (in various forms) over one hundred times. He saw it as central to the gospel message he was preaching. Although in some places Paul used this Greek word to mean the kind of right living believers should practice (see 1 Timothy 6:11), in this context the word certainly means the righteousness that God gives to believers (see Romans 4:3, 22). God's old agreement makes us guilty, while God's new agreement "makes us right."

God alone is truly righteous. No one is righteous before God (Romans 3:10). But God mercifully gives his own righteousness to those who believe in his Son (Romans 5:17). This way, all those who believe in Jesus are declared righteous before God (Romans 3:20-22). Believers, in turn, begin to alter their behavior one step at a time because the Holy Spirit lives within them, guiding them in paths of righteousness (see Romans 8:4, 10).

This sentence, therefore, sums up the difference between the old covenant and the new covenant Paul had preached to the Corinthians: The old, by pointing out sin, brings God's judgment; but the new, through Jesus' innocent life and death, brings God's righteousness to the believer.

3:10-11 **In fact, that first glory was not glorious at all compared with the overwhelming glory of the new covenant.**[NLT] The old covenant was *glorious*. Not only did Moses' face shine, but thunder, lightning, earthquakes, dense clouds, blazing fire, and a deafening trumpet blast accompanied its inauguration at Mount Sinai (Exodus 19:16-20). The Israelites were terrified. They were forbidden from standing on the mountain or even on its boundaries. If they did, they would die. The glory of God inspired fear and reverence. The brilliance of Moses' face was only a slight reflection of God's glory; the people knew this, for they had seen God shake the very foundations of Mount Sinai.

> If the church could be aroused to a deeper sense of the glory that awaits her, she would enter with a warmer spirit into the struggles that are before her. *J. H. Thornwell*

Paul did not discount the glory of the old covenant. He fully acknowledged it, but he made it clear that it *was not glorious at all compared with the overwhelming glory of the new covenant*. The new ministry of the Spirit is even more glorious. The changed hearts and lives of believers is an even more miraculous work of God than lightning, thunder, and earthquakes. In fact, this greater glory was eclipsing the glory of the old covenant. Just as the bright light of the sun makes a flashlight useless, so the surpassing glory of the new covenant renders the lesser glory useless.

So if the old covenant, which has been set aside, was full of glory, then the new covenant, which remains forever, has far greater glory.[NLT] Paul reiterated the greater glory of the new covenant. The fact that the *old covenant* was temporary, had *been set aside,* and was being superseded by the new covenant, once again underscored the more perfect nature of the new. It showed

far more of God's glory, for it would not only be everlasting, but
it would also impart eternal life to anyone who believes in Jesus.

Indeed, the new covenant had already shown God's glory.
Jesus Christ, in his perfect life, had revealed God to human
beings. Jesus was God in a human body, and his death on the
cross revealed God's loving nature. God was willing to sacrifice
his only Son to save people from their own sins. Jesus' life was
truly a glorious revelation, but the glory of the new covenant did
not end there. On the day of Pentecost, the Holy Spirit overwhelmed Jesus' followers, empowering them to be his witnesses.
The people who heard the disciples speaking in different languages were in awe (Acts 2:12-13). Something even more amazing—and more glorious—occurred over the next months and
years. Those who put their trust in Christ would receive the Holy
Spirit and their lives would be changed as a result. God's saving
of human souls is greater than anything we consider great in this
world—big houses, fat bank accounts, fame, or power and influence.

God's merciful work in people's lives goes largely unnoticed
by many. They take it for granted. But this is the work that brings
the most glory to God—a glory that all the fire, smoke, and lightning of the old covenant could not surpass.

3:12-13 **Since, then, we have such a hope, we act with great boldness.**[NRSV] From his discussion on the superiority of the new covenant over the old, Paul concluded that the new inspires *great
boldness.* The Greek word translated "boldness" is the word that
the Greeks used to speak of the right to free speech. Here Paul
used this word to indicate the public nature of his ministry. He
would boldly preach the mysteries of salvation that had been
obscured for centuries. Although the Jews had God's promises
regarding the coming Savior and Messiah in the Scriptures, not
even their well-educated rabbis could fathom exactly what God
planned to do. But to the apostles, God had revealed this mystery: God had planned long ago to offer salvation to both Jews
and Gentiles through the death of the Messiah (see Ephesians
3:6). Openly and publicly, Paul was proclaiming this great mystery in the cities all over the Roman world.

Paul's boldness was an outgrowth of his *hope* in the new covenant—the glorious, permanent ministry of the Holy Spirit in the
lives of believers. Unlike the present-day use of the term "hope,"
Paul did not mean "wishful longings." As Paul explained in his
letter to the Romans, Christian hope is a confident expectation
that God will do what he promises to do. Just as Abraham fully
expected that God would make him a father of many nations

(Romans 4:18-21), Christians, too, can confidently expect that
God will give them eternal salvation (Romans 5:5). This type of
confidence in the faithfulness of God inspired Paul to publicly
proclaim the Good News of salvation.

FREEDOM OF SPEECH
Because Paul had hope in what God has in store, he witnessed
boldly. Boldness is not to be confused with cockiness or
insensitivity. Rather, it is an ability to confidently communicate
what you know to be true even when present circumstances
would point in another direction. How would those who know
you best evaluate you in terms of boldness in your ministry? If
you lack the boldness you feel God has entitled you to, what
would account for living below your means? Lack of knowledge
of what God has promised? Lack of trust in what he claims?
Lack of preparation in communicating it?

**We are not like Moses, who would put a veil over his face to
keep the Israelites from gazing at it while the radiance was
fading away.**NIV Paul interpreted the *veil over [Moses'] face* as
an effort on Moses' part to conceal the fact that the *radiance* of
his face *was fading away.* In the fading away of this brilliance,
Paul saw a sign that the old covenant, which Moses presented to
the people, would also fade.

Thus, Paul's boldness in his ministry lay in the eternal nature
of the new covenant. Paul could act with greater confidence than
the spiritual giant Moses, for Paul had been given an eternal message to proclaim to all nations. God's plan for salvation was no
longer hidden. It was not only a time to celebrate God's great
mercy, it was also a time for boldness. It was a time to declare
God's glory to all the nations, making disciples of whoever
turned to God for the gift of salvation.

3:14-16 **But their minds were made dull, for to this day the same veil
remains when the old covenant is read. It has not been
removed, because only in Christ is it taken away. Even to this
day when Moses is read, a veil covers their hearts.**NIV Apparently, it bothered Paul that not many Jews turned to Christ when
the gospel was announced to them. Paul's common practice when
he first went to a city was to preach to the Jews who would
gather in the local synagogue (as he did in Corinth, see Acts 18:1-
4). But the Jews rejected his message of salvation (Acts 18:6-7).
At times, Jews even pursued Paul to other cities to try to silence
him (see Acts 14:1, 19). Paul most frequently found welcome
with the God-fearing Gentiles (Acts 17:4).

In his letter to the Romans, Paul focused on why the Jews had rejected Jesus, to whom all of the Scriptures (the Old Testament) pointed. Jesus was Israel's Messiah, the person who fulfilled God's promises to Israel. The Jews, if anyone, should be rejoicing. Instead, their hearts were hardened, their *minds were made dull* to what was occurring (see Romans 9–11, especially 10:1-3). But Paul knew that the rejection of the gospel by the Jews was part of God's mysterious plan so that his free offer of salvation could extend to the Gentiles (see Romans 11:28). God had let the Jews' hearts become hardened and rebellious so he could clearly show that he was a God of mercy to all people—both Gentile and Jew had rebelliously rejected him at one time (see Romans 11:29-31). God, however, had mercifully included believing Gentiles as his people. In Romans, Paul used the analogy of grafting a limb onto a tree. In the same way, God had broken off those unbelieving Jews and had grafted a foreign limb—the Gentiles—into his tree of faith (see Romans 11:17-21). Yet Paul still refused to believe that God had completely abandoned Israel—God's chosen people. One day, God would once again shower his mercy on the Jews (Romans 11:32).

This passage in 2 Corinthians gives a short summary of Paul's teaching on why the Jews had rejected the gospel. This passage pictures the reading of the Law and the Prophets in the synagogue. As Paul's travelogue in Acts reveals, he had been in these services many times. These verses express what was going through Paul's mind at the time. He was astonished that the Jews could not understand the One to whom the Scriptures were pointing: Jesus Christ. A real *veil* covered their minds and their hearts—the very center of their intellectual, social, and spiritual selves—so that they could not understand the truth.

But *in Christ* the veil is miraculously lifted. Just as Christ had opened Paul's spiritual eyes to the truth about Jesus, the Holy Spirit would also open believers' eyes to how Jesus fulfilled the Scriptures.

But whenever anyone turns to the Lord, the veil is taken away.[NIV] Moses and his veil illustrate the fading of the old system and the veiling of the Jews' minds by their pride, hardness of heart, and refusal to repent. The veil kept many Jews from understanding the references to Christ in the Scriptures they heard every week.

When Moses turned to God, he removed the veil (see Exodus 34:34). In the same way, when a person turns to Christ—God's only Son—*the veil is taken away* by Christ himself. The veil represents the sin that clouds the person's understanding about God's great plan of salvation. The idea of turning implies repen-

tance—a conscious rejection of one's old ways and a turning to
God and his ways. The image of turning to God in the Old Testament always implies turning away from false gods (2 Chronicles
34:2; Psalm 53:3; Jeremiah 17:5).

When anyone *turns to the Lord* and becomes a Christian,
Christ removes the veil, giving that person not only understanding of the true meaning of the Scriptures but also eternal life
and freedom from trying to be saved by keeping laws. Christ
saves the person not only from sin but from the ignorance that his
or her sin has created.

**3:17-18 Now the Lord is the Spirit, and where the Spirit of the Lord is,
there is freedom.**NRSV In rabbinical tradition, a teacher would
update the language of the Scripture for his audience. Paul, following his own rabbinical training, updated the language of Exodus for
his Christian audience. It wasn't God the Father who had removed
the veil from the Corinthians' hearts but Christ the Lord. As the life-
giving Spirit in resurrection (1 Corinthians 15:45), Christ can live
in his people (13:5) and free them from their blindness.

Next, Paul introduced another reason why the new covenant is
better than the old: It is a ministry of *freedom.* Paul used this
description as a defense of his ministry, assuming that his readers
knew the full extent of his teaching on Christian freedom. It
relates to the concept of boldness in 3:12. Christ's death on the
cross bought freedom for anyone who believes (1 Corinthians
6:20). He frees us from sin and the condemnation that results
from trying to obey the law (Romans 8:1-4; Galatians 3:21-24).
He frees us from the fear of death, the penalty for our sins
(Romans 5:17-18). Jesus even frees us from the evil powers of
the age (Galatians 1:4). This passage cites another trap from
which Christ frees believers: an ignorance of God's plan of salvation. Christ frees believers from the same mental veil that covered many of the Jews to whom Paul was preaching (3:14).

When we trust Christ to save us, Jesus removes that heavy burden of trying to please him. His light dispels our ignorance, giving us a clear understanding of the gospel. By trusting Christ, we
are loved, accepted, forgiven, and freed to live for him.

**And all of us have had that veil removed so that we can be
mirrors that brightly reflect the glory of the Lord.**NLT Here
Paul resumed his interpretation of Moses' actions with his veil.
Just as Moses took off his veil when he went into the Lord's presence, so too all Christians can behold God's glory without any
veil covering them. Unlike the Jews, who had to rely on priests to
mediate between them and God, Christians through Christ's sav-

ing work on the cross have direct access to the Father (Ephesians 2:18).

The Greek word translated "mirrors" can be interpreted in two different ways. It can either mean "to behold oneself in a mirror" or "to reflect as a mirror does." Some scholars suggest that the primary contrast Paul was making here is that Christians can behold God's glory, unlike their Jewish counterparts who rejected Christ. The New Living Translation, however, translates the idea that Christians functioned like a mirror. Thus, under the new covenant, all believers can *reflect the glory of the Lord.* In contrast, under the old covenant only Moses had access to the Lord's presence and thus could reflect his glory. But now all Christians can be like Moses. Thus, when Christians, who are given access to the Father through Christ's work, look at God's glory, they begin to reflect his holy character in their lives. As a result of this encounter with God, they are forever changed.

And as the Spirit of the Lord works within us, we become more and more like him and reflect his glory even more.[NLT] The glory that the Spirit imparts to the believer is more excellent and lasts longer than the glory that Moses experienced. By gazing at the nature of God with unveiled minds, all of us Christians can be more like him. "Become more and more like him" is literally in Greek "are being transformed." The same word appears in Matthew 17:2 and Mark 9:2, where it refers to Jesus' transfiguration, and also in Romans 12:2, where it refers to Christians' moral transformation.

The gospel reveals the truth about Christ, and *the Spirit of the Lord works within us,* transforming us morally as we understand and apply it. Through learning about Christ's life, we can understand how wonderful God is and what he is really like. As our knowledge deepens, the Holy Spirit works within us to help us to change to become more like Christ (for more on moral transformation, see Jeremiah 31:33; Ezekiel 36:25-27; Romans 6:1-4; 2 Corinthians 5:17; Galatians 6:15).

Becoming Christlike is a progressive experience (see Romans 8:29; Galatians 4:19; Philippians 3:21; 1 John 3:2). "Becoming more and more" expresses the Greek tense of the verb Paul used here. Being transformed into Christ's likeness is a continual process. "Reflect his glory even more" translates Paul's literal phrase in Greek: "glory to glory." Thus, Paul was saying that as the Holy Spirit works through our lives, we—step-by-step—come closer to God's perfect way of living. It occurs little by little as the Holy Spirit points out more areas of our lives that need to be submitted to God's will; and we, then, freely submit to God. The Holy Spirit works through the preaching of God's Word, the reading of Scripture, our prayer life, and the wise guidance of other mature believers to lead believers on God's wonderful path of righteousness.

God works in his own timing. The Holy Spirit brings about change in our lives and hearts through a slow process. So never give up if you don't see the spiritual progress you desire. The Holy Spirit works in his own way and his own timing.

2 Corinthians 4

Paul was under attack at Corinth. His authority and honesty were being questioned. Charges of duplicity were circulating in the church. Paul was facing a church in revolt.

How did Paul handle opposition? At every step, he deflected criticisms of his abilities. He simply refused to defend himself. He even submitted to his opponents a list of his weaknesses and the trials he had endured. Why did Paul do this? He knew that this list would focus the Corinthians on what was important: God's glorious plan of salvation. God had commissioned Paul to tell Jews and Gentiles alike the Good News. He was sent to minister to them. Paul's apostolic authority was mercifully given to him by Jesus. Paul was hoping that the Corinthians would recognize his God-given authority. Listing his own abilities, accomplishments, and credentials and defending himself would encourage the Corinthians to evaluate him and other preachers in the same way. By responding to criticism this way, Paul was encouraging the Corinthians to evaluate all preachers in the light of the truths of God's Word.

One way to handle conflict in the church is to keep bringing the church back to the truth that God has called all believers to work together for the cause of Christ. There will be disagreements and differences in the church. Personalities will conflict. People will have different agendas. In the end, however, believers must recommit to their fundamental purpose for gathering together: to further Christ's kingdom.

4:1 Therefore, since we have this ministry, as we have received mercy, we do not lose heart.^{NKJV} With grand language and persuasive analogies in the last chapter, Paul painted an appealing picture of what it means to be a Christian minister. This chapter comes down to reality. What does all this mean for everyday life? How does God's plan of salvation change anything?

First of all, it imparts courage to *not lose heart*. The Greek for this phrase can mean anything from not becoming discouraged to not acting like a coward. In other words, the glorious plan of God gave Paul hope and courage to face his day with great confidence in God (see 3:4, 12; 5:6-8).

Paul underscored, again, that his confidence was not in his own abilities (see 1:12; 3:4-6, 12). Instead, he was a minister of the gospel only because of the *mercy* of God. Before his conversion, Paul had hunted down believers, vowing to imprison them and destroy the budding church. Despite Paul's anger and hatred of Christians, God showed him mercy (Ephesians 2:4; Titus 3:5). Even though Paul was a self-proclaimed enemy of Jesus, God was patient with him. Christ himself stopped Paul on the road to Damascus, rescuing him from the path that leads to eternal death. Christ also commissioned him to preach the gospel (Acts 9:1-19). Paul deserved none of this, and he knew it (see 1 Timothy 1:12-16). Only God's kindness allowed him to serve.

4:2 We reject all shameful and underhanded methods.[NLT] Earlier, Paul had spoken of his opponents as "hucksters . . . who preach just to make money" (2:17 NLT). This verse contrasts the way Paul preached with the methods of some of the traveling preachers who had come to Corinth. These preachers had sought a platform on which to speak and ask for monetary support. Most likely, these were the ones who had been leading the attack on Paul's travel plans (1:23-24), honesty (1:12), and credentials (3:1-3). This verse (as well as 1:12 and 12:16) answered Paul's opponents' accusation that he had somehow tried to mislead the Corinthians.

In 2 Corinthians, Paul categorically denied using any dubious techniques in his preaching. He and his fellow evangelists had rejected *all shameful and underhanded methods.* This expression denotes methods, motives, and actions that are shrouded in secrecy because they are intrinsically scandalous. The implication is that some of the preachers who had visited Corinth had greedy motives. Paul could perceive their hidden motives because of the havoc and confusion these men were causing in Corinth.

We do not try to trick anyone, and we do not distort the word of God.[NLT] One of the telltale signs of the impure motives of these preachers was the way they handled God's Word. Instead of a straightforward presentation of the truths of the gospel, they used tricks to captivate their audience. In so doing, they were twisting God's Word.

The Greek phrase translated "trick" (see 11:3, where the same Greek phrase is used) literally means "to walk in ways that are capable of anything." In other words, these teachers would do anything to get what they wanted. They would even *distort the word of God* for their own benefit. The Greek word translated "distort" was commonly used for tampering with merchandise in order to make it more profitable. Some merchants of the first century would cheat their customers by diluting wine or changing the accuracy of scales. In Ephesians 4:14, Paul wrote of false teachers as cheating gamblers who loaded the dice to trick people. The false teachers who had visited Corinth were diluting God's Word or twisting it to serve their own selfish purposes.

We tell the truth before God, and all who are honest know that.^{NLT} Paul had rejected such deceptive and cunning ways when he preached to the Corinthians. He had "walked" by faith instead of placing his trust in the ingenious, deceptive ways of the world (see 5:7). In others words, Paul always reminded himself of the spiritual realities that were behind his ministry. When he preached the truths of God's Word, he reminded himself that he was preaching it *before God*. He stood in the presence of God. The Lord God, the One who knows all secrets, could look into Paul's heart and discern his motives. Because God was always watching him, Paul was careful to preach for the right reasons. He consciously submitted his motivations to God's scrutiny, so that no shameful act or motive could disqualify him as a minister. Paul opened up his entire life and honestly told the Corinthians the *truth*. He hid nothing.

Because Paul's preaching and motives had been called into question by the Corinthians, he pleaded with them to evaluate his behavior among them to see if he had been devious. Paul was confident that if they fairly judged him, he would be judged innocent of all of the charges against him.

TWISTERS
Paul condemned those who twist God's Word. Preachers, teachers, and anyone else who talks about Jesus Christ must remember that they stand in God's presence—he hears every word. Many Christian ministers and leaders twist Scripture in their attempt to motivate audiences. Others take Scripture out of context to promote their own views. When you tell people about Christ, be careful not to distort the message to please your audience. Proclaim the truth of God's Word.

4:3-4 And even if our gospel is veiled, it is veiled to those who are perishing.^{NIV} Paul took up the charge that his message was obscure or unclear—a charge he had repeatedly defended himself against in the first part of his letter (see 1:12; 3:12-18). In the previous section, Paul had explained at length that his *gospel* was a straightforward presentation of God's plan of salvation, while

Moses' ministry concealed parts of God's plan in order to prepare the people for Jesus and his greater message (see 3:7-18).

Although the message Paul preached was a clear presentation of salvation, he admitted that the gospel would be *veiled,* or obscure, to some. He explained that there are two types of people—those who will receive eternal life and *those who are perishing.* Paul had already explained that the fragrance of his message would be the smell of death to those who were dying (2:15); this verse states that their understanding will be obscured (4:3). The gospel will confuse and confound them. In 1 Corinthians, Paul had already explained how the wisdom of God is foolishness to the wise of this world (1 Corinthians 1:18). The same idea is being expressed here. Those who stubbornly refuse to believe in Christ and insist on placing their trust in their own abilities and intellect will never understand the truth of the gospel.

The god of this age has blinded the minds of unbelievers, so that they cannot see the light of the gospel of the glory of Christ, who is the image of God.[NIV] Paul's description here of the way Satan blinds unbelievers is reminiscent of his conversion experience on the Damascus road. Although Paul could see perfectly well, he had been *blinded* to spiritual truth. Naively and zealously, he had persecuted the Christians, vowing to destroy them in any way possible. Unknowingly, Paul had been an instrument of Satan. In one magnificent moment, however, Christ had broken through Satan's deception and had revealed the truth to Paul. A glorious vision of Christ finally had opened Paul's eyes to the truth. Appropriately, Paul had been physically blinded for a while (Acts 9:1-18).

Why can't everyone understand the truth of the gospel? Out of his own experience, Paul answered this question. It is because the *god of this age has blinded the minds of unbelievers*—and, at one time, had blinded him—to *the light of the gospel of the glory of Christ.*

The "god of this age" is a title for Satan, the great deceiver. This present world is in Satan's grasp. But Jesus' life and death began an all-out war on Satan. The church—the community of believers—is awaiting Jesus' victorious return, when Satan will finally be imprisoned and Jesus will reign forever (2 Thessalonians 1:7-10). In the meantime, however, Satan continues to try to trap believers in sin (1 Timothy 3:7). A Christian's refuge and defense is in the victor, Jesus. He will guard believers from the evil one (2 Thessalonians 3:3). Believers can be certain of Jesus' protection by reading God's Word and praying for his protection

(Ephesians 6:17-18). Then they will be able to feel safe from the attacks and deceptions of their spiritual enemies.

Instead of being blinded by Satan like unbelievers are, believers recognize that Jesus is the exact visible representation of God, the *image of God* (see also Colossians 1:15). God the Father as spirit is invisible (1 Timothy 6:16). God's Son, however, is God's visible expression. Jesus not only reflects the Father, but, as God, he reveals God to us (John 1:18; 14:9; Hebrews 1:1-2). Christ's glory expresses divine glory. Jesus is not a copy but the very embodiment of God's nature. He is "the reflection of God's glory and the exact imprint of God's very being" (Hebrews 1:3 NRSV). To know Jesus is to know God (see John 10:30; Philippians 2:6).

BLINDED
The gospel is open and revealed to everyone except those who refuse to believe. Satan is "the god of this age." His work is to deceive, and he has blinded those who don't believe in Christ (see 11:14-15). The allure of money, power, and pleasure blinds people to the light of Christ's gospel. Those who reject Christ and prefer their own pursuits have unknowingly made Satan their god. Do you know someone Satan has blinded? Pray that the light of Christ will penetrate their darkened minds.

4:5 For we do not preach ourselves, but Jesus Christ as Lord, and ourselves as your servants for Jesus' sake.^{NIV} The focus of Paul's preaching was on Christ and not himself. In 1 Corinthians Paul had already reminded the Corinthian believers that he had not concentrated on trying to present the gospel with his own profound ideas or with particularly eloquent phrases. Instead, Paul had preached Jesus Christ and his death on the cross. Paul had stuck to the essential truths of the gospel: Christ's death on the cross provides salvation for all those who believe in him (1 Corinthians 2:1-2). This verse underscores another central aspect of Paul's message: Jesus is Master, or *Lord,* of all believers.

Since his own authority was under attack, Paul could have written that he was their God-appointed leader and teacher (as he did in 1 Timothy 2:7). Instead, Paul emphasized that he and his fellow evangelists were the Corinthians' *servants.* Several times in his New Testament letters, Paul wrote of himself as a servant or even a slave of Christ (11:23; Romans 1:1; Galatians 1:10) and even called all believers to be slaves to God (Romans 6:22). Here Paul underscored that he was also a servant of the people he ministered to—in this case, the Corinthians. Throughout 2 Corinthians, Paul reiterated that he was not trying to exercise arbitrary

2 CORINTHIANS 4:6   330

authority over their faith (1:24). On the contrary, Paul was merely serving them as Christ's appointed messenger, faithfully delivering the truths of the gospel to them.

A SERVANT'S HEART
Paul willingly served the Corinthian church, even though the people must have deeply disappointed him. Serving people requires a sacrifice of time and personal desires. Being Christ's follower means serving others, even when they do not measure up to our expectations. Rather than promote your own importance, serve others and help them grow. Discover their needs and concerns. Treat their interests as more important than your own.

4:6 **For God, who said, "Let there be light in the darkness," has made us understand that this light is the brightness of the glory of God that is seen in the face of Jesus Christ.**^{NLT} Paul returned to the image of *light* and *darkness,* which he had introduced in 4:4. The image symbolizes the stark difference between good and evil, between God and Satan. The Old Testament psalm writers and prophets frequently used the image of light to describe God's Word and God's deliverance of his people (see Psalm 119:105; Isaiah 9:2; 42:16; Daniel 2:22).

This verse makes it clear that this imagery of light and darkness came from the Creation story itself (Genesis 1:2-5). Just as God had brought order out of the chaos of darkness by ordering, *"Let there be light in the darkness,"* so God was piercing the chaos of evil with the light of his truth. The light of Christ exposes falsehood and evil for what it is: a perversion of the good (Ephesians 5:13-14). Those who believe in Jesus become children of the light. They live in the light, allowing it to judge all of their actions (see Ephesians 5:8; 1 Thessalonians 5:5).

This passage emphasizes that the light *is the brightness of the glory of God that is seen in the face of Jesus Christ.* The light of Christ illumines a believer's understanding. Only those who allow their minds to be clouded by Satan's dark deceptions think the message is obscure. God illumines the minds of believers so that they know with certainty that in Jesus' face they see the glory of God. The implication is that those who look for God's glory only in the old covenant, in the face of Moses, are being deceived by Satan (compare with 3:15-17).

If and when doubts plague you, ask the Holy Spirit to illumine your heart. Then spend time reading God's Word and submitting your questions to God.

4:7 But we have this treasure in clay jars, so that it may be made clear that this extraordinary power belongs to God and does not come from us.[NRSV] People keep treasures in safety deposit boxes and vaults. But God places his glorious *treasure*—the message that frees people from sin—in fragile, cheap, and ordinary *clay jars*. In Paul's day, clay pots had many uses. Made cheaply, these pots held everything from food to fuel. They could be seen just about everywhere—in window openings, near cooking fires, and in marketplaces. If they broke—and they broke easily—they would be discarded.

JARS OF CLAY
Fragile earthenware jars were common in Paul's day. Thus, they provided an apt metaphor for illustrating the fragility of human messengers in contrast to the valuable treasure of the message of salvation. The light of the gospel is the treasure that even Satan cannot take away. Clay pots leak, they chip, they aren't very attractive. By design they are simply functional. Their plain appearance doesn't detract from their contents. Often, we are discouraged by our imperfections. Feeling inadequate, we feel ineffective. This verse teaches, however, that our imperfect humanity is no hindrance to God's holy purpose. A person's flaws, scars, chips, and cracks allow the presence of an all-sufficient God to leak out. List everything about you that you wish were different. In what areas of your life do you feel inadequate? Can you thank God for the way he has "wired" you? Many will see Christ in you and be drawn to him because they relate more easily to someone who isn't perfect.

Paul compared his life, and that of his fellow evangelists, to these cheap clay jars. In contrast, the message of freedom that God had entrusted to them was a treasure of great worth—an eternal treasure that would last much longer than their frail bodies. Why would God do this? Because he delights in empowering the weak in order to confound the strong. The Lord loves to answer the prayers of the needy and bring down those who take pride in themselves (see Luke 1:51-55; Jeremiah 20:13). God works through the weak and powerless so that it is clear that *this extraordinary power belongs to God and does not come from* people (1 Corinthians 2:3-4). In fact, God was choosing the weak and powerless among the citizens of Corinth to demonstrate the power of the Holy Spirit within. Today, the church seems weak, unable to withstand the tidal wave of immorality in society. The fact that God loves to work through weakness should inspire the same courage that Paul possessed (see 4:1). Weakness and powerlessness should provide the basis for a renewed hope in God. The Lord loves to deliver, rescue, and save. He loves those who consciously remember to praise him for his acts of mercy. For a Christian, powerlessness is never a limitation but an opportunity for God to work in mighty and powerful ways.

The supremely valuable message of salvation in Jesus Christ has been entrusted by God to frail and fallible human beings ("clay jars"). Paul's focus, however, was not on the perishable container but on its priceless contents—God's powerful presence indwelling his people. Though his people are weak, God uses them to spread his Good News, and he gives them the power to do his work. Knowing that the power is his should keep believers from pride and motivate them to keep daily contact with God, their power source. Believers' responsibility is to let people see God through their lives.

4:8-9 **We are hard pressed on every side, but not crushed; perplexed, but not in despair; persecuted, but not abandoned; struck down, but not destroyed.**^{NIV} Yet Paul refused to stoop to comparing his credentials to those of his opponents. Wisely, he steered away from boasting in himself. Instead, he recounted his sufferings (see 11:23-33 for a list of the experiences to which Paul here alludes). He freely admitted he had been *hard pressed* and *perplexed*. Few teachers would admit to being confused because they might lose the respect of their audience. Paul did not shrink from admitting his own weaknesses. At times, the pressures of his ministry had left him feeling surrounded and trapped. At times, he did not know which way to turn, where to go, or what to do (see Acts 16:6-10; 22:10). Then there is the *but . . .* the "but God." The Lord did not abandon Paul to his own inadequacies. God had saved Paul from being *crushed* by his responsibilities and from reaching utter despair.

The next two entries speak of external opposition: Paul had been *persecuted* and *struck down*. Paul had received most of his opposition from Jews. They had persecuted him, even following him to different cities to malign him (see Acts 14:19). The word Paul used for "persecuted" means "tracking down a prey." Thus, Paul was picturing himself as being hunted down. God never *abandoned* him, however. God always came to his rescue, not leaving him to be devoured by his enemies. Paul had even been struck down. This may have been an allusion to the time the citizens of Lystra dragged him outside of the city and stoned him, leaving him for dead. But the Lord enabled the bloodied and bruised Paul to live—to get up and continue preaching in the name of Jesus (Acts 14:19-20).

DOWN BUT NOT OUT
Paul reminds us that though we may think we are at the end of
the rope, we are never at the end of hope. Our perishable
bodies are subject to sin and suffering, but God never
abandons us. Because Christ has won the victory over death,
we have eternal life. All our risks, humiliations, and trials are
opportunities for Christ to demonstrate his power and presence
in and through us. We must ask ourselves, "Could I handle the
suffering and opposition that Paul did?" The American success
syndrome is a great enemy of effective ministry. From an
earthly perspective, Paul was not very successful. Like Paul,
we must carry out our ministry, looking to God for strength.
When opposition, slander, or disappointment threaten to rob
you of the victory, remember that no one can destroy what God
has accomplished through you.

4:10-12 **We always carry around in our body the death of Jesus, so
that the life of Jesus may also be revealed in our body. For we
who are alive are always being given over to death for Jesus'
sake, so that his life may be revealed in our mortal body.**NIV
The Christians at Corinth, like many believers today, were
impressed with eloquence, skill, and power. Although the Corinthians were searching for God's work among those who spoke
eloquently and showed powerful signs, Paul tried to redirect their
thoughts to hardships, distress, and failures. It was in those times
when weakness became painfully obvious that God would work
in marvelous ways.

Paul could have listed his successes in ministry: the more than
a dozen churches that he had founded in the Mediterranean world
(4:8-9). Instead, he focused on his own weakness to reiterate his
point: God had entrusted his glorious message of salvation to
fragile people—mere clay jars—in order to demonstrate his surpassing glory (4:7).

Jesus himself was Paul's model. Although Jesus had all the glories of heaven—all of its power and privilege—he gave it all up
to suffer humiliation, insults, and finally death (see Philippians
2:5-11). Paul saw his own sufferings for the cause of Christ as
connected to Jesus' sufferings on earth. Of course, Jesus' suffering was of a qualitatively different nature. Jesus died on the cross
to save believers from their sins (5:16-21; Romans 3:21-26; 8:2;
1 Corinthians 1:18-31; Galatians 1:4; Colossians 1:23-24). Only
Jesus' death can save because only he lived a perfect life. Yet
Jesus had warned his followers they could also expect suffering
and hardship: "If they persecuted me, they will persecute you
also" (see John 15:20-21 NIV). The suffering of Jesus' followers
would be merely an extension of Jesus' own suffering.

CALLED TO SUFFER

Paul never feared suffering, for he knew that God was in control, that his suffering helped others to be more courageous in spreading the gospel, and that through suffering, he was revealing Christ himself, who also suffered.

Speaker	Reference	Words about Suffering
Jesus	Matthew 5:10-12	Those who are persecuted are called "blessed."
Jesus	Matthew 10:23	The Son of Man will return and end all suffering.
Jesus	John 15:20	Jesus was persecuted; we will be persecuted.
The Apostles	Acts 5:41	We can rejoice for being considered worthy to suffer for Christ.
Jesus	Acts 9:16	Paul was called to suffer for Jesus' name.
Paul	Romans 8:17	As children and heirs, we will share in Jesus' suffering.
Paul	2 Corinthians 1:3-7	God gives comfort in suffering.
Paul	2 Corinthians 7–12	Paul suffered so that others might be saved.
Paul	2 Corinthians 6:4-5, 9-10	Paul suffered yet rejoiced.
Paul	Philippians 1:20-21	Our sufferings can glorify God.
Paul	Philippians 1:29	Suffering for Christ's name is a privilege.
Paul	2 Timothy 1:12	We must not be ashamed of suffering; trust Christ.
Paul	2 Timothy 2:10	Paul suffered for the sake of other believers.
Paul	2 Timothy 3:11	God will rescue us from suffering—now or in eternity.
Paul	2 Timothy 4:5	We are called to endure hardship.
Author of Hebrews	Hebrews 10:32-34	We can face suffering because we know we have God's inheritance.
James	James 1:2	We can consider it pure joy to face trials.
Peter	1 Peter 1:6-7	Our suffering is refining our faith.
Peter	1 Peter 2:21	We suffer because Christ suffered.
Peter	1 Peter 3:13-14	We are blessed for suffering for what is right.
Peter	1 Peter 4:1, 13, 16	We suffer yet rejoice because we suffer for Christ.
Jesus	Revelation 2:10	We must be faithful even to death; the crown of life awaits us.

Paul had been specifically called by Jesus to suffer for his name (Acts 9:15-16). He considered his many sufferings as a badge, or proof, of his authority as an apostle of Christ (Galatians 4:12-15; Philippians 1:29-30; 4:14-15; 1 Thessalonians 1:6; 3:1-15; 2 Timothy 1:8, 11-12). So as a traveling evangelist, Paul did

carry around the suffering and humiliation that is symbolized in
the *death of Jesus.* For Paul, Jesus' death symbolized the believers' death to their former selfish and wicked ways (Romans 6:11;
Galatians 2:20). So Paul, *always being given over to death for
Jesus' sake,* did this *so that [Christ's] life may be revealed in
[Paul's] mortal body.* Paul, and many others with him (see the
chart), endured suffering and scarcity in order to further the cause
of the truth.

**So we live in the face of death, but it has resulted in eternal
life for you.**[NLT] The wonderful part of Paul's analogy with Jesus'
life and death is that it does not end with Jesus' death on the
cross. *Death* does not have the final word. Three days later, Jesus
was alive. He was raised from the dead, as the great Victor over
sin and death. Although most of Jerusalem only saw a humiliated
and weak man dying on a cross, Jesus' followers saw the risen
and glorified Lord (Luke 23–24).

Paul lived *in the face of death.* The pressures of the world
wore on him. His opponents at Corinth saw his weaknesses as a
reason to gloat over him and his eventual downfall. Just as the
Jews and Romans in power thought that putting Jesus to death
would get rid of him, so Paul's opponents thought that his failures, weaknesses, and death would silence him. Paul, however,
knew that something greater than life on this earth was working
through him. His sufferings and death would never spell the end
for the life-giving message of the gospel. In fact, God was working so that Paul's suffering would result in *eternal life for* those
who believe in Jesus. This passage reminded the Corinthians that
Paul's sufferings, which the Corinthians were presently ashamed
of, had brought the message of eternal life to them in the first
place. Paul had courageously endured the insults of the Jews in
order to deliver the gospel to them—the message that would
result in their eternal salvation (Acts 18:6).

4:13-14 **It is written: "I believed; therefore I have spoken." With that
same spirit of faith we also believe and therefore speak.**[NIV] In
this passage, Paul identified himself with the writer of Psalm 116.
Paul, like the psalmist, had experienced the "terrors of the
grave." "Death had its hands around [Paul's] throat" (Psalm
116:3 NLT). In the midst of troubles and in the face of death, Paul,
like the psalmist, had cried out to God (Psalm 116:4). The psalmist believed that God would answer his prayers (compare 1:11 to
Psalm 116:1). In fact, his prayers were his only defense. For this
reason, the psalmist vowed to pray as long as he had breath
(Psalm 116:2). His prayers were not the only expression of his

faith in God; he also promised to thank and praise God, telling others of what God had done for him (see Psalm 116:14, 17-18).

In this psalm, Paul saw an extraordinary expression of faith, which he endeavored to imitate. The psalmist had refused to let his circumstances dictate to him what he should believe. Even death could not frighten him, for he had placed his trust solidly in the God who was stronger than death. Paul knew that faith is the way a person receives God's free gift of salvation (Romans 3:24-25). In Ephesians, he wrote: "For it is by grace you have been saved, through faith—and this not from yourselves, it is the gift of God" (Ephesians 2:8 NIV). Even faith is a gift from God. Not only is faith the way to eternal salvation, it is also a way of life for believers. Christians are called to walk by faith (5:7; Galatians 2:19-20). Believers are to look beyond the troubles of this world to God and his eternal glory. That will give them hope.

Because we know that the one who raised the Lord Jesus from the dead will also raise us with Jesus and present us with you in his presence.NIV Although Paul was experiencing the sufferings and death of Christ on this earth (4:10-12), he placed his hope in the God *who raised the Lord Jesus from the dead.* Although Paul was facing suffering, he wasn't discouraged, because he knew that Jesus would return. At that time, Paul and the Corinthian believers would celebrate their Savior in his presence because God would also raise them *with Jesus.* Paul had already told the Corinthians that he was looking forward to taking pride in the maturity of their faith, and he hoped that they, in turn, would take pride in him (1:13-14).

Because of his faith in Christ, Paul had access to the same great power that raised Jesus from dead (Philippians 3:10). This truth motivated Paul to endure hardship and persist in preaching the gospel. He had explained this in 1 Corinthians. The believers in Corinth had been struggling with the doctrine of the Resurrection, so Paul had written much to explain why the Resurrection is a central doctrine of the Christian faith. It was important that Christ had been raised from the dead, because without that truth, their faith would be utterly useless. Jesus would not be interceding before God for them; Jesus would only be a human being who had modeled a good life. If that were the case, there would be no reason for evangelists, much less believers, to endure hardship for the cause of Christ (1 Corinthians 15:30-34).

With his sights always set on the glories of God's kingdom, Paul didn't have any reason to be ashamed (Romans 1:16; see also Hebrews 12:2). Instead, he boldly and confidently could preach the gospel and tell others of what God had done for him (4:1).

4:15-16 Yes, everything is for your sake, so that grace, as it extends to more and more people, may increase thanksgiving, to the glory of God.^{NRSV} This letter continues to remind the Corinthians of Paul's servant role. He had been sent by Jesus to serve them (4:1, 5; see 1 Corinthians 3:5). All of the trials and difficulties he had endured were for their benefit—*for* their *sake* (see 1:6). He had planned to visit them twice because he wanted to serve them on two occasions (1:15). He had refused monetary support when he had ministered among them in order to serve them free of charge (11:8). As a servant, Paul was careful not to control the Corinthians' faith but instead to assist them in maturing in the Christian faith. Although Paul was obviously insulted on his last trip to Corinth, he had ignored the insult and had forgiven the offender for the Corinthians' sake (2:10). At the beginning of 2 Corinthians, Paul had even insisted that his recent troubles in Asia Minor had been for the sake of the Corinthians (1:5-7).

This passage explains that all he endured, all he said, and all he did benefited the Corinthians. As more people heard of and accepted the *grace* of God—that is, God's gift of salvation—more people would join the grand celebration before God, praising and thanking him (4:14). *Thanksgiving* would begin to overflow toward God. This would benefit the Corinthian Christians, for—through their prayers—they also had participated in Paul's work of spreading the gospel (see 1:11). Ultimately, God would be glorified through all this. All praise and *glory* would be solely his, for he is the One who sacrificed his own Son for the benefit of all who believe.

LOOKING AHEAD
Paul had faced sufferings and distress as he preached the Good News. But he knew that one day his trials would be over and that he would obtain God's rest and rewards. As we face great troubles, it's easy to focus on the pain rather than on our ultimate goal. Just as athletes concentrate on the finish line and ignore their discomfort, we too must focus on the reward for our faith and the joy that lasts forever. No matter what happens to us in this life, we have the assurance of eternal life, when all suffering will end and all sorrow will flee away (Isaiah 35:10).

Therefore we do not lose heart. Though outwardly we are wasting away, yet inwardly we are being renewed day by day.^{NIV} Paul and his colleagues would *not lose heart* because they knew the great power behind their message (3:16-18).

This passage contrasts the outward with the inward. Most people automatically read into this passage a distinction between

the material, physical body with the inner soul. This idea, however, is more of a Western idea. It is clear from the context that
Paul was contrasting the temporary with the eternal. He was not
merely talking about how his physical body was beginning to
waste away. Instead, he was speaking about how all the things of
this life—his wealth, his influence, his power—were deteriorating. These were temporary in the first place, so this could be
expected. Troubles were besieging him. Opponents were attacking him. In the midst of it all, Paul saw his inner soul—the part of
himself that was destined for eternal life—as *being renewed day
by day* (see Isaiah 40:31; Colossians 3:10). The hardships of
Paul's ministry were real and were having their effect. Paul, however, did not gripe or complain about how much he was giving up
in order to preach the gospel. Instead, he knew that every trouble,
hardship, and difficulty endured for Christ's sake was making
him spiritually new. This occurred day by day, trouble by trouble.
Paul saw every difficulty as an opportunity to mature in the faith.

FINISHING STRONG
It is easy to lose heart and quit. We have all faced problems in
our relationships or in our work that have caused us to want to
think about laying down the tools and walking away. Instead of
giving up when persecution wore him down, Paul allowed the
Holy Spirit to strengthen him within (Ephesians 3:16). Don't let
fatigue, pain, or criticism force you off the job. Renew your
commitment to serving Christ. Don't forsake your eternal
reward because of the intensity of today's pain. Your very
weakness allows the resurrection power of Christ to strengthen
you moment by moment.

4:17-18 **For this slight momentary affliction is preparing us for an
eternal weight of glory beyond all measure, because we look
not at what can be seen but at what cannot be seen; for what
can be seen is temporary, but what cannot be seen is eternal.**NRSV Present-day society is constantly changing. Change is
expected, and people spend their lives trying to keep ahead of the
changes in their workplace. This passage highlights what is permanent, something on which believers can plant their feet and
know that it is solid. It will always be there, no matter what
changes. It is the gospel message that is preparing all believers
for eternity with their loving Creator.

Paul knew that nothing in this life lasts forever. Paul knew that
the hardship he endured was a *slight momentary affliction* in comparison to how long he would enjoy God's presence. He concluded, therefore, that the troubles of this world are an extremely

light burden compared to the *eternal weight of glory.* Millions, billions, and trillions of years do not even compare to the length of infinite time.

What really matters—what is eternal and permanent—cannot be seen, touched, or measured. Only with the eyes of faith can people *look . . . at what cannot be seen.* Only with eyes of faith can they begin to understand, with God's help, the eternal significance of their actions. A believer's hope is not in this world. A Christian's hope is not in the power and wealth that can be accumulated on earth. Instead, a Christian's hope is in Christ—someone who cannot be seen at the present moment (Romans 8:24; Hebrews 11:1). Nevertheless, Jesus Christ and his significance to every person's life is real enough. That is why Paul encouraged the Corinthians to live by faith and not by sight (5:7). The Corinthians were to take their eyes off of this world—for *what can be seen is temporary*—and place them on the Almighty, the One who possessed all power. They were to invest in what was permanent and *eternal* and would withstand the unpredictable changes of life, in heavenly treasures that would never deteriorate (see Luke 12:33).

THE OPPORTUNITIES IN TRIALS

Our troubles should not diminish our faith or disillusion us. We should realize that there is a purpose in our suffering. Problems and human limitations have several benefits:

- They remind us of Christ's suffering for us.
- They keep us from pride.
- They cause us to look beyond this brief life.
- They prove our faith to others.
- They give God the opportunity to demonstrate his power.
- They bring an eternal reward.

See your troubles as opportunities!

Our ultimate hope when we are experiencing terrible illness, persecution, or pain is the realization that this life is not all there is—there is life after death! Knowing that we will live forever with God in a place without sin and suffering can help us live above the pain we face in this life.

---

2 Corinthians 5:1–6:2

As a Christian evangelist in the first century, Paul was insulted, ridiculed, and taunted. For the cause of the gospel, he faced angry mobs, irate local officials, and conceited philosophers. He spent many anxious nights in prayer and long hours working to support himself and studying the Scriptures. He received no applause, no reward, no appreciation.

Why did he do this? Paul answered this question for the Corinthians. He measured all of his troubles in the light of eternity. Paul knew that he would experience infinite happiness and unending joy in the next life. This confident hope was Paul's motivation to never stop preaching the truth to all who would listen.

5:1 Now we know that if the earthly tent we live in is destroyed, we have a building from God, an eternal house in heaven, not built by human hands.NIV Paul knew the Corinthians were wondering how he could endure so many hardships and difficulties (see 4:8-10), so he outlined his hope: the resurrection of his body to heavenly glory.

The Corinthians had difficulty understanding the resurrection and its place in the Christian worldview. Greeks did not believe in a bodily resurrection (notice how the Greek philosophers in Athens sneered at Paul when he spoke of a bodily resurrection; see Acts 17:32). Most Greeks thought that only the soul would survive death. They thought of the soul—the essence of a person—as imprisoned in a physical body, a body that was intrinsically evil. Upon death the soul would be released from its imprisonment. According to the Greeks, only the soul would enter an eternal state. Because of the strong Greek influence in the church, some believers in Corinth had begun teaching there was no bodily resurrection from the dead (see 1 Corinthians 15:12, 35). Thus, Paul had thoroughly explained the doctrine of the resurrection to them (see 1 Corinthians 15:12-57). Paul underscored its significance and made it clear that denying the resurrection of believers was tantamount to denying the resurrection of Jesus himself and, thus, the Christian faith (1 Corinthians 15:12-

34). Paul did not mince words: "If Christ has not been raised, then your faith is useless" (1 Corinthians 15:17 NLT). Paul would not risk his life for a futile and meaningless message (1 Corinthians 15:30).

In 2 Corinthians, in the middle of discussing his own sufferings for the gospel, Paul once again broached the subject of the resurrection. His confident hope that he would be given an *eternal* body by God inspired him to consider his present troubles as nothing, in light of the heavenly glory he would enjoy forever and ever (see 4:17-18). Paul compared his present *earthly* body to a *tent,* a temporary structure designed to be dismantled (see also 2 Peter 1:13-15). Although the image of a tent may suggest that the physical body covers the soul, the point of this passage is to contrast the temporary nature of earthly bodies to the permanent nature of heavenly bodies. Paul never conceded in his New Testament writings that the physical, mortal body was a covering for the immortal soul. Instead, he consistently taught the Jewish concept of the soul as the source of a person's life. The soul and the body are not separate identities. That is why Paul could speak of the "redemption of our bodies" (Romans 8:23 NIV). Not only are believers' souls saved, but their bodies will also be redeemed from the tragic consequences of sin.

And when this earthly tent *is destroyed*—a reference to physical death—believers will be given *an eternal house in heaven,* an eternal body. The contrast is clear. Our earthly bodies are like temporary, flimsy tents, while our eternal bodies will be permanent buildings. In the same way, earthly troubles are temporary, while the glory and joy of heaven are eternal (compare with 4:17-18).

Life in this earthly body makes believers "groan" for their perfect heavenly bodies (see 5:2-3 and the commentary on the following verses for more on the nature of spiritual bodies; see also Romans 8:22-23). Although these spiritual bodies will somehow be associated with our old physical bodies (Romans 8:23), they will be of an entirely different nature. They will be imperishable, glorious, and eternal (see Paul's discussion in 1 Corinthians 15:42-44). They will be perfect bodies for our new eternal existence with Jesus Christ.

5:2 For in this tent we groan, longing to be clothed with our heavenly dwelling.^{NRSV} Although Paul was loaded down with all sorts of troubles in this world (see 1:8; 4:8, 16-17), he did not despair. The Greek word Paul used for "groan" can either mean "to moan," as in the way people groan after being struck, or it can mean "to sigh," as in the way people breathe heavily when they yearn for something. Paul may have had both ideas in mind: He was groaning over his trials, but his troubles inspired him to yearn for heaven. Romans 8:21-23 states that all of creation groans under the decay that resulted from sin, and these verses indicate that believers also join in that moaning. The imagery in Romans 8:21-23 is extremely similar to the imagery here. This "groaning" is the hope by which we were saved, the hope that we will be raised to eternal life with Jesus Christ (Romans 8:24-25).

When Paul spoke of wanting to be *clothed* with a *heavenly dwelling,* he was referring to his longing to receive a resurrected body. This image depicts the glorious truth that the earthly bodies of Christians will be transformed into eternal, heavenly bodies.

5:3 If indeed, having been clothed, we shall not be found naked.^{NKJV} The believers in Corinth probably had been influenced by the Greek idea that death would free the soul from the prison of the body. Often, the Greeks would speak of death as stripping the soul and leaving it naked. The Greeks looked forward to this nakedness of the soul. This idea was probably the reason some Corinthians had begun to deny a bodily resurrection in the first place (1 Corinthians 15:12). This verse clearly repudiates the idea that believers' earthly bodies will be stripped off to reveal their naked souls. Instead, believers' earthly bodies would be covered with perfect, heavenly bodies.

5:4 For while we are in this tent, we groan and are burdened, because we do not wish to be unclothed but to be clothed with our heavenly dwelling, so that what is mortal may be swallowed up by life.^{NIV} This verse adds another image to this list of images about the heavenly body. In addition to speaking of it as a permanent building and overcoat, Paul depicted it as an animal consuming its prey. The eternal and permanent—*life* itself—will swallow up the temporary and the decaying—the *mortal.* The fact that Paul piled image upon image and repeated himself indicates his concern that the Corinthians understand the bodily resurrection. It will not be a matter of stripping off one's eternal body, as the Greeks commonly assumed; it would be a matter of being *clothed*—that is, "being clothed over" (see verse 2)—with the eternal and the perfect.

Paul had already described, in detail, to the Corinthians their resurrected bodies (1 Corinthians 15:46-58). This passage might be a clarification of his earlier teachings on the subject (compare it with 1 Corinthians 15:50-55). He had used several images to describe the difference between earthly and spiritual bodies. He had compared the difference between earthly and heavenly flesh to the difference between the flesh of animals and that of fish

(1 Corinthians 15:39-40). To describe the transformation that would result, Paul had compared the earthly body to a seed that had been planted in the ground. The small seed has to "die" in order to grow into a living, beautiful plant. In the same way, the earthly body has to be sown in weakness, decay, and even die before it yields the glorious, resurrected body (1 Corinthians 15:42-44).

Through these analogies and images, Paul was trying to emphasize what the resurrection meant for the Corinthians. Being "clothed" or "covered" with eternal bodies indicates that when Christians die, they will not lose their personalities or even their recognizable characteristics. As Jesus' own resurrection body shows, believers will have bodies that to some degree correspond with their own physical bodies. Their bodies will be redeemed (Romans 8:24). Through Christ's saving work, their resurrected bodies will be better than they can imagine.

Few details are given about the Christian's resurrected body, but the Bible does say it will be perfect, without sickness, disease, or pain (see Philippians 3:21; Revelation 21:4). Knowing this should affect the way Christians live on earth. Although believers will be transformed on the last day, they will retain the character that they have developed here on earth. The Corinthians had foolishly begun to live as if death would change everything: "Let us eat and drink, for tomorrow we die" (1 Corinthians 15:32 NIV). But Paul was trying to impress on them that what they did in this life did matter. In light of the certainty of a bodily resurrection, Paul encouraged the Corinthians to "stop sinning," and that "bad company corrupts good character" (1 Corinthians 15:33-34 NIV). Paul's exhortation applies today. Develop your character in this life, for every one of your actions here on earth has eternal consequences.

HOPE

Paul's knowledge that his mortality would be swallowed up with eternal life (5:4) is a universal hope we all have. According to the writer of Ecclesiastes, God "has planted eternity in the human heart" (Ecclesiastes 3:11 NLT). Human beings have an innate sense of transcendence and longing for ultimate reality experienced only in the eternal presence of God. This spiritual desire is addressed by every world religion and cult and (at least secretly) desired by every person. What occurrences in daily life can provide you an opportunity to witness God's solution to this universal spiritual search? A baby's birth, a parent's death, or the death of a dream all can be springboards for sharing the hope you have in Christ. Spread the Good News!

5:5 Now it is God who has made us for this very purpose and has given us the Spirit as a deposit, guaranteeing what is to come.NIV Paul's yearning for his heavenly body was not a desperate hope. God had determined long ago that believers in his Son would inherit eternal glory. This picks up the idea expressed in 4:17 that the Lord God had planned not only to justify believers through his Son's sacrificial death, but he also had planned to glorify them with heavenly bodies (see Romans 8:28-30 for Paul's explanation of how God is shaping believers into Christ's likeness).

Part of God's wonderful plan to save those who believe in his Son includes the Holy *Spirit*. On the day of Pentecost, God had sent his Holy Spirit to believers to empower them to be witnesses (Acts 2). Jesus had promised this would happen: The Spirit would come to remind them of the truth (John 14:26; Acts 1:5-8). Paul saw the Spirit at work in his life (Romans 15:18-19; 1 Corinthians 12:13) and in the lives of the Corinthians (1 Corinthians 2:12; 3:16; 6:19; 12:7, 13) as proof of his and their eternal destiny with God the Father. The Spirit was a *deposit*. The Greek word for "deposit" is *arrabon,* a business term meaning "guarantee" (see 1:22) or down payment. In other words, the Spirit is God's guarantee that he will one day pay up in full. Paul envisioned Christ, on one glorious day, coming to complete the process that had already begun, with the help of the Holy Spirit, within the Corinthians' lives (see 4:16; see also Romans 8:23; Ephesians 1:13-14). Through his death, Jesus will not only save believers, he will also clothe them in heavenly glory so that they can celebrate their salvation in God's presence (Romans 8:30; 9:23). The Holy Spirit within believers is a trustworthy guarantee that God will give Christians everlasting bodies at the resurrection (1:22). Christians have eternity within them now!

IT'S ALREADY BEGUN
The Holy Spirit is God's "guarantee" of what will come. When a cold lingers, a person may need antibiotics. When the medicine does its job, the person can feel the healing begin. In the dead of winter, a trip to a warm climate does wonders. The sunshine thaws the winter cold. But consider the work of the Holy Spirit. His work assures believers that the healing process will be thoroughly completed in Christ's presence. Each time the Holy Spirit reminds you of Scripture, convicts you of sin, restrains you from selfish behavior, or prompts you to love, you have evidence that he is present. You have the Spirit within you beginning the transformation process. Whether you deal with aches and pains or even disabling limitations, trust God that his total renovation of your body and soul is in process.

5:6-7 So we are always confident, knowing that while we are at home in the body we are absent from the Lord.^{NKJV} **So we are always confident, knowing that while we are at home in the body we are absent from the Lord.**^NKJV Paul was not afraid to die because he was *confident* of spending eternity with Christ. He wasn't going to lose heart in the face of all the trials and sufferings he was facing (4:8-9, 17). Although he couldn't physically see *the Lord* Jesus while he was still on earth, Paul remained confident in God and his plan of salvation. One day, Jesus would return to gather all of those who believe in him to bring them to their eternal home. Paul was confident and would speak the Good News boldly (3:12).

Of course, facing the unknown may cause anxiety, and leaving loved ones hurts deeply. But because Christians believe in Jesus, they can share Paul's hope and confidence of eternal life with Christ.

For we walk by faith, not by sight.^NRSV Walking around with your eyes closed is dangerous. Running into walls and tripping over objects would be a constant risk. Paul was saying it would be ludicrous for Christians to pattern their lives around this material world. Christians believe there is a greater spiritual reality that determines how they will live in eternity. To base life on what can be seen—the realities of this world—would be foolish indeed. This world will pass away, but the truth of God's Word will never pass away (Matthew 24:35; 2 Peter 3:10).

Instead of ordering their lives on the realities of this world, Christians are obligated to evaluate everything they do in light of eternity. This requires *faith*. The beginning point of faith is believing in God's character—he *is* who he says he is. The end point is believing in God's promises—he will *do* what he says he will do. When Christians believe God will fulfill his promises, even though they don't see those promises materializing yet, they demonstrate true faith (see John 20:24-31). God has promised eternal life, blessings, and rewards. Faith believes these realities are as real as the elements of the world that can be seen. Faith allows Christians to live in a God-honoring way and to make God-honoring decisions because these can be based on spiritual realities that are not seen. This confidence in the realities that are unseen allows believers to persevere in this faith, regardless of persecution, opposition, or temptation (see Hebrews 11:6; 1 Peter 1:8-9).

5:8 Yes, we do have confidence, and we would rather be away from the body and at home with the Lord.^NRSV This verse straightforwardly asserts that to be *away from the body* means being *at home with the Lord*. Paul also wrote in his letter to the Philippians that departing from this life means to "be with

Christ" (Philippians 1:23 NIV). These passages have been the subject of much debate over the exact state of believers at death—what theologians call the "intermediate state" between being at home in the body (5:6) and at home with the Lord. Since Paul wrote about the bodily resurrection occurring when Jesus returns (see 1 Corinthians 15:51-54) and also of believers being with Jesus immediately after they die, several theories have been proposed to explain this transitional state of the believer. In recent years, all of the theories about the disembodied state have been severely criticized. Many commentators have pointed out that these theories are based more on philosophical ideas about a person's soul than on Scripture. Some of the confusion is due to very little scriptural explanation.

There are four main views of the "intermediate state":

1. *Soul sleep*—This view is held by Seventh-Day Adventists and Jehovah's Witnesses. They believe that the soul rests in unconsciousness or oblivion until the resurrection. They base this view on verses where death is referred to as "sleep" (see Acts 7:6; 13:36; 1 Corinthians 15:6; 1 Thessalonians 4:13-15, and even Jesus' words in John 11:11). Some have modified this view to say that believers are "with Christ," but not in a conscious state. However, Scripture teaches the believer's immediate presence with the Lord at death in Jesus' words in Luke 23:43 to the thief on the cross, "I assure you, today you will be with me in paradise" (NLT) and in his final prayer, "Father, I entrust my spirit into your hands!" (NLT). Stephen, the first Christian martyr, said right before he died, "Lord Jesus, receive my spirit" (NLT).

2. *Purgatory*—This is the Roman Catholic view that at death those who have died in their sins and rejected Christ go to Hades for eternal punishment; those who died in a perfect state of grace go directly to heaven. Those who are not spiritually perfect go to purgatory for a refining process and purification of sin. This view has developed largely from church theologians and church councils rather than the Bible itself, although 1 Corinthians 3:15 has been used by Catholics to justify this view: "If the work is burned up, the builder will suffer loss; the builder will be saved, but only as through fire" (NRSV).

3. *Immediate resurrection*—This view states that at death there is an immediate separation from the earthly body and an immediate reclothing or reconstituting of the resurrection body. Proponents teach that in 1 Corinthians 15 and 1 Thessalonians 4, Paul believed in the resurrection of the

body at the Second Coming and fully believed that believers would see it in their lifetime. After Paul's brush with death and the reality that he might die before Christ returns, Paul explained what would be the case for those who died in the interval. Romans 8:19 and Colossians 3:4 are used to argue that believers are already resurrected but will be "revealed" or glorified at the Second Coming.

4. *Incomplete resurrection*—This view is the most commonly accepted view of Paul's words in the New Testament. There is a conscious, personal existence for the believer after death. At death, a believer goes to a place and condition of blessedness. The time interval between the believer's death and the full resurrection of the body will be imperceptible to the Christian. No anxiety or discomfort will mar this condition. Most do not believe this will be a bodiless existence because of Paul's teaching that he abhorred nakedness (5:3-4). However, it is true that the body will not be in its complete and final form because Paul points to a future resurrection as a specific event (Philippians 3:20-21; 1 Thessalonians 4:16-17), as does Jesus (John 5:25-29). At death we will assume a different expression or condition of the bodily self; then, at the Second Coming, this will be exchanged or reconstituted as the resurrection body.

In the final analysis, Christians can only affirm exactly what the Bible says: (1) When a believer dies, he or she will be with Jesus (see also Philippians 1:23). Believers will not float in a limbo state. Instead, they will have a personal encounter with the Savior. (2) When Jesus returns in all his glory, all believers will be given heavenly bodies that will be perfect and will last forever (see 1 Corinthians 15:51-54; 1 Thessalonians 4:16-18). A believer's life in eternity will involve some type of bodily existence. We have the example of our Lord's resurrected body as he appeared on earth. (3) The Spirit imparted to believers in this life not only guarantees that they will be resurrected to eternal glory but also begins that transformation within believers' souls (see 4:16; 5:5).

Although this verse, along with others, has provoked much speculation, Paul's point is abundantly clear: A believer's destination—his or her eternal home with Jesus—should inspire *confidence* and courage in the face of life's difficulties. Although Christians may moan under the strain of persecution, their problems should never push them to despair. Like a woman in labor, believers endure the pain and suffering joyfully, because they know it is temporary and will lead to something much better: a perfect and eternal home.

5:9-10 So our aim is to please him always, whether we are here in this body or away from this body.^{NLT} Unlike unbelievers, who are still blinded to the truth (see 4:4), believers know beyond a shadow of doubt where they are going after death: to be with Jesus. For those who believe in Christ, death is only a prelude to eternal life with him. Knowing that when you die you will be with Jesus should inspire you to live *to please* your Lord and Savior, Jesus Christ *always*. Just as you live for Christ's sake on this earth, you will continue to live for him in heaven. The transformation that the Holy Spirit is working within you now will finally be completed: You will become like Jesus (Romans 8:29-30). Let this hope give you confidence and inspire you to faithful service.

THE BIG TEST
According to Paul, all Christians will stand before the judgment seat of Christ. An evaluation of all thoughts, words, and deeds awaits them in the future. School teaches students to prepare for tests that gauge their achievement. Employers motivate employees by regular performance reviews. Doctors remind patients of annual physical exams. Evaluations are a part of life. Although eternal salvation is not dependent on personal moral achievement, believers will be called to account for their resourcefulness, faithfulness, and loving behavior (or lack of it) for purposes of rewards. If you stood before the Lord today, and he handed you a report card, what grade would do you think you would receive in moral purity? in financial integrity? in teachableness? in humility? in compassion? in perseverance in the faith? Use this future test as a motivation for present godly living.

For we must all stand before Christ to be judged. We will each receive whatever we deserve for the good or evil we have done in our bodies.^{NLT} Eternal life is a free gift given on the basis of God's grace (Ephesians 2:8-9), but Christians' lives will still be *judged* by Christ. Salvation is never obtained by works (Romans 4:4-5), and this judgment before Christ will not determine believers' eternal destiny. Instead, at this judgment, Christ will reward Christians for how they have lived on earth. God's gracious gift of salvation does not free Christians from the requirement of faithful obedience to Christ. All Christians must give account for how they have lived in this body (see the chart in the Life Application Bible Commentary *Matthew* 16:27; see also Acts 10:42; Romans 14:10-12; 1 Corinthians 3:10-15).

Some Corinthians thought their freedom in Christ allowed them to do anything (see 1 Corinthians 6:12), but Paul had already warned them in 1 Corinthians 6:20 that they were to

DON'T FORGET TO DO GOOD

We are saved by faith in Jesus Christ, but faith ought to result in a changed life and a willingness to do good to others.

What Jesus said . . .	Matthew 5:14-16; 6:1; 16:27; John 3:21
What Paul said . . .	2 Corinthians 9:8; Ephesians 2:10; 2 Thessalonians 2:16-17; 1 Timothy 6:17-19; 2 Timothy 3:16-17; Titus 3:14
What the writer of Hebrews said . . .	Hebrews 13:16
What James said . . .	James 1:22; 2:14-26; 3:13
What Peter said . . .	1 Peter 1:17; 2:12
What John said . . .	1 John 2:6; Revelation 14:13

honor God with their bodies because God had redeemed them with a price. Here the Corinthians are warned again with the prospect of appearing before the judgment seat of Christ. Paul had been dragged before Gallio's judgment seat (Greek *bema*) for preaching the gospel in Corinth (in fact, a stone structure remains even today in the ruins of Corinth, which is known as the *bema*). The believers would face Christ on his judgment seat (see Acts 18:12-13). Christ would render an accounting of what all Christians had done for him, just as the master in Jesus' parable had evaluated the performance of his servants (see Matthew 25:14-29). Christian service should be motivated by a love for Christ for the way he has graciously laid down his life for us (13:14; 1 Corinthians 16:22; Ephesians 6:24). It also should be motivated by an appropriate fear of God (see 5:11 for more on this).

Throughout 2 Corinthians, Paul was telling the Corinthians how he had been careful about his speech and behavior among them because he knew Jesus was hearing what he had said and was judging it (1:14; 2:10, 17; 3:18; 4:2, 14). This passage warns the Corinthians that their speech and behavior will also be judged, and they would *receive whatever* they deserved *for the good or evil* they had *done in* their *bodies*. This is a sober reminder to all Christians that we must evaluate all we do from God's perspective. The fact that we, as Christians, will meet Jesus should inspire both joy and a holy fear—joy that we will finally be with our Savior and fear that Jesus will hold us accountable for our actions.

BE RECONCILED TO GOD / 5:11–6:2

The first step to resolving a dispute is asking the other person for forgiveness, but no one enjoys taking that initial step. Whether it is a conflict between a husband and wife or a brother and sister, the first step toward reconciliation is difficult because no one wants to admit that he or she was wrong.

This passage points out that God has graciously taken the first step—in fact, the first stride—toward reconciliation with human beings. This in no way implies that God is somehow guilty or at fault. Ever since Adam and Eve's rebellion in the Garden of Eden, people have consistently rebelled against God, ignoring his ways and depriving him of the worship he deserves (Romans 3:23). God has done nothing wrong. In fact, he has only given people chance after chance to return to him. Although all human beings have persisted in their rebellion, God has not destroyed them. Instead, he has provided everything to sustain life—from the air they breathe to the rains that make their crops grow (Matthew 5:45). Through his only Son, God the Father has reached out even further to his rebellious people. Through Christ's death, God canceled our debts and forgave our sins (Colossians 2:13). He even places his Holy Spirit in our hearts so we can live according to his perfect ways (Galatians 5:16-18). Through Jesus, God has taken the initial step toward reconciliation, and he offers the free gift of salvation to all people. Anyone can come to accept his free gift (Ephesians 2:8-9; Revelation 22:17). Take advantage of God's free gift. What a profound truth and great news!

5:11-12 **It is because we know this solemn fear of the Lord that we work so hard to persuade others. God knows we are sincere, and I hope you know this, too.**[NLT] After reminding the Corinthians that everyone will appear before Christ's judgment seat, Paul explained that he had evaluated his own motives and actions in light of this sobering fact. He knew—and reminded himself of the fact—that God saw his motivations. His life was an open book to God. Paul didn't have to prove to God that he was *sincere,* for God already knew it. Paul hoped that the Corinthians, also, would understand that his actions were motivated by a healthy respect for God—not by greed or any other sinful motivation.

Paul feared God. The Greek word Paul used for "fear" is *phobos,* the root of our English word "phobia." *Phobos* can refer to anything from terror to reverential awe. In an age where independence, courage, and self-reliance are consistently lauded, it is difficult for people today to understand why they should fear anything. Preachers tend to skip over fear as a motivation for serving God and instead emphasize how love should motivate Christians (see 5:14).

But many forget that fear isn't fundamentally bad. Fear keeps people from jumping out of airplanes without a parachute. Fear can be anything from a healthy respect for natural laws to a respect for the laws of a nation. The Bible says that those who do not fear God will inevitably be judged (Psalm 36:1-12; 55:19-23). But on the other hand, the fear of God gives a person wisdom and helps that person avoid evil (Proverbs 15:33; 16:6). Thus, fear of God means having a proper respect for his perfect nature and great power. For those who have persisted in evil and rebellious ways, contemplating God should inspire dread. Their ways have been condemned by God, and their path leads to death (see 2:14-16). Believers who contemplate God should be filled with reverential awe, standing in wonder and amazement at his greatness.

Having a *solemn fear of the Lord* does not mean that believers become paralyzed. On the contrary, knowing God's perfection and that he will judge everyone's actions should spur Christians to good deeds, to what pleases our God (Proverbs 8:13). The fear of the Lord also frees believers from all of life's anxieties and worries. Knowing that God Almighty is "for us" (Romans 8:31) can keep believers unafraid of all earthly powers—people, governments, or the forces of nature (Proverbs 3:25-26). God takes care of his own. Ironically, the fear of God, in the end, inspires an uncommon courage in the face of the vicissitudes of life.

We are not commending ourselves to you again, but giving you an opportunity to boast about us, so that you may be able to answer those who boast in outward appearance and not in the heart.NRSV In this letter, Paul has been extremely cautious about bragging about himself to the Corinthians. Several times he has explicitly denied doing any such thing (see 3:1; 10:18). Paul knew that in the process of *commending* himself, he could easily fall into the trap of doing just what the false preachers were doing: bragging about their own spirituality and their own accomplishments.

Paul's Corinthian critics were more concerned about getting ahead in this world (see 2:17). They were preaching the gospel for money and popularity. They were boasting in *outward appearance:* eloquent speeches (11:5-6; 1 Corinthians 2:1), formal letters of recommendation (3:1), and impressive presentations (see 10:10-11). In contrast, Paul and his companions were preaching out of concern for eternity and to please the ultimate Judge, God himself. The Corinthians had been dazzled by these magnificent and impressive shows. They had been captivated by their astonishing rhetoric. Subtly, they had given up striving to find God's perspective.

Don't be captivated by spectacles and shows as the Corinthians were. Instead, judge a preacher or teacher by God's Word.

Find out about the person's character and integrity. If the preacher is more concerned about himself than about Christ, avoid that person and his message.

5:13 **If we are out of our mind, it is for the sake of God; if we are in our right mind, it is for you.**NIV Exactly what Paul meant by being *out of our mind* is not entirely clear. Some have suggested that since Paul used the Greek word *ekstasis* for "out of our mind" (the root of the English word "ecstasy"), he was speaking about visions and other ecstatic spiritual experiences. It is obvious from 1 Corinthians that the Corinthians had become so infatuated by one ecstatic spiritual gift—speaking in tongues—that they were neglecting more important matters: love and building up each other in Christ (see 1 Corinthians 13:1–14:5). In this verse Paul was saying that if he experienced ecstatic experiences, it was for his private edification—not something to show off to others.

Others have suggested that the Greek *(ekstasis)* for "out of our mind" means simply that Paul was "mad." Mark used the Greek word in this sense to describe how Jesus' family thought he was "mad" (see Mark 3:21). Perhaps the Corinthians had begun to think that Paul had a mental problem. He welcomed all kinds of trials, difficulties, and sufferings and even listed them (see 4:7-9). Later, Festus would call Paul mad because of his unquenchable zeal to preach the gospel (see Acts 26:22-24). Paul had already warned the Corinthians in 1 Corinthians that the gospel and its messengers would appear foolish to the wise of this world (1 Corinthians 2:7-16). If this was the idea that Paul was trying to express, then he was saying that he was acting like a fool because of his zeal for God and the gospel.

Although Paul didn't clarify his meaning, his point is abundantly clear. Paul's actions were not motivated by self-interest or a quest for power. Everything he did—whether he was out of his mind or in his *right mind*—was for God and for the spiritual welfare of the Corinthians.

5:14 **For Christ's love compels us, because we are convinced that one died for all, and therefore all died.**NIV Everything that Paul and his companions did was to honor God. Not only did fear of God motivate them (see 5:11), but Christ's love controlled their actions. The Greek word for "compels" means "to hold fast." In other words, the love of Christ was constraining them to certain courses of action. They knew that Jesus, out of his great love, had given up his life for their sakes. He had not acted out of his own self-interest, selfishly holding on to the glory of heaven that he already possessed (Philippians 2:6). Instead, Jesus had willingly *died* on the cross.

Jesus died for *all* because on the cross he—the perfect Son of God—bore the curse that lay on *all* sinners. Thus, when Christ died on the cross, God saw *all* sinners, along with their sins, die on the cross (John 3:16-17; Romans 5:8). That is why those who accept this truth and believe in Jesus can receive God's forgiveness for their sin.

5:15 And he died for all, that those who live should no longer live for themselves but for him who died for them and was raised again.^{NIV} Because Christ was willing to make the ultimate sacrifice, to die for *all,* those who believe in Jesus should be willing to abandon their old, selfish ways in order to live for Christ (Romans 6:6-14; Galatians 2:20; Colossians 2:20). Like Paul, we should no longer live to please ourselves. We should die to ourselves and live for Christ, who is alive today and interceding with God on our behalf (Romans 6:22).

COUNTERCULTURAL CHRISTIANITY
In light of Christ's death, Paul is insistent that Christians have no right to live selfishly (5:14). This biblical idea attacks today's culture head-on. In the middle of the twentieth century, popular magazine titles were generically named *Life, Look,* and *Time.* As the new millennium approached, magazine titles reflected an increasingly ego-driven society: *People, Us,* and *Self.* Imagine that you have been approached to come up with a name and format for a new magazine whose content reflects a Christlike lifestyle. What titles would you suggest? What articles would you feature in this magazine? As an editor, what lifestyle issues would you want to address? In what ways would you encourage Christians to counter society's values?

5:16-17 So from now on we regard no one from a worldly point of view. Though we once regarded Christ in this way, we do so no longer.^{NIV} At one time, Paul had evaluated Jesus *from a worldly point of view*—in Greek, literally, "after the flesh," meaning "according to human standards." As an educated Jew, Paul was looking forward to the Messiah. But the Jews of his time were looking for a political Messiah, a powerful person who would free them from Roman rule. Instead, Jesus had died, even suffering the Romans' most cruel punishment: crucifixion. Because Deuteronomy 21:23 says "anyone who is hung on a tree is under God's curse" NIV, the Jews considered dying on a cross a sign of God's disapproval. According to human standards, Jesus was an insignificant man who died like a criminal—not a person who deserved worship.

Paul's encounter with the risen Christ on the Damascus road

radically changed his thinking (Acts 9:1-15). All of his learning and all of his training under the teachers of the law and the respected Gamaliel had not led him to the truth. The wisdom of the world had not pointed him to the Savior of the world (see 1 Corinthians 2:1-16 for Paul's explanation of why God circumvented human wisdom in his plan of salvation).

Only this personal encounter with Jesus convinced Paul that he needed to reevaluate his own life in light of what Jesus had accomplished on the cross. Jesus had given up his life for others—not only for the Jews, but also for the Gentiles (see Acts 10:34-44 for Peter's discovery of this). As a Pharisee, Paul had strictly followed Jewish law and its traditions, which limited contact with unbelieving Gentiles (see Acts 10:12-16, 28-29 for Peter's reaction to entering a Gentiles' house). In light of Christ's work, however, Paul abandoned those scruples and began calling Gentiles to faith in Jesus Christ (Romans 11:13; 15:16). He regarded everyone—both Jew and Gentile—as completely unworthy sinners before God (Romans 3:9). Anyone who acknowledged this fact, repented, and believed in Jesus as their Lord and Savior would enter the Christian community, whether Jew or Gentile (Ephesians 3:6). Paul no longer was looking on the outward appearances—whether a person was from a certain ethnic or racial origin. Instead, he evaluated people through Christ's perspective.

So if anyone is in Christ, there is a new creation: everything old has passed away; see, everything has become new![NLT] Christians are brand-new people. The Holy Spirit gives them new life, and they are not the same anymore. Christians are not reformed, rehabilitated, or reeducated—they are recreated *(a new creation),* living in vital union with Christ (Colossians 2:6-7). At conversion, believers are not merely turning over a new leaf; they are beginning a new life under a new Master.

In addition to recreating individual Christians, Jesus is incorporating them into an entirely new order. This new creation that Christ has begun constructing through his work on the cross includes the community of faith and all of creation (see Romans 8:20-21; Ephesians 1:9-10). This recreation of all the earth was something the prophet Isaiah had predicted (see Isaiah 65:17). An important aspect of this completely new creation is how people are reconciled to their Creator and even to other people. The distinction between Jew and Gentile is abolished. In its place is the new creation (see Galatians 6:15). *Everything old has passed away.* The old order of sin and death has gone; the selfish, sinful human nature has been dealt a death blow (see Galatians 5:16-21, 24). Old ways of thinking, old distinctions, have been abolished for those who are *in Christ*. In its place, the new has come. To draw attention to the coming of this new order, Paul announced it with the word "see."

NEW LIFE
Paul proclaimed a whole new creation in Christ. Too often this verse has been individualized so that the main point is blurred. Many preach, "If anyone is in Christ, *that person* is a new creation." While this is true, Paul is saying much more. Not only are believers changed from within (mysterious new creations in Christ), but a whole new order of creative energy began with Christ. There is a new covenant, a new perspective, a new body, a new church. All of creation is being renewed.

So sit up. Take notice. The old, worn-out ways are being replaced with *new*. This is not a superficial change that will be quickly superseded by another novelty. This is an entirely *new* order of all creation under Christ's authority. It requires a new way of looking at all people and all of creation. Does your life reflect this new perspective?

5:18 **All this is from God, who reconciled us to himself through Christ and gave us the ministry of reconciliation.**NIV This new creation is not of any human doing. God himself has begun the work. Only God can allow people to approach him. Only God can satisfy his own righteous demands. Only God can save. God is the Author and Finisher of salvation (see Hebrews 12:2). God brought his people to himself—in other words, *reconciled us*—by blotting out our sins (see also Ephesians 2:13-18) and making us righteous. When they trust in Christ, believers are no longer God's enemies. Through Christ's self-sacrificial work on the cross, God has made believers part of his family. Jesus died in our place so that we might enjoy fellowship with God (1 Corinthians 15:3).

Because believers have been reconciled to God, we have the privilege of encouraging others to accept God's free gift, to become reconciled as well. This is called *the ministry of reconciliation*. Since Paul experienced reconciliation through Christ, it became his mission to preach that message: "For if, when we were God's enemies, we were reconciled to him through the death of his Son, how much more, having been reconciled, shall we be saved through his life!" (Romans 5:10 NIV). Today, the church owes it to the world to keep on spreading the message.

5:19 **For God was in Christ, reconciling the world to himself, no longer counting people's sins against them. This is the wonderful message he has given us to tell others.**NLT This is a quick summary of what his "ministry of reconciliation" entails. God had given Paul and other Christian evangelists the *wonderful message* of how God through Christ saves sinners. Just in case the Corinthians had forgotten the heart of Paul's message to them, he repeated it to them: Christ was reconciling the world to God by *no longer counting people's sins against them.* Paul used a Greek word for "counting" that was commonly used when a Greek spoke of calculating the debt of a person. Thus, God was no longer calculating people's debt to him; instead, he was actively giving them more: the precious gift of salvation.

The Greek word for "sins" *(paraptomata)* literally means "fall beside," in other words, a "failing." Paul used it to express anything that deviated from God's ways. But God, through Christ's death on the cross, was bringing back all people—Jews and Greeks alike—who had fallen (Romans 5:10; Ephesians 2:14-17). Although we were enemies of God, Christ reached out to us, saving us from certain destruction. He even washed us in order that we might approach God with clean hearts (Colossians 1:21-22).

5:20-21 **We are therefore Christ's ambassadors, as though God were making his appeal through us. We implore you on Christ's behalf: Be reconciled to God.**[NIV] Ambassadors are official representatives of one country to another. In the first century, an ambassador was an elderly man of high rank who would travel to another country with messages from the monarch of his country. These messages might be simply congratulations at appropriate occasions, or it could be an official censure. Paul described himself and his coworkers as *Christ's ambassadors,* representatives of Christ to the world (5:19).

Paul was a spokesmen for *God.* The message he preached was, in fact, God's *appeal* to the world. Paul obtained his authority to preach from God himself. God had not given this authority to Paul because he was an especially gifted speaker or had the right credentials. God simply had chosen Paul to deliver God's appeal. If Paul ever deviated from God's message, he would lose his authority to speak (see 1 Corinthians 12:3).

What was Paul's message that he had to deliver *on Christ's behalf?* It was to *be reconciled to God.* Paul phrased this command in the passive tense. He wasn't commanding people to reconcile themselves; they were incapable of doing that. Instead, Paul was announcing that they could be reconciled to God and that they should accept God's free gift of reconciliation. Paul did not announce this message halfheartedly. He implored—even urged and pleaded—everyone who would listen to him to accept God's free gift of salvation. It was extremely urgent, for it would change their eternal destiny.

God made him who had no sin to be sin for us.^{NIV} Although

Jesus was completely innocent, *God made* him *who had no sin to be sin for us*. There are three views on what Paul meant by this:
(1) Jesus was made a sinner when he died on the cross. This, of course, is not true. Jesus did not break the law at any point. He could not be a sinless sacrifice (Hebrews 7:26) and a sinner at the same time. Rather it was "for us" that he bore the consequences of our sin: death. (2) Still others have seen this as a reference to the Jewish sacrificial system. God made Jesus (1 Corinthians 5:7), although perfect and unblemished, into a sin offering for all humanity (see Romans 3:25; Hebrews 13:11-14). Although Paul does teach that Christ was a sin offering for us, and the Greek word for "sin," *hamartia,* can also be used for sin offering, it would have been confusing for Paul to say "he who had no sin offering became a sin offering." (3) Most likely the meaning is that Christ bore the consequences of, or punishment for, our sins, as stated in Galatians 3:13:

> *Christ redeemed us from the curse of the law by becoming a curse for us, for it is written: "Cursed is everyone who is hung on a tree."* (NIV)

In other words, God made Jesus, who was completely innocent and perfect, identify himself with sin so he could take it away.

In life, rarely will anyone claim perfection. Sin is a part of life, so much so that many people simply expect to encounter dishonesty, self-centeredness, and greed in other people. If they don't, they are surprised. That is why many people in Jesus' day expressed surprise at Jesus' life. They could not find anything wrong with him (see Pilate's words in Luke 23:4-22, the centurion's words in Luke 23:41-48, and God's testimony in Matthew 3:17; 17:5). The disciples, Jesus' closest friends and followers, did not find any evil in his actions (see Peter's testimony in 1 Peter 2:22 and John's testimony in 1 John 3:5). Here Paul used the Greek word meaning "to know" in a personal way in the expression *had no sin*. Thus Paul was asserting that Jesus never knew what it meant to sin: He always followed God's ways.

So that in him we might become the righteousness of God.^{NIV}
Jesus bore the consequences of believers' sin for their sakes. Since Jesus, who was perfect and innocent, took on the penalty of sin—death itself, Jesus can now give those who believe in him his *righteousness*. His perfect righteousness can cover our corrupt and imperfect lives. When people trust in Christ, they make an exchange—their sin for his righteousness. Believers' sin was

placed on Jesus at his crucifixion. His righteousness is given to believers at their conversion. This is what Christians mean by Christ's atonement for sin.

If it were not for the reality contained in 5:21, all of Christianity would be wishful thinking, a "hope so" religion. Here, Paul clarified the eternal transaction whereby each believer is passed "from death to life" (John 5:24 NIV). How grateful we should be for God's kindness to us.

6:1-2 As God's fellow workers we urge you not to receive God's grace in vain.^{NIV} What does Paul mean when he says that he and his *fellow workers* urged the believers in Corinth *not to receive God's grace in vain?* "Grace" is God's undeserved favor. People receive God's totally undeserved gift by believing in Jesus. Even a person's ability to believe is a gift from God (Ephesians 2:8). God has paved the way for people to be reconciled to him. All they need to do is respond to the announcement of this Good News.

So how can anyone accept God's favor "in vain"? Commentators have explained this in a variety of ways—from seeing this as an appeal to unbelievers not to ignore God's grace (see Hebrews 2:2-4) to interpreting it as an exhortation to nominal Christians to mature in their faith (see Matthew 13:18-23). Most likely, however, Paul was urging the Corinthians to take God's grace seriously: to live up to the gospel's demands.

In 1 Corinthians, Paul had warned the Corinthians not to build hay and stubble on the sure foundation he himself had laid: the gospel truth that Jesus Christ saves. Paul even warned that their work would be put through the fire of judgment. A person whose work was destroyed would still be saved but would suffer great loss (see 1 Corinthians 3:10-15).

In this letter, Paul had already mentioned how he was carefully evaluating all of his actions because he knew he would have to stand before Jesus (see 5:10). The end of this letter urges the Corinthians to test themselves to see if their faith was genuine (13:5-6) and, at the same time, exhorts them to not sin (13:2-3, 7). Thus, in this passage, Paul was most likely imploring the Corinthians, who had already accepted Jesus, to live up to their profession of faith (see 5:14).

Paul has cautiously described how he was the Corinthians' servant (4:5) and how everything he did was for their sake (1:6-7, 15; 2:10; 5:13). Here he began to instruct the Corinthians based on his authority as Christ's ambassador (see 5:14-21). Still Paul was cautious. Instead of commanding as he did in his previous letter (1 Corinthians 7:10; 14:37), he "urged." The Greek for "urge" was used in the first century by authority figures who could command but who were diplomatically asking. So in this passage, Paul began to assert his apostolic authority. As an ambassador of Christ, he was obligated to guide believers in the truth.

For he says, "In the time of my favor I heard you, and in the day of salvation I helped you." I tell you, now is the time of God's favor, now is the day of salvation.^{NLT} The prophet Isaiah predicted a *time of* God's *favor*—a time of God's own choosing—when he would save his people: God would release them from bondage and clear a path for them to return to their land and restore their fortunes (see Isaiah 49:8-12, 23-26). God would do all this so that the whole world would know that he was Israel's Savior and Redeemer (Isaiah 49:26). The Hebrews who had heard Isaiah's message long ago would have understood this as a prediction that God would one day bring the Israelites back out of their exile in Babylon. This did occur (see Ezra 1).

PRECIOUS MOMENTS
Now is the time of God's favor, according to Paul. *Now* is the day of salvation. Paul could be called a *"now* Christian." For Paul, *today* is what matters most to God. A classic comic strip shows two children debating the merits of remembering, anticipating, and living life. The little girl finally says, "Yesterday is past. Tomorrow is future. All we have is today. Today is a gift. That is why it is called 'the present.'" God's mercies and presence are available moment by moment. Although there is reason to glance over the shoulder or sneak a peek at future possibilities, the Lord of the *now* calls us to celebrate life without regrets. What regrets hold you hostage to the past? What dreams expend the energy you need to obey God today? What can you do today to sanctify it as a holy moment never to be repeated? Once you have identified what to do, let that act call you to worship.

Paul, however, understood Isaiah's prediction as also being fulfilled in his day. God had sent Jesus to the earth. It was the time of God's favor. Moreover, Jesus died on the cross to save all who believe in him (John 3:16-17). It was the *day of salvation*. So Paul, being God's messenger just as Isaiah was, echoed Isaiah's message with even more urgency. Paul announced that what Isaiah was looking forward to had occurred.

God offers salvation to all people. Many people put off making a decision to receive God's salvation, thinking that there will be a better time—but they could easily miss their opportunity altogether. There is no time like the present to receive God's forgiveness. *Now*—that is, today—is the day when God has revealed his great plan of salvation.

2 Corinthians 6:3–7:1

"For better or for worse, for richer, for poorer, in sickness and in health, to love and to cherish, till death us do part." At a wedding, a couple exchanges their vows. These vows list a variety of situations in which they promise to love the other. Paul did something similar for the Corinthians. He listed the different situations he had endured in order to remain faithful to Christ and his divine calling to preach the Good News. Paul had demonstrated his willingness to suffer all kinds of hardships—beatings, imprisonments, poverty, and even insults—for Jesus. He had a single-hearted commitment to Christ. This extraordinary commitment, demonstrated by the sufferings he had endured, was proof of his apostolic authority. Instead of submitting a list of successes and accomplishments, Paul submitted a list of difficult situations that he had endured for Christ.

6:3-5 **We are putting no obstacle in anyone's way, so that no fault may be found with our ministry.**NRSV Paul knew that unbelievers and believers alike were watching his life. God had entrusted Paul with the message of truth; he, in turn, had to live up to God's ways. That is why he was careful to be straightforward, honest, and upright (see 1:12). Any wrongdoing—or anything that was perceived to be wrong—might distract from the gospel message (4:2; 1 Corinthians 1:17). It might even be an *obstacle* that would cause people to find *fault* with Paul's *ministry.* Paul did not want any of his actions to discredit God or the gospel. The last thing he wanted to do was bring ridicule on God's glorious plan of salvation. All Christians should show this kind of care. As God's children, Christians should live like they belong to God.

But as servants of God we have commended ourselves in every way: through great endurance, in afflictions, hardships, calamities.NRSV *In every way* imaginable Paul had diligently served God. He had proven to be Christ's trustworthy servant.

The Corinthians, however, had begun to doubt Paul's credentials and, more importantly, his authority over them (see 12:11). So Paul listed the different situations in which he had served

God. Similar to his weaknesses in 4:8-10, this list includes predicaments that most preachers would not catalog for their audiences.

Difficult situations and worrisome predicaments teach *endurance* (see Paul's explanation in 1:6). This passage indicates that with that same patient endurance Paul had faced all kinds of *afflictions*. The word "afflictions" is a general term referring to all types of hardships. When calling Paul to be an evangelist, Christ warned him that he would suffer greatly (see Acts 9:15-16). At key junctures in Paul's ministry, the Holy Spirit had warned him of all types of *hardships* that he would face in the towns, villages, and cities in which he would preach. Paul, however, was not concerned about these difficulties or even about his own life. He continued to focus on his mission. He wanted to fulfill the task that God had given him: to announce the Good News (see Acts 20:23-24). He knew that nothing—neither hardship, persecution, hunger, nor nakedness—could separate him from Christ's love (see Romans 8:37-39). By faith, Paul faced all *calamities* with resolute courage. Although Paul could expect suffering in this world, he knew that one day he would finish the race and be with his wonderful Savior, Jesus (4:17-18).

We have been beaten, been put in jail, faced angry mobs.[NLT] After describing in general terms what he had endured for Jesus, Paul started naming some of the specific situations in which he had served God. Chapter 11 describes some of these difficulties in even more detail.

For preaching Christ, Paul had been *beaten*. In 11:23-25, Paul recalls that he had been whipped five times by the Jews. He also had been beaten with rods by the civil authorities on three separate occasions. Luke recorded in the book of Acts that Paul and Silas suffered this punishment at Philippi (see Acts 16:23-24).

Paul had *been put in jail* in Philippi (Acts 16:23). In almost every city, Paul had *faced angry mobs,* usually stirred up by resentful Jews. In Pisidian Antioch, Jews stirred the high-ranking men and women of the city to expel him from that city (Acts 13:49-52). In Iconium, the citizens plotted to stone Paul to death (Acts 14:5-6). In Lystra, an angry mob did stone him, and, miraculously, he survived it and went to the next town to preach the Good News (Acts 14:19). At Philippi, a mob seized Paul and Silas and had them imprisoned (Acts 16:19-24). At Thessalonica, a crowd looking for Paul surrounded Jason's house (Acts 17:5). At Ephesus, an enraged mob of silversmiths seized Paul's traveling companions (Acts 19:23-41). Even during Paul's ministry among the Corinthians, the Jews of Corinth seized Paul and brought him before the governor (see Acts 18:12-17). Everywhere Paul preached the gospel, he was met with incensed mobs. He expected opposition, but he also expected Jesus to see him through those difficult situations (see 1:3-7).

IMPRISONED BUT NOT INACTIVE
Being imprisoned would cause many people to become bitter or to give up, but Paul saw imprisonment as one more opportunity to spread the Good News of Christ. Paul realized that his current circumstances weren't as important as what he did with them. Turning a bad situation into a good one, he reached out to the Roman soldiers who made up the palace guard and encouraged Christians who were afraid of persecution. We may not be in prison, but we still have plenty of opportunities to be discouraged—times of indecision, financial burdens, family conflict, church conflict, or the loss of our jobs. How we act in such situations will reflect what we believe. Like Paul, look for ways to demonstrate your faith even in bad situations. Whether or not the situation improves, your faith will grow stronger.

Worked to exhaustion, endured sleepless nights, and gone without food.^{NLT} After listing some of the involuntary hardships he faced, Paul mentioned the hardships he had endured voluntarily in order to further the cause of the gospel. Paul not only dutifully faced all kinds of opposition for Christ, he also made personal sacrifices so that he could continue to announce the Good News.

Paul had *worked to exhaustion* so as not to become a burden to the people he was preaching to, especially the Corinthians (see 11:9). In Thessalonica, he worked night and day; perhaps this caused some of those *sleepless nights* Paul *endured* (1 Thessalonians 2:9; 3:8). Perhaps some of those voluntary sleepless nights were not spent in physical labor but in prayer for all the churches (see 11:28; see Romans 1:10; Ephesians 1:16; Philippians 1:4 for some of Paul's prayers). Moreover, Paul had *gone without food.* He may have done this in order to not be a financial burden for the people to whom he was ministering (see 11:7-10).

6:6-7 We have proved ourselves by our purity, our understanding, our patience, our kindness, our sincere love, and the power of the Holy Spirit.^{NLT} In the middle of his list of the difficult situations he faced for the cause of Christ, Paul listed five character traits of an effective minister of the gospel.

First, he and his coworkers had acted in *purity.* To be pure means to be free of any contamination. Paul's actions (1 Timothy 5:22) and thoughts (Philippians 4:8) were pure. Paul may have had in mind a phony preacher's motivations—such as greed and self-interest—which were contaminating the messages of many preachers who had visited Corinth (see Paul's description of these traveling preachers in 4:2).

Second, he and his coworkers had *understanding*. This does not refer to a wealth of information. Instead, it means a clear understanding of the gospel message. Christ had revealed to Paul the mysteries of salvation (Ephesians 3:6). Paul understood the gospel and knew he had to communicate it clearly (1:12).

Third, they had *patience*. Paul had learned patience through all of these difficult situations. In the end, however, any patience he had was from the Holy Spirit, for in Galatians Paul explicitly stated that "the fruit of the Spirit is love, joy, peace, patience, kindness, goodness, faithfulness, gentleness and self-control" (Galatians 5:22-23 NIV). *The Holy Spirit* empowered all of Paul's efforts. Even Paul's character traits were not of his own doing but a product of the Holy Spirit dwelling within him.

Fourth, they treated others with *kindness*. Through the Spirit's power, Paul had learned to consider others' needs above his own. Realizing how much God had done for him, Paul sought to show that same type of mercy to others.

Finally, they had *sincere love*. The self-sacrificial love that Jesus had shown to the Corinthians when he died for them on the cross (see Romans 5:5) was the type of love Paul attempted to emulate in his ministry.

We have faithfully preached the truth. God's power has been working in us.NLT Although Paul encountered all kinds of opposition when he preached the Good News, he did not give up preaching the word of truth. Although traveling preachers were deceiving the Corinthians with a false gospel (see 4:2; 11:4), Paul would continue to preach *the truth* so that *God's power* might be demonstrated (see 1 Corinthians 2:1-4).

LIVING PROOF
Paul said that his life proved his message. In everything he did, Paul always considered what his actions communicated about Jesus Christ. If you are a believer, you are a minister for God. In the course of each day, non-Christians observe you. Don't let your careless or undisciplined actions be another person's excuse for rejecting Christ.

We have righteousness as our weapon, both to attack and to defend ourselves.NLT A Roman soldier would arm himself with a full-length shield in his left hand and a spear in his right hand. In

the original Greek, Paul literally wrote "we have weapons of righteousness of the right and of the left." Thus, the NLT translators
made it clear what Paul's readers would have known: that weapons
in the right hand were *to attack,* while weapons in the left were *to
defend.* No Roman soldier was fully prepared for battle without
both weapons: his shield on his left and his spear on his right.

Ephesians 6:10-18 lists, along with *righteousness,* the other
spiritual weapons. They consist of the gospel message itself, the
truth of God's Word, and faith. In order to resist the devil, Christians need to not only immerse themselves in the truths of God's
Word and the gospel itself, they need to put their faith into action.
The righteousness God gives Christians through faith in Christ
should be evident in the way they live. Then Christians will be
able to withstand Satan's attacks.

6:8-10 **We serve God whether people honor us or despise us, whether
they slander us or praise us.**NLT A pastor's job is to confront
people with the truths of the gospel. But sometimes this responsibility is neglected because a pastor is more concerned about
being liked. The traveling preachers in
Corinth were like this. They had told
the Corinthians what they wanted to
hear. They did this to advance their
careers and to obtain money and letters
of recommendation (see 3:1; 4:2).
Some of them had completely wan-
dered from the truth and were preaching a different gospel (11:4). They were
even attacking Paul's authority in order

> A Christian man is the
> most free lord of all, and
> subject to none; a
> Christian man is the most
> dutiful servant of all, and
> subject to everyone.
> *Martin Luther*

to wield power in the Corinthian church (for the specific attacks
on Paul, see 10:10-11).

Instead of worrying about the reaction of his audience, Paul
focused on whom he was serving: God (6:4). He would *serve
God whether* he was honored or despised, whether he was slandered or praised. No flattery or insult would distract Paul from
preaching the Good News.

**We are honest, but they call us impostors. We are well known,
but we are treated as unknown.**NLT This passage contrasts how
God evaluated Paul's ministry with how his critics saw it. God's
evaluation mattered most to Paul, for he had his sights set on eternity, not on the temporary conditions of the present (see 5:1-10).

The paradox was that though Paul and his coworkers were
completely *honest,* they were still being accused as *impostors.*
They had renounced all deceptive means to communicate the
holy message of God (see 4:2). They used no tricks or games.

Instead, Paul preached the truth with a genuine frankness and with the power of God himself (see 1 Corinthians 2:4).

Paul's preaching and actions were *well known* to many, but in contrast, the powerful and wise of this world *treated* him *as unknown.* They considered his message as foolishness (see Acts 17:18-21, 32-33; 1 Corinthians 2:6-10). They were thoroughly unacquainted with Paul's arguments. (See Gallio's reaction to the Corinthian Jews who brought Paul before him, in Acts 18:14-17).

We live close to death, but here we are, still alive.^{NLT} Second Corinthians began with an explanation of how Paul had faced *death* in Asia Minor (present-day Turkey; see 1:8). Some commentators have suggested that 1:8 refers to Paul's imprisonment in Ephesus when he faced the death penalty in association with the riot that had occurred there (see Acts 19:21-41). *But,* even so, he was *still alive.* After being stoned, Paul miraculously got up and went to the next city to preach the gospel (for the story, see Acts 14:19-20). Whether this is an allusion to Paul's being *close to death* in Lystra or in Asia Minor, this verse summarizes what happened. Although he had been left for dead, Paul continued to live and preach.

We have been beaten within an inch of our lives.^{NLT} This translation makes the verse reiterate the same thought as the previous sentence. This may very well be the case, for Paul had been beaten and whipped on numerous occasions for preaching the gospel (see 6:5; 11:23-24). In the first century, often people would die of a beating at the hands of the authorities. The Jews used whips with metal pieces, which would tear into the flesh. The Roman authorities beat offenders with rods. Both beatings could be severe enough to kill a person.

NO COMPROMISE!
What a difference it makes to know Jesus! He cares for his own in spite of what the world thinks. Christians don't have to give in to public opinion and pressure. Paul stood faithful to God whether people praised him or condemned him. He remained active, joyous, and content in the most difficult hardships. Don't let circumstances or people's expectations control you. Be firm as you stand true to God.

The Greek also has another connotation. The Greek word used for "beaten" is commonly used by New Testament writers for divine chastisement (see also 1 Corinthians 11:32). Paul may have been saying, therefore, that his many sufferings were not an indication that God was displeased with his ministry, as his critics at Corinth were claiming. On the contrary, Paul's sufferings were a mark of his apostolic authority. Christ had called him to suffer for the gospel (see 1:5-7; Acts 9:16).

Our hearts ache, but we always have joy.NLT In addition to hardships, Paul's ministry involved mental anguish. Paul had agonized over the Corinthians' spiritual welfare, as well as the welfare of other churches. He had spent night and day in prayer, committing these churches and their congregations to the Lord (see Romans 10:1; Philippians 1:9; 1 Thessalonians 3:10; 2 Thessalonians 1:11). Although the *hearts* of him and his coworkers would *ache* over the churches, they were filled with *joy* because they knew what their spiritual struggles would accomplish. Jesus had already triumphed over Satan and his evil forces (Colossians 2:5). All of those who had placed their faith in Jesus, the One whom Paul preached, would join him in celebration on the fabulous day when Christ would return (see Paul's hope for the Corinthians in 1:14).

We are poor, but we give spiritual riches to others. We own nothing, and yet have everything.NLT Paul had no earthly riches. He had worked long hours as a tentmaker in order to preach the gospel free of charge to the Corinthians (see Acts 18:1-5). He had even gone without sleep and food in order to further the cause of the gospel (11:27). Being *poor* was one of the hardships Paul was enduring in order to preach to the Gentiles throughout the Mediterranean world. Through his deprivation, Paul had learned to be content with what God had given him (Philippians 4:12). Paul was placing his *riches* in a kingdom that would last forever (see Matthew 6:19-21).

THE SECRET OF GIVING
Paul wrote that he was poor and yet capable of making many others rich. Christians today have that same privilege. The rewards of teaching others the truths of God's Word cannot be measured. Even if we never make more than a modest income, the satisfaction we receive knowing we have invested in the spiritual development of another person is worth more than a diversified stock portfolio. With whom are you currently spending time as a Christian mentor? What areas of personal growth has God used you to facilitate? Pray for these individuals by name. Ask God to help them see how wealthy they are in the economy of the kingdom of God.

6:11-13 We have spoken freely to you, Corinthians, and opened wide our hearts to you.NIV Paul had been completely straightforward with the Corinthians. His transparent honesty is mentioned at numerous places in this letter (1:12-13, 23-24; 2:17; 4:1-2; 5:11).

Critics at Corinth were accusing Paul of some sort of deception. Paul hoped that the very fact that he was cataloging his own weaknesses and sufferings before the Corinthians would testify to his openness. Who would submit a list of failures to one's critics (see Paul's list at 4:8-10)? What preacher would admit he was perplexed and troubled? But Paul did, even though his severest critics resided at Corinth. He had opened up his life and ministry not only to God but also to the Corinthians (see 5:11). He submitted it to their inspection and examination. But he knew that God was his final judge (see 5:9-10; 1 Corinthians 4:5).

We are not withholding our affection from you, but you are withholding yours from us. As a fair exchange—I speak as to my children—open wide your hearts also.[NIV] Paul had revealed his true feelings for the Corinthian believers—he and his coworkers were *not withholding [their] affection* from them. The Corinthians, however, were reacting coldly to Paul. They criticized his preaching (11:6; 1 Corinthians 2:1-4), his writing (1:13), and his demeanor among them (10:9-10). Although Paul, along with Silas and Timothy, had founded the Corinthian church, the church was rejecting its founder (see 1:14).

As Paul would explain in this letter, any harsh words he had for the Corinthians came from his deep love for them (see 7:8-13). He wanted them to grow in the faith. Paul hoped his sincerity in this letter—the way he opened up his life to the Corinthians' examination—would prompt them to also *open* their *hearts* to him.

As founder of the church, Paul had fatherly affections for the Corinthians. He had spent hours agonizing over the believers' spiritual welfare (11:28) and had worked hard for them. But like rebellious youth, the Corinthians had returned Paul's concern with a cold heart. Although Paul could have commanded and disciplined them, he merely pleaded with them. He wanted to give them a chance to reform their ways (see Paul's attitude in 2:1-4; 13:5).

DON'T HOLD BACK
Paul confronted the Corinthians for withholding their affections. They had let suspicions and misconceptions ruin their relationship with Paul. Instead of accepting him, they were becoming mean-spirited and hard-hearted. In close relationships, like those in families, withholding affection can become a tool for one person to control another. Those types of people use love and affection to induce others to go their way or to punish those who don't. Keep your heart and mind open, even when people disappoint you. Don't use love as a weapon.

BE SEPARATE FROM UNBELIEVERS / 6:14–7:1

Counselors use the triangle to explain hostility in relationships.
For instance, a daughter might have a wonderful relationship
with her mother. The daughter, however, can easily poison that
relationship by having a girlfriend whom the mother dislikes. The
aversion for this friend will inevitably affect the mother's relationship with her own child. The harmony of the family will be
disrupted until the mother changes her feelings for the friend or
the child ends the friendship. This occurs because all three are
tied together in a triangular relationship. Each relationship—the
mother's relationship to the child and the friend and, conversely,
the child's relationship to the mother and the friend—are inter-
connected.

This passage seems to be describing the same type of phenomenon. If the Corinthians wanted to be reconciled to God (5:20),
they had to separate themselves from unbelievers (6:14). It was
that simple. A partnership with those who worship other gods
would poison a relationship with the one true God.

Many have wondered how the discussion about holiness in
6:14–7:1 relates to the preceding and following passages. Paul's
appeal to the Corinthians to "open wide" their hearts to him is
abruptly interrupted at 6:14 and then taken up again at 7:2. How
would the Corinthians' association with unbelievers (6:14) dis-
turb Paul's relationship with them (6:14)?

Scholars have debated the source of this passage for years.
Although some have suggested that this passage may have been
inserted by a later editor, there is no manuscript evidence that
2 Corinthians ever existed without these verses. The same lack of
manuscript evidence also excludes another prominent theory—
namely, that this passage might be a separate letter from Paul to
the Corinthians (see the Introduction).

The unique Greek writing style of 6:14–7:1 indicates that Paul
most likely was quoting an early Christian sermon, perhaps even
a Jewish sermon. He had already exhorted the Corinthians to be
reconciled to God (5:20-21; 6:1-2) and was pleading with them
to open their hearts to him as God's messenger (6:11-12). In this
short sermon quote, Paul was reminding the Corinthians what reconciliation to God means. If they were to open their hearts to him
as God's messenger (6:13), they had to separate themselves from
the wickedness of unbelievers. Their pagan neighbors would only
tempt them to reject God's Word and God's ways.

6:14-15 Do not be yoked together with unbelievers.[NIV] After passionately appealing to the Corinthians to open their hearts to him,
Paul exhorted them to *not be yoked together with unbelievers.* He

LIGHT VERSUS DARKNESS

In many places in Scripture, the realm of God and the realm of evil are contrasted by the differences between light and darkness.

Darkness	Light	Reference
A condition of despair	The appearance of hope	Isaiah 9:2
Unable to recognize the light	Able to enlighten the world	John 1:4-5, 9
The power of Satan	The power of God	Acts 26:18
Evil deeds	Good deeds	Romans 13:12-14
Natural heart condition	Given by God to shine in our hearts by knowing Jesus Christ	2 Corinthians 4:6
Fruitless works	Source of all that is good, right, true	Ephesians 5:8-11
Spiritual forces of evil	Armor of God	Ephesians 6:12-13
Powerful captivity	Kingdom of the Son, redemption, forgiveness	Colossians 1:12-14
Cannot exist in God's presence	God's presence, fellowship with God, cleansing of sin	1 John 1:5, 7
Passing away	Lasting forever	1 John 2:8-11

urged them not to form binding relationships with nonbelievers because this might weaken their Christian commitment, integrity, or standards.

Earlier, Paul had explained that not associating with unbelievers did not mean isolation from nonbelievers (see 1 Corinthians 5:9-10). The Corinthians were even to remain with their unbelieving spouses (1 Corinthians 7:12-13). In order to witness to their neighbors, believers were to adopt some of the customs of the people to whom they were witnessing: "I try to find common ground with everyone so that I might bring them to Christ" (1 Corinthians 9:22 NLT).

So what did it mean to avoid being "yoked together with unbelievers"? The Greek for "yoked together" was used in the first century for the act of harnessing animals together. It was against God's law to yoke together animals with different degrees of strength, such as an ox and a mule, because the plow would be pulled unevenly or the weight being carried would be spilled (see

Deuteronomy 22:10). In the same way, a believer and an unbeliever are categorically different. Partnering with unbelievers would lead to disaster.

In 1 Corinthians, Paul had forbidden the Corinthians from submitting their disputes to a secular judge (6:1-6). He had admonished them to refrain from sexual immorality, especially the prostitution of the Greek temples (see 6:12-20). He had even expressed astonishment that they hadn't expelled a member of the church who had persisted in having an affair with his stepmother (5:1-13). Moreover, he had told them to refrain from participating in feasts that honored local gods (see 10:6-22). Any of these specific issues, especially the feasts to local gods, could be considered as being *yoked together with unbelievers.* Apparently the Corinthian church was having a difficult time separating themselves from the immoral practices of their unbelieving neighbors. Paul was telling the Corinthians to avoid any situation that would compromise their faith or their Christian morals. While this verse applies to all partnerships and alliances, marriage certainly comes under this teaching.

MARRIAGE YOKE
Paul said, "Do not be yoked together with unbelievers." This certainly applies to marriage. While Paul didn't want the new believers to divorce their unbelieving spouses (see 1 Corinthians 7:12-13), he certainly did not encourage single believers to enter into marriage with unbelievers. Such marriages cannot have unity in the most important issue in life—commitment and obedience to God. Because marriage involves two people becoming one, faith may become an issue, and one spouse may have to compromise beliefs for the sake of unity. Many people discount this problem only to regret it later. Don't allow emotion or passion to blind you to the ultimate importance of marrying someone with whom you can be united spiritually.

For what do righteousness and wickedness have in common? Or what fellowship can light have with darkness?[NIV] These two rhetorical questions highlight the ethical difference between believers and unbelievers. The first question emphasizes that Christians, as recipients of God's *righteousness* through Jesus, are to live righteous lives here on earth. In contrast, unbelievers do not pay attention to God's law and are dedicated to *wickedness.* Obviously, they have nothing *in common.*

The second question emphasizes that Christians are committed to the truth. In Scripture, "light" often refers to God's truth, his gospel message, which had penetrated the darkness of this world (4:4-

5; see 1 Corinthians 4:5). John called Jesus the light of the world, a term Jesus had used to describe himself (see John 1:4-7; 3:19-21). And John used the image of light to describe God's salvation (John 1:5; 3:19; 8:12). In contrast, "darkness" refers to the chaos that reigns when lies and deceptions pass for the truth, when evil is considered good and good is considered evil (see Romans 1:25-26). Obviously, light and darkness cannot have any *fellowship*.

What harmony can there be between Christ and the Devil? How can a believer be a partner with an unbeliever?[NLT] Paul continued his series of rhetorical questions with two questions that underscore the religious differences between believers and unbelievers.

BUSINESS PARTNERS
What would Paul say about a Christian in a business partnership with an unbeliever? Much of what Paul said about marriage in 1 Corinthians 7:12-13 would apply. If we are already in a partnership, we should not disrupt it. When entering into a new partnership, however, we must be very careful.

We court disaster when we enter into partnership with unbelievers, because our very foundations differ. While one serves the Lord, the other does not recognize God's authority. Inevitably, the one who serves God is faced with the temptation to compromise values. When that happens, spiritual disaster results.

There are important basic guidelines for partnerships. Before entering into a partnership, ask
- What are my motives?
- What problems am I avoiding by seeking this partnership?
- Is this partnership the best solution, or is it only a quick fix to my problem?
- Have I prayed or asked others to pray for guidance?
- Are my partner and I really working toward the same goals?
- Am I willing to settle for less financial gain in order to do what God wants?

The third rhetorical question contrasts the great difference *between Christ* and *the Devil*. The Greek word *beliar* is translated "the Devil." This is the only place that this Greek word is used in the New Testament, although Jewish literature from the first century commonly used it for Satan. The Greek word is derived from a Hebrew word that means "worthlessness" or "lawlessness."

Since believers are intimately connected to Jesus Christ (5:20-21), they cannot have any fellowship with the things of the Devil. Unbelievers, in contrast, are being deceived and enticed by Satan

(4:3-4). Their motivations and actions come from their own self-interest and not from a profound reverence for God (Romans 2:8).

The fourth rhetorical question reiterates that believers and unbelievers can never truly *partner* together. In Greek, the word for "partner" means to hold some property, such as land, in common. Thus, with these penetrating questions, Paul seemed to be advising the Corinthians to be wary of entering into associations that by their very nature might compromise their Christian morals.

6:16-18 What agreement is there between the temple of God and idols? For we are the temple of the living God.^{NIV} In his earlier letter to the Corinthians, Paul had used the image of *the temple* of God to designate the community of believers in Corinth (1 Corinthians 3:16). Later, Paul also used the image of the "temple of the living God" to refer to individual believers (1 Corinthians 6:18-20). In this passage, however, Paul used the plural.

Thus, in Paul's fifth rhetorical question, he was referring not to individual believers but to the community of faith as *the temple of God.* As building blocks of this glorious temple, each individual had to maintain a holy life, set apart to God. There was no room for any mixed loyalties. No compromise or agreement had been made between the true God and other so-called gods.

With these five short rhetorical questions, Paul was emphasizing the absurdity of Christians continuing to associate with idols or idol worship.

LIVING CHURCH
Quoting from the prophet Isaiah, Paul asserted that the church is the temple of the living God. Corinth had an abundance of temples of pagan deities, so the recipients of his letter were able to visualize the contrast the apostle intended. Those who follow Christ are not known by a building or the address where their worship services are held. They are known as those in whom the Spirit of God lives. It is easy to become identified with a place of worship. But the church is not where believers go; it is who they are. God is not waiting for his people in some stained-glass setting. He is always with them. That is a sobering and yet a comforting thought. How does your behavior reflect on the God you represent? How does the knowledge of God being in you at all times give you boldness to articulate your faith with confidence?

As God has said: "I will live with them and walk among them, and I will be their God, and they will be my people."^{NIV} Several Old Testament quotes illustrate how the church at Corinth was a fulfillment of God's promises long ago. When God

brought the Israelites out of Egyptian bondage, he made them his
holy people. He had them construct a tabernacle, where his glori
ous presence would reside in its inner sanctuary. In this sense,
God would *live with them*—even *walk among them.* He wasn't
going to be a far-off God, who watched the Israelites from a distance. The Israelites were his people, and he would be intimately
connected to them (see Leviticus 26:11-12).

The prophet Ezekiel also prophesied of a time when God
would live among his people forever (see Ezekiel 37:26-28). By
quoting this passage, Paul was saying that Ezekiel's prophecy
was being fulfilled in the Corinthian church. Jesus, a descendant
of David and the Son of God himself, had defeated Satan. He had
begun his reign as the King of a heavenly kingdom. As believers,
the Corinthians were part of this spiritual kingdom. Jesus, as God
in human form, had literally shown people what God was like
(Matthew 1:23; John 1:14). In a real sense, God had lived among
his people. After Jesus' resurrection and ascension, God sent his
Holy Spirit to the believers who had gathered in Jerusalem on the
Day of Pentecost. From that day to the present, every believer
has God living within his or her spirit (Romans 8:9; 1 Corinthians 6:19; 2 Timothy 1:14).

**"Therefore come out from them and be separate, says the
Lord. Touch no unclean thing, and I will receive you. I will be
a Father to you, and you will be my sons and daughters, says
the Lord Almighty."**[NIV] After his first negative command to the
Corinthians—to not partner with unbelievers—Paul quickly gave
them a positive command. Instead of partnering with unbelievers,
they were to *be separate* from anything that was *unclean* or anything sinful.

To emphasize his point, Paul strung together several Old Testament quotes. He loosely quoted Isaiah 52:11: "Depart, depart, go
out from there! Touch no unclean thing!" (NIV). Originally this
was a command for the exiles to come out of Babylon and to
abandon any object associated with pagan worship. In this passage, Paul interpreted this command as also a command to Christians to separate themselves from the immorality of the pagan
peoples around them.

Paul continued his comparison of the Corinthian Christians
with the returning Israelite exiles. The phrase "I will receive you"
is an adaptation of Ezekiel's prophecy that God would gather all
of Israel's exiles together (see Ezekiel 20:34). Finally, Paul
adapted God's promise to be the Father of David's Son (see
2 Samuel 7:14; see also Hebrews 1:5, where the author interpreted this verse as a prophecy about Jesus) to also refer to believ-

ers. Christians would become the *sons and daughters* of God (see Isaiah 43:6 where Isaiah prophesied of a time when God would gather all his sons and daughters together). Through Christ's death, believers have become part of God's loving family (see Galatians 4:1-7).

SEPARATION
Separation from the world involves more than keeping our distance from sinners; it means staying close to God (see 7:1-2). More than avoiding entertainment that leads to sin, it extends into how we spend our time and money. There is no way to separate ourselves totally from all sinful influences. Nevertheless, we are to resist the sin around us, without either giving up or giving in. When you know what God wants you to do, make a clean break with sinful practices.

7:1 Because we have these promises, dear friends, let us cleanse ourselves from everything that can defile our body or spirit.[NLT] Because God has given *these promises:* to live with his people (6:16), to welcome them as his people (6:17), and to act like a loving Father toward them (6:18), Christians are to *cleanse* themselves of *everything that* can *defile.* In 1 Corinthians, Paul used the word "defile" to describe how eating food sacrificed to idols made a conscience impure. Paul was primarily worried about the way the Corinthians were still participating in some of the pagan feasts. Paul explained to the Corinthians that participating in such feasts would be wrong and would provoke God (see 1 Corinthians 10:14-22). By abstaining from these feasts, the Corinthians would begin to *cleanse*—or more literally, "to purify" or "to prune"—evil out of their lives. The Corinthians were to have nothing to do with paganism. They were to make a clean break with their past and give themselves to God alone.

And let us work toward complete purity because we fear God.[NLT] What does the phrase "work toward complete purity" mean? Was Paul advocating perfectionism? Did he expect the Corinthians to become perfect in this life? "Work toward complete purity" literally means "perfecting holiness." The Greek word connotes "becoming mature" or "becoming complete." Thus, Paul wasn't suggesting that the Corinthians could become sinless in this life. Instead, he was prodding the Corinthians to work at maturing in their faith. God had provided them with all the resources they needed, and Christ's Spirit would empower them to become Christlike (see Romans 8:2).

In his letter to the Philippians, Paul categorically denied that he was perfect (Philippians 3:12). But being imperfect was never a reason for Paul to become apathetic about his own spiritual walk. Instead, he saw his imperfection as a reason to press on, to strive harder to become more and more like Christ (Philippians 3:13-15). Paul knew that only the Spirit within him could provide the power to pursue spiritual maturity (Romans 8:2). Believers will finally reach perfection at Christ's return. Until then, they are commanded to cooperate with the Holy Spirit, maturing them in the faith (Jude 1:24-25).

Paul exhorted the Corinthians to pursue purity out of *fear* of *God*. "Fear" means to keep respect or awe for God. He is the almighty Creator. Just as we show proper respect to presidents and sports heroes, we should show even greater respect to the King of kings. Genuinely honoring and loving God means obeying him (see John 14:15). Thus, obeying God's commands and pursuing spiritual maturity are the best ways to show respect for God (see commentary on 5:11 for more on fear as a motivation).

PERFECTIONISM
How can we become perfect? In this life, we certainly cannot be flawless, but we can aspire to be as much like Christ as possible because we have the Spirit of Christ within us. We are to separate ourselves from the world's sinful values. We are to be devoted to God's desires rather than to our own and carry his love and mercy into the world. We can't achieve Christlike character and holy living all at once, but we must grow toward maturity and wholeness. Just as we expect different behavior from a baby, a child, a teenager, and an adult, so God expects different behavior from us, depending on our stage of spiritual development. Let us love others as completely as God loves us.

---

2 Corinthians 7:2-16

Affectionate greetings, loud laughter, hugs, and kisses usually accompany family get-togethers. Lavish meals and late-night conversations signify the excitement and delight of close friends and families gathering together. These gatherings are filled with joy, and even more so when somebody has good news to share—a new baby, a promotion at work, an engagement, or a graduation.

This passage describes Paul's meeting with Titus. Although Paul had faced strong opposition in Macedonia (7:5), Titus's arrival had filled him with joy and encouragement. Titus had brought good news from Corinth: The believers were growing in their faith and confronting some of the persistent problems in their congregation. Knowing that the church he had founded in Corinth was maturing and furthering the cause of the gospel was the best kind of news Paul could have hoped for. His joy—and his praise for God—knew no bounds.

The fact that Paul here resumed his story about his recent travel plans (7:5) after several chapters (see 2:13 for the last mention of his trip to Macedonia) has caused much speculation about the section in between (2:14–7:4). Some have suggested that 2:14–7:4 may have been added by a later editor or may be a separate letter from Paul inserted awkwardly after 2:13, but there is no manuscript evidence for those theories. Clearly Paul, concerned about the accusations against his authority and his ministry circulating in Corinth, spent these chapters (2:14–7:4) explaining and defending his ministry to the Corinthians. He ended this extended defense by appealing to the Corinthians to not only reconcile themselves to God but also to reconcile themselves to himself as God's messenger (see 6:13 and 7:2). So this (7:3) was a logical place to resume a description of his latest travels (from 2:13), for Titus had told Paul of the Corinthians' steps at reconciling themselves to Paul. The joy of meeting Titus had been accompanied by an even greater joy: Paul had been delighted to hear that the Corinthians were sorry about the distressing incident that occurred on his last visit and that they longed for him to visit them again (see 7:7). This was not only a reunion between Titus and Paul, but also a spiritual reunion between Paul and the Corinthians. It was appropriate, therefore, for Paul to describe this meeting, after his appeal to the Corinthians to "make room" for him in their hearts (7:2 NIV).

7:2-4 Make room in your hearts for us.NRSV This repeats Paul's plea for the Corinthians to "open wide your hearts" (6:13 NIV). Here Paul phrased it as making *room* in their *hearts* for Paul and his coworkers. This appeal logically follows Paul's exhortation to the Corinthians to separate themselves from relationships with unbelievers that would compromise their loyalty to Christ (see 6:14–7:1). By separating themselves from the entanglements of evil, they could effectively *make room* in their hearts for Paul and his message from God.

We have wronged no one, we have corrupted no one, we have taken advantage of no one.NRSV This appeal is coupled with three denials. Most likely, Paul was responding to accusations that the Corinthians had been repeating. Not one person among the Corinthians had been *wronged, corrupted,* or *taken advantage of.* All three words are translations of Greek words that were commonly used for deceitful and exploitative financial dealings. Paul's critics may have been criticizing the collection for the Jerusalem church (see 8:1-7). The end of this letter contains a strong defense against this charge—that is, the charge of financially exploiting the believers (12:13, 17-18 NIV).

OPEN HEARTS
Paul insisted that the Corinthians "make room in their hearts" for him. He knew how much those who comprise the church of Jesus Christ need one another. If fellowship was necessary in Paul's day, it is all the more crucial today, when time is more valuable than money. Each day holds barely enough time to care for personal and family needs, let alone to meet the needs of others. Yet the activities that occupy our time and usurp our energy are not as important as the community described in these verses. Paul's intention is not "coffee and donuts between church" fellowship. We need accountability that comes from lives intertwined by the cords of commitment and love. If you are not in a small group Bible study, take the first steps. The next time you are invited over for coffee, dessert, or a meal by fellow Christians, accept the opportunity enthusiastically.

I do not say this to condemn you, for I said before that you are in our hearts, to die together and to live together.NRSV Paul had spent considerable time defending his ministry (see the previous verse and 1:23-23; 3:1-6; 4:1-2, 8-10; 5:6-10; 6:3-13). Moreover, he had appealed to the Corinthians to open their hearts to him (6:13; 7:2). Some in the Corinthian church could have interpreted this as a stern rebuke. The believers at Corinth may even have thought that Paul was abandoning them or dismissing them as genuine Christians. Here Paul assured the Corinthians that this was not his intent.

On the contrary, Paul considered himself so intimately connected to the Corinthians that not even death could separate them. In Christ, he would *live* for the Corinthians and even *die* for them.

I often boast about you; I have great pride in you; I am filled with consolation; I am overjoyed in all our affliction.NRSV Like a loving father, Paul had boasted to Titus of the Corinthians and hoped to boast about them before Jesus (see 1:14; 7:14). Paul possessed *great pride* in them, and that hope had been realized by Titus's recent report (see 7:14). Moreover, even though Paul had recently faced many *afflictions,* knowing that the Corinthians were maturing in the faith had brought him great *consolation* and joy (see Paul's description of his trials and God's comfort in 1:3-11).

7:5-7 For when we came into Macedonia, this body of ours had no rest, but we were harassed at every turn—conflicts on the outside, fears within.NIV Here Paul resumed the story that he left off in 2:13 of how he had forsaken some exciting evangelistic opportunities in Troas in order to look for Titus in *Macedonia.* He knew that Titus had visited Corinth and would have some news of how the Corinthians were progressing in their faith. So like a father who was anxious to hear news of his children, Paul had hurried ahead to find out how the Corinthians were doing.

But by leaving Troas, Paul did not escape the troubles he had encountered in Asia Minor (present-day Turkey, see 1:8-11). Instead, he continued to be *harassed* by *conflicts* and hardships everywhere he turned. Paul's first visit to Macedonia had been a tumultuous one, and it appears that this one was also. On his first visit, a group of Jews from Thessalonica had followed him all over the province of Macedonia, opposing his teaching (see Acts 17:13). Perhaps it was those determined opponents in Thessalonica who "harassed" Paul on this journey. Paul's letters to the Thessalonians reveal that the church was enduring much persecution (see 1 Thessalonians 1:6-8; 2 Thessalonians 1:4).

Paul was also beset by *fears.* He had already told the Corinthians that he was concerned about Titus's and the Corinthians' welfare (see 2:13). Most likely, Paul's fears were a profound concern over the spiritual maturity of the churches he had founded (see

1 Thessalonians 3:1-5). He spent hours committing this to God in prayer (see 1 Thessalonians 3:10). This may account for his lack of sleep (11:27) and *rest*. In fact, he would tell the Corinthians that every day he was burdened with his concern over the spiritual fate of the churches (see 11:28).

But God, who encourages those who are discouraged, encouraged us by the arrival of Titus. His presence was a joy, but so was the news he brought of the encouragement he received from you.^{NLT} The previous verses state that the Corinthians had brought Paul great joy. Paul began describing his meeting with Titus to illustrate how the Corinthians could bring him joy (see 7:4). Though Paul still had many problems to face in Macedonia, God had *encouraged* him at the right time with *the arrival of Titus*. This may be the same comfort that Paul had described at the beginning of his letter (see 1:3-4). Merely being reunited with a fellow laborer in Christ probably brought Paul *joy*. Paul made it clear that Titus's message also brought him great joy.

Titus had been sent on a difficult mission. He had to deliver a stern letter from Paul that exhorted the Corinthians to right some wrongs. No one knew—especially Paul, who was greatly concerned about the whole matter (see 2:13)—how the Corinthians would react. Titus brought word that the Corinthians had welcomed him and his unpleasant message. He had been welcomed as an emissary of Paul.

Moreover, the Corinthians had given Titus *encouragement;* as a result, Titus could encourage Paul. This passage, as in chapter 1, emphasizes the interrelationships between Paul and the Corinthian believers. Previously Paul had mentioned how the Corinthians' prayers had helped his ministry (1:11). In turn, he could encourage them because God had comforted him through their prayers (1:6-7). This passage, however, describes how the Corinthians had encouraged Paul. This description of the meeting provides a real-life illustration of how the church as a body works together to build each other up in the faith, something Paul had encouraged the Corinthians to do in an earlier letter (see 1 Corinthians 12:24-26; 14:12).

When he told me how much you were looking forward to my visit, and how sorry you were about what had happened, and how loyal your love is for me, I was filled with joy!^{NLT} According to Titus's report, the Corinthians were truly *sorry* about the incident and wanted to reaffirm their commitment to Paul and let him know of their *loyal love* for him. They were even *looking forward* to Paul's next *visit*. Naturally, such a report would encourage any leader. After a rocky period between Paul and the

Corinthians, the church was correcting some of the problems that had arisen in their congregation. They were ready for Paul to visit them.

7:8-9 I am no longer sorry that I sent that letter to you, though I was sorry for a time, for I know that it was painful to you for a little while.^NLT Paul's previous *letter* to the Corinthians was the one he had cried over because he had to censure them (see 2:1-4 for a discussion of this letter). It has become generally accepted that 1 Corinthians was not the letter to which Paul was here alluding, primarily because 1 Corinthians as a whole does not reflect the extreme sorrow described by Paul here and in 2:4.

Paul was merely alluding to the circumstances around this letter ("the one who did the wrong" in 7:12); he had described the situation in more detail in 2:5-11. On his last trip to Corinth, some person had publicly offended Paul (see 2:5). Some believe that the offense was the persistent incest in the church (described in 1 Corinthians 5:1-5), but many commentators discount this interpretation because the majority of 2 Corinthians is devoted to defending Paul's apostolic authority, not exhorting the Corinthians to sexual purity (see also 3:1-4; 5:17-18; 6:1-11; 13:3). Thus, the letter referred to in this verse probably has been lost to us.

CHEERFUL EARFUL
The Corinthians were caused sorrow by an earlier letter Paul had written them. But the apostle is quick to say he was *not* sorry for what he had written. This caring pastor had confronted a wayward congregation in love, much like a loving parent would discipline a rebellious child. The bitter taste of the medicine that Paul had prescribed achieved the desired outcome. The Scripture calls believers to express tough love with the hope that the depth of a relationship will minimize the inevitable pain of healing. "Wounds from a friend can be trusted, but an enemy multiplies kisses" (Proverbs 27:6). As you quietly sit before the Lord, ask him to point out someone who is in need of reproof by you. Rehearse what you will write or say to that person in an effort to speak the truth in love.

Apparently Paul had written this "stern letter" to the Corinthians soon after his "painful visit" with them. In this letter, he had exhorted the Corinthians to discipline their members who persisted in error—specifically, the one who had publicly opposing Paul's authority (see 2:1-4; 7:8; 13:1-4). At first, Paul was sorry that he had sent that letter. He had written it with a great amount of anguish (see 2:4), knowing that his tone and his message would be *painful* to the Corinthian believers. But Titus's report that they were still anxiously awaiting his visit and had reaffirmed their loyalty to him had caused Paul to change his mind. The letter had produced its desired effect. Although harsh, it had produced a change of heart in the Corinthians, the repentance that God desired.

Yet now I am happy, not because you were made sorry, but because your sorrow led you to repentance. For you became sorrowful as God intended and so were not harmed in any way by us.^{NIV} Paul quickly explained the source of his happiness—he didn't want his critics to twist his words. Paul wasn't happy about the Corinthians' sorrow; on the contrary, he never wanted to grieve them. Paul knew, however, that it was necessary to make the Corinthians *sorry* in order to prompt them to *repentance*.

The repentance Paul wanted was not merely anguish over the acrimonious situation or a regret that it had ever happened. Godly repentance implies a reorientation of the entire person away from sins and toward God's ways. It is a "turning around." The type of sorrow that compels a person to change his or her direction is what God wants—not "sorrow" that paralyzes or becomes resentful. Part of "the fears" that had plagued Paul in Macedonia must have been how the Corinthians had received his latest letter (7:5). Just as Paul was concerned that the disciplined offender might be overwhelmed by sorrow (see 2:6-7), so he had been worried that the Corinthians' sorrow over the letter might lead to more strife. Instead, the disciplinary letter had caused no harm. Paul had wisely administered the right amount of discipline so that the church had not been *harmed*— literally, "had not experienced any loss."

ON THE RECEIVING END
Paul affirmed the Corinthians for their right response to the correction he had given them. It's difficult to accept criticism, correction, or rebuke with poise and grace. It is much more natural to be defensive and then counterattack. We can accept criticism with self-pity, thinking we don't really deserve it. We can be angry and resentful. But a mature Christian should graciously accept constructive criticism, sincerely evaluate it, and grow from it.

7:10-11 **For God can use sorrow in our lives to help us turn away from sin and seek salvation. We will never regret that kind of sorrow. But sorrow without repentance is the kind that results in death.**^{NLT} Many people are sorry only for the effects of their sins or for being caught. In the original Greek, "sorrow without repentance" literally means "the sorrow of the world." When people do not channel their grief over their behavior into life-changing actions, it is unproductive grief. It leads to self-pity. But godly sorrow is practical and action-oriented. When a person realizes what he or she has done wrong, that person should not only regret the error but also turn back to God. Only God can empower people to change their ways. Only God can save people from the way sin imprisons them and paralyzes them. Only God can *help us turn away from sin and seek salvation.*

Compare the stories of Peter and Judas. Both handled the events surrounding Jesus' death in a wrong way. Judas brazenly betrayed Jesus with a kiss (Mark 14:43-46). Peter denied knowing Jesus three different times (John 18:15-27). Both were overcome with grief over their actions (Matthew 26:75; 27:3). Although Peter was distraught, he had the humility and the courage to admit his failure, reform his behavior, and rededicate his life to Jesus' cause (see John 21:15-19). In contrast, Judas let his remorse eat at his soul. Eventually overcome by guilt, he committed suicide. Judas wasn't able to learn from his sin and repent. He didn't submit his sins to Christ and beg to be forgiven. He was too proud to cry out for salvation, so his stubbornness led to death.

See what this godly sorrow has produced in you: what earnestness, what eagerness to clear yourselves, what indignation, what alarm, what longing, what concern, what readiness to see justice done. At every point you have proved yourselves to be innocent in this matter.[NIV] Titus's encouraging report from Corinth gave Paul the evidence that the Corinthians had responded appropriately to his stern letter—with *earnestness* and an *eagerness to clear* themselves. At every point, the Corinthians had proved their blamelessness. They were completely *innocent.* They were absolved of what had occurred on Paul's last visit (see 13:1-2).

Titus had explained the Corinthians' reaction to Paul's letter step-by-step; and Paul listed those steps here, approving each one. The letter had inspired appropriate *indignation,* or displeasure, about what had been happening among them. It had also caused *alarm.* Perhaps the Corinthians were fearful of God's divine judgment or Paul's discipline. Their intense *longing* and great *concern* to restore their damaged relationship with Paul had led them to take prompt action against the offender *to see justice done* (see 2:5-11). They were so earnest about clearing themselves they might have been too harsh on the offender. So Paul told how to show love to the offender and welcome him back into the community of faith, lest Satan take that opportunity to entice him away (see 2:5-11). Although the Corinthians may have punished the offender too harshly, Paul did not offer any words of correction. Instead, he praised them in glowing terms. Their zeal to right wrongs and to change their behavior was exactly the kind of *godly sorrow* that could mold them into a holy people.

INSTITUTE OF CORRECTION
It is difficult to be confronted with our sin, and even more difficult to get rid of sin. Paul praised the Corinthians for clearing up an especially troublesome situation (see 2:5-11). Do you tend to be defensive when confronted? Don't let pride keep you from admitting your sins. Accept correction as a tool for your growth, and do all you can to correct problems that are pointed out to you.

7:12-13 So even though I wrote to you, it was not on account of the one who did the wrong or of the injured party, but rather that before God you could see for yourselves how devoted to us you are.[NIV] Paul stated the purpose of his last letter, the letter he had written with tears (2:4). He *wrote* it so that the Corinthians would realize *how devoted* they truly were to their founder. Paul's primary purpose was to save the deteriorating relationship between himself and the Corinthians; and according to the previous verse, the letter had done just that.

Although the Corinthians knew the identity of the *one who did the wrong,* Paul discreetly didn't mention his name because more than likely his letter would be circulated in all the churches of southern Greece. Since Paul was instructing the Corinthians to restore this man to Christian fellowship, Paul didn't want his name to be unnecessarily despised. The anonymity of this man has given scholars throughout the centuries much to write about. Traditionally, scholars have identified this offender as the incestuous man Paul spoke of in 1 Corinthians 5:1-5. But since 2 Corinthians doesn't address sexual immorality, this is unlikely. Instead, most commentators have agreed that the offender in some way challenged Paul's apostolic authority (see 13:1-2) on his last visit to Corinth (see 1:23–2:11). Paul spent a considerable amount of time explaining and defending his ministry in this letter (see 1:12-24; 3:1-6; 4:5-18; 5:11-21; 6:3-13; 10:1-18; 13:1-4). Therefore, most commentators have come to the conclusion that the offender was someone who challenged Paul's authority on his last visit to Corinth.

What was more important to Paul than exactly who the offender was and what he had done was the furtherance of the cause of the gospel in Corinth. Paul reminded the Corinthians

PRINCIPLES OF CONFRONTATION IN 2 CORINTHIANS

Sometimes rebuke is necessary, but it must be used with caution. The purpose of any rebuke, confrontation, or discipline is to help people, not hurt them.

Method	Reference
Be firm and bold.	7:9; 10:2
Affirm all you see that is good.	7:4
Be accurate and honest.	7:14; 8:21
Know the facts.	11:22-27
Follow up after the confrontation.	7:13; 12:14
Be gentle after being firm.	7:15; 13:11-13
Speak words that reflect Christ's message, not your own ideas.	10:3; 10:12-13; 12:19
Use discipline only when all else fails.	13:2

that their relationship to him wasn't trivial. Everything he did would benefit them in some way; their prayers and actions would, in turn, encourage him in his task of preaching the gospel (see 1:6-7, 11; 7:4). They were so interdependent because everything each of them did was *before God*—in fact, in his presence (2:10, 17; 3:4; 4:14). They were all part of God's family.

By all this we are encouraged. In addition to our own encouragement, we were especially delighted to see how happy Titus was, because his spirit has been refreshed by all of you.NIV The Corinthians' appropriate reaction to Paul's disciplinary letter had encouraged Paul. In addition, he was encouraged by the way Titus had *been refreshed by all of* the Corinthians. Even though the church in Corinth was in turmoil, Titus had taken on the challenge of delivering the disagreeable news to the Corinthians. No one—not even Paul—knew how the Corinthians would respond. Yet Titus was pleasantly surprised. The Corinthians welcomed him and his message.

7:14-16 I had told him how proud I was of you—and you didn't disappoint me. I have always told you the truth, and now my boasting to Titus has also proved true!NLT Although Paul refused to boast in his own accomplishments in this letter (3:1; 5:12; 10:12, 18), he didn't hesitate to boast in God's accomplishment through him (1:12; 6:4; 10:8, 13-17; 11:30). Here he even boasts in the Corinthians (see also his boasts to the Macedonians in 9:2-3), just as he anticipated the day when he would boast of them before Jesus (see 1:14).

Even though the Corinthians had caused Paul so much pain and grief (see 2:4; 8:16; 11:28), Paul still was *proud* of his spiritual children. He refused to focus on their weaknesses and failures; instead, he praised their strengths (see how he praised the Corinthians at 8:7; 1 Corinthians 14:12).

And his affection for you is all the greater when he remembers that you were all obedient, receiving him with fear and trembling. I am glad I can have complete confidence in you.[NIV] Here Paul went to great lengths to emphasize Titus's respect and devotion for the Corinthians. Paul emphasized their relationship with Titus because he was sending Titus back to them to collect money for the Jerusalem church (8:16-18).

At the same time, Paul praised the Corinthians for welcoming Titus, obeying him as an official representative of Paul himself. The Corinthians had also welcomed Titus *with fear and trembling* because of the seriousness of his mission.

2 Corinthians 8

Letters in the mail, telethons on the radio, and even homeless people on the street—appeals for money come from almost every direction. Sometimes they prick the conscience; sometimes they simply annoy.

The next two chapters are a tactful appeal for money. They provide us with the two best chapters in the Bible for teaching stewardship today.

Even though some of the Corinthians were questioning his authority, Paul bravely asked for money for the impoverished Jerusalem Christians. About a year before the writing of 2 Corinthians, the believers in Corinth had started collecting money for the poor in Jerusalem (see 8:10). First Corinthians instructed the Corinthians to set aside money every week for the offering (see 1 Corinthians 16:1-4). But that collection had floundered (see 8:10-11). It appears that greedy, traveling preachers (2:17) had suggested that Paul had invented the collection to extort money from the congregation. They asserted this, even though Paul had taken no money from the Corinthians to support his own ministry (7:2; 11:7-9; 12:14-17). He had supported himself as a tentmaker when he was in Corinth (Acts 18:1-4). These traveling preachers may have very well wanted to divert the money to themselves (2:17). In any case, one of the purposes of 2 Corinthians was to encourage the Corinthians (in a diplomatic way) to finish the collection they had started a year ago (8:10-11; 9:1-3). Paul was sending Titus as his official representative to lead these efforts (8:16-17). Paul's skill in tactfully presenting the need and how the Corinthians could meet that need is one example of how to appropriately ask for financial assistance.

It was only after he had thoroughly explained his ministry to the Corinthians that Paul ventured to ask for money. He had defended his honesty and integrity (1:12-14). He had explained his calling from God and his message to the Gentiles (see 3:7-18; 5:11-21); and he had described the hardships and sufferings that he had endured because of his single-hearted devotion to Christ (4:7-9; 6:3-9).

It was only after he had given the Corinthians an admirable

illustration of true generosity that he appealed to the Corinthians to emulate their example (see 8:1-5). The Macedonians had given out of their poverty. They had given out of their devotion to Christ and had even begged Paul for the opportunity to give.

Paul accompanied his appeal for money with a detailed explanation of the precautions he had taken to ensure that the money would not be mishandled. Two representatives from the churches would accompany Titus to Corinth to guarantee that the money would reach its intended recipients. These representatives would even accompany Paul when he delivered the money to the Jerusalem church (see 8:16-24).

Apparently, Paul's fund-raising efforts were successful, for he wrote to the Romans about the Jerusalem collection. He explained to them that the collection was not only an expression of Christian charity but also an expression of gratitude to the Jewish Christians who had endured persecution in order to preach the Good News of salvation to them (see Romans 15:25-27). In the end, Paul was more concerned about the unity of the church—whether Jews would accept the Gentiles into the church—than any specific amount of money (see Acts 17:1-26, where Paul defends the Gentiles' faith when he hands over the money).

8:1 **We want you to know, brothers and sisters, about the grace of God that has been granted to the churches of Macedonia.**NRSV Paul's great tact with the Corinthians should be noted. Although Paul planned to ask the Corinthians to collect money for the impoverished Jerusalem Christians, he first presented them with an illustration of admirable generosity: the giving of the Macedonians.

From the start, Paul gave *God* the glory for the ability and the desire to give. Human nature motivates people to hoard wealth. The common excuse for accumulating great amounts of money is to make one's future entirely secure (see Luke 12:18-21). Only when Christians completely trust God for all their needs, as they should (see Matthew 6:28-34), can they begin to freely give out of what God has given them (see Matthew 10:8). Not only are material possessions gifts from God, but also the willingness to give is a gift from God. God's free *grace*--his undeserved favor—motivates us to give our time, money, and talents more generously to others.

Paul, writing from *Macedonia* (2:13; 7:5), hoped that news of the generosity of these churches would encourage the Corinthian believers to also give generously. Macedonia was a Roman province located in present-day northern Greece; Corinth was the capital of the southern province of Greece, called Achaia at the time. Although all of present-day Greece had been united by Philip of

Macedon in 338 B.C., the two neighboring provinces, under Roman rule, had become rivals. By using the Macedonian Christians as an illustration of praiseworthy giving, Paul was consciously appealing to the Corinthians' competitive spirit (8:8). He knew they wanted to excel in everything (see 8:7; see also 1 Corinthians 14:12), so he encouraged them also to excel in giving to others.

8:2 **For during a severe ordeal of affliction, their abundant joy and their extreme poverty have overflowed in a wealth of generosity on their part.**[NRSV] Paul had founded the Macedonian churches on his second missionary journey. At Philippi, Paul and Silas had been harassed, stripped, and severely beaten (see Acts 16:22-24). At Thessalonica, a mob had searched the city for Paul and Silas. Fortunately, they didn't find them. Instead, they had dragged Jason, a prominent Thessalonian believer, before the city council (see Acts 17:5-7). The Thessalonian Jews who had stirred up trouble for Paul in their city had followed Paul to Berea, trying to silence him (Acts 17:13-15). So although Jesus had called Paul and his fellow evangelists to Macedonia, they had experienced opposition to the preaching of the gospel at every turn (see Acts 16:6-10).

From Paul's letters to the Thessalonians and to the Philippians, it appears that this persecution did not subside after Paul's initial visit. In spite of *a severe ordeal of affliction* at the hands of their own people, the Macedonian Christians had grown in their Christian faith, endeavoring to imitate Jesus in every situation (see Philippians 1:29-30; 1 Thessalonians 1:6; 2:1-2, 14). Because of their endurance, the Thessalonians had become a model for Christians throughout Greece (1 Thessalonians 1:7). Paul boasted of their perseverance in the faith in the face of great persecution (2 Thessalonians 1:4). The mention of them to the Corinthians here is only one of the occasions when he commended the Macedonian believers. He also spoke of their generosity to the Roman Christians (see Romans 15:26). The persecution had not abated by the time Paul visited Macedonia on his third missionary journey, for he described in this letter how he was plagued by all types of troubles when he traveled through the region (see 7:5).

Although the Macedonians had experienced great affliction and *extreme poverty,* they still gave generously. They were filled with *abundant joy* because they possessed the message of salvation (see 1 Thessalonians 1:6) and had faith in God (see Philippians 1:25-26). Their joy *overflowed in a wealth of generosity.* They considered their monetary gifts to the Jerusalem Christians as a small token of their appreciation to God for their eternal salvation. Jesus had said, "Freely you have received, freely give"

(Matthew 10:8 NIV; see also the poor widow's example in Mark 12:41-44). The Corinthians were doing just that.

Paul said the Macedonians *overflowed* in a wealth of generosity. The Greek word for "generosity" *(aplotetos)* can also mean sincerity, singleness, and simplicity. In the generosity of their giving, the Macedonians not only shared their wealth but also received a wealth of blessing in their hearts as they gave.

JOY OF HELPING
During his third missionary journey, Paul had collected money for the impoverished believers in Jerusalem. The churches in Macedonia—Philippi, Thessalonica, and Berea—had given money even though they were poor (8:1), and they had given more than Paul expected. This was sacrificial giving—they were poor themselves, but they wanted to help. The point of giving is not so much the amount given, but why and how it is given. God does not want gifts given grudgingly. Instead, he wants his people to give as these churches did—out of dedication to Christ, love for fellow believers, and the joy of helping those in need, as well as the fact that it was simply the good and right thing to do. How well does your giving measure up to the standards set by the Macedonian churches?

8:3-4 **For I testify that they gave as much as they were able, and even beyond their ability. Entirely on their own, they urgently pleaded with us for the privilege of sharing in this service to the saints.**[NIV] Paul continued to praise the Macedonians for their attitude about giving. Apparently, the Macedonians had calculated how much they could give and then tried to exceed that amount. Their giving was *beyond* what Paul could expect. In fact, Paul had been reluctant to ask for money for the Jerusalem Christians. It was the Macedonians who had *urgently pleaded* with Paul to take their money also.

Paul used three key Greek words to describe Christian generosity. First, it is a Christian's *privilege.* The Greek word translated here as "privilege" is *charis,* the word commonly translated "grace" (see 8:1). The opportunity to give out of one's wealth is entirely a gift from God. Second, it is *sharing* of the Christian's life. The Greek word here is *koinonia,* the word commonly translated "fellowship." Just as the Corinthians were sharing in Paul's ministry by praying for him (1:11; see also Philemon 1:6), the Macedonians knew that by giving they could "share" their great joy for their salvation with other believers. In essence, this is "fellowship": Christians sharing with each other their enthusiasm for Jesus, their Savior. Finally, Paul described the Macedonians' giving as a *service.* The Greek word here is *diakonias,* the word from which the English word "deacon" is derived. Giving money is a way to serve others.

BEYOND YOUR CIRCLE
The kingdom of God spreads through believers' concern and eagerness to help others. This passage (8:1-2) tells of several churches joining to help others beyond their own circle of friends and their own city. Explore ways you might link up with a ministry outside your city by supporting them either through your church or through a Christian organization. By joining with other believers to finance God's work, you increase Christian unity and help Christ's kingdom grow. Reevaluate your giving. Is it the bare minimum or is it the best of your ability?

8:5 Best of all, they went beyond our highest hopes, for their first action was to dedicate themselves to the Lord and to us for whatever directions God might give them.[NLT] The Macedonians' giving was not motivated by a desire for praise from Paul or others. Their generosity was fundamentally motivated by their desire to serve *the Lord* Jesus. They *first* dedicated themselves to God and expressed the desire to follow God wherever that may lead. Their generosity and charity wasn't for its own sake. They were not looking for congratulations from others. They weren't doing it to feel good about themselves. They gave because they knew they were God's. Everything they had—even their very souls—were God's. Knowing this, they devoted themselves to serving Jesus and his kingdom in anyway they could.

GIVING OURSELVES
Paul realized the undergirding of the Macedonian Christians' generosity was that they "gave themselves first to the Lord" (8:5 NIV). What impressed Paul was not how much money they gave but how willing they were to give themselves and their possessions to the Lord. The impoverished believers in northern Greece recognized to whom they belonged (and thus who owned all their belongings). Those who surrender their lives to the Lord are in a position to give beyond their ability. Believers' wealth and possessions are not theirs to keep. They are to be managed on behalf of their true owner. That is what the word "stewardship" means. As a symbolic act of sacrifice, open your Bible to this section of 2 Corinthians and place your wallet, watch, and personal calendar on top. Spend a few moments in prayer releasing your time, money, and commitments to the Lord. Listen for what he might want you to do today with those three areas of resources.

8:6 **So we have urged Titus, who encouraged your giving in the first place, to return to you and encourage you to complete your share in this ministry of giving.**^{NLT} This passage explains why Paul was describing the way the Macedonians were giving to the Jerusalem collection. He would send Titus back to *return to* Corinth *and encourage* the believers *to complete their share in this ministry of giving*—in other words, to finish the collection efforts there.

On his previous visit (or possibly a visit sometime before the one in which Titus delivered the "severe letter"), Titus had encouraged the Corinthians to continue collecting sums of money every week for the Jerusalem church (see 8:6), for Paul had instructed the Corinthians to do just that in an earlier letter (see 1 Corinthians 16:1-4). Apparently, the Corinthians' giving had dwindled, perhaps in light of some of the criticisms circulating in the church about Paul and his authority (see Paul's defense of himself throughout this letter: 7:2; 11:7-9; 12:14-17).

8:7 **Since you excel in so many ways—you have so much faith, such gifted speakers, such knowledge, such enthusiasm, and such love for us—now I want you to excel also in this gracious ministry of giving.**^{NLT} Paul once again appealed to the Corinthians' competitive spirit. They had striven to *excel in so many ways,* and God had responded to their *enthusiasm* by giving them a wealth of spiritual gifts (see 1 Corinthians 1:4).

Knowing that the Corinthians had a great amount of enthusiasm for spiritual gifts, Paul placed *giving* alongside other gifts. Paul wanted the Corinthians *to excel also in this gracious ministry of giving,* in being concerned for other people's welfare. If they could compete at giving to others, their energies might be directed away from the spiritual gifts that were causing quarrels in their church (see 1 Corinthians 3:3).

THE MINISTRY OF GIVING
Paul encouraged the Corinthians to excel in the grace of giving (8:7). Too often, stewardship of money is given a different status than other aspects of discipleship. Most believers would not want growth in faith, knowledge, or love to stop at a certain level. Yet many decide a fixed percentage to give and stay there for life. True discipleship includes growing in the mature use of all resources, so giving should expand as well. God can give you the desire and enable you to increase your capacity to give. Don't miss this opportunity for growth.

8:8 I am not commanding you, but I want to test the sincerity of your love by comparing it with the earnestness of others.^{NIV} Giving is a natural response of Christian love. Paul did not order the Corinthians to give; he encouraged them to prove the *sincerity* of their *love* for Christ *by comparing it with the earnestness of others*. When you love someone, you want to help that person. You want to give your time, your attention, and your possessions to enrich that person. If you refuse to help, your love is not as sincere as you say it is.

8:9 For you know the grace of our Lord Jesus Christ, that though He was rich, yet for your sakes He became poor, that you through His poverty might become rich.^{NKJV} The Corinthian church—a wealthy church—had pledged a great deal of money, but they had not yet given any of it. Paul was concerned that they might never get around to giving what they had promised, so he gave them two models of generous giving. In the previous verse and first part of this chapter (8:1-5, 8), Paul had given them the first model: the poor Macedonian Christians who had enthusiastically given beyond what they could afford. Then in this verse, Paul gave the Corinthians another model: Jesus himself. Although the Macedonians had shown a great amount of generosity in past, their sacrifice couldn't compare with Jesus' giving of himself. Jesus' action was the ultimate model for the Corinthians.

Jesus became *poor* for the Corinthians' *sakes* by generously giving up his rights as God and becoming human. Although he was God and possessed all the privileges, power, and wisdom of God (John 1:1-14), the Son of God relinquished all that. He voluntarily became a man named Jesus of Nazareth. The Lord became *poor* when he became human because he set aside so much. He was a heavenly King, and he humbled himself to become a servant of lowly human beings. He even voluntarily surrendered himself to death on a cross—the most cruel and humiliating death known at that time. Yet by doing so, he made all who believe in him *rich*. Christians have not only been saved through his self-sacrificial actions, they have also been accepted into God's family (5:8, 18). That means that they have a glorious, eternal inheritance in heaven (4:18; 5:1).

8:10-11 And here is my advice about what is best for you in this matter: Last year you were the first not only to give but also to have the desire to do so. Now finish the work, so that your eager willingness to do it may be matched by your completion of it, according to your means.^{NIV} Paul was careful not to command the Corinthians (8:8); he only gave *advice*.

This passage also appeals to the Corinthians' competitive spirit (see also 8:1-2, 6-8). They had been the *first* in two ways! They had started the fund for the relief of the Jerusalem Christians and were the first to contribute substantially to the fund. At this point, Paul asked the Corinthians to *finish the work* and fulfill their commitments so that their *eager willingness* at the beginning would be *matched by [their] completion of* the task (see also 9:5). He challenged the Corinthians to act on their plans and give *according to* their *means* (8:14).

Four principles of giving emerge in the following verses:

1. Your willingness to give cheerfully is more important than the amount you give (8:12; 9:5).
2. You should strive to fulfill your financial commitments (see also 9:5).
3. If you give to others in need, they will, in turn, help you when you are in need (8:14).
4. You should give as a response to Christ, not for anything you can get out of it (8:9; 9:13).

How you give reflects your devotion to Christ. Don't rush into a commitment to give. Evaluate your finances, so that you will be able to keep your promise.

SECOND HALF
Like a coach in the locker room at halftime, Paul called the Corinthians to finish what they had begun (8:11). They had distinguished themselves as winners thus far, but the game wasn't over yet. The excitement of starting must be matched by the determination of completion. It is easy to make promises when making them enhances a person's image. When the spotlight leaves and the cost of the vow seems to compound daily, enthusiasm wanes. It becomes easy to forfeit honor by forgetting what was promised. To whom did you recently say, "I'll pray for you!" Have you? It sounded spiritually mature and caring, but did you mean it? Have you made a financial pledge to a Christian organization or your church that you have yet to fulfill? God will empower you to finish your pledge.

8:12 If you are really eager to give, it isn't important how much you are able to give. God wants you to give what you have, not what you don't have.^{NLT} Paul wasn't as concerned about the total amount the Corinthians would raise, but he wanted them to be *eager* in giving. When he spoke of the Macedonians' giving, he did not tell the Corinthians *how much* the Macedonians had given but *how* they had given: They gave with great joy, out of their devotion to Christ (8:2-3, 5). Paul was more concerned

about the Corinthians' attitude than whether he reached a certain
goal in his fund-raising.

Although what the Corinthians possessed was a gift from God
in the first place (1 Corinthians 4:7), Paul asked them to *give* of
what they had, *not what* they didn't *have*. Sacrificial giving must
be responsible.

8:13-14 **Of course, I don't mean you should give so much that you suffer from having too little. I only mean that there should be
some equality. Right now you have plenty and can help them.
Then at some other time they can share with you when you
need it. In this way, everyone's needs will be met.**[NLT] Paul
wanted the Corinthians to give generously but not to the extent
that those who depended on the givers (their families, for example) must *suffer from having too little.* Give until it hurts, but
don't give so that it hurts your family or relatives who need your
financial support.

The Jerusalem Christians had been poor for some time. About
a decade before this collection, the believers in Antioch had sent
Paul and Barnabas with some monetary relief for the church at
Jerusalem. Palestine had been hit with a severe famine, and apparently the believers in Jerusalem were in great need (see Acts
11:27-30). Most likely, the Jerusalem Christians remained
extremely poor because of their social ostracism. Right from the
start, the Jews (headed at that time by Paul himself) had under-
taken an intense campaign of persecution against Jewish Christians (see Acts 5:17-18; 7:54-60; 8:1-3). The early Christians had
to flee Jerusalem to avoid imprisonment or a worse fate. Naturally, persecution of that sort would disrupt the businesses of
those Christians. Apparently, the Christians in and around Jerusalem had limited ways to support themselves—even a decade later.

Paul considered the poverty of the Jerusalem Christians as an
opportunity for Gentile believers. They could dispel any doubts
about the genuineness of their faith by demonstrating it through
giving generously to the Jerusalem church—the church that had
sacrificed in the beginning to send evangelists throughout the
Roman world (see Paul's explanation of the collection in Romans
15:25-27). Paul hoped their generosity would smooth over some
of the hesitancy of some Jewish Christians to accept Gentiles into
the church (see Acts 21:15-25 for Paul's defense of his ministry
with the Gentiles at the presentation of the gift).

In the end, the giving and the receiving of money would tie the
entire church together. Each would be dependent on the other.
Just as the Gentiles had been dependent on the Jewish Christians
for the wonderful message of salvation, the Jews would be depen-

dent on the Gentiles for financial support. Each part's *need* would be *met* with the other's strength, so the entire church would be built up. Paul appealed to the principle of *equality,* or the principles of fair shares. Each church should provide for other churches as the need arose. Each church should help the others out of the resources God had given it. If one church was wealthy, it could meet the others' needs. When conditions reversed, the formerly poor church might be able to return the favor.

As a result, members of the church would become interdependent on each other. But more importantly, they would become dependent on Christ (see Paul's discussion of the church as the body of Christ in 1 Corinthians 12:12-26).

Churches today should reconsider the principle of "fair shares" and take the initiative to help poor churches. Many urban churches suffer from a chronic lack of financial support. Most pastors around the world live at what would be considered poverty level in North America. The wealthier churches should help them.

8:15 Do you remember what the Scriptures say about this? "Those who gathered a lot had nothing left over, and those who gathered only a little had enough."^{NLT} Paul quoted Exodus 16:18 to illustrate how everyone's needs would be met. In the wilderness, the Israelites could not find enough food to feed all of their number. So God provided food from heaven: manna. These thin, white flakes appeared on the ground every morning. God told the Israelites to gather as much as they needed for the day. Some gathered more than others, but each had enough for the day. Those who were greedy tried to store the manna for the next day. They didn't trust God for what they needed. Their lack of trust was rewarded with a smelly, maggot-ridden mess (see Exodus 16:19).

PRINCIPLES OF GIVING
How do you decide how much to give? Paul gave the Corinthian church several principles to follow:

- Each person should follow through on previous promises (8:10-11; 9:3).
- Each person should give as much as he or she is able (8:12; 9:6).
- Each person must make up his or her own mind how much to give (9:7).
- Each person should give in proportion to what God has given him or her (9:10).

God gives to you so that you can give to others.

Although God didn't supply the first-century Christians' needs the same way, Paul saw the same principles at work. God would provide everyone with what they needed. Although some had more and others had less, everyone's needs would be met in the end. Some may have had more than others, but everyone's needs would be met. God wanted the wealthy to give out of their surplus so that the needy could have enough. It wasn't a matter of exact equality; instead, it was a matter of fairness or justice.

8:16-17 **I am thankful to God that he has given Titus the same enthusiasm for you that I have. He welcomed our request that he visit you again. In fact, he himself was eager to go and see you.**[NLT] The rest of chapter 8 is, in essence, a letter of recommendation for Titus and two anonymous "brothers." Titus was an official representative of Paul, while the "brothers" were representatives of churches who had contributed to the Jerusalem fund (see 8:18, 22).

Paul first commended Titus to the Corinthians. He had already emphasized how encouraged Titus was after his initial visit with them (see 7:13-15). The Corinthians had welcomed Titus, had respected his message to them, and had even provided for his needs (see 7:7, 15). When Paul asked him to visit Corinth again, Titus *welcomed* Paul's *request that he visit* the Corinthians again. He himself had been *eager to go and see* them. He had the same *enthusiasm* as Paul did. Like Paul, Titus wanted to spur the Corinthians to excel in giving (see 8:7). Appropriately, Paul thanked *God* for Titus's earnest attitude. Titus's eagerness to head up the collection efforts in Corinth was as much a gift from God as the ability to give in the first place (see 8:1).

8:18-19 **And we are sending along with him the brother who is praised by all the churches for his service to the gospel. What is more, he was chosen by the churches to accompany us as we carry the offering, which we administer in order to honor the Lord himself and to show our eagerness to help.**[NIV] Paul took some steps to guard the integrity of the Jerusalem collection. A *brother* had been *chosen by the churches* to ensure that the money would be given to its intended recipients. Paul didn't want any allegations of financial impropriety, especially the sort of allegations that were already circulating in Corinth (see Paul's defense in 12:16-18).

Who was this brother? Ancient commentators assumed the person was Luke because they took "his service to the gospel" to mean that this person had written a Gospel book. Recent commentators, however, uniformly deny that Paul ever used the Greek word for "gospel" to refer to a Gospel book. Other commentators have suggested that Apollos or Barnabas may have been this anonymous brother. But the Corinthians would have known both of these men, and thus they would not have needed an introduction. Most commentators suggest that this brother was a representative from the Macedonian churches. Thus, Sopater from Berea or Aristarchus and Secundus from Thessalonica could be possibilities (see Acts 20:4-5). Other commentators insist that the fact that Paul stated that Macedonians were accompanying him later implies that this brother was not a Macedonian. These scholars, therefore, offer Tychicus and Trophimus as possibilities (see Acts 21:29).

In any case, this brother would function as a representative for the churches to ensure that the money of the Jerusalem collection would be handled properly. Paul did not want anyone to accuse him of mishandling this gift for the Jerusalem Christians, for that would defeat his entire purpose. The gift was to promote unity in the early church, not division (see Paul's explanation of this in Romans 15:25-27).

8:20-21 By traveling together we will guard against any suspicion, for we are anxious that no one should find fault with the way we are handling this generous gift. We are careful to be honorable before the Lord, but we also want everyone else to know we are honorable.NLT Paul didn't want anyone to be suspicious of his handling of the money. Therefore, he was *careful* that his actions were not only *honorable before the Lord,* who saw all things, but also before people, who look on the appearance of things (see Proverbs 3:4). That is why he had refused any kind of financial support from the Corinthians when he had first ministered among them (see 1 Corinthians 9:12). He didn't want anyone to think he was preaching for money (see 1 Corinthians 9:19).

Paul's concern about how things appeared to others continued with the Jerusalem collection. In his initial instructions to the Corinthians about this (see 1 Corinthians 16:1-4), Paul advised the leaders of the Corinthian church to collect the money every week. He did not want anything to do with collecting the money. In addition, the Corinthians were to appoint representatives from their own church to take the money to Jerusalem. Paul didn't even want to deliver the money, for he wanted to remain above suspicion. After writing 1 Corinthians, however, Paul had changed his mind. He had become convinced by the Holy Spirit that he should also go to Jerusalem (see his later explanation of his actions in Acts 20:22-24; 21:11-14).

In order to finish the collection without *any suspicion,* Paul continued to refrain from collecting the money himself. Instead, he sent someone whom the Corinthians respected and trusted: Titus. Accompanying Titus were two other representatives from

the churches who contributed to the fund to oversee how the
money was handled.

ABOVE BOARD
Paul was aware that when Christians publicly profess
allegiance to the living God, what they do automatically reflects
on him. When non-Christians find reason to be critical of
believers, they are also critical of Christ. So Paul used every
safeguard to maintain integrity in the collection of money for the
Jerusalem church. Those outside the church can view
skeptically the way believers handle money in the church.
Financial scandals among high-profile ministries have alerted
the nonbelieving world to the unethical gimmicks that some
Christians use.

It is possible to avoid mismanagement of God's resources.
Does your church or organization have a system of checks and
balances that prevent wrongful behavior? Are there financial
practices in your ministry that need to be reviewed? Christians
must have the highest standard of financial responsibility.

**8:22 In addition, we are sending with them our brother who has
often proved to us in many ways that he is zealous, and now
even more so because of his great confidence in you.**[NIV] Paul
recommended the third *brother* to the Corinthians in these verses.
Again, this brother remains anonymous; he could be any one of the
people mentioned above (in the commentary on 8:18). Although
Paul didn't mention this person's name, he made it clear that the
man had proven himself. The Greek for "proved" means "to test."
This man's zeal for Christ had been tested in *many ways,* and he
had passed these tests. Besides, this man had evidently heard about
the Corinthians from Paul and Titus, and he possessed the same
confidence that Paul had in them (see 7:13-16).

**8:23 As for Titus, he is my partner and fellow worker among you;
as for our brothers, they are representatives of the churches
and an honor to Christ.**[NIV] The last two verses of this chapter
summarize Paul's recommendation of Titus and his two traveling
companions. Although Paul called Titus his son in the faith in
Titus 1:4, here he called Titus a *partner and fellow worker* in the
preaching of the gospel. Paul did this in order to emphasize
Titus's authority among the Corinthians. Titus was Paul's official
representative to the Corinthians to collect the money for the
relief of the Jerusalem Christians (8:6).

The two *representatives of the churches* who accompanied Titus
were also recommended by Paul to the Corinthians (the complete
list of representatives is given in Acts 20:4). The Greek for "representatives" is *apostoloi*—literally, apostles. In the Gospels, this

Greek word is only used for the Twelve. Paul in his letters, however, used the term for any representative of a church commissioned for some special task (Barnabas in 1 Corinthians 9:5; James
in Galatians 1:19). *Apostolos* literally means "the one sent forth."

**8:24 Therefore show these men the proof of our love and the rea-
son for our pride in you, so that the churches can see it.**NIV
Paul told the Corinthians to shower their Christian *love* on these
fellow believers, just as they had welcomed Titus before (see 7:7,
13). They had proven Paul's boasting about them true on Titus's
first visit (see 7:14); now Paul encouraged them to do the same
for these two other representatives. These men were representing
the other *churches;* therefore, the Corinthians should conduct
themselves in an appropriate way, for their conduct would be
broadcasted to other churches by these representatives. The fact
that Paul spent so much time recommending these emissaries and
their mission to the Corinthians might indicate that Paul was a
little apprehensive of how the Corinthians would treat them.
Paul's last visit was especially painful (see 2:1-4). Perhaps that
visit was still on his mind, even though Titus had given him an
encouraging report (7:6-7).

In any case, Paul was preparing the Corinthians for his next visit.
It wouldn't be a casual visit. Titus had already prepared the way by
delivering Paul's stern letter (see 2:3-4). But Titus was returning
with another letter from Paul (2 Corinthians) and two more representatives to ensure that everything would be in order. Afterwards,
Paul would come with even more representatives from the Macedonian churches (see 9:4). If there was any confrontation like the one
that occurred on the last visit (see 13:1-3), Paul would have several
unbiased witnesses from a number of churches. They would be
able to testify to the integrity of Paul's handling of the situation.

LIVING PROOF
The Corinthian congregation was admonished to show the
proof of their love to those who traveled on behalf of the
apostle Paul (8:24). The congregation was known as a loving
group, but love is not real love until it acts. If the proof of the
pudding is in the tasting, the proof of professed love is in the
living out of it. We prove our love when we find tangible ways to
give it away each day. List five ways you can express your love
before the day is over. It could include making a phone call,
sending a letter, asking forgiveness of someone, sending a
check or a bouquet of flowers, making a pot of soup for an
elderly friend, or leaving your briefcase at the office tonight so
you can spend quality time with your family.

2 Corinthians 9

This passage reminds the Corinthians of their initial enthusiasm for the Jerusalem collection, their delight that God could use them to help other believers. Their enthusiasm was contagious. The Macedonians had heard of their eagerness and had also eagerly responded to the appeal for money. As Paul was preparing to collect the last of the contributions, however, the Corinthians' enthusiasm had waned. The collection had grounded to a halt. Paul was worried that when he came to Corinth the Corinthians would give grudgingly. Paul was worried they had forgotten what a privilege it was to be involved in God's work. God wants cheerful givers and enthusiastic team players (9:7). He can do without selfish and disgruntled givers.

9:1-2 **There is no need for me to write to you about this service to the saints. For I know your eagerness to help, and I have been boasting about it to the Macedonians, telling them that since last year you in Achaia were ready to give; and your enthusiasm has stirred most of them to action.**^{NIV} Paul was not sending Titus and his representatives to Corinth (8:16-24) in order to explain the collection and how it would benefit the Jerusalem Christians. A *year* before, they were one of the first to begin *this service* (see 8:10). In fact, Paul had been *boasting* to the Christians in Macedonia about the Corinthians' *eagerness to help*. It was word of the Corinthians' eagerness that *stirred* the Macedonians to want to give so generously (see Paul's description of their giving in 8:1-5).

By describing how their own *enthusiasm* had incited the Macedonians to give, Paul was, in effect, prodding the Corinthians to rekindle their initial enthusiasm for giving. Paul wasn't naive about human behavior. The start and end of a marathon are much more thrilling than the miles in between. It takes stubborn determination and perseverance to keep on running—to run, in spite of the blisters, sore muscles, and exhaustion.

Paul also knew that it took a community to persevere. Just as teammates will cheer their runner on in a race, so Paul was sending Titus and two other believers to the Corinthians to cheer them on. The efforts at collecting the funds in Corinth had been side-tracked by greedy, traveling preachers, who were consolidating their power in the church by criticizing Paul (see 2:17; 12:14-18). Paul hoped his description of how the Macedonians had given out of their extreme poverty (see 8:2-3) would also "stir" the Corinthians to action, just as word of the Corinthians' eagerness had stirred the Macedonians. To ensure this, Paul was sending Titus and two others to oversee the collection efforts (see 9:4-5).

Because Paul appears to be reintroducing the topic of the collection in 9:1, some have speculated that 9:1-15 is a separate letter recommending Titus to the churches throughout the province of *Achaia* (the province of southern Greece, of which Corinth was the capital; see 9:2). According to this theory, the previous passage (8:1-24) is a letter of commendation for Titus exclusively to the church in Corinth. These scholars believe the way chapter 9 repeats much of chapter 8 supports this hypothesis. No manuscripts have been found, however, to support this theory. Moreover, it is based on the spurious judgment that chapters 8 and 9 do not follow each other logically. A closer examination of these chapters reveal the interdependence of the two chapters. Paul had just exhorted the Corinthians to show their Christian love to Titus so that he would not be proven wrong in his boasting about them (see 8:24). In 9:1-5, Paul told the Corinthians exactly what he had been boasting about: their eagerness to give since last year (9:2). Moreover, Paul explained that they could avoid embarrassment by giving the generous gift they had promised last year (8:11). Thus it is better to view chapter 9 as a further explanation of why and how the Corinthian church, along with the churches in Achaia, could give, rather than a separate letter to Achaia.

9:3 But I am sending these brothers just to be sure that you really are ready, as I told them you would be, with your money all collected. I don't want it to turn out that I was wrong in my boasting about you.[NLT] Paul didn't want his boasts about the Corinthians to be proven *wrong*—literally, in Greek, "to be empty." That was why Paul decided to send Titus with two other representatives *(brothers)*. In several months, Paul would return to Jerusalem with the money (see Acts 20:1-5, 22-24; 24:17); therefore, the final contribution had to be *ready* when he came to Corinth (9:4). Titus's job was to inspire the Corinthians to diligently set aside money as Paul had instructed them in his earlier letter (see 1 Corinthians 16:1-4). The representatives who accompanied Titus, on the other hand, were to ensure that all the money was collected. In sharp contrast to the false teachers who had infiltrated the Corinthian church, no underhanded methods would be used (2:17). Respected and trustworthy representatives from the churches would witness the entire process (see 8:20).

9:4 I would be humiliated—and so would you—if some Macedonian Christians came with me, only to find that you still weren't ready after all I had told them!NLT Paul, accompanied by delegates from the Macedonian churches, would follow Titus. The Macedonian church representatives would exert a little friendly peer pressure on the Corinthians. They would certainly compare the generosity of their own churches to that of the Corinthians. Paul *had told* the Macedonians how the Corinthians had eagerly wanted to give from the beginning (about a year ago). But since then, much had changed. Paul was taking precautions just in case the Corinthians were to challenge his apostolic authority on this visit (see 13:1-4). These *Macedonian Christians* would act as witnesses to how Paul had handled any confrontation that might occur. Paul was giving the Corinthians plenty of warning about his coming. In this passage, he skillfully warned the Corinthians of how he would be *humiliated* if the Corinthians were unprepared for his visit. On the surface, Paul was speaking about the Jerusalem collection, but he certainly may have been warning the Corinthians of his other concerns. Paul was hoping that the Macedonians would not find the Corinthian church in spiritual disorder. That would be even more embarrassing. The end of this letter will state it more bluntly, where Paul would sternly warn the Corinthians to prepare themselves for his visit by examining their hearts before God. When he came, he would mediate their disputes and even discipline those who were sinning (see 13:1-5). If they doubted his authority, he would give them convincing proof of his authority from God (see 13:3-4).

Of course, Paul hoped for the better, that the presence of so many representatives from the churches would silence his critics. He hoped that this letter (2 Corinthians) delivered by Titus himself would prompt the Corinthians to make the necessary changes in the way they lived out their faith. Paul also knew human nature, however, so he took the necessary precautions, sending Titus to prod them on—not only in collecting the funds but also in their spiritual maturity. Paul's reference in this verse to being humiliated was a gentle goad to the Corinthians.

9:5 So I thought it necessary to urge the brothers to go on ahead to you, and arrange in advance for this bountiful gift that you have promised, so that it may be ready as a voluntary gift and not as an extortion.NRSV Evidently, the Corinthians had pledged a great deal of money a year ago, for Paul called the *gift* a *bountiful* one. Paul wasn't asking for more money; he was merely reminding the Corinthians to fulfill the commitments they had already made (see 8:10-12).

Paul, however, didn't want this substantial amount of money to be collected under pressure or in a short time period. Otherwise, his appearance at Corinth would be associated with frenzied collection efforts. Instead, Paul wanted the money to be given voluntarily, not coerced in any way (see Philemon 1:8-9). The Greek word Paul used for "extortion" connotes some type of cheating or defrauding. If the money was raised in a short time, it might give the appearance of some type of scam. Paul wanted the Corinthians to remember that they were giving to God. This required some advance planning. Titus and the two traveling *brothers* would go to Corinth before Paul's visit to *arrange in advance* the collection of the funds. Proper preparation could ensure that the people would give cheerfully.

ADVANCE WORK
Paul urged some of his friends to visit Corinth in advance of his visit, in order to finish the arrangements for the offering being taken for the church in Jerusalem (9:5). What might seem to be merely a spontaneous response to an announced dilemma was much more. Organization, preparation, and follow-through are necessary tracks on which the train of God's purposes travels. When Billy Graham agrees to hold a crusade in a city, his organization sends an advance team that spends months making contacts, negotiating contracts with facilities, and training volunteers—all for only a few days of evangelistic meetings. For those who attend the crusade, everything seems to happen without much effort; but partly because of the efforts expended beforehand and behind the scenes, the Graham crusades consistently achieve their goal of winning people to Christ.

9:6 Remember this: Whoever sows sparingly will also reap sparingly, and whoever sows generously will also reap generously.[NIV] The people of this time were intimately familiar with the principles of an agricultural economy. Planting, weeding, and harvesting were common, everyday tasks. Everyone would have known of a foolish neighbor who had used too much of his grain instead of saving it as seed for his fields. Lavishly scattering seeds all over one's fields was a risk. What if birds ate it up? What if the soil was inferior and wouldn't produce a harvest? Keeping more seeds in storage might appear to be wise, a way to ensure against future disasters. But the farmer who scattered his seed meagerly inevitably would have a small harvest. A farmer

NEEDS FOR A FUND-RAISING PROJECT

The topic of fund-raising is not one to be avoided or one that should embarrass us, but all fund-raising efforts should be planned and conducted responsibly.

who refused to risk his grain on the next year's harvest would lose.

This piece of agricultural wisdom contains a profound truth about Christian giving (see Proverbs 11:24-26; 22:8-9 for similar sayings). Those who are like the foolish farmer who sowed *sparingly*—those who refuse to trust God with their future financial security—will inevitably lose out on God's rich blessings. Those who sow *generously* will invest in an eternal harvest that will exceed their expectations.

9:7 Each of you must give as you have made up your mind, not reluctantly or under compulsion, for God loves a cheerful giver.NRSV Each Corinthian believer was to decide how much God wanted him or her to give. It wasn't to be an impulsive decision but a deliberate one. They were to assess their own ability to give and plan accordingly. This was to be intentional, planned giving, for Paul had already told them to lay aside some money every week (1 Corinthians 16:1-4). This was one reason for Paul sending Titus ahead. He wanted someone to organize the weekly collections so that no one would fall short of how much they had pledged the year before (9:5). It seems that although they had already pledged the money, they had not given it yet.

Paul didn't want to use urgent appeals or pressure tactics to coerce the Corinthians to give. Even though he was the one appealing for the money, he was careful to give the Corinthians enough time to think and to pray about how much God wanted them to give. Paul didn't want anyone giving *reluctantly or under compulsion*. Paul knew that God weighs the heart and not the amount of money; he looks at the giver and not the gift. A *cheer-ful giver,* who gives out of a sincere gratitude for what God has done, is the type of giver God cherishes. God multiplies those gifts beyond measure (9:11).

ATTITUDE
A giving attitude is more important than the amount given (9:7). The person who can only give a small gift shouldn't be embarrassed. God is concerned about *how* a person gives from his or her resources (see Mark 12:41-44 for Jesus' commendation of a poor widow's generosity). According to that standard, the giving of the Macedonian churches would be difficult to match (8:3). God himself is a cheerful giver. Consider all he has done for us. He is pleased when we who are created in his image give generously and joyfully. Do you have a difficult time letting go of your money? It may reflect your ungratefulness to God.

9:8 And God is able to make all grace abound to you, so that in all things at all times, having all that you need, you will abound in every good work.[NIV] The biggest obstacle that people have to overcome in order to give is worry. What if I will not have enough money next year for my retirement? What if some emergency comes up? What if I lose my job? These verses reassure the Corinthians that God is able to meet *all* their needs. He is the Almighty. He owns *all* of the world; moreover, he blesses those who give back to him.

Paul emphasized *all* in this verse. Christians who give back to God will lack nothing. God's favor—his *grace*—will be showered on people who give. They will have everything they *need* in the various situations in which they find themselves. In the Old Testament, God even invited the Israelites "to test" him in this. If they brought all the required tithes to him, God promised to "throw open the floodgates of heaven and pour out so much blessing that [they] will not have room enough for it" (Malachi 3:10 NIV).

The purpose of God's overwhelming blessing is always to equip his people to do *every good work.* This text doesn't imply that Christian giving is a contract with God, where the one who gives gets. Instead, it says that God will provide whatever a Christian needs to do good. Thus, in the end, a Christian's good works will bring praise and glory to God (see chart in the Life Application Commentary *Hebrews* 13:16).

9:9 As the Scriptures say, "Godly people give generously to the poor. Their good deeds will never be forgotten."[NLT] Just as a farmer has to scatter the seed on the ground in order to reap an abundant harvest, so Christians must scatter what they possess among *the poor* in order to reap God's blessing. Paul already made it clear that God's blessing does not always include an increase of riches. All of God's gifts, both spiritual and material, are intended to help a Christian do good works (9:8). This quote from Psalm 112:9 demonstrates this truth. Although the psalmist does speak of material blessings for the righteous person in that psalm (Psalm 112:3), Paul quotes a line that emphasizes the spiritual benefits of generosity to the poor. Those who are blessed by God with financial resources should give generously to help those with less. Memory of this righteousness *will never be forgotten.* Those who receive this person's gifts will remember the generosity for a long time, but, more importantly, God will never forget the person's benevolence.

9:10 Now he who supplies seed to the sower and bread for food will also supply and increase your store of seed and will enlarge the harvest of your righteousness.NIV God *supplies* both the *seed* and the *bread,* both the surplus to invest and the resources to support one's family every day. The resources that God gives Christians are not to be hoarded, foolishly devoured, or thrown away. God gives gifts to his people for their own use and for investing back into God's work. Instead of squandering these gifts, Christians need to cultivate them in order to produce more good works (9:8).

God does not limit himself to merely giving more resources—in other words, more seed. He blesses what you sow. He showers the seed with gentle rain. He gives the seed that is sown everything it needs to grow into a healthy, thriving plant. Although the seed is small, it has great potential if it has the right conditions to grow (see Jesus' parables on seeds in Matthew 13:1-9, 18-23, 31-32).

In the same way, God blesses believers' feeble efforts at generosity so that they *enlarge the harvest.* This harvest does not consist of personal wealth and riches. It is a harvest *of your righteousness.* God will take inadequate efforts at good works and increase them so that they bless many people. All a person has to do is give.

9:11-12 Yes, you will be enriched so that you can give even more generously. And when we take your gifts to those who need them, they will break out in thanksgiving to God. So two good things will happen—the needs of the Christians in Jerusalem will be met, and they will joyfully express their thanksgiving to God.NLT Giving generously to those in need causes *two good things* to *happen.* First, through those *gifts* given *to those who*

need them, God meets their *needs* (here, specifically, the needs of
the *Christians in Jerusalem*). Second, the recipients of these generous gifts will *break out in thanksgiving to God, joyfully* expressing it! Their celebration over these gifts will lead to heartfelt
praise to God, for they will know that it is God who enables the
giver to give in the first place.

So, in Paul's eyes, giving is not a strategy for financial growth
but another way to bring praise and honor to God, who supplies
everyone's needs. Christians shouldn't give to others in order to
receive personal rewards. They should give liberally to the poor
in order to see God work.

STINGY CHRISTIANS?
Paul wanted his readers to be generous on every occasion. As
he appealed to the Corinthians to give sacrificially to aid the
Jerusalem congregation, he reminded them that God is the
source of everything good (9:10). Believers are called to be
generous because of the example of the Lord of life. A stingy
Christian should be an extinct species. Generosity proves that
a person's heart has been cleansed of self-interest and filled
with the servant spirit of Jesus himself. That is why acts of
generosity result in God being praised. When those through
whom God works give freely, his undercover operation is
exposed and applauded. Do neighbors see generosity in your
actions?

**9:13 You will be glorifying God through your generous gifts. For
your generosity to them will prove that you are obedient to
the Good News of Christ.**^{NLT} In addition to the normal advantages that come through Christian giving (see 9:11-12), Paul
hoped that the Jerusalem collection would have extra benefits:
He hoped that through this gift from Gentile Christians Jewish
and Gentile believers would be drawn closer together in Christian
fellowship.

During the early decades of the church, Jewish Christians had
grave doubts about whether the Gentiles' faith was sincere. Even
the apostle Peter was surprised that God wanted him to break
Jewish ceremonial law in order to preach the gospel to Cornelius,
a Gentile centurion (see Acts 10:1-33). But he did; Cornelius and
his household not only came to faith in Christ but also received
the Holy Spirit (10:34-46). This development wasn't welcomed
by some of the Jewish believers in Jerusalem (see Acts 11:3).
Only after Peter had defended his actions did the believers in
Jerusalem finally agree that salvation had been extended to the
Gentiles also (Acts 11:18). Unfortunately, this wasn't the end of

CONCERN FOR THE POOR

Concern and care for the poor is essential to true biblical Christianity.

We are not to take advantage of the needy . . . . . Exodus 22:25-27

We are not to charge interest or make a
profit on food sold to them . . . . Leviticus 25:35-37

Every third year the tithe was to be
given to poor people . . . . Deuteronomy 14:28-29

We are instructed to give generously
to the poor . . . . Deuteronomy 15:11;
                                                      Matthew 6:2-4

Jesus had special concern for the
place of the poor . . . . Luke 4:18-19; 6:20-21

Paul was eager to remember the poor . . . . Galatians 2:10

The Bible teaches that Christians should care for the poor, so what can you do?

Feed the poor.
• Contribute to a food relief organization.
• Volunteer to help in a community program.
• Work through your church to develop a project to help the needy.
• Consider giving extra tithe to help ministries that assist the poor.

Secure justice for the poor.
• Help widows, orphans, strangers, and the oppressed.
• Help agencies that work for housing, education, and job opportunities for needy people.

Uphold the cause of the poor.
• Stand against oppression.
• Intercede for even one person.
• Write to Christian missions and encourage them to support the cause of the poor.

---

the controversy. Later, some Jewish believers from Judea went to Antioch to inform Gentile believers that they had to be circumcised in order to be saved (see Acts 15:1). Even Peter tacitly joined in their hypocrisy because he was afraid of what this group would say (see Galatians 2:11-13). The controversy that erupted out of this was resolved at a meeting in Jerusalem. There the leaders of the early church agreed that salvation was only through faith in Jesus, not through the law (see Acts 15:6-19; Galatians 3:6-7, 13-14; Ephesians 2:8). Even though the issue had been resolved, it kept coming up. Jewish legalists misled the Gentile believers in Galatia (Galatians 3:1-5); and, apparently, decades after Peter's first meeting with Cornelius, there were still Jewish believers in Jerusalem who doubted the genuineness of the Gentiles' faith.

Paul viewed the collection for the destitute Jerusalem believers as concrete evidence that the Gentile believers were *obedient to the Good News of Christ*. One of the directives of the Jerusalem Council was that Gentile Christians shouldn't forget the poor (see Galatians 2:10). The Gentiles' generous gift to the Jerusalem poor would prove that they were obeying this directive. Paul never viewed the Jerusalem collection as a rite of initiation for the Gentiles. He was always perfectly clear that salvation came only through faith in Jesus (Galatians 3:26). Giving back to God, however, is one of many signs that a person's faith is authentic (see also James 2:14-18).

9:14 And they will pray for you with deep affection because of the wonderful grace of God shown through you.[NLT] The collection for the Jerusalem believers would not only demonstrate the sincerity of the Corinthians' faith, it would also tie the Christian community of faith closer together. Jewish Christians would view the monetary gift as an indication of God's *wonderful grace* working in the Corinthians' lives. Why would any Gentile— whether a Galatian or a Greek—give generously to the Jews in Jerusalem? Many of the Jews were not even citizens of the Roman Empire. They were a poor, minority group within the empire, with not much clout. Only God's undeserved grace in their lives could motivate them to give (see 8:8-9).

Some Jewish Christians in the first century still found it difficult to accept Gentiles into the community of faith. This generous gift might be the one thing that would prompt these Jews to start praying for the Corinthian believers for the first time. Just as the Corinthians' prayers for Paul made them partners with him in sharing the gospel (1:11), so these prayers of Jewish Christians would make them partners with Gentile believers. Through the Jerusalem collection, Jesus would begin to unite Jews and Gentiles into one body, the church (see Galatians 3:28). They were all becoming part of Jesus' body; each was dependent on the other. The Gentiles had relied on the Jews to tell them the wonderful Good News of Jesus, while the Jews were relying on the Gentiles to support them financially (see Paul's explanation of the offering at Romans 15:26-27). Through this, the entire community of faith—Jewish and Gentile Christians—would be built up in love.

9:15 Thanks be to God for His indescribable gift!^{NKJV} Paul ended his appeal for giving with fervent praise to God. The source of all this—the ability to give, the desire to give, even the reconciliation that would occur between Jewish and Gentile believers— was solely from God's hands. God is the ultimate Giver.

This verse may be saying that the whole process from giver to recipient is an *indescribable gift* from God. But since Paul used the Greek word for "gift" that is commonly used for Jesus' gift of righteousness (see Romans 5:15), Paul certainly was thanking God here for Jesus' gift of salvation. That God freely saves all those who believe in Jesus is truly an "indescribable gift." God's extraordinary gift of salvation should motivate you to give generously to others. Spend time meditating on how much God has given you. Then evaluate your generosity in light of God's generosity to you.

THANKFUL
Thankfulness puts everything in the right perspective; God gives what is needed for service, comfort, expression, and recreation.

Thankful people can worship wholeheartedly. Gratitude opens our hearts to God's peace and enables believers to put on love.

To increase your thankfulness, take an inventory of all you have (include your relationships, memories, abilities, and family, as well as material possessions). Use the inventory for prayers of gratitude. Before worship, pause and reflect on reasons for thanks. Celebrate God's goodness.

---

2 Corinthians 10

We will punish those who remained disobedient after the rest of you became loyal and obedient. (2 Corinthians 10:6 NLT)
We will be just as demanding and forceful in person as we are in our letters. (2 Corinthians 10:11 NLT)

Paul's message in the last four chapters of 2 Corinthians is obvious: The Corinthians had better shape up before his next visit (10:6, 11; 13:2, 10). Clearly chapter 10 introduces a drastic change of tone in 2 Corinthians: from conciliatory to severe. In the first nine chapters, Paul was careful to congratulate the Corinthians for their obedience to his latest directives (2:5-11; 7:2-15). The last four chapters, however, warn the Corinthians in no uncertain terms to reform their ways (10:6, 11; 13:2, 5). The first half of the letter uses diplomatic language (see 3:1; 5:12), while the second half contains scathing sarcasm (11:7-8, 19).

Because of this drastic change in tone, some commentators have asserted that the last four chapters of 2 Corinthians are in reality the "severe letter" spoken of in 7:8 (see the introduction). Even though this theory has gained popularity, there are other ways to explain the differences in tone. First, Paul may have been using the time-honored strategy of complimenting a person before criticizing him or her. In 2 Corinthians, Paul first commended the Corinthians for their obedience to his recent instructions so they would be open to changing their behavior in other areas. The commendation would prepare them to accept the more harsh aspects of what he had to say: for example, the fact that on his next visit he would discipline those who oppose his authority (see 2 Corinthians 13:1-3). Another way to explain the change of tone is to assume that there was an extended pause in the writing of 2 Corinthians at 10:1. During this pause, Paul received distressing news of what was occurring in Corinth, and he appropriately addressed those issues with a more severe tone.

In any case, it is clear that the first nine chapters of 2 Corinthians have a cautious and measured tone that points to an uneasy relationship between Paul and the Corinthians. Paul had to explain the intent of what he was saying (3:1-2; 5:12-14; 7:3-4), had to defend his recent travel plans (1:17), and had to beg for the Corinthians' affection (6:11-12; 7:2). Although Paul and the Corinthians had been reconciled to a certain extent (see 7:7, 12-16), there were persistent problems in their relationship. Whatever the exact cause of Paul's change of tone in chapter 10, it is obvious that certain difficulties in the Corinthian church deserved a more harsh tone. Paul had already cautiously defended his authority (3:1-6), his ministry (5:19-21), and his integrity (8:20). He had already commended the Corinthians for their hospitality (7:13) and their eagerness to give (9:2). At this point in 2 Corinthians, Paul was ready to admonish the Corinthians to change their ways (11:3-4, 12-14; 13:5).

10:1 Now I, Paul, plead with you. I plead with the gentleness and kindness that Christ himself would use, even though some of you say I am bold in my letters but timid in person.[NLT] Although most of the Corinthian congregation sided with Paul (as is evident from 7:8-16), a persistent minority continued to slander him. (This group of critics may have been associated with the repentant offender of 2:5-11, but no one knows for certain.) The group impugned Paul's integrity by pointing out that he was *bold* in his letters but *timid in person*—in other words, reluctant to exercise any authority when he visited them. Paul's critics saw this as duplicity and an indication that Paul truly didn't possess the spiritual authority he claimed. Chapters 10 through 13 are Paul's direct response to his critics in Corinth.

Rarely did *Paul* use his own name in the middle of a letter (for the exceptions, see Colossians 1:23; Philemon 1:19). Paul commonly identified himself at the beginning and the end of his letters (see 1 Corinthians 1:1; 16:21; Colossians 1:1; 4:18; 2 Thessalonians 1:1; 3:17). But he identified himself at this point in 2 Corinthians because his own reputation and the truth of what he preached were under attack.

This harsh section of 2 Corinthians (chapter 10 through 13) begins with kind and gentle words. Paul used the Greek verb *parakalo* for "plead" that officials within the Roman Empire, who had full authority to order and command, used to ask someone in a polite way to do something. By using this word, Paul was in no way conceding anything to his opponents: He *did* have the authority to command. Yet Paul consciously refused to exercise his authority in an overbearing manner. Instead of commanding, he asked. (Paul used this same strategy in 2:8; 6:1; 12:18; see also Romans 12:1; 1 Corinthians 1:10; 4:13, 16; 16:15; 1 Thessalonians 4:1.) Because he refused to act authoritatively, his opponents accused him of being timid and cowardly.

Jesus *Christ* was Paul's model in the approach he took here. Although Jesus possessed complete heavenly authority, he came to this earth as a servant (Philippians 2:5-11). Instead of commanding obedience and respect, Jesus simply asks for people to believe in him. Following Christ's example, the apostle Paul, who possessed full authority from Jesus (2:17; 5:19), merely pleaded with the Corinthians. In this way, Paul was showing them Christ's *gentleness and kindness.* The Greek word for "gentleness" has the idea of "forbearance"—like that of a benevolent judge being lenient on the guilty. "Kindness" speaks of friendliness and cheerfulness. In other words, Paul wasn't going to act like a harsh and overbearing judge. He already had reputed any idea that he was trying to be a "lord" over their souls (see 1:24).

10:2 I beg you that when I come I may not have to be as bold as I expect to be toward some people who think that we live by the standards of this world.^{NIV} Here Paul explained why he was writing this letter. He was hoping and praying that when he came, everything would be in order in the church (see 13:7). Paul had already said that he wasn't writing to condemn them (see 7:3). Instead, he was writing so that when he came to Corinth, he wouldn't have to be *bold.* Paul didn't want to spend his time disciplining the errant members of the Corinthian church when he could be building them up and encouraging them (see 13:10). This was the same reason that Paul had postponed his visit to Corinth in the first place (2:1-2). He wanted to give the Corinthians enough time to deal with the difficulties in their church on their own.

Paul was acting like a wise and patient father, sensibly giving the Corinthians time and space to sort out what was right versus what was wrong, what was true versus what was false. Paul didn't leave them without guidance, however. He sent official representatives, such as Titus, with stern warnings (2:3-4). In the end, he wanted to give the Corinthians an opportunity to mature in the faith on their own. Second Corinthians was Paul's last warning to the church (see 13:1-5). Within short order, he was going to visit Corinth. Titus was traveling ahead to deliver this letter and prepare the Corinthians for Paul's visit (8:16-24). If the believers didn't resolve the disputes within their church (13:1) and punish those who persisted in sin (13:2) before Paul came, he would do it himself. Titus and the representatives from the Macedonian churches would act as witnesses to all that Paul would do (see 9:4).

This verse also clearly identifies Paul's critics: *some people who think that we live by the standards of this world.* Apparently, Paul's opponents in Corinth were accusing him of making decisions and preaching according to worldly standards instead of God's holy standards. In the first chapter of 2 Corinthians, Paul had already defended his recent travel plans from just such an accusation (see 1:17).

10:3 We are human, but we don't wage war with human plans and methods.NLT In this verse the Greek word *sarx,* commonly translated "flesh," is translated here as "human plans and methods." With this word, Paul was clearly contrasting human standards with God's standards.

Paul freely admitted that he was *human.* Paul lived in a human body that was susceptible to all kinds of difficulties, oversights, and weaknesses. Yet he refused to admit that he waged spiritual *war with human plans and methods.* As he would do in his letter to the Ephesians, Paul equated the Christian life to a war. This war isn't "against flesh and blood, but against the rulers, against the authorities, against the powers of this dark world and against the spiritual forces of evil in the heavenly realms" (Ephesians 6:12 NIV). The Christian life is a spiritual battle against spiritual forces aligned against Christ. Fighting this spiritual battle with weapons of the world—with physical strength, worldly strategies, and material wealth—would be foolish. A spiritual battle requires spiritual weapons that can only come from God.

10:4-5 We use God's mighty weapons, not mere worldly weapons, to knock down the Devil's strongholds. With these weapons we break down every proud argument that keeps people from knowing God. With these weapons we conquer their rebellious ideas, and we teach them to obey Christ.NLT According to Paul's Epistle to the Ephesians, *God's mighty weapons* are faith, truth, righteousness, the gospel message, and the Word of God. The Holy Spirit equips Christians for the struggle, providing the weapons they need (see 6:6; Ephesians 6:10-20).

Worldly weapons—wealth, fame, and political might—may wield some power on this earth, but they are useless in spiritual battles. Trickery and deception may be effective in dealing with other people, but only truth will achieve success in the spiritual realm. Cynicism may protect a person from betrayal, but only faith in God will empower a believer in his or her spiritual struggles. A willingness to flout conventional morality might gain someone a following in this world, but only persistently following God's righteous ways will ensure victory in the spiritual realm.

Paul didn't consider the mighty Roman armies and the extraordinary affluence of the Roman emperor as the true *strongholds* of evil (see Proverbs 21:22 for an allusion to strongholds). Instead, he saw the strongholds of evil as being *proud arguments* against Christianity, and *rebellious ideas.* The world of ideas is the real battleground for God and the Devil. In Greek, the words for "proud argument" connotes logic or reasoning that attempts to divert people from the gospel. *Rebellious ideas* in Greek is "high things raised up." The wording recalls the story of Babel, where people attempted to build a high tower to celebrate their own greatness (Genesis 11:1-9). Paul described these "high things" as being raised up "against the knowledge of God" (NRSV). Paul wasn't referring to a tall building here, but to every complex theory or philosophy that blocks people from knowing the truth about God and worshiping him. These false philosophies that divert glory from God and hide the truth are the *Devil's strongholds.* Just as an army would attack a fortress, so Christians must take apart and defeat these false and evil arguments.

In Corinth, where advances in Greek philosophy were held in high esteem, the believers were tempted to evaluate the gospel with the various tools of Greek philosophy. In an earlier letter, Paul had already told the Corinthians that the gospel would appear as foolishness to those who saw the world through the lenses of secular Greek philosophy (see 1 Corinthians 1:22). Paul had experienced this himself. When he had presented the gospel to the philosophers who gathered in Athens, they had responded with insults and taunts (see Acts 17:32). To these philosophers, the gospel was pure folly.

GOD'S WAR
Like Paul, we are merely weak humans, but we don't need to use human plans and methods to win our battles. God's mighty weapons are available to us as we fight against Satan's "strongholds" (10:4). The Christian must choose whose methods to use, God's or the world's. Paul assures us that God's mighty weapons—prayer, faith, hope, love, God's Word, the Holy Spirit—are powerful and effective (see Ephesians 6:13-18)! These weapons can break down the proud human arguments against God and the walls that Satan builds to keep people from finding God. When dealing with the pride that keeps people from a relationship with Christ, you may be tempted to use human weapons and methods. But only God can break down these barriers.

10:6 And we will punish those who remained disobedient after the rest of you became loyal and obedient.^{NLT} This spells out what this divine arsenal would mean to the Corinthian church. Paul wouldn't hesitate on his next visit to use those spiritual weapons entrusted to him to *punish those who remained disobedient.*

But notice how Paul attached a condition to his exercising of his authority. He would not do so until *the rest of* the Corinthian believers recommitted themselves to be *obedient* to the gospel. According to Titus's recent report, the majority of the Corinthians had already

> Faith and obedience are bound up in the same bundle. He that obeys God, trusts God; and he that trusts God obeys God. *Charles H. Spurgeon*

done this. They had been filled with godly sorrow about the recent problems in their church and had made the necessary steps toward reconciling themselves to Paul (see 7:7-13). From the way Paul carefully defended his ministry in this letter (see 1:12-18; 3:1-5; 5:11-17), it is clear that there was still a rebellious minority in the church (see 2:17). At the end of this letter, Paul promised to deal sternly with this minority on his next visit. Paul couldn't stand by and watch these "false apostles" (11:13) mislead the church anymore.

UNHEALTHY THOUGHTS
Spirit-empowered believers must capture every thought and yield it to Christ (10:5). An old saying contends that you can't keep the birds from flying overhead, but you can keep them from building a nest in your hair. When exposed to ideas or opportunities that can easily engage your imagination, you have a choice. You can recognize the danger and turn away, or you can allow unhealthy thoughts to take you captive. Your thoughts need not control your choices if they are laid before the One who gives you the mind of Christ. You capture your fantasies and desires when you honestly admit them to the Lord and ask him to redirect your thinking. Ask God to give you the spirit of discernment to keep your thoughts focused on his truth.

10:7 You are looking only on the surface of things.^{NIV} Paul encouraged the Corinthians to adjust their perspective. They had been *looking only on the surface of things*—listening intently to the false teachers who were boasting of themselves—their own authority (10:12-13), their perfect Hebrew heritage (11:21-22), and their visionary experiences (12:11-12). All of their loud boasts and extravagant displays of power had dazzled the Corinthians so much that they had become blind to the simplicity of

the gospel message that Paul had preached to them in the first
place (1 Corinthians 2:1-3).

**You must recognize that we belong to Christ just as much as
those who proudly declare that they belong to Christ.**NLT The
false teachers who had infiltrated the Corinthian church were
claiming to be teachers of Christ. Since they were from Judea
(11:21-22), their claims may have included some knowledge or
acquaintance with Jesus during his ministry on earth. In any case,
Paul matched their claim to belong *to Christ.* The Corinthians
would have certainly known about Paul's personal encounter
with Jesus on the Damascus road, the encounter that had changed
Paul forever (see Acts 9:1-10).

Here Paul challenged those who were doubting his authority to
consider carefully the evidence for Paul's own relationship to
Jesus: First, the undeniably changed lives of people who believed
in the message he preached (3:1-5); second, the integrity with
which he faithfully presented the gospel message (4:1-5); third,
the hardships he had endured for the cause of Christ (6:3-10;
11:23-29); and finally, the fact that Christ himself had commissioned him to be an apostle to the Gentiles (1:21-22; 5:20-21; 6:1-
2; 10:8; 12:2-4).

10:8 **For even if I boast somewhat freely about the authority the
Lord gave us for building you up rather than pulling you down,
I will not be ashamed of it.**NIV Although Paul's opponents had portrayed him as weak and powerless, Paul reminded the Corinthians
that he did possess God-given *authority* (see 1:21-22; 5:20-21).
False teachers were encouraging the believers to ignore Paul, but
he maintained that what he had written in his letters was to be taken
seriously. Paul possessed the authority from *the Lord* to exhort the
Corinthians. Although he would not boast in himself or compare
himself to other preachers, he would boast in the Lord and in the
authority that Jesus had given him to preach the gospel that saves
(see 10:12-13, 17-18; see also 1 Corinthians 1:31).

Unlike the false teachers who had come to Corinth, Paul knew
the limits of his authority (compare with 10:13-14). He wasn't
given the authorization to pull down the church. His mission was
to build up the church throughout the world. When Paul had first
visited Corinth to preach the gospel, he was faithful to his mission. He had built the Corinthian church on the gospel truths relating to Jesus (1 Corinthians 3:9-13; see also Acts 18:4-6). Paul's
mission was constructive, not destructive. That is why he had hes-
itated to visit them. Paul was afraid that his visit would cause
more pain than was necessary (1:23-24; 12:19-21).

10:9 I do not want to seem to be trying to frighten you with my letters.^{NIV} Apparently Paul's critics at Corinth had attacked Paul's letters as not only being hard to understand (see Paul's defense of the straightforwardness of his letters in 1:13) but also written *to frighten* them. Paul's last letter to the Corinthians had been harsh. Paul had even cried over it (2:3-4). The letter was necessary, however, because Paul had to work through some troublesome situations in the church.

10:10 For some say, "His letters are weighty and forceful, but in person he is unimpressive and his speaking amounts to nothing."^{NIV} Greece was known for its eloquent and persuasive orators. Corinth, a prominent Greek city at this time, was filled with trained speakers. Apparently, some of the Corinthian believers (perhaps encouraged by the false teachers among them) were judging Paul's speaking ability. He had already admitted to the Corinthians that he had consciously avoided dependence on rhetoric or human philosophy when he had presented the gospel of salvation to them (see 1 Corinthians 2:1-3). He wanted the message to speak for itself, unencumbered by such distractions.

10:11 Such people should realize that what we are in our letters when we are absent, we will be in our actions when we are present.^{NIV} In the past, Paul had refrained from disciplining members of the Corinthian church in person. He had warned them to stop sinning (see 13:2) on several occasions and had written letters encouraging them to discipline persistent sinners (see 1 Corinthians 5:1-5). Paul had used these indirect methods to encourage the leaders of the Corinthian church to take charge of the situation and discipline their own members. Paul even had promised to go along with the judgments they used to make (see 1 Corinthians 1:5; see also 2:6-10). Because his more accommodating approach wasn't working with the Corinthians, however, Paul assured them that on his next visit he would exercise his authority (13:3-4), punishing those who had not taken his warnings to heart earlier (13:1-2).

10:12 We do not dare to classify or compare ourselves with some of those who commend themselves. But when they measure themselves by one another, and compare themselves with one another, they do not show good sense.^{NRSV} Here Paul went on the offensive. Although his critics had dared to *commend themselves,* Paul would *not dare* compare himself with them or anyone else. Any ability he possessed was a gift from God; therefore, God deserved the full credit for it.

GOD'S STANDARD
Paul criticized the false teachers who were trying to prove their goodness by comparing themselves with others rather than with God's standards (10:12). Those who compare themselves with others may feel pride because they think they're better. But when measured against God's standards, it becomes obvious that no one has any basis for pride. Don't worry about other people's accomplishments. Instead, continually ask: How does my life measure up to what God wants? How does my life compare to that of Jesus Christ?

Yet Paul's opponents in Corinth didn't shrink from measuring and comparing themselves *with one another.* In so doing, they were robbing God of the glory that was due to him (10:17). Instead of waiting for God to commend them, they were lavishly praising themselves. Because the Corinthians tended to focus on appearances (see 5:12, 16; 10:7), they had been successfully duped by the false teachers' slick presentation (11:4, 19-20). Meanwhile, Paul, who appropriately refrained from any boasting, was accused by the Corinthians of being "unimpressive" (10:10 NIV). Although the Corinthians claimed to be wise, they didn't recognize that the pretentious boasts of Paul's opponents did *not show good sense* (10:17-18). Because of the power these false teachers were consolidating in the congregation, Paul was finally forced to spell it out: These teachers were foolish, loud-mouthed braggarts!

MEASURING UP
It was unthinkable for the apostle Paul to compare himself with other so-called leaders who spent their time commending themselves (10:12). Paul understood that his task as a messenger of the gospel demanded humility. He knew his weaknesses, both physically and rhetorically, and he was quite confident of his strengths. But even his abilities were gifts of God for which he could not take full credit. It is senseless to compare oneself and one's ministry with what others are achieving. Each person has been assigned his or her own task and his or her own abilities. As you look in the mirror tomorrow morning, take a long, close look. That person looking back at you is unlike any other person God has created. You are unique. So are your talents and abilities. Your accomplishments are filtered through a sieve of an imperfect personality and mixed motives. So too is that person whose ministry you envy. Your ministry is hindered when you compare yourself with others. Spend a few moments confessing your envy and jealousy. Then thank the Lord for creating you the way he did.

10:13 **We, however, will not boast beyond limits, but will keep within the field that God has assigned to us, to reach out even as far as you.**NRSV Because the Corinthians had listened to these false teachers, they were forcing Paul to *boast* in order to silence his critics (see 11:1–12:13). Here Paul explained the grounds on which he was boasting. To boast in himself and in his own accomplishments would have been entirely inappropriate. Only God deserved honor, for he had given Paul his abilities.

What could Paul boast about? Paul could only boast in God and in the tasks God had assigned him. Paul regarded his assignment at Corinth as within his proper *limits*. Apparently, Paul saw the false teachers as invading his *field*—in other words, usurping the responsibilities God had *assigned* to him. Paul was expressing that Corinth was well within the field or territory that God had measured out to him.

10:14 **For we were not overstepping our limits when we reached you; we were the first to come all the way to you with the good news of Christ.**NRSV How did Paul know that God had given him Corinth as part of his responsibility? It was because Paul and his companions *were the first to come all the way to* the Corinthians with the gospel: He was the founder of the Corinthian church, and as such could exercise authority over the congregation. That should have been obvious to the believers in Corinth. But Paul had another reason for considering the Corinthians well within his *limits*. The Holy Spirit had commissioned him as a missionary to the Gentiles (Acts 22:21). The Christian leaders in Jerusalem had confirmed his commission:

> *They saw that I had been entrusted with the task of preaching the gospel to the Gentiles, just as Peter had been to the Jews. (Galatians 2:7* NIV*)*

This confirmation by the Jerusalem elders amounted to a division of evangelistic labor: Paul was to preach to the Gentiles, while Peter was to preach to the Jews. Paul had stayed within his limits. Had these teachers who had come from Judea (see 11:22) stayed within their limits?

Although Paul might have been concerned about these teachers from Judea breaking his agreement with the Jerusalem elders, it is clear that Paul's primary concern was that these teachers were misleading the believers in Corinth. Paul had welcomed in the past any teacher of the truth, such as Apollos, to build on the foundation he had laid (see 1 Corinthians 3:5-13). In the final analysis, however, the Corinthians had only one founder: Paul himself (see 1 Corinthians 4:14-16). If anyone could claim authority over the Corinthian congregation, he could. Ironically, it was his authority that was being called into question.

10:15-16 We do not boast beyond limits, that is, in the labors of others.^{NRSV} Paul refused to *boast* in the fruit of the *labors* of other evangelists, as the false teachers were doing with the Corinthians (the fruit of Paul's hard labor among them).

Paul used a Greek word for "labors" that connoted physically demanding labor. Paul had indeed supported his own evangelistic efforts in Corinth by making tents out of goat-hair cloth (see Acts 18:1-3). He didn't even shrink from persecution at the hands of the Jews (Acts 18:12-17). The Corinthian church had been established because of Paul's willingness to suffer hardship.

But our hope is that, as your faith increases, our sphere of action among you may be greatly enlarged, so that we may proclaim the good news in lands beyond you, without boasting of work already done in someone else's sphere of action.^{NRSV} Unlike the traveling preachers who had come to live off the Corinthian congregation (see 2:17), Paul envisioned his evangelistic ministry as expanding into unevangelized regions. He would never plan on invading regions that had already been evangelized by some other teacher. In order to do this, however, the Corinthians' *faith* had to increase. As they matured in the faith, Paul could enlarge his *sphere of action*. Paul might have been implying that as the Corinthians matured in their faith, he could spend less time guiding them in their Christian walk. As mature Christians, they would not only be less dependent on Paul to solve their congregation's problems, but they would also start supporting Paul as he launched evangelistic missions *beyond* them into completely unevangelized areas. From Paul's letter to the Romans, we know that Paul's vision included reaching Spain with the Good News (see Romans 15:24).

10:17-18 "Let the one who boasts, boast in the Lord." For it is not those who commend themselves that are approved, but those whom the Lord commends.^{NRSV} The following chapters list some of Paul's ministerial credentials and accomplishments. Paul was extremely cautious about boasting about himself; first of all, so that he might not rob the honor that God deserved (11:30-31), and secondly so that he might not be misunderstood as praising himself (see 5:12-13; 10:13; 11:16-18). The situation in Corinth, however, had forced Paul to set aside his scruples about boasting in order to save the Corinthian church from ruin. By touting his credentials—the credentials the Corinthians should have recog-

PAUL'S CREDENTIALS

One of Paul's biggest problems with the church in Corinth was his concern that they viewed him as no more than a blustering preacher; thus, they were not taking seriously his advice in his letters and on his visits. Paul addressed this attitude in the letter of 2 Corinthians, pointing out his credentials as an apostle of Christ and why the Corinthians should take his advice.

1:1, 21; 4:1	Commissioned by God
1:18; 4:2	Spoke truthfully
1:12	Acted in holiness, sincerity, and dependence on God alone in his dealings with them
1:13-14	Was straightforward and sincere in his letters
1:22	Had God's Holy Spirit
2:4; 6:11; 11:11	Loved the Corinthian believers
2:17	Spoke with sincerity and Christ's authority
3:2-3	Worked among the Corinthians and changed their lives
4:1, 16	Did not lose heart
4:2	Taught the Bible with integrity
4:5	Had Christ as the center of his message
4:8-12; 6:4-5, 9-10	Endured persecution as he taught the Good News
5:18-20	Was Christ's ambassador, called to tell the Good News
6:3-4	Tried to live an exemplary life so that others would not be kept from God
6:6	Led a pure life, understood the gospel, and displayed patience with the Corinthians
6:7	Was truthful and filled with God's power
6:8	Stood true to God first and always
7:2; 11:7-9	Never corrupted or exploited anyone
8:20-21	Handled the Corinthians' offering for the Jerusalem believers in a responsible, blameless manner
10:1-6	Used God's weapons, not his own, for God's work
10:7-8	Was confident that he belonged to Christ
10:12-13	Boasted not in himself but in the Lord
10:14-15	Had authority because he taught them the Good News
11:23-33	Endured pain and danger as he fulfilled his calling
12:2-4	Was blessed with an astounding vision
12:7-10	Was constantly humbled by a "thorn in the flesh" that God refused to take away
12:12	Did miracles among the Corinthians
12:19	Was always motivated to strengthen others spiritually
13:4	Was filled with God's power
13:9	Was always concerned that his spiritual children become mature believers

nized in the first place—Paul hoped to discredit the false teachers who had infiltrated the church (11:12).

Paul paraphrased Jeremiah 9:24 in order to emphasize to the Corinthians that he knew he was treading on shaky ground. The Old Testament passage was especially relevant because it was an indictment against false teachers who took pride in their wisdom and their speaking abilities (10:9-10):

> *This is what the Lord says: "Let not the wise man gloat in his wisdom, or the mighty man in his might, or the rich man in his riches. Let them boast in this alone: that they truly know me and understand that I am the Lord who is just and righteous, whose love is unfailing, and that I delight in these things. I, the Lord, have spoken!" (Jeremiah 9:23-24 NLT)*

Only those who seek after God and make it a priority to know and love him are *approved* by God. Only those who bring honor and praise to God, instead of themselves, are those people in whom God delights; and, in the end, only God's approval counts. In light of eternity, it really doesn't matter how other people judge us.

SELF-ACCLAMATION
When those who do something well seek recognition and receive it, they can become proud. How much better it is to seek the praise of God rather than the praise of people. Then, when praise comes, you will be free to give God the credit. What should you change about the way you live in order to receive God's commendation?

---

2 Corinthians 11

Because the Corinthians were easily impressed by résumés (11:21-23), articulate and persuasive speakers (11:6), and shows of spiritual power (12:12), they had been duped by a group of false teachers. By consistently criticizing and accusing Paul, this group of upstart teachers had undermined Paul's authority in Corinth. Paul felt obligated to respond to their criticisms, point by point (11:21). He had founded the church and had the responsibility to keep the church on the right course (1 Corinthians 4:15).

11:1 I hope you will be patient with me as I keep on talking like a fool. Please bear with me.[NLT] Paul asked the Corinthian believers to *be patient* and *bear with* him as he spoke of his apostolic credentials. He felt foolish repeating his credentials because it was through his evangelistic efforts that he had founded the Corinthian church. There shouldn't be any reason for the Corinthians to question him; he was their father in the Christian faith (see 1 Corinthians 4:15). But because the Corinthians had been mesmerized by the rhetoric of these false teachers, dazzled by their claims to ecstatic spiritual experiences, and duped by their logic, Paul was forced to talk like a *fool,* to remind them of what he had done for the cause of Christ. It was against his principles to do this, for all honor, glory, and even boasts belonged to God (see 10:17). Yet Paul was in a dilemma. If he didn't speak up, the false teachers in Corinth might continue to lead the Corinthian believers astray. Paul had hoped that the believers would discern the emptiness of these false teachers' boasts, but they had not. As a spokesman for the truth, therefore, Paul couldn't stay silent; he had to speak up. In this case, speaking up for the truth meant defending his own credentials. If his own ministry was discredited, the gospel he preached would also be discredited.

11:2 I am jealous for you with the jealousy of God himself. For I promised you as a pure bride to one husband, Christ.[NLT] Paul was anxious that the Corinthian church's love should be reserved for Christ alone, just as a chaste virgin saves her love for her groom. In the first century, an engagement was a serious commitment, similar to a contract. If the *bride* wasn't a virgin on the wedding day, it was considered a breach of the engagement contract. Ensuring the bride's purity and virginity until the wedding day was partially her father's responsibility.

Paul had already described himself as the Corinthians' spiritual father (see 1 Corinthians 4:15). This passage depicts his concern for the Corinthians as a father's concern for the purity of his daughter. Paul had already *promised* the Corinthians *as a pure bride to one husband, Christ.* He was anticipating that wonderful day when he would present them proudly to Jesus. That day when Christ returns will be like a great wedding feast, an image that Jesus himself had used for his second coming (see Matthew 25:1-11). To guarantee that he would not be embarrassed at Christ's return, Paul took the necessary steps to discourage the Corinthians not to stray from their pure devotion to Christ (11:3). He was willing to indulge in some foolish boasting in order to make the Corinthians come back to their senses and ignore the diversions of these false teachers, who had invaded Corinth preaching a different Jesus (11:4).

JEALOUSY
Paul was jealous for the Corinthian church (11:2). Jealousy is not always wrong. Righteous jealousy is an overwhelming desire for another's well-being, based on sincere love, not on self-gratification. Jealousy is portrayed in the Old Testament when God refuses to let his rebellious people self-destruct. It is the jealous love that Paul attributed to God in Romans 8:38-39: "For I am convinced that neither death nor life, neither angels nor demons, neither the present nor the future, nor any powers, neither height nor depth, nor anything else in all creation, will be able to separate us from the love of God that is in Christ Jesus our Lord" (NIV). With this kind of jealous fervor, Paul watched over those with whom God had entrusted him. Believers, too, must show concern for others. Of those who have come to Christ under your tutelage, how many are still growing in their faith? If they still look to you as their primary spiritual advisor, when is the last time you had contact with them? Are you aware of outside influences that are competing for their time and energy? Don't let the day conclude without spending time in prayer for them.

Thus, the *jealousy* that motivated Paul wasn't a jealousy for his own reputation or his own power. This can be clearly seen in Paul's words: He boasted in his weaknesses, trials, and difficulties, instead of in his strengths, accomplishments, and successes (see especially 11:30-33). This jealousy was a godly jealousy for the Corinthians: that they might wholeheartedly follow Christ, their Savior (11:3-4).

Although Paul welcomed any godly teacher, such as Apollos, to instruct the Corinthians in the essentials of the Christian faith (see his praise of Apollo's work in 1 Corinthians 3:6), he opposed any teacher who preached a different Christ or a different gospel, as the false teachers in Corinth had been doing.

11:3 But I am afraid that as the serpent deceived Eve by its cunning, your thoughts will be led astray from a sincere and pure devotion to Christ.^{NRSV} Eve represents innocence and purity. This passage compares the serpent's temptation to the temptation of the false teachers' enticing message. The Corinthians had begun their Christian walk with a sincere and pure devotion to Christ. But false teachers were luring Corinthian believers away from the truth. Paul didn't want the believers' single-minded love for Christ to be corrupted. The Greek word Paul used for "led astray" actually means "to ruin." The Corinthians weren't merely wandering slightly from the path; they were soiling their purity.

Although some commentators see an allusion in this passage to the sexual immorality that may have persisted in the Corinthian church (see 1 Corinthians 6:9-20), the focus here is on the Corinthians' *thoughts*. Sin begins with thoughts. The serpent first tried to convince Eve that God's law was not the best for her, that the advantages of disobeying God outweighed the advantage of obeying him. The serpent's deception was primarily directed against what Eve thought about God and his instructions (Genesis 3:1-6). Satan knew that once the mind was convinced, actions would soon follow. Eve was persuaded by Satan's lies and subsequently reached out to pluck the forbidden fruit. In the same way, the false teachers were Satan's servants, deceiving the Corinthians to abandon their wholehearted devotion to Christ (see 11:14-15). Paul knew that thoughts are the primary battleground for spiritual warfare (see 10:5). That is why he took these false teachers so seriously. Paul equated the false teachers' success with Satan's victory in the spiritual war that was being waged in the Corinthian church.

LISTENING
The Corinthian believers fell for smooth talk and messages that sounded good and seemed to make sense (11:3). Today, many false teachings seem to make sense. Don't believe someone simply because he or she sounds like an authority or says words you like to hear. Search the Bible and check each message against God's Word. The Bible should be your authoritative guide. Don't listen to any "authoritative preacher" who contradicts God's Word.

Just as Eve lost her focus by listening to the serpent, believers too can lose their focus by letting their lives become crowded and confused. Is there anything that weakens your commitment to keep Christ first in your life?

11:4 For if someone comes and proclaims another Jesus than the one we proclaimed, or if you receive a different spirit from the one you received, or a different gospel from the one you accepted, you submit to it readily enough.^{NRSV} The false teachers who had come to Corinth had distorted the truth about Jesus and ended up preaching a different *Jesus,* a *different spirit* than the Holy Spirit, and a *different gospel* than God's way of salvation.

Exactly how the false teaching was different from the gospel Paul preached has intrigued biblical scholars for centuries. Because Paul spent most of his time in this letter defending his authority instead of addressing any doctrinal errors, 2 Corinthians offers few clues.

Some commentators have suggested that this "different gospel" was the legalism preached by Judaizers to the Galatians (see Galatians 3:1-6). Galatians 1:6-9 describes this legalist teaching as a different gospel. As evidence for this view, these commentators point to how Paul carefully differentiated the new covenant from the old, the gospel of Christ from the message of Moses (see Galatians 3:7-18). The false teachers in Corinth were certainly Jews who were bragging about their Jewish heritage (11:22). Moreover, Paul called them "servants of righteousness" (11:15), an apt term for the legalistic Jews who were enslaving Gentiles with a righteousness that was obtained from the law. Thus, according to this view, the "other Jesus" that the false teachers preached was a Jesus who taught obedience to Jewish laws as the way to salvation.

But many commentators don't believe that Paul's opponents in Corinth were legalists because Paul didn't discuss the law in 2 Corinthians. Instead of discussing the law, Paul reinforced over and over that his credentials as an apostle came directly from Christ. And as proof of his authority, Christ had demonstrated his power through Paul's weaknesses (3:1-5; 4:8-12; 6:3-10; 11:16-33). Apparently the false teachers were boasting of their superior credentials (3:1; 11:22), their speaking ability (10:10; 11:6), and their ecstatic spiritual experiences (12:1, 12). They had begun to compare their ministry to Paul's, denigrating his abilities and credentials in order to highlight their own competence.

The Greeks were known for the way they valued polished oratory and erudition. (See 1 Corinthians 1:22, where Paul described

the Greek infatuation with their own wisdom.) The Isthmian
Games, held at Corinth, featured many speech contests in which
contestants would extemporaneously speak on a given subject.
The speaker who could impress the audience with his polished
delivery would win. It could be conjectured that the false teachers who had come to Corinth from Judea (11:22) were thoroughly
familiar with Greek ways. They knew Greek customs and the
Greek language so well that they could present themselves to
Corinthians as polished Greek orators. Although they were Jewish, they imitated the Greek teachers who traveled throughout the
Mediterranean world, trying to impress their audience and earn
money by doing so. In fact, Paul had accused them in 2:17 of
being peddlers of God's Word. Thus the false teachers were teaching "another Jesus," one who, like them, was a powerful speaker
and a wonder worker—not the suffering and crucified Jesus
whom Paul preached (see 1 Corinthians 1:23; Philippians 2:5-11).

Because of the sparse amount of evidence in 2 Corinthians, the
exact form of the false teachers' erroneous teaching cannot be
known. But whether it was a heresy dealing with the Jewish law
or a heresy dealing with Greek wisdom and knowledge (see
1 Corinthians 1:21-25), clearly the teaching was a different gospel and a different spirit than what Paul preached. The false teachers were distracting the Corinthians from the grace of God, the
only thing that could save them (see Paul's emphasis on grace in
1:12; 6:1; 9:8; 12:9). These false teachers' rhetoric, reasoning,
and boasts were drawing attention to themselves instead of pointing the Corinthians to God.

**11:5-6 But I do not think I am in the least inferior to those "super-
apostles." I may not be a trained speaker, but I do have
knowledge. We have made this perfectly clear to you in every
way.**NIV Paul, a brilliant thinker, was not trained in Greek rhetoric. He probably wasn't a spellbinding speaker. Although Paul's
preaching ministry was effective (see Acts 17), he had not been
trained in the Greek schools of oratory and speechmaking, as the
false teachers evidently had been. In fact, Paul avoided fine-
sounding arguments and lofty ideas in order to preach the simple
gospel message (see 1 Corinthians 1:17). Some of the Corinthians had begun to think that Paul's plain speaking style indicated a
simple-mindedness.

When confronted with these accusations, Paul didn't study
Greek rhetoric in order to compete with these trained orators.
Instead, he explained to the Corinthians that the gospel was a
scandal, a stumbling block (1 Corinthians 1:23). It wouldn't fit
into their preconceived notions of excellence. It was pure folly to

the wise of this world. God made the gospel simple because he
loves to circumvent the powerful in order to show how much he
can accomplish with those who are weak, powerless, inarticulate,
and foolish. Paul couldn't compete with the polished orators at
Corinth, and he didn't want to. Their message would be
applauded, while his simple message would be scorned (see the
response of the Greek philosophers in Acts 17:32). But it didn't
matter how the world responded to the gospel. No matter what
the response, the gospel Paul preached was still the message of
God's salvation, a message that the Holy Spirit would use to save
people from their sins and transform their lives (see Romans
1:16; 1 Corinthians 2:1-8).

Despite what his accusers *(those "super-apostles")* said, Paul
claimed that he did possess *knowledge,* but it wasn't the knowledge of the world and its ways. It was knowledge of the gospel
and how someone can become saved (Ephesians 3:3-6). Paul had
made every effort to preach this message in a *clear* and straightforward way (see 1:12-14; 1 Corinthians 2:4-5). He didn't want
to use sophisticated rhetoric or intricate arguments in order to persuade people. He simply wanted to preach the gospel.

SELF-ASSESSMENT
Paul conceded that he was not a trained speaker (11:5-6). But
that acknowledgment didn't undermine his message. He knew
that what mattered most was the knowledge he had to share,
not the package—not his ability to speak brilliantly. Teaching
the truths of the gospel was far more important. God's Word
stands on its own merit and is not dependent on imperfect
human beings to create its own hearing. Many people feel that
if they can't sing, speak, teach, or preach as well as their
idolized heroes, they are insecure about saying or doing
anything. Don't apologize for your inadequacies. Accept your
limitations with the same humility that you accept the strengths
God has given you to communicate.

**11:7 Was it a sin for me to lower myself in order to elevate you by
preaching the gospel of God to you free of charge?**[NIV] The
Corinthians evaluated a speaker by how much money he
demanded from his audience. A good speaker would charge a
large sum; a fair speaker would be cheaper; a poor speaker would
speak for free. Since Paul hadn't asked for money when he
preached in Corinth, some were accusing him of being an ama-
teur speaker.

In 1 Corinthians Paul had made it clear that he could have
demanded a wage or financial support, but he had chosen to

forego any payment in order to offer the gospel free of charge.
Jesus himself had taught that godly ministers could expect to be
supported by the people to whom they ministered (Matthew
10:10).

The reason why Paul hadn't asked for support when he first
came to Corinth was because he thought he would be misunderstood. Many teachers traveled the Roman Empire hoping to make
a good profit from their own speaking abilities (2:17), and Paul
thought that he might appear like one of them. Moreover, a
preacher or teacher who received substantial support from any
one person was expected to show gratitude to the patron. Usually
this amounted to preaching only what a patron approved. Paul
may have been wary of taking money from a person because he
thought he would be identified as a spokesmen for one group or
another. Paul was extremely careful to protect his freedom to
preach the unadulterated gospel message and let it speak for itself.

Instead of asking for a fee, as a professional speaker would do,
Paul supported himself by manual labor, working as a tentmaker
with Priscilla and Aquila (see Acts 18:1-3). Prominent Greeks
considered manual labor as beneath them. In Greco-Roman society, it was more honorable for a traveling teacher to beg than it
was for him to stoop to demeaning manual labor. In contrast, the
Jews respected manual labor. In fact, Jewish rabbis, teachers of
the law, were required to support themselves with some kind of
trade. Thus, when Paul supported himself as a tentmaker, he was
following his rabbinical training. The sophisticated teachers at
Corinth attacked Paul for doing this, trying to discredit his ministry by drawing attention to this fact. How could Paul, a mere
lower-class worker, teach them?

**11:8-9 I robbed other churches by receiving support from them so as
to serve you. And when I was with you and needed something,
I was not a burden to anyone, for the brothers who came
from Macedonia supplied what I needed. I have kept myself
from being a burden to you in any way, and will continue to
do so.**NIV Paul's language in these verses evokes a military metaphor. The Greek word for "support" was used in the first century
for a soldier's pay. The Greek word for "robbed" is a military
term that depicts how a first-century soldier would "strip bare"
his enemies. Thus, Paul was saying that in order to *serve* the
Corinthians he had, in effect, plundered the churches in *Macedonia* for his wages. This strong language may reflect the accusations of Paul's critics.

Although Paul had never taken any money from the Corinthians for his ministry (and was being criticized for that, 11:7), his

critics were (amazingly and somewhat ironically) also accusing
him of trying to rob the Corinthian church with the "ruse" of the
Jerusalem collection (see 8:16-21; 12:16-18). Paul must have
anticipated some of these problems, for from the start he had
refused to collect any money for the collection himself. Instead,
he had told the Corinthians to appoint people to collect the
money and deliver it. Paul wouldn't handle any of the money
(see 8:18-21; 1 Corinthians 16:1-3). He wouldn't make himself a
burden to the Corinthians, no matter what the situation was,
whether he *needed* support or not.

Why did Paul accept support from the Macedonian Christians
and refuse it from the Corinthians? Part of the answer to this
question is that the Macedonians were giving cheerfully (8:1-5).
The Corinthians, on the other hand, were accusing Paul of trying
to "exploit" them (12:17 NIV). The Macedonians wanted to give
freely with no strings attached; the Corinthians were using their
money to gain influence and power. So there would be no question about his motivations, Paul would *continue* to refuse com-
pensation. The Macedonians weren't questioning his authority,
but the Corinthians were.

**11:10-11 As surely as the truth of Christ is in me, nobody in the
regions of Achaia will stop this boasting of mine. Why?
Because I do not love you? God knows I do!**^{NIV} Paul knew that
the fact he hadn't taken any money from the Corinthians was the
strongest rebuttal to the false teachers, for their whole purpose in
preaching was to gather a following who would support them
(see 2:17). More than likely, they were the ones who had slowed
the collection for the Jerusalem Christians in order to divert the
funds to themselves. Paul hoped that his consistent integrity with
money would be one of the indicators that he was a preacher of
the truth, while his opponents were greedy peddlers of falsehoods
(2:17).

Why did Paul refuse support? Why did he boast in his own
integrity? Why did he oppose the false teachers? It was because
of his deep *love* for the Corinthians. As the founder of the
church of Corinth, Paul was concerned for the Corinthians' spiritual welfare. He was jealous for their spiritual purity (1:6, 23;
2:10).

**11:12 And what I do I will also continue to do, in order to deny an
opportunity to those who want an opportunity to be recognized as our equals in what they boast about.**^{NRSV} In order to
set the record straight, Paul wouldn't stop boasting that he had
preached the gospel free of charge (see 6:10; 7:2; 11:27; 12:16-
18; 1 Corinthians 9:3-18). Eventually, the Corinthians would

wake up to the fact that these false teachers, unlike Paul, were more interested in the money of the Corinthians than in their spiritual welfare.

Although Paul was being forced to boast foolishly about his own ministry, it was his consistent honesty and integrity—the way he had conducted himself around the Corinthians—that would silence his critics and answer their charges against him. These new preachers wanted to be recognized as "super-apostles" (11:5); but in reality, they could not be considered Paul's *equals.* They weren't willing to suffer, as Jesus had, to present the gospel free of charge.

LOVE 'EM OR LEAVE 'EM
Paul loved those to whom he was writing (11:11). What he wrote (as challenging and harsh as it is) must be understood against the backdrop of his undying commitment to their best interests. Those being taught can easily detect whether a pastor or teacher declaring God's Word has a sincere interest in their lives or only in disseminating information. People who know they are loved respond to truth and open their hearts to be filled by the Spirit. Do you love those to whom you open God's Word? Ask the Lord to make you tender to those you serve. As you stand before those faces, contemplate the fact that each face has a name and each name a story that explains their idiosyncrasies. Make mention on occasion how much you appreciate them. Publicly thank God for the privilege to serve this group of people.

11:13 **For such boasters are false apostles, deceitful workers, disguising themselves as apostles of Christ.**[NRSV] Paul reserved some of the harshest language for those who were boasting about their ministry among the Corinthians: They were *false apostles* and *deceitful workers.* How could Paul be so confident that these teachers were *disguising themselves as apostles?*

One of the first signs that a teacher is false is that that teacher tries to discredit true Christian teachers and preachers. That was what was occurring at Corinth: Paul's credentials, authority, and speaking abilities were being questioned by these self-serving teachers (11:5-6). By discrediting Paul's authority, these teachers were trying to build up their own following in the congregation Paul had founded (10:13-18).

A second sign of a false teacher is that teacher's self-serving methods. The teachers at Corinth were boasting of their own credentials, comparing themselves to Paul (3:1; 10:12). Their methods (their loud boasts) should have been a clue that these teachers were not looking out for the Corinthians' spiritual welfare but

instead for their own financial welfare. They wanted to consoli-
date power over the congregation, and the way they handled their
authority revealed their greedy goals (2:17). They were very overbearing (11:20).

A third sign that these teachers were false and deceitful is
that their methods were causing division and conflict in the
church. Paul would warn the Romans about such people, those
who love to divide (see Romans 16:17). Instead of building
the Corinthians up in the faith as Paul hoped to do (13:10),
these teachers were tearing the church down in order to put
together their own following (10:12-18). They were not building on the solid foundation: the gospel of Jesus Christ
(1 Corinthians 3:10-13).

The final sign that these were false teachers is the message
they preached. The conflict they caused in the church, their self-
serving methods, and their criticism of God's teachers should
have prompted the Corinthians to inspect the message thoroughly. A careful analysis would have revealed that it was "different" from the true gospel that Paul, Silas, Timothy, and Apollos
had preached (11:4-5).

The Corinthian believers should have tested the teachers to see
whether they believed Jesus is the Son of God (1 John 4:1-2).
The Corinthians had failed to do this and had even let these teachers wreak havoc in their congregation. Paul was disappointed
with the Corinthians' lack of discernment (11:4, 19-20), and he
felt compelled to expose the teachers for who they were: false
apostles.

**11:14 And no wonder, for Satan himself masquerades as an angel
of light.**[NIV] Paul wasn't amazed that false teachers were disguising themselves as preachers of God, for *Satan* himself had
deceived God's people in similar ways.

Paul had already warned the Corinthians to not give Satan any
chance to tempt them or disrupt their congregation (see 2:11;
1 Corinthians 7:5). Here, Paul compared the false teachers' deception with Satan's actions.

Although the Old Testament doesn't describe Satan as *an
angel of light,* Jewish writings do. Paul may have been thinking
of the stories in the *Life of Adam and Eve* and the *Apocalypse of
Moses* when he wrote this verse. For instance, the *Life of Adam
and Eve* describes Satan as taking on the appearance of an angel
who pretends to console Eve as she grieves. Nothing could be
more deceitful than Satan, the prince of darkness (Ephesians
6:12; Colossians 1:13), disguising himself as an angel of light. In

the same way, false teachers, claiming to represent the truth, are
extremely deceptive.

SATAN'S MEN
Satan and his servants can deceive people by appearing to be
attractive, good, and moral. Many unsuspecting people follow
smooth-talking, Bible-quoting leaders into cults. Don't be fooled
by external appearances. Impressions alone are not an
accurate indicator of who is or isn't a true follower of Christ, so
it helps to ask these questions:
- Do the teachings confirm Scripture (Acts 17:11)?
- Does the teacher affirm and proclaim that Jesus Christ is
  God who came into the world as a man to save people from
  their sins (1 John 4:1-3)?
- Is the teacher's lifestyle consistent with biblical morality
  (Matthew 12:33-37)?

11:15 **It is not surprising, then, if his servants masquerade as servants of righteousness. Their end will be what their actions
deserve.**[NIV] Although these false teachers claimed to be *servants
of* God's *righteousness,* they were servants of Satan, the god of
this age (4:4). Their actions betrayed them. Instead of bringing
glory to God, they were boasting in their own achievements
(10:17-18). Instead of preaching in response to God's call (compare 2:17 with 4:1-2, 5; 5:20), they were preaching for money.
Instead of guarding the spiritual welfare of their followers, they
were consolidating power over their followers (compare 1:23-24;
10:8; 11:21 with 11:18-20). Instead of preaching the gospel of
Jesus Christ clearly (11:6-7), they were preaching a twisted gospel of another Jesus (11:4). In the *end,* their fraud would be
exposed for what it was: a ruse to divert Christians from their
devotion to God. And they will get *what their actions deserve—*
God's judgment.

JUST DESSERTS
Paul reminds the Corinthians that everyone will one day
receive what they deserve. Here Paul is speaking about false
teachers and hypocritical leaders. But the principle applies to
all who speak on God's behalf. The apostle James said that
teachers will be judged by the Lord with closer scrutiny than will
those who sit under their teaching (James 3:1). If it is not
already your practice, each time you sit down with the
Scriptures to prepare a lesson or a sermon, spend some quiet
moments in prayer asking the Holy Spirit to make them real in
your life.

PAUL'S MANY TRIALS / 11:16-33

"Are they servants of Christ? . . . I am more." (11:23 NIV). This was Paul's ultimate rebuttal.

If the greedy teachers of Corinth questioned Paul's authority, he questioned their devotion to Christ. They were enjoying the luxuries of one of the most prominent cities in the Roman Empire, while Paul, as he noted in this passage, was enduring all kinds of hardships to preach the gospel to those who hadn't heard it. These teachers had been careful to collect correct references, respected credentials, and impeccable recommendations; but they, unlike Paul, had failed to offer their entire lives in service of Christ, wherever that brought them. Paul's long list of hardships he had endured couldn't be matched by any of the teachers who were criticizing him.

11:16-18 **I repeat: Let no one take me for a fool. But if you do, then receive me just as you would a fool, so that I may do a little boasting. In this self-confident boasting I am not talking as the Lord would, but as a fool. Since many are boasting in the way the world does, I too will boast.**^{NIV} Clearly, Paul was extremely reluctant to do any *boasting*. He knew that pride in one's own accomplishments eventually leads to destruction (Psalm 12:13; Proverbs 16:18). Boasting robs God of the honor he deserves (Psalm 96:8; 97:6). Only God, the source of all wisdom, skill, and strength, can accept glory and praise (Psalm 44:8; 1 Corinthians 1:31).

But faced with the persistent faultfinding of his critics, Paul felt compelled to list his accomplishments for the Corinthians. He wasn't primarily concerned with his own reputation but, instead, with the spiritual welfare of the Corinthian believers. If his critics' attacks went unanswered, the believers might turn away from Christ (11:3-4, 12). Paul had to speak up in order to quiet the gossip and slander circulating in the Corinthian church.

Defending oneself against false accusations, however, isn't always the Christian response to slander. Jesus himself remained silent in the face of his accusers (Mark 14:61), and sometimes Christians have to remain silent in the face of outlandish accusations in order to advance the cause of Christ. In this case, Paul thought a hardy defense of his actions would be appropriate.

Even though Paul knew he had to defend himself, he was extremely careful. He cautiously explained to the Corinthians that although he was not a *fool,* he was going to act like a *fool* in order to silence those false teachers who were *boasting in the way the world does* (see 11:1-5). It was only because the Corinthians were still evaluating people as *the world does*—according to appearances—that these false teachers had gained a foothold in the congregation in the first place (see 5:16-17; 10:7).

Paul wanted to make it clear to the Corinthians that such boasting wasn't the proper behavior for the minister of the *Lord*. In effect, he was turning the tables on his critics by boasting in his weaknesses instead of his strengths (11:30). He simply refused to enter into a bragging contest with his opponents (10:12). By freely admitting his weaknesses, Paul hoped to stop the foolish boasting and the competitive spirit that pervaded the Corinthian congregation (see 1 Corinthians 3:18-23).

11:19 **After all, you, who think you are so wise, enjoy listening to fools!**NLT With biting sarcasm, Paul reprimanded the Corinthians for putting up with these arrogant false teachers. Apparently, the Corinthians, like their nearby neighbors the Athenians, tried to keep up on all the new ideas in the Roman Empire. Therefore, they thought they were being *wise* when they welcomed itinerant teachers and listened to their new ideas. If these teachers were godly, like Apollos, Paul applauded this generous hospitality. The most recent teachers, however, were introducing a different gospel and were discrediting Paul in the process (11:4). Even though this was happening, the Corinthians continued to listen to them.

11:20 **You put up with it when they make you their slaves, take everything you have, take advantage of you, put on airs, and slap you in the face.**NLT The Corinthians continued to listen to the false teachers even when it became clear that they were trying to enslave the Corinthians. Paul went on to explain the nature of this enslavement, with four evocative images of exploitation.

"Take everything" is a translation of a Greek verb commonly used to describe how animals "devour" their prey. "Take advantage" is from a Greek verb used to describe how a hunter "catches" animals with a trap or a bait. The imagery of a hunter and prey suggests that the false teachers' primary sin was their motives. They were traveling preachers looking for a gullible group of people to support them. They were literally preying on the Corinthians, trying to exploit the relationship for all that it was worth. Ironically, the Corinthians thought they were wise by welcoming their teacher when, in reality, these itinerant teachers were making the Corinthians into fools.

The oppressive methods of these false teachers should have tipped off the Corinthians to their questionable motives. With arrogant boasts, they paraded their credentials and achievements. *Put on airs* is literally "to lift up" high. Paul used the same word to describe anything that was exalted above the knowledge of God (see 10:5). The false teachers were exalting themselves with their hollow boasts against not only Paul's authority among the Corinthians but also against God himself.

Finally, Paul described these false teachers as slapping the Corinthians *in the face*. In the first century, it was common for religious authorities to slap the face of a person who blasphemed (see Acts 23:2). Apparently, these false teachers had concentrated their power in Corinth, so much so that they had the audacity to slap those who opposed them.

11:21 To my shame I admit that we were too weak for that! What anyone else dares to boast about—I am speaking as a fool—I also dare to boast about.^{NIV} Paul was probably quoting what his critics said about him when he wrote that he was *too weak* to take advantage of the Corinthians, to take their money, and to physically discipline them. Even though Paul would refrain from doing that, he was going to *dare to boast,* just as his opponents did. Once again, Paul issued a disclaimer. He felt foolish talking as he did, listing his accomplishments.

FOOLISH BRAGGING
Paul reluctantly stooped beneath his usual dignity to boast of his qualifications as an apostle (11:21). Everyone has a pedigree of experience. And Paul was no exception. In fact, his résumé was far and away above that of those who dared criticize his credentials. Even though educational degrees, personal achievements, and family background don't qualify a person for salvation, they definitely explain his or her orientation toward the world. A person's achievements and failures prepare that person for the task to which God has called him or her. Take a moment to think through your unique qualifications for ministry. List the major turning points in your life, including educational degrees, areas of service, or professional achievements. Offer this list to the Lord, thanking him for what he has allowed you to experience and asking him to use you to advance his kingdom.

11:22 They say they are Hebrews, do they? So am I. And they say they are Israelites? So am I. And they are descendants of Abraham? So am I.^{NLT} These statements address the charges Paul's opponents had leveled against him point by point.

First of all, these traveling preachers from Judea were bragging about being *Hebrews* and *Israelites*—God's chosen people. Paul had been born in Tarsus; and thus, in his opponents' eyes, he had a questionable heritage. Was Paul a pure Jew? Did he consider Judea his home? Did he understand the Hebrew language? Paul unequivocally said yes. He was also one of the *descendants of Abraham*. He was descended from the tribe of Benjamin and thus was an Israelite. He had been circumcised eight days after he was born—a physical sign of his Israelite heritage. He had been trained by one of the most respected Pharisees of that day, Gamaliel. As a Pharisee, he had spent hours poring over the Hebrew Bible and had been scrupulously careful to observe Jewish law (Philippians 3:4-6). No one could question Paul's credentials as a Jew and as an expert in the Hebrew Scriptures.

11:23 Are they servants of Christ? (I am out of my mind to talk like this.) I am more. I have worked much harder, been in prison more frequently, been flogged more severely, and been exposed to death again and again.[NIV] Although Paul had conceded to his opponents their Jewish heritage, he would not agree with them that they were *servants of Christ*. Paul had already described these people as "false apostles." These teachers were not from Christ, as they claimed. To prove his point, Paul listed all the trials he suffered for Christ. Could his opponents, who boasted in achievements, accomplishments, and credentials, produce an even more extensive list of suffering and persecution endured for Christ's name? Were they willing to follow Jesus' way of the cross, his life of suffering? Were they willing to take up their crosses daily for Christ (Matthew 10:38)?

Paul had demonstrated his willingness to endure suffering for his Lord, just as Jesus had called him to do (see Jesus' words in Acts 9:15-16). Paul had suffered the hardship of imprisonment, including floggings (Acts 16:22-24). He had faced *death* on a number of occasions (see Acts 14:19, when Paul was stoned by a crowd). In fact, at the beginning of this letter, Paul explained that he had come dangerously close to *death* in his recent travels in Asia Minor (1:9). Since this letter was written during Paul's third missionary journey (Acts 18:23–21:17), his trials weren't over. He would experience further difficulties and humiliations for the cause of Christ (see Acts 21:30-33; 22:24-30). Paul was sacrificing his life for the gospel, something the false teachers would never do.

11:24 Five times I have received from the Jews the forty lashes minus one.[NRSV] To utterly silence his opponents, Paul listed in detail what he had endured for the cause of the gospel.

According to the Jewish law, *forty lashes* was the maximum number the Jews could prescribe (Deuteronomy 25:3). The rabbis, however, would only allow thirty-nine, so that if the flogger miscounted he wouldn't accidentally sin by administering more than forty. These beatings were carried out in the synagogues and were for either moral or religious offenses. The lashes were made of several straps of leather, sometimes with bone or metal tied to the ends to inflict more pain. In Paul's case, the punishment would have been for preaching the gospel, what Jews commonly considered blasphemy. None of these beatings are recorded in Acts, but the adamant opposition of the Jews to the gospel message is recorded (Acts 13:45, 50; 14:2; 18:6, 12).

11:25 Three times I was beaten with rods. Once I received a stoning.NRSV Only the Romans could administer beatings with rods. Yet Paul *was beaten with rods* at Philippi (Acts 16:22). Apparently, government officials had beaten him on two other occasions (these weren't recorded in the book of Acts, however). Finally, at Lystra, Paul had survived a *stoning* (Acts 14:8-20).

Three times I was shipwrecked; for a night and a day I was adrift at sea.NRSV Sea travel was not as safe as it is today. Paul had been *shipwrecked* three times, and he would face another accident on his voyage to Rome (Acts 27). By this time, Paul had probably made at least eight or nine voyages; thus, given the danger of first-century sea travel, he could have certainly experienced that many disasters at sea. The fact that Paul survived twenty-four hours *adrift* at sea would have been considered miraculous in the first century, a sign of God's hand on his life.

11:26 On frequent journeys, in danger from rivers, danger from bandits, danger from my own people, danger from Gentiles, danger in the city, danger in the wilderness, danger at sea, danger from false brothers and sisters.NRSV The sea did not present the only *danger* Paul faced on the many *journeys* he took in order to present the gospel all over the Mediterranean world. *Bandits* were a constant problem in the ancient world. The rocky road from Jerusalem to Jericho was one of the many roads considered especially dangerous. That is why Jesus set his parable of the Good Samaritan on that road (Luke 10:30-37). The Corinthians, too, would have known of the dangers from bandits, for the road that stretched from their city to Athens was known to harbor bandits, especially in the *wilderness* areas.

In addition, Paul's *own people,* the Jews, were trying to orchestrate his downfall. When Paul first visited Corinth, the Jews had dragged him before the governor of Achaia in order to stop him from preaching (Acts 18:12-17). The *Gentiles* also had opposed Paul in Philippi and in Ephesus (Acts 16:19-24; 19:23-31). These dangerous situations each occurred in a *city.*

Paul's list of dangers climaxes in *false brothers and sisters,* and his point is abundantly clear. Since he had bravely faced all sorts of dangers for Christ, he certainly would have enough courage to face those false teachers who were discrediting his author-

ity and his name in Corinth. On past visits, Paul had not been as
aggressive with those who opposed him (10:1). He was planning
to confront his critics on his next visit (13:1-5).

GOD'S PROTECTION
Ministry for Paul was synonymous with danger. This passage
makes eight references to dangerous occurrences Paul had
faced in every imaginable place. God did not shield Paul from
risky situations, but the Lord was always with him. Even in a
technologically advanced society we are surrounded by danger
every day of our lives. The certainty of suffering is a theme that
runs throughout the Old and New Testaments. Even Jesus said
before leaving earth, "In this world you will have trouble." But we
must remember the way the Savior concluded his prediction. "But
take heart! I have overcome the world" (John 16:33 NIV). When
you face trials and suffering, go to Jesus for strength and
patience. He understands your needs and is able to help.

**11:27 I have labored and toiled and have often gone without sleep;
I have known hunger and thirst and have often gone without
food; I have been cold and naked.**NIV Paul had begun his
résumé by recounting the persecution and danger he had faced
involuntarily as a preacher of the gospel (11:22-26). Here Paul
started recounting the hardships he had willingly endured in
order to further the cause of Christ.

First, in order to place his ministry beyond reproach, Paul had
supported himself by working at a manual trade. Life as an itinerant laborer in the first century was difficult. As an outsider, Paul
would have been given the most strenuous and difficult work (see
1 Thessalonians 2:9; 2 Thessalonians 3:8). At Corinth, he had
labored and toiled as a tentmaker (Acts 18:1-3). It was only in
his spare time that he preached and taught. Because Paul wasn't
able to dedicate himself completely to the ministry, he had willingly gone *without sleep*. Because of the low wages of itinerant
laborers and the hardships of first-century travel, Paul wouldn't
have been a stranger to *hunger, thirst,* and *cold*. But Paul had
endured all these hardships cheerfully to preach the gospel, to tell
men and women all over the Roman Empire that Jesus could save
them from their sins.

**11:28 Then, besides all this, I have the daily burden of how the
churches are getting along.**NLT Not only had Paul faced beatings,
dangers, and all kinds of hardships, every day he thought about the
spiritual health of the churches he had founded. There were so
many pitfalls and traps into which a young congregation could fall.
Persecution could force the church to compromise its theology;

quarreling and inner strife could distract the church from its purpose; false teachers could deceive a church. Paul was concerned
that the churches wouldn't persevere in the faith. One indication of
his *burden* was his dedication and persistence in praying for them.
Many of his New Testament letters indicate that he was praying for
those to whom he was writing (see 13:7-9; Romans 1:10; Philippians 1:4; 1 Thessalonians 1:2; 2 Thessalonians 1:11-12).

Paul even wrote down several of his prayers (see Ephesians
1:16-18; 3:14-19; Colossians 1:3-14). Paul's prayers reveal his
concerns. His primary concern was that the churches be firmly
rooted in Jesus Christ, not wavering from the faith (Ephesians
1:16-17). He also wanted them to experience all of the benefits of
being a child of God—the wisdom, knowledge, and power available through the Spirit that lives within them (Ephesians 3:16-
17). Moreover, he wanted them to live up to their calling as
Christians, producing good works so that Jesus would be honored
(13:7-9; Colossians 1:10). Presumably, Paul was praying the
same way for the Corinthians.

**11:29 Who is weak without my feeling that weakness? Who is led
astray, and I do not burn with anger?**NLT If Paul heard of any
individual who was *weak* in the faith, he sympathized with that
person. He encouraged stronger believers to help weaker ones
(1 Thessalonians 5:14). If any individual strayed from the faith,
Paul commonly placed the blame on Satan and his evil designs.
Paul's concern for the faith of those led astray can be seen clearly
in 2:5-11, where he encouraged the Corinthians to restore the
offender as soon as possible.

HEARTBEAT
Paul was concerned for more than just the congregation in
Corinth. His heart beat with compassion and concern for all the
churches with whom he had personal contact (11:28). Granted,
Paul was an apostle, and that job description (like that of a
superintendent or a bishop) included maintaining contact with
several churches. But apostles are not the only ones called to
have a concern for Christians in other churches. In fact, in his
high priestly prayer, Jesus asked his Father that all Christians
would be unified in love (John 17). How well are you connected
to Christians outside of your local church? Perhaps your church
can start a ministry to pray for other churches in your
community.

**11:30 If I must boast, I will boast of the things that show my weak-
ness.**NRSV Although the Corinthians had forced Paul to defend his
own integrity and his apostolic authority, this letter focuses on

Paul's *weakness*. Paul paraded his sufferings, trials, and weaknesses before his opponents. He didn't boast in his accomplishments, as they did; thereby, he defused some of their criticisms. If
they were accusing him of being incompetent, Paul freely admitted that no one was competent to preach the gospel; his competence came from Christ (3:4-6). Paul's résumé was a list of
failures—nothing in comparison to the list of accomplishments of
his opponents (4:7-10; 6:3-10; 11:22-29).

How could Paul expect to reassert his authority with such self-
debasement? He knew that his authority didn't rest in his abilities
but in his appointment. Christ had called him to be an apostle to
the Gentiles (Romans 1:1, 5; 11:13). The only way Paul could
show his authority was to point out how God had worked through
his weaknesses. These were the telltale signs of God's work in
his life.

**11:31 The God and Father of the Lord Jesus, who is to be praised
forever, knows that I am not lying.**^{NIV} Paul had already called
on God as a witness to his truthfulness three other times in this
letter: when he asserted his integrity in
his recent travel plans (1:18), when he
denied taking any money from the
Corinthians (11:10), and when he
asserted his genuine love for them
(11:11). Paul didn't hesitate to use oaths
when he believed something he was
saying would be doubted (see also Galatians 1:20). Here Paul may have
thought that the Corinthians would doubt either the following
action-filled story about his escape from Damascus (11:32-33) or
the recounting of his vision of the third heaven (12:1-5).

> Christians are like tea
> bags. You never know
> what kind you are until
> you are in hot water.
> *Eleanor Searle Whitney*

**11:32 When I was in Damascus, the governor under King Aretas
kept guards at the city gates to catch me.**^{NLT} Most likely, the
Roman Emperor Caligula (A.D. 37–41) had given *King Aretas* IV,
the king of the Nabateans from 9 B.C. to A.D. 40, the authority to
appoint a *governor* to oversee the Nabatean population in Damascus. The Jews in Damascus had been able to enlist this governor
to help them try to *catch* Paul (see Acts 9:22-25).

**11:33 But I was lowered in a basket through a window in the city
wall, and that's how I got away!**^{NLT} The way the passage builds
up to this story indicates that Paul saw this as a seminal event.
Although Paul would run from his persecutors on other occasions
(Acts 14:5-6; 17:10, 14), this was this first time he was forced to
do so. Paul had come to Damascus with his head held high. The

high priest had given him the authority to arrest Christians in that city. After his conversion, Paul was forced to sneak out of the city under the cover of darkness. He couldn't even walk through the city gates, much less command the authority and respect of the city elders (compare Acts 9:1-2 with 9:23-25).

Although Christ had predicted that Paul would suffer much for him (Acts 9:15-16), this was probably the first time Paul had realized to what extent he would have to suffer. Hunted as a common criminal, he couldn't stand up to his accusers and defend himself with integrity. Instead, he had to run away. For Paul, fleeing would have been considered a coward's reaction. This was probably one of the weakest moments he had experienced in his life, and admitting this to his opponents in Corinth would have been extremely difficult for him to write.

2 Corinthians 12

God had granted Paul a vision of the highest heaven. Paul had heard words that couldn't be repeated and had seen sights that couldn't be recounted. But because of this experience, God had given him a "thorn"—a weakness that continually reminded him of his utter dependence on God. Paul had experienced what others would never experience in this life. Instead of being able to boast about it, Paul had to suffer because of it.

12:1 I must go on boasting. Although there is nothing to be gained, I will go on to visions and revelations from the Lord.NIV Paul felt compelled to move to the next category about which his opponents had been *boasting: visions and revelations.* It is clear from the frequency of disclaimers about boasting in this section (11:30; 12:1, 5-6, 9-11) that Paul thought of bragging about revelations as the height of folly. A revelation by definition was purely God's work. The Lord freely chooses to reveal mysteries and truths to those he wants to, not to those worthy of it. Paul's vision on the Damascus road proved that point. He was opposing Christ with all his strength—plotting the destruction of Christ's followers. Despite his intentions, Christ appeared to him (Acts 9:1-19). There wasn't any redeemable quality in Paul. There was no room for bragging. It was a surprise. Jesus chose to appear to Paul.

Yet apparently, Paul's critics were boasting in revelations. In effect, they were saying that they had been judged worthy of these revelations. Only a fool boasts in something that is so clearly the work of God.

12:2 I know a person in Christ who fourteen years ago was caught up to the third heaven.NRSV In this sentence, Paul switched to the third person, speaking of the event as if another person had told him about it. It is obvious, however, that Paul is, in fact, the *person in Christ* who *was caught up to the third heaven.* In 12:7, Paul would explain that God had given him a "thorn in the flesh" in order to keep him from becoming arrogant about this revelation.

So why did Paul recount the revelation as if he were an observer and not a participant in these revelations? There are two
common explanations: (1) Some have asserted that Paul was trying to express the way he felt during the vision, as an observer of
what was happening. (2) Others understand this as a technique
Paul used to distance himself from the boasting he felt he had to
do. This is the most likely reason Paul did this, for he seems to be
expressing that sentiment in 12:5: "I will boast about a man like
that, but I will not boast about myself, except about my weaknesses" (2 Corinthians 12:5 NIV). Although he felt compelled to
tell the Corinthians about this revelation in order to prove his
apostolic authority, Paul used the technique of speaking in the
third person to avoid bragging directly about this revelation. Paul
was willing to risk obscurity in his writing in order to guard
against pride.

Although Paul didn't give many details about this ecstatic
experience, he did write that he was "caught up to the third
heaven." What does this mean? In Paul's day, the notion of multi-
ple heavens—from three to seven heavens—was common. Scholars who have systematically analyzed the use of the words
"heaven" and "heavens" in the Old and New Testament believe
that the Scriptures use the word "heaven" to refer to three separate places. The first heaven is the earth's atmosphere (see Acts
1:9-10); the second heaven is the entire universe, which contains
all the stars (see Genesis 1:14). The third heaven, beyond these
two heavens, is where God himself lives (1 Peter 3:22). This is
the "heaven of heavens" (Nehemiah 9:6; Psalm 68:33 NKJV).
Whether or not Paul had this three-fold division of the heavens in
mind, it is clear that he considered the third heaven as the highest
heaven. Paul saw his revelation as an extraordinary and unique
revelation (12:7). Nothing less than going to the heaven above all
heavens would silence those who boasted in their own revelations.

It was *fourteen years* ago that Paul experienced this revelation.
Although Luke records a number of visions and trances Paul
received (Acts 9:3-7; 16:9; 22:17-21), including the one Paul
experienced while visiting Corinth (Acts 18:9-10), none of those
visions fit the description here. Paul was not alluding to the
Damascus road vision, for he clearly stated that he was already
"in Christ" (i.e., a Christian) when this vision was given. The
visions and revelations in Corinth and Troas (Acts 16:9) had
occurred several years before he wrote this letter. The trance that
Paul experienced in Jerusalem came close to the time period, but
in that trance Paul wasn't lifted up to heaven. Instead, God simply gave Paul a clear command (Acts 22:17-21). In contrast, Paul

described this revelation as such a rapturous experience that he heard words he could not repeat (12:4). The fact that Paul couldn't express what he heard might explain the silence about this revelation in the book of Acts.

Fourteen years before the writing of 2 Corinthians would be around A.D. 40, close to the beginning of Paul's ministry. Paul may have experienced this revelation when he was in Arabia (see Galatians 1:17; 2:2), or when he was in Antioch (Acts 13:1-3), or when he was stoned outside of Lystra and assumed dead (Acts 14:19-20).

Whether in the body or out of the body I do not know; God knows.[NRSV] Apparently, the Corinthians valued visions and revelations and would have been interested in the technicalities of the type of vision and how it could be categorized. Paul discouraged any extensive debate over the vision he had experienced by admitting his own ignorance about such details and reminding the Corinthians of God's omniscience. God is the only one who knows the mysteries surrounding Paul's vision. The fact that Paul admitted the possibility that he could have been *in the body* was perhaps a rebuttal of the Greek notion that only one's soul could ascend to God. The Corinthians most likely were strongly influenced by these Greek notions, for Paul had to explain at length the Christian concept of a bodily resurrection (see 1 Corinthians 15:1-58, especially verses 35-44).

12:3-4 And I know that this man—whether in the body or apart from the body I do not know, but God knows—was caught up to paradise.[NIV] This verse repeats the thought of 12:2. Some commentators assert that Paul was referring to a different revelation than the "third heaven" vision, but it seems that "paradise" is used as a synonym. For Paul to equate the third heaven with paradise would have not been unheard of in the first century. The Jewish apocryphal book the *Apocalypse of Moses* equates the two. Thus, in this sentence, Paul was merely repeating that he had actually been transported to heaven, though he didn't know how.

Jesus also had used the word "paradise" as a synonym for heaven. He had promised the thief on a cross next to his that he would meet the thief in paradise on that very day (Luke 23:43). Then, in Revelation 2:7, Jesus promised the tree of life, the one in paradise, to all those who overcome. The latter reference is an obvious allusion to the Garden of Eden, where the tree of life and the tree of the knowledge of good and evil stood in the middle of the garden (see Genesis 2:9). In fact, the root meaning of the Greek word *paradeisos,* translated here as "paradise," is "enclosure" and had come to refer to an enclosed park. Thus the word implied a restored Garden of Eden, the beautiful place God was preparing for his people, the immediate resting place of the righteous dead and the ultimate place where believers will dwell after the resurrection.

And heard things so astounding that they cannot be told.^{NLT} Given the extraordinary nature of this revelation (12:4), this is a surprisingly brief description of it. All Paul revealed was that he had been transported to heaven and had heard some *things*. He was *not permitted to tell* the Corinthians what he heard!

What Paul saw and heard in heaven was meant for his own edification. Most likely, God was strengthening and encouraging him for the extraordinary trials and suffering he would have to face in order to preach the Good News (see Acts 9:15-16). Paul mentioned it here only to invalidate the claims of his opponents in Corinth.

The emphasis here is instructive. Although accounts of revelations and visions typically focus on what a person has seen, Paul highlighted what he had *heard*. For Paul, listening to God and responding to his Word was extremely important (see Romans 10:14, 17; Galatians 3:5; Ephesians 1:13).

12:5-6 **That experience is something worth boasting about, but I am not going to do it. I am going to boast only about my weaknesses. I have plenty to boast about and would be no fool in doing it, because I would be telling the truth. But I won't do it. I don't want anyone to think more highly of me than what they can actually see in my life and my message.**^{NRSV} Paul sensed he was on shaky ground when he started referring to a revelation that he couldn't describe. He didn't want anyone to mistakenly think that he was boasting about himself in this revelation. Therefore, he once again issued a disclaimer that he wasn't boasting in himself.

If the Corinthians thought Paul was boasting, then they shouldn't consider him a *fool,* for, unlike his critics, he was telling *the truth* (see 11:13-15). Paul hadn't broadcasted his vision, because he wanted people to judge his integrity and the truthfulness of the gospel for themselves. They could evaluate the evidence from what they had seen and heard. Anyone could claim to have a vision from God. Paul had experienced one of the highest order. But he had refused to base his authority and his message on his spiritual experiences. Instead, he had determined to put all this away and preach the clear message that Christ had been crucified for people's sins (1 Corinthians 2:2). Paul wanted the Corinthians and all those who heard him to judge his message on its own merits and on the way in which the Holy Spirit was using the message to transform people's lives (1 Corinthians 2:3).

In this passage, Paul turned attention away from his vision and to his *weaknesses*. Paul, no doubt, was alluding to his "thorn in the flesh," which he would discuss in 12:7-10. The thorn in the flesh was another occasion for God's direct intervention in Paul's life (see 11:30-33 for Paul's recounting of another experience in which he considered himself weak).

PROUD OF WEAKNESS
Even though he had an enviable list of credentials and supernatural encounters, Paul only boasted about his weaknesses (12:5). It's obvious that Paul didn't live in our day. Contemporary culture marches to the cadence of strength, power, prestige, and control. But Paul knew something many in today's society don't. Acknowledging weaknesses not only draws a person closer to God, it draws the person closer to other people. Weakness is the great leveler. Only a few ascend the heights of success, but everybody has known disappointments, setbacks, and suffering. The pain of defeat and the gnawing ache of insecurity reminds people that they need a Savior. Believers must be convinced of that truth before they can articulate that need to others. As you identify weaknesses in your life, surrender them to the One who is your strength.

12:7 **To keep me from becoming conceited because of these surpassingly great revelations, there was given me a thorn in my flesh, a messenger of Satan, to torment me.**[NIV] Paul's *thorn in the flesh* is not known, because he never reveals it. Because the Greek word for "flesh" can refer either to one's physical body or one's carnal self, there have been numerous conjectures concerning what the "thorn in the flesh" was.

The Greek word for "thorn" can also mean "stake." The word is used in the Greek Old Testament for Israel's neighbors who had become a temptation and a snare to the Israelites (Numbers 33:55). Some interpret Paul's use of the word here as a veiled reference to people who opposed the gospel—whether the false teachers who were deceiving the Corinthians or the Jews who were actively opposing his preaching.

Others argue that this type of external opposition wouldn't have humbled Paul, as he clearly stated the thorn did. According to these commentators, the thorn had to be some type of temptation of the flesh. Medieval commentators usually suggested a sexual temptation, while commentators of the Reformation suggested a spiritual temptation. In any case, this sort of explanation suggests that Paul would have viewed this temptation as a hindrance to the gospel and would have been humbled by his weakness.

Another set of commentators insist that the thorn in the flesh is a reference to a physical weakness, not to a persistent temptation. The earliest commentators on 2 Corinthians suggested that this ailment could have been severe headaches. These interpreters viewed the thorn in the flesh as a description of symptoms. In other words, "it feels like a bar going through my head." Some doctors think Paul may have had recurrent malarial fever, a disease that includes migraine headaches.

Many commentators, however, continue to insist that the thorn in the flesh is simply a general metaphor for Paul's physical weaknesses (especially in his eyes), and not a description of the symptoms. Some see hints in Paul's letter to the Galatians of a type of eye disease that impaired his vision. Paul wrote:

> *Even though my illness was a trial to you, you did not treat me with contempt or scorn. Instead, you welcomed me as if I were an angel of God, as if I were Christ Jesus himself. What has happened to all your joy? I can testify that, if you could have done so, you would have torn out your eyes and given them to me. (Galatians 4:14-15 NIV)*

The fact that the Galatians would have taken out their own eyes and given them to Paul is strong evidence for eye problems. Moreover, the fact that Paul described his writing as so large also supports this theory (see Galatians 6:11). Whatever the thorn was, it is clear that it was a chronic and debilitating problem, which at times kept Paul from working and attending to his ministerial responsibilities.

Yet this passage in 2 Corinthians does not focus on the exact problem Paul faced—he purposely didn't explain the nature of the problem in detail. The important point was why the thorn was given to him. Jesus had given Paul *surpassingly great revelations* in order to invigorate him for his mission to the Gentiles. But to keep Paul *from becoming conceited* about his unique vision, God had allowed *Satan* to *torment* him with some hardship or temptation. This thorn continually reminded Paul of his dependence on God and steered him away from pride, arrogance, and self-sufficiency. In this way, God would use Satan's evil designs for good, just as he had with Joseph and his brothers (Genesis 50:19-20).

The Bible describes God using Satan to test believers in several different places. According to the book of Job, Satan harassed Job with all kinds of catastrophes, including illness. But God limited Satan. He placed restrictions on what Satan could do (see Job 1–2). In 1 Thessalonians 2:17-18, Paul described how Satan hindered him from returning to Thessalonica (see Acts 17:1-10; see also Romans 17:17). We must always remember that

Satan has no power over Jesus (John 14:30-31) and that even the demons must obey Christ's will (Mark 1:21-28; 5:1-13). Moreover, Jesus gave this authority over the demons to the disciples (Mark 6:7).

Paul had to explain the reason for his thorn, because the Corinthians valued success instead of failure, power instead of weakness. Those who are so often dazzled by success need to learn the same lesson. Christ loves to work through weakness (1 Corinthians 1:26-29).

12:8 Three times I appealed to the Lord about this, that it would leave me.[NRSV] Because this thorn was a hindrance to his ministry, Paul saw it as caused by Satan (12:7). Appropriately, Paul responded to these demonic-inspired attacks with prayer, the chief weapon of the Christian against evil (Luke 22:40; Ephesians 6:12, 18). Paul prayed for the thorn's removal so he could be free to preach the Good News and build up others in the faith. Paul was persistent in his prayers, twice earnestly asking Christ to remove the problem. Even though Paul didn't receive a response, he determined to ask a third time. Believers should follow Paul's example. Three, however, is not a magic number for how many times to pray. Paul didn't say why he only prayed three times. Jesus was tempted three times, and he also prayed three times in the garden of Gethsemane. Paul may have followed Jesus' example in this situation (see Matthew 26:36-45).

But in the end, perseverance in prayer—much more than fervency—indicates a person's concern over an issue and acknowledgment that only Jesus can help. In his wisdom, however, the Lord does not always remove problems, as he didn't do in this situation (see 12:9). Sometimes he denies requests so that his people will depend on his abundant grace.

DEPEND ON CHRIST
God had used the "thorn" to teach Paul humility. Those who are strong in their own abilities or resources are tempted to do God's work on their own, and that can lead to arrogance. Those who struggle with weaknesses tend to rely on Christ's power. Only then can they become stronger than they could ever be on their own. Christ does not want his people to try to be weak, passive, or ineffective: Life provides enough hindrances and setbacks. Nor should they feign humility or timidity in order to gain his help. When obstacles come, they must depend on Christ. Only his power will make them effective for him and will help them do work that has lasting value.

GOD'S SOVEREIGNTY
Three times Paul prayed for healing and did not receive it. He
received, however, something far greater because he received
greater grace from God, a stronger character, and an ability to
empathize with others. God, according to his sovereign plan,
doesn't heal some believers of their physical ailments. We don't
know why some are spared and others aren't. God chooses
according to his divine purposes. Our task is to pray, to believe,
and to trust. Paul is living proof that holy living and courageous
faith do not ensure instant physical healing. When we pray for
healing, we must trust our bodies to God's care. We must
recognize that nothing separates us from his love (Romans
8:35-39) and that our spiritual condition is always more
important than our physical condition.

12:9 **And He said to me, "My grace is sufficient for you, for My
strength is made perfect in weakness."**NKJV Jesus' answer to
Paul's prayer is the theme of 2 Corinthians: Christ's *grace* is
what empowers Paul's ministry, despite his own inadequacies
and failures (1:3-4; 3:4-6; 4:1, 5, 7-12, 16-17; 6:3-10; 7:5-6;
10:17; 11:23-30; 13:9; see also 1 Corinthians 15:9-10). Christ's
grace gives all believers the strength also to bear temptations, trials, and difficulties.

Although Paul's request wasn't granted, Jesus assured him that
he would continue to work through Paul *in* his *weakness.* In fact,
Christ's *strength* was *made perfect in* Paul's weakness. The
Greek word for "weakness" means the frailty of human existence—the shortcomings we encounter in our bodies.

Thus Christ's strength is brought to completion when it shows
itself through human weakness. Personal success and self-sufficiency obscures God's work. When there is no adversity, Jesus'
power can be overlooked or taken for granted. Obvious weakness
shows Jesus' power in full relief.

**Therefore I will boast all the more gladly about my weak-
nesses, so that Christ's power may rest on me.**NIV Paul restated
Jesus' answer to him as a principle for his own life. Instead of
continuing to ask God to take away his "thorn," Paul wholeheartedly accepted Jesus' answer to his prayer. Paul accepted that
Jesus, in his divine wisdom, knew what was best for him.

Even if Jesus' way involved suffering, humiliation, and *weaknesses,* Paul would submit. In fact, he would *gladly*—that is, with
great pleasure—*boast* in his weaknesses, for it was through his
weaknesses that Christ could powerfully work through him.
Christ's power could be fully displayed—not in Paul's strength,
not in Paul's wisdom, and not in arrogant boasts—but in weak-

ness. It was only in Paul's weakness that Christ's power could fully *rest on* Paul—literally, in Greek, act as "a shelter over" Paul. In other words, Paul didn't want to wander away from the protection and support that was in Christ by relying on his own strength. He wanted Christ's power to overshadow everything he did; only then would his work be truly effective.

Jesus had taught his disciples this principle years before: "I am the vine, you are the branches. Those who abide in me and I in them bear much fruit, because apart from me you can do nothing" (John 15:5 NRSV). It is only when believers remain in Christ and rely on Christ's power that they become truly effective.

12:10 Since I know it is all for Christ's good, I am quite content with my weaknesses and with insults, hardships, persecutions, and calamities. For when I am weak, then I am strong.NLT Although Christ did not remove Paul's affliction, he promised to demonstrate his power in Paul's *weaknesses.* Knowing this, Paul welcomed times when he appeared weak or even powerless. He saw *insults* and *hardships* in a different light. They gave him opportunities to grow closer to Jesus in prayer. For when he was at his wits' end— when he had no options left—he would be forced to run to Jesus— to rely on Christ's help. Paul's utter dependence on Christ came into clear light. This was not the only benefit of the *persecutions* and *calamities.* At those times, Paul would look for Christ working in a marvelous and mighty way. Christ's clear manifestation of his power in Paul's weakness would become a source of inspiration and a reason to praise and glorify Jesus.

THE TAPESTRY OF LIFE
What God allowed Paul to experience was for "Christ's good" (12:10). This means that the kingdom over which Christ rules was served by the circumstances the apostle encountered. Even though daily hardships and failure are not easily graphed on a chart of personal achievement, they are by no means wasted. Consider the underside of a handmade tapestry. The elaborate coordinated threads on the exterior side of the fabric, woven with precision and creativity, produce a work of art intended by the weaver. The side that will not be seen, however, is a tangled mess of thread, yarn, and knots. How similar to life! Christ uses what appears to be random circumstances with no meaning—simply knots and tangles—and makes something beautiful out of them. We must not draw undue attention to ourselves, even in our suffering. He can produce spiritual renewal out of great difficulty and conflict.

The fact that Christ's power is displayed in weak people should give believers courage. Instead of relying on their own energy, effort, or talent, they should turn to Christ for wisdom and strength. Weakness not only helps a person develop Christian character; it also deepens that person's worship, because admitting weakness affirms Christ's inexhaustible strength.

PAUL'S CONCERN FOR THE CORINTHIANS / 12:11-21

Toward the end of 2 Corinthians, Paul begins to sound like a father who is profoundly disappointed in his children. Paul was disappointed that the Corinthians hadn't defended him when others had maligned his reputation (12:11-12). He was disappointed that they were questioning his motives (12:16-18). He was disappointed that they hadn't shown him the same kind of love he had showered on them (12:15). Paul was planning to visit Corinth, but he was clearly apprehensive about it. Would he find all kinds of disorders, just as if the Corinthians were his children running wild? Would he find them arguing and fighting (12:20)? Paul hoped that everything would be in order; then he could congratulate the Corinthians instead of disciplining them.

12:11 **I have made a fool of myself, but you drove me to it. I ought to have been commended by you.**[NIV] The Corinthians should have defended their founder when malicious rumors about him had begun to circulate in their congregation. After all, Paul was their spiritual father (1 Corinthians 4:15; 9:1; 11:2-4). The very existence of the gathering of believers, whose lives had been changed by the Holy Spirit, was evidence of Paul's faithfulness to the truth (3:1-5).

For I am not in the least inferior to the "super-apostles," even though I am nothing.[NIV] In an earlier letter, Paul had called himself "the least of the apostles" because he had at one time persecuted the church (1 Corinthians 15:9-10 NIV). Apparently, Paul's critics in Corinth had seized upon this admission and had tried to impugn his apostolic authority. Here Paul made it clear that he definitely wasn't the least of those who called themselves *"super-apostles."* The "super-apostles" weren't the true apostles of Christ—Peter, James, and John; instead, they were those traveling preachers who had come to Corinth and claimed to be apostles superior to Paul (2:17; 11:5). Thus, he sarcastically calls them "super-apostles." Actually, these people weren't even apostles at all but were false apostles sent by Satan (see 11:13-14). They claimed to be servants of Christ, but they refused to face suffering, indignities, and hardship for Christ's sake. (See how Paul compared himself to them in 11:23-27.) They were more concerned about their money and their reputation than about Christ (2:17; 3:1).

THE MIRACLES OF PAUL

Paul, as a spokesman for God and an energetic evangelist to the Gentiles, performed miracles wherever he went. God gave Paul the power to heal, to exorcise, and to perform other wonders in order to verify the truth of his message (Romans 15:17-19; 1 Corinthians 2:4-5). In 12:12, Paul reminded the Corinthians of all the miracles he had done among them. That and their transformed lives should have been proof enough that God was speaking through him.

In Paphos, Paul blinded Elymas the sorcerer
for opposing the gospel . . . . Acts 13:6-12

In Iconium, Paul performed many miraculous
signs and wonders. . . . . Acts 14:1-3

In Lystra, Paul enabled a crippled man to walk. . . . . Acts 14:8-10

To the council in Jerusalem, Paul described all
the miraculous signs and wonders God had
done among the Gentiles . . . . Acts 15:12

In Philippi, Paul exorcised a demon from
a slave girl . . . . Acts 16:16-18

In Ephesus and throughout Asia Minor, Paul
performed all kinds of miracles; even handker-
chiefs that touched Paul could be empowered
by God to heal someone . . . . Acts 19:11-12

In Troas, Paul brought Eutychus back to life
after his deadly fall. . . . . Acts 20:9-12

In Malta, Paul healed Publius's father and other
sick people on the island . . . . Acts 28:1-10

Paul never thought he would have to defend himself against these conniving preachers, but the Corinthians had forced him to do so. In order to address these critics, he had to answer their criticisms in their own language: foolish boasts.

12:12 The signs of a true apostle were performed among you with utmost patience, signs and wonders and mighty works.NRSV When Paul was in Corinth, he had acted according to his calling as an apostle of Christ. He had been careful to be completely honest in all his dealings so that no one could impugn his name (1:12). He had faithfully preached the gospel (5:11, 19-21; 1 Corinthians 1:23; 9:16-18), and his preaching in Corinth had been accompanied by *signs and wonders and mighty works*. Paul used the Greek word *dunamis* for "mighty works." This word refers to the great acts of God. The Greek word for "wonders" was typically used for phenomena that inspire fear, while the Greek word *semeion,* translated "signs" here, refers to miraculous signs. John's Gospel describes Jesus' miracles with this Greek word on a number of occasions (John 4:54; 6:14; 12:18). Jesus' ministry, like Paul's, was authenticated by all kinds of miracles (Acts 2:22).

In fact, Paul had performed miracles in almost every city he had visited—from Lystra (Acts 14:8-10) to Ephesus (Acts 19:11-12). Through these signs, the Spirit of God had clearly demonstrated to the Corinthians Paul's apostolic authority and the truthfulness of the gospel message he preached (Romans 15:17-19; 1 Corinthians 2:4).

12:13 **How have you been worse off than the other churches, except that I myself did not burden you? Forgive me this wrong!**NRSV The only practice Paul refrained from doing that these "super-apostles" did was charging money for his teaching. Building on the Greek notion that manual labor was beneath teachers and preachers, these false teachers had asserted that one of the signs of an apostle was demanding payment for his services (2:17). The fact that Paul had spent long hours sewing tents together disqualified him as an apostle in the eyes of these false teachers. In 1 Corinthians, Paul had explained that earning a living as a preacher was the right of every apostle (see 1 Corinthians 9:11-12), but Paul hadn't taken advantage of this right because he didn't want to owe anything to any one person. He wanted the freedom to preach the gospel to everyone—no matter if they were Jew or Greek, slave or free (1 Corinthians 9:19-23).

Paul's message was not just another teaching that could be bought and sold in the marketplace of ideas. It was the truth; it was free. Paul's policy of preaching free of charge served him well when problems arose in the Corinthian congregation. It was the one behavior that Paul's opponents could never imitate, for the whole purpose of their ministry was to take people's money. By consistently pointing out this difference between himself and his critics, Paul hoped the Corinthians would finally wake up to the scam (2:17; 11:7-12). Paul's rhetorical question in this verse is sarcastic. The Corinthian church was better off than other churches, for Paul hadn't asked for their financial support.

ON TRIAL
Paul was not merely revealing his feelings; he was defending his authority as an apostle of Jesus Christ (12:1-12). Paul was hurt that the church in Corinth doubted and questioned him, so he defended himself for the cause of the gospel, not to satisfy his ego. When you are put on trial, do you think only about saving your reputation? Or are you more concerned about what people will think about Christ?

12:14-15 Now I am ready to visit you for the third time, and I will not be a burden to you, because what I want is not your possessions but you.^{NIV} Paul had founded the church in Corinth on his first visit there (Acts 18:1). He had subsequently made a short and painful visit. That second visit was when he had warned those who were persistent in sinning to repent of their sin (2:1; 13:2). After this visit, he had abandoned plans for another visit and had instead written a stern letter, warning the Corinthian congregation that it was the church's responsibility to punish the wrongdoer (2:1-4; 7:8-13). Now he was planning to visit them. This would be his *third* visit (see also 13:1).

Paul explained that, as on his previous visits, he didn't want to be paid or fed. The Corinthian church was too divided; accusations might result from him accepting any money. Paul didn't want their *possessions* anyway; rather, he wanted their allegiance and friendship.

After all, children should not have to save up for their parents, but parents for their children. So I will very gladly spend for you everything I have and expend myself as well. If I love you more, will you love me less?^{NIV} Paul had been the Corinthians' spiritual parent. As their father, he had promised his spiritual children—the Corinthians—as a pure bride to Christ (see 11:2). But Paul was concerned: Were the Corinthians abandoning their devotion to Christ (11:2-3)? These doubts were the reason for much of his stern admonishment in this letter (10:1-7; 11:3-4, 16-21; 12:20-21; 13:2, 5).

As a parent naturally loves his or her child, so Paul loved the Corinthians. As their spiritual father, he wasn't going to ask for money on this visit. Paul, like a father, would *gladly spend* on them. Fathers in the first century were expected to support their children, saving money and possessions as an inheritance for their sons and a dowry for their daughters. The fact that he refused financial support wasn't a sign of his rejection of the Corinthians but a sign of his great affection for them (see also 11:11). Paul was willing to go beyond storing money for them; he was willing to *expend* himself—to completely exhaust his finances, time, and energy—on them. Paul's love for them was more than a parental love, it was a self-sacrificial love.

After expressing his love for the Corinthians, Paul asked what any parent would ask his or her children: "Will you love me after I have spent all my life loving you?"

12:16-17 Some of you admit I was not a burden to you. But they still think I was sneaky and took advantage of you by trickery. But how? Did any of the men I sent to you take advantage of

you?[NLT] Paul's boast that he had never accepted any money from
the Corinthians was a direct challenge to the false teachers. Ever
since they had arrived in Corinth, they had tried to find ways to
extort more money from the church (2:17; 11:7-12). The false
teachers had to discredit Paul in some way, and they had done so
by casting doubt on the collection for the destitute Jerusalem
Christians (see 8:1–9:15). "Was this Paul's devious way of collecting even more money for himself?" "Would he dip his hand
into the pot once it was all collected?" According to them, the
Jerusalem collection was Paul's way of taking advantage of them.

From the start, however, Paul had guarded against such accusations. The Corinthians had proposed the collection in the first
place (8:10). At the time, Paul had told them to set aside money
every Sunday when he was gone. Also, Paul would have nothing
to do with collecting the money. Moreover, he wouldn't even
deliver the collection to Jerusalem (see 1 Corinthians 16:1-3).
Paul wasn't going to have any contact with the money.

Finally, Paul asked the Corinthians a legitimate question: How
could he trick them out of their money?

**12:18 I urged Titus to go, and sent the brother with him. Titus did
not take advantage of you, did he? Did we not conduct ourselves with the same spirit? Did we not take the same
steps?**[NRSV] Titus had earned the respect of the Corinthians (7:13-
16). Paul had given Titus the difficult job of delivering the severe
letter to the Corinthians (see 7:7-9). Titus had accepted the
challenge and had done a masterful job of exhorting the Corinthians and smoothing over their relationship with Paul (7:7).

Since the Corinthians admired Titus, Paul reminded them that
Titus was functioning as his representative. If they had found
nothing wrong with Titus's conduct, how could they find anything wrong with him, the very person Titus was representing?
Titus had learned what *steps* to take from Paul. How could Paul's
own steps be any different?

This appeal would have been even more persuasive because
Titus himself was delivering the epistle known as 2 Corinthians.
His impeccable behavior among them would be a continual rebut-
tal to the gossip of those who were discrediting Paul.

**12:19 Have you been thinking all along that we have been defend-
ing ourselves before you? We are speaking in Christ before
God.**[NRSV] Paul was worried that the Corinthians might get the
impression that he was trying defend his own reputation. Here
Paul corrected this impression, if it existed.

It wasn't before the Corinthians that Paul was speaking, it was
before *God* himself. By clearly stating that he was speaking

before God at various points in this letter (see 1:12-14, 23; 2:10; 3:4; 4:2; 5:10-11; 10:18; 11:11, 31), Paul was trying to impress on the Corinthians the gravity of their actions. This wasn't merely a debate between two teachers, so the Corinthians could judge who had spoken with the most poise. This was a dispute that was being held in the throne room of God. The Lord himself would judge who was his trustworthy representative (see 5:20; 6:3-10).

Everything we do, beloved, is for the sake of building you up.^{NRSV} Paul was confident that he would pass God's judgment because God knew that all that he had done was for the Corinthians' benefit. Paul's chief concern was for the Corinthians, that they become firmly grounded in the faith. All of his efforts were dedicated to *building up* the Corinthians in the faith and were directed to this purpose, whether it was delaying a visit (1:23-24) or writing a stern letter of warning (7:8-9), whether it was his willingness to endure suffering (1:6) or his refusal to take money (11:7; 12:14-15). Paul knew that God himself could see his motives, that everything he did was out of love for the Corinthians (11:11) and concern for their spiritual welfare (11:2-3).

12:20 **For I am afraid that when I come to visit you I won't like what I find, and then you won't like my response.**^{NLT} On his last visit to Corinth, Paul had warned those who were persisting in sin to repent of their ways (13:2). He had even postponed his plans to visit Corinth in order to give them time to put their church in order (1:23–2:4). According to Titus's report, the Corinthians had made some progress in this. They had taken appropriate action against the anonymous offender (2:5-11; 7:11). Their discipline was so severe that Paul had become concerned that the offender might leave the Christian faith altogether (2:7-11).

I am afraid that I will find quarreling, jealousy, outbursts of anger, selfishness, backstabbing, gossip, conceit, and disorderly behavior.^{NLT} Even with all this progress, Paul was still apprehensive that the church might not be ready for his visit. He was concerned that the Corinthians might not have taken the appropriate steps to rid their church of sin. The fact that Paul was writing this letter so soon after Titus's report on the Corinthians may indicate that Titus, although genuinely encouraged by the Corinthians (7:13-16), may have noticed some ongoing problems in the congregation.

Paul was worried that the Corinthians might still be *quarreling* (in Greek, the word can mean "strife" or "contention"; the word is also used in the list of sins in Romans 1:29; 13:13). In his earlier letter, Paul had already warned the Corinthians of dividing into factions and competing for power in the church (see 1 Corinthians 1:10-13; 3:3).

One of the key problems in the church was the Corinthians' *jealousy* of each other (1 Corinthians 3:3-5). Instead of concentrating on what they could each do for God, they were enviously eyeing one another, coveting the abilities and resources God had given their fellow brothers and sisters in Christ (see also Romans 13:13).

It was the Corinthians' *selfishness* (literally, in the Greek, their "selfish ambition"; see also Galatians 5:20) that was also causing problems in the church. In 1 Corinthians 4:6-7, Paul had described how they were boasting in themselves, and he had already warned them to focus their energies on preserving Christ's honor—not their own reputation.

These evil attitudes were resulting in *outbursts of anger* in the church. Evidently, tempers were short because of the division and jealousy in the Corinthian church. Instead of growing into a supportive community of faith (1 Corinthians 12:12-13), the Corinthians were dividing into factions and fighting each other. In the process, they were tearing down the church, the very temple of God (1 Corinthians 3:16-17).

These disputes were not one-time affairs. They were ongoing quarrels, where church members on each side began *backstabbing* each other. The Greek word used by Paul here literally means "evil speech" or "slander" (see Romans 1:30 and James 4:11 for more on slander). In this way, the Corinthians were impugning the reputation of their fellow brothers and sisters in Christ (1 Corinthians 5:11; 6:10).

Not only were they slandering each other, but they did so in secret. They continued to maliciously *gossip* about each other— and also, presumably, Paul (see 1 Corinthians 5:11; 6:10). The Greek word for "gossip" is literally "whisperer" (see Paul's use of the word in Romans 1:29).

Instead of building each other up in the Christian faith (1 Corinthians 12:7), the Corinthians were simply growing conceited (see 1 Corinthians 4:6; 8:1). The Greek word Paul used for "conceit" means "inflated." The Corinthians had become inflated with pride (see Paul's similar description in 1 Corinthians 8:1). Evidently, members in the Corinthian church were especially gifted; therefore, many of them aspired to rise to prominence in the growing church (1 Corinthians 12:27–3:1; 14:12). But their arrogance had become a formidable obstacle to God and his work. If they would only seek after God's honor instead of their own glory, then God could establish his kingdom among them.

Finally, Paul warned the Corinthians of *disorderly behavior,* just as he had done in 1 Corinthians (6:1-8; 11:20-22, 33-34; 14:32-33, 40). Paul was speaking about any behavior that disrupted worship services or contributed to the disunity of the church.

THE IMPORTANCE OF LOVE
Quarreling, jealousy, outbursts of anger, selfishness, backstabbing, gossip, conceit, and disorderly behavior. Every church in Paul's day (and ever since) could be described with those words. After all, the church is made up of imperfect, forgiven yet sin-prone people. Even Paul never achieved his lifelong ambition to pastor a congregation where all were well-behaved, Christlike saints. Congregations like this one in Corinth were spiritually gifted and full of potential but fraught with problems that kept Paul in prayer. It's helpful to remember that Paul's eloquent treatise on love (1 Corinthians 13) was written for this group of people in an attempt to address their selfishness. The absence of God's enabling love in any person or church will result in conflict, greed, and self-absorption. Read through 1 Corinthians 13 with an eye for how you will approach people this week.

12:21 I fear that when I come again, my God may humble me before you.^{NRSV} Paul had already told the Corinthians that he was concerned that he might be humiliated when he came to Corinth. Some Macedonian Christians were accompanying him. If Paul found the church in disorder and the Corinthians refusing to participate in the Jerusalem collection, then Paul would be humiliated in the presence of the devout Christians from Macedonia (see 9:3-5).

And that I may have to mourn over many who previously sinned and have not repented of the impurity, sexual immorality, and licentiousness that they have practiced.^{NRSV} Paul hinted here that finding the Corinthian congregation in disorder would mean more than his own humiliation. He would also have to *mourn over* those who stubbornly refused to repent of their sins.

The sins Paul listed here are sexual sins (as compared to sins relating to pride in 12:20). The Greek for "impurity" means "unclean." The word suggests that those who participate in sexual perversions are "unclean" before God. The Greek for "sexual immorality" is *porneia* (the word is the root for the English word "pornographic"). *Porneia* refers to illicit sexual intercourse and is commonly translated "fornication." Finally, the Greek for "licentiousness" means "excess" or "absence of restraint." The word connotes shameful conduct, the type of sexual deviance that occurred at religious orgies in Corinth.

Paul had already warned them to resist the sexual temptations that were commonplace in Corinth (1 Corinthians 6:18-20). The church was to discipline those church members who persisted in sexual immorality (1 Corinthians 5:9-12). Those who claimed to worship Christ simply couldn't imitate the impure sexual practices of the society around them. In 1 Corinthians, Paul had given the church specific instructions on how to treat one member who was committing incest: The church was to remove him from fellowship (1 Corinthians 5:2).

Paul was afraid that his directions had not been heeded. The fact that he would have to mourn over those who hadn't repented of their sexual sins implied that Paul was going to carry out the discipline he had told the Corinthians to impose. On his visit, he would have to remove these people from fellowship. He didn't want to discipline them, for it would cause him great sorrow. That is why Paul wrote in a stern manner, hoping that the church leaders would straighten out the situation before he arrived. As Christians, they had to live in a different way than unbelievers, not letting pagan society dictate their behavior. The same is true for believers today. They can't let the moral laxity of our times dictate their own behavior and habits. They must live up to their calling as God's people.

2 Corinthians 13

True Christian love sometimes demands confrontation. Throughout 2 Corinthians, Paul had expressed his great love for the Corinthians (11:11; 12:15). He had spent most of the letter taking the time to address their concerns and their accusations (1:12-14, 17, 23; 4:1-2; 5:11-13; 6:11-12; 12:16-18). But at the end of this letter—in this last chapter—Paul didn't hesitate to warn the Corinthians sternly (13:2). Although they had begun to reject his authority, Paul continued to seek them out and affirm them (2:3; 7:4, 16). Yet at the same time, Paul warned them that everything they did was before God, the great Judge. If they wouldn't take his advice, he encouraged them to examine themselves. Did they measure up? Were they living as if Christ was living in them (13:5)?

13:1-2 This is the third time I am coming to visit you.[NLT] Paul had first visited Corinth on his second missionary journey. In that city known for its vigorous commerce and, also, for its gross immorality, Paul had gathered together a small group of believers. He spent a year and a half with them, instructing them in the Christian faith (see Acts 18:1-17). During his second visit, a painful incident had occurred (2:1, 5). Therefore, Paul's next *visit* was the *third time* he would have been in Corinth.

The relationship between Paul and the Corinthian believers had been a long one. In addition to spending a year and a half with them, Paul had sent several emissaries there, including Timothy (1 Corinthians 4:17), Titus, and an unknown brother (12:18). Obviously, Paul had invested a large amount of time in the Corinthians because he saw their congregation as a key base for his future missionary efforts to the West (see 10:16). Subsequently, it had to be disappointing for Paul to have to write letters of warning to a church for which he had such high hopes.

As the Scriptures say, "The facts of every case must be established by the testimony of two or three witnesses." I have already warned those who had been sinning when I was there on my second visit. Now I again warn them and all others, just as I did before, that this next time I will not spare

them.NIV Paul quoted Deuteronomy 19:15 as a stern legal summons to the Corinthians. Throughout 2 Corinthians, he had explained and defended his actions (see 2:1-4; 11:22-31). Finally here, at the end of his letter, Paul stopped defending himself and directly confronted the Corinthians. He wasn't coming to them in a "timid" manner, as he had done before (10:1 NIV). He wouldn't merely issue warnings. Instead, he would exercise his apostolic authority in full measure.

The exact reason why Paul quoted Deuteronomy 19:15 has been the subject of some debate among commentators. During his ministry, Jesus had endorsed the Old Testament principle that all accusations had to be established on the testimony of two or three witnesses (Matthew 18:15-17). By quoting this law, Paul may have been implying that this time he would be coming to the Corinthians as a judge. He would settle their disputes and quarrels, but everything had to be done in a proper order: All disputes would have to be presented to him with two or three witnesses.

Other commentators suggest that Paul was quoting Deuteronomy 19:15 because he considered his third visit as the final witness against the Corinthians. He had visited them on two separate occasions and had warned them at least two times—during his last visit and also in this letter, 2 Corinthians. He had taken the appropriate steps before disciplining them. He had warned them enough times and had waited long enough for repentance. His next visit would be the third one, the time he would come in judgment. Paul didn't specify in 2 Corinthians exactly what kind of discipline he would use. One type of early church discipline was to confront publicly those who persisted in their sins. Another common form of punishment was to prohibit such people from participating in the fellowship of the church, specifically the eating and drinking of Communion (1 Corinthians 5:11). If Paul had to take such drastic measures on this visit, he would be fully prepared because Titus and an entourage of Macedonian Christians would be there to be his witnesses (8:16-19; 9:4).

In the final analysis, Paul may have been quoting Deuteronomy 19:15 to indicate both ideas, that he had already given them three warnings and that they could bring disputes before him with three witnesses. Jesus' teaching in Matthew 18:15-17 supports both interpretations. Jesus had instructed his disciples to confront a fellow Christian with three warnings—one in private, one with two other witnesses, and one in front of the church (Matthew 18:15-17). There were to be not only three different witnesses before anyone could pass judgment on a believer but also three separate occasions when the believer was to be warned of his or her sin.

13:3 **I will give you all the proof you want that Christ speaks through me. Christ is not weak in his dealings with you; he is a mighty power among you.**^{NLT} Some of the Corinthians had been asking for *proof* that Paul was truly speaking on behalf of *Christ,* that he was truly an apostle. Influenced by Greek ideas, these Corinthians understood speaking ability, persuasiveness, and reports of visions as evidence of Christ working through a teacher or speaker (see 11:5; 12:12).

Paul did not censure their critical attitude. They certainly were to judge their teachers to ascertain whether they preached that Jesus is Lord (see 1 Corinthians 12:2-3). But the Corinthians were judging Paul by the wrong standards. Instead of judging whether his message pointed to Jesus as Lord and Savior, the Corinthians were criticizing Paul for his lack of eloquence, his weaknesses, and his timidity (10:1; 11:5; 12:7-10).

In this verse, Paul directly challenged the Corinthians. If they were looking for proof and *mighty power,* then they would most assuredly experience Christ's power on his next visit. Jesus' power among them, however, would not be the type of power the Corinthians were expecting. He wouldn't present spectacular wonders through Paul so that the Corinthians could sit back, watch, and judge them. When Christ came in mighty power, he wouldn't be coming to prove himself to the Corinthians but instead to judge the false teachers among them. Instead of demanding all kinds of proof and power, the Corinthians should have spent that time testing themselves to see if they were following Jesus completely.

13:4 **Although he died on the cross in weakness, he now lives by the mighty power of God. We, too, are weak, but we live in him and have God's power—the power we use in dealing with you.**^{NLT} Paul's consistent message to the Corinthians was that Christ *died on the cross* (1 Corinthians 1:23), a message of Christ's *weakness.* In spite of this emphasis in the gospel, the Corinthians had been impressed with the false teachers' display of spiritual "strength." Though they still worshiped Jesus Christ, who came in human weakness (see Philippians 2:6-11), the Corinthians sought out powerful and persuasive teachers.

Paul reminded the Corinthians that *God's power* demonstrated itself through weakness, not through power (12:9). Christ's own life was testimony of this fact. Jesus had refused Satan's tempting offers to wield power over people's lives. He rejected the opportunity to impress people and create a large following by jumping from the top of the temple and miraculously surviving (Matthew 4:5-7). He even refused Satan's offer to rule over the entire world

(Matthew 4:8-10). Instead, Jesus obediently took the more difficult road that God had laid out for him—the road of suffering, humiliation, and a criminal's death on the cross. Instead of wielding power over the world (the authority that was his right as the Son of God), Jesus had come to serve and even lay down his life for others (see Matthew 20:28). Through Christ's weakness, God worked in a powerful way. Through Christ's death on the cross, God provided salvation for all those who believe (John 3:16-18).

Just as God had demonstrated his power through Christ's weakness, he was doing the same in Paul's life. It was through hardships, persecutions, and even a stoning that God had shown his power (see Paul's three lists in 4:7-10; 6:3-10; 11:23-33). The power that God gave Paul was the strength to serve the church. As an apostle of Jesus, Paul's mission was the same as Jesus' mission: to be a servant (compare 4:5; 6:4; 11:23 with John 13:12-17). In contrast, the false teachers who had infiltrated the Corinthian church were not acting as servants but as masters (see 11:19-21).

IN HIM
Paul said "we live in him and have God's power" (13:4 NLT). That knowledge was a comfort to the apostle. It should be to all believers as well. Christians are not playing church. They are not in this angry ocean of a world in a rubber raft and a plastic paddle. They are passengers on His Majesty's finest vessel, driven by the indwelling power of the Holy Spirit. There is always the temptation to underestimate their ability to accomplish what Christ desires. It is to easy to forget that he is the vine and we are simply the branches (John 15:5). Branches that are attached to the vine naturally accomplish the fruit-producing purposes for which they were created. As you pray, thank God that he desires to work through you as you make your time, resources, and abilities available to him.

13:5 Examine yourselves to see whether you are in the faith; test yourselves. Do you not realize that Christ Jesus is in you—unless, of course, you fail the test?[NIV] The Corinthians had insisted on testing Paul, the one who had introduced them to the gospel of salvation in the first place. This letter responds to the Corinthians and answers some of their questions (see 1:12-24; 3:4-6; 11:22-23; 12:16-18). Now that Paul had withstood their investigation, he asked the Corinthians to *examine* themselves, to *test* whether they were acting in accordance with the Christian *faith*.

At the outset, Paul had expressed confidence in the Corinthian believers (7:4, 16). He genuinely believed *Christ Jesus* was *in* them (Romans 8:10-11; Colossians 1:27). He never expressed doubts about their faith, for on his initial missionary visit Christ had certainly acted powerfully in their lives (1:21-22; 3:1-3; 1 Corinthians 1:26-29; 2:4; 3:16, 23; 6:19-20). But if they didn't believe in the fundamental truths of the Christian faith, then they would *fail* the test.

13:6 And I trust that you will discover that we have not failed the test.NIV If the Corinthians did pass their own self-examination, then, by implication, Paul would have, also, passed the *test*. The fact that their lives had been changed by the gospel Paul had preached to them in the first place was Paul's letter of recommendation (see 3:1-3). Paul had founded the Corinthian church. How could the Corinthians, of all people, question him? The fact that they were persevering in the faith was a reflection of the effectiveness of his ministry. Although it was completely absurd for the Corinthian church to question their own founder, they were doing just that! Here Paul tactfully reminded the Corinthians that their Christian faith was a result of his ministry, the same ministry that they were now questioning.

CHECKUPS
Paul challenged the Corinthians to examine and test themselves to see if they really were Christians (13:5). This passage urges believers to give themselves spiritual checkups. They should look for a growing awareness of Christ's presence and power in their lives. Only then will they know if they are true Christians, or merely impostors. If you're not taking active steps to draw closer to God, you are moving further away from him.

13:7-8 We pray to God that you will not do anything wrong.NLT Paul was a man of prayer. He was deeply concerned about the spiritual growth of the Christian church (11:28), so he spent his nights and days praying about those who had accepted Christ as a result of his ministry (see Paul's prayers in Ephesians 1:18-21; 3:16-20; Philippians 1:9-11; Colossians 1:9-14; 1 Thessalonians 3:10; 2 Thessalonians 1:11-12). Although the Corinthians had caused him much trouble and grief (2:4), Paul had never stopped praying for them. He prayed that God might give them the wisdom and the power to do what was right.

We pray this, not to show that our ministry to you has been successful, but because we want you to do right even if we ourselves seem to have failed. Our responsibility is never to oppose the truth, but to stand for the truth at all times.NLT Paul didn't want to be misunderstood. He wasn't praying for their

success, so that, in turn, he would appear *successful.* He wasn't
acting in the same way as those false teachers who preached for
profit—those preachers who looked for good recommendations
from successful churches (2:17–3:1). His prayer was for the
Corinthians' success, even if it meant that people might consider
him to be a failure. Just as Christ was willing to suffer insults and
die on a cross in order to serve all of humanity, Paul was willing
to become a failure in order to serve the Corinthians and the *truth*
of the gospel (13:4). Do you have the same commitment?

**13:9 We are glad to be weak, if you are really strong. What we
pray for is your restoration to maturity.**^{NLT} Just as parents will
make great sacrifices for their children's welfare, so Paul didn't
hesitate to make sacrifices for the Corinthians. Paul wanted the
Corinthians to grow in the faith and to become *strong* Christians.
If he had to exhaust himself, deplete his own resources, and
appear *weak,* he would do so for their sakes (see also 1:6; 12:14-
15). He had invested much in them, spending over a year instructing them in the faith. He wanted the Corinthians to continue to
grow in the faith. For this reason, Paul spent hours committing
them to God in prayer. In addition to praying that the Corinthians
wouldn't do anything wrong (13:7), he prayed for their *restoration to maturity.* The Greek for "restoration to maturity" has the
idea of "putting into proper condition." Thus, Paul's prayer was
that the church would be in order when he arrived (see 1 Corinthians 14:29-33 for an example of the disorder in the Corinthian
congregation).

As you share the gospel, your goal should be not merely to see
others profess faith or begin attending church but to see them
grow into mature Christians. Don't set your sights too low. Pray
for the people to whom you speak about the gospel.

**13:10 I am writing this to you before I come, hoping that I won't
need to deal harshly with you when I do come. For I want to
use the authority the Lord has given me to build you up, not
to tear you down.**^{NLT} In Paul's day, when someone began explaining why he or she had written, it was a clear sign that the author
was ending the letter. The same is true in Paul's New Testament
letters.

Paul had written 2 Corinthians and was sending it with Titus
(8:16, 23) so that when he came he would find the Corinthian
church in order. He wouldn't have to use the *authority* God had
given him to discipline the church, as he was threatening (13:1-
4). Instead, Paul and the Corinthians could encourage each other
in the faith and build one another up (1:23-24; 2:1-3; 10:8). Thus,
this letter, although at times a bit severe (for instance, see 11:3-5,

19-21), was an expression of Paul's great love for the Corinthians (11:11; 12:15). Just as a concerned parent would warn an out-of-control child before the child gets hurt or severely punished, so Paul was warning the Corinthians before it was too late. Paul didn't want to *deal harshly* with them, but he would be forced to take drastic measures if certain ones persisted in sin (13:2-3).

Yet Paul still hoped and prayed for the best. Throughout the letter, he expressed his confidence in the Corinthians. He knew they could handle all the difficult and troublesome situations in their congregation. (Notice how Paul endorsed the Corinthians' actions against the offender in 2:5-11; 7:7-13.) By delaying his visit to Corinth and sending Titus instead (2:1; 7:6-8; 8:16-17), Paul was giving the Corinthians time to respond to his warnings appropriately. Even though the Corinthians were doubting Paul's apostolic authority, he was giving them the benefit of the doubt. Paul was hoping that this letter would prepare the Corinthians for his visit.

GOOD FOUNDATIONS
The authority Paul received from the Lord was for building up, not tearing down, the church (13:10). He wanted the people of God to identify themselves as a holy people among whom God lived. At times critical and confrontational, Paul was always building up people. His example informs this cynical age. Insults and put-downs are common currency. Sarcasm is one of the most popular forms of humor. Even in the church, Christians quickly turn on each other with less than loving comments. But Christians are the temple of the Holy Spirit and the dwelling place of the most high God. There is no room in the household of faith for the deprecation of a fellow worker. Before the week is over, write a note of encouragement to several people in your sphere of influence who probably aren't being built up by others in the church. Remind them how much their presence and abilities are needed in your congregation. Tell them you appreciate them.

13:11 Finally, brothers and sisters, farewell. Put things in order, listen to my appeal.^{NRSV} Paul typically would end his letters with a short list of exhortations (see Colossians 4:2-6; 1 Thessalonians 5:12-22). In 2 Corinthians, he did the same.

"Put things in order" repeats Paul's command in 13:9 (the NIV translates the Greek word in this verse and in 13:9 with the English word "perfection"). Foremost in Paul's mind was that the church leaders of the Corinthian congregation would take charge by disciplining the unrepentant (13:2), silencing the false teachers in their congregation (11:13), and restoring the repentant to church fellowship (2:7).

Paul had already warned the Corinthians and told them what to do. All they had to do at this point was to *listen* to him. His *appeal* in 2 Corinthians was to reject the false gospel of his opponents (11:2-5) and to stay faithful to the gospel he had preached to them (6:1-2; 13:5).

Agree with one another, live in peace; and the God of love and peace will be with you.NRSV Paul knew that the disruption the false teachers had caused in the Corinthian church would create disunity. In fact, the Corinthian church from the start hadn't been unified. It had been plagued with quarrels and disruptions (1 Corinthians 1:11-13). In 1 Corinthians, Paul had carefully explained to the Corinthians that each member of the church was part of the body of Christ. In the same way that the parts of a person's body work together, the Corinthians should work together as members of Christ's body. They should seek opportunities to build each other up in the faith (1 Corinthians 1:10; 12:7, 12-14). With his brief commands to *agree* and to *live in peace,* this verse sums up Paul's exhortations in his earlier letter for the Corinthians to unite as one congregation under Christ (see 1 Corinthians 12:27). They were to put their disputes aside and join together under Christ's leadership to advance his heavenly kingdom. What differences with fellow believers do you need to put aside in order to work with them for Christ's purposes in your church and community?

A TRUE FIX

Paul's closing words—what he wanted the Corinthians to remember about the needs facing their church—are still fitting for the church today. When these qualities are not present, there are problems that must be dealt with. These traits do not come to a church by glossing over problems, conflicts, and difficulties. They are not produced by neglect, denial, withdrawal, or bitterness. They are the by-products of the extremely hard work of solving problems. Just as Paul and the Corinthians had to hammer out difficulties to bring peace, so believers must apply the principles of God's Word and not just hear them.

13:12-13 **Greet one another with a holy kiss. All the saints send their greetings.**NIV Just as present-day writers would typically end their letters with a "sincerely," so in Paul's day letter writers would end their letters with an exchange of greetings. In these verses, Paul used this letter-writing convention (just as he did in Romans 16:3-16; 1 Corinthians 16:19-21; Philippians 4:21-23).

Paul encouraged the Corinthians to *greet* each other with a

kiss. He had done the same in his earlier letter to them (see
1 Corinthians 16:20). In Paul's day, a kiss on a person's cheek or
shoulder was a common greeting, a gesture of friendship. Such a
kiss is similar to a hearty handshake or a hug in present-day society. Paul was evidently encouraging the Corinthians to greet one
another warmly as the first sign of their commitment to agree
with one another and to live in peace.

By alluding to the *greetings* of *all the saints,* Paul was remind-
ing the Corinthians that other congregations throughout the
Roman Empire were trying, along with the Corinthians, to be uni-
fied under Christ. There were congregations across the eastern
Mediterranean that shared the same faith and the Spirit that the
Corinthians had. Although these believers were miles apart, all
Christians were united through the Holy Spirit under Jesus
Christ's authority.

The saints who were with Paul at the time—specifically, the
Macedonian Christians—were sending their greetings to the
Corinthians as an expression of their love and concern for the
believers in Corinth.

**13:14 May the grace of the Lord Jesus Christ, and the love of God,
and the fellowship of the Holy Spirit be with you all.**[NIV] Paul's
final blessing on the Corinthians invokes all three members of the
Trinity—the Father (God), the Son (Lord Jesus Christ), and the
Holy Spirit. Although the term "Trinity" is not explicitly used in
the Bible, verses such as this one show that early Christians
believed that there were three persons in the Godhead: God the
Father, Jesus the Son, and the Holy Spirit (for more verses on the
Trinity, see Matthew 3:17; 28:19; Luke 1:35). Denying that *Jesus*
is God would mean denying that his death on the cross could provide God's unmerited *grace* to those who believe in Jesus. Denying that the *Holy Spirit* is God would mean denying that the
Spirit could provide believers *fellowship* with God and each other.

With this final Trinitarian benediction, Paul was giving the
Corinthians a model from the Godhead of how to be unified in
love. Through the Spirit's empowering, they, too, could begin to
imitate in their congregation the grace, love, and fellowship that
the Godhead already enjoyed.

Paul had every right to refuse to communicate with the Corinthians until they reformed their ways. Instead, Paul loved them
and mercifully reached out to them with visits and letters, again
and again. This type of persistent love was the type of grace Jesus
had shown Paul. Although Paul had persecuted the church (1 Timothy 1:13), Jesus had graciously shown him mercy. In the same
way, Paul didn't withdraw himself from the Corinthians when

they began to reject him. He didn't exclude them from fellowship. Instead, he expressed love and concern for them. He prayed for them. He even lovingly warned them about the false teaching and the immorality in the congregation. It was by his commitment to the Corinthians—through good times and bad, through rejection and acceptance—that Paul hoped to bring the Corinthians back into the full enjoyment of Christ and Christian unity.

BIBLIOGRAPHY

Barrett, C. K. *The First Epistle to the Corinthians.* New York: Harper & Row, 1968.

————. *The Second Epistle to the Corinthians.* Black New Testament Commentary. Peabody, Mass.: Hendrickson Publishers, 1973.

Belleville, Linda L. *Second Corinthians.* The IVP New Testament Commentary Series. Downers Grove, Illinois: InverVarsity Press, 1996.

Erickson, Millard J. *Christian Theology.* Grand Rapids: Baker Book House, 1985.

Fee, Gordon D. *God's Empowering Presence: The Holy Spirit in the Letters of Paul.* Peabody, Mass.: Hendrickson Publishers, 1994.

————. *The First Epistle to the Corinthians.* Grand Rapids: Eerdmans, 1987.

Harris, Murray. "2 Corinthians" in *The Expositor's Bible Commentary,* vol: 10. Frank E. Gaebelein, ed. Grand Rapids: Zondervan, 1976.

Hawthorne, Gerald F., Ralph Martin, and Daniel Reid. *Dictionary of Paul and His Letters.* Downers Grove, Illinois: InterVarsity Press, 1993.

Hughes, Philip E. *Paul's Second Epistle to the Corinthians.* Grand Rapids: Eerdmans, 1962.

Kruse, Colin. *Second Corinthians.* Tyndale New Testament Commentaries. Grand Rapids: Eerdmans, 1987.

Mare, W. Harold. "1 Corinthians." In *The Expositor's Bible Commentary,* vol. 10. Frank E. Gaebelein, ed. Grand Rapids: Zondervan, 1976.

Martin, Ralph P. *Second Corinthians.* Word Biblical Commentary. Waco, Texas: Word, 1986.

Morris, Leon. *First Corinthians.* Tyndale New Testament Commentaries. Grand Rapids: Eerdmans, 1988.

INDEX

Paul's suffering for the gospel, 274–277,
332–338, 361–368, 379–380,
438–446
application for today, 275, 333, 335, 337,
338, 363, 443, 455
Trinity, 43
Troas, 298–301
Trustworthiness
needed in God's servants, 57–58
application for today, 57, 285
Unity importance in the church, 24–29,
179–180
in the church, Christ's body, 174–180
Lord's Supper shows, 144
application for today, 25, 27, 145, 176,
177, 179, 302
Veil, 316, 320–323, 327–329
Weak/Strong Believers, 117–119
Chart: Stronger and Weaker Believers,
116
Wealth
God's versus the world's, 61–64
Widowhood
Paul's advice about, 97–98, 109–110
Wilderness
Israel in, 135–138

Wisdom God's versus the world's, 30–37,
39–40, 55–56
gift of, 170–171
application for today, 33, 41
Witnessing
application for today, 29, 32, 35, 38, 46,
128, 280, 327
Women
head covering in worship in Corinth,
153–159
in worship in Corinth, 212–213
roles of men and women, 157–158
application for today, 158, 159
Words
importance of, 282–285
application for today, 283, 285
Worship
as a theme of 1 Corinthians, 11
in an orderly way, 207–215
women in, 212–213
application for today, 204, 207, 212, 215,
358
Chart: What the Bible Says about
Worship, 208–209
Yeast, 71–73